The Netherlands

Ryan Ver Berkmoes
Karla Zimmerman

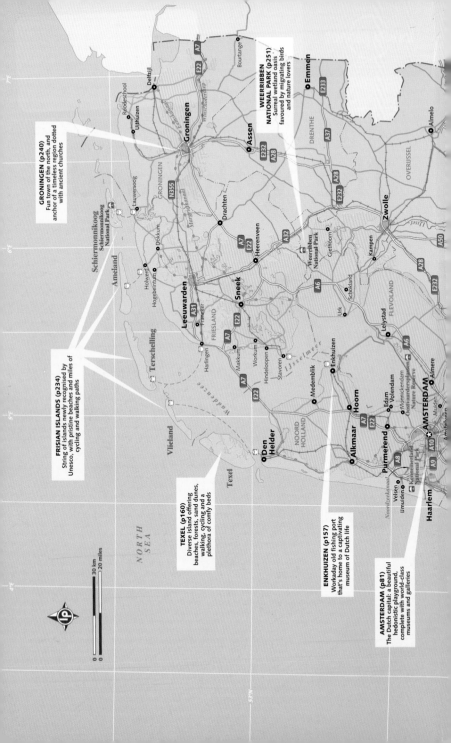

GRONINGEN (p240)
Fun town of the north, and anchor of a timeless region dotted with ancient churches

WEERRIBBEN NATIONAL PARK (p251)
Surreal wetland oasis favoured by migrating birds and nature lovers

FRISIAN ISLANDS (p234)
String of islands newly recognised by Unesco, with pristine beaches and miles of cycling and walking paths

TEXEL (p160)
Diverse island offering beaches, forests, sand dunes, walking, cycling and a plethora of comfy beds

ENKHUIZEN (p157)
Workaday old fishing port that's home to a captivating museum of Dutch life

AMSTERDAM (p81)
The Dutch capital: a beautiful hedonistic playground, complete with world-class museums and galleries

NORTH SEA

30 km
20 miles

Left C Company canoeing on adventure training in Bavaria.

Below A recce platoon patrol on the Tigris.

WO2 Falconer (*centre*).

A view from the roof of CIMIC House.

Training for a petrol-bomb attack.

A view from the top sangar of CIMIC House, looking east.

Night fighting from the roof of CIMIC House, August 2005.

An 81mm mortar in action.

Stand-off in Al Amarah. This photograph probably shows 1LI, from whom 1PWRR took over in April 2004.

Left Captain Ross
'Rosco' Noott
and an Iraqi
policeman.

Centre Corporal Palmer
QRL training Iraqi
police recruits.

Bottom Iraqi police.

Hearts and minds.

Private Lee O'Callaghan's body is repatriated from Basra.

Major Coote and WO2 Falconer of C Company.

A soldier of the Household Cavalry Regiment scans the horizon on the Iraqi border.

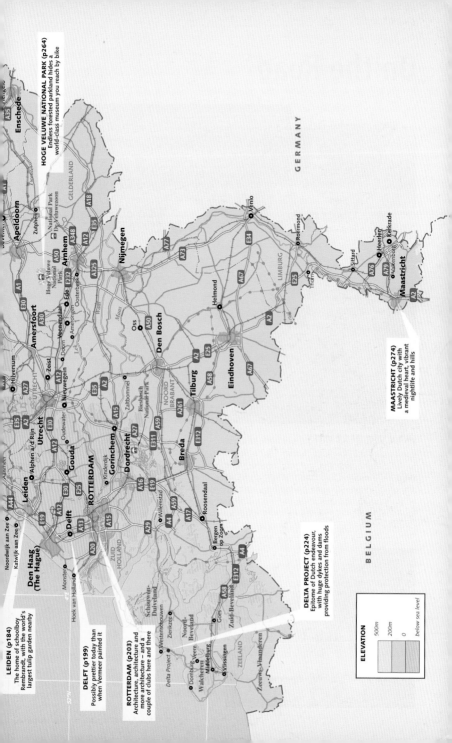

LEIDEN (p184)
The home of schoolboy Rembrandt, with the world's largest tulip garden nearby

HOGE VELUWE NATIONAL PARK (p264)
Endless forested parkland hides a world-class museum you reach by bike

DELFT (p199)
Possibly prettier today than when Vermeer painted it

ROTTERDAM (p203)
Architecture, architecture and more architecture – and a couple of clubs here and there

DELTA PROJECT (p224)
Epitome of Dutch endeavour, with huge dykes and dams providing protection from floods

MAASTRICHT (p274)
Lively Dutch city with a medieval heart, vibrant nightlife and hills

ELEVATION

500m
200m
0
below sea level

GERMANY

BELGIUM

GELDERLAND

LIMBURG

NOORD BRABANT

ZUID HOLLAND

ZEELAND

UTRECHT

Enschede
Apeldoorn
Arnhem
Nijmegen
Venlo
Roermond
Sittard
Heerlen
Kerkrade
Maastricht
Vaals
Valkenburg

Hilversum
Amersfoort
Zeist
Nieuwegein
Utrecht
Gouda
Doorn
Veenendaal
Ede
Oosterbeek
Helmond
Oss
Den Bosch
Zaltbommel
Eindhoven
Tilburg
Breda
Roosendaal
Bergen op Zoom
Gorinchem
Dordrecht
Kinderdijk
Willemstad
ROTTERDAM
Delft
Den Haag (The Hague)
Leiden
Katwijk aan Zee
Noordwijk aan Zee
Monster
Hoek van Holland
Alphen a/d Rijn
Oudewater
Amerongen

Hoge Veluwe National Park
De Veluwezoom

Biesbosch Nationaal Park

Schouwen-Duiveland
Westenschouwen
Zierikzee
Noord-Beveland
Walcheren
Domburg
Veere
Middelburg
Vlissingen
Zuid-Beveland
Goes
Zeeuws-Vlaanderen
Delta Project
Zuthpen
Thorn

On the Road

RYAN VER BERKMOES Coordinating Author

It was a dark and stormy day. Squalls blew in from the North Sea causing the windmills at Zaanse Schans (p146) to shake, rattle and, well, spin. Straining against the winds, the ancient timbers creaked like old sailing ships. My favourite is a windmill that still grinds paint pigments just as was done for Rembrandt, Vermeer and other worthies. The park is a short day trip northwest of Amsterdam and is easily reached by train or bike. Afterwards, you raise a little flag and a small boat picks you up for a short jaunt to the pretty village of Zaandijk. On this day, however, we might as well have been on a wave-tossed journey to the New World.

KARLA ZIMMERMAN Here's a quintessential Amsterdam moment – lock up the bike, gaze at the canal, and walk over the bridge to the cafe on the other side, where a frothy beer awaits.

For full author biographies see p318.

The Netherlands Highlights

It's easy to explore the Netherlands and the rewards far outweigh the effort. A Renaissance masterpiece is found around the corner of a museum, a chance stop for a snack becomes a memorable vignette or a national icon is seen in a new light. The nation is compact and easy to get around, especially by bike, so you can toss the itinerary into the nearest recycling bin and let your trip be shaped by whim, mood or mere random opportunity.

FRANS LEMMENS

1 AMSTERDAM CANALS

A lot of the charm of Amsterdam (p81) lies in its streets, canals and old houses. The city centre is small and compact, and you'll bump into a lot of old churches and stuff.

sheriff_truman, Traveller

DELFT

Delft (p199) is like a mini-Amsterdam; it's got lots of historic sites, a characteristic, cute, old city centre, canals (and canal boats), little cafes and nice shops. It's also known for Delftware ceramics, and you can still visit one of the original factories – or plenty of little galleries and shops where they sell it.

Lotte Vester, Lonely Planet Staff

ROTTERDAM

Walk across the modern Erasmus bridge to the south and have lunch at the Hotel New York (p211), then head next door to the photography museum located in an old harbour warehouse. It was from this area that the land movers used to emigrate from Holland to the west (New York). Eat and drink in the bars, pubs and coffeeshops in the street called 'Witte de Withstraat'.

Dutchcruz, Traveller

WINDMILLS

Holland is known for its eternal war against the water. In this respect I always like the trip along the river Lek. Head to Kinderdijk (p215) to watch the windmills. On the dyke it is easy to see that the level of the water in the river is above the level of the land on the other side of the dyke. I find this more indicative of Holland than the red light districts in a number of cities.

Liberat, Traveller

WADLOPEN

Wadlopen (mudflat-walking; p246) is smelly, cold, wet, filthy, exhausting and heaps of fun. We walked about 20km (more than five hours!) in the North Sea, from Pieterburen to pretty Schiermonnikoog, where we warmed up on the beach with beer and hot *bitterballen, kroketten* and *frites*.

Fergie Munn, Traveller

6

FRANS LEMMENS

MARTIN MOOS

5

ART IN THE NETHERLANDS

Wherever you look, art seems to permeate Dutch culture. It all goes back to the era when fine paintings were as common as chickens and, though respected, were sometimes traded for fowl.

Karla Zimmerman, Lonely Planet Author

WILL SALTER

7

DUTCH DELIGHTS

One of the first things I do when I go back to the Netherlands is savour some *oude goudse kaas* (old Gouda cheese). You can buy it anywhere around the country, just make sure you try some – bread or crackers optional!

Craig Kilburn, Lonely Planet Staff

FRANS LEMMENS

HOGE VELUWE NATIONAL PARK

If the weather is OK, visit the Hoge Veluwe National Park (p264). You can rent a bicycle at the entrance, enjoy the nature and visit the Kröller-Müller Museum in this park, with a substantial Van Gogh collection!

Arizona, Traveller

8

RAW HERRINGS

Raw herrings are delicious, especially when you cover them in onion and pickle and wrap them in a soft white bun. The flavour is surprisingly subtle, given the smell, and the texture is like raw tuna but smoother. If you have a drink from a bottle of water to wash it down then don't even think about drinking from that same bottle later on – you will get a rude fishy flashback.

Katherine Watson, Traveller

9

O.D. VANDE VEER/AL

WILL SAI

10

LANGUID LIVING

I lazed under a tree on a Dutch river bank on a sultry day watching river traffic go by. It felt like a scene from an 18th-century Dutch landscape painting, only I wasn't wearing frumpy woollen clothes and a funny hat. And I smelled better – I think.

Ryan Ver Berkmoes, Lonely Planet Author

Contents

Regional Map Contents

Destination the Netherlands

The Netherlands is a very big, small country. So much of this sea-battered, windswept, flat-as-a-pancake place has played an oversized role in history that it seems hardly possible that it is only 135th in the league table of nations' size, right after Switzerland and Bhutan.

In the world of art it's given us Rembrandt and Van Gogh. Sure, there's also Frans Hals, Hieronymus Bosch and Piet Mondrian, but when you've got the first two, why worry about the rest? OK that Vermeer guy, he's big…

Then there are icons. Classic windmills, the ultimate green machines that are back in vogue a century after the Dutch used the twirling beasties to pump the country dry. And clogs? Renewable. Affordable. Floatable (if the dykes break). And tulips? The Dutch have made a fortune from little bulbs that go in the ground, then burst forth with beauty that's universally loved. Compare that to countries who have made a fortune planting, say, landmines in the ground.

The Dutch themselves seem oversized. (Actually they are, being statistically the tallest nationality on the planet.) Gregariousness, thrift, good sense and wry humour are all national traits, as is no-holds-barred honesty. This is not the country for the neurotic to ask: 'Do you think I look fat?'

Language is another trait where they excel. Yes, the Dutch language often makes the uninitiated suspect that the speaker needs a spittoon, but at the merest hint of your native tongue the Dutch smoothly shift to flawless English, and even toss in a joke to let you know that they didn't just learn it in a book.

But the most defining aspect of the Dutch, and one that also defines the Netherlands, is the ingrained devotion to tolerance. Most non-Dutch don't realise that the country is roughly divided between Protestants and Catholics. And unlike other places where this is the case and where it's resulted in no end of trouble, it hasn't been a cause of strife here for hundreds of years.

These days, as well as tolerance, it's probably because the rather unreligious Dutch simply don't care. But go back 100 years to when people were more

FAST FACTS

Population: 16.5 million

Area: 41,526 sq km

Land in tulip bulbs: 110 sq km

Per capita GDP: €35,400

Unemployment rate: 6.8% (2009)

Inflation: 2% (2009 average)

Waterways: 5046km (navigable for ships over 50 tonnes)

Number of windmills: 1180

MORE DUTCH FAST FACTS

The Dutch love statistics and they're a favourite topic of conversation. Here are some esoteric stats to get you ready for any conversational gambit in a cafe. We suggest you break the ice by asking: 'Were you born at home?' (Should you want more, the government agency Statistics Netherlands has a vast amount of data on its website, www.cbs.nl.)

- The Netherlands hosted 8 million foreign overnight guests in 2008; 1.5 million were from Britain.
- From 2005 to 2008, 29% of births in the country were home deliveries.
- One person out of 50 in the Netherlands is of Moroccan descent.
- The nation exported more than 689 million kilos of cheese in 2008, which adds up to 42kg per inhabitant.
- In 2020, one in five people in the Netherlands will be aged over 65.
- Seven out of eight locals had home internet access in 2008 – the highest percentage in the EU.
- One-third of Dutch internet users won't shop online.
- One in 10 Dutch youth aged 15 to 20 years has smoked pot in the past 30 days, one of the lowest rates in Europe.

HOLLAND VS THE NETHERLANDS: WHAT'S THE DIFFERENCE?

'Holland' is a popular synonym for the Netherlands, yet in reality it only refers to the combined provinces of Noord (North) and Zuid (South) Holland. The rest of the country (Utrecht, Limburg, Friesland etc) is not Holland, even if the Dutch themselves make the same mistake – although those doing this often seem to be from a certain two provinces…

devout and wandered around the dykes saying prayers while dressed in black, and the Dutch found a typically sensible way to deal with possible religious strife: tolerance. You don't bother me and I won't bother you.

Tolerance influences every aspect of Dutch life. For decades the nation has been governed by broad coalitions embracing parties on the right and left. Extremist parties appear, get 6% of the vote, and disappear at the next election. If you're gay you can get married; if you want to smoke pot you can. If you want to dress up like a leprechaun and have somebody ride you like a stallion, well you can do that too.

But in a country where seeking the middle ground is paramount (possibly due to a lack of high ground?), even tolerance has been found to have its limits. After political provocateur Theo van Gogh was murdered in 2004 by an immigrant angered over his anti-Muslim rhetoric, the official response was to require prospective residents to take lessons in the role of tolerance in Dutch society.

The Dutch discovered they were intolerant of the intolerant. And the 'things to be intolerant of' list has been growing. When a convicted human trafficker sentenced to 7½ years in prison was let out so he could 'take care of personal business' and then didn't return to serve the rest of his time (surprise!), there was anger over his jailers being too tolerant.

The famous coffeeshops where you can order your pot and hash off a menu are also under fire, as are the legal red light districts. The 'smart bars' where you could order magic mushrooms are already gone and even liberal governments, such as those in Amsterdam and Rotterdam, are talking about closing 50% of coffeeshops and making the rest Dutch-only.

It seems the Dutch are fed up with drug and sex tourists, and the gangs and underworld figures that profit off them. Whether this is a temporary, conservative shift fuelled by troubled times or whether it represents a fundamental change in tolerance remains to be seen.

For Amsterdam – the entire city a Dutch icon like the ones mentioned earlier – these upheavals will merely create more ripples in a city used to waves of change. Misunderstood by many, the virtual heart of the Netherlands is not what many people expect on their first visit. The sex and drugs are mostly kept to one 'hood (convenient to the train station) while the rest of the city keeps to its own beauty along the murky canals.

Amsterdam wears its rich history proudly, even if it doesn't put on the airs it could as one of the world's great cities – that would be very un-Dutch. But if you only stay in Amsterdam you will misunderstand the rest of this big, small place. Other places as old as Amsterdam have evocative beauty and come in a variety of sizes: Edam, Haarlem, Delft and Deventer to name just some.

Perhaps the best way to get to the heart of the Netherlands is to do as the Dutch do. Join them in the city centres of classic towns as far flung as Groningen, Maastricht and Den Bosch, lively places filled with cafes that heave with happy Dutch socialising on a sunny day. Or join them on the thousands of kilometres of bike routes as they add not a molecule of carbon to the atmosphere while riding through the lush countryside and past sweeping watery vistas at sea (or is it see?) level.

You don't have to travel far to find a lot.

Getting Started

The Netherlands is an easy place to visit. Up-to-date information is plentiful, almost every Dutch person speaks decent English, transport links are swift, distances are short, and there's an abundance of sights and activities. All this means you can be spontaneous and not worry about a huge amount of preparation or endless planning.

That said, a bit of foresight is essential to pinpoint sights that match your interests, and to get the timing right – the tulip fields aren't much to look at before the blossoms open or after the stems are denuded. And during the busy summer you'll probably want to book your Amsterdam accommodation, as Amsterdam's best (and sometimes worst) hotels book up well in advance, and other towns may have limited sleeping options.

WHEN TO GO

The Netherlands has a typical maritime climate, with cool winters and mild summers. Be prepared for blustery and changeable weather and limited sunny days in summer – although climate change may be changing that. Precipitation (79cm a year) is spread rather evenly over the calendar.

See Climate, p285, for more information.

Like much of Europe, the high season runs from June to August, which is known for its hot, sticky spells but isn't quite the Riviera shown in some tourist brochures. In fact the moderate climes mean that the typical fan-free, non-air-conditioned hotel room can roast. Hordes of tourists pulse through the Netherlands at this time, but these are the best months to sit by the canals drinking and chatting. Many Dutch take a summer holiday, and the last weekend in July is deadly for traffic. You may be surrounded by other foreigners in August, but the month is crammed with events – see p287.

Mid-March to May, and September to mid-October are the shoulder seasons. Spring is wonderful, as the bulbs are in bloom – April for daffodils, May for tulips. Easter is busy in Amsterdam, but if you can visit during Koninginnedag (30 April, see p116) it's worth fighting the crowds. Early October with its Indian summer can be an excellent time to come.

As the temperature drops, so does the number of tourists – things are calmest from mid-October to mid-March. Museums are quiet (and many are closed; note the listings in this book) and you can mingle with the 'real' Dutch in cosy pubs during this time. Accommodation rates fall, though some

---

DON'T LEAVE HOME WITHOUT...

- Converter for European plugs
- Earplugs to counteract fellow hotel guests and street noise
- Abandoning your diet *(frites!)*
- Decent rain jacket
- Plans to tiptoe through the tulips
- Open mind to drugs and sex
- Thick skin for Dutch honesty/bluntness
- Taste for bad '80s music, because you won't be able to escape it
- Quick reflexes to avoid cyclists and dodge dog poo
- A smaller bag than you thought – you can buy anything you forget to pack

hotels might be closed. The short days of winter (December to February) see periods of slushy snow and temperatures close to freezing – this is a challenging time for those on a cycling holiday.

School holidays are staggered according to region but fall around mid-February, early May, July and August, and the end of October (see p288).

COSTS & MONEY

The Netherlands really isn't a budget buy, but neither is it the most expensive European destination. If you're happy eating chips, sleeping in hostels and walking around, it's possible to hang in the country for under €50 per day. Those who prefer a couple of solid meals a day, a comfy bed with private facilities, a few cafe drinks and travelling by public transport are looking at €100 per day as a starting point. Add-ons such as museums, treats, nicer digs, day trips etc will quickly lift your budget.

There are a lot of free activities to stretch your budget, especially in Amsterdam in summer, and discount passes in large cities can yield lots of discounts (see p286). And don't underestimate the pleasure of simply wandering around Dutch cities soaking up their history and beauty. It's free – at least until you yield to the temptation of that beguiling cafe.

HOW MUCH?

Size 37 plain/painted clogs €17.50/20.50

2/15 strip card for public transport €1.60/6.70

One day's parking in Amsterdam €50

One day's bike hire €6-10

Cinema ticket €7.50

TRAVELLING RESPONSIBLY

One of the best ways you can travel responsibly in the Netherlands is to provide your own transport power: there is no better place in the world for cycling (see p67). But even if you're not peddling away, the superb public transport system can get you almost everywhere you need to go (and most of the trains run on electricity). Cars are not needed and are a major pain to park or even simply to manoeuvre around the pedestrian-friendly city centres.

Otherwise your best way to travel responsibly is to simply mimic the locals. The Netherlands has a deep commitment to recycling and sustainability. Hotels, restaurants and other businesses tend to reflect the same national green vibe.

TRAVEL LITERATURE

Girl with a Pearl Earring, by Tracy Chevalier, explores the conflict between duty and sexuality. Set in Delft, the story was made into a Hollywood movie starring Colin Firth (as Jan Vermeer) and Scarlett Johansson (as a maid in his employ), and offers insights into a painter's life during the Golden Age.

Xenophobe's Guide to the Dutch, by Rodney Bolt, takes an irreverent look at all things Dutch and strikes a fine balance between humour and truth. A quick, fun read.

The Dutch, I Presume?, by Martijn de Rooi, Jurjen Drenth and friends, is another book that attempts to explain the peculiarities of the Dutch psyche, and the Dutch people's love affair with windmills, wooden shoes and shelf toilets. It has more facts than insights, but it's still an interesting read and the photos are inspired.

Amsterdam, by Geert Mak, interweaves tales of ordinary citizens with the bigger picture of cultural, social and economic history. It also delves into the Dutch psyche: for instance, why the Dutch eschew nationalism for business reasons.

The UnDutchables, by Colin White and Laurie Boucke, is a point of reference for virtually anyone who goes to live in the Netherlands. These two Americans have observed foibles that many Dutch themselves seem not to recognise.

The Embarrassment of Riches, by Simon Schama, is an epic account of Dutch culture in the Golden Age, using art to mirror a nation with all its

TOP 10

United Kingdom · Amsterdam · Germany

MUST-SEE FILMS

The following is a shortlist of critically acclaimed Dutch films worth seeing before your trip.

1 *Antonia* (Antonia's Line), directed by Marleen Gorris, 1995. A strong-willed Dutch woman recalls life in a colourful village. Won an Oscar for best foreign film.

2 *De Aanslag* (The Assault), directed by Fons Rademakers, 1986. A physician spends his adult life investigating why his neighbours betrayed his family in WWII.

3 *De Tweeling* (Twin Sisters), directed by Ben Sombogaart, 2004. Touching story of twins separated in the Netherlands and Germany during WWII.

4 *Fanfare*, directed by Bert Haanstra, 1958. Classic satire about two amateur brass bands vying for a government grant in a small Dutch town.

5 *Interview*, directed by Theo van Gogh, 2003. Low-key account of a war correspondent conducting an interview with a soap-opera actress.

6 *Shouf Shouf Habibi* (Hush Hush Baby), directed by Albert ter Heerdt, 2004. Comedy about a Moroccan family finding its way in Dutch society.

7 *Simon*, directed by Eddy Terstall, 2004. A complicated friendship develops when a hetero hash dealer hits a gay man with his car.

8 *Turks Fruit* (Turkish Delight), directed by Paul Verhoeven, 1973. A distressed sculptor (Rutger Hauer) picks up numerous women to forget the loss of his wife; a modern classic.

9 *Zus & So*, directed by Paula van der Oest, 2001. Comedy about three sisters who plot to sabotage the engagement of their gay brother for material gain.

10 *Zwartboek* (Black Book), directed by Paul Verhoeven, 2006. This action-packed story explores some of the less heroic aspects of the Dutch resistance in WWII.

MEMORABLE MUSEUMS

The Netherlands is peppered with exceptional museums. The following are some of our favourites:

1 Kröller-Müller Museum (p265) One of the world's best for art, set in a vast park.

2 Rijksmuseum (p105) *The* museum for Dutch art.

3 Van Gogh Museum (p104) The man and his art.

4 Anne Frank Huis (p102) The book's setting is perfectly presented.

5 Frans Hals Museum (p141) The artist's work is shown in a setting that reflects his life.

6 Zaanse Schans (p146) Fun setting for windmill-mania.

7 Zuiderzeemuseum (p157) Amazing open-air museum of Dutch life.

8 Mauritshuis (p191) Art 101 in a palace.

9 Museum Boijmans van Beuningen (p205) Fun-filled museum with art through the ages.

10 Maritime & Beachcombers Museum (p162) Flotsam and jetsam are just some of the highlights.

resident neuroses and religious idiosyncrasies. Masterfully written and full of offbeat themes such as the popularity of breakfast paintings.

Tulip Fever, by Deborah Moggach, offers a feel for Amsterdam proper around the time when Rembrandt was at his peak and tulips were worth more than their weight in gold. A nice bonus is the reproductions of Dutch paintings found in some editions.

INTERNET RESOURCES

See p68 for internet resources you can use while on a cycling holiday.

Dutch Ministry of Foreign Affairs (www.minbuza.nl) Wealth of background facts and information, but not officious.

Dutch News (www.dutchnews.nl) Daily headlines and news stories in English.

Expatica (www.expatica.com/holland) Entertaining all-round guide to life in the Netherlands, with daily news, listings and even singles ads.

Google Translate (translate.google.com) Many Dutch websites have English-language pages; for those that don't Google supplies instant translation.

Learn Dutch (www.learndutch.org) Online Dutch course; learn to say 'hello, my name is Hans Brinker' in under a minute.

Lonely Planet (www.lonelyplanet.com) General information on the Netherlands and links to various useful Dutch sites.

Netherlands Tourism Board (www.holland.com) Attractions, cultural articles and loads of practical stuff among the PR; good search function.

Uitburo (www.uitburo.nl) Events site for the Netherlands. It's in Dutch but is easy to navigate.

Windmill Database (www.molendatabase.com) Pick out your favourite icon in advance.

Itineraries
CLASSIC ROUTES

THE LAY OF THE LOWLANDS
One Week / Amsterdam to Kinderdijk

Begin in **Amsterdam** (p81). Visit the **Van Gogh Museum** (p104) and the **Rijksmuseum** (p105) and rent a bicycle to explore the pretty neighbourhood of **Jordaan** (p100). On the second day board a **canal boat tour** (p114) and walk the **Red Light District** (p97) before hitting a brown cafe or coffeeshop.

Head west to the town of **Haarlem** (p140) – stroll the compact old quarter, and view the masterpieces at the **Frans Hals Museum** (p141) and the stained glass of the **Grote Kerk van St Bavo** (p141).

Spend a day in **Leiden** (p184) with its old-world splendour. In tulip season (April and May) witness the unbelievable colours of the **Keukenhof gardens** (p189), north of town. Then spend a day in **Den Haag** (p189), being sure not to miss the **Mauritshuis** (p191) collection, with five-star works from everyone from Vermeer to Warhol.

In the remaining time take a harbour boat tour in **Rotterdam** (p203) and visit the **Museum Boijmans van Beuningen** (p205) and the **Maritiem Museum Rotterdam** (p208). The next morning, do a walking tour of the city's **modern architecture** (p209) before departing for **Kinderdijk** (p215) and its gaggle of Unesco-recognised windmills.

This popular route from Amsterdam through the historic Dutch cities of Haarlem, Den Haag and Rotterdam is a mere 103km; the sheer variety of charms will make a week flash by.

SOUTHERN SOJOURN   Two Weeks / Amsterdam to Utrecht

If you've two weeks to spare, start in **Amsterdam** (p81), but extend your stay to three days, and as well as a visit to the city's big museums, take time out to relax in **Vondelpark** (p106), the capital's English-style park. Once again, discover the delights of the district of **Jordaan** (p100) and add the **Southern Canal Belt** (p103), then take a load off in **Hoppe** (p127), a grand cafe on the Spui, and browse the exotic wares in the **Albert Cuypmarkt** (see the boxed text, p134). Learn about the glories of the Dutch East India Company at the renovated **Nederlands Scheepvaartmuseum** (p109) then plunge into the city's celebrated **nightlife** (p129). Escape the city by bicycle to enjoy the windmills and seascapes of the **Waterland Region** (p147).

Continue on as in the one-week tour to Haarlem, Leiden (and Keukenhof, in season), Den Haag and Rotterdam, but add a day for **Delft** (p199) and its Vermeer splendour. Take the ferry to see the windmills at **Kinderdijk** (p215), then head for **Middelburg** (p220), Zeeland's prosperous capital, and the nearby **Delta Project** (p224). Take trains through the Netherlands' southern provinces, stopping for the hidden canals of lovely **Den Bosch** (p268), before continuing to **Maastricht** (p274), a city with more panache than most; two days should be enough to sample some great cuisine and meander through the medieval centre. Head north to visit Hanseatic **Deventer** (p253) and then head east to the excellent **Kröller-Müller Museum** (p265). Polish off your trip in the cosmopolitan yet deeply historic city of **Utrecht** (p173).

A two-week tour covering 700km that passes through some of Holland's classic cities, and allows an exploration of the country's astounding Delta Project and a world-class museum.

CIRCUMNAVIGATING THE IJSSELMEER

**Two Weeks / Amsterdam
to Amsterdam**

A practical place to start this tour is **Amsterdam** (p81); three days in the capital will whiz by in a blur of museums, parks, canal tours and nightlife. From here, head north along the IJsselmeer coast through the **Waterland Region** (p147) to the tiny fishing village of **Marken** (p149). Cycle the dykes around the inland sea to cute-as-a-button **Edam** (p150), which comes second only to Haarlem as the prettiest town in Noord Holland. Stay overnight here before reaching **Alkmaar** (p152) early to experience its kitsch but fun cheese market, then spend the afternoon wandering through Enkhuizen's enthralling **Zuiderzeemuseum** (p157).

The next morning catch a bus to **Den Helder** (p160), and from there a ferry to **Texel** (p160). Spend two days (or the entire two weeks…) dividing your time between the beach and bike exploration, then take another ferry to **Vlieland** (p235) to appreciate the wilder side of the Frisian Islands. From Vlieland, a ferry will take you back to the mainland and dump you at **Harlingen** (p232), from where **Leeuwarden** (p228) is only a short train ride away. Friesland's capital is an entertaining place, as are the nearby chain of captivating coastal towns highlighted by **Hindeloopen** (p233) on the IJsselmeer.

Break the train trip from Leeuwarden to Amsterdam at beguiling **Zwolle** (p255) and add more stops in **Naarden** (p166) and **Muiden** (p165), two of Noord Holland's historical fortress towns.

This two-week trip, covering 570km, provides a taste of Dutch life on the sea. It passes through historically important nautical towns, holiday islands and old fortresses.

ROADS LESS TRAVELLED

ISLAND ESCAPES   One to Two Weeks / Amsterdam to Schiermonnikoog

The necklace of low-lying Wadden Islands (Texel, Vlieland, Terschelling, Ameland and Schiermonnikoog) is recognised by Unesco and makes for good island-hopping, preferably with your bicycle in tow. Some ferry links require advance planning; with precise planning you can link all five by boat (p235) but for most there will be connections via the mainland. From Amsterdam, head to **Texel** (p160). Hop on your bike and snake along the island's western coast from sleepy Den Hoorn through dark copses to the **Ecomare** (p161) seal and bird refuge. Comb the eastern side of the island, admiring pretty thatched houses in Oosterend and visiting the superb **Maritime & Beachcombers Museum** (p162) in Oudeschild.

From De Cocksdorp at the northern end of Texel, board the morning ferry to car-free **Vlieland** (p235) to explore its nature and hiking trails before catching the boat to **Terschelling** (p236), Friesland's main tourist island. Hole up in peaceful **Oosterend** (p236) and cycle the untouched dunes, then hightail it by ferry to **Harlingen** (p232), a pretty little port on the Frisian coast, and on to **Holwerd** (p231), to ferry across to somnolent **Ameland** (p237). Stay in the whaling port of **Nes** (p237). Return via the ports of Holwerd and **Lauwersoog** (p245) and back on a ferry to **Schiermonnikoog** (p237), the smallest of the Frisian Islands and featuring a windswept, evocative national park.

This hop along the Wadden Islands covers just 200km, but you will be tempted to spend from one to two weeks soaking up the island's wild, enchanting beauty.

EASTERN EXPERIENCE

One Week / Groningen to Dordrecht

The Netherlands' eastern expanse is largely ignored by tourists who settle for the big guns of the Dutch lowlands, but there are myriad highlights among the *polders* (strips of farmland separated by canals) waiting to be discovered.

Begin your trip in **Groningen** (p240), a vibrant city filled with students, bars, cafes and a couple of fine museums. Cycle southeast to **Bourtange** (p247), a perfectly preserved 17th-century fortified town on the border with Germany, before moving on to Borger and its prehistoric **hunebedden** (see the boxed text, p249), stone arrangements once used as burial chambers. Cycle through the woods to **Kamp Westerbork** (p248) and encounter its moving, horrible heritage. Catch a train to **Zwolle** (p255), a compact, easygoing town. A bike trip through the beautifully natural expanse of nearby **Weerribben National Park** (p251) should include renting a canoe.

From Zwolle it's only a short train ride to **Deventer** (p253), an unhurried Hanseatic town that's ideal for backstreet meanders. Next, explore the **Hoge Veluwe National Park** (p264), a natural oasis that's home to one of the finest art museums in the country. Then head for **Den Bosch** (p268), a city ringed by unusual canals and defensive walls. **Breda** (p272) is your next stop, where a day and a night can be spent appreciating the city's cafe-filled centre. Go back to nature at **Biesbosch National Park** (p218) before finishing up on the lovely old streets and canals of **Dordrecht** (p216).

This seven-day excursion through the Netherlands' eastern provinces covers 550km and touches on the country's less-visited towns, cities and natural attractions.

TAILORED TRIPS

FAMILY FORAYS

Aside from canal tours and bike rides, **Amsterdam** (p113) is filled with family attractions. The **Nederlands Scheepvaartmuseum** (p109), with its tall-ship replicas, and **Tropenmuseum** (p108), featuring a separate children's section, will spark imaginations young and old, while excess energy can be spent running wild in **Vondelpark** (p106) or **TunFun** (p100), a large underground playground. Then kids can settle back down with the butterflies in **Hortus Botanicus** (p107).

Close to the capital, the windmills and boat rides of **Zaanse Schans** (p146) will surely delight, as will the sand dunes and pristine beaches of the **Zuid-Kennemerduinen National Park** (p145).

Further north, the old toys you can try at the **Zuiderzeemuseum** (p157) in Enkhuizen are fun, while kids love bidding for apples at **Museum Broeker Veiling** (p155) in Broek op Langedijk.

In Gelderland, shiver with the critters at Arnhem's well laid-out **Burgers' Zoo** (p262). The cute seals and interactive nature displays of Texel's **Ecomare** (p161) and Pieterburen's **Zeehondencreche** (p246) never fail to please.

Efteling (p272), with scary rides aplenty, is the 'Dutch Disneyland'. Enjoy a pint-sized Holland at **Madurodam** (p193) or **RailZ Miniworld** (p208). Maastricht's spooky **underground caves** (see the boxed text, p277) are perfect for the entire family, as is the **Waterland Neeltje Jans** (p223).

ADULT ENTERTAINMENT

There is no denying that the Netherlands is a playground for grown-ups. Breweries, brown cafes, coffeeshops, red light districts, world-class clubbing, and the old masters' art are just waiting to be enjoyed.

Start in Amsterdam. Its centre overflows with **brown cafes** (p127), but to get straight to the source, go for a quality beverage at **Brouwerij 't IJ** (p129), a small brewery with potent beers. With scores of **coffeeshops** (p129), the capital offers ample opportunity to partake in a spliff or two, and no one, but no one (unless they suffer from erythrophobia) should miss a stroll through the legendary **Red Light District** (p97). **Clubs** (p131) abound, as do museums devoted to great masters, such as Rembrandt and Van Gogh.

Rotterdam's **clubbing scene** (p212) is renowned, as are its **summer festivals** (p209), and Groningen's **nightlife** (p244), fuelled by thousands of students, is a lively hedonistic mix. **Utrecht** (p178) has a rollicking nightlife thanks to its ancient university.

Beer is also a Dutch delight. **Maastricht** (p279), close to Belgium and Trappist breweries, should be the first stop for a beer connoisseur, while the best of the Low Countries' amber brew can be sampled at Alkmaar's **Nationaal Biermuseum** (p153). Small, local breweries, such as Texel's **Bierbrouwerij** (p162) and Nijmegen's **De Hemel** (p261), dot the country.

History

For centuries the rich and turbulent history of the Netherlands, complete with wave after wave of invaders and invading waves, was inseparable from that of neighbouring Belgium and Luxembourg. This trio was long known as the Low Countries, and the founding of the modern Netherlands only took place in 1579, while its current borders were set as late as 1830.

FOREIGN DOMINATION

The territory that became the Netherlands has been inhabited since prehistoric times; *hunebedden* (p249) – stone structures used as burial mounds – are clear evidence of this. The first invaders to take note of the locals were the Romans, who, under Julius Caesar, conquered a wide region along the Rijn (Rhine) and its tributaries by 59 BC. Celtic and Germanic tribes initially bowed to Caesar's rule. Utrecht became a main outpost of the empire, but the soggy territory of Friesland was left to its own devices, and its early settlers built homes on mounds of mud (called *terpen*) to escape the frequent floods; Hogebeintum (p231) has a surviving example.

As Roman power began to fade, the Franks, an aggressive German tribe to the east, began to muscle in. By the end of the 8th century, the Franks had completed their conquest of the Low Countries and began converting the local populace to Christianity, using force whenever necessary. Charlemagne, the first in a long line of Holy Roman emperors, was by far the most successful Frankish king. He built a palace at Nijmegen (p259), but the empire fell apart after his death in 814.

For the next 200 years Vikings sailed up Dutch rivers to loot and pillage. Local rulers developed their own fortified towns and made up their own government and laws – even though, strictly speaking, they answered to the Pope in Rome.

Over time local lords, who were nominally bound to a German king, began to gain power. When one lord struggled with another for territory, invariably their townsfolk would provide support, but only in return for various freedoms. By the beginning of the 12th century these relationships were laid down in charters – documents that not only spelt out the lord's power but also detailed other bureaucratic matters, such as taxation. Around the same time, Dutch towns with sea access, such as Deventer and Zwolle, joined the Hanseatic League (a group of powerful trading cities in present-day Germany, including Hamburg and Rostock; p255). These federal towns grew wealthy through the league's single-minded development of laws, regulations and policies that promoted trade.

Hans Brinker, who supposedly stuck his finger in a dyke and saved the Netherlands from a flood, is an American invention and unknown in the Netherlands. He starred in a 19th-century children's book.

TIMELINE

59 BC	800	1150–1300
The Romans extend their empire to what is today the Netherlands. Over the next four centuries the Romans build advanced towns, farms and the straight roads that still shape the landscape.	Christianity arrives in the Low Countries by force. It replaces various Celtic belief systems and those who don't convert are killed. Charlemagne builds a church, parts of which survive in Nijmegen.	Dams are built to retain the IJ River between the Zuiderzee and Haarlem, a key start to the ongoing tug-of-war with the sea.

Meanwhile the many little lords met their match in the dukes of Burgundy, who gradually took over the Low Countries. Duke Philip the Good, who ruled from 1419 to 1467, showed the towns of the Low Countries who was boss by essentially telling them to stuff their charters. Although this limited the towns' freedom, it also brought a degree of stability to the region that had been missing during the era of squabbling lords. By this time Utrecht had become the ecclesiastical centre of the Low Countries, whereas Amsterdam was but a modest trading post.

The 15th century ushered in great prosperity for the Low Countries. The Dutch became adept at shipbuilding in support of the Hanseatic trade, and merchants thrived by selling luxury items such as tapestries, fashionable clothing and paintings – but also more mundane commodities such as salted herring and beer.

With their wealth tapped through taxes, the Low Countries were naturally coveted by a succession of rulers. In 1482 Mary of Burgundy, Philip's grand-daughter, passed the Low Countries on to her son, Philip the Fair.

The family intrigues that followed are worthy of a costume drama. Philip married Joanna, the daughter of King Ferdinand and Queen Isabella of Spain. In 1530 Philip bequeathed the Low Countries to his son Charles, now a member of the powerful Habsburg dynasty. Charles V was crowned Holy Roman Emperor, making him monarch of most of Europe.

Fortunately, the rule of Charles V did not stand in the way of the Low Countries' growing wealth. But this all changed in 1555, when Charles handed over Spain and the Low Countries to his son, Philip II.

THE FIGHT FOR INDEPENDENCE

Philip II of Spain was a staunch Catholic and suffered under a slight case of theomania. Conflict with the Low Countries was inevitable; the Protestant reformation had spread throughout the colony, fuelled by the ideas of Erasmus and the actions of Martin Luther. However, before the Spanish arrived the religious landscape of the Low Countries was quite diverse: Lutherans wielded great influence, but smaller churches had their places too. For instance, the Anabaptists were polygamists and communists, and nudity was promoted as a means of equality among their masses (in the warmer seasons). In the end it was Calvinism that emerged in the Low Countries as the main challenger to the Roman Catholic Church, and to Philip's rule.

A big believer in the Inquisition, Philip went after the Protestants with a vengeance. Matters came to a head in 1566 when the puritanical Calvinists went on a rampage, destroying the art and religious icons of Catholic churches in many parts of the Netherlands. Evidence of this is still readily apparent in the barren interiors of Dutch churches today.

This sent Philip into action. The Duke of Alba was chosen to lead a 10,000-strong army to the Netherlands in 1568 to quell the unruly serfs; as the Duke

---

Thomas C Grattan's recently updated *Holland: The History of the Netherlands* takes a detailed – if somewhat academic – look at the past of the Dutch, from the invasion of the Romans to the beginning of the 20th century.

A helpful site for those tracing their Dutch heritage is www.godutch .com. It has a comprehensive, step-by-step guide.

1200

The age of city-states is in full bloom as lords rule in many riverside towns, such as Den Bosch and Rotterdam. Trading between the towns is the source of wealth and a powerful inducement against war, despite frequent strife.

1275

Amsterdam is founded after the count of Holland grants toll-free status to residents along the Amstel. The city gains its first direct access to the ocean via the Zuiderzee, now the IJsselmeer.

1287

The Zuiderzee floods during a storm and 50,000 to 80,000 people are killed. Except for a few port cities around its periphery, the sea is frequently regarded as a source of trouble.

wasn't one to take prisoners, his forces slaughtered thousands, and so began the Dutch war of independence, which lasted 80 years.

The Prince van Oranje, Willem the Silent (thus named for his refusal to argue over religious issues), was one of the few nobles not to side with Philip, and he led the Dutch revolt against Spanish rule. Willem, who had been Philip's lieutenant in Holland, Zeeland and Utrecht, began to rely on the Dutch Calvinists for his chief support. He championed the principle of tolerance, and this philosophy became part of the foundation of an independent Dutch state. The rebels' cause, however, was hampered by lack of money and patchy support from towns.

Changing tack in 1572, Willem hired a bunch of English pirates to fight for his cause. Known as the Watergeuzen (Sea Beggars), they sailed up the myriad Dutch rivers and seized towns such as Leiden (p184) from the surprised and land-bound Spanish forces. The strategy worked like a charm, and by the end of the year Willem controlled every city except Amsterdam.

The Spanish responded by sacking the Duke of Alba and sending in a new commander, Alessandro Farnese, who was a more able leader. Much of the 1570s saw a constant shift of power as one side or the other gained temporary supremacy.

The *Flying Dutchman* is a mythical 17th-century ship cursed to sail the seas forever, unable to go home. The story has myriad variations, many added to by grog-addled seamen.

THE UNION OF UTRECHT

The Low Countries split for good in 1579 when the more Protestant and rebellious provinces in the north formed the Union of Utrecht. This explicitly anti-Spanish alliance became known as the United Provinces, the basis for the Netherlands as we know it today. The southern regions of the Low Countries had always remained Catholic and were much more open to compromise with Spain. They eventually became Belgium.

Although the United Provinces had declared their independence from Spain, the war dragged on. In 1584 the United Provinces suffered a major blow when their leader, Willem the Silent, was assassinated in Delft. The Dutch once again turned to the English for help, and Elizabeth I lent assistance, but it was the English victory over the Armada in 1588 that proved the most beneficial. In a series of brilliant military campaigns, the Dutch drove the Spanish out of the United Provinces by the turn of the 17th century. Trouble with Spain was far from over, however, and fighting resumed as part of the larger Thirty Years' War throughout Europe. In 1648 the Treaty of Westphalia, which ended the Thirty Years' War, included the proviso that Spain recognise the independence of the United Provinces, ending the 80-year conflict between the Netherlands and Spain.

In the early 1600s the Dutch East India Company flooded the local market with cheap porcelain from China. The Dutch responded with what's known today as Delftware. Today most 'Delftware' is cheap imports from China.

THE GOLDEN AGE

Throughout the turmoil of the 15th and 16th centuries, Holland's merchant cities (particularly Amsterdam) had managed to keep trade alive. Their skill at

1419	1452	1519
The beginning of the end of the powerful city states. The dukes of Burgundy consolidate power and unify rich trading towns under one geographic empire. Freedoms suffer under central rule.	Fire devours the timber frames and thatch of central Amsterdam. New building laws decree that only brick and tile be used in future. Similar conflagrations in other towns leads to the 'Dutch' look prized today.	Spain's Charles V is crowned Holy Roman Emperor. Treaties and dynastic marriages make Amsterdam part of the Spanish empire, with Catholicism the main faith. Protestants are tolerated in a broad area comprising Holland and the northeast.

TULIPMANIA

A bursting economic bubble is not a modern phenomenon. The first occurred between 1636 and 1637 in the Netherlands, and over a flower everyone associates with the Dutch – the tulip.

Tulips originated as wildflowers in Central Asia. They were first cultivated by the Turks ('tulip' is Turkish for turban) and made their way to Europe via Vienna in the mid-1500s. By the beginning of the 17th century Holland was enthralled by the beautiful flower, which flourished in the country's cool climate and fertile delta soil.

It was not long before trading in tulips started to get out of hand. In late 1636 a tulip-trading mania swept the Netherlands; speculative buying and selling made some individual bulbs more expensive than an Amsterdam house, and even ordinary people sank their life's savings into a few bulbs. Speculators fell over themselves to outbid each other in taverns. At the height of Tulipmania, in early 1637, a single bulb of the legendary *Semper augustus* fetched more than 10 years' worth of the average worker's wages. An English botanist bisected one of his host's bulbs and landed in jail until he could raise thousands of florins in compensation.

The bonanza couldn't last. When some bulbs failed to fetch their expected prices in Haarlem in February 1637, the bottom fell out of the market. Within a matter of weeks a wave of bankruptcies swept the land, hitting wealthy merchants as well as simple folk. Speculators were stuck with unsold bulbs, or bulbs they'd reserved but hadn't yet paid for (the concept of financial options, incidentally, was invented during Tulipmania). The government refused to get involved with a pursuit they regarded as gambling.

The speculative froth is gone, but passion for the tulip endures. It remains a relatively expensive flower, and cool-headed growers have perfected their craft. To this day the Dutch are the world leaders in tulip cultivation and supply most of the bulbs exported to Europe and North America. For an explosion of blooms, visit Keukenhof gardens near Leiden in season (p189). To see wealth in bloom, visit the flower market at Aalsmeer (p165).

The Embarrassment of Riches by Simon Schama is a thoughtful look at the tensions generated between vast wealth and Calvinist sobriety in the Golden Age, with implications for modern society.

business and sailing was so great that, even at the peak of the rebellion, the Spanish had no choice but to use Dutch boats for transporting their grain. However, with the arrival of peace the cities began to boom. This era of economic prosperity and cultural fruition came to be known as the Golden Age.

The Dutch soon began to expand their horizons, and the merchant fleet known as the Dutch East India Company was formed in 1602. It quickly monopolised key shipping and trade routes east of Africa's Cape of Good Hope and west of the Strait of Magellan, making it the largest trading company of the 17th century. It became almost as powerful as a sovereign state, with the ability to raise its own armed forces and establish colonies.

Its sister, the Dutch West India Company, traded with Africa and the Americas and was at the very centre of the American slave trade. Seamen working for both companies discovered (in a very Western sense of the word) or conquered lands including Tasmania, New Zealand, Malaysia, Sri Lanka and Mauritius. English explorer Henry Hudson landed on the island

1555	**1566–68**	**1579**
In the first major assault on Dutch tolerance, Philip II cracks down on Protestants in favour of Catholics. Religious wars follow and Calvinists pillage Catholic churches, stripping them of their decor and wealth.	The Low Countries revolt against a lack of religious freedom and the repressive acts of Philip II of Spain, launching the Eighty Years' War. In Friesland the rebels win their first battle, which would be immortalised in the Dutch national anthem.	With scores of Dutch towns captured by Calvinist brigands, known as Watergeuzen (Sea Beggars), a Dutch republic made up of seven provinces is declared by Willem the Silent at the Union of Utrecht.

of Manhattan in 1609 as he searched for the Northwest Passage, and Dutch settlers named it New Amsterdam. (The Netherlands sponsored rousing celebrations of the 400th anniversary in New York City that were attended by scores of Dutch and all but ignored by blasé Manhattanites.)

Culturally, the United Provinces flourished in the Golden Age. The wealth of the merchant class supported numerous artists, including Jan Vermeer, Jan Steen, Frans Hals and Rembrandt (see p39). The sciences were not left out: Dutch physicist and astronomer Christiaan Huygens discovered Saturn's rings and invented the pendulum clock; celebrated philosopher Benedict de Spinoza wrote a brilliant thesis saying that the universe was identical to God; and Frenchman René Descartes, known for his philosophy 'I think, therefore I am', found intellectual freedom in the Netherlands and stayed for two decades.

The Union of Utrecht's promise of religious tolerance led to a surprising amount of religious diversity that was rare in Europe at the time. Calvinism was the official religion of the government, but various other Protestants, Jews and Catholics were allowed to practise their faith. However, in a legacy of the troubles with Spain, Catholics had to worship in private, which led to the creation of clandestine churches. Many of these unusual buildings have survived to the present day.

Politically, however, the young Dutch republic was at an all-time low. The House of Oranje-Nassau fought the republicans for control of the country; while the house wanted to centralise power with Prince van Oranje as *stadhouder* (chief magistrate), the republicans wanted the cities and provinces to run their own affairs. Prince Willem II won the dispute but died suddenly three months later, one week before his son was born. Dutch regional leaders exploited this power vacuum by abolishing the *stadhouder,* and authority was decentralised.

International conflict was never very far away. In 1652 the United Provinces went to war with their old friend England, mainly over the increasing strength of the Dutch merchant fleet. Both countries entered a hotchpotch of alliances with Spain, France and Sweden in an effort to gain the upper hand. During one round of treaties the Dutch agreed to give New Amsterdam to the English (who promptly renamed it New York) in return for Surinam in South America. In 1672 the French army marched into the Netherlands and, as the Dutch had devoted most of their resources to the navy, found little resistance on land. The country appealed to the House of Oranje, which appointed Willem III as general of the Dutch forces.

In a single stroke Willem improved relations with the English by marrying his cousin Mary, daughter of the English king James II. Perhaps sensing he was no longer welcome in England – his opponents feared that he would restore the Roman Catholic Church there – James fled to France, and Willem and Mary were named king and queen of England in 1689. Using his strong diplomatic skills, Willem created the Grand Alliance that joined England,

The Dutch *bought* (a concept foreign to North American tribes at the time) the island of Manhattan from the Lenape in 1626 for the equivalent of US$24 worth of beads.

1596	**1688**	**1700**
A Dutch trade expedition to Indonesia loses half its crew but brings back cargo that's sold for a profit. This leads to the formation of the Dutch East India Company and the colonisation of the archipelago.	Willem III of Orange repels the French with the help of Austria, Spain and Brandenburg (Prussia). Willem then invades England, where he and his wife, Mary Stuart, are proclaimed king and queen.	The effective end of the Golden Age as wars empty the Dutch treasury, floods become common and the ruling class becomes caught up in conspicuous consumption instead of creating wealth.

the United Provinces, Spain, Sweden and several German states to fight the expansionist ambitions of France's Louis XIV.

The Grand Alliance defeated the French several times. In 1697 Louis XIV agreed to give up most of the territory France had conquered. As if to drive the point home, the Dutch again joined the English to fight the French in the War of the Spanish Succession, ending with the Treaty of Utrecht in 1713.

Tulipomania: The Story of the World's Most Coveted Flower by Mike Dash is an engaging look at the bizarre bulb fever that swept the nation in the 17th century.

DUTCH DECLINE & FRENCH RULE

Financially weakened by the ongoing wars with France, the United Provinces began to spiral downwards. Its maritime fleet, left battered and bleeding from the wars, lost valuable trading routes to the British, while domestically the population was decreasing. The dykes were also in a sorry state – there was little money to repair them, and widespread floods swept across the country. Merchants were more likely to spend their profits on luxuries than on sensible investments in their businesses, which in turn contributed to the country's overall economic decline.

Politically, the United Provinces were as unstable as the dykes. A series of struggles between the House of Oranje and its democratic opponents led to a civil war in 1785; the dispute was settled three years later when the *stadhouders* agreed to limit their own powers. When the French revolutionary forces invaded in 1795, with the aid of those eager for constitutional reform in the United Provinces collapsed and became the Batavian Republic. It survived only until 1806, when Napoleon renamed it the Kingdom of Holland and installed his brother, Louis Bonaparte, as king.

The Dutch National Archive (www.nationaal archief.nl) has almost a thousand years of historical documents, maps, drawings and photos.

Louis proved to be not quite the kind of king Napoleon would have liked. He actually seemed to like his subjects and often favoured them over France; in 1810 Napoleon declared Louis the weakest link and bounced him out of office. With Napoleon's attention diverted in Russia, though, the supporters of the House of Oranje invited Prince Willem VI back. He landed at Scheveningen in 1813 and was named prince sovereign of the Netherlands; the following year he was crowned King Willem I, beginning a monarchy that continues to this day (opposite).

INDEPENDENT KINGDOM & WWI

With the defeat of Napoleon, Europe celebrated with the Congress of Vienna in 1815. It was here that the Kingdom of the Netherlands – the Netherlands in the north and Belgium in the south – was formed. However, the marriage was doomed from the start. The partners had little in common, including their dominant religions (Calvinist and Catholic), languages (Dutch and French) and favoured way of making money (trade and manufacturing). Matters weren't helped by Willem, who generally sided with his fellow northerners.

In 1830 the southern states revolted, and nine years later Willem was forced to let the south go. In a nice historical twist, Willem abdicated one

1795	1813–14	1830
French troops install the Batavian Republic, named after the Batavi tribe that rebelled against Roman rule. The fragmented United Provinces become a centralised state, with Amsterdam as its capital.	The French are overthrown, and Willem VI of Orange is crowned as Dutch king Willem I. The protestant north and Catholic south are joined as the United Kingdom of the Netherlands.	With help from the French the southern provinces secede to form the Kingdom of Belgium. The country is not formally recognised by the Dutch government until 1839.

THOSE 'DULL' DUTCH ROYALS

Not yet 200 years in power, the House of Orange has roots back to the 16th century. Unlike a certain royal family to the west across the Channel, the Dutch royals have proved to be of limited value to tabloid publishers or others hoping to profit from their exploits.

The most notable was Queen Wilhelmina, who took a page from Britain's Queen Victoria and approached her job as if she were a general. Although some faulted her for fleeing the Germans in WWII, she ended up winning praise for her stalwart support of her people. During the postwar years, the family were a mostly low-key and benign presence (they have no substantive power within the Dutch government) with the exception of Prince Bernhard, who was caught up in a bribery scandal in the 1970s with the US defence firm Lockheed.

The present queen Beatrix (born 1938) took the throne in 1980. The third female monarch in a row, she shows no sign of relinquishing power by abdicating to her son, Prince Willem-Alexander, suggesting he 'needs to spend time with his family'. In this case that is his wife, Princess Maxima, a former banker he met at a party in Spain. Although her Argentine roots raised a few eyebrows, Maxima has won praise for her work on immigrant issues and support of gay rights.

Royal gossip has been minimal (with the exception of a niece who accused the Queen Beatrix of drinking too much red wine) and the Dutch people seem to prefer this. Although the richest woman in the world with a US$5.5 billion fortune, Beatrix and her brood are seen as being modest. The one day most Dutch think of the House of Orange is on Koninginnedag (Queen's Day, 30 April) when they wear the national colour, and drink. The celebrations were scarred in 2009 when a deranged man unsuccessfully attacked the family in Apeldoorn, killing himself and seven others in the process.

---

year later so that he could marry – surprise! – a Belgian Catholic. It's not known if he ever spoke French at home.

His son, King Willem II, granted a new and more liberal constitution to the people of the Netherlands in 1848. This included a number of democratic ideals and even made the monarchy the servant of the elected government. This document remains the foundation of the Dutch government in the present day. Its role on the world stage long over, the Netherlands played only a small part in European affairs and concentrated on liberalism at home.

During WWI the Netherlands remained neutral, although its shipping industry was damaged by both the Allies and the Germans. It did, however, gain economic and financial ground by trading with both sides.

Following WWI the country, like some of its European counterparts, embarked on innovative social programs that targeted poverty, the rights of women and children, and education. Industrially, the coal mines of south Limburg were exploited to great success, Rotterdam became one of Europe's most important ports and the scheme to reclaim the Zuiderzee was launched in 1932.

The official website of the Dutch royal family, www.koninklijkhuis.nl, features mini-biographies and virtual tours of the palaces.

1865–76	1914–20	1932
A period of rapid economic and social change. The North Sea Canal is dug, the Dutch railway system expanded and socialist principles of government are established.	The Netherlands remains neutral in WWI while trading with both sides. Food shortages cripple the country, leading to strikes, unrest and growing support for the Dutch Communist Party.	After centuries of schemes, dyke-building and floods, the Zuiderzee reclamation begins, spurred on by a deadly 1916 storm surge. The completion of the mammoth Afsluitdijk begins the land-reclamation process.

WWII

The Dutch tried to remain neutral during WWII, but in May 1940 the Germans invaded anyway. The advancing Nazis levelled much of Rotterdam in a raid designed to force the Dutch to surrender. They obliged. The War and Resistance Museum in Rotterdam (Oorlogs Verzets Museum, p208) documents the attack and surrender.

DUTCH JEWS

The tale of Jews in Europe is often one of repression, persecution and downright hatred. In the Netherlands, it is more a tale of acceptance and prosperity, until the coming of the Nazis.

Amsterdam is the focus of Jewish history in the Netherlands, and Jews played a key role in the city's development over the centuries. The first documented evidence of Jewish presence in the city dates back to the 12th century, but numbers began to swell with the expulsion of Sephardic Jews from Spain and Portugal in the 1580s.

As was the case in much of Europe, guilds barred the newcomers from most trades. Some of the Sephardim were diamond cutters, however, for whom there was no guild. Others introduced printing and tobacco processing or worked as street retailers, bankers and doctors. The majority eked out a living as labourers and small-time traders on the margins of society. Still, they weren't confined to a ghetto and, with some restrictions, could buy property and exercise their religion – freedoms unheard of elsewhere in Europe.

The 17th century saw another influx of Jewish refugees, this time Ashkenazim fleeing pogroms in Central and Eastern Europe. The two groups didn't always get on well and separate synagogues were established, helping Amsterdam to become one of Europe's major Jewish centres.

The guilds and all restrictions on Jews were abolished during the French occupation, and the Jewish community thrived in the 19th century. Poverty was still considerable, but the economic, social and political emancipation of the Jews helped their middle class move up in society.

All this came to an end with the German occupation of the Netherlands. The Nazis brought about the almost complete annihilation of the Dutch Jewish community. Before WWII the Netherlands counted 140,000 Jews, of whom about two-thirds lived in Amsterdam. Fewer than 25,000 survived the war, and Amsterdam's Jewish quarter was left a ghost town. Many homes stood derelict until their demolition in the 1970s, and only a handful of synagogues throughout the country are once again operating as houses of worship.

Estimates put the current Jewish population of the Netherlands at between 41,000 and 45,000, almost half living in Amsterdam.

Jewish history is recounted at several museums across the country, including the following:

- Anne Frank Huis in Amsterdam (p102), a must-see for visitors.
- Joods Historisch Museum in Amsterdam (p100), which covers the sweep of the Dutch Jewish experience.
- Kamp Westerbork in the east near Groningen (p248), where most Dutch Jews were held during WWII before being sent to German death camps.

1940	1944–45	1958
Germany invades the Netherlands. Rotterdam is destroyed by the Luftwaffe, but Amsterdam suffers only minor damage before capitulating. Queen Wilhemina sets up a Dutch exile government in London.	The Allies liberate the southern Netherlands, but the north and west of the country are cut off from supplies. The British Operation Market Garden fails and thousands of Dutch perish in the bitter 'Winter of Hunger'.	The Delta project is launched following the great floods of Zeeland in 1953.

TROPICAL NETHERLANDS

The Kingdom of the Netherlands has shrunk even more with the end of the Netherlands Antilles. Really nothing more than a grab-bag of Dutch holdings in the Caribbean, islanders always saw themselves as residents of their island first. Aruba flew the coop first, in 1986, and never looked back. It is an independent country within the Netherlands, which effectively means it's autonomous but saves a lot of money on operating embassies, having its own military and the like. The other five island-nations within the Netherlands Antilles began holding votes and talks about their future in 2005. Curaçao and Sint Maarten are going the route of Aruba. Bonaire, Saba and St Eustatius are staying much closer to the Netherlands and will effectively be municipalities within the nation, nice warm ones popular with Dutch tourists at that.

Queen Wilhelmina issued a proclamation of 'flaming protest' to the nation and escaped with her family to England. The plucky monarch, who had been key in maintaining Dutch neutrality in WWI, now found herself in a much different situation and made encouraging broadcasts to her subjects back home via the BBC and Radio Orange. The Germans put Dutch industry and farms to work for war purposes and there was much deprivation. Dutch resistance was primarily passive and only gained any kind of momentum when thousands of Dutch men were taken to Germany and forced to work in Nazi factories. A far worse fate awaited the country's Jews (opposite).

The heir to the Dutch throne, Crown Prince Willem-Alexander, and his wife Princess Maxima have three young daughters: Catharina-Amalia, Alexia and Ariane.

The 'Winter of Hunger' of 1944–45 was a desperate time in the Netherlands. The British-led Operation Market Garden (p264) had been a huge disaster and the Allies abandoned all efforts to liberate the Dutch. The Germans stripped the country of much of its food and wealth, and mass starvation ensued. Many people were reduced to eating tulip bulbs for their daily subsistence. Canadian troops finally liberated the country in May 1945.

POSTWAR RECONSTRUCTION

The Netherlands faced major concerns in the postwar years both at home and abroad. Domestically, it had to restore its money-making businesses while rebuilding its battered infrastructure, which it did very well; trade took off once again, new wealth followed the discovery of large natural gas fields in the North Sea off the Dutch coast, and Dutch farmers became some of the most productive in Europe.

The Dutch were still using their army to hold onto revolutionary Indonesia in 1948. But the US and other countries threatened to withhold postwar aid and the Dutch quit the following year.

Overseas, the colonies began to clamour for independence. The Dutch East Indies declared itself independent in 1945, and after four years of bitter fighting and negotiations the independence of Indonesia was recognised at the end of 1949. Surinam also became independent in 1975. In the Caribbean, the Netherlands Antilles disbanded but none of the islands severed ties completely (above).

1960s	1975	1980
Social upheaval sweeps the Netherlands leading to the creation of the Provos, a provocative underground countercultural movement.	The Netherlands' drugs laws distinguish soft from hard drugs; possession of small amounts of marijuana is decriminalised. Amsterdam's Nieuwmarkt district becomes a battleground for squatters and police over the construction of the metro.	The coronation of Queen Beatrix is disrupted by a smoke bomb and riot on the Dam. The term 'proletarian shopping' (ie looting) enters the national lexicon.

THE PROVOCATIVE PROVOS

The 1960s were a breeding ground for discontent and anti-establishment activity, and in the Netherlands this underground movement led to the formation of the Provos. This small group of anarchic individuals staged street 'happenings' or creative, playful provocations (hence the name) around the Lieverdje (Little Darling) on Amsterdam's Spui (p85).

In 1962 an Amsterdam window cleaner and self-professed sorcerer, Robert Jasper Grootveld, began to deface cigarette billboards with a huge letter 'K' for *kanker* (cancer) to expose the role of advertising in addictive consumerism. Dressed as a medicine man, he held get-togethers in his garage and chanted mantras against cigarette smoking (but under the influence of pot).

This attracted yet more bizarre characters. Poet 'Johnny the Selfkicker' bombarded his audience with frenzied, stream-of-consciousness recitals. Bart Huges drilled a hole in his forehead – a so-called 'third eye' – to relieve pressure on the brain and expand his consciousness.

The group gained international notoriety in March 1966 with its protests at the marriage of Princess (now Queen) Beatrix to German Claus von Amsberg. Protestors jeered the wedding couple as their procession rolled through Amsterdam, and bystanders chanted 'bring my bicycle back' – a reference to the many bikes commandeered by the retreating German soldiers in 1945. This was broadcast live to the world.

In the same year the Provos gained enough support to win a seat on Amsterdam's city council. The group began developing 'White Plans', pro-environment schemes including the famous White Bicycle Plan to ease traffic congestion with a fleet of free white bicycles – they were soon stolen. The movement dissolved in the 1970s, but it left a lasting legacy: the squatters' movement, which encouraged the poor to occupy uninhabited buildings, in turn forced the government to adopt measures to help underprivileged tenants.

The same social upheavals that swept the world in the 1960s were also felt in the Netherlands. Students, labour groups, hippies and more took to the streets in protest. Among the more colourful were a group that came to be known as the Provos (above). A huge squatters' movement sprung up in Amsterdam, and homeless groups took over empty buildings – many of which had once belonged to Jews – and refused to leave.

Tolerance towards drug use and homosexuals also emerged at the time. The country's drug policy grew out of practical considerations, when a flood of young people populated Amsterdam and made the policing of drug laws impracticable (see p289 for the current drug policy). Official government policy became supportive of homosexuals who, since 2001, may legally marry.

Queen Beatrix ascended the throne in 1980 after her mother, Juliana, abdicated (see the boxed text, p29, for more on the royal family).

All governments since 1945 have been coalitions, with parties mainly differing over economic policies. However, coalitions shift constantly based on the political climate, and in recent years there have been winds of change. Tension between different political colours and creeds had never been a problem

John Lennon and Yoko Ono took to bed at the Amsterdam Hilton for a week in 1969 and invited the world's press to join them. Rather than salacious entertainment, however, they offered bromides about world peace.

2001	2002	2003
Same-sex marriage is legalised in the Netherlands, the first country in the world to do so. In the next few years Belgium, Spain, Canada and South Africa follow suit.	Leading politician Pim Fortuyn, a hardliner on immigration and integration, is assassinated. The ruling Dutch parties shift to the right after suffering major losses in the national election.	Her Royal Highness Catharina-Amalia Beatrix Carmen Victoria, second in line to the throne, is born.

THE LEGACY OF THEO & PIM

If the 2004 assassination of Theo van Gogh rocked the Netherlands, it was the assassination of Pim Fortuyn two years earlier that gave the initial push.

The political career of the charismatic Fortuyn (pronounced fore-town) lasted a mere five months, yet his impact on the Netherlands has proved indelible. His campaign for parliament in 2002 is best remembered for his speeches on immigration: particularly that the Netherlands was 'full' and that immigrants should not be allowed to stay without learning the language or integrating. Thousands of white, low-income earners in Fortuyn's home base of Rotterdam and other cities rallied round the gay, dandyish former university professor. Fortuyn was feted as the next prime minister, even as his opponents accused him of pursuing right-wing, racist policies.

Just days before the general election in May 2002, Fortuyn was assassinated by an animal-rights activist in Hilversum, some 20km from Amsterdam. Riots erupted outside parliament, and for a brief instant the threat of anarchy hung in the air. Fortuyn's political party, the Lijst Pim Fortuyn (LPF), had a number of members elected to parliament and was included in the next coalition, but without the dynamic Fortuyn it sputtered in search of a leader. In the 2003 election, voters all but deserted the LPF, which voted itself out of existence in 2007.

Enter Theo van Gogh, a filmmaker and provocateur whose 11-minute documentary *Submission Part 1* featured four short stories about Koranic verses that could be interpreted as justifying violence against women. The film was a collaboration with Ayaan Hirsi Ali, a Muslim-born woman who had emigrated from Somalia to escape an arranged marriage and eventually became a member of parliament. Hirsi Ali had become an outspoken critic of Islamic law and declared herself an atheist.

The documentary aired on Dutch TV in 2004, and Van Gogh was shot and his throat slashed as he was cycling down an Amsterdam street in rush hour. A letter threatening the nation, politicians, and Hirsi Ali in particular, was impaled on a knife stuck in Van Gogh's chest. Hirsi Ali went into hiding. The killing was all the more shocking to locals because the 27-year-old killer, while of Moroccan descent, was born and raised in Amsterdam. He proclaimed that he was acting in defence of Islam and would do the same thing again if given the chance, and he was sentenced to life imprisonment (one of only a few dozen life sentences in the Netherlands since WWII). The Dutch government continues to spend more than €3 million per year protecting Hirsi Ali from threats.

---

in the Netherlands, until the murders of Theo van Gogh and Pim Fortuyn stirred emotions and struck fear into the hearts of some (see above).

The leading political parties in the Netherlands responded with a shift to the right. In 2006 the government passed a controversial immigration law requiring newcomers to have competency in Dutch language and culture before they could get a residency permit (see p37). Although anti-immigrant parties captured 6% of the vote in elections held late that year, the Socialists scored the biggest gains and the Christian Democratic Union (CDA) continued its usual role, forming a broad coalition government.

Meanwhile Den Haag stays in the news as war-crimes trials move forward for people such as Radovan Karadzic in the city's various international courts.

The largest political party in the Netherlands is the Christian Democratic Union (CDA). Nominally centre-right, it has a historic streak of pragmatism that has seen it often moderate its views to reflect popular opinion.

2004

Activist filmmaker Theo van Gogh, a critic of Islam, is assassinated in Amsterdam, sparking intense debate over the limits of Dutch multiculturalism and the need for immigrants to adopt Dutch values.

2005

The Dutch – usually fairly enthusiastic supporters of the EU – resoundingly reject the EU constitution in a June referendum.

2008

Start of the snuff out. Amsterdam announces plans to clean up the Red Light District and close coffeeshops, citing gang criminality. Other cities follow suit and the 'smart shops' selling mushrooms are closed.

The Culture

THE NATIONAL PSYCHE

Make no mistake, the Dutch have a flair for social engineering. The same nation that built its living rooms on a drained seabed also invented *verzuiling* (pillarisation), a social order in which each religion and political persuasion achieved the right to do its own thing, with its own institutions. This meant not only more churches, but also separate radio stations, newspapers, unions, political parties, sport clubs and so on. The idea got a bit out of hand with pillarised bakeries, but it did promote social harmony by giving everyone a voice.

Although the pillars are less distinct today, they left a legacy of tolerance. In fact tolerance is as Dutch as herring and ice skating, and what's more it's good for business, whether it be tourism or trade. The same applies to *gezelligheid* (conviviality, see opposite), that easy intimacy that comes out at the drop of a hat. Where other nations struggle to get the words out, the Dutch are irrepressibly voluble. Sit alone in a pub and you'll soon have a few merry friends.

The Dutch also have a moralistic streak (coming from the Calvinists) and a tendency to wag the finger in disapproval. The Dutch may seem stunningly blunt, but the impulse comes from the desire to be direct and honest.

On sex and drugs, the ever-practical Dutch argue that vice is not going to go away, so you might as well control it. Sex is discussed openly (newspaper coverage of breast enhancement or genital piercing with full-on photos, for example). But promiscuity is the last thing on Dutch minds. It is perhaps revealing that only about 5% of customers frequenting the red light district are Dutch (traditionally, the biggest group has been the Brits).

By the same token, marijuana and hashish are legal. You want to get high? Go ahead. Yet if you think everyone here gets stoned, you're wrong. Only a fraction of the population smokes dope, fewer people than in Britain, the USA and France, where drug policies are much stricter. On the other hand, the 'harder' drugs such as heroin, LSD, cocaine and ecstasy are outlawed, and dealers are prosecuted.

The Dutch have a great love of detail. Statistics on the most trivial subjects make the paper (eg the number of pigeons on the Dam this year, incidence of rubbish being put out early), and somewhere down the line this feeds mountains of bureaucracy.

Last but not least, the Dutch are famously thrifty with their money – and they often don't know what to think of this. In one breath they might joke about how copper wire was invented by two Dutchmen fighting over a penny, and in the next, tell you that they don't like being called cheap.

LIFESTYLE

Many Dutch live independent, busy lives, divided into strict schedules. Notice is usually required for everything, including visits to your mother, and it's not done to just 'pop round' anywhere. Socialising is done mainly in the home, through clubs and in circles of old friends, which can make it tough for foreigners to 'break in' at first. However, if you're invited to join a family party, you've crossed a major threshold – the Dutch don't invite just *anybody* into their homes, and chances are you've made a friend for life. Birthdays are celebrated in a big way, with oodles of cake and cries of well-wishing loud enough to wake the dead.

Most Dutch families are small, with two or three children. Rents are high, so Junior might live with his family well into his 20s or share an apartment.

The site www.wooden shoes.nl is devoted to a foundation of Dutch culture, *klompen* (clogs).

Arguably, no household item represents Dutch thrift better than the popular *flessenlikker* (bottle-scraper). This miracle tool has a disk on the business end and can scrape the last elusive smears from a mayonnaise jar or salad-dressing bottle.

GEZELLIGHEID

Variously translated as snug, friendly, cosy, informal, companionable and convivial, *gezelligheid* is a particular trait of the Dutch, and it's best experienced rather than explained. To do so, grab a table with friends in the sun outside a cafe, hang out for a few hours (preferably the entire day), and you'll soon understand the concept.

However, Dutch housing policies have made it easier in recent years to get a mortgage.

On average the Dutch are fairly well off – they may not flaunt it, but they now earn more per capita than the Germans (€27,519 versus €24,123). Consumer spending is healthy, especially for travel to warm climates. New cars abound and after a 2009 economic stimulus scheme purchased old clunkers, few people chug around in old bombs.

Gays and lesbians enjoy considerable freedom and respect among people of all ages. Discrimination on the basis of sexual orientation is not only illegal, but morally unacceptable; the police advertise in the gay media for applicants; the armed forces admit homosexuals on an equal footing. Most significantly, in 2001 the Netherlands became the first country in the world to legalise same-sex marriages, although this is a privilege reserved for local couples.

ECONOMY

The Netherlands has an extraordinarily strong economy for its size. The world's largest corporation, Royal Dutch Shell, is headquartered in Den Haag. It's 2008 revenues of US$458 billion would place it at No 24 on the World Bank list of nations ranked by annual gross domestic product (GDP), just below Saudi Arabia and ahead of Norway (the Netherlands is at No 16).

The country is a leader in service industries such as banking and electronics (Philips) and has a highly developed horticultural industry dealing in bulbs and cut flowers. Agriculture plays an important role, particularly dairy farming and glasshouse fruits and vegetables. Rotterdam harbour handles the largest shipping tonnage in Europe, a vital facility in a country that provides more than one-third of the continent's shipping and trucking. Large supplies of natural gas are tapped and refined on the northeastern coasts.

Dutch business is largely dependent on exports and has been caught in the worldwide recession. But while the downturn had its bite, Dutch unemployment was at 6.8% when the US and much of Europe were in double digits.

POPULATION

The need to love thy neighbour is especially strong in the Netherlands, where the population density is the highest in Europe (396 per square kilometre). Nearly half of the country's 16.5 million residents live in the western hoop around Amsterdam, Den Haag and Rotterdam; the provinces of Drenthe, Overijssel and Zeeland in the southwest are sparsely settled, in Dutch terms

DOS & DON'TS

Do give a firm handshake or triple cheek kiss.

Do take a number at the post office counter.

Do show up five to 15 minutes late on social occasions.

Do dress casually unless it's an overtly formal affair.

Do say *'goedendag'* when you enter a shop.

Don't smoke dope or drink on the streets.

Don't be late for official appointments.

Don't ask about a person's salary.

Don't forget someone's birthday.

HEAD & SHOULDERS ABOVE THE REST

The Dutch are the tallest people in the world, averaging 1.81m (5ft, 11in) for men and 1.68m (5ft, 6in) for women, according to Statistics Netherlands. Copious intake of milk proteins, smaller families and superior prenatal care are cited as likely causes, but researchers also suspect there is some magic fertiliser in the Dutch gene pool. Whatever the reason, the Dutch keep growing, as do their doorways. Today, the minimum required height for doors in new homes and businesses is 2.315m (7ft, 6in).

at least. Since 2002, people living in towns and cities outnumber those living in rural areas.

More than 80% of the population are of Dutch stock; the rest is mainly made up of people from the former colonies of Indonesia, Surinam and the Netherlands Antilles, plus more recent arrivals from Turkey, Morocco and countries throughout Africa.

SPORT

The Netherlands is one sport-happy country. About two-thirds of all Dutch engage in some form of sporty activity, and the average person now spends 20 minutes more a week getting sweaty than in the 1970s. Sport is organised to a fault: about five million people belong to nearly 30,000 clubs and associations in the Netherlands.

Soccer, cycling and skating are the favourites, but Dutch sporting aptitude was shown to be wide-ranging in 2009 when the national baseball and cricket teams scored surprise victories in international competitions.

Football (Soccer)

Football is the Dutch national game, and they're pretty good at it. The national football team competes in virtually every World Cup (2006 saw them knocked out in a steamy match against Portugal) and Euro Cup (in 2008 they lost to Russia in the quarter finals). 'Local' teams such as Ajax, Feyenoord and PSV enjoy international renown. The country has produced world-class players, such as Ruud Gullit, Dennis Bergkamp and the legendary Johan Cruyff. The unique Dutch approach to the game – known as Total Football (in which spatial tactics are analysed and carried out with meticulous precision) – fascinated viewers at its peak in the 1970s.

Passion for football runs so high it's almost scary. The national football association counts a million members, and every weekend professional and amateur teams hit pitches across the country. Many pro clubs play in modern, high-tech stadiums, such as Amsterdam ArenA (p132), assisted by a modern, high-tech police force to counteract hooligans.

Cycling

To say the Dutch are avid cyclists is like saying the English don't mind football. In sporting terms there's extensive coverage of races in the media, and you'll see uniformed teams whiz by on practice runs in remote quarters. Joop Zoetemelk pedalled to victory in the 1980 Tour de France after finishing second six times. The biggest Dutch wheel-off is the Amstel Gold Race around hilly Limburg in late April, while the five-day Tour de Nederland, which speeds through the country at the end of August, attracts thousands of fans.

Leontien van Moorsel is one of the best Dutch athletes ever. She won scores of cycling championships in the 1990s. At the 2000 and 2004 Olympics she won a combined total of four golds, one silver and one bronze.

Skating

Ice skating is as Dutch as *kroketten* (croquettes; p47), and thousands of people hit the ice when the country's lakes and ditches freeze over. When the lakes aren't frozen, the Netherlands has dozens of ice rinks with Olympic-sized tracks and areas for hockey and figure skating. The most famous amateur event is Friesland's 220km-long Elfstedentocht (p234).

The Dutch generally perform well in speed skating at the Winter Olympics; in 2006 all of its nine medals (three of which were gold) were won on the ice. International competitions are held at the Thialf indoor ice stadium in Heerenveen, Friesland.

Traditional Dutch toilets come with a shelf where deposited goods sit until swept away by a flush of water. The reason is tied to health and the supposed benefit of pondering what comes out as carefully as what goes in. Not, as some wags say, because the Dutch can't bear to see anything underwater.

For a virtual peek into the world of the Netherlands' most famous football team, Ajax, check out www.ajax.nl.

Brilliant Orange: the Neurotic Genius of Dutch Football by David Winner has interviews with players about their personal experiences, and ties in Dutch architecture, social structure, sense of humour and even Calvinist history in a highly readable attempt to explain the Dutch psyche.

Swimming

Swimming is the most popular sport when it comes to the raw number of practitioners, edging out even football and cycling. One-third of all Dutch swim in the pools, lakes or sea, and fancy aquatic complexes have sprung up in many cities to meet demand.

Legendary Dutch swimmer Inge de Bruin won a total of eight medals at the 2000 and 2004 Olympics. In 2008 the Dutch women's water polo team sunk all competition and took the gold.

Tennis

Tennis has been incredibly popular since the long-retired Richard Krajicek fell to his knees after clinching the 1996 Wimbledon final. The national tennis club is the country's second largest sporting club after football, and many people book time on courts in all-weather sports halls.

Burgundian duke Philip the Good most likely invented the tennis racquet in Holland in around 1500.

MULTICULTURALISM

The Netherlands has a long history of tolerance towards immigration and a reputation for welcoming immigrants with open arms. The largest wave of immigration occurred in the 1960s, when the government recruited migrant workers from Turkey and Morocco to bridge a labour gap. In the mid-1970s, the granting of independence to the Dutch colony of Surinam in South America saw an influx of Surinamese.

COFFEESHOPS

Ground zero for many a visitor, the humble *koffieshop* is an establishment unique to the Netherlands: a place to buy cannabis and, to a lesser extent, actual coffee.

Every major town (and a few minor ones) has a handful of coffeeshops, and the touristy joints are easy to spot: just look for the telling hemp leaves, Rastafarian colours (red, yellow and green) or *X-Files* alien adorning the facade. However, the better, more comfortable – and far more appealing – shops can be hard to differentiate from a regular *koffiehuis* (espresso bar or sandwich shop) or cafe, and usually cater to a discerning local crowd. Very few serve alcohol, which is a blessing in disguise as it's not always wise to mix the two drugs.

The range of marijuana on sale can be quite daunting, so it's best to get the advice of someone behind the bar. Be honest – if you're a novice, don't be afraid to 'fess up; it's better to start with something light (like Thai) than end up getting ill after smoking some Skunk or White Zombie. Prerolled joints are available for anything between €2 and €5, and these are handy for sampling various types. Most people buy small bags of dope, though, which go for around €4 to €12 (the better the quality, the less the bag will contain). Price and quality are generally OK – you won't get ripped off in a coffeeshop.

Space cakes and cookies (and even chocolate!) are sold in a rather low-key fashion, mainly because of their potency and the time it takes for them to kick in; some take an hour to work, in which time you've probably consumed a couple more because you're not feeling anything… Ask the staff how much you should take and heed their advice. If you do it right, you'll have a very gentle, pleasant ride for up to six hours.

Most cannabis products used to be imported, but these days the country has top-notch home produce, so-called *nederwiet* (*nay*-der-weet), developed by diligent horticulturists and grown in greenhouses with up to five harvests a year. Even the police admit it's a superior product, especially the potent Superskunk with up to 13% of the active substance THC (Nigerian grass has 5% and Colombian 7%). The value of the pot crop is put at €2 billion annually and much of it is thought to be controlled by gangs. Concerns over criminality are causing the Dutch to rethink their tolerant attitudes to coffeeshops and many of the 700 licenced outlets are under threat of closure.

For more information legal matters, plus how much you can buy and at what age you can smoke, see p289.

DOUBLE DUTCH

For better or for worse, the Dutch have maintained close ties with the English for centuries, and this intimate relationship has led to a menagerie of 'Dutch' catchphrases in the English language. Here are some of the more well known:

- Double Dutch – nonsense or complete gibberish; a jump-rope game using two skipping ropes. 'Going double Dutch' refers to using two types of contraceptive at the same time.

- Dutch courage – strength or confidence gained from drinking alcohol.

- Dutch oven – large, thick-walled cooking pot with a tight-fitting lid; the act of farting in bed, then trapping your partner – and the stench – under the covers.

- Dutch uncle – a person who sternly gives (often benevolent) advice.

- Dutch wife – pillow or frame used for resting the legs on in bed; a prostitute or sex doll.

- Going Dutch – splitting the bill at a restaurant. Also known as Dutch date or Dutch treat.

- Pass the dutchie – not a phrase as such, but the title of a top-10 hit by Musical Youth in 1982. 'Dutchie' refers to an aluminium cooking pot supposedly manufactured in the Netherlands and used throughout the West Indies.

In the past few years, however, the country's loose immigration policy has been called into question. Politically, there has been a significant swing to the right and consequently a move towards shutting the door on immigration. The assassinations of Pim Fortuyn and Theo van Gogh (see the boxed text, p33) caused tensions to rise between the Dutch and Muslim immigrants, and made many Dutch consider whether immigrants were doing enough to learn the traditions of their newly adopted country.

In recent years concern that immigrant communities are not becoming 'Dutch' has only increased and there is now a government Ministry of Integration. Strongly urging people to take classes in the Dutch language and culture, where concepts such as tolerance are emphasised, is official policy. And some municipalities have gone further, suggesting that social benefits will be reduced for immigrants who don't take the classes.

How the paradoxical concept of forcing people to learn to be tolerant will play out remains to be seen.

MEDIA

The Dutch value freedom of expression, and the media have an independent, pluralistic character that is guaranteed by the constitution. Newspapers, TV and radio are free to decide on the nature and content of their programs.

The Netherlands first set up a public broadcasting system in the 1920s. In an approach that's all Dutch, the airwaves are divided up in an attempt to give everyone a say, and broadcasts are still linked to social or religious groups (air time is allocated in line with their membership numbers). The state-owned networks are Ned 1, Ned 2 and Ned 3, who battle it out with commercial channels such as NET5 and the RTL empire.

The Radio Netherlands website, www.radio netherlands.nl, has articles in English on topical social issues.

Amsterdam's *De Telegraaf* is the country's biggest-selling newspaper and the closest thing to a tabloid you'll find. The *NRC Handelsblad* is the intellectual paper, while readers of the *Volkskrant* are decidedly left of centre. *Het Parool* is Amsterdam's afternoon newspaper. *Metro*, *Spits* and *De Per* are free papers distributed from train-station stands.

RELIGION

For centuries, religious preference was split between the two heavyweights of Western society, Catholicism and Protestantism, and if you were Dutch you were one or the other. Today, 43% of the population over the age of 18 claims to have no religious affiliation, and the number of former churches that house offices, art galleries and shops is an obvious sign of today's attitude to religion.

The old faith may have suffered a heavy blow in recent decades, but it's far from dead: 27% of the population follows Catholicism, 27% Protestantism. Vestiges exist of a religious border between Protestants and Catholics; the area north of a line running roughly from the province of Zeeland in the southwest to the province of Drenthe is home to the majority of Protestants, while anywhere to the south is predominantly Catholic.

The church has little or no influence on societal matters such as same-sex marriage, euthanasia and prescription of cannabis for medical purposes, all of which are legal in the Netherlands.

The latest religion to have any great impact on Dutch society is Islam. Today, approximately 5.8% of the population classes itself as Muslim and the number is steadily increasing, especially in multicultural Rotterdam.

WOMEN IN THE NETHERLANDS

Dutch women attained the right to vote in 1919, and by the 1970s abortion on demand was paid for by the national health service. Dutch women are a remarkably confident lot; on a social level, equality is taken for granted and women are almost as likely as men to initiate contact with the opposite sex. It's still a different story in the workplace – fewer women than men are employed full time, and fewer still hold positions in senior management. About 68% of Dutch women work part time, less than 25 hours a week.

ARTS

The arts flourished in the Netherlands long before Rembrandt put brush to canvas. The country takes great pride in its world-class museums, the variety of classical and innovative music, and the many theatre productions staged every season. It always seems as though there's room for another arts festival to spring into being, and the variety boggles the mind.

Painting
THE EARLY DAYS

The Netherlands has spawned a realm of famous painters, starting with Jan van Eyck (1385–1441), who is generally regarded as the founder of the Flemish School and credited with perfecting the technique of oil painting. Hot on his heels was the wonderfully named Hieronymous Bosch (1415–1516), whose 15th-century religious works are as fearful as they are fascinating, and are charged with drama, distorted creatures and agonised victims. Pieter Brueghel the Elder (1525–69) is another highly acclaimed painter from Holland's early generation, and his allegorical scenes of Flemish landscapes and peasant life are instantly recognisable even by those with a minimal interest in art.

Easily the greatest of the 17th-century Dutch painters was Rembrandt (see the boxed text, p40), a man of unearthly talent whose plays of light and shadow created shimmering religious scenes. Another great of the era was Frans Hals (1581–1666), who devoted himself to portraits; his expressive paintings can be seen in the Rijksmuseum (p105) in Amsterdam and the Frans Hals Museum (p141) in Haarlem.

A discussion of 17th-century art would not be complete without a mention of Johannes Vermeer (1632–75) of Delft. He was the master of genre painting, such as *View of Delft* and historical and biblical scenes, and he recently gained celluloid fame through *Girl with a Pearl Earring*, a dramatised account of the

Orange, as the national colour, has ties to the Dutch monarchy. The House of Orange (p29) traces its legacy back to Willem of Orange, leader of the resistance against the Spanish in the 16th century.

REMBRANDT

Painting is the grandchild of nature. It is related to God.

Rembrandt van Rijn

The son of a miller, Rembrandt van Rijn (1606–69) was the greatest and most versatile of all 17th-century artists. In some respects Rembrandt was centuries ahead of his time, as shown by the emotive brushwork of his later works.

Rembrandt grew up in Leiden and was a student at the Latin School (p185), where he became good at chiaroscuro, the technique of creating depth through light and darkness. In 1631 he moved to Amsterdam to run a painting studio, where he and his staff churned out scores of profitable portraits, such as *Anatomy Lesson of Dr Tulp*. The studio work was also good for his personal life; he married the studio owner's niece, Saskia van Uylenburgh.

After Rembrandt fell out with his boss he bought the house next door, now the Museum het Rembrandthuis (p99). Here he set up his own studio, employing staff in a warehouse in Amsterdam's Jordaan to cope with the demand for 'Rembrandts'. His paintings became all the rage and the studio became the largest in the country, despite his gruff manners and open agnosticism.

As one of the city's main art collectors, Rembrandt often sketched and painted for himself. Amsterdam's Jewish residents acted as models for dramatic biblical scenes.

Business went downhill after Saskia died in 1642. Rembrandt's innovative group portrait, *Nightwatch*, may have won over the art critics – but his subjects had all paid good money and some were unhappy to appear in the background. The artist's love affairs and lavish lifestyle marred his reputation, and he eventually went bankrupt. His house and art collection were sold and, with the debtors breathing down his neck, Rembrandt took a modest abode on the Jordaan's Rozengracht.

Rembrandt ended life a broken man (see the achingly sad self-portrait at Den Haag's Mauritshuis, p191) and passed away a year after the death of his son Titus, largely forgotten by the society he once served. Four centuries later, his status could not be more different. His name is synonymous with 'masterpiece' and any museum guard will tell you that the most common question they hear is 'where are the Rembrandts?'

To see a swathe of Rembrandt's work, visit the Rijksmuseum in Amsterdam, which has kept them on temporary display while the rest of the museum is rebuilt – they wouldn't dare put them away.

---

painting of his famous work of the same name, made into a movie based on Tracy Chevalier's 1999 novel. Both paintings are on display at the Mauritshuis (p191).

Jan Steen (1626–79) skilfully captured the domestic chaos of ordinary Dutch life. Lively and bold, his paintings are not only artistically eye-catching but also fun; *The Merry Family,* on display at the Rijksmuseum, is a classic example, showing adults enjoying themselves around the dinner table, blissfully unaware of the children pouring themselves a drink in the foreground.

If you were to prompt passers-by to name the first painter to pop into their head, a large majority would probably blurt out Vincent van Gogh. Although he spent much of his life in Belgium and France, he is very much claimed by the Dutch as one of their own (for more, see the boxed text, opposite).

DE STIJL & BEYOND

An Amersfoort-born painter named Piet Mondriaan (1872–1944) changed the direction of 20th-century art when he introduced the cubist De Stijl movement in 1917. De Stijl aimed to harmonise all the arts by returning artistic expression to its essence, and the artist – who changed the spelling of his name to Mondrian after moving to Paris in 1910 – did this by reducing shapes to horizontal and vertical lines. His paintings came to consist of bold rectangular patterns using only the three primary colours (red, yellow and blue), a style known as neoplasticism. Mondrian's moving ode to the USA entitled *Victory Boogie Woogie* is considered the flagship work of the genre. When open, Amsterdam's Stedelijk Museum (p106) has other examples in its collection, such as *Composition with Red, Black, Blue, Yellow and Grey*. The movement influenced a generation of sculptors and designers such as Gerrit Rietveld, who planned the Van Gogh Museum and other buildings along De Stijl lines.

The last century also saw the perplexing designs of Maurits Cornelis (MC) Escher (1902–72), whose impossible images continue to fascinate to this day. A waterfall feeds itself, people go up and down a staircase that ends where it starts, a pair of hands draw each other. He was also a master of organic tile patterns that feed into one another while subtly changing the picture into something else; his work can be viewed at the Escher in het Paleis (p193) in Den Haag when it reopens.

After WWII, artists rebelled against artistic conventions and vented their rage in abstract expressionism. Karel Appel (1921–2006) and Constant (1920–2005) drew on styles pioneered by other European artists, exploiting bright colours to produce works that leapt off the canvas. In Paris they met up with Danish Asger Jorn (1914–73) and the Belgian Corneille (1922–), and together these artists formed the CoBrA group (Copenhagen, Brussels and Amsterdam). Much of their work can be seen at the CoBrA Museum (p110).

Contemporary Dutch artists are usually well represented at international events. Look out for the installations of Jan Dibbets (1941–) and Ger van Elk (1941–), who mix photography, painting and sculpture, as well as the wry graphic illustrations of Marthe Röling (1939–). Among the younger generation, the artist duo Liet Heringa (1966–) and Maarten Van Kalsbeek (1962–) are known for their moody, free-form sculptures, Michael Raedecker (1963–) for his dreamy, radiant still lifes and Roger Braun (1972–) for industrial realism.

VINCENT VAN GOGH

Without a doubt the greatest 19th-century Dutch painter was Vincent van Gogh (1853–90). His striking use of colour, coarse brushwork and layered contours put him in a league all his own yet, astonishingly, he was self-taught and his painting career lasted less than 10 years, from 1881 to 1890. In this time he produced a staggering 900 paintings and 1100 drawings.

Born in Zundert near the Belgian border, the young Van Gogh had a hard time settling into life, but by 1880 he had found his true calling and threw himself into painting with abandon.

He spent much of his early career in the Low Countries, where he produced dark, heavy paintings, such as his celebrated *Potato Eaters* (1885). In the mid-1800s he moved to Paris to live with his brother Theo, a constant support for the troubled artist. It was here that his contact with Impressionists, such as Gauguin, transformed the Dutchman's painting into blazing depictions of flowers, portraits and the wide-open spaces of Paris.

In 1888 Van Gogh moved to Arles, but depression and hallucinations began to haunt him. In a deranged moment, he cut off his left ear lobe and sent it to a prostitute. Poor mental health forced him into a psychiatric hospital, but in his lucid moments he continued to paint. Unable to quell his personal demons, however, he shot himself, dying on 29 July 1890.

His paintings were only appreciated towards the end of his life (he sold one painting while alive, *Red Vineyard at Arles*) and he lived a life of poverty. Today his paintings fetch millions; his *Portrait of Dr Gachet* is one of the top 10 most expensive painting ever sold, going for a cool US$82.5 million in 1990. Van Gogh's works now hang in galleries from New York to Moscow, but a number can be seen in Amsterdam's Van Gogh Museum (p104), which has *Potato Eaters,* and at the Kröller-Müller Museum (p265) near Arnhem.

Music

The old, dour Calvinists of the 17th century were never fans of music, dismissing it as frivolous. They only began to allow church organ music because they realised it kept people out of pubs.

Despite this inauspicious start, the music scene in the Netherlands is renowned. Dutch musicians excel in the classics, techno/dance and jazz, and the high level of music appreciation means there's a steady stream of touring talent.

There has, however, been a revival in '80s music in recent years. You'll hear it in restaurants, bars and even clubs, where '80s nights are all the rage. While we're not bashing the music of more than two decades ago (who doesn't like early Depeche Mode?), after a week or two of listening to '80s pop you'll be ready to listen to *anything* else.

CLASSICAL MUSIC

The Holland Festival Oude Muziek (p177) is held each year in Utrecht, and celebrates the Top 40 hits of the 16th and 17th centuries.

The Netherlands has many orchestras based in cities throughout the country. Den Haag, Rotterdam and Maastricht have a full calendar of performances by local orchestras and groups, but Amsterdam's Royal Concertgebouw Orchestra (p130) towers over them all, thanks in no small part to the near-perfect acoustics of its winning concert hall, the Concertgebouw.

If you're looking for Dutch home-grown talent, you can hardly do better than the mop-topped pianist Ronald Brautigam, who has performed around the country and all over the world. Violinist-violist Isabelle van Keulen founded her own chamber music festival in Delft, and brings in the crowds wherever she appears. The country's leading cellist is Pieter Wispelwey, known for his fiery temperament and a challenging repertoire.

Pianist Wibi Soerjadi is one of the country's most successful classical musicians, famous for his sparkling interpretations of romantic works and his Javanese-prince looks. Soprano Charlotte Margiono is known for her interpretations of *Le Nozze de Figaro* and *The Magic Flute*. Mezzo-soprano Jard van Nes has a giant reputation for her solo parts in Mahler's symphonies.

The Nederlandse Opera is based in Amsterdam's Stopera (officially called the Muziektheater; p130), and stages world-class performances, though its forays into experimental fare stir up inevitable controversy.

JAZZ

The Beatles have the most hits (16) on the all-time list of No 1 songs in the Netherlands. No 2 with 14 hits is Marco Borsato, who sings Italian pop songs in Dutch.

The Dutch jazz scene has produced some mainstream artists in recent years. Among gifted young chanteuses are Fleurine, Ilse Huizinga and the Surinam-born Denise Jannah, who records for Blue Note and is widely recognised as the country's best jazz singer. Jannah's repertoire consists of American standards with elements of Surinamese music.

Astrid Seriese and Carmen Gomez operate in the crossover field, where jazz verges on, or blends with, pop. Father and daughter Hans and Candy Dulfer, tenor and alto saxophonists respectively, are a bit more daring. Dad, in particular, constantly extends his musical boundaries by experimenting with sampling techniques drawn from the hip-hop genre. Candy is better known internationally, thanks to her performances with Prince, Van Morrison and Pink Floyd, among others, which have introduced her to a wide audience.

Trumpeter and Jordaan native Saskia Laroo mixes jazz with dance, but still earns respect in traditional circles. Other leading jazzers are bass player Hein van de Geyn, guitarist Jesse van Ruller and pianist Michiel Borstlap, winner of the Thelonius Monk award.

An effervescent soloist on the flute is Peter Guidi, who set up the jazz program at the Muziekschool Amsterdam and leads its big band, Jazzmania.

The Willem Breuker Kollektief is another big band of note, enjoying a reputation for experimentation.

The phenomenal success of the North Sea Jazz Festival (p210) every summer in Rotterdam has helped drive the scene. Amsterdam's leading jazz club, Bimhuis (p130), is *the* jazz venue to head to.

POP, ROCK & DANCE

Chances are you've heard old hits by Dutch bands such as 'Radar Love' by Golden Earring, 'Venus' by Shocking Blue or 'Hocus Pocus' by Jan Akkerman's Focus.

The highest-profile Dutch rock star, Herman Brood, burst onto the scene with *His Wild Romance* at the end of the '70s. He became a real-life, drug-addled, self-absorbed rock star, until he threw himself off the top of the Amsterdam Hilton in 2001. After his death, his remake of *My Way* went to number one in the Netherlands.

The Dutch were pioneers of club music, fusing techno and industrial into the dark, hyperactive beat that became known as 'gabber' in the early 1990s.

Nowadays Amsterdam is the pop capital of the Netherlands, and talent is drawn to the city like moths to a flame. It is a major hub of the DJ trade, not just for the Netherlands but for the world. Top names on the international circuit include Tiësto, Armin van Buuren, Marco V and Ferry Corsten. You can find them at venues large and small in Amsterdam and Rotterdam, which also has a vaunted club scene.

Pop scene regulars include the Britpop-inspired Moke, singer-songwriter Marike Jager, guitar-pop band Johan, retro-soul singer Alain Clark and dance-rock mavens, the Melomanics. Successful Dutch rappers include the Moroccan-Dutch artist Ali B, and Brainpower and Blaxtar, who both rap in their native Dutch. Hardcore rappers Osdorp Posse were the first on the local scene, and they remained popular until hanging up their microphones in 2009.

Pop festivals come out of the woodwork in the warmer months: Den Haag's gargantuan Parkpop (p194), draws around 350,000 ravers to the city in June, while Dance Valley (www.dancevalley.nl) in Spaarnwoude near Amsterdam pulls up to 100 live acts and DJs in mid-July.

American author John Irving set his novel *A Widow for One Year* in Amsterdam's Red Light District; British novelist Irvine Welsh's *The Acid House* is a short-story collection about Amsterdam's drug underworld.

WORLD MUSIC

Cosmopolitan Amsterdam offers a wealth of world music. Surinam-born Ronald Snijders, a top jazz flautist, is a frequent highlight, as is the venerable Chris Hinze.

Fra-Fra-Sound plays jazz and 'paramaribop', a contraction of Paramaribo (the capital of Surinam) and bebop. What you'll hear is traditional Surinamese *kaseko,* itself a banquet of African, European and American music.

Zuco 103, a Dutch-Brazilian outfit, combines bossa nova and samba with DJ rubs on the turntable. The equally eclectic New Cool Collective blends jazz with drum 'n' bass and '60s Go-Go.

Amsterdam's Roots Music Festival (p115) of world music happens at different locations every year in June, but centres around the Oosterpark area.

Literature

In the Middle Ages Dutch literature stuck to epic tales of chivalry and allegories. But that changed in the 16th century with Erasmus, a name familiar to school children across the globe. The leading Dutch humanist wrote a satire on the church and society called *His Praise of Folly.*

In her book *Dutch Women Don't Get Depressed,* Dutch psychologist Ellen de Bruinand uses scientific studies to show that women in the Netherlands are a whole lot happier than women elsewhere in the world. She says that personal choice and freedom is the key.

The literary lights of the Golden Age included Spinoza, an Amsterdam Jew who wrote deep philosophical treatises. Spinoza rejected the concept of free will, contending that humans acted purely out of self-preservation.

Dutch literature flourished in the 17th century with writers such as Vondel (the Dutch Shakespeare), Bredero and Hooft. Postwar literature was dominated by Willem Frederik Hermans, Harry Mulisch and Gerard Reve and, later, Jan Wolkers, Maarten 't Hart and Frederik van der Heijden.

Today there are many Dutch writers earning acclaim.

Xaviera Hollander, author of *The Happy Hooker*, a 1972 classic based on her life as a sex worker, now runs a B&B in Amsterdam, Xaviera's Happy House (p121).

RECOMMENDED READS

▪ *Diary of Anne Frank (Het Dagboek van Anne Frank)* by Anne Frank. Possibly the most famous book penned in the Netherlands; a moving account of a young Jewish girl's thoughts while hiding from the occupying Germans. Her hiding place should not be missed (see p102).

▪ *The Discovery of Heaven (De Ontdekking van de Hemel)* by Harry Mulisch. Two friends find they were conceived on the same day, and share love, hate, a woman and a child who is destined to return the Ten Commandments to God. Made into a film of the same name in 2001.

▪ *A Dutchman's Slight Adventures* by Simon Carmiggelt. An amusing collection of vignettes from the author's column in the newspaper *Het Parool*. Carmiggelt was a master of local colour, often writing his observations from pubs and park benches in Amsterdam.

▪ *First Gray, Then White, Then Blue (Eerst Grijs, Dan Wit, Dan Blauw)* by Margriet de Moor. An intense tale of passion and deception in which a woman reappears after a two-year absence from her husband, with no explanation or remorse.

▪ *The Following Story (Het Volgende Verhaal)* by Cees Nooteboom. Award-winning contemporary Dutch writer tackles a schoolmaster's journey through memory and imagination in the final seconds of his life.

▪ *A Heart of Stone (Een Hart van Steen)* by Renate Dorrestein. A terrifying Gothic-style tale of violence, childhood and madness told from inside the minds of three troubled children of a superficially idyllic family.

▪ *In a Dark Wood Wandering (Het Woud der Verwachting)* by Hella Haase. Quirky historical novel set during the Hundred Years' War, with a cast of believable characters based on great figures from mad Charles VI to Joan of Arc.

▪ *Lost Paradise* by Cees Nooteboom. An allegorical tale of angels and humans, of Brazilians in Australia and a literary critic in Austria. One of the Netherlands' most prolific writers, Nooteboom also wrote *The Following Story*, winner of the Aristeion European Prize for Literature in 1991.

▪ *Max Havelaar* by Multatuli. An indictment of colonial forced-labour policy in the Dutch East Indies (present-day Indonesia), written in 1860. Multatuli – Latin for 'I have suffered greatly' – was the pen name of Eduard Dekker, a colonial bureaucrat.

▪ *Netherland* by Joseph O'Neill. The acclaimed 2008 novel by the Irish-born, Dutch-raised author. A Den Haag–born narrator explores life in New York and London after 9/11.

▪ *Parents Worry* by Gerard Reve. A contemporary classic, a tragicomic novel about a day in the ravaged life of a singer and poet with one hell of a case of writer's block. Reve, who passed away in 2006, was acknowledged as one of the great 20th-century Dutch authors.

▪ *The Two Hearts of Kwasi Boachi (De Zwarte met het Witte Hart)* by Arthur Japin. The true story of two West African princes sent to study in Holland in the 1830s, and what becomes of them in the ensuing years.

▪ *The Vanishing (Het Gouden Ei; The Golden Egg)* by Tim Krabbé. Gripping psychological thriller following a man's hunt for his missing girlfriend, and a study of the banality of evil. Made into the Dutch-French film *Spoorloos* and remade as the American film *The Vanishing*.

Cinema & Television

The Netherlands' film industry is humble, producing around 20 feature films a year. Yet the Dutch have won three Best Foreign Language Film Academy Awards, including Marleen Gorris with 1995's *Antonia's Line*. Recent nominees include Paula van der Oest's *Zus & Zo* (2002) and Ben Sombogaart's *Twin Sisters* (2003).

Decades before, Joris Ivens won an international peace prize for *Song of the Rivers* (1954), a global comparison of workers' conditions.

Dutch filmmakers who have made it big in Hollywood include Paul Verhoeven *(Robocop, Basic Instinct, Starship Troopers)* and Jan de Bont *(Speed, Lara Croft II)*. The former, however, has produced better work at home, such as the violent erotic thriller *De Vierde Man* (The Fourth Man), and *Turks Fruit* (Turkish Delight), a provocative tale of love and sex.

The murder mysteries of Dick Maas, a former cartoonist, have been compared with Dario Argenti's – fascinating to look at, but riddled with plot flaws. *Amsterdammed* (1988) features a murderer who uses Amsterdam's canals to escape.

Dutch TV tends not to travel well abroad, mostly due to the language, but foreign-language remakes of Dutch shows are enormously popular. Many visitors expect Dutch TV to be stuffed to the gills with porn, but it just ain't the case (unless you tune in to hotel pay TV channels).

The reality-TV craze began here with *Big Brother,* produced by Endemol, now based in Amsterdam. *Big Brother* was swiftly copied in the UK, Germany, Australia and the USA – and has spread to places as diverse as Brazil, Mexico and Africa. Endemol is also behind international hits such as *Fear Factor; Extreme Makeover: Home Edition; Ready, Steady, Cook; Deal or No Deal* and the splash-filled obstacle-course show *Wipeout*.

See news of the Dutch film industry unspool at www.hollandfilm.nl.

Photography

Portraiture is a major theme of contemporary Dutch photography. The most famous living photographer from the Netherlands is probably Anton Corbijn (1955–), known for his portraits of celebrities and musicians. Corbijn has also made film clips for bands such as Nirvana and Coldplay. His feature film *Control*, based on the life of Joy Division frontman Ian Curtis, earned rave reviews at the Cannes film festival in 2007.

Rineke Dijkstra (1959–) creates unflinching head-on portraits, both analytical and empathetic, of common people such as soldiers carrying rifles and folks in bathing suits on the beach. Hellen van Meene's (1972–) portraits are more intimate. Vinoodh Matadin (1961–) creates shots for exhibitions and advertising campaigns, at turns grim and glamorous.

Amsterdam-based Aernout Mik (1962–) has exhibited in Europe and North America with film installations known for combining studies in group dynamics with a sculptor's sense of space. Marijke van Warmerdam (1959–), based in Amsterdam and New York, creates absurdist loops of everyday life in repeating sequences – eg the Japanese technique of bowing.

The Netherlands has a tradition of photography committed to social themes. The first World Press Photo exhibition (www.worldpressphoto .org) was held in Amsterdam in 1975, and the exhibition still opens in the city before touring the globe.

The Nederlands Fotomuseum (p208) has excellent special exhibitions, as do most other major museums in the country.

The Amsterdam Fantastic Film Festival (www .afff.nl) is devoted to European and international fantasy, horror and science-fiction movies.

Predictable outrage was stirred in advance of the Dutch reality TV special *The Big Donor Show*, in which three dying people vied for a donor kidney. Only later was it revealed that the show was a fake, designed to show the plight of people waiting for organ transplants. It won an Emmy.

Theatre

The Netherlands has a rich theatrical tradition going back to medieval times. In the Golden Age, when Dutch was the language of trade, companies from

The Dutch version of the Oscar is the Golden Calf, awarded each year at the Netherlands Film Festival (www.filmfestival.nl) in Utrecht. Sadly it didn't exist in 1956 when it could have been awarded to Charlton Heston for *Ben Hur*.

the Low Countries toured the theatres of Europe. Some highlights of the era – Vondel's tragedies, Bredero's comedies and Hooft's verses – are still performed today, albeit with a contemporary voice.

A modern troupe to watch for is **Warner & Consorten** (www.warnerenconsorten.nl), a collective that stages unexpected performances in unusual places around town. The dialogue-free shows inject humour into everyday situations and objects, while music is generated with weird materials.

English-language companies often visit Amsterdam, especially in summer. Glitzy musicals play to full houses in the Koninklijk Theater Carré (p132) or other large venues. The comedy scene is led by English-language outfits such as Boom Chicago (p131).

Dance

The Dutch are world leaders in modern dance. Den Haag's Nederlands Dans Theater (p195) troupe was established in 1959, melding modern dance with classical ballet. It is an offshoot of Amsterdam's Het Nederlands Ballet, which performs mainly classical ballets, as well as modern Dutch works.

Food & Drink

Like many other countries in northern Europe, the Netherlands has never had a reputation for outstanding, or even fine, cuisine. Hearty, hefty, filling, stodgy – these are the adjectives with which Dutch cooking is usually tagged. This, however, has a historical context; traditionally, the Dutch never paid that much attention to food, as there was too much work to be done and little time to cook. It is quite revealing that, during the Golden Age, spices such as pepper were more of a currency than a culinary ingredient.

In recent years, however, these attitudes have been transformed by a culinary revolution sweeping the Netherlands. Fresh winds are blowing through the Dutch traditional kitchen, breathing new life into centuries-old recipes by giving them a contemporary twist. Creative Dutch chefs are taking concepts from the rest of Europe and the world and melding them with excellent meats, seafood and vegetables sourced locally.

Dutch Cooking: Traditions, Ingredients, Tastes & Techniques by Janny de Moor is a recent cookbook that reflects all the good trends sweeping through Dutch cuisine.

STAPLES & SPECIALITIES

The Dutch start the day with a filling, yet unexciting, breakfast of a few slices of bread accompanied by jam, cheese and a boiled egg. Coffee is always involved. Lunch tends to be more of a snack, especially for the working crowd, taken between noon and 2pm. A half-hour is common for the midday break, just long enough for employees to snag a quick sandwich or empty their lunchbox. Dinner is the main meal of the day and is usually a substantial serving, whether it be traditional Dutch cuisine or something from beyond the Netherlands' borders.

DUTCH

Van Gogh perfectly captured the main ingredient of traditional Dutch cooking in his *Potato Eaters*. Typically boiled to death, these 'earth apples' are accompanied by meat – and more boiled vegetables. Gravy is then added for flavour. It's certainly not fancy, but it is filling.

Few restaurants serve exclusively Dutch cuisine, but many places have several homeland items on the menu, especially in winter. Some time-honoured favourites:

Access a collection of Dutch recipes in English, and online shopping for Canadian and US citizens who absolutely need Dutch products, at www .dutchmarket.com.

- *stamppot* (mashed pot) – a simple dish of potatoes mashed with kale, endive or sauerkraut and served with smoked sausage or strips of pork. Perfect in winter.
- *hutspot* (hotchpotch) – similar to *stamppot,* but with potatoes, carrots, onions, braised meat and more spices.
- *erwtensoep* (pea soup) – plenty of peas with onions, carrots, smoked sausage and bacon. And the perfect pea soup? A spoon stuck upright in the pot should remain standing. (Not served in summer.)
- *asperge* (asparagus) – usually white and often crunchy; very popular when it's in season (spring); served with ham and butter.
- *kroketten* (croquettes) – dough balls with various fillings that are crumbed and deep-fried; the variety called *bitterballen* are a popular pub snack served with mustard.
- *mosselen* (mussels) – cooked with white wine, chopped leeks and onions, and served in a bowl or cooking pot with a side dish of *frites* or *patat* (French fries); they're popular, and are best eaten from September to April.

Dutch Cooking: The New Kitchen by Manon Sikkel and Michiel Klonhammer is a fresh perspective on traditional Dutch cuisine, in which age-old recipes are given a modern makeover.

Lamb is prominently featured on menus, and when you are near the coast – really near – seafood is on every menu. It is also eaten as a snack, in which form it is everywhere. *Haring* (herring) is a national institution, eaten lightly salted or occasionally pickled but never fried or cooked (see opposite); *paling* (eel) is usually smoked.

Typical Dutch desserts are fruit pie (apple, cherry or other fruit), *vla* (custard) and ice cream. Many snack bars and pubs serve *appeltaart* (apple pie), which is always good. Amazingly, some Dutch eat *hagelslag* (chocolate sprinkles) on bread for breakfast.

Finally, most towns have at least one place serving *pannenkoeken* (pancakes), which come in a huge number of varieties. The mini-version, covered in caster sugar, is *poffertjes*.

INDONESIAN

Indonesian cooking, a piquant legacy of the colonial era, is a rich and complex blend of many cultures: chilli peppers, peanut sauce and curries from Thailand, lemon grass and fish sauce from Vietnam, intricate Indian spice mixes, and Asian cooking methods.

In the Netherlands, Indonesian food is often toned down for sensitive Western palates. If you want it hot *(pedis,* pronounced 'p-*dis'),* say so, but be prepared for watering eyes and burnt taste buds. You might play it safe by asking for *sambal* (chilli paste) and helping yourself. *Sambal oelek* is red and hot; the dark-brown *sambal badjak* is onion-based, mild and sweet.

Julius Caesar was a big fan of Dutch cheese.

The most famous Indonesian dish is *rijsttafel* (rice table), an array of spicy savoury dishes such as braised beef, pork satay and ribs served with white rice. *Nasi rames* is a steaming plate of boiled rice covered in several rich condiments, while the same dish with thick noodles is called *bami rames*.

SURINAMESE

Dishes from this former colony have Caribbean roots, blending African and Indian flavours with Indonesian influences introduced by Javanese labourers. Chicken, lamb and beef curries are common menu items. *Roti,* a chickpea-flour pancake filled with potatoes, long beans, bean sprouts and meat (vegetarian versions are available), is by far the favoured choice of the Dutch.

DISTINCTLY CHEESY

Some Dutch say it makes them tall; others complain it causes nightmares. Whatever the case, the Netherlands is justifiably famous for its cheese *(kaas)*. The Dutch – known as the original cheeseheads – consume 16.5kg of the stuff every year.

Nearly two-thirds of all cheese sold is Gouda. The tastier varieties have strong, complex flavours and are best enjoyed with a bottle of wine or two. Try some *oud* (old) Gouda, hard and rich in flavour and a popular bar snack eaten with mustard. Oud Amsterdammer is a real delight, deep orange and crumbly with white crystals of ripeness.

Edam is similar to Gouda but slightly drier and less creamy. Leidse or Leiden cheese is another export hit, laced with cumin or caraway seed and light in flavour.

In the shops you'll also find scores of varieties that are virtually unknown outside the country. Frisian Nagelkaas might be made with parsley juice, buttermilk, and 'nails' of caraway seed. Kruidenkaas has a melange of herbs such as fennel, celery, pepper or onions. Graskaas is 'new harvest' Gouda made after cows begin to roam the meadows and munch grass.

Lower-fat cheeses include Milner, Kollumer and Maaslander. One has to start somewhere: the stats show that the Dutch are gaining weight despite all that cycling.

Try all these and possibly empty your wallet at Alkmaar's legendary cheese shop De Tromp Kaaswinkel (p154) or Gouda's 't Kaaswinkeltje (p198).

TASTY TRAVEL

Raw fish isn't that bad – sushi and sashimi, for instance, are delectable morsels that make the world a better place. However, the sight of a local slowly sliding a raw herring head first (thankfully head*less*) down their gullet looks, well, wrong. But the Dutch love this salted delicacy and are eager for visitors to try it. If an entire fish is too much to stomach, it can be cut into bite-sized pieces and served with onion and pickles. You'll find vendors the length and breadth of the country – look for the words *haring* or *Hollandse niuewe* and dig in.

Another acquired taste in Holland is *drop*. This so-called sweet is a thick, rubbery liquorice root and Arabic gum concoction the Dutch go crazy for – a reputed 30 million kilos of the stuff is consumed each year. Its bitter taste is reminiscent of childhood medicine and some foreigners have trouble taking a second bite. There's also a liquid version; look for a bottle of Dropshot in supermarkets.

DRINKS
Nonalcoholic

More coffee is consumed per capita in the Netherlands than in any other European country bar Denmark. Ordering a *koffie* will get you a sizeable cup of the black stuff and a separate package or jug of *koffiemelk*, a slightly sour-tasting cream akin to condensed milk. *Koffie verkeerd* is similar to latte, served in a big mug with plenty of real milk. If you order espresso or cappuccino, you'll be lucky to get a decent Italian version. Don't count on finding decaffeinated coffee; if you do it may be instant.

> The Dutch drink on average 140L of coffee each per year.

Tea is usually served Continental-style: a cup or pot of hot water with a tea bag on the side. Varieties might be presented in a humidorlike box for you to pick and choose. If you want milk, say *met melk, graag.* Many locals prefer to add a slice of lemon.

Alcoholic

Lager beer is the staple drink, served cool and topped by a head of froth so big it would start a brawl in an Australian bar. Heineken tells us that these are 'flavour bubbles', and requests for no head will earn a steely response. *Een bier* or *een pils* will get you a normal glass; *een kleintje pils* is a small glass and *een fluitje* is a tall but thin glass – perfect for multiple refills. Some places serve half-litre mugs to please tourists. See p50 for more delightful details.

> Amsterdam's Brouwerij De Prael (www.deprael.nl) brews a range of beers named after dead Dutch singers. All are very worthy memorials to their namesakes and are sold at better pubs and cafes around the country.

Dutch *jenever* (gin) is made from juniper berries and drunk chilled from a shot glass filled to the brim. Most people prefer *jonge* (young) *jenever,* which is smoother; the strong juniper flavour of *oude* (old) *jenever* can be an acquired taste. The aptly named *kopstoot* (head butt) is a double-whammy of *jenever* and a beer chaser. The palette of indigenous liqueurs includes *advocaat* (a kind of eggnog) and the herb-based *Beerenburg*, a Frisian schnapps.

Wine seems to be an afterthought in the Netherlands – but an afterthought that is slowly taking hold. Plenty of European and New World varieties are available, but take a second look at the prices, as Dutch import duties normally keep them high.

CELEBRATIONS

The Dutch sweet tooth really comes out during the annual holidays and festivities. Early December is a good time to sample traditional treats such as spicy *speculaas* biscuits or *pepernoten,* the little crunchy ginger nuts that are handed out at Sinterklaas. *Oliebollen* are small, spherical donuts filled with raisins or other diced fruit, deep-fried and dusted with icing sugar; you can buy these calorie bombs from street vendors in the run-up to New Year.

A TASTY BREW

The Dutch love beer. It's seen as the perfect companion for time spent with friends in the sun or out partying till the small hours. And they've had plenty of time to cultivate this unquestioning love – beer has been a popular drink since the 14th century, and at one time the Dutch could lay claim to no fewer than 559 brewers. Most Dutch beer is pilsner (or lager), a clear, crisp, golden beer with strong hop flavouring.

Heineken is the Netherlands' (and possibly the world's) best-known beer. However, like Fosters in Australia, it has a poor name at home – 'the beer your cheap father drinks', to quote one wag. Amstel (owned by Heineken) is also well known, and Grolsch and Oranjeboom can also claim a certain amount of international fame. Most beers contain around 5% alcohol, and a few of those cute little glasses can pack a strong punch.

While the big names are ubiquitous, the Netherlands has scores of small brewers worth trying, including Gulpen, Haarlem's Jopen, Bavaria, Drie Ringen, Leeuw and Utrecht. La Trappe is the only Dutch Trappist beer, brewed close to Tilburg. The potent beers made by Amsterdam's Brouwerij 't IJ (p108) are sold on tap and in some local pubs – try the Columbus brew (9% alcohol).

Other local breweries worth trying include Texelse Bierbrouwerij (p162) on Texel, Rotterdam's Stadsbrouwerij De Pelgrim (p211), Utrecht's Oudaen (p177) and De Hemel in Nijmegen. In addition almost every town has at least one cafe or bar serving a huge range of beers. We list many in this book, including one of the best, Take One (p279) in Maastricht.

If you're around in spring or autumn, don't pass up the chance to sample Grolsch's seasonal bock beers, such as Lentebok (spring bock) and Herfstbok (autumn bock). Sample many – and possibly suffer the consequences – at Utrecht's Café Ledig Erf (p178), which has a bock beer fest over an autumn weekend.

And on a hot summer day, the seasonal fruity red beers by the major brewers are a refreshing treat.

Muisjes (little mice) are sugar-coated aniseed sprinkles served on a round *beschuit* (rusk biscuit) to celebrate the birth of a child – blue and white for a boy; pink and white for a girl.

WHERE TO EAT & DRINK

Restaurants abound and they cater to a wide variety of tastes and budgets. Their biggest competitors are *eetcafés*, affordable publike eateries with a huge local following.

The official website of the Dutch can-collectors' association is www .blik-op-blik.nl. Hunt for that rare Dutch beer can here.

When the Dutch say cafe they're referring to a pub, also known as a *kroeg*, and there are more than 1000 of them in Amsterdam alone. Coffee is served, but as a sideline. Many cafes and pubs also serve food, but few open before 9am. A fixture in many cafes is an outdoor terrace that may be covered and heated in winter. Here the Dutch soak up the outdoor atmosphere and pass the time chatting, people-watching or simply taking a break from everything.

The most famous type of cafe is the *bruin café* (brown cafe). The true specimen has been in business for a while; expect sandy wooden floors and an atmosphere perfect for deep conversation. The name comes from the smoky stains on the walls, although newer aspirants just slap on some brown paint.

Grand cafes are more spacious than brown cafes or pubs and have comfortable furniture. They're all the rage, and any pub that puts in a few solid tables and chairs might call itself a grand cafe. Normally opening at 10am, they're marvellous for a lazy lunch or brunch.

At www.lekker.nl you can read reviews and listings for more than 9000 restaurants and cafes.

Falling within the 'other' category are theatre cafes, which attract a trendy mix of bohemian and chic; *proeflokalen*, or tasting houses, which once were attached to distilleries (good for sampling dozens of *jenevers* and liqueurs); trendy bars with cool designer interiors; and the ubiquitous Irish pubs.

Quick Eats

Broodjeszaken (sandwich shops) or snack bars proliferate. The latter offer multicoloured treats in a display case, usually based on some sort of meat and spices, and everything is dumped into a deep-fryer when you order.

FEBO-style snack bars have long rows of coin-operated windows à la the Jetsons and are the lifeblood of late-night partiers. The *frikandel* (€1.40) is worrisomely addictive. A *kaas soufflé* has a lavalike pocket of gooey goodness.

The national institution, *Vlaamse frites* (Flemish fries), are French fries made from whole potatoes rather than the potato pulp you will get if the sign only says *frites*. They are supposed to be smothered in mayonnaise (though you can ask for ketchup, curry sauce, garlic sauce or other gloppy toppings). Heed the words of Vincent Vega *(Pulp Fiction)*: 'You know what they put on french fries in Holland? Mayonnaise. And I don't mean a little bit on the side – they fuckin' drown 'em in it.'

Seafood is everywhere. The most popular – aside from raw herring (see the boxed text, p49) – is *kibbeling* (deep-fried cod parings), while smoked eel has legions of fans.

Lebanese and Turkish snack bars specialise in *shoarma,* a pitta bread filled with sliced lamb from a vertical spit – also known as a *gyros* or doner kebab.

Frinkandels, the staple of late-night snack stands and FEBOs, looks like a sort of brown extruded hot dog (we're being polite), and like a hot dog is best not pondered too deeply, especially given it's 'economical' ingredients. Instead let its greasy, spicy goodness seduce you. Then go into detox.

VEGETARIANS & VEGANS

For all their liberalism and openness, it's surprising to note that the Dutch are slow on the vegetarian uptake. Outside the major metropolises you'll be hard-pressed to find a strictly vegetarian-only restaurant in the small town you're visiting; in this case, you'll be relying on the couple of veg options available on most restaurant menus. Check their purity before ordering, though, as often you can't be sure whether they're 100% meat- or fish-free (meat stock is a common culprit).

Once you do track down a vegetarian restaurant, you'll be happy to find that they rely on organic ingredients and often make everything in-house, from the bread with your starter to your cake for dessert.

EATING WITH KIDS

Children are welcome in all but the most formal restaurants. In fact, the trend towards stylish bistro-style eateries with high ceilings and a slightly raucous atmosphere are all the better for little ones, who may enjoy a dish of raucousness with their meal. Everyone is pretty tolerant of any antics children may get up to during a meal. You'll see Dutch families enjoying meals inside and out at cafes, pubs and restaurants, as well as sitting on benches sharing a quick repast from a fish stall or *frites* joint.

Kids' menus are common and tend to have the deep-fried treats that always go down well. You can also reasonably ask for high-chairs and even crayons in many restaurants.

See p285 for more tips and information.

HABITS & CUSTOMS

At first take, it looks as though the Dutch aren't all that fussed about food. Meals tend to be rushed, and quantity appears to win over quality. But these habits are fading fast as younger Dutch – having enjoyed wonderful meals abroad on holiday – demand similar experiences at home. Social events are in a class of their own, and diners with something to celebrate might camp out in a restaurant for an entire evening.

Dinner usually takes place between 6pm and 9.30pm. Popular places fill up by 7pm because the Dutch eat early; if this doesn't suit, aim for the second sitting from around 8.30pm to 9.30pm, when films, concerts and other

FAVOURITE PLACES TO EAT

High-brow, low-brow, no-brow: our favourite places for a meal or a snack span every budget and style. The unifier? Terrific eats!

The following are all in Amsterdam.

- **Pancakes!** (p125) – locals and tourists grace the blue-tile tables for the ultimate tasty cliché.
- **Tempo Doeloe** (p125) – fab Indonesian fare with a fine sampling of the country's flavours.
- **Van Dobben** (p125) – white-coated counter men specialise in snappy banter while serving tasty traditional Dutch fare at all hours.
- **Gartine** (p123) – slow-food credentialed and serving breakfast pastries, sandwiches and salads from produce grown in its own garden.
- **Marius** (p127) – foodies swoon over the Dutch Chez Panisse and inventive fresh creations of chef Kees.

For some beloved Amsterdam snack spots, see p124.

The following are our picks for the rest of the Netherlands, in the order they appear in this guidebook.

- **IJssalon W Laan** (p154), Alkmaar – there's nothing cheesy about this legendary ice-cream vendor.
- **Van Der Star** (p164), Texel – deli with the best smoked fish in the country.
- **Blauw** (p178), Utrecht – the place for stylish Indonesian food with a side of vintage art and hip minimalism.
- **Mangerie De Jonge Koekop** (p188), Leiden – fresh and inventive fare and starlit dining.
- **Les Ombrellas** (p195), Den Haag – at a confluence of canals, enjoy superb seafood.
- **Kamphuisen** (p198), Gouda – as brown a cafe as you'll find, with excellent lamb, steak, fish and more.
- **De Ballentent** (p211), Rotterdam – the city's best waterfront pub-cafe is the place for *bals*, huge, homemade meatloafy meatballs.
- **Spinoza's** (p230), Leeuwarden – enjoy regional specialities in the courtyard or candle-lit interior.
- **Muller** (p244), Groningen – watch drama of the good kind in the kitchen while you savour the region's best seasonal menu.
- **Poppe** (p257), Zwolle – the open kitchen issues forth a steady stream of superb seasonal dishes.
- **Jan de Groot** (p270), Den Bosch – the crowds know this bakery is the place to get the local speciality – creamy *Bossche bols* (Den Bosch balls).
- **Sjieke** (p278), Maastricht – this cosy corner spot turns out traditional Dutch fare with colour and flair; in summer there are tables in the park across the street.

Dutch Delights by Sylvia Pessireron, Jurjen Drenth and friends is a playful look at the eating habits of the Dutch. It's easy to digest and filled with superb photos.

performances start. Bear in mind that many kitchens close by 9pm, although full-service restaurants in the largest cities *may* serve past midnight.

A *dagschotel* (dish of the day) is good value, but don't expect a culinary adventure. The trend in some places is to change menus with the seasons to reflect what's fresh; this is a sign of an enlightened kitchen and should be encouraged.

Coffee breaks are a national institution and occur frequently throughout the day. Restaurants will serve a single cookie or biscuit with coffee, but in homes you'll be offered one per cup.

Many restaurants don't accept credit cards; for tipping advice, see p290.

DOS & DON'TS

- Do round up the bill by 5% to 10% (unless the service is bad).
- Do split the costs.
- Do reserve ahead, especially at weekends.
- Do take children to pubs and restaurants.
- Do bring flowers or wine when invited home.
- Don't ask to go 'Dutch'.
- Don't ask for a doggie bag.
- Don't cut off a tip on the cheese cart (always slice).
- Don't make loud complaints about the service (it's usually counterproductive).

EAT YOUR WORDS

Dutch restaurants are skilled in serving foreigners, so bilingual or English menus are practically the norm. Refer to the Language chapter (p309) for tips on pronunciation and some handy phrases.

Food Glossary

appelmoes	*a-*puhl*-*moos	apple sauce
beenham	*bayn-*ham	leg ham
belegd broodje	buh-*lekht broa-*chuh	filled sandwich
biologisch	bee-yo-*lo-*khees	organic
boerenomelet	*boo-*ruhn-oa-muh-*let*	omelette with vegetables and ham
dagschotel	*dakh-*skhoa-tuhl	dish of the day
drop	drop	liquorice
frikandel	free-kan-*del*	deep-fried meat snack, like a sausage
hagelslag	*haa-*khuhl-slakh	chocolate sprinkles
Hollandse nieuwe	ho-lant-suh *nee-*wuh	salted herring, first of the season
hoofdgerecht	*hoaft-*khuh-rekht	main course
kaas	kaas	cheese
kroket	kroa-*ket*	meat croquette
nagerecht	*naa-*khuh-rekht	dessert
pannenkoek	*pa-*nuhn-kook	pancake
patat	pa-*tat*	chips/French fries
poffertjes	*po-*fuhr-tyuhs	mini pancakes
speculaas	*spay-*ku-laas	spiced biscuit
tosti	*tos-*ti	toasted sandwich
uitsmijter	*öyt-*smay-tuhr	fried egg, ham and cheese on bread
Vlaamse frites	*vlaam-*suh freet	thick chips/fries made from whole potatoes
vlammetjes	*vla-*muh-tyuhs	spicy spring rolls
voorgerecht	*voar-*khuh-rekht	starter

COOKING TERMS

gaar	khaar	well done
gebakken	khuh-*ba-*kuhn	baked/fried
gebraden	khe-*braa-*duhn	roasted
gefrituurd	khuh-free-*turt*	deep fried
gegratineerd	khuh-khra-tee-*nayrt*	browned on top with cheese
gegrild	khuh-*khrilt*	grilled
gegrild aan 't spit	khuh-*khrilt* aant spit	spit-roasted
gekookt	khuh-*koakt*	boiled

Windmills in my Oven by Gaitri Pagrach-Chandraby is a mix of Dutch baking, social commentary and regional customs, and a few tasty recipes are thrown in for good measure.

The ban on smoking has been relaxed for small bars and cafes where the only workers are also the owners.

gepaneerd	khuh·pa·*nayrt*	coated in breadcrumbs
gepocheerd	khuh·po·*shayrt*	poached
gerookt	khuh·*roakt*	smoked
geroosterd	khuh·*roas*·tuhrt	toasted
gesauteerd	khuh·soa·*tayrt*	sautéed
gestoofd	khuh·*stoaft*	braised
gestoomd	khuh·*stoamt*	steamed
gevuld	khuh·*vuhlt*	stuffed
half doorbakken	half doar·*ba*·kuhn	medium
rood	roat	rare

peper	*pay*·puhr	pepper
suiker	*söy*·kuhr	sugar
zout	zowt	salt

DESSERTS

amandelbroodje	a·*man*·duhl·broa·chuh	sweet roll with almond filling
appelgebak	*a*·puhl·khuh·bak	apple pie
cake	kayk	cake
ijs	ays	ice cream
slagroom	*slakh*·roam	whipped cream
taart	taart	tart, pie, cake
vla	vlaa	custard
wafel	*waa*·fuhl	waffle

DRINKS

bier	beer	beer
brandewijn	*bran*·duh·wayn	brandy
jenever (or *genever*)	yuh·*nay*·vuhr	Dutch gin
jus d'orange/sinaasappelsap	zhu do·*ranzh*/*see*·nas·a·puhl·sap	orange juice
koffie	*ko*·fee	coffee
koffie verkeerd	*ko*·fee vuhr·*kayrt*	latte
melk	melk	milk
met melk/citroen	met melk/see·*troon*	with milk/lemon
rood/wit	roat/wit	red/white
spa blauw (a brand)	spaa blow	still mineral water
spa rood (a brand)	spaa roat	fizzy mineral water
thee	tay	tea
water	*waa*·tuhr	water
wijn	wayn	wine
zoet/droog	zoot/droakh	sweet/dry

FRUIT, VEGETABLES, STAPLES & SPICES

aardappel	*aart*·a·puhl	potato
appel	*a*·puhl	apple
artisjok	ar·tee·*shok*	artichoke
asperge	as·*per*·zhuh	asparagus
aubergine	oa·ber·*zheen*	eggplant/aubergine
boon	boan	bean
champignon	sham·pee·*nyon*	mushroom
courgette	koor·*zhet*	zucchini/courgette
erwt	ert	pea
groene paprika	*khroo*·nuh *pa*·pree·ka	green pepper (capsicum)
groente	*khroon*·tuh	vegetable
kers	*kers*	cherry

knoflook	knof·loak	garlic
komkommer	kom·kom·uhr	cucumber
kool	koal	cabbage
maïs	ma·ees	sweet corn
olijf	o·layf	olive
peer	payr	pear
perzik	per·zik	peach
peterselie	pay·tuhr·say·lee	parsley
pompoen	pom·poon	pumpkin
prei	pray	leek
pruim	pröym	plum
rijst	rayst	rice
rode paprika	roa·duh pap·ree·ka	red pepper (capsicum)
selderij	sel·duh·ray	celery
sinaasappel	see·nas·a·puhl	orange
sla	slaa	lettuce
spinazie	spee·naa·zee	spinach
spruitje	spröy·chuh	Brussels sprout
ui	öy	onion
witlof	wit·lof	chicory
wortel	wor·tuhl	carrot

MEAT & POULTRY

beenham	bayn·ham	ham on the bone
eend	aynt	duck
ei	ay	egg
everzwijn	ay·vuhr·zwayn	boar
fazant	fa·zant	pheasant
gevogelte	khuh·voa·khuhl·tuh	poultry
hert	hert	venison
kalfsvlees	kalfs·vlays	veal
kalkoen	kal·koon	turkey
kip	kip	chicken
konijn	ko·nayn	rabbit
lamsvlees	lams·vlays	lamb
lever	lay·vuhr	liver
paard	paart	horse
parelhoen	paa·ruhl·hoon	guinea fowl
ribstuk	rip·stuk	rib steak
rookworst	roak·worst	smoked sausage
rundvlees	runt·vlays	beef
schapenvlees	skhaa·puhn·vlays	mutton
slak	slak	snail
spek	spek	bacon
tong	tong	tongue
varkensvlees	var·kuhns·vlays	pork
vlees	vlays	meat
vleeswaren	vlays·waa·ruhn	cooked/prepared meats, cold cuts
wild	wilt	game
worst	worst	sausage

SEAFOOD

ansjovis	an·shoa·vis	anchovy
baars	baars	bream
forel	foa·rel	trout

garnaal	khar·*naal*	shrimp, prawns, scampi
haring	*haa*·ring	herring
inktvis	*ingt*·vis	squid
kabeljauw	kaa·buhl·*jow*	cod
krab	krap	crab
kreeft	krayft	lobster
maatjes	*maa*·chuhs	herring fillets
makreel	ma·*krayl*	mackerel
oester	*oos*·tuhr	oyster
paling	*paa*·ling	eel
rivierkreeft	ree·*veer*·krayft	crayfish
roodbaars	*roat*·baars	red mullet
St Jacobsschelp	sint·*yaa*·kop·skhelp	scallop
schol	skhol	plaice
tong	tong	sole
tonijn	to·*nayn*	tuna
vis	vis	fish
zalm	zalm	salmon
zeebaars	*zay*·baars	bass/sea bream

INDONESIAN DISHES

ayam	*a*·yam	chicken
babi pangang	*baa*·bee *pang*·gang	suckling pig with sweet and sour sauce
bami goreng	*baa*·mee *goa*·reng	stir-fry dish of noodles, vegies, pork and shrimp
daging	*da*·ging	beef
gado–gado	*gaa*·doa *gaa*·doa	vegetables with peanut sauce
goreng	*goa*·reng	fried
kroepoek	*kroo*·pook	deep-fried prawn crackers
loempia	*loom*·pee·ya	spring roll
nasi	*na*·see	rice
nasi goreng	*na*·see *goa*·reng	fried rice with meat and vegies
pedis	*pay*·dis	very spicy
pisang	*pee*·sang	banana
rendang	*ren*·dang	stewed beef in dry hot sauce
rijsttafel	*rays*·taa·fuhl	a selection of spicy meats, fruits, vegetables and sauces served with rice
sambal	*sam*·bal	chilli paste
saté	sa·*tay*	peanut sauce
seroendeng	*se*·roon·deng	fried coconut
taugé	tow·*zhay*	bean sprouts

Architecture

The Dutch are masters of architecture and use of space, but this is nothing new. Through the ages, few countries have exerted more influence on the discipline of art and construction than the Netherlands. From the original sober cathedrals to the sleek modern structures, their ideas and designs have spread not only throughout Europe but also to the new world.

The wonderful thing about Dutch architecture is that you can time-travel through a thousand years of beautiful buildings in one city alone. The weird thing about Dutch architecture – with all its influence, cleverness and internationally renowned architects – is that you're not going to find bombastic statements such as St Peter's cathedral or the Louvre. But, then again, ostentation was never in keeping with the Dutch character. It's the little surprises that charm most: a subtle joke, a flourish on a 17th-century gable or that seemingly unending flight of stairs that seems far too tight to be at all practical but still manages to transport you to the 4th floor…

ROMANESQUE

Romanesque architecture, which took the country (and Europe) by storm between 900 and 1250, is the earliest architectural style remaining in the country, if you discount the *hunebedden* (p249). Its main characteristics are an uncomplicated form, thick walls, small windows and round arches.

The oldest church of this style in the Netherlands is the Pieterskerk (p174) in Utrecht. Built in 1048, it's one of five churches that form a cross in the city, with the cathedral at its centre. Runner-up is Nijmegen's 16-sided Sint Nicolaaskapel (p259), which is basically a scaled-down copy of Charlemagne's chapel in Aachen, Germany. Another classic example of Romanesque is the Onze Lieve Vrouwebasiliek (p275) in Maastricht; its fortresslike tower with round turrets evokes images of Umberto Eco's novel of monastic intrigue, *The Name of the Rose*.

Holland's countryside is also privy to this style of architecture. The windy plains of the north are filled with examples of sturdy brick churches erected in the 12th and 13th centuries, such as the lonely church perched on a manmade hill in Hogebeintum (p231) in Friesland.

GOTHIC

By around 1250 the love affair with Romanesque was over, and the Gothic era was ushered in. Pointed arches, ribbed vaulting and dizzying heights were trademarks of this new architectural style, which was to last until 1600. Although the Dutch buildings didn't match the size of the French Gothic cathedrals, a rich style emerged in Catholic Brabant that could compete with anything abroad. Stone churches with soaring vaults and buttresses, such as Sint Janskathedraal (p269) in Den Bosch and Breda's Grote Kerk (p272), were erected. Both are good examples of the Brabant Gothic style, as it was later known. Note the timber vaulting and the widespread use of brick among the stone.

Stone is normally a constant fixture of Gothic buildings, but in the marshy lands of the western Netherlands it was too heavy (and too scarce) to use. The basic ingredients of bricks – clay and sand – were in abundance, however. Still, bricks are not exactly light material, and weight limits forced architects to build long or wide to compensate for the lack of height. The Sint Janskerk (p197) in Gouda is the longest church in the country, with a nave of 123m, and it has the delicate, stately feel of a variant called Flamboyant Gothic.

The Nederlands Architectuur Instituut (www.nai.nl) in Rotterdam (p207) is the top authority on the latest developments.

Stone Gothic structures do exist in the western stretches of Holland, though: Haarlem's Grote Kerk van St Bavo (p141) is a wonderful example.

If Gothic tickles your fancy, take a peek at the town halls in Gouda (p196) and Middelburg (p220), both of which are nearly overwhelming in their weightiness and pomp.

MANNERISM

The ultimate in early functionalism, windmills have a variety of distinctive designs and their characteristic look makes them national icons. See the boxed text, p215, for details.

From the middle of the 16th century the Renaissance style that was sweeping through Italy steadily began to filter into the Netherlands. The Dutch naturally put their own spin on this new architectural design, which came to be known as mannerism (c 1550–1650). Also known as Dutch Renaissance, this unique style falls somewhere between Renaissance and baroque; it retained the bold curving forms and rich ornamentation of baroque but merged them with classical Greek and Roman and traditional Dutch styles. Building facades were accentuated with mock columns (pilasters) and the simple spout gables were replaced with step gables (see the boxed text, opposite) that were richly decorated with sculptures, columns and obelisks. The playful interaction of red brick and horizontal bands of white or yellow sandstone was based on mathematical formulas designed to please the eye.

Hendrik de Keyser (1565–1621) was the champion of mannerism. His Zuiderkerk (p100), Noorderkerk (p100) and Westerkerk (p102) in Amsterdam are standout examples; all three show a major break from the sober, stolid lines of brick churches located out in the sticks. Their steeples are ornate and built with a variety of contrasting materials, while the windows are framed in white stone set off by brown brick. Florid details enliven the walls and roof lines.

GOLDEN AGE

After the Netherlands became a world trading power in the 17th century, its rich merchants were able to splash out on lavish buildings.

More than anything, the new architecture had to impress. The leading lights in the architectural field, such as Jacob van Campen (1595–1657) and the brothers Philips and Justus Vingboons, again turned to ancient Greek and Roman designs for ideas. To make buildings look taller, the step gable was replaced by a neck gable, and pilasters were built to look like imperial columns, complete with pedestals. Decorative scrolls were added as finishing flourishes, and the peak wore a triangle or globe to simulate a temple roof.

A wonderful example of this is the Koninklijk Paleis (Royal Palace; p85) in Amsterdam, originally built as the town hall in 1648. Van Campen, the architect, drew on classical designs and dropped many of De Keyser's playful decorations, and the resulting building exuded gravity with its solid lines and shape.

This new form of architecture suited the city's businessmen, who needed to let the world know that they were successful. As sports cars were still centuries away, canal houses became showpieces. Despite the narrow plots, each building from this time makes a statement at gable level through sculpture and myriad shapes and forms. Philips and Justus Vingboons were specialists in these swanky residences; their most famous works include the Bijbels Museum (Biblical Museum; p103) and houses scattered throughout Amsterdam's western canal belt.

The capital is not the only city to display such grand architecture. Den Haag has 17th-century showpieces, including the Paleis Noordeinde (p193) and the Mauritshuis (p191), and scores of other examples line the picture-perfect canals of Leiden, Delft and Maastricht, to name but a few.

From the mid-17th century onwards Dutch architecture began to influence France and England, and its colonial styles can still be seen in the Hudson River Valley of New York state.

GABLES & HOISTS

Travel the length and breadth of the Netherlands and there is one architectural phenomenon you simply can't escape – the elegant gable. These eye-catching vertical triangular or oblong sections at the top of a facade are as important to Dutch architecture as *gezelligheid* (conviviality, cosiness) is to the Dutch psyche.

The original purpose of a gable was entirely practical – it not only hid the roof from public view but also helped to identify the house (this changed when the occupying French introduced house numbers in 1795). The more ornate the gable, the easier it was to spot. Other distinguishing features included facade decorations, signs and cartouches (wall tablets).

There are four main types of Dutch gable. The simple spout gable – a copy of the earliest wooden gables – is characterised by semicircular windows or shutters and looks not unlike an upturned funnel; it was used mainly for warehouses from the 1580s to the early 1700s. The step gable, which literally looks like steps, was a late-Gothic design favoured by Dutch Renaissance architects from 1580 to 1660. The neck gable, also known as the bottle gable because it resembled a bottle spout, was introduced in the 1640s and proved most durable, featuring occasionally in designs of the early 19th century. Some neck gables incorporated a step. The graceful slopes of the bell gable first appeared in the 1660s and became popular in the 18th century.

From the 18th century onwards many new houses no longer had gables but rather straight, horizontal cornices that were richly decorated, often with pseudo-balustrades.

If you find yourself wondering whether many canal houses are tipping forward, or you've simply had too much to drink or smoke, don't worry. A lot were built with a slight forward lean to allow goods and furniture to be hoisted into the attic without bumping into the house (and windows). A few houses have huge hoist-wheels in the attic with a rope and hook that run through the hoist beam.

FRENCH INFLUENCE

By the 18th century the wealthy classes had turned their backs on trade for more staid lives in banking or finance, which meant a lot of time at home. Around the same time, Dutch architects began deferring to all things French; dainty Louis XV furnishings and florid rococo facades became all the rage. It was then a perfect time for new French building trends to sweep the country. Daniel Marot (1661–1752), together with his assistants Jean and Anthony Coulon, was the first to introduce French interior design with matching exteriors. Good examples of their work can be found along the Lange Voorhout in Den Haag, near the British embassy. Rooms were bathed in light, thanks to stuccoed ceilings and tall sash windows, and everything from staircases to furniture was designed in harmony.

Rotterdam's 12-storey Witte Huis (built 1898) was Europe's first 'skyscraper'.

NEOCLASSICISM

Architecture took a back seat during the Napoleonic Wars in the late 18th century. Buildings still needed to be built, of course, so designers dug deep into ancient Greek and Roman blueprints once more and eventually came up with neoclassicism (c 1790–1850). Known for its order, symmetry and simplicity, neoclassical design became the mainstay for houses of worship, courtyards and other official buildings. A shining example of neoclassicism is Groningen's town hall (p241); of particular note are the classical pillars, although the use of brick walls is a purely Dutch accent. Many a church was subsidised by the government water ministry and so was named a Waterstaatkerk (state water church), such as the lonely house of worship in Schokland (p170).

LATE 19TH CENTURY

From the 1850s onwards, many of the country's large architectural projects siphoned as much as they could from the Gothic era, creating neo-Gothic.

Soon afterwards, freedom of religion was declared and Catholics were allowed to build new churches in Protestant areas. Neo-Gothic suited the Catholics just fine, and a boom in church-building took place; Amsterdam's Krijtberg (p104) is one of the most glorious examples.

Another wave of nostalgia, neo-Renaissance, drew heavily on De Keyser's earlier masterpieces. Neo-Renaissance buildings were erected throughout the country, made to look like well-polished veterans from three centuries earlier. For many observers, these stepped-gable edifices with alternating stone and brick are the epitome of classic Dutch architecture.

One of the leading architects of this period was Pierre Cuypers (1827–1921), who built several neo-Gothic churches but often merged the style with neo-Renaissance, as can be seen in Amsterdam's Centraal Station (p97) and Rijksmuseum (p105). These are predominantly Gothic structures but have touches of Dutch Renaissance brickwork.

Frank Lloyd Wright acolyte William Dudok's stunning town hall is the one good reason to visit Hilversum (p167).

BERLAGE & THE AMSTERDAM SCHOOL

As the 20th century approached, the neo styles and their reliance on the past were strongly criticised by Hendrik Petrus Berlage (1856–1934), the father of modern Dutch architecture. He favoured spartan, practical designs over frivolous ornamentation; the 1902 Beurs van Berlage (p96) displays these ideals to the full. Berlage cooperated with sculptors, painters and tilers to ensure that ornamentation was integrated into the overall design in a supportive role, rather than being tacked on as an embellishment to hide the structure.

The website of who's who in Holland's architectural scene is www.dutch architects.com.

Berlage's residential designs approached a block of buildings as a whole, not as a collection of individual houses. In this he influenced the young architects of what became known as the Amsterdam School, though they rejected his stark rationalism and preferred more creative designs. Leading exponents were Michel de Klerk (1884–1923), Piet Kramer (1881–1961) and Johan van der Mey (1878–1949); the latter ushered in the Amsterdam School (c 1916–30) with his extraordinary Scheepvaarthuis (p109), which now houses a museum.

Brick was the material of choice for such architects, and housing blocks were treated as sculptures, with curved corners, oddly placed windows and ornamental, rocket-shaped towers. Their Amsterdam housing estates, such as De Klerk's 'Ship' in the west, have been described as fairy-tale fortresses rendered in a Dutch version of art deco. Their preference for form over function meant their designs were great to look at but not always fantastic to live in, with small windows and inefficient use of space.

The Guide to Modern Architecture in the Netherlands by Paul Groenendijk and Piet Vollaard is a comprehensive look at 20th-century architecture, arranged by region, with short explanations and photos.

Housing subsidies sparked a frenzy of residential building activity in the 1920s. At the time, many architects of the Amsterdam School worked for the Amsterdam city council and designed the buildings for the Oud Zuid (Old South, p104). This large-scale expansion – mapped out by Berlage – called for good-quality housing, wide boulevards and cosy squares; it was instigated by the labour party, but the original designer didn't get much of a chance to design the buildings, as council architects were pushing their own blueprints.

FUNCTIONALISM

While Amsterdam School–type buildings were being erected all over their namesake city, a new generation of architects began to rebel against the school's impractical (not to mention expensive) structures. Influenced by the Bauhaus school in Germany, Frank Lloyd Wright in the USA and Le Corbusier in France, they formed a group called 'the 8'. It was the first stirring of functionalism (1927–70).

CYCLING THROUGH ARCHITECTURE

For a firsthand view of how Dutch cities have developed through the ages and how they effortlessly merge with the surrounding countryside, hire a bike in Amsterdam and cycle to Haarlem (two hours).

Start in the very heart of the capital among its gabled houses and grand buildings, then head west through its spacious, modern suburbs and on to the unhurried outer business parks punctuated by wide roads and glass-and-steel constructions; before you know it, you'll have smoothly arrived in the countryside. An hour of gentle riding is before you until it all starts again, but in reverse; Haarlem's business parks greet you first, followed by contemporary suburbs, and suddenly you're savouring a beer in the shadow of the glorious Gothic Grote Kerk.

Architects such as B Merkelbach (1901–61) and Gerrit Rietveld (1888–1965) believed that form should follow function and sang the praises of steel, glass and concrete. Their spacious designs were practical and allowed for plenty of sunlight; the Rietveld-Schröderhuis (p176) is the only house built completely along functionalist De Stijl lines.

After the war, functionalism came to the fore and stamped its authority on new suburbs to the west and south of Amsterdam, as well as war-damaged cities such as Rotterdam. High-rise suburbs were built on a large scale yet weren't sufficient to keep up with the population boom and urbanisation of Dutch life. But functionalism fell from favour as the smart design aspects were watered down in low-cost housing projects for the masses.

Bart Lootsma's Super Dutch *is a slick book covering contemporary Dutch design from the country's most influential architects.*

MODERNISM & BEYOND

Construction has been booming in the Netherlands since the 1980s, and architects have had ample opportunity to flirt with numerous 'isms' such as structuralism, neorationalism, postmodernism and supermodernism. Evidence of these styles can be found in Rotterdam (p207), where city planners have encouraged bold designs that range from Piet Blom's startling cube-shaped Boompjestorens to Ben van Berkel's graceful Erasmusbrug.

In fact the whole city is a modern architectural showcase where new 'exhibits' are erected all the time. The tallest building in the country, the MaasToren, topped out at 165m, and just a short distance away the rising De Rotterdam will be the largest building in the country. The latter is designed by Rotterdam's own Rem Koolhaas, one of the world's most influential architects.

Striking examples in Amsterdam include the NEMO science centre (p108), which recalls a resurfacing submarine, and the recent Eastern Docklands housing estate, where 'blue is green' – ie the surrounding water takes on the role of lawns and shrubbery.

The shores along Amsterdam's IJ River are a good place to see the vaunted Dutch traditions of urban design in action. Northwest of Centraal Station lies the Westerdokeiland, an imposing clutch of flats, offices and cafes embracing a pleasure harbour; to the northeast is Oosterdokeiland, an A1 office location with housing and home to the new Openbare Bibliotheek. Across the river in Amsterdam-Noord there's Overhoeks, a housing estate on the old Shell Oil compound that will soon border the future Filmmuseum. And so a new city rises where once there was marsh, the story of the Netherlands.

The website www .emporis.com is a great place to get the basics on recent Dutch buildings, who designed them and what else the architects have done.

Rotterdam is home to MVRDV, a firm known for its space-saving schemes such as designing 40-storey pig farms.

Environment

There's no arguing with the fact that the Netherlands is a product of human endeavour, and a well-manicured one at that. Everywhere you look, from the neat rows of *polders* (strips of farmland separated by canals) to the omnipresent dykes, everything looks so, well, planned and organised. 'God created the world, but the Dutch created the Netherlands', as the saying goes.

Much of this tinkering with nature has been out of necessity – it's hard to live underwater for any length of time. But all this reorganisation has put a strain on the Dutch environment. Whether it's from pollution, deforestation or flooding, the cumulative dangers to natural and artificial environments are pressing. Nearly one-third of the country's surface is devoted to agriculture, while much of the rest serves towns and industry.

Since the mid-20th century Dutch awareness of the environment has grown by leaps and bounds. Citizens dutifully sort their rubbish, support pro-bicycle schemes, and protest over scores of projects of potential detriment. City-centre congestion has been eased by cutting parking spaces, closing roads, erecting speed bumps and initiating park-and-ride programs. Country roads tend to favour bike lanes at the cost of motor vehicles.

The Dutch now tend to monitor pollution as they do their dykes – with extreme vigilance.

THE LAND

A third of the dairy cattle in the world are Holstein Friesian, a high-yielding black and white variety from the north of the Netherlands.

Flanked by Belgium, Germany and the choppy waters of the North Sea, the land mass of the Netherlands is to a great degree artificial, having been reclaimed from the sea over many centuries. Maps from the Middle Ages are a curious sight today, with large chunks of land 'missing' from Noord Holland and Zeeland. The country now encompasses 41,526 sq km, making it roughly half the size of Scotland or a touch bigger than the USA's state of Maryland.

Twelve provinces make up the Netherlands. Almost all of these are as flat as a Dutch pancake, for want of a better term; the only hills to speak of in the entire country rise from its very southern tip, near Maastricht. The soil in the west and north is relatively young and consists of peat and clay formed less than 10,000 years ago. Much of this area is below sea level, or reclaimed land.

The efforts of the Dutch to create new land – which basically equates to reclaiming it from the encroaching sea – are almost super-human. Over the past century alone four vast *polders* have been created through ingenious engineering: Wieringermeer in Noord Holland; the Noordoostpolder (Northeast *polder*) in Flevoland; and the Noordpolder (North *polder*) and Zuidpolder (South *polder*) on the province-island of Flevoland. Much of this, just over 1700 sq km, was drained after a barrier dyke closed off the North Sea in 1932 (see p169). In total, an astounding 20% of the country is reclaimed land.

Polders (areas of drained land) form 60% of the Netherlands landscape.

It's impossible to talk about the Dutch landscape without mentioning water which covers 20% of the entire country. Most Dutch people shudder at the thought of a leak in the dykes. If the Netherlands were to lose its 2400km of mighty dykes and dunes – some of which are 25m high – the large cities would be inundated. Modern pumping stations run around the clock to drain off excess water.

The danger of floods is most acute in the southwestern province of Zeeland, a sprawling estuary for the rivers Schelde, Maas, Lek and Waal. The latter two are branches of the Rijn (Rhine), the final leg of a watery journey that begins in the Swiss Alps. The Maas is another of Europe's major rivers to cross the country. It rises in France and travels through Belgium before depositing its load in the North Sea in the Delta region.

WILDLIFE

Human encroachment has played a huge role in the wildlife of the Netherlands. Few wildlife habitats are left intact in the country, and more than 10% of species are imported; since 1900, the number of imported species has doubled.

While Holland's flora and fauna will always be in constant change, one thing remains the same – birds love the place. A great depth of species can be seen the entire year round, and bird-watching enthusiasts will be all aflutter at the abundance of opportunities to spot our feathered friends.

Animals

The Netherlands is a paradise for birds and those who love to follow them around. The wetlands are a major migration stop for European birds, particularly Texel's Duinen van Texel National Park (p160), Flevoland's Oostvaardersplassen Nature Reserve (p170) and the Delta (p224). Just take the geese: a dozen varieties, from white-fronted to pink-footed, break their V-formations to winter here.

Along urban canals you'll see plenty of mallards, coots and swans as well as the lovely grebe with its regal head plumage. The graceful blue heron spears frogs and tiny fish in the ditches of the *polder* lands, but also loiters on canal boats in and out of town. Other frequent guests include the black cormorant, an accomplished diver with a wingspan of nearly 1m.

A variety of fish species dart about the canals and estuaries. One of the most interesting species is the eel, which thrives in both fresh and salt water. These amazing creatures breed in the Sargasso Sea off Bermuda before making the perilous journey to the North Sea (only to end up down someone's gullet). Freshwater species such as white bream, rudd, pike, perch, stickleback and carp also enjoy the canal environment. You can admire them up close at Amsterdam's Artis zoo (p108), in an aquarium that simulates an Amsterdam canal.

In the coastal waters there are 12 crustacean species including the Chinese mitten crab. This tasty little guy from the Far East has adapted so well to the Dutch estuaries that it's become a hazard to river habitats. Further out, the stock of North Sea cod, shrimp and sole has suffered from chronic overfishing, and catches are now limited by EU quotas.

Larger mammals such as the fox, badger and fallow deer have retreated to the national parks and reserves. Some species such as boar, mouflon and red deer have been reintroduced to controlled habitats. Herds of seals can be spotted on coastal sandbanks. Introduced muskrats are common in the countryside, while their cousins, the water vole and the brown rat, find shelter in the canalside nooks and crannies of cities.

Plants

Mention plant life in the Netherlands and most people think of tulips. Indeed, these cultivated bulbs are in many ways representative of much of

Where to Watch Birds in Holland, Belgium and Northern France by Arnoud van den Berg and Dominique Lafontaine is a regional guide to the best places to see your favourite species, with the locations of observation hides.

The site www.dutch birding.nl is the online home of the Dutch Birding Society.

HIGHS & LOWS

There's no arguing that the Netherlands is a low, flat country (Netherlands in Dutch means 'low land'), but it does have some dips and bumps. Its lowest point – the small town of Nieuwerkerk aan den IJssel, near Rotterdam – is 6.74m below sea level, while its highest point, the Vaalserberg in Limburg, is a meagre 321m above.

BIRD-WATCHING FOR BEGINNERS

Seen through an amateur bird-watcher's eyes, some of the more interesting sightings might include the following:

■ Avocet – common on the Waddenzee and the Delta, with slender upturned bill, and black and white plumage.

■ Black woodpecker – drums seldom but loudly. To see it, try woodlands such as Hoge Veluwe National Park.

■ Bluethroat – song like a free-wheeling bicycle; seen in Biesbosch National Park, Flevoland and the Delta.

■ Great white egret – cranelike species common in marshlands. First bred in Flevoland in the early 1990s.

■ Marsh harrier – bird of prey; often hovers over reed beds and arable land.

■ Spoonbill – once scarce, this odd-looking fellow has proliferated on coasts in Zeeland and the Wadden Islands.

■ White stork – nearly extinct in the 1980s, numbers have since recovered. Enormous nests.

---

the country's flora in that they were imported from elsewhere and then commercially exploited. A range of other flowers and fruit and vegetables – such as tomatoes and sweet peppers (capsicum) – fit this profile.

Of course, the flowers of the Netherlands are not limited to exotic types. There are also thousands of wild varieties on display, such as the marsh orchid (with a pink crown of tiny blooms) or the Zeeland masterwort (with bunches of white, compact blooms).

> The Netherlands is planted with 228 sq km of flower bulbs, the equivalent of around 32,500 football fields.

Much of the undeveloped land is covered by grass, which is widely used for grazing. The wet weather means that the grass remains green and grows for much of the year – on coastal dunes and mudflats, and around brackish lakes and river deltas. Marshes, heaths and peatlands are the next most common features. The remnants of oak, beech, ash and pine forests are carefully managed. Wooded areas such as Hoge Veluwe National Park are mostly products of recent forestation, so trees tend to be young and of a similar age.

NATIONAL PARKS

With so few corners of the Netherlands left untouched, the Dutch cherish every bit of nature that's left, and that's doubly true for their national parks (www.nationaalpark.nl). But while the first designated natural reserve was born in 1930, it wasn't until 1984 that the first publicly funded park was established.

> The site www.nationaal park.nl provides a comprehensive list of national parks in the Netherlands.

National parks in the Netherlands tend to be small affairs – for an area to become a park, it must only be bigger than 10 sq km (and of course be important in environmental terms). Most of the 20 national parks in the country average a mere 6400 hectares and are not meant to preserve some natural wonder, but are open areas of special interest. A total of 1289 sq km, or just over 3%, of the Netherlands is protected in the form of national parks; the most northerly is the island of Schiermonnikoog, and the most southerly is the terraced landscape of De Meinweg.

Some national parks are heavily visited, not only because there's plenty of nature to see but also because of their well-developed visitors centres and excellent displays of contemporary flora and fauna. Hoge Veluwe, established in 1935, is a particular favourite. Once the country retreat of the wealthy Kröller-Müller family, it's now open to the public, who can explore the sandy hills and forests that once were prevalent in this part of the Netherlands.

NOTABLE NATIONAL PARKS & NATURE RESERVES OF THE NETHERLANDS			
Name	Features	Activities	Best time to visit
Biesbosch NP (p218)	estuarine reed marsh, woodland	canoeing, hiking, bird-watching, cycling	Mar-Sep
Duinen van Texel NP (p160)	dunes, heath, forest	hiking, cycling, bird-watching, swimming	Mar-Sep
Hoge Veluwe NP (p264)	marsh, forests, dunes	hiking, cycling, art-viewing	year-round
Oostvaardersplassen NR (p170)	wild reed marsh, grassland	hiking, cycling, bird-watching, fishing	year-round
Schiermonnikoog NP (p237)	car-free island, dunes, mudflats	hiking, mudflat-walking, bird-watching	Mar-Sep
Weerribben NP (p251)	peat marsh	kayaking, canoeing, hiking, bird-watching	year-round
Zuid-Kennemerland NP (p145)	dunes, heath, forest	hiking, bird-watching, cycling	Mar-Sep

Of the 19 remaining national parks, Weerribben in Overijssel is one of the most important as it preserves a landscape once heavily scarred by the peat harvest. Here the modern objective is to allow the land to return to nature, as is the case on the island of Schiermonnikoog in Friesland, which occupies a good portion once used by a sect of monks and which gained Unesco recognition in 2009. Biesbosch, near Rotterdam, was formerly inhabited by reed farmers.

The most interesting national parks (NP) and nature reserves (NR) are detailed in the boxed text, above.

ENVIRONMENTAL ISSUES

As a people, the Dutch are more aware of environmental issues than most. But then again, with high population density, widespread car ownership, heavy industrialisation, extensive farming and more than a quarter of the country below sea level, they need to be.

As early as the 1980s a succession of Dutch governments began to put in motion plans to tighten the standards for industrial and farm pollution, and also made recycling a part of everyday life.

King Car

While people are happy to recycle, they're not so happy to give up their precious cars. Despite good, reasonably cheap public transportation, private car ownership has risen sharply over the past two decades. Use of vehicles is now about 50% above the levels of the late 1980s. Some critics warn that unless action is taken the country's streets and motorways will become gridlocked (as they already are at rush hour around the Randstad). Stiff parking fees (Amsterdam's, at €50 per day, are the highest in the world), the distinct lack of parking spaces, pedestrian spaces and outlandish fines have helped curb congestion in the inner cities. Outside of town centres, minor roads are being reconfigured to put cyclists first, with drivers reduced to shared single lanes. Such schemes, plus the aggressive building plan for separate cycling routes, have made some headway in slowing the growth in car use. Although when a country driver blows past you on a dyke road doing 120km/h and scattering all before him, it's obvious that the concept of modest car use has not been universally adopted.

Troubled Waters

The effects of climate change are obvious in the Netherlands. Over the past century the winters have become shorter and milder. The long-distance ice-skating race known as the Elfstedentocht (see the boxed text, p234) may die

Leiden and Amsterdam have both voted to ban SUVs from their city centres on the grounds that the gas-hogs emit too much pollution.

Dutch Light is an award-winning documentary available on DVD that takes an illuminating look at the play of natural light on the Dutch environment. Is it really as special as so many – including many a famous artist – have said?

out because the waterways in the northern province of Friesland rarely freeze hard enough (the last race was in 1997). The Dutch national weather service KNMI predicts that only four to 10 races will be held this century. Although damp and cold, winter in the Netherlands today is not the ice-covered deep freeze you see in Renaissance paintings.

The lack of ice over winter is simply annoying; a rise in sea levels would constitute a disaster of epic proportions. If the sea level rises as forecast, the country could theoretically sink beneath the waves, like Atlantis, or at least suffer annual flooding. Funds have been allocated to extend the dykes and storm barriers (completed only in 1997).

Normally agreeable Belgium is in high-dudgeon over a Dutch dragging of feet to dredge channels in the south to allow much larger ships to reach Antwerp. The Dutch cite all sorts of environmental worries.

The possibility of a watery onslaught is very real, and not just from the sea. Glaciers in Switzerland are melting and that water finds it way into the Rhine and eventually becoming the Rijn in the Netherlands. River flows are expected to increase by 12.5% in the next decade. However, in a break from the past the Dutch are now planning to work with the waters, as it were, not fight them. Although sure to be contentious in the coming years, plans are being made to dedicate vast swathes of land in the southern plains. Instead of fighting to keep all water out, seasonal surges will be accommodated on land that has been stripped of housing and is simply used for seasonal agriculture.

Jump online and check out these conservation organisations: Dutch Friends of the Earth, www.milieudefensie .nl; Society for Nature and Environment, www .snm.nl; and Greenpeace, www.greenpeace.org.

Growing Trouble

The Dutch chicken population hovers around 100 million, one of the largest concentrations in the industrialised world (or six chickens for every citizen). Such industrialised farming has been the cornerstone of Dutch agriculture since WWII and has brought much wealth to the country. Who hasn't seen the brilliant red Dutch tomato waiting to be sold in a supermarket in the dead of winter? (These tasteless lumps are gassed while green, which turns them red, and then flown at great expense all over the world.)

But with concerns about ground-water quality (the government recently allocated €660 million to clean up sites leaching pollution into ground water), intensive farming and all the artificial fertilisers, chemicals and animal waste that come with it are under scrutiny.

More attention is being paid to sustainable development. Bowing to pressure from both the government and green organisations such as Greenpeace, Dutch companies are shouldering more responsibility for the impact of their operations on society and the environment. Organic *(biologische)* food is rapidly gaining in popularity and the huge agriculture industry is realising that profits can be made from more sustainable practices and by going green – and we don't just mean ungassed tomatoes.

Cycling in the Netherlands

If you're a cycling aficionado you'll be in heaven in the Netherlands. The nation where everyone rides bikes to commute, to visit friends, to shop or just to have fun is perfectly designed for cyclists to enjoy the pursuit. And it's flat – mostly.

No matter what shape you're in – or what age you are – the Netherlands is a perfect country to explore by *fiets* (bicycle). Even if it's only a day pedalling along Amsterdam's canals, or a couple of hours rolling through green *polder* (strips of farmland separated by canals) landscape, it's more than worth it, and you'll be rewarded with the sense of freedom (and fun) only a bicycle can offer.

With more than 20,000km of dedicated bike paths *(fietspaden)*, there's even more reason to hop on a bike and do as the locals do. And every local seems to be doing it; the Netherlands has more bicycles than its 16 million citizens. You'll see stockbrokers in tailored suits riding alongside pensioners and teenagers, and mutual tolerance prevails.

Major roads have separate bike lanes and, except for motorways, there's virtually nowhere bicycles can't go. That said, in places such as the Delta region and along the coast you'll often need stamina to combat the North Sea headwinds.

You can have a great holiday cycling in the Netherlands. Whether you spend an entire trip cycling around the country, or do a series of day trips, or even just the occasional jaunt, you'll find that riding a bike here can be the highlight of your trip. And there are many places where riding a bike is simply the only way to get around, such as the national parks, the coastal beaches and the Frisian Islands.

LF ROUTES

While the Netherlands is webbed with bike routes great and small, one series stands out as the motorways of cycling: the LF routes. Standing for *landelijke fietsroutes* (long-distance routes) but virtually always simply called LF, this growing network of routes criss-cross the country and – like motorways – are designed to get you from one locale to another. So far there are more than 25 routes comprising close to 7000km. All are well marked by distinctive green-and-white signs.

LF routes (called 'national bike routes' in this book) mostly use existing bicycle lanes and rural roads, which often run beside dykes. A whole series of guidebooks has sprung up around them, including a range with one title for each route.

See p70 for some of our favourite LF routes.

INFORMATION

Cycling information is copious and widely available. Your biggest challenge will be limiting yourself.

Maps & Books

All tourist offices stock a huge range of maps and guidebooks for cycling. In addition they are adept at handling questions from cyclists about routes etc. The one exception is Amsterdam, where the sheer volume of tourists means that the tourist office doesn't have a lot of time. In the capital, head to one of

Bicycle Touring Holland by Katherine Widing details more than 50 bike excursions throughout the country; it's heavy on practical information and very comprehensive.

the bookshops (p83) for your references. You can also purchase maps and books at **ANWB** (www.anwb.com), the Dutch motor club's offices.

The best maps are found only in the Netherlands and not through international sources such as generic online bookshops.

The best overall maps are the widely available Falk/VVV *Fietskaart met Knooppuntennetwerk* (cycling network) maps, a series of 20 that blanket the country in 1:50,000 scale, and cost €8. The keys are in English and they are highly detailed and very easy to use. Every bike lane, path and other route is shown, along with distances.

Beyond these maps, there is a bewildering array of regional and specialist bike maps, some as detailed as 1:30,000. Many are only available at the local tourist offices of the region covered.

The site www.fietsplatform.nl is run by the Dutch National Cycling Platform, the organisation responsible for the LF routes. It has info on the routes, publications, tours and more.

Websites

There are many online resources. Here are some excellent starting points (go to translate.google.com to instantly translate Dutch sites into English):

- holland.cyclingaroundtheworld.nl – Superb English-language site with a vast amount of useful and inspiring information.
- www.landelijkefietsroutes.nl – Dutch site that lists all the LF routes and gives basic details and an outline of each.
- fiets.startpagina.nl – Dutch site that lists every conceivable website associated with cycling in the Netherlands.

PLANNING

Experienced cyclists will know how far they are comfortable riding each day. In general, people used to being on their bikes say that 80km to 100km of riding each day is both comfortable and allows them plenty of time to stop and see the sights, or as is especially true in the Netherlands, smell the flowers.

If you have no idea how far you can or want to ride a day, then you need to find out! First-time tourers are often comfortable at 50km a day, which is easy in the Netherlands as you rarely even have to ride that far from one interesting town to the next. If you really have no idea what will work for you, then don't plunge in with an overly ambitious point-to-point itinerary. Rather, try a few circular day trips to start. The Waterland Route at the end of this chapter (p71) is 37km long and a perfect introduction to Dutch bike riding. Try it – or one of the other circular routes we list (p70) – and see how you go.

CLOTHING & EQUIPMENT

Wind and rain are all-too-familiar features of Dutch weather. A lightweight nylon jacket will provide protection, and a breathable variety (Gore-Tex or the like) helps you stay cool and dry. The same thing applies to cycling trousers or shorts.

USING THIS BOOK

In the Getting There & Away section for every city, town and attraction in this book, relevant cycling information is listed. This can include the following types of information:

- Whether the train station has a bike shop.
- Useful independent bike shops.
- Which LF routes pass through or near the city.
- Cycling details and distances to nearby towns and attractions.
- Ideas for day trips.

A standard touring bike is ideal for the Netherlands' flat arena, and for toting a tent and provisions. Gears are useful for riding against the wind, or for tackling a hilly route in Overijssel or Limburg – though the Alps it ain't. Other popular items include a frame bag (for a windcheater and lunch pack), water bottles and a handlebar map-holder so you'll always know where you're going. Very few locals wear a helmet, although they're sensible protection, especially for children.

Make sure your set of wheels has a bell: paths can get terribly crowded (at times with blasé pedestrians who don't move) and it becomes a pain if you have to ask to pass every time. Another necessity is a repair kit. Most rental shops will provide one on request.

GETTING A BIKE

Your choices are hiring a bike, buying a bike or using your own. Each has pros and cons.

Hire

Rental shops are available in abundance. Many day trippers avail themselves of the train-station bicycle shops, called **Rijwiel shops** (www.ov-fiets.nl), which are found in more than 100 train stations. Details are noted throughout this book.

Operating long hours (6am to midnight is common), the shops hire out bikes from €6 to €8 per day with discounts by the week. Many have a selection of models. You'll have to show a passport or national ID card, and leave a credit-card imprint or pay a deposit (usually €25 to €100).

The shops also usually offer repairs, sell new bikes and have secured bike parking (from per day/week €1.10/4.40).

Private shops charge similar rates but may be more flexible on the form of deposit. In summer it's advisable to reserve ahead, as shops regularly hire out their entire stock, especially on places such as the nearly car-free Frisian Islands where everybody arriving wants a bike.

You normally have to return your bike to the place you rented it. Given that distances are short, you can easily just hop a train back to your starting point.

Purchase

Your basic used bicycle (no gears, with coaster brakes, maybe a bit rickety) can be bought for around €75 from bicycle shops or the classified ads. Count on paying €100 or more for a reliable two-wheeler with gears. Stolen bikes are available on the street for as little as €15, but it's highly illegal and the cash usually goes straight into a junkie's arm. Good new models start at around €200 on sale, but top-of-the-line brands can cost €1000 or more. Bike shops are everywhere.

Your Own Bike

If you love your bike, it may be the ideal mechanical companion for your trip. But there are drawbacks. First, there's the hassle of getting your bike to the Netherlands. See p296 for what to take into consideration when flying with your bike. See p297 for information on riding in over the border and see p298 for how to come from the UK on a ferry.

More importantly, the odds of your bike being stolen in Amsterdam, and to a lesser extent Rotterdam, are high.

More than 150,000 bikes are stolen each year in Amsterdam. Good reason not to leave your prized racer from home outside (even if it's locked).

ON THE TRAIN

You may bring your bicycle onto any train as long as there is room; a day pass for bikes (*dagkaart fiets;* €6) is valid in the entire country regardless of the distance involved. There are no fees for collapsible bikes so long as they can be considered hand luggage.

Dutch trains often have special carriages for loading two-wheelers – look for the bicycle logos on the side of the carriage. Bicycles are prohibited on trains during the weekday rush hours (6.30am to 9am and 4.30pm to 6pm), except for the Hoek van Holland boat train. There are no restrictions on holidays, at weekends or during July and August.

ROAD RULES & SECURITY

Most major roads have separate bike lanes with their own signs and traffic lights. Generally, the same road rules apply to cyclists as to other vehicles, even if few cyclists seem to observe them (notably in Amsterdam). In theory, you could be fined for running a traffic light or reckless riding, but it rarely happens. Watch out at roundabouts, where right of way may be unclear.

Be sure you have one or two good locks. Hardened chain-link or T-hoop varieties are best for attaching the frame and front wheel to something solid. However, even the toughest lock won't stop a determined thief, so if you have an expensive model it's probably safer to buy or hire a bike locally. Many train-station bike-hire shops also run *fietsenstallingen,* secure storage areas where you can leave your bike (per day/week approximately €1.10/4.40). In some places you'll also encounter bicycle 'lockers' that can be accessed electronically.

Don't ever leave your bike unlocked, even for an instant. Secondhand bikes are a lucrative trade, and hundreds of thousands are stolen in the Netherlands each year. Even if you report the theft to the police, chances of recovery are virtually nil.

For more on cycling road rules, see p111.

TOURS

Amsterdam has several outfits offering bike tours of the city; see p114 for details. For multiday trips around the country, see p302 for a few ideas. There are many bike-touring operators.

ACCOMMODATION

Apart from the camping grounds listed in this book, there are plenty of nature camp sites along bike paths, often adjoined to a local farm. They tend to be smaller, simpler and cheaper than the regular camping grounds, and many don't allow cars or caravans. The **Stichting Natuurkampeerterreinen** (Nature Campsites Foundation; www.natuurkampeerterreinen.nl) has more than 130 locations throughout the Netherlands.

You may also wish to try *trekkershutten,* basic hikers' huts available at many camping grounds. See p281 for more information.

Many hostels, B&Bs and hotels throughout the country are well geared to cyclists' needs; often those on some of the more popular cycle routes, particularly along the coastline, market directly to tourists on two wheels. As always, tourist information offices can help here.

ROUTES

To give you an idea of what's possible, here are some of our favourite cycling routes.

Important LF Routes

Among the nearly 30 routes are these:

- LF1 North Sea – Follows the coast of Holland from the Belgian border 280km north to Den Helder; jogs inland briefly near Den Haag and Haarlem.

About 85% of Dutch people own at least one bike, far and away the highest rate in the world.

- LF2 Cities Route – From the Belgian border (it starts in Brussels) runs via Dordrecht, Rotterdam and Gouda to Amsterdam.
- LF3 – A 500km marathon route that runs north from Maastricht through Nijmegen to Arnhem, then to Zwolle via Deventer and finally to Leeuwarden and the north coast.
- LF4 Central Netherlands Route – Starts at the coast at Den Haag and runs 300km east through Utrecht and Arnhem to the German border.
- LF7 Overland Route – Runs 350km northwest from Maastricht through Den Bosch, Utrecht and Amsterdam to Alkmaar.

Good Day Trips

Just a smidgen of what's possible (see the relevant sections of the book for details):

- Amsterdam to Haarlem (p144) A return trip to a great day-trip town that can include a side jaunt to the beach.
- Amsterdam to Waterland (below).
- Den Haag to Gouda (p198) A classic day trip through lush Dutch countryside to a cute little cheesy town.
- Rotterdam to Kinderdijk (p215) See the heritage-listed windmills.
- Dordrecht to Biesbosch National Park (p218) A trip to a beautiful park that fully reveals its charms to those able to explore by bike.

Three Long-Distance Faves

Each of these can be done in a week by a rider of average ability, and you'll still have lots of time to stop off and see things along the way. Add more time to turn them into longer, circle routes, or do your return journey by train. Another option is to avoid the surrounding Amsterdam hassle, take the train to the first town and pick up your bike there.

- Old Holland – Amsterdam–Haarlem–Leiden–the coast/tulips–Den Haag–Delft–Dordrecht.
- North Holland – Amsterdam–Waterland–Marken–Edam–Enkhuizen–Alkmaar–the coast–Den Helder–Texel.
- Classic Holland – Amsterdam–Muiden–Utrecht–Amersfoort–Hoge Veluwe National Park–Arnhem–Deventer–Zwolle.

Waterland Route

37km, 3½ to five hours

The eastern half of Waterland is culture-shock material: 20 minutes from central Amsterdam you step centuries back in time. This is an area of isolated farming communities and flocks of birds amid ditches, dykes and lakes.

It takes a few minutes to get out of town. First, take your bike onto the free Buiksloterwegveer ferry behind Amsterdam's Centraal Station across the IJ River. Then continue 1km along the west bank of the Noordhollands Kanaal. Cross the second bridge, continue along the east bank for a few hundred metres and turn right, under the freeway and along Nieuwendammerdijk past Vliegenbos camping ground. At the end of Nieuwendammerdijk, do a dogleg and continue along Schellingwouderdijk. Follow this under the two major road bridges, when it becomes Durgerdammerdijk, and you're on your way.

The pretty town of Durgerdam looks out across the water to IJburg, a major land-reclamation project that will eventually house 45,000 people. Further north, the dyke road passes several lakes and former sea inlets – low-lying, drained peatlands that were flooded during storms and now form important bird-breeding areas. Colonies include plovers, godwits, bitterns, golden-eyes, snipes, herons and spoonbills. Climb the dyke at one of the viewing points for uninterrupted views to both sides.

Fiets-Fun (www.fiets-fun .nl) runs popular and economical bicycle tours lasting one or two weeks that stop each night in rural, car-free camping grounds. Camping equipment is provided.

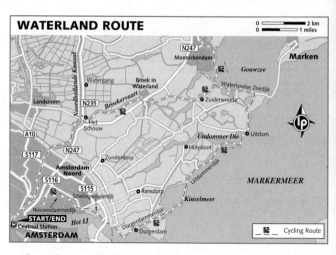

WATERLAND ROUTE

The road – now called Uitdammerdijk – passes the town of Uitdam, after which you turn left (west) towards Monnickendam (p148). Alternatively, you could turn right and proceed along the causeway to the former island of Marken (p149). After visiting Marken, you could take the summer ferry to Volendam (p149) and backtrack along the sea dyke to Monnickendam. Or you could return over the causeway from Marken and pick up our tour again towards Monnickendam. These diversions to Marken and (especially) Volendam would add significantly to the length of your trip (55km, seven to 10 hours).

From Monnickendam, return the way you came (if you came by the first route, not by one of the Marken diversions), but about 1.5km south of town turn right (southwest) towards Zuiderwoude. From there, continue to Broek in Waterland (p147), a pretty town with old wooden houses. Then cycle along the south bank of the Broekervaart canal towards Het Schouw on the Noordhollands Kanaal. Cross the Noordhollands Kanaal (the bridge is slightly to the north); bird-watchers may want to head up the west bank towards Watergang and its bird-breeding areas. Otherwise, follow the west bank back down to Amsterdam-Noord. From here it's straight cycling all the way to the ferry to Centraal Station.

THE SURPRISING NETHERLANDS

Everybody seems to have a favourite stereotypical image of the Netherlands, and obviously only having one means that the picture is far from complete. Even if people just traded their clichés, a fuller picture would emerge: a dyke for a bike for a windmill for a Rembrandt for a coffeeshop for a… Add them together and you get a rollicking, fascinating kind of place. It may be little but it's really quite big.

GLENN VAN DER KNIJFF

Cycling

The Dutch have not only raised cycling to an art, it's a way of life. It's how you commute to work, go to the shop, pay a visit to your lover and any other trip you might like to take. And the country is built for it: flat lands ribboned with bike routes.

Author Tip
Travellers can cycle the length and breadth of the Netherlands, just like the Dutch do. You can hire bikes anywhere and ride them everywhere. No country is more ideal for the ultimate pedal-powered green holiday. See p67 for details.

❶ Bike Parking Lots
Along city streets and outside big train stations is a scene that gives every first-timer pause: a veritable sea of bikes jammed together in one shiny, multicoloured tangle. It's like a Jackson Pollock vision (he *wasn't* a Dutch painter by the way).

❷ Everyone Cycles
There you are puffin' along on your first Dutch bike ride when a person of indeterminate advanced years zips right past, sitting all erect and proper on their one-speeder. Everyone cycles here; it's greener than driving, way faster than walking.

❸ Rolling Through Nature
The Netherlands has 20 national parks, all best enjoyed by bike. Off the north coast, the Wadden Islands are now Unesco-recognised and ideally suited for cycling. Some are car-free and you can ride endless bike routes alongside sand and sea.

❹ Cycling is Fun
Take a highly individualistic activity like riding a bike and add it to a highly individualistic city like Amsterdam and you get street theatre. It's not just a way to get from point A to point B but a personal expression in a place where tolerance of the bizarre is a credo.

Masterpieces & Masterworks

Dutch painters are rightfully legends: Bosch, Rembrandt, Vermeer, Van Gogh and Mondrian to name a few. Their works move, entertain, confound, surprise, illuminate and more. And some Dutch artists haven't been constrained by canvas – in evidence from the achingly beautiful old canals of Amsterdam to the architectural playground that is modern Rotterdam.

Author Tip
See the best of Dutch art in one beautiful small space at Den Haag's Mauritshuis (p191). See windmills turn in the wind at Zaanse Schans (p146) and Kinderdijk (p215). See Rotterdam's architecture from a boat (p209).

❶ Ever a Masterpiece
You can walk tiny Delft in an hour but the impressions will last for years. Vermeer may have left us barely three dozen paintings, but it's easy to see where he got a lifetime's worth of inspiration in this beautiful little town.

❷ Fabled Gables
Look up as you wander around the ancient canals of an old Dutch town (but don't fall in!) and enjoy the passing parade of 16th- and 17th-century facades, each surmounted by its own artfully stepped gable. Like faces in a crowd, no two are alike.

❸ The Real Rembrandt
'He's so good, he's a Rembrandt'. In the Netherlands you can see the real thing in Amsterdam and at smaller museums across the country. Look at the expressions in the Rijksmuseum's *Nightwatch* and you'll see what all the fuss is about.

❹ Sculpture That's 50 Storeys Tall
Buildings and bridges that are surprising, shocking and amusing are the highlight of modern Rotterdam, where the world's best architects are in the midst of a decades-long competition to claim 'mine's more stunning than yours'.

Urban Life

Amsterdam has been a vibrant centre of Dutch life for hundreds of years and no place better combines a gorgeous sweep of history with an ever-changing up-to-the-second vibe. And other cities capture the same energy, even when only on a small scale.

1

❶ Individual Character(s)
Maybe it's something in the water – or something in the air – but the capital can seem like one endless performance of street theatre. People flock here from all over the world to be exactly who they want to be all the time.

❷ Wit by the Kilo
Dry, playful humour underpins much Dutch discourse and it's easy for visitors to get caught up until they see the twinkle of an eye. Rotterdam decided the perfect public sculpture for its main shopping district is *Santa with Butt Plug*.

❸ Something in the Window
Strolling the narrow, canal-bordered streets of Amsterdam you'll find an array of shops and markets as idiosyncratic as their customers. Things you didn't know were for sale will have a tiny store or stall catering to buyers.

Drinking like the Dutch

When it's sunny the Dutch seem to multiply by the thousands and spread over entire squares of outdoor cafes. Actually, they do that when it's cloudy, or about to rain, or at night or, well, anytime. Having a drink in the Netherlands, whether it's coffee (Java was once a colony), a frothy beer or something more exotic, is a pleasurable part of life.

1 RICHARD NEBESKY; 2 MARTIN MOOS

❶ From Pub to Club

Partiers flock from all over Europe to Amsterdam and Rotterdam for endless nights in booming, moving, flashing clubs. DJs with worldwide reputations spin magic after midnight and way past dawn.

❷ Go Brown

The Dutch have turned dodgy weather into a benefit as it sends you indoors for a drink. *Bruine cafés* (brown cafes) are an institution. Amid the timeless charm, candles flicker and mirth prevails.

❸ When Clichés Collide

Beer and cheese go together beautifully. And the Dutch have a lot more interesting beer than the brands that conquered the world. Interesting ales from microbreweries are best enjoyed with a plate of aged Gouda, where complex flavours lurk in every bite.

Amsterdam

In many ways, Amsterdam today resembles Amsterdam of yore. The pale-yellow light Rembrandt loved still bathes 17th-century homes. Boats still glide along curved canals. And candles still burn in smoked-stained cafes. Of course, no one was skating in a rhinestone-studded jockstrap or biking along with a blow-up sex doll back then...

Amsterdam is revered for its progressive mindset. Coffeeshops sell cannabis. Prostitutes join the local union. The mayor marries gay couples. Tolerance has been a core Dutch value from the get-go, though there has been some soul-searching in recent years over whether it should have limits.

Meanwhile, the city grooves onward. Art lovers will be hard-pressed to find more riches per square kilometre than the mega-collections at the Rijks, Van Gogh, Rembrandt House and Hermitage Amsterdam museums. Foodies can chow hot-spiced ethnic eats and traditional Dutch treats, much of it locally sourced. Music fans can tune in to concert halls booked solid with entertainment from all over the globe. And outdoor enthusiasts? Look no further than your bicycle, to ride to the lush parks and cow-dotted outer districts.

While other cities in Europe's premier league are monumental, Amsterdam, by contrast, is irreverent, intimate and accessible: you can walk across town in 30 minutes. Late April through to September are good times to visit, when parades and festivals take over streets and stages. Actually, Amsterdam parties any time of year, rain or shine. Pack an umbrella, and you're good to go.

HIGHLIGHTS

- Admire the vivid swirls of a tortured genius at the **Van Gogh Museum** (p104)
- Experience a young girl's hidden life at **Anne Frank Huis** (p102)
- Visit the Golden Age painter's inner sanctum at **Museum Het Rembrandthuis** (p99)
- Feel *gezelligheid* (a cosy sense of wellbeing) in the lanes and cafes of the **Jordaan** (p100)
- Lose yourself in a sea of humanity at **Albert Cuypmarkt** (p107), where Amsterdam's diversity comes together

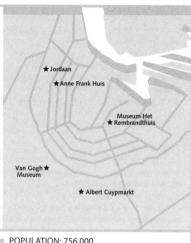

- TELEPHONE CODE: 020
- POPULATION: 756,000

AMSTERDAM

HISTORY

Around 1200, a fishing community known as Aemstelredamme – 'the dam across the Amstel River' – emerged at what is now the Dam. On 27 October 1275 the count of Holland waived tolls on locks and bridges for those who lived by the weir, and the town of Amsterdam was born. It soon developed into a major seaport.

Calvinist brigands captured Amsterdam in 1578, and soon declared the seven northern provinces – led by Holland and Zeeland – a republic, with Amsterdam at its core. The stage was set for the Golden Age, when merchants and artisans flocked to Amsterdam and a new class of moneyed intellectuals made their mark.

By the late 17th century Holland couldn't match the might of France and England, but when the country's first railway opened in 1839 the city was revitalised in a stroke.

During the latter part of that century, Amsterdammers were certainly buoyant and in a feisty mood, as the Eel Riot of 1886 proves. At the time, the sport of eel pulling was very popular throughout the city. The rules were simple: a rope would be suspended over a canal, with a live eel attached to it. Underneath, competitors in boats would try to grab the poor creature, with the ever-present threat of landing in the water adding a frisson to the proceedings.

When the authorities made the game illegal – denouncing it as a 'cruel, popular amusement' – the Jordaan erupted in riots so intense that 25 people died from gunshot wounds inflicted by the police.

The first part of the 20th century was characterised by more trouble, as WWI and the Great Depression took their toll. WWII brought hardship and hunger (see p30), but the city bounced back in the postwar years with the help of US aid and newly discovered natural gas fields off the Dutch coast.

By 1955 local life was humming along enough for French philosopher Albert Camus to write, 'Have you noticed that Amsterdam's concentric canals resemble the circles of hell? The middle-class hell, of course, peopled with bad dreams'.

How incredible, then, to see the next few decades unfold.

In the 1960s students occupied the administrative centre of the University of Amsterdam, and the women's movement began a campaign that fuelled the abortion debate throughout the next decade. Meanwhile pranksters, anarchists and radicals began a systematic program to derail conservative attitudes – with a peculiarly Amsterdammer dose of absurdism.

AMSTERDAM IN...

Two Days

Do your duty first: spin through the **Rijksmuseum** (p105) or **Van Gogh Museum** (p104) before the crowds arrive, then snack your way along **Albert Cuypmarkt** (p107) or grab a late Turkish breakfast at **Bazar Amsterdam** (p126). Stroll the Canal Belt and poke around the offbeat boutiques in the **Negen Straatjes** (p102). Sign up for a canal tour with the **St Nicolaas Boat Club** (p114) – it will actually take place on day two, but reservations must be made in person in advance. At twilight, venture through the **Red Light District** (p97) and have a drink at one of the cafes around **Nieuwmarkt** (p99). Afterwards, do elegant Dutch for dinner at **Hemelse Modder** (p124).

On the second morning visit the **Anne Frank Huis** (p102), have lunch at **Pancakes!** (p125), then hop aboard your canal tour. Check at the **Uitburo** (p131) for concert or show tickets, or hit the bars and clubs around the Leidseplein.

Four Days

On the third day fuel up in the morning at **Gartine** (p123), then hire a **bike** (p136) and see where you end up – **Vondelpark** (p106) is good for people-watching, or pedal to the **Eastern Islands and Eastern Docklands** (p108) to check out the mod architecture. Have a *gezellig* (cosy) dinner in the **Jordaan** (p124).

On day four visit a **coffeeshop** (p129) if you haven't done so already, and check out any museums you've missed such as the **Museum het Rembrandthuis** (p99) or **Hermitage Amsterdam** (p103).

Nowhere was this more evident than in the antics of the Provos, whose members included poet Johnny the Selfkicker and Bart Huges, an 'open-minded' fellow who drilled a hole in his forehead to achieve enlightenment (see the boxed text, p32).

During that decade, Amsterdam became Europe's 'Magic Centre': hippies smoked dope on the Dam, camped in Vondelpark and tripped at clubs such as the Melkweg, an abandoned dairy barn. In 1972 the first coffeeshop opened and in 1976 marijuana was decriminalised, to free up police resources for combating hard drugs. With soaring housing prices, squatters began to occupy buildings left empty by speculators; in the process, they helped save several notable historical structures from demolition.

Since the 1990s squatting has become more subdued and the city's economy has shifted to white-collar jobs, a thriving service industry and increasing gentrification. The ethnic make-up has changed too, with non-Dutch nationalities (particularly Moroccans, Surinamese and Turks) comprising more than 45% of the population.

In the first years of the 21st century, two high-profile murders and protests over immigration caused citywide anxiety. The government swiftly mounted a unity campaign called 'We Amsterdammers', which pulled the populace together, more or less. City residents have recently turned their attention to a new metro line, massive artificial suburban islands and other grand urban projects, as well as the Red Light District clean-up (see the boxed text, p99).

ORIENTATION

Centraal Station is the city's hub. From here the streets radiate outwards across the network of canals. The Dam is the heart, a 10-minute walk southwest of the station. Continuing on for another kilometre or so brings you to Leidseplein, the centre of mainstream nightlife. Nieuwmarkt (southeast of the station) is a vast cobblestone square with open-air markets and popular pubs. The Red Light District glows between the Dam and Nieuwmarkt, just south of the station.

Beyond the city centre is the Canal Belt, whose main waterways include the Singel, Herengracht, Keizersgracht and Prinsengracht, all adorned with lush, 17th-century homes. Outside the belt is the Jordaan, filled with quirky shops, bohemian bars and art galleries to the west, and the posh, museum-laden Old South

(Oud Zuid) to the (yes) south. Multicultural De Pijp sits next door to the east, followed by the garden district known as the Plantage. It segues into the old warehouses of the Eastern Islands and Eastern Docklands, which are now modern Dutch architectural showcases.

The main tourist office at Centraal Station sells a detailed street map (€2).

For further information on getting around, see p136.

INFORMATION
Bookshops
For gay-oriented bookshops, see p118.

American Book Center (Map pp88-9; ☎ 625 55 37; Spui 12) Amsterdam's biggest selection of English-language books, travel guides, newspapers and magazines.

Book Exchange (Map pp88-9; ☎ 626 62 66; Kloveniersburgwal 58) Secondhand books, many in English.

Pied á Terre (Map pp92-3; ☎ 627 44 55; Overtoom 135; ☽ closed Sun) A classy travel-book shop, with hiking and cycling guides and maps.

Selexyz Scheltema (Map pp92-3; ☎ 523 14 11; Koningsplein 20) Largest bookshop in town, with many foreign titles.

Discount Card
Students and seniors regularly get a few euros off museum admission; bring ID. For discount cards useable Netherlands-wide, such as the useful Museumkaart, see p286.

I Amsterdam Card (per 24/36/72hr €38/48/58) Available at VVV offices and some hotels. Provides admission to many museums, canal boat trips, and discounts and freebies at shops, attractions and restaurants. Also includes a GVB transit pass.

Emergency
Emergency (☎ 112) Police, ambulance, fire.

Police headquarters (Map pp92-3; ☎ 0900 88 44; Elandsgracht 117) Nonemergency help.

Internet Access
Internet cafes are scattered around town, with the largest concentration in the city centre. Costs are roughly €1.50 to €2 per hour. Or try the main library (p84) for free access. Cafes and coffeeshops also often have computers and/or wi-fi.

The Internet Café (Map pp88-9; ☎ 620 12 92; www .internetcafe.nl; Martelaarsgracht 11; ☽ 9-1am Sun-Thu, to 3am Fri & Sat) Near Centraal Station.

Internet City (Map pp88-9; ☎ 620 12 92; Nieuwendijk 76; ☽ 9am-midnight) More than 100 terminals near the main coffeeshop drag.

Internet Resources

Amsterdam Hotspots (www.amsterdamhotspots.nl) Highlights hip places to eat, drink, smoke, sleep and party down.

Backpackers on High Heels (www.bonhighheels .com) Stylish local girls give good shopping and sight-seeing tips.

I Amsterdam (www.iamsterdam.com) Excellent city-run portal providing sightseeing, accommodation, transport and event info.

SpecialBite (www.specialbite.com, in Dutch) Sends out 'spotters' to review what's new and cool on the dining scene.

Left Luggage

At Centraal Station there's a left-luggage desk downstairs from track 2, near the southeast-ern corner of the station. Storage costs around €5 for 24 hours.

Libraries

Centrale Bibliotheek (Map p95; ☎ 523 09 00; www .oba.nl; Oosterdokskade 143; 🕑 10am-10pm) The mod main library is a great place to pop in and take a load off – especially the top-floor cafe, with views over the city and water. Loads of couches, chairs, free internet terminals and free wi-fi grace every floor.

Media

For more on national media, see p38.

Het Parool (www.parool.nl, in Dutch) Amsterdam's favourite newspaper for culture and politics; the Saturday *PS* section has good entertainment listings.

Time Out Amsterdam (www.timeout.com/amsterdam) Monthly English-language magazine with cultural features and useful listings.

Medical Services

Dam Apotheek (Map pp88-9; ☎ 624 43 31; Damstraat 2; 🕑 8.30am-5.30pm Mon-Fri, 10am-5pm Sat, noon-5pm Sun) Pharmacy just off the Dam.

Onze Lieve Vrouwe Gasthuis (Map pp86-7; ☎ 599 91 11; Oosterparkstraat 1) A 24-hour public hospital.

Money

Banks stick to official exchange rates and charge a sensible commission, as does **GWK Travelex** (☎ 0900 05 66; Centraal Station Map pp88-9; 🕑 8am-10pm Mon-Sat, 9am-10pm Sun; Leidseplein Map pp92-3 Leidseplein 31a; 🕑 9.30am-5.30pm Mon-Sat, 10.30am-5.30pm Sun; Schiphol airport 🕑 24hr).

Post

Main post office (Map pp88-9; ☎ 330 05 55; Singel 250; 🕑 9am-7pm Mon-Fri, to noon Sat)

Telephone

For information about mobile phones, phone codes, public telephones and phonecards, see p291.

Toilets

Apart from the redolent public urinals for men in places such as the Red Light District, there are no public toilets in Amsterdam. Your best bet is to slip into a department store, where you'll pay the toilet attendants around €0.50.

Tourist Information

The **Amsterdam Tourist Office** (VVV; ☎ 0900-400 40 40; www.iamsterdam.com) has several branches that provide maps and help with museum, tour and hotel bookings. Note there's usually a service charge involved, and the offices are quite busy. There are several branches:

Centraal Station (Map pp88-9; Track 2; 🕑 11am-7pm) Located inside.

Centraal Station (Map pp88-9; Stationsplein 10; 🕑 9am-7pm) Located outside, behind the tram stops.

Leidseplein (Map pp92-3; Stadhouderskade 1; 🕑 10am-6pm)

Schiphol airport (🕑 7am-10pm)

Travel Agencies

Joho (Map pp88-9; ☎ 517 13 57; www.joho.nl; Taksteeg 8; 🕑 10am-6pm Mon-Sat) Sells travel services, guide-books and offers advice on work and volunteering.

DANGERS & ANNOYANCES

Theft is rare in hotel rooms, but it's always wise to deposit valuables for safekeeping at the reception desk or, where available, in your in-room safe. Theft is more common at hostels; bring your own lock for your locker.

Watch out for pickpockets in crowded markets and on trams. Violent crime is rare, especially involving foreigners, although there have been a small number of gay-bashing in-cidents recently.

Cars with foreign registration are popular targets for smash-and-grab theft. Don't leave valuable items in the car; remove registration and ID papers and the radio/stereo if possible.

There are occasionally some junkie types around the Zeedijk and Gelderskade, and also on the Nieuwendijk near Centraal Station. Generally, they won't bother you if you don't bother them.

Bicycles are numerous and can be danger-ous for pedestrians. When crossing the street look for speeding bikes as well as cars; don't stray into a bike lane without looking both ways. Cyclists, meanwhile, should take care to watch out for unwitting foreign tourists, and to lock up their bikes.

Drugs

Don't light up joints just anywhere without asking permission. In general, stick to coffeeshops. Drugs are technically illegal but tolerated. See p289 for laws relating to hard and soft drugs.

SIGHTS

If you want top-line attractions, Amsterdam delivers. The classical art circuit is an obvious route: with the Van Gogh Museum, Rijksmuseum, Stedelijk Museum and Hermitage outpost within easy reach, you'll be spoilt for choice. Then there are the theatres, coffeeshops, Golden Age facades, brown cafes – we could tailor itineraries for you until the cows come home. But, ultimately, take our tip and just wander (see the boxed text, p101).

Most of Amsterdam's major sights are in the city centre or within a few kilometres, such as the big-ticket attractions in the Old South neighbourhood. Note the top museums can get jam-packed and require a bit of preplanning; see the boxed text, p96, for details.

For a more in-depth exploration of the city, pick up Lonely Planet's *Amsterdam* city guide.

City Centre

Amsterdam's heart beats in its medieval core, as well as in the centuries-old Red Light and Nieuwmarkt districts. All visitors end up here at some point, whether to see the Royal Palace, Rembrandt's abode or near-naked women beckoning from windows. Centraal Station is the main landmark. Damrak, the core's main thoroughfare, slices south from the station to the Dam (Amsterdam's central square). The road then becomes Rokin (in the throes of metro construction in 2010) as it continues south.

MEDIEVAL CENTRE

The **Dam** (Map pp88–9) is the very spot from which the city sprouted, where a group of fisherfolk built a barrier across the Amstel River around 1200. Today pigeons, tourists and the occasional fun fair besiege the square.

Facing the Dam, the **Koninklijk Paleis** (Royal Palace; Map pp88-9; ☎ 620 40 60; www.paleisamsterdam .nl; Dam; adult/child €7.50/6.50; ⏰ 11am-5pm Jun-Aug, noon-5pm Tue-Sun Sep-May) is the official residence of Queen Beatrix, although she actually lives in Den Haag. Built as a grand city hall in 1665, the building later became the palace of Napoleon's brother, Louis. In a classic slip-up in the new lingo, French-born Louis told his subjects here that he was the 'rabbit (konijn) of Holland', whereas he meant 'king' (konink). Napoleon dismissed him two years later. The opulent, chandelier- and mural-filled interior sparkles after a major renovation completed in 2009.

Behind the palace stands the **Nieuwe Kerk** (New Church; Map pp88-9; ☎ 638 69 09; www.nieuwekerk .nl; Dam; adult/child €4/3; ⏰ 10am-5pm), the historical stage for Dutch coronations. The 15th-century, late-Gothic basilica is only 'new' in relation to the Oude Kerk (p97). A few monumental items dominate the otherwise spartan interior – a magnificent carved oak chancel, a bronze choir screen, a massive organ and enormous stained-glass windows. The building is now used for exhibitions and organ concerts. Opening times and admission fees can vary, depending on what's going on.

The **Nationaal Monument** (Map pp88–9) on the eastern side of the Dam commemorates those who died during WWII; the fallen are honoured in a Remembrance Day ceremony here every 4 May. The statues around the white obelisk stand for war, peace and resistance. In the 1960s hippies used to camp out here before being shooed away by police.

To the south, the square called **Spui** (Map pp92–3) is a popular meeting spot, ringed by pubs and bookshops. It holds a book market on Friday, followed by an art market on Sunday. And just so you know: it's pronounced 'spow' (rhymes with 'now').

The **Begijnhof** (Map pp88-9; ☎ 622 19 18; www .begijnhofamsterdam.nl; admission free; ⏰ 8am-5pm), a 14th-century former convent, hides behind the walls north of the Spui. It's a surreal oasis of peace, with tiny houses and postage-stamp gardens around a well-kept courtyard. The Beguines were a Catholic order of unmarried or widowed women who cared for the elderly and lived a religious life without taking monastic orders.

(Continued on page 96)

GREATER AMSTERDAM

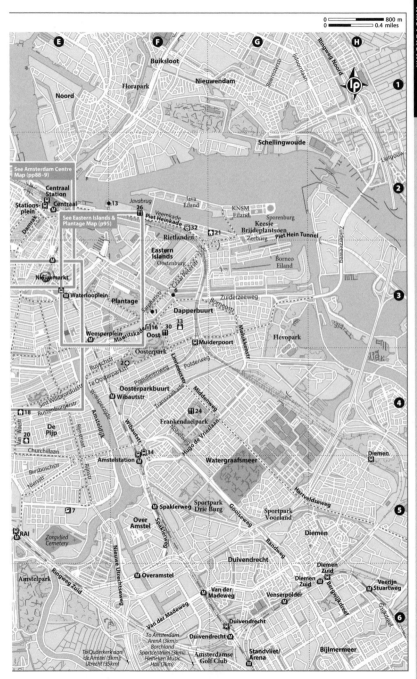

0 |=========| 800 m
0 |=========| 0.4 miles

Buiksloot

Florapark

Nieuwendam

Noord

Schellingwoude

See Amsterdam Centre
Map (pp88–9)

Centraal
Station

Stations-
plein

Centraal

●13

Javabrug

26

Java
Eiland

KNSM
Eiland

Sporenburg

Damrak

Piet Heinkade

Veemkade

32

21

Keesje
Brijdeplantsoen

Zeeburg

Piet Hein Tunnel

See Eastern Islands &
Plantage Map (p95)

Rietlanden

Zuiderzeeweg

Nieuwmarkt

Eastern
Islands

Oostenburg

Borneo
Eiland

Waterlooplein

Plantage

● 1

Dapperbuurt

Zuiderzeeweg

Weesperplein

Mauritskade

16

30

Oost

33

Flevopark

Muiderpoort

Oosterpark

De Pijp

18

20

Churchillaan

Oosterparkbuurt

Wibautstr

Middenweg

24

Frankendaelpark

Hugo de Vrieslaan

Amstelstation

34

Watergraafsmeer

Diemen

7

Spaklerweg

Sportpark
Drie Burg

Gooiseweg

Sportpark
Voorland

RAI

Over
Amstel

Diemen

Zorgvlied
Cemetery

Duivendrecht

Amstelpark

Ringweg Zuid

Overamstel

Duivendrecht

Diemen
Zuid

Veerijn

Stuartweg

Van der
Madeweg

Venserpolder

Van der Madeweg

Duivendrecht

Standvliet/
Arena

Bijlmermeer

To Amsterdam
ArenA (3km);
Borchland
Sportcentrum (3km);
Heineken Music
Hall (3km)

To Ouderkerk aan
de Amstel (5km);
Utrecht (35km)

Amsterdamse
Golf Club

AMSTERDAM

AMSTERDAM CENTRE

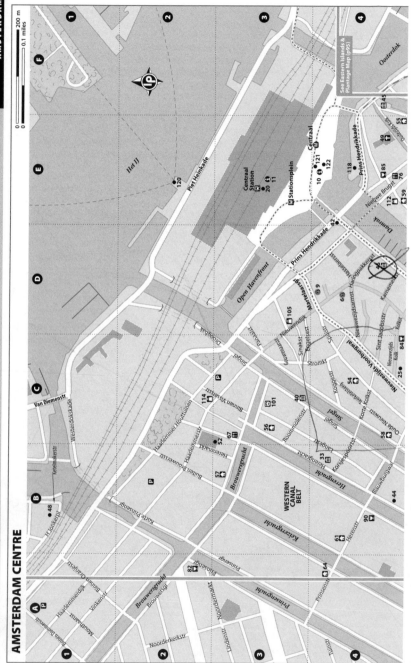

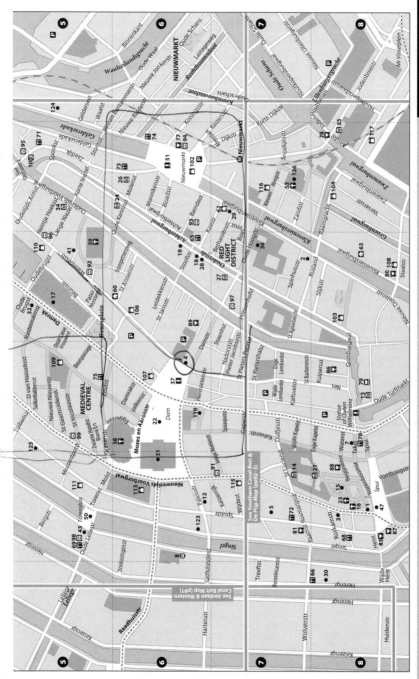

AMSTERDAM CENTRE (pp88–9)

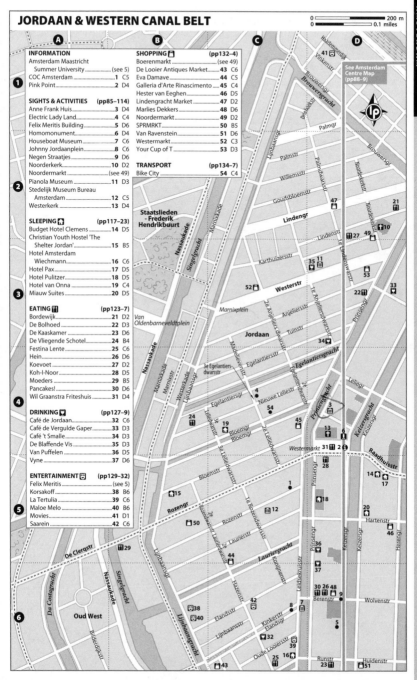

JORDAAN & WESTERN CANAL BELT

0 — 200 m
0 — 0.1 miles

See Amsterdam
Centre Map
(pp88–9)

INFORMATION
Amsterdam Maastricht
  Summer University .... (see 5)
COC Amsterdam **1** C5
Pink Point **2** D4

SIGHTS & ACTIVITIES   (pp85–114)
Anne Frank Huis **3** D4
Electric Lady Land **4** C4
Felix Meritis Building **5** D6
Homomonument **6** D4
Houseboat Museum **7** C6
Johnny Jordaanplein **8** C6
Negen Straatjes **9** D6
Noorderkerk **10** D2
Noordermarkt ....(see 49)
Pianola Museum **11** D3
Stedelijk Museum Bureau
  Amsterdam **12** C5
Westerkerk **13** D4

SLEEPING   **(pp117–23)**
Budget Hotel Clemens **14** D5
Christian Youth Hostel 'The
  Shelter Jordan' **15** B5
Hotel Amsterdam
  Wiechmann **16** C6
Hotel Pax **17** D5
Hotel Pulitzer **18** D5
Hotel van Onna **19** C4
Miauw Suites **20** D5

EATING   **(pp123–7)**
Bordewijk **21** D2
De Bolhoed **22** D3
De Kaaskamer **23** D6
De Vliegende Schotel **24** B4
Festina Lente **25** C6
Hein **26** D6
Koevoet **27** D2
Koh-I-Noor **28** D5
Moeders **29** B5
Pancakes! **30** D6
Wil Graanstra Friteshuis **31** D4

DRINKING   **(pp127–9)**
Café de Jordaan...........................**32** C6
Café de Vergulde Gaper **33** D3
Café 't Smalle **34** D3
De Blaffende Vis **35** D3
Van Puffelen **36** D5
Vyne **37** D6

ENTERTAINMENT   **(pp129–32)**
Felix Meritis ....(see 5)
Korsakoff **38** B6
La Tertulia **39** C6
Maloe Melo **40** B6
Movies **41** D1
Saarein **42** C6

SHOPPING   **(pp132–4)**
Boerenmarkt ....(see 49)
De Looier Antiques Market........**43** C6
Eva Damave **44** C5
Galleria d'Arte Rinascimento **45** C4
Hester van Eeghen **46** D5
Lindengracht Market **47** D2
Marlies Dekkers **48** D6
Noordermarkt **49** D2
SPRMRKT **50** B5
Van Ravenstein **51** D6
Westermarkt **52** C3
Your Cup of T **53** D3

TRANSPORT   **(pp134–7)**
Bike City **54** C4

AMSTERDAM

SOUTHERN CANAL BELT & DE PIJP

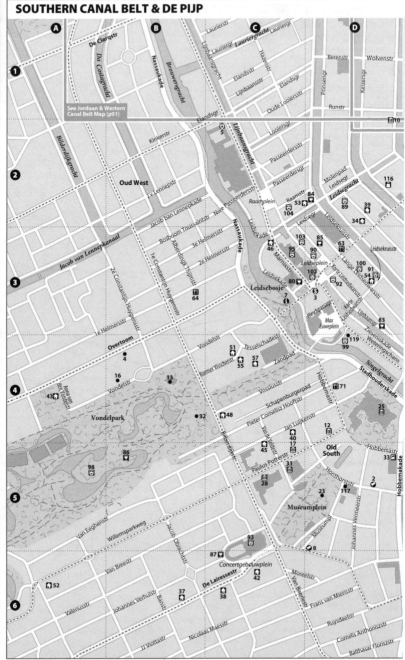

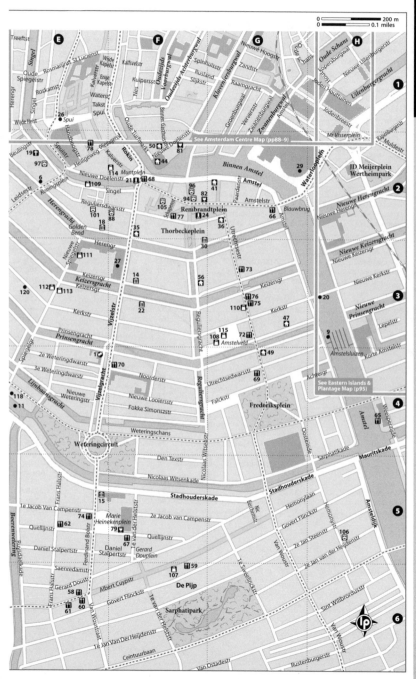

SOUTHERN CANAL BELT & DE PIJP (pp92–3)

EASTERN ISLANDS & PLANTAGE

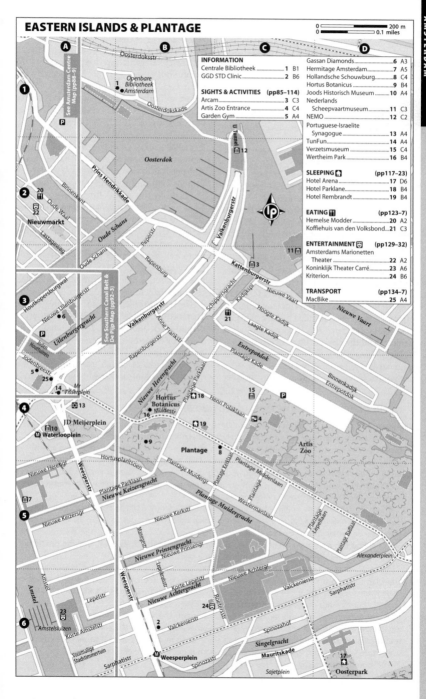

INFORMATION	
Centrale Bibliotheek	**1** B1
GGD STD Clinic	**2** B6

SIGHTS & ACTIVITIES	(pp85–114)
Arcam	**3** C3
Artis Zoo Entrance	**4** C4
Garden Gym	**5** A4

Gassan Diamonds	**6** A3
Hermitage Amsterdam	**7** A5
Hollandsche Schouwburg	**8** C4
Hortus Botanicus	**9** B4
Joods Historisch Museum	**10** A4
Nederlands	
Scheepvaartmuseum	**11** C3
NEMO	**12** C2
Portugese-Israelite	
Synagogue	**13** A4
TunFun	**14** A4
Verzetsmuseum	**15** C4
Wertheim Park	**16** B4

SLEEPING	(pp117–23)
Hotel Arena	**17** D6
Hotel Parklane	**18** B4
Hotel Rembrandt	**19** B4

EATING	(pp123–7)
Hemelse Modder	**20** A2
Koffiehuis van den Volksbond	**21** C3

ENTERTAINMENT	(pp129–32)
Amsterdams Marionetten	
Theater	**22** A2
Koninklijk Theater Carré	**23** A6
Kriterion	**24** B6

TRANSPORT	(pp134–7)
MacBike	**25** A4

(Continued from page 85)

There are two churches here: the **Begijnhof Kapel** (Map pp88–9), a clandestine chapel where the Beguines were forced to worship after their Gothic church was taken away by the Calvinists; and the **Engelse Kerk** (English Church; Map pp88–9), built around 1392. It was eventually rented out to the local community of English and Scottish Presbyterian refugees – the Pilgrim Fathers worshipped here – and still serves as the city's Presbyterian church. Also note the house at No 34; it dates from around 1425, making it the oldest preserved wooden house in the Netherlands.

The fascinating **Amsterdams Historisch Museum** (Amsterdam Historical Museum; Map pp88–9; ☎ 523 18 22; www.ahm.nl; Kalverstraat 92; adult/child €10/5; ☉ 10am-5pm Mon-Fri, 11am-5pm Sat & Sun) resides in the former civic orphanage (which was here till 1960). Begin with the large-screen TV showing an aerial view of Amsterdam's evolution, from tiny settlement on the Amstel to canal-crossed metropolis. Exhibits include religious objects, porcelains, a detailed history of Dutch trading, bicycle use, WWII, gay rights, civic projects and the city's drug policies.

From the orphanage's courtyard (note the cupboards where the orphans used to store their possessions), walk through to the **Civic**

Guard Gallery (Map pp88–9; ☎ 523 18 22; Kalverstraat 92; admission free; ☉ 10am-5pm Mon-Fri, 11am-5pm Sat & Sun), where the group portraits of medieval, ruffled-collar gents are in stark contrast to Rembrandt's more dynamic *Nightwatch* – the most famous of the group-portrait Dutch paintings in the Rijksmuseum. This is one of the world's largest collections of such group portraits, and it's free. Don't miss it.

The street that fronts the museum and gallery is **Kalverstraat**, a shopping mecca of designer jeans and striped sneakers, sleek leather boots and pot-leaf-logoed underwear. It's a far cry from its 17th-century days as a cattle market.

Those in the mood for a giggle should head to the **Sexmuseum Amsterdam** (Map pp88–9; ☎ 622 83 76; www.sexmuseumamsterdam.nl; Damrak 18; admission €3; ☉ 9.30am-11.30pm). Ogle replicas of Pompeian porn, 14th-century Viennese erotica and some of the world's earliest nude photographs, along with plastic derrières that fart at passers-by and an animatronic flasher. It's good, silly fun.

The **Beurs van Berlage** (Map pp88–9; ☎ 530 41 41; www.beursvanberlage.net, in Dutch; Damrak 243; ☉ 10am-6pm) is the old stock-and-commodities exchange designed by renowned architect HP Berlage. The functional lines and chunky square clock tower are landmarks of Dutch urban architecture. Today the building is home to the Netherlands

---

QUEUES & DISCOUNTS: THE MUSEUM LOWDOWN

Amsterdam's world-class museums draw millions of visitors each year, and queues at the Van Gogh Museum, Rijksmuseum, Anne Frank Huis and Hermitage Amsterdam can be outrageous, particularly in summer. Want to beat the crowds and save money at these sights? Here's how.

Tip 1: You've heard it ad nauseum, but it's true – if you go to the big attractions in the morning, during their first hour of operation, you're going to get in quickly. The same goes for evening hours. The Rijks and Van Gogh museums are open late on Friday, the Hermitage on Wednesday and the Anne Frank house every night in summer.

Tip 2: Buy your tickets online. Most sights sell e-tickets (you'll need to be able to print them out), and there's little to no surcharge. Online ticket holders then get to enter via a separate, faster queue (usually) than everyone else.

Tip 3: You can also buy advance tickets at tourist information offices (p84), but the problem is that the queues there are often as lengthy as the ones at the sights.

Tip 4: Think about getting a discount card. The Museumkaart (Museum Card) works well if you plan to be in the Netherlands a while. For €35, you get free entry to some 400 museums nationwide for a year. After five or six museums the card will have paid for itself. Plus card holders typically get to jump queues at museums and enter via a special 'fast lane'.

If you are making just one quick trip to Amsterdam, consider the I Amsterdam Card (per 24/48/72hr €38/48/58). It includes many of the same venues as the Museumkaart, plus a GVB transit pass. You'll need to move fast (ie visit three or so museums per day) to make it pay for itself. Note I Amsterdam Card holders typically do not get fast-track entry to sights.

For more details on the cards, see p286.

Philharmonic Orchestra and hosts occasional museum exhibitions. Roam the premises, or grab a bite and ponder the murals in the cafe.

The **Allard Pierson Museum** (Map pp88-9; ☎ 525 25 56; www.allardpiersonmuseum.nl; Oude Turfmarkt 127; adult/ child €6.50/3.25; ☉ 10am-5pm Tue-Fri, 1-5pm Sat & Sun), run by the University of Amsterdam, shows a rich archaeological collection, including an actual mummy, ancient Greek and Mesopotamian vases, a wagon from the royal tombs at Salamis (Cyprus), and galleries stuffed to the wainscoting with other fascinating items.

Beyond being a transport hub, **Centraal Station** (Map pp88–9) is a sight in itself. The turreted marvel dates from 1889 and was the work of AL Ghent and Pierre Cuypers, the master architects who also designed the Rijksmuseum and the Concertgebouw. The station's resemblance to the Rijksmuseum is easy to spot: a central section with Gothic towers and wings.

St Nicolaaskerk (Map pp88-9; ☎ 624 87 49; Prins Hendrikkade 73; admission free; ☉ noon-3pm Mon, 11am-4pm Tue-Fri, 11am-3pm Sat, services 12.30pm Mon-Sat, 10.30am & 1pm Sun), built in 1887, is the city's main Catholic church. The impressive interior features black marble pillars and an ethereal bluish aura in the soaring dome. St Nicholas is the patron saint of seafarers, so the church became an important symbol for Amsterdam.

Speaking of seafaring: the small brick tower behind the church is the **Schreierstoren** (Map pp88-9; Prins Hendrikkade 94-95), where English captain Henry Hudson set sail to find a northern passage to the East Indies (and ended up buying Manhattan instead).

The **Munttoren** (Mint Tower; Map pp92-3; cnr Rokin & Singel) is another prominent tower. When the French occupied the country in the 1670s, the national mint was transferred here from Dordrecht for safekeeping. The French got the money anyway when they later took Amsterdam.

RED LIGHT DISTRICT

Amsterdam's famous Red Light District retains the power to make your jaw go limp, even if near-naked prostitutes propositioning passers-by from backlit windows is the oldest Amsterdam cliché.

The district, known locally as De Wallen, has for centuries been the undoing of countless souls with its houses of ill repute and distilleries. Changes are afoot, however, as the city government has decided to convert many of the prostitution windows to art galleries to clean up the area (see Put Out the Red Light?, p99). It's possible big swathes could be gone by the time you're reading this.

While the ambience is still somewhat seamy, it's far less threatening than in sex districts elsewhere. Young couples, Salvation Army volunteers, drunks, the police and respectable old-age pensioners all live, work and socialise here, in stride with the surrounding commerce.

And remember: unless you want to end up in a canal along with your camera, don't take photos of the window women.

Warmoesstraat (Map pp88–9) forms the district's western boundary. Here rough-edged bars, hotels and sex shops luridly rub shoulders with some great old architecture and cafes.

East off Warmoesstraat is the city's oldest surviving building (from 1306), the mighty **Oude Kerk** (Old Church; Map pp88-9; ☎ 625 82 84; www .oudekerk.nl; Oudekerksplein 23; adult/child €5/4; ☉ 11am-5pm Mon-Sat, 1-5pm Sun), built to honour the city's patron saint, St Nicholas (the inspiration for red-suited Saint Nick). In one of Europe's great moral contradictions, the tower, arguably Amsterdam's most beautiful, commands a magnificent view – one that includes the Red Light District. See for yourself on a **tower tour** (admission €6; ☉ every 30min, 1-4.30pm Apr-Sep). But maybe the view's no contradiction at all: some of the 15th-century carvings on the choir stalls are downright naughty. There's also a stunning Müller organ, gilded oak vaults and stained-glass windows from 1555. As in the Nieuwe Kerk, many famous Amsterdammers are buried under worn tombstones, including Rembrandt's first wife, Saskia van Uylenburgh.

Outside, embedded in the cobblestones near the church's main entrance, look for the 'golden torso' plaque of a naked woman held by a groping, padlocked hand. The torso mysteriously appeared one day, was removed by police and then put back as most people seemed to like it.

Around the corner, the **Prostitution Information Centre** (Map pp88-9; ☎ 420 73 28; www.pic-amsterdam.com; Enge Kerksteeg 3; ☉ from 4pm Sat or by appointment), established by a former sex worker, provides frank information and advice about prostitution to anyone who wants it – those in the business, those buying its services and those who are just visiting. The centre's small store sells enlightening reading material and maps, but best of all is its excellent, hour-long walking tour (5pm Sat,

RED LIGHT DISTRICT FAQS

- Year prostitution was legalised in the Netherlands: 1810
- Year brothels were legalised: 2000
- Percentage of working prostitutes born in the Netherlands: 5%
- Estimated percentage of prostitutes working illegally in the Netherlands: less than 5%
- Average rental cost per window (paid by prostitute): €75 to €150 per eight-hour shift, depending on location
- Typical base cost for sex (aka a 'quickie'): €50
- Typical duration of encounter with prostitute: 15 minutes
- Nation that provides the most clients: Great Britain
- Most likely time to see prostitutes with Dutch patrons: Monday morning (when many businesses and most shops are closed)
- Do prostitutes pay taxes? Yes
- Are condoms required by law? No, but it's virtually impossible to find a prostitute who'll work without one
- Is there a union? Yes
- Are medical checkups required? No
- Is pimping legal? No
- Is trafficking in prostitutes legal? No
- Penalty for either of the above: Maximum of six years' imprisonment
- Are accommodations made if a patron can't perform? No
- What happens if a patron gets violent? Prostitutes' quarters are equipped with a button that, when pressed, activates a light outside. The offender had better hope that the police get there before the Hell's Angels do.
- Why red light? Because it's flattering. Especially when used in combination with black light, it makes teeth sparkle. Even as early as the 1300s, women carrying red lanterns met sailors near the port. Try it for yourself sometime.

€12.50 per person, no reservations needed), which takes you around the neighbourhood and into a prostitute's working room. Proceeds go to the nonprofit centre.

Another holy site rises nearby: the **Museum Amstelkring** (Map pp88-9; ☎ 624 66 04; www.museum amstelkring.nl; Oudezijds Voorburgwal 40; adult/child €7/1; ☺ 10am-5pm Mon-Sat, 1-5pm Sun), which hides a secret church. Ons' Lieve Heer op Solder (Our Dear Lord in the Attic), as it's known, was a Catholic chapel set up c 1578 after the Calvinists seized power and outlawed other religions. Inside you'll find the city's richest collection of Catholic art, a labyrinth of tiled staircases, cubbyhole quarters and the unexpectedly grand worship room itself. The museum is being renovated through to 2011, but remains open to visitors.

Oudezijds Achterburgwal is a rich vein for only-in-Amsterdam sights. The **Cannabis College** (Map pp88-9; ☎ 423 44 20; www.cannabiscollege .com; Oudezijds Achterburgwal 124; admission free; ☺ 11am-7pm) educates visitors on where to find coffeeshops that sell organic weed, tips for having a positive smoking experience and the lowdown on local cannabis laws. You can also try out a vaporiser (bring your own smoking material) and visit the mondo plants growing sky-high in the basement garden (€3 to see them; photos permitted).

The **Hash, Marijuana & Hemp Museum** (Map pp88-9; ☎ 623 59 61; www.hashmuseum.com; Oudezijds Achterburgwal 148; admission €9; ☺ 10am-11pm) features simple exhibits that cover dope botany, the relationship between cannabis and religion, and the history of Amsterdam coffeeshops. Queen Victoria used marijuana for menstrual cramps, it says here... Admission also includes the Hemp Gallery, filled with hemp art and historical items, in a separate building a few doors down.

The **Erotic Museum** (Map pp88-9; ☎ 624 73 03; Oudezijds Achterburgwal 54; admission €5; ☺ 11am-1am) has an assortment of bondage exhibits, erotic photos and cartoons. Although this museum has the advantage of location, it's less entertaining than the Sexmuseum Amsterdam (p96).

The block's most famous club is **Casa Rosso** (Map pp88-9; ☎ 627 89 54; www.janot.nl; Oudezijds Achterburgwal 106-108; admission with/without drinks €45/30; ☺ 8pm-2am), where live sex shows mount the stage each evening.

Zeedijk (Map pp88-9) bounds the Red Light District on the northeast side and marks the location of Amsterdam's old sea wall. Since the late 19th century the street has been the hub of Amsterdam's Chinatown, but it's also a symbol of urban rebirth: in the 1980s it was a major junkie hangout, but it's now home to a Buddhist temple, hole-in-the-wall eateries and some excellent bars.

The aforementioned temple is the **Guan Yin Shrine** (Fo Guang Shan He Hua Temple; Map pp88-9; ☎ 420 23 57; www.ibps.nl; Zeedijk 106-118; admission free; ☺ noon-5pm Tue-Sat, 10am-5pm Sun, plus noon-5pm Mon Jun-Aug), Europe's first Chinese-imperial-style Buddhist temple (completed in 2000). It is dedicated to Guan Yin, the Buddhist goddess of mercy, and it's worth a peek inside.

NIEUWMARKT

Nieuwmarkt (New Market) is a district as historic as anything you'll find in Amsterdam.

Rembrandt painted canalscapes here, and Jewish merchants generated a fair share of the city's wealth with diamonds and other ventures. Today this square east of the Red Light District is a bright, relaxed place ringed with cafes, shops and restaurants – arguably the grandest spot in town after the Dam.

The centre of attention is the imposing, fairy-tale **Waag** (Weigh-house; Map pp88-9), which dates from 1488, when it was part of the city's fortifications. From the 17th century onward it was Amsterdam's main weigh house, and later a spot for public executions. A bar-restaurant occupies it today, lit to great effect by medieval candle-wheels. Nieuwmarkt square itself hosts a variety of markets and events.

You almost expect to find the master himself at the **Museum het Rembrandthuis** (Rembrandt House Museum; Map pp88-9; ☎ 520 04 00; www.rembrandthuis .nl; Jodenbreestraat 4-6; adult/child €8/1.50; ☺ 10am-5pm), where Rembrandt van Rijn ran the Netherlands' largest painting studio, only to lose the lot when profligacy set in, enemies swooped and bankruptcy came a-knocking. The museum has almost every etching he made (around 250) and holds etching demonstrations several times daily. Expect to see between 20 and 100 etchings on display, depending on the exhibit. There's also a mind-boggling collection of Rembrandt's possessions: seashells, weaponry, Roman busts and military helmets. Ask for the free audio guide at the entrance. You can buy advance tickets online, though it's not as vital here as at some of the other big museums.

PUT OUT THE RED LIGHT?

They say it's not about morals but crime. In early 2008, Amsterdam's city officials announced the launch of Project 1012 to clean up the Red Light District (1012 is the area's postal code).

The first component is to halve the number of prostitution windows over the next few years (exact dates are fuzzy in the plan). The city wants to move prostitution away from Oudekerksplein and zone it to Oude Nieuwstraat and Oudezijds Achterburgwal and its side streets. The empty windows will become fashion and art galleries, and indeed this already has happened to many sites.

Coffeeshops are the other big target. Of the 76 in the area, 26 are slated for closure when their licences expire over the next three to six years.

Officials claim the two vices, which are not illegal themselves, attract elements of organised crime, and that pimps, traffickers and money launderers have entered the scene and set the neighbourhood on a downward spiral.

Opponents say the government is using crime as an excuse, because it doesn't like Amsterdam's current reputation for sin. They also point to a growing local conservatism, which prompted the city to ban tobacco smoking and magic mushrooms, too, over the past few years.

How far the city will take its clean-up efforts, and how serious it will be about enforcement, remains to be seen.

IN A TIGHT SPOT

Amsterdam is chock-full of slender homes because property used to be taxed on frontage – the narrower your facade, the less you paid.

Witness the narrow house (Map pp88–9) at Oude Hoogstraat 22, east of the Dam. It's 2.02m wide, 6m deep and several storeys tall, occupying a mere 12 sq metres per storey. This could well be the tiniest (self-contained) house in Europe.

The Kleine Trippenhuis (Map pp88–9) at Kloveniersburgwal 26 is 2.44m wide. It stands opposite the mansion once owned by the wealthy Trip brothers and, so the story goes, their coachman exclaimed: 'If only I could have a house as wide as my masters' door!'

The streets around Rembrandt House are prime wandering territory: a vibrant mix of old Amsterdam, canals and quirky shops and cafes.

Waterlooplein lies to the south. The square was once known as Vlooienburg ('flea town'), a good description for the knick-knacks on offer here today at the browse-worthy **Waterlooplein Flea Market** (Map pp88-9; 9am-5pm Mon-Sat).

The hulking **Stopera** (Map pp92-3; ☎ 551 81 17; Waterlooplein 22) complex – which houses both the city hall and the opera – opened in 1986 after nearly two decades of controversy. One critic remarked that the building 'has all the charm of an Ikea chair'. See p130 for details of performances in the Muziektheater. There are usually free lunchtime concerts on Tuesdays from 12.30pm to 1pm from October to June.

Just east is the **Joods Historisch Museum** (Jewish Historical Museum; Map p95; ☎ 626 99 45; www.jhm.nl; JD Meijerplein 2-4; adult/child €7.50/3; 11am-5pm), a beautifully restored complex of four Ashkenazic synagogues from the 17th and 18th centuries. Displays show the rise of Jewish enterprise and its role in the Dutch economy, and the history of Jews in the Netherlands. The English-language audio tour is excellent (no extra charge). There's also a kosher cafe serving Jewish specialities.

The majestic **Portuguese-Israelite Synagogue** (Map p95; ☎ 624 53 51; www.esnoga.com; Mr Visserplein 3; adult/child €6.50/5; 10am-4pm Sun-Fri Apr-Oct, 10am-4pm Sun-Thu, 10am-3pm Fri Nov-Mar) stands nearby. Built for the Sephardic community in the 17th century, the synagogue was Europe's largest at the time and was based on the Temple of Solomon.

Ask about the discount ticket if you plan to visit both the Jewish museum and synagogue.

Under the Mr Visserplein traffic circle, **TunFun** (Map p95; ☎ 689 43 00; www.tunfun.nl; Mr Visserplein 7; adult/child free/€7.50; 10am-6pm) is a kids' playground built in an old underpass. It has slides, ball pools, trampolines, a minicinema, a soccer field and a snack bar – even a children's disco. An adult must accompany children.

A short walk northeast of Waterlooplein, **Gassan Diamonds** (Map p95; ☎ 622 53 33; www.gassandiamonds.com; Nieuwe Uilenburgerstraat 173-175; admission free; 9am-5pm) demonstrates how an ungainly clump of rock is transformed into a girl's best friend. You'll get a quick primer in assessing the gems for quality, and see diamond cutters and polishers in action. The one-hour tour is the best of its kind in town – which is why so many tour buses stop here. Don't worry: the line moves fast.

The **Zuiderkerk** (Southern Church; Map pp88-9; ☎ 552 79 87; Zuiderkerkhof 72; admission free; 9am-4pm Mon-Fri, noon-4pm Sat) climbs the heavens between Nieuwmarkt square and Waterlooplein. Built in the early 1600s, it was the first custom-built Protestant church in Amsterdam (based on a Catholic design). During the 'Hunger Winter' of WWII it served as a morgue. Now it's a city-run info centre for Amsterdam's various urban expansion plans, shown in intriguing exhibits.

Jordaan

Originally a stronghold of the working class, the Jordaan is now one of the most desirable areas to live in Amsterdam. It's a pastiche of modest old homes and a few modern carbuncles, squashed into a grid of tiny lanes peppered with bite-sized cafes and shops. Its intimacy is contagious, and nowadays the average Jordaan dweller is more likely to be a gallery owner than a blue-collar labourer.

The name 'Jordaan' may be a corruption of the French *jardin* (garden), as many French Huguenots settled here in what used to be the market gardens. Other historians contend that the name had biblical connotations and referred to the Jordan River.

The **Noorderkerk** (Map p91; ☎ 626 64 36; www.noorderkerk.org; Noordermarkt 48; admission free; 10.30am-3pm Mon, 11am-1pm Sat, 1.30-5.30pm Sun) was a Calvinist church for Jordaan's 'common' people. It's shaped like a Greek cross – four arms of equal length – around a central pulpit.

DIY AMSTERDAM

Follow the canals, the crowds or that cobbled side street. Pursue that strain of violin music, or the sweet smell in the air. Push the odd wooden door that says 'open to the public'. You never know what you'll find: a hidden garden, an old building tucked out of sight, a delicious bakery or cafe.

Amsterdam is ripe for rambling, its compact core laced by atmospheric lanes and quarters. You'll see it best without your nose stuck in a book or map. So go ahead and put away this guide. We don't mind a bit.

A sculpture near the entrance commemorates the bloody Jordaan riots of July 1934, when five people died in protests over government austerity measures.

The **Noordermarkt** (Map p91), on the plaza in front of the Noorderkerk, hosts a flea market on Monday morning and a *boerenmarkt* (farmers market) on Saturday morning.

The offbeat **Houseboat Museum** (Map p91; ☎ 427 07 50; www.houseboatmuseum.nl; Prinsengracht opposite No 296; adult/child under 152cm €3.50/2.75; ☒ 11am-5pm Tue-Sun Mar-Oct, 11am-5pm Fri-Sun Nov-Feb, closed most of Jan) is aboard a sailing barge (23m long by 4m wide) from 1914. The displays are rather minimal, but you'll get a real feel for how cosy life can be on the water when you see the sleeping, living, cooking and dining quarters. In case you were wondering: houseboat toilets, until this century, could drain directly into the canals, but they now must hook up to the city sewerage system.

The colourful square beside the museum is **Johnny Jordaanplein** (Map p91; cnr Prinsengracht & Elandsgracht), named for a popular musician in the mid-1900s who sang the nostalgic tunes known as *levenslied*, or tears-in-your-beer-style ballads, which were popular in the district.

At the **Pianola Museum** (Map p91; ☎ 627 96 24; www.pianola.nl; Westerstraat 106; adult/child €5/3; ☒ 2-5pm Sun) you can hear concerts of player pianos from the early 1900s, with rare classical or jazz tunes composed especially for the instrument. The curator gives demonstrations with great zest.

Blink and you might walk right past the unobtrusive **Stedelijk Museum Bureau Amsterdam** (Map p91; ☎ 422 04 71; www.smba.nl; Rozenstraat 59; admission free; ☒ 11am-5pm Tue-Sun), a 'project space' of the Stedelijk Museum (p106). Exhibits here

– from painting and sculpture to new media and installation pieces – mix contemporary artists who have Amsterdam connections with some 'international context'.

For art of an entirely different ilk, visit **Electric Lady Land** (Map p91; ☎ 420 37 76; www.electric-lady-land.com; 2e Leliedwarsstraat 5; admission €5; ☒ 1-6pm Tue-Sat), the world's first museum of fluorescence. Even if you didn't eat a space cake before arriving, you're gonna feel like it, as grey-ponytailed artist and owner Nick Padalino takes you to his shop's basement and shows you all kinds of glow-in-the-dark objects, from psychedelic sculptures to luminescent rocks.

Western Canal Belt

Bordered by the Brouwersgracht and Leidsegracht (to the north and south respectively), the Singel to the east and the Prinsengracht to the west, the Western Canal Belt is one of Amsterdam's most gorgeous areas, filled with grand old mansions and quirky little speciality shops.

In 1613, authorities decided the city had become too crowded, so they embarked on an ambitious project to expand Amsterdam's area with semicircular and radial waterways on the western and southern sides, along with bridges and connecting roads. By 1625, the Western Canal Belt was ready for action.

Each canal had a different personality. The **Brouwersgracht** (Brewers' Canal) was named after the breweries that used to operate along the water. It's one of the most picturesque canals today and a great place for a stroll, although it wasn't always so: throughout most of its history it was an industrial canal full of stinky warehouses, workshops and factories.

The **Herengracht** (Gentlemen's Canal) was named after the '17 Gentlemen' of the United East India Company. The first section south from Brouwersgracht shows how these bigwigs sunk their profits into showpiece residences. Almost as swanky was the **Keizersgracht** (Emperor's Canal), a nod to Maximilian I, ruler of Habsburg and later the Holy Roman Empire.

Prinsengracht, named after Prince Willem van Oranje, was designed as a slightly cheaper canal and provided a barrier against the crusty, working-class Jordaan. Today it's peppered with cafes and shops rather than stately offices and banks, and the houses are smaller and narrower. Houseboats line the quays.

ANNE FRANK

The Anne Frank Huis is where the Jewish Frank family hid to escape deportation during WWII. As the German occupiers tightened the noose around Amsterdam's Jewish inhabitants, Otto Frank – together with his wife, two daughters and several friends – moved into the rear annexe in July 1942, and the entrance was concealed behind a revolving bookcase.

The Franks were betrayed to the Gestapo in August 1944 and deported via Kamp Westerbork in Drenthe (p248); Anne died in Bergen-Belsen concentration camp in March 1945, just weeks before it was liberated. Her father Otto was the only one of their group to survive. After the war Anne's diary was found among the litter in the annexe, and her father published it. The diary, which gives a moving account of wartime horrors seen through a young girl's eyes, has sold more than 25 million copies and has been translated into 60 languages.

Addressed to the fictitious Kitty, the diary traces the teenager's development through puberty and persecution, and displays all the signs of a gifted writer in the making.

The **Anne Frank Huis** (Anne Frank House; Map p91; ☎ 556 71 05; www.annefrank.org; Prinsengracht 267; adult/child €8.50/4; ♼ 9am-9pm mid-Mar–Jun, 9am-10pm Jul & Aug, 9am-7pm Sep–mid Mar) is the Western Canal Belt's übersight, drawing almost a million visitors annually. With its reconstruction of Anne's melancholy bedroom and her actual diary – sitting alone in its glass case, filled with sunnily optimistic writing tempered by quiet despair – it's a powerful experience. The focus of the museum is the *achterhuis* (rear house), also known as the secret annexe, a dark and airless space where the Franks and others observed complete silence during the daytimes, outgrew their clothes, pasted photos of Hollywood stars on the walls and read Dickens, before being mysteriously betrayed and sent to their deaths. The house stays open later on some Saturdays.

The venue does not accept the I Amsterdam Card or the Museumkaart, and queues can easily involved an hour-plus wait at peak times. Come before 10am or after 6pm to avoid the crowds. Or buy tickets online a few days in advance (€.50 surcharge), which allows you to skip the queue and use the ticket-holders' entrance to the left of the main door.

The **Westerkerk** (Map p91; ☎ 624 77 66; www.westerkerk.nl; Prinsengracht 281; church admission free, tower €6 by tour only; ♼ church 11am-3pm Mon-Fri Apr-Jun & Sep, 11am-3pm Mon-Sat Jul & Aug, tower 10am-5.30pm Mon-Sat Apr-Sep) is the main gathering place for Amsterdam's Dutch Reformed Church community. Rembrandt, who died bankrupt in 1669 at nearby Rozengracht, is buried somewhere in the church – perhaps near the grave of his son Titus, where there's a commemorative plaque. A highlight is the bell tower, Amsterdam's highest church tower at 85m. It's topped by the imperial crown that Habsburg emperor Maximilian I bestowed to the city's coat of arms in 1489. The climb (186 steps) during the 60-minute tour is steep and claustrophobic, but there are periodic landings where you can rest while the guide describes the bells and other workings of the massive carillon.

The pink granite triangles of the **Homomonument** (Map p91; cnr Keizersgracht & Raadhuisstraat), at Westermarkt behind the church, commemorate gays and lesbians who were persecuted by the Nazis; citizens lay out flowers on Liberation Day (4 May).

To the south are the **Negen Straatjes** (Nine Little Streets; Map p91; www.de9straatjes.nl), the tic-tac-toe board of Amsterdam shopping. The straatjes are full of quirky little shops dealing in antiques, fashions, housewares and one-offs including everything from toothbrushes to antique eyeglass frames.

The 100-plus-year-old Dutch cheesemaker **Reypenaer** (Map pp88-9; ☎ 320 63 33; www.reypenaer.com; Singel 182; tastings with/without wine pairings €10/7.50; ♼ 2pm & 4pm Wed-Sun) offers tastings in a rustic, wood-tabled classroom under its shop. The hour-long session includes six cheeses, plus optional wine and port pairings. It's a unique experience and you'll leave a *kaas* (cheese) connoisseur.

Heading east across the Singel is **Torensluis** (Map pp88–9), one of the oldest and widest bridges in the city. The big moustached bust is of Multatuli, the pen name of the brilliant 19th-century author Eduard Douwes Dekker, who exposed colonial narrow-mindedness in a novel about a coffee merchant. The nearby **Multatuli Museum** (Map pp88-9; ☎ 638 19 38; www.multatuli-museum.nl; Korsjespoortsteeg 20; admission free; ♼ 10am-5pm Tue, noon-5pm Sat & Sun, closed Sat Jul & Aug) tells his story.

Also on the Singel is the **Poezenboot** (Cat Boat; Map pp88-9; ☎ 625 87 94; www.poezenboot.nl; Singel, opposite No 40; admission by donation; ☯ 1-3pm, closed Wed & Sun), one of Amsterdam's more unusual flea markets. The barge began life as a shelter for hundreds of homeless cats in the 1960s. It's now a registered charity – pat and pet the current feline inhabitants for a small donation.

The **Felix Meritis building** (Map p91; ☎ 623 13 11; www.felix.meritis.nl; Keizersgracht 324) stands south along the Keizersgracht. It was built in 1787 for the Felix Meritis organisation (Latin for 'Happiness through Achievement'), a society of wealthy residents who promoted the ideals of the Enlightenment through science, arts and commerce. Composers such as Brahms, Grieg and Saint-Saëns performed in its oval concert hall, and it's still a theatre today (see p131). The adjoining cafe is exceptional.

The **Bijbels Museum** (Bible Museum; Map pp92-3; ☎ 624 24 36; www.bijbelsmuseum.nl; Herengracht 366-368; adult/child €7.50/3.75; ☯ 10am-5pm Mon-Sat, 11am-5pm Sun) has model temples, freshly restored 18th-century ceiling frescos by Jacob de Wit, and several centuries of the good book, including a Delft bible, printed in 1477. On the ground floor you can sniff scents mentioned in the good book and stroll through a garden of biblical trees.

The landmark **Westindisch Huis** (Map pp88-9) on Herenmarkt is the former head office of the West India Company. When Admiral Piet Heyn captured the Spanish silver fleet off Cuba in 1628, the booty was stored here.

Haarlemmerstraat (Map pp88-9), at the canal belt's northern tip, is another hip shopping and eating street, but with more of an edge than the Negen Straatjes. It links to Haarlemmerdijk, booming with further stylish wares on into the Jordaan.

Southern Canal Belt

If the Western Canal Belt is upmarket and refined, the Southern Canal Belt is more diverse and populist, though no less stately. It spans the area from the Leidsegracht in the west to the Amstel in the east, anchored by two key nightlife districts: Leidseplein and Rembrandtplein. In between are the antique and art shops of the Spiegel quarter and the city's gay nightlife centre around Reguliersdwarsstraat.

The **Hermitage Amsterdam** (Map p95; ☎ 530 87 51; www.hermitage.nl; Amstel 51; adult/child under 16 €15/free; ☯ 10am-5pm, to 8pm Wed) has fast become one of the city's most popular attractions since its 2009 opening. The long-standing ties of Russia and Holland – remember Czar Peter the Great learned shipbuilding here in 1697 – led to this local branch of St Petersburg's State Hermitage Museum. Prestigious exhibits, such as treasures from the Russian palace or masterworks by Matisse and Picasso, change about twice per year, and they're as well-curated as you'd expect. Come before 11am daily or on Wednesday after 5pm (the museum's late night) to avoid the lengthiest queues. At the time of writing, there was no online ticketing.

Amsterdam has specialised in flower markets since the 17th century, so if they interest you, make your way to the southern side of the Singel between Koningsplein and Vijzelstraat for the **Bloemenmarkt** (Flower Market; Map pp92-3; ☯ 9am-5pm, closed Sun Dec-Feb), which offers bulbs galore.

In the district's southwestern corner is **Leidseplein**, one of Amsterdam's liveliest squares. It was once the gateway for travellers heading south towards Leiden; the oil lamps have given way to screaming neon signs, but street musicians and artists are still drawn to the cobblestone square. There's something for everyone here: cinemas, cafes, pubs and nightclubs, and a smorgasbord of restaurants. Check at the Uitburo (p131) in the **Stadsschouwburg** (City Theatre; Map pp92-3; ☎ 624 23 11; Leidseplein 26) for last-minute tickets to various venues.

The corner of Herengracht and Vijzelstraat is dominated by the colossal **Stadsarchief** (Municipal Archives; Map pp92-3; ☎ 251 15 11; www.stadsarchief.amsterdam.nl; Vijzelstraat 32; admission free; ☯ 10am-5pm Tue-Fri, 11am-5pm Sat & Sun), occupying a 1923 bank building. When you step inside head to the left, to the enormous tiled basement vault and displays of archive gems such as the 1942 police report on the theft of Anne Frank's bicycle. A small cinema at the back shows vintage films about the city. Upstairs, a fantastic bookshop sells city-oriented tomes.

Across the street from the Stadsarchief's southeastern corner is **FOAM** (Fotografie Museum Amsterdam; Map pp92-3; ☎ 551 65 00; www.foam.nl; Keizersgracht 609; adult/child €7.50/free; ☯ 10am-6pm Sat-Wed, to 9pm Thu & Fri), an impressive museum devoted to photography. Two storeys of changing exhibitions feature world-renowned photographers such as Sir Cecil Beaton, Annie Leibovitz and Henri Cartier-Bresson. Simple, functionalist and large galleries, some with skylights or grand windows for natural light, provide the setting for this impressive museum – accessible and inspiring, yet always critical.

Across the Keizersgracht from FOAM is **Museum Van Loon** (Map pp92–3; ☎ 624 5255; www.museum vanloon.nl; Keizersgracht 672; adult/child €6/4; ☑ 11am-5pm, closed Tue), an opulent 1672 residence that was first home to painter Ferdinand Bol and later to the wealthy Van Loon family. The house recalls canalside living in Amsterdam when money was no object. Inside there are important paintings such as *Wedding Portrait* by Jan Miense Molenaer and a collection of some 150 portraits of the Van Loons.

A couple of unusual museums lie along the Herengracht. The **Tassenmuseum Hendrikje** (Museum of Bags & Purses; Map pp92–3; ☎ 524 64 52; www .tassenmuseum.nl; Herengracht 573; adult/child €6.50/free; ☑ 10am-5pm) displays half a millennium's worth of handbags – the largest collection in the Western world. The **Kattenkabinet** (Cats Cabinet; Map pp92–3; ☎ 626 53 78; www.kattenkabinet.nl; Herengracht 497; adult/child €5/2.50; ☑ 10am-4pm Tue-Fri, 1-5pm Sat & Sun) is devoted to the feline presence in art and includes works largely from Dutch and French artists (Theopile-Alexandre Steinlen, 1859–1923, figures prominently) as well as a small Rembrandt (a Madonna and Child with cat and snake) and Picasso's *Le Chat*.

The Herengracht here, between Leidsestraat and Vijzelstraat, is known as the **Golden Bend** (Map pp92–3), which had some of the largest private mansions in the city during the Golden Age. Most now belong to bankers, lawyers and financial advisers. French culture was all the rage among the city's wealthy class, so most styles are Gallic with a Dutch twist.

At the corner of Herengracht and **Reguliersgracht**, canal tour boats halt for photos at the beautiful 'canal of the seven bridges', cut in 1664. The arches are illuminated at night and reflect dreamily on the rippling water.

Nearby is **Thorbeckeplein**, with a statue of Jan Rudolf Thorbecke, the liberal politician who created the Dutch parliamentary system in 1848.

Just north of Thorbeckeplein is the raucous (or 'tacky', if you like) **Rembrandtplein**, focused around the hulking statue of the *Nightwatch* artist (Map pp92–3). The grassy square is lined with pubs, grand cafes and restaurants, and is usually buzzing with good-time guys 'n' gals looking for high times and potent toxins.

A night out on Rembrandtplein is best preceded by a meander down **Utrechtsestraat**. It's relaxed, as shopping streets go, with the occasional tram going past cosy restaurants and unique stores.

Continue east to the Amstel and you'll see the **Amstelsluizen** (Map pp92–3). These sluices allowed the canals to be flushed with fresh river water, and they were still operated by hand until a few years ago. Across the river stands the **Koninklijk Theater Carré** (Map p95), originally built as a circus but now the city's largest theatre. To the left is the **Magere Brug** (Map pp92–3), the most photographed drawbridge in the city. Often mistranslated as the 'Skinny Bridge', it was actually named after the Mager sisters, who lived on opposite sides of the canal. As the sweet tale goes, the sisters had a footbridge built so that they could visit with ease.

The soaring turrets of the **Krijtberg** (Chalk Mountain; Map pp92–3; ☎ 623 19 23; www.krijtberg.nl; Singel 446; ☑ 1-5pm, closed Mon & Fri) rise in the Southern Canal Belt's northwest corner. It's one of the city's most beautiful Gothic churches (built 1883), thanks largely to its colourful interior – a stark contrast to spartan Calvinist churches. A house here belonged to a chalk merchant, hence the name.

Nieuwe Spiegelstraat, lined with swish antique shops and art galleries, begins at the Herengracht. The extension of this street, the pretty **Spiegelgracht**, leads past more antiques and paintings en route to the Rijksmuseum.

Old South (Oud Zuid)

This genteel, wedge-shaped neighbourhood, often called the Museum Quarter, holds some of Amsterdam's biggest draws. The Rijksmuseum, Van Gogh Museum and Stedelijk Museum all cluster around the busy **Museumplein** (Map pp92–3), which hosted the World Exhibition of 1883. It's now a park, with an underground Albert Heijn supermarket (handy for picnics), a skate ramp and a large pond that becomes a festive ice rink in winter.

The Old South also features many fine examples of Amsterdam School architecture, with porthole windows, mock prows and other maritime motifs gracing the facades of weighty apartment complexes. Keep an eye out as you wander around.

VAN GOGH MUSEUM

Opened in 1973 to house the collection of Vincent's younger brother Theo, the outstanding **Van Gogh Museum** (Map pp92–3; ☎ 570 52 00; www.vangoghmuseum.nl; Paulus Potterstraat 7; adult/child

FREE THRILLS

It's possible to spend a fortune in Amsterdam, but many enjoyable sights and activities cost nothing.

- **Red Light District** (p97) Keep your eyes on the architecture and you needn't spend a cent.
- **Civic Guard Gallery** (p96) Stroll through this monumental gallery of city defenders by the Amsterdams Historisch Museum.
- **Concertgebouw**, **Muziekgebouw** and **Muziektheater** (p130) Treat yourself to great musicians playing great numbers gratis at lunchtime.
- **Gassan Diamonds Tour** (p100) Don't know your princess from marquise, river from top cape? Get the bling lowdown here.
- **Cannabis College** (p98) Will you graduate with honours after your vaporiser test?
- **Stadsarchief** (p103) Examine Anne Frank's bike-theft report, vintage films and more at the city's extensive archives.
- **Ferry ride to NDSM-werf** (p110) Sail from Centraal Station to northern Amsterdam's edgy art community.
- **Markets** (p134) Books, antiques, organic cheeses – Amsterdam is chock-full of markets and they're always free to browse.
- **Brouwerij 't IJ Brewery Tour** (p108) Learn how the brewery makes its organic beer, then quaff a glassful under the local windmill.

€12.50/2.50; 10am-6pm Sat-Thu, to 10pm Fri) consists of 200 paintings and 500 drawings by Vincent and his contemporaries, such as Gauguin, Monet, Toulouse-Lautrec and Bernard.

Van Gogh's career lasted less than a decade, ending in 1890 at age 37 when he committed suicide. The museum shows his works in chronological order on the 1st floor, from his moody Brabant canvases (*The Potato Eaters*) to the famous works from his French period (*The Yellow House in Arles, The Bedroom at Arles* and several self-portraits). Sunflowers and other blossoms display his knack for using Mediterranean light and colour. *Wheatfield with Crows* is an ominous work that he painted shortly before he died.

Designed by Gerrit Rietveld, the exhibition spaces are generous enough to accommodate insane crowds without obscuring the paintings. The sleek rear annexe hosts changing exhibitions and is an attraction in its own right, looking very much like an enormous clam (it's nicknamed 'the mussel').

Come before 11am or on Friday night (when the museum hosts special cultural events) to avoid the longest queues. I Amsterdam Card holders have a separate 'fast' lane for entry, but it can be almost as long as the regular queue. Advance ticket holders and Museumkaart owners get in quickest via their dedicated lane. You can get advance tickets online, with no surcharge.

RIJKSMUSEUM

The **Rijksmuseum** (National Museum; Map pp92-3; ☎ 674 70 00; www.rijksmuseum.nl; Stadhouderskade 42; adult/child €11/free; 9am-6pm, to 8.30pm Fri) is the premier art museum of the Netherlands, and no self-respecting visitor to Amsterdam can afford to miss it. Though most of the building is closed for renovations until 2013, there is an excellent collection of around 200 masterpieces – a sort of 'best of' group – exhibited in a side section, the Philips wing.

Pride of place is taken by Rembrandt's *Nightwatch* (1650), showing the militia led by Frans Banningh Cocq, a future mayor of the city. The painting only acquired its name over time with a layer of grime (it's nice and clean now). Other 17th-century Dutch masters include Jan Vermeer (*The Milkmaid* and *Woman in Blue Reading a Letter*), Frans Hals (*The Merry Drinker*) and Jan Steen (*The Merry Family*).

Other good sections are Sculpture and Applied Art (delftware, dollhouses, porcelain, furniture), Dutch History and Asiatic Art. The museum's famous print archives have some 800,000 prints and drawings.

The Rijksmuseum building was completed in 1885 to a design by Pierre Cuypers. The exterior remains a feast for the eyes, with tiled murals, faux-Gothic towers and glints of gold harking back to the fortunes of the Golden Age.

To avoid the most outrageous queues, come before 10am or on Friday night, when the museum stays open late. I Amsterdam card holders must wait in the regular queue. Advance ticket holders and Museumkaart owners can jump into the separate 'fast lane' (look for the sign northeast of the Philips wing entrance). Advance tickets are available online, with no surcharge.

STEDELIJK MUSEUM

Built in 1895 to a neo-Renaissance design by AM Weissman, the **Stedelijk Museum** (Map pp92-3; ☎ 573 29 11; www.stedelijk.nl; Paulus Potterstraat 13) is the permanent home of the National Museum of Modern Art. The modern classics here are among the world's most admired, amassed with great skill by postwar curator Willem Sandberg. The permanent collection includes all the blue chips of 19th- and 20th-century painting – Monet, Picasso and Chagall among them – as well as sculptures by Rodin, abstracts by Mondrian and Kandinsky, and much, much more.

When we visited, the museum was finishing up its years-long renovation and expansion (the latter bit dubbed 'the Bathtub' by locals), scheduled for completion in spring 2010. Call for admission prices and hours.

CONCERTGEBOUW

The 1888, neo-Renaissance **Concertgebouw** (Concert Bldg; Map pp92-3; ☎ 671 83 45; www.concertgebouw .nl; Concertgebouwplein 2-6) is the world's busiest concert hall. Under the 50-year guidance of composer and conductor Willem Mengelberg (1871–1951), the Koninklijk Concertgebouw Orkest (Royal Concert Building Orchestra) developed into one of the world's finest. Dozens of landmark performances have been recorded in the Main Hall's near-perfect acoustics; the lure of playing in the venue is so strong that local musicians accept pay that's lower than that in many other countries. For concert details, including free shows on Wednesdays at lunchtime, see p130.

DIAMOND AND GIN MUSEUMS

The Old South also holds a couple of smaller-scale attractions. The **House of Bols** (Map pp92-3; ☎ 570 85 41; www.houseofbols.com; Paulus Potterstraat 14;

admission €11.50; ☻ noon-6pm Wed-Mon) is a *jenever* (Dutch gin) museum run by the Bols distillery. The hour-long, self-guided tour includes a confusing sniff test, a company history and a cocktail made by one of the bartenders who train at the academy upstairs. You must be aged 18 or over to visit.

The **Diamond Museum** (Map pp92-3; ☎ 305 53 00; www .diamantmuseum.nl; Paulus Potterstraat 8; adult/child €7.50/5; ☻ 9am-5pm) explores the trade's history and Amsterdam's shining role in it. The museum is fairly low-tech, and those who are economically minded might want just to go next door to Coster Diamonds (the company owns the museum and is attached to it) and take a free factory tour, where you can see gem cutters at work and hear about the process. Gassan Diamonds (p100) is another tour option.

Vondelpark

Right next to the Old South's museum hubbub is **Vondelpark** (Map pp92-3; www.vondelpark.nl), and on a sunny day there's no place better to make your escape. As people from all walks of life descend on this sprawling equivalent to New York City's Central Park, a party atmosphere ensues. Some kick back by reading a book, others hook up with friends to share a spliff or cradle a beer at one of the three outdoor cafes, while others trade songs on beat-up guitars. The park was named after poet and playwright Joost van den Vondel, the 'Dutch Shakespeare'.

The English-style layout offers an abundance of ponds, lawns, thickets and winding footpaths that encourage visitors to get out and explore. For bicycle rentals, the outlet of MacBike (p136) at Weteringschans is relatively close to Vondelpark's main entrance. For in-line skate rentals, try De Vondeltuin (p112), near the south entrance.

The **Filmmuseum** (Map pp92-3; ☎ 589 14 00; www .filmmuseum.nl; Vondelpark 3) isn't a museum per se but presides over a priceless archive of films screened in its two theatres, sometimes with live music. The museum's grand Café Vertigo is a popular meeting place and an ideal spot to people-watch; on summer evenings it shows free films on the outdoor terrace. At the time of writing the Filmmuseum was expected to relocate to a sleek new building in Amsterdam-Noord in 2011.

The culture continues at the park's Openluchttheater (p131), which puts on free summer concerts.

Built in 1882, the **Hollandsche Manege** (Map pp92-3; ☎ 618 09 42; www.dehollandschemanege.nl; in Dutch; Vondelstraat 140; ☒ 2-11pm Mon-Fri, from 9am Wed, 9am-6pm Sat, 9am-5pm Sun) is an indoor riding school inspired by the famous Spanish Riding School in Vienna. Upstairs is a cafe where you can sip a beer or coffee while watching the instructor put the horses through their paces. Opening times vary, so ring ahead.

The **Electrische Museumtramlijn Amsterdam** (Tram Museum Amsterdam; Map pp86-7; ☎ 673 75 38; www .museumtramlijn.org; Amstelveenseweg 264; return ticket adult/ child €4/2; ☒ 11am-6pm Sun mid-Apr–Oct) isn't really a museum but a starting point for historical trams that clang to the Amsterdamse Bos recreation area – a worthwhile 1¼-hour outing. The museum is just southwest of Vondelpark in the former Haarlemmermeer train station.

De Pijp

This district, lying south of the broad Stadhouderskade, supposedly got its name from its straight, narrow streets that resemble the stems of old clay pipes. The area was Amsterdam's first 19th-century slum, but it's now undergoing a determined gentrification. De Pijp is often called the Quartier Latin, thanks to its lively mix of people: labourers, intellectuals, new immigrants, prostitutes, young urban professionals, gays, lesbians – the whole kit and caboodle, really.

The best place to marvel at the multicultural scene is the **Albert Cuypmarkt** (Map pp92-3; www.albertcuypmarkt.nl; Albert Cuypstraat btwn Van Woustraat & Ferdinand Bolstraat; ☒ 10am-5pm Mon-Sat), Amsterdam's largest and busiest market. Stalls cater to Surinamese, Moroccan and Indonesian clientele, and cheese lovers wherever they may hail from. Vendors loudly tout their odd gadgets and their arrays of fruit, vegetables, herbs and spices. They sell clothes and other general goods too, often cheaper than anywhere else. And then there are the snack vendors, tempting passers-by with herring sandwiches, egg rolls, donuts and *stroopwafels* (two cookielike waffles with caramel syrup filling). If you have room after all that, the surrounding area teems with cosy cafes and eateries, many with an exotic flavour.

The district's other draw is the **Heineken Experience** (Map pp92-3; ☎ 523 96 66; www.heineken experience.com; Stadhouderskade 78; admission €15; ☒ 11am-7pm, last ticket sales at 5.30pm). On the site of the company's old brewery, the newly renovated attraction let's you take a self-guided tour that's tantamount to brew-worship. Learn the history of the Heineken family, watch Heinie commercials from around the world, visit the horse stables and make your own music video. In the Experience's crowning glory – a multimedia exhibit where you actually 'become' a beer – you'll get shaken up, sprayed with water and subjected to heat. Afterward you get to down a couple of cold ones (though we should point out the suds are dismissed as 'old man's beer' by many locals, while being sold at a premium abroad). Allow 75 minutes for the visit, and expect lots of company; come before noon to beat the crowds. Those on a budget who want a brewery tour will do better at Brouwerij 't IJ (p108), a small, organic sudsmaker with a free tour.

South of Albert Cuypstraat is the **Sarphatipark**, an English-style park named after 19th-century Jewish doctor, chemist and businessman Samuel Sarphati. With its ponds, fountains and abundant bird life, it's an eminently agreeable spot for a picnic lunch.

Plantage

In the 19th century the Jewish elite began to move from the city's centre to the Plantage (Plantation), where they built imposing villas. Until then the Plantage had been a district of parks and gardens.

Established in 1638, the **Hortus Botanicus** (Botanical Garden; Map p95; ☎ 625 90 21; www.dehortus .nl; Plantage Middenlaan 2A; adult/child €7/3.50; ☒ 9am-5pm Mon-Fri, 10am-5pm Sat & Sun, to 7pm daily Jul & Aug, to 4pm daily Dec & Jan) became a repository for tropical seeds and plants brought by Dutch ships from the East and West Indies. From here, coffee, pineapple, cinnamon and palm-oil plants were distributed throughout the world. The 4000-plus species are kept in wonderful structures, including the colonial-era seed house and a three-climate glasshouse. The 300-year-old cycad is possibly the world's oldest potted plant. The butterfly house is a hit with kids and stoned adults. Guided tours (additional €1) are held at 2pm Sunday year-round.

Across the road is **Wertheim Park** (Map p95), a lovely, willow-shaded spot for canalside lounging. The green space also holds a reflective Auschwitz memorial sculpture.

Around the corner, the **Verzetsmuseum** (Resistance Museum; Map p95; ☎ 620 25 35; www.dutch resistancemuseum.org; Plantage Kerklaan 61; adult/child €6.50/3.50; ☒ 10am-5pm Tue-Fri, 11am-5pm Sat-Mon) describes the daily realities of the Dutch resistance during WWII using photos, documents and audio clips. Topics include the concepts of active and passive resistance, how the illegal press operated, how 300,000 people were kept in hiding and how all this could be funded.

The **Hollandsche Schouwburg** (Holland Theatre; Map p95; ☎ 626 99 45; www.hollandscheschouwburg.nl; Plantage Middenlaan 24; admission free; ⌚ 11am-4pm) played a tragic role during WWII. After 1942 the theatre became a detention centre for Jews awaiting deportation. Up to 80,000 people passed through here on their way to the death camps. Little more than the facade is left standing today, and there is a memorial room and an exhibition room with videos and documents on the building's history.

The oldest zoo on the European continent, **Artis** (Map p95; ☎ 523 34 00; www.artis.nl, in Dutch; Plantage Kerklaan 38-40; adult/child €18.50/15; ⌚ 9am-6pm Apr-Oct, to 5pm Nov-Mar) has an alphabet soup of wildlife: alligators, birds, chimps and so on up to zebras. The layout is full of delightful ponds, statues, and leafy, winding pathways. Themed habitats such as African savannah and tropical rainforest are pretty convincing. For many, the aquarium complex is the highlight, featuring coral reefs, shark tanks and an Amsterdam canal displayed from a fish's point of view. There's also a planetarium and a kids' petting zoo.

East of Artis zoo stands the 18th-century **De Gooyer Windmill** (Map pp86–7), a former grain mill and the sole survivor of five windmills that once churned in this corner of the city. The structure alongside that used to be public baths, but now houses the **Brouwerij 't IJ** (Map pp86-7; ☎ 622 83 25; Funenkade 7; ⌚ 3-8pm), a small brewery producing potent, organic beers under the distinctive ostrich label. It's a picture-perfect spot to sit and sip a cold one. There's a free tour on Friday at 4pm.

Oosterpark

The Oosterpark district (Map pp86–7), named after the lush park at its core, was built in the 1880s for diamond-industry workers. Many of them were Jewish families who had the means to leave the cramped centre.

The **Tropenmuseum** (Tropics Museum; Map pp86-7; ☎ 568 82 15; www.tropenmuseum.nl; Linnaeusstraat 2; adult/child €7.50/4; ⌚ 10am-5pm) is the star attraction. It houses a three-storey collection of colonial artefacts, presented with insight, imagination and a fair amount of multimedia.

You can stroll through an African market or a Central Asian yurt (traditional felt hut), see ritual masks and spiky spears, and listen to recordings of exotic musical instruments. There's a children's section, a great gift shop and two cafes serving global foods. It's a grand place to spend a lazy Monday, when many other museums are closed. The attached Tropeninstituut Theater screens films and hosts music, dance and plays by visiting international artists.

The park sits behind the museum and is where filmmaker Theo van Gogh was murdered in 2004 (see the boxed text, p33). A silvery monument titled *De Schreeuw* (The Scream) honours him in the southeast corner.

Eastern Islands & Eastern Docklands

If you're looking for one place to see the cutting edge of Dutch – and indeed European – architecture, this district east of Centraal Station is it.

The city constructed the three Eastern Islands (Kattenburg, Wittenburg and Oostenburg) back in the 1650s to handle the rapidly expanding seaborne trade. The Dutch East India Company set up on Oostenburg, private shipyards and dockworkers' homes dominated Wittenburg, and admiralty offices sprung up on Kattenburg. The Eastern Docklands, a onetime shipyard and warehouse district, arose to the islands' north and east.

Toward the end of the 20th century, architects took to the area and began transforming it into a playground for slick modern design. Note the district is less compact than other neighbourhoods, so it's easiest to cover it by bicycle. **Eastern Docklands Amsterdam** (www.eastern docklands.com) is a good resource for further information and DIY walking and cycling tours.

The bold **Muziekgebouw aan 't IJ** (Music Bldg on the IJ; Map pp86-7; Piet Heinkade 1) is the area's most sparkling eye candy. Its Star Ferry cafe (p129) makes a great stop for drinks and harbour views. For concert details, see p130.

The green, shiplike building on the eastern harbour is **NEMO** (Map p95; ☎ 531 32 33; www .e-nemo.nl; Oosterdok 2; adult/child €12.50/6.50; ⌚ 10am-5pm Tue-Sun, plus Mon Jun-Aug), designed by big-name architect Renzo Piano. It's a science museum with loads of interactive exhibits to entertain kids, such as drawing with a laser, 'antigravity' trick mirrors, and a 'lab' where

COOL RIDES

Beyond carrying you from museum to museum, Amsterdam's public transport system provides sweet, low-cost sightseeing journeys. For fares and other details, see p137.

■ Tram 10 runs from near Westerpark, around the perimeter of the canal loop and out to the Eastern Docklands, passing 19th-century housing blocks, the Rijksmuseum and De Gooyer Windmill along the way.

■ Tram 5 starts at Centraal Station and cuts south through the centre past most of Amsterdam's major landmarks. The GVB offers a free English podcast tour for the route; download it from the 'Tourist Guide' section of www.gvb.nl.

■ The Stop/Go bus is top-notch for canal gazing, as it hugs pretty Prinsengracht en route from Waterlooplein to Centraal Station to Oosterdok (opposite the main library).

■ Free ferries sail from the dock behind Centraal Station. The best is the 15-minute ride to NDSM-werf (see p110). Or try the five-minute trip to Buiksloterweg.

you can answer questions such as 'How black is black?' and 'How do you make cheese?' NEMO's stepped roof (admission free) is the city's largest summer terrace, and worth a stair climb for its fantastic views.

On the walk down to NEMO, you'll pass a whole collection of restored cargo ships. The pièce de résistance is the replica of the *Amsterdam* (admission €5, or €2 if you've paid the NEMO entrance), a historical square-rigger moored alongside the museum. Climb aboard, peruse the captain's quarters and watch actors re-create life at sea. The boat usually floats at the Nederlands Scheepvaartmuseum (below), but it's at NEMO during the Scheepvaartmuseum's renovation.

Next door is **Arcam** (Map p95; ☎ 620 48 78; www.arcam.nl; Prins Hendrikkade 600; admission free; ⏰ 1-5pm Tue-Sat), the Amsterdam Architecture Foundation's stunning facility, which should be the first port of call for architecture and urban-design fans. It offers changing exhibits on the city's buildings, and reference materials on just about anything built in town, from early history to the very latest housing development. Among the best titles are *Twenty-five Buildings You Should Have Seen* and *Eastern Docklands Map*.

Around the corner is the **Nederlands Scheepvaartmuseum** (Netherlands Shipping Museum; Map p95; ☎ 523 22 22; www.scheepvaartmuseum.nl; Kattenburgerplein 1), occupying a building that was once the Dutch navy's headquarters. Early shipping routes, naval combat, fishing and whaling are all explained in loving detail, and there are 500 models of boats and ships. At the time of writing the museum was shut until mid-2011 for a major renovation.

Westerpark & Western Islands

A stone's throw northwest of the Jordaan, Westerpark and the Western Islands offer eating and drinking options and architectural sights, all about a 20-minute walk west of Centraal Station.

The busy road to Haarlem led through the **Haarlemmerpoort** (Haarlem Gate; Map pp86–7) on Haarlemmerplein, where travellers heading into town had to leave their horses and carts. The impressive gateway was built for King Willem II to pass through on the way to his 1840 coronation.

If you go through the gate and head west along busy Haarlemmerweg, you'll come to **Westergasfabriek** (Map pp86-7; ☎ 586 07 10; www.wester gasfabriek.nl; Haarlemmerweg 8-10), a late-19th-century Dutch Renaissance complex. It was the city gasworks until it was all but abandoned in the 1960s, its soil contaminated. Now the soil has been replaced with lawns, a long pool suitable for wading (bring the kids), sports facilities and even child care. As you move west away from town, reedy wilderness, with marshes and shallow waterfalls, begins to take over. The site is surrounded by the long and varied **Westerpark**; bike on in and stay a while. Inside the main buildings are cinemas, cafes, restaurants, nightclubs and offices.

Just north of Westerpark over the train tracks is **Het Schip** (Map pp86-7; ☎ 418 28 85; www .hetschip.nl; Spaarndammerplantsoen 140; admission €7.50; ⏰ 1-5pm Wed-Fri, plus Tue Jul & Aug, 11am-5pm Sat & Sun). This remarkable housing project (1920) is a flagship of the Amsterdam School of architecture (see p60). The triangular block, loosely resembling a ship, was designed by Michel de Klerk for railway employees. Het Schip now hosts a small museum in three parts: you can poke around the delightful old post office, walk through a worker's apartment (complete with period furniture) and enjoy a snack in the lunchroom. Architecture buffs will want to make the pilgrimage. Bus 22 ends its route right at Het Schip's front door.

The Western Islands were raised from the riverbed to accommodate warehouses for Dutch colonial goods. The district is a world unto itself, cut through with canals and linked by small drawbridges. It's home to artists' studios and some unique restaurants. **Prinseneiland** and **Realeneiland** are the prettiest of the tiny archipelago.

Amstelveen & Around

The quiet dormitory town of Amstelveen lies south of Amsterdam proper. Its star attraction is the **Amsterdamse Bos** (Amsterdam Woods; Map pp86-7; www.amsterdamsebos.nl; Bosbaanweg 5; admission free; park 24hr, visitors centre noon-5pm), a vast tract of lakes, woods and meadows that draws many Amsterdammers looking for a leafy good time. In the densest thickets you can forget you're near a city at all (though actually you're right by Schiphol airport), and it's a wonderful place to let kids run free.

Get your bearings with a map from the visitors centre by the main entrance. You can rent bikes (€4.50/9.50 per hour/day; open 10am to 6pm, closed Monday) or gear up for a kid-friendly tree-top **climbing park** (adult/child €19.50/14.50; noon-6pm Mon-Fri, 10am-7pm Sat & Sun), both by the main entrance. You can also rent

kayaks (€6 per hour) in the interior to paddle through the wetlands. Perhaps the most delightful attraction is **De Ridammerhoeve** (645 50 34; 10am-5pm Wed-Mon Mar-Oct, Wed-Sun Nov-Feb), an organic working goat farm where kids can feed bottles of milk to, well, kids. The cafeteria sells goat's-milk smoothies and ice cream, as well as cheeses made on the premises. Take bus 170 or 172 from Centraal Station, or ride the historical tram (p107) from the Haarlemmermeer Station on summer Sundays.

Nearby is the fascinating, two-storey **CoBrA Museum** (off Map pp86-7; 547 50 50; www.cobra -museum.nl; Sandbergplein 1; adult/child €9.50/5; 11am-5pm Tue-Sun). Formed by artists from Copenhagen, Brussels and Amsterdam after WWII, the CoBrA movement (p41) vented the fury of abstract expressionism. The modern paintings, ceramics and statues on display here still polarise audiences today. The museum is opposite the Amstelveen bus terminal; take bus 170 or 172 from Centraal Station in Amsterdam.

The **Amsterdam RAI** (Map pp86-7; 549 12 12; www .rai.nl; Europaplein 22), an exhibition and conference centre, is the largest complex of its kind in the country. From boats and caravans to fashion shows, few events are beyond its reach.

ACTIVITIES
Cycling

Fiets (bicycles) are everywhere in Amsterdam, where they outnumber cars. But there aren't elaborate mountain bikes rolling through the city's dedicated lanes. Instead, virtually

---

DETOUR: NDSM-WERF

Hop on the ferry behind Centraal Station and set sail for a different world. **NDSM-werf** (Map pp86-7; 330 54 80; www.ndsm.nl) looks like the set from a post-apocalyptic film – abandoned boats and trams rust by the water's edge, graffiti is scrawled across every surface, smoke stacks belch in the distance, and huge carved wooden tiki heads gaze over it all.

The area is actually a city-sponsored art community called Kinetisch Noord that has taken over a derelict shipyard. Participants converted an old warehouse to hold more than 100 studios, as well as theatres and a skateboard hall, and it has quickly become a centre for underground culture and events, such as the Over het IJ Festival (p116). MTV thought the area was so cutting-edge that it, too, revamped one of the old industrial buildings and made it its European headquarters.

True, unless an event is going on, there's not much to do besides wander around and ogle the recycled-junk street-art (which is pretty damn cool). **Café Noorderlicht** (Map pp86-7; 492 27 70; TT Neveritaweg 33; 11am-late), in a Tibetan-prayer-flag-draped greenhouse, provides food and drinks in a funky ambience. To find it, look for signs posted from the ferry dock.

Speaking of which: the free ferry to NDSM-werf leaves from Platform 1 behind Centraal Station from 9am to midnight, at 15 minutes and 45 minutes past the hour. The trip takes 15 minutes and you can bring your bike (also free).

BICYCLE RULES

The heavy traffic can be intimidating, but observe a few basics and soon you'll be freewheeling like a native:

- When riding, watch for cars. Cyclists have the right of way, except when vehicles are entering from the right, although not all motorists respect this.
- Watch for pedestrians, too. Tourists tend to wander in and out of bike paths with no idea they're in a dangerous spot.
- By law, after dusk you need to use the lights on your bike (front and rear) and have reflectors on both wheels. If your bike does not have lights, you need to use clip-on lights, both front and rear.
- It's polite to give a quick ring of your bell as a warning. If someone's about to hit you, a good sharp yell is effective.
- Watch out for tram tracks – if your wheel gets get caught in one, you'll break your bones.
- Always lock your bike securely, since bike theft is rampant. Most bikes come with two locks, one for the front wheel (attach it to the frame) and the other for the back. One lock should also be attached to a fixed structure.
- Try to stick to the city's 400km of bike paths, identified by signage and their reddish colour.

---

everyone rides sturdy, two- or three-gear (often no gear) granny rattlers (Gazelle or Sparta brands). There's no need for the fancy stuff in a city that's as flat as a pancake. Also, a 21-speed racer will probably be stolen within an hour of being parked: 150,000 bikes are nicked in Amsterdam per year. See the boxed text, above for tips on city cycling. See p136 for a list of bike-rental shops.

Gyms

Fitness First (Map pp88-9; ☎ 530 03 40; www.fitness first.nl; Nieuwezijds Kolk 15; day passes €18; ☻ 7am-10pm Mon-Thu, to 9pm Fri, 9am-4pm Sat & Sun) Cardio and weightlifting equipment, group classes, sauna, and steam and aroma rooms.

Garden Gym (Map p95; ☎ 626 87 72; www.health garden.nl; Jodenbreestraat 158; day passes €9.50-13; ☻ 9am-10.30pm Mon, Wed & Fri, noon-11pm Tue & Thu, 9am-5.30pm Sat & Sun) Has been rated Amsterdam's best gym for women, with aerobics, sauna, massage and physiotherapy.

Saunas

Saunas are mixed and there's no prudish swimsuit nonsense, so check your modesty at the front desk (or pick up an extra towel). For information about gay saunas, see the boxed text, p118.

Hammam (Map pp86-7; ☎ 681 48 18; www.hammam amsterdam.nl; Zaanstraat 88; admission €17; ☻ noon-9pm Tue-Fri, to 8pm Sat & Sun, last entry 2½hr before closing) Attractive, female-only, Turkish-style place.

Koan Float (Map pp88-9; ☎ 555 00 33; www.koanfloat .nl; Herengracht 321; floating 45/60min €32.50/38.50; ☻ 9.30am-11pm) No sauna – saltwater flotation tanks and massages instead; good for jet lag.

Sauna Deco (Map pp88-9; ☎ 623 82 15; www.saunadeco .nl; Herengracht 115; admission noon-3pm Mon-Fri €17, all other times €19.50; ☻ noon-11pm Mon-Sat, from 3pm Tue, 1-7pm Sun) Scandinavian-style sauna in a lovely building.

Skating
ICE

When the canals freeze over (which, to skaters, doesn't happen often enough), Amsterdam resembles an old Dutch painting as skaters cut up tracks, scarves trailing in the headwind. Beware, though: this oil painting bites – drownings happen each year. Stay away from the ice unless you see large groups of people, and be very careful at the edges and under bridges – areas with weak ice.

In winter you can skate on the pond at Museumplein (Map pp92–3) for a modest fee.

IN-LINE

Amsterdammers are very keen on in-line skating. Check out **Friday Night Skate** (www.friday nightskate.com), a 15km careen through town in the company of hundreds of fellow skeelers. You needn't be a pro, but braking skills and protective gear are essential. Assemble at 8pm near the Filmmuseum (Map pp92–3) in the Vondelpark for an 8.30pm departure. The skate is cancelled if the streets are wet.

AMSTERDAM

Vondelpark itself is a good bet for a spot of in-line skating. Rent skates and gear at **De Vondeltuin** (Map pp86-7; ☎ 062 756 55 76; Vondelpark 7; skate rental per 1hr/2hr/day €5/7.50/10; ☼ 11am-8pm Mar-Oct), near the Amstelveenseweg entrance.

SKATEBOARDING
There's a half-pipe on the Museumplein (Map pp92–3). Skateboarders are advised to bring their own gear to Amsterdam as rentals are thin on the ground.

Swimming
Amsterdam has many indoor pools, and outdoor pools open in summer. Ring ahead: hours can vary from day to day or season to season, few are open past 7pm, and there are often restricted sessions – nude (of course), children, women, seniors, clubs, lap swimming etc.
De Mirandabad (Map pp86-7; ☎ 536 44 44; De Mirandalaan 9; admission €3.55) Indoor and outdoor pools, twisting slides, a beach, a wave machine, squash courts, a fitness room; kids will love it.
Zuiderbad (Map pp92-3; ☎ 678 13 90; Hobbemastraat 26; adult/child €3.10/2.75) Venerable indoor pool (built 1912) restored to original art deco splendour; it's a stone's throw from the Rijksmuseum.

Tennis & Squash
Borchland Sportcentrum (off Map pp86-7; ☎ 563 33 33; Borchlandweg 6-12; per hr €9-15; ☼ 8am-11pm) Tennis, squash and badminton courts, bowling alleys and a restaurant. It's next to the Amsterdam ArenA stadium, well south of town (metro: Strandvliet).
Squash City (Map pp88-9; ☎ 626 78 83; Ketelmakerstraat 6; day pass €10-12; ☼ 7am-midnight Mon-Thu, to 11.30pm Fri, 8.45am-8pm Sat & Sun) Closest squash option to the city centre; also has a fitness centre and sauna.

CANAL APPRECIATION WALKING TOUR

WALK FACTS
Start The Dam
Finish Crea Café
Distance 3.75km
Duration 1.5 hours

Amsterdam has more canals than Venice. This tour ambles by the Canal Belt's 17th-century waterways, as well as hallowed historical sites.

Start at **The Dam** (**1**; p85), the very spot where Amsterdam was born. It's flanked by the **Koninklijk Paleis** (**2**; p85), Queen Beatrix's pad (though she's rarely here), and the **Nieuw Kerk** (**3**; p85), the stage for Dutch coronations.

Heading west, the Singel is the first canal from the centre; it originally was a moat that defended Amsterdam's outer limits. The **Torensluis** (**4**; p102), Amsterdam's oldest bridge, crosses it. A statue of Multatuli, the Dutch literary giant, gazes over the scene; the **Multatuli Museum** (**5**; p102) is a few blocks north.

Amsterdam's wealthiest residents once lived along the **Herengracht** (**6**; p101), named after the Heeren XVII (17 Gentlemen) of the United East India Company. It soon intersects with the pretty **Brouwersgracht** (**7**; p101), or Brewers' Canal, which took its name from the sudsmakers here in days of yore. Where the canals meet offers one of our favourite views, with boats passing in three directions. To the north is the Herenmarkt, with the landmark **Westindisch Huis** (**8**; p103), the former head office of the Dutch West India Company.

Turning south, cross the Brouwersgracht to the **Keizersgracht** (**9**; p101), or Emperor's Canal, where imposing old warehouses now hold modern living and working quarters.

At peaceful Leliegracht, turn west toward **Prinsengracht** (**10**; p101). You'll pass the **Anne Frank Huis** (**11**; p102) and the soaring tower of the **Westerkerk** (**12**; p102). Behind it is Karin Dann's quietly moving **Homomonument** (**13**; p102) and the **house** (**14**; Westermarkt 6) where René Descartes stayed during his sojourn in Amsterdam; it's marked with a plaque.

Prinsengracht is known for its groovy houseboats, which you'll see as you continue strolling down the street. Climb aboard one and explore the cramped, er, cosy interior at the **Houseboat Museum** (**15**; p101).

Back on Keizersgracht, you can't miss the quirky **Felix Meritis building** (**16**; p103), a onetime enlightenment society turned alternative theatre. After WWII the monumental edifice served as the Dutch Communist Party's head office.

You've got some walking to do to reach our final destination. En route you'll pass the **Spui** (**17**; p85), hosting late-week book and art markets. Your goal is **Crea Café** (**18**; p127). What better way to conclude than to sit canalside with well-priced beer in hand, watching a parade of boats float by?

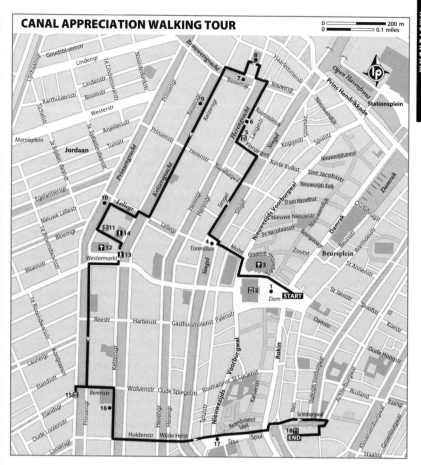

CANAL APPRECIATION WALKING TOUR

AMSTERDAM FOR CHILDREN

The extroverted monkeys, shimmying fish and planetarium at Artis (p108) will keep young eyes shining. Tykes can feed goats and climb trees in Amsterdamse Bos (p110), south of the city. But start with a sure-fire thrill: a pedal-powered canal bike (paddleboat) ride (p136) through the city's waterways.

Science and technology centre NEMO (p108) answers questions such as 'How black is black?' and 'How do you make cheese?' among its hands-on exhibits. Floating next to it is a replica of the 16th-century ship *Amsterdam*, staffed by costumed pirates who welcome kids aboard. The bell-clanging tram rides at the Electrische Museumtramlijn Amsterdam (p107) also are also a hit with wee ones.

The Amsterdams Marionetten Theater (p131) near the Nieuwmarkt gives captivating shows such as Mozart's *The Magic Flute*, and over Christmas there's usually a circus in Koninklijk Theater Carré (p132).

For more culture, check out the Tropenmuseum (p108), with its children's section and activities focusing on exotic locations (although shows tend to be in Dutch). The Joods Historisch Museum (p100) also has a children's section about Jewish life in Amsterdam.

The Old South (p104) is a fine neighbourhood for cycling with the kids in tow – wide streets, parks and fine old residential areas. The Vondelpark (p106) is great for picnics and has ducks and a children's playground.

Finally, the underground TunFun (p100) playground is good for soaking up excess energy, as is De Mirandabad (p112), where there are swimming pools, slides, a beach and a wave machine.

TOURS
Bicycle Tours
The companies below also rent bikes. For more, see p136.

Mike's Bike Tours (Map pp92-3; ☎ 622 79 70; www .mikesbikeamsterdam.com; Kerkstraat 134). Highly recommended four-hour tours (per person €22) around the centre of town and into the countryside, with stops at windmills and cheese farms.

Orange Bike (Map pp88-9; ☎ 528 99 90; www.orange bike.nl; Geldersekade 37) Traditional city cycling tours cover the major sights, but it also offers the fun Culinaire Snack Tours (per person €32.50, three hours, needs a minimum of four people to run), which include trying Dutch *bitterballen* (mini croquettes with meat), cheeses and *jenever*. Also at Singel 233 (Map pp88-9).

Yellow Bike Tours (Map pp88-9; ☎ 620 69 40; www .yellowbike.nl; Nieuwezijds Kolk 29) Choose from two- and three-hour city tours (per person €18.50 to €21.50) or a four-hour countryside tour (€27.50) through the pretty Waterland district north of central Amsterdam. Tours are less youth-oriented than Mike's, and limited to 15 participants. Reservations recommended.

Boat Tours
Sure they're touristy, but canal tours are also a delightful way to see the city. Several operators depart from moorings at Centraal Station, Damrak, Rokin and opposite the Rijksmuseum – just hop on board. To avoid the steamed-up glass window effect, look for a boat with an open seating area.

Blue Boat Company (Map pp92-3; ☎ 679 13 70; www .blueboat.nl; Stadhouderskade 30; ☺ every 30min 10am-6pm & 7pm Apr-Sep, every hr 10am-5pm Oct-Mar) Blue Boat's main tour (adult/child €12/6) clocks in at 75 minutes. Evening cruises (adult/child €15/10) are offered three times a night from April to September, and at 8pm the rest of the year. The Blue Boat dock is near the Rijksmuseum.

Canal Bus (Map pp92-3; ☎ 623 98 86; www.canal.nl; Weteringschans 26; day pass adult/child €20/10) Offers a unique hop-on, hop-off service visiting most of the big destinations. Routes vary depending on where you want to visit.

St Nicolaas Boat Club (Map pp92-3; www.amsterdam boatclub.com) By far the best boat tour in the city. The open-air, 10-seat boats can manoeuvre into the narrowest canals. Patrons are allowed to smoke dope and drink beer on board, while the captains amuse with stories about alternative Amsterdam. Rides last 60 to 90 minutes. There

is no set fee, just a suggested donation of €10. Departure times vary according to numbers; sign up at the bar at Boom Chicago (p131).

Wetlands Safari (Map pp88-9; ☎ 686 11 66; www .wetlandssafari.com; per person incl transport & picnic €38; ☺ 9.30am Mon-Fri, 10am Sun) This exceptional 5½-hour tour meets in town and buses you just north of the city where you canoe through boggy, froggy wetlands and past windmills and 17th-century villages. Meet at the VVV tourist office opposite Centraal Station.

Walking Tours
Cannabis Tour (2hr tour €15) Learn about smoky places from the Orange Bike (left) folks.

Daklozentour (Homeless person tour; ☎ 0643 64 30 47; www.daklozentour.nl; €10) Ed de Boer was homeless for many years and offers tours in and around the Red Light District, with fascinating insights into the city and life on the streets. Call for details about exact tour times – most run just over an hour.

Mokum Events (Map pp88-9; ☎ 427 29 09; www .mokumevents.com; Damrak 44; from €13) City tours that go beyond the norm, with themes such as Jewish Amsterdam, Courtyards of the Jordaan and Coffeeshops. They offer bus, bike and boat tours, too.

Prostitution Information Centre Tour (Map pp88-9; ☎ 420 73 28; www.pic-amsterdam.com; Enge Kerkstraat 3; €12.50; ☺ 5pm Sat) The Prostitution Information Centre (p97) offers fascinating one-hour tours of the Red Light District explaining the nitty-gritty of the window business. Just show up; no reservations are necessary.

Randy Roy's Redlight Tours (Map pp88-9; ☎ 06 4185 3288; www.randyroysredlighttours.com; €12.50; ☺ 8pm Sun-Thu, 8pm & 10pm Fri & Sat) The darkest secrets of Mike Tyson, Quentin Tarantino and other celebs feature in this lively 1½-hour tour of the Red Light District. Meet in front of the Victoria Hotel, opposite Centraal Station.

FESTIVALS & EVENTS
February
Commemoration of the February Strike (25 Feb) In memory of the 1941 anti-Nazi general strike.

March
Stille Omgang (Silent Procession; Sun closest to 15 Mar) Catholics walk along the Holy Way to commemorate the 1345 Miracle of Amsterdam.

April
Koninginnedag (Queen's Day; www.koninginnedag amsterdam.nl; 30 Apr) Celebrated countrywide, but especially in Amsterdam (see the boxed text, p116).

Amsterdam Fantastic Film Festival (www.imagine filmfestival.nl) European and international fantasy, horror and science-fiction movies.

AN INSIDER'S GUIDE TO AMSTERDAM: PETER MOSKOS *As told to Simon Sellars*

Peter Moskos, along with Toine Rikken, founded the St Nicolaas Boat Club (opposite) in 1997. It's a boat-tour company that provides an alternative angle on Amsterdam and its waterlogged history. We asked Peter to regale us with his unique perspective.

Favourite area of Amsterdam? On a boat in the IJ. There's no better place to understand the importance of water and shipping to Amsterdam's history – plus it's beautiful out there.

And your least favourite? Any big, ugly road with too many cars, although architecturally every place has something interesting and can tell you something about urban planning.

What's the biggest misconception about Amsterdam? That it's the world's sex capital. It's not – the Dutch just have the sense to put it all out in the open and capitalise on it. And while it may be the world's recreational-drug capital, stop bingeing and enjoy it like you live here year-round.

What's your favourite 'Amsterdam experience'? Biking and boating. And Koninginnedag (Queen's Day; see the boxed text, p116) – the biggest drunk garage sale in the world.

Least favourite? The weather – especially the winter weather. Or the winter weather in the summer. And the rain that never stops.

What Amsterdam-specific film or book would you recommend? The film *Amsterdammed* is fun, with a great high-speed boat chase, but it doesn't depict anything of reality. *Simon* is the best Amsterdam film ever – and maybe the best-ever Dutch movie. Jan-Willem van der Wettering's cop stories are pretty good, but Geert Mak's *Amsterdam* is the single best book about the city.

Your favourite Amsterdam bar and coffeeshop? Any brown cafe in the Jordaan is great – get a *jenever* (Dutch gin) and a beer and talk with the locals. The coffeeshop De Rokerij has a super-cool atmosphere – sort of how I imagine a 19th-century Chinese opium den would have been. And of course my brother's bar at Boom Chicago (p131), because that's the home base for our boats.

Favourite local slang or swear words? I'm trying to get *spetterend* back into the vocab – it's a very uncool way of saying 'cool'. But the Dutch have a shortage of swear words, so they often resort to English.

What's your strangest Amsterdam bike story? A guy wearing a jockstrap on rollerblades. He used to be everywhere, even in the cold weather. He disappeared a couple of years ago. Perhaps he caught pneumonia and passed on.

How has living in Amsterdam changed you? It's made me realise that bikes are the best form of urban transit possible. And that, basically, this is a city that works. There's something to be said for literally living on top of each other and in close-knit surroundings. It's given me the opportunity to see how a large city can allow everyone to do their own thing without getting all bent out of shape about it.

Describe the St Nicolaas Boat Club for someone new to it. We're a friendly entry point to understanding Amsterdam from the greatest perspective of all: the canals. We offer cosy rides with knowledgeable pilots, and all we ask for is a donation at the end.

World Press Photo (www.worldpressphoto.org; late Apr-May) The world's best photojournalists display their pix at the Oude Kerk.

May

Herdenkingsdag (Remembrance Day; 4 May) For the fallen of WWII. Queen Beatrix lays a wreath on the Dam and the city observes two minutes' silence at 8pm.

Bevrijdingsdag (Liberation Day; 5 May) The end of German occupation in 1945 is commemorated with street parties, a free market and live music, especially in Vondelpark.

Luilak (Lazy Bones) In the early hours on the Saturday before Whit Sunday, children go around ringing door bells, making noise and waking people up. Luilak is a remnant of a pre-Christian festival celebrating the awakening of spring.

Art Amsterdam (www.artamsterdam.nl; mid-May) Four-day art fair for buyers with deep pockets.

June

Holland Festival (www.hollandfestival.nl) For most of June, the country's biggest extravaganza for theatre, dance, film and pop music has a justified claim to cutting-edge innovation.

Vondelpark Open-Air Theatre (Jun-late Aug) Free events held 'for the people'. There's high drama and concerts across the genres from pop and world to classical and jazz.

Roots Music Festival (www.amsterdamroots.nl; late Jun) World music and culture with performances, parades, workshops and a market, most of it occurring in Oosterpark.

ORANGE DAY

One Amsterdam event not to miss is Koninginnedag – or Queen's Day, or Orange Day – which is held in celebration of Queen Beatrix's birthday on 30 April, when over a million revellers make the city seem like the freakingest place on the planet. People descend from all over the country, clogging and choking the train system to its breaking point.

The whole shebang is basically an excuse for a gigantic drinking fest and to wear ridiculous outfits, all in orange, the country's national colour. It's quite a sight to see the entire city awash in orange fake afros, orange beer, orange balloon animals, more orange beer, orange dope, yet more orange beer, orange leather boys, orange skater dykes, orange roller coasters, orange clogs, orange fashion victims, orange grannies and grandpas, even more orange beer, orange Red Bull... Wear something orange.

There's also a free market throughout the city, where anyone can sell anything they like, as well as street parties and live music.

To get you in the mood for Koninginnedag, the website **Expatica** (www.expatica.com) supplies a helpful 'orange vocabulary', which you can bandy about on 30 April at your leisure. Try this on for size with the nearest reveller: say 'Hey man/woman, I've got...'

- *oranjegekte:* orange madness
- *oranjekoorts:* orange fever
- *oranjestemming:* orange mood
- *oranjeeuforie:* orange euphoria
- *oranjesfeer:* orange atmosphere
- *oranjemania:* orange mania

Most likely they'll look at you with pity, replying, 'Man/woman, you've really got the *oranjeziekte* (orange sickness)'.

July

Over het IJ Festival (www.overhetij.nl) Big performing-arts events (dance, theatre, music) take place for 10 days around at the NDSM shipyards in Amsterdam-Noord.

Julidans (www.julidans.nl) Dance festival that gets some 20,000 visitors; remarkable given that it takes place in small venues.

5 Days Off (www.5daysoff.nl, in Dutch) Indoor electronica dance parties at various venues, including Paradiso and the Heineken Music Hall.

Robeco Summer Concerts (www.robecozomer concerten.nl, in Dutch; mid-Jul–Aug) A quality line-up of 80-odd classical, jazz and world-music concerts at Amsterdam's top concert venue, the Concertgebouw.

Amsterdam International Fashion Week (www.amsterdamfashionweek.com; late Jul) Five days of fashion festivities, with many events at the Westergasfabriek.

August

De Parade (www.deparade.nl, in Dutch; 1st 2 weeks of Aug) Carnivalesque outdoor theatre festival, held in the Martin Luther King Park, with unforgettable ambience.

Grachtenfestival (Canal Festival; www.grachtenfestival.nl; late Aug) Five days of free classical concerts in courtyards and private canalside homes, as well as on the canals themselves.

Hartjesdagen Zeedijk (3rd Mon of Aug and weekend leading up to it) Dating back to medieval times, this festival showcases street theatre; there's a parade and all kinds of music along the Zeedijk and in Nieuwmarkt.

Uitmarkt (www.uitmarkt.nl, in Dutch; late Aug) The reopening of Amsterdam's cultural season, with three days of free concerts and information booths around the Eastern Docklands.

September

Monumentendag (www.openmonumentendag.nl; 2nd weekend of Sep) Registered historical buildings open their doors to the public.

Jordaan Festival (www.jordaanfestival.nl, in Dutch; 3rd weekend of Sep) This street festival also sees hundreds of small boats take to the canals.

Dam Tot Damloop (www.damloop.nl, in Dutch; 3rd Sun of Sep) A 16km foot race between the Dam in Amsterdam and the Dam in Zaandam, with around 20,000 runners and many more spectators.

October

Amsterdam Marathon (www.amsterdamarathon.nl; mid-Oct) Thousands of runners loop through the city, starting and finishing at the Olympic Stadium (Map pp86–7).

Amsterdam Dance Event (www.amsterdam-dance
-event.nl; late Oct) A club music powwow, with 700 DJs
and 80,000 dancers attending parties citywide.

November

Cannabis Cup (www.hightimes.com; last half of Nov)
Marijuana festival hosted by *High Times* magazine, with
awards for best grass, biggest spliff and so on, plus there's
a hemp expo and a fashion show.

International Documentary Film Festival (www
.idfa.nl; late Nov) Ten days dedicated to screening fascinating true stories from all over the world.

SLEEPING

Book well ahead for weekends and in summer.
It's worth paying a bit extra for something
central so you can enjoy the nightlife without
resorting to night buses or taxis. Also consider the Old South and Vondelpark areas:
both offer quality digs that are close to the
museums and only a short walk from the action at Leidseplein.

Many lodgings cater specifically to party
animals, with flowing booze, pot smoking and
general mayhem around the clock. Others
exude old-world charm, particularly around
the Canal Belt. Any hotel with more than 20
rooms is considered large, and many rooms
are on the snug side. Note that wi-fi is nearly
universal, but air-conditioning and lifts are not.
Prepare to carry your luggage up steep staircases, or else request a lower-floor room.

Rates listed are nondiscounted rack rates;
prices usually drop from October to April.
Rates include breakfast unless stated otherwise. Most of the quoted rates also include
a 5% city-hotel tax; however, this is sometimes added separately to the bill, so ask
before booking. If you're paying by credit
card, some hotels add a surcharge of up to
5% (ouch).

For short-term apartment rentals try
Citymundo (www.citymundo.com), a reliable broker
that offers houseboats, studios and apartments
for a minimum of three nights. You can also
check www.expatica.com and www.craigslist
.com for sublets, swaps and other options.

City Centre

BUDGET

Aivengo Youth Hostel (Map pp88-9; ☎ 421 36 70; www
.aivengoyouthhostel.com; Spuistraat 6; dm €15-25; 4-bed room per
person €20-35; 🖳 🛜) Funky Aivengo has a quiet,
respectful vibe and is spread out across two
buildings – one with a Middle Eastern interior,

the other with exposed wood beams. Rates include linen and towels as well as a safety deposit
box, but there's no breakfast or common rooms.
Note there is a 4am to 6am lockout.

Stadsdoelen Youth Hostel (Map pp88-9; ☎ 624 68
32; www.stayokay.com; Kloveniersburgwal 97; dm €20-28,
s €27-38, d €36-72; 🖳 🛜) Efficient Stadsdoelen
is always bustling with backpackers and we
can understand why. The staff is friendly,
and the mix of 11 ultraclean, single-sex and
co-ed rooms (each with up to 20 beds and free
lockers) offers some privacy. There's a big TV
room, a pool table and laundry facilities. Wi-fi
(lobby only) costs €3 per hour.

Hotel/Hostel Winston (Map pp88-9; ☎ 623 13 80; www
.winston.nl; Warmoesstraat 123; dm €32-42, s €77-100, d €90-
120) With rock'n'roll rooms, an attached busy
club, beer garden and smoking deck, this place
hops 24/7. Group dorm rooms sleep up to
eight. Most private rooms are 'art' rooms: local
artists were given free rein, with results from
super-edgy (entirely stainless steel) to playful
and raunchy. Wi-fi is in the lobby only.

MIDRANGE

Hotel Luxer (Map pp88-9; ☎ 330 32 05; http://hotelluxer
.tobook.com; Warmoesstraat 11; s €50-100, d €80-150;
❄ 🖳 🛜) This smart little number is probably
the best option for your money in the thick of
the Red Light District, with vast numbers of
pubs within staggering distance. Rooms are
small but well equipped (air-conditioning!)
and at night the breakfast area becomes a chic
little bar. Breakfast costs €10.

our pick **Hotel Brouwer** (Map pp88-9; ☎ 624 63 58;
www.hotelbrouwer.nl; Singel 83; s/d €63/100; 🖳 🛜) Our
favourite hotel in this price range, Brouwer
has just eight rooms in a house dating to
1652. Rooms are named for Dutch painters,
are furnished simply, and all have canal views.
There's a mix of Delft-blue tiles and early-
20th-century furniture, and – get this – a tiny
elevator. Staff dispense friendly advice. Reserve
well in advance. No credit cards accepted.

Hotel Résidence Le Coin (Map pp92-3; ☎ 524 68 00;
www.lecoin.nl; Nieuwe Doelenstraat 5; s €110, d €133-147;
🛜) This shiny inn owned by the University
of Amsterdam offers 42 small, high-class
apartments spread over seven historical
buildings, all equipped with designer furniture, wood floors and kitchenettes – and all
reachable by lift. It's in the thick of things,
and just a five-minute stroll to Nieuwmarkt's
action. Breakfast costs €11.50 and wi-fi costs
€5 per day.

GAY & LESBIAN AMSTERDAM

Information

The **Gay & Lesbian Switchboard** (☎ 623 65 65; www.switchboard.nl, in Dutch) is a comprehensive info source, while **COC Amsterdam** (Map p91; ☎ 626 30 87; www.cocamsterdam.nl; Rozenstraat 14) is Amsterdam's gay and lesbian social centre.

Pick up the *Bent Guide,* published in English, at the **Pink Point** (Map p91; www.pinkpoint.org; ⌚ 10am-6pm), a kiosk near the Homomonument (p102) that's a goldmine of queer info.

Gay News Amsterdam (www.gayamsterdam.nl) is a free paper and *Gaymap Amsterdam* is a free map. Gay radio station MVS broadcasts 7pm to 8pm Monday to Saturday on 106.8FM (cable 103.3FM).

For gay books, try **Intermale** (Map pp88-9; ☎ 625 00 09; www.intermale.nl; Spuistraat 251), with 1½ floors of photo books, sexy mags, videos and porno postcards.

Vrolijk (Map pp88-9; ☎ 623 51 42; www.vrolijk.nu; Paleisstraat 135; ⌚ closed Sun Oct-Dec) stocks major gay and lesbian magazines, as well as novels, guidebooks, postcards, art, poetry and DVDs.

Sleeping

The majority of hotels in town are lesbian and gay friendly, but some cater specifically to queer clientele:

Amistad (Map pp92-3; ☎ 624 80 74; www.amistad.nl; Kerkstraat 42; s/d without bathroom from €75/94, with bathroom from €100/130; 🖳 🛜) Rooms at this bijou hotel are dotted with designer Philippe Starck chairs, CD players, chic soft furnishings and computers (no need to bring your own!). The breakfast room (with ruby-red walls and make-a-friend communal tables) becomes a gay internet cafe later.

Black Tulip Hotel (Map pp88-9; ☎ 427 09 33; www.blacktulip.nl; Geldersekade 16; s €125, d €145-195; 🖳 🛜) This small hotel has more bondage gear than you can crack a whip at. Everything is fashionable and most rooms contain sling and bondage hooks; a few contain bondage chairs and steel cages. There's a three-night minimum on weekends.

Golden Bear (Map pp92-3; ☎ 624 47 85; www.goldenbear.nl; Kerkstraat 37; s/d without bathroom from €63/88, with bathroom from €90/105; 🛜) The oldest gay hotel in Amsterdam has been operating since 1948. Straddling two 18th-century buildings, rooms are done up in bright colours, mod-furnishings and minifridges.

Orfeo Hotel (Map pp92-3; ☎ 623 13 47; www.hotelorfeo.com; Leidsekruisstraat 14; dm from €35, s with bathroom €60-70, d with/without bathroom €85/125; 🖳 🛜) A convenient cheap option for gay fellas, central Orfeo has simple, small, wood-panelled rooms and the flirtiest breakfast room in town.

Entertainment

Amsterdam's gay scene is among the world's largest. Four hubs party hardest: Warmoesstraat in the Red Light District hosts the infamous, kink-filled leather and fetish bars. Rembrandtplein

Misc Eat Drink Sleep (Map pp88-9; ☎ 330 62 41; www.misc eatdrinksleep.com; Kloveniersburgwal 20; d €155-235; 🖳 🛜) Steps from Nieuwmarkt, the Misc's six themed rooms range from 'baroque' (quite romantic) to the 'room of wonders' (a modern Moroccan escapade). Canal-view rooms cost more, but the garden-view rooms are equally charming (and bigger). Bonus: all snacks and nonalcoholic beverages from the minibar are free.

TOP END

Hotel de l'Europe (Map pp92-3; ☎ 531 17 77; www.leurope .nl; Nieuwe Doelenstraat 2-8; s/d €360/445; 🛄 🖳 🛜 🎗) Oozing Victorian elegance, L'Europe welcomes you with a glam chandelier, marble lobby, 100 gloriously large rooms (some have terraces, most have canal views) and smart

extras like boats for canal cruises. There's an elegant smoking lounge with killer water views. Wi-fi costs €16 per day. You can designate your stay to be carbon-neutral.

Jordaan

BUDGET

Christian Youth Hostel 'The Shelter Jordan' (Map p91; ☎ 624 47 17; www.shelter.nl; Bloemstraat 179; dm €16.50-29.50; 🖳 🛜) OK, we'll put up with the 'no-everything' (no drinkin', partyin', stumblin' in clearly stoned) policy at this small hostel because it's such a gem, on a quiet block yet conveniently near the tram line. Single-sex dorms are quiet and clean, breakfasts (especially the fluffy pancakes) are beaut, and the garden patio is a relaxing retreat. Wi-fi costs €2.50 per hour.

is for traditional pubs and brown cafes, some with a campy bent. Leidseplein has a smattering of venues. The classiest act is Reguliersdwarsstraat, located one street down from the flower market, which draws the beautiful crowd.

Some possibilities:

ARC (Map pp92-3; ☎ 689 70 70; www.bararc.com; Reguliersdwarsstraat 44) The cool minimalist interior at this bar-restaurant is sooo right for beautiful media types (predominantly gay, though also lesbian and straight).

Argos (Map pp88-9; ☎ 622 65 95; www.argosbar.com; Warmoesstraat 95) Amsterdam's oldest leather bar. Dress code for the regular 'SOS' (Sex On Sunday) party: nude or seminude.

Bingo at De Spijker (Map pp92-3; ☎ 620 59 19; www.spijkerbar.nl; Kerkstraat 4; ☆ 6pm Sat) This friendly leather bar hosts the hottest game in town.

De Engel Van Amsterdam (Map pp88-9; ☎ 427 63 81; www.engelamsterdam.nl; Zeedijk 21; ☆ from 1pm) The 'Angel' draws a cruisey terrace crowd. On Sundays there's a meet-and-greet with a singalong party.

Getto (Map pp88-9; ☎ 421 51 51; www.getto.nl; Warmoesstraat 51; ☆ closed Mon) This groovy, long restaurant-bar is loved for its open, welcoming attitude, great people-watching from the front, and a rear lounge where you can chill.

Montmartre (Map pp92-3; ☎ 620 76 22; www.cafemontmartre.nl; Halvemaansteeg 17) Beneath outrageous ceiling decorations, patrons sing loudly to Dutch ballads and top-40 songs. It's like a gay Eurovision. Regarded by many as the Benelux's best gay bar.

Queen's Head (Map pp88-9; ☎ 420 24 75; www.queenshead.nl; Zeedijk 20) A beautiful, canal-view, old-world-style cafe once run by legendary drag queen Dusty. It' a mixed gay-straight crowd now, with drag shows on Tuesdays.

Saarein (Map p91; ☎ 623 49 01; www.saarein.nl; Elandsstraat 119; ☆ closed Mon) This one-time feminist stronghold is still a meeting place for lesbians, although gay men are welcome too. The building dates from the 1600s. There's a small menu with tapas and soups.

Soho (Map pp92-3; ☎ 616 13 12; www.pubsoho.eu; Reguliersdwarsstraat 36) Kitsch, huge, two-storey bar throbbing with a young, flirty, pretty clientele.

Thermos Day Sauna (Map pp92-3; ☎ 623 91 58; www.thermos.nl; Raamstraat 33; admission €19; ☆ noon-8pm) Sprawling, popular place for sexual contact: porn movies, darkrooms, roof deck, hair salon and restaurant.

Festivals

The biggest single party is the **Roze Wester** thrown at the Homomonument on Queen's Day (30 April), with bands and street dancing. The **Amsterdam Pride Festival** (first Saturday in August; www.amsterdampride.nl) is the only water-borne gay parade in the world, with lots of pride showing on the outlandish floats.

International Budget Hostel (Map pp92-3; ☎ 624 27 84; www.internationalbudgethostel.com; Leidsegracht 76; dm €18-32, tw €65-80; 🖳) Reasons to stay: canalside location in a former warehouse; close to nightlife; four-person limit in rooms; cool mix of backpackers from around the world; clean rooms with lockers; staff who are more pleasant than they need to be; low off-season rates. Reason not: your money will go further elsewhere as breakfast isn't included.

Hotel Van Onna (Map p91; ☎ 626 58 01; www.hotelvanonna.nl; Bloemgracht 102-108; r per person €45; 🖳) Even if the 43 rooms here won't win any design awards, they're reasonably priced and you're in a gorgeous section of the Jordaan, within earshot of the Westerkerk's bells (get a back room if you're sensitive to noise). Rooms

sleep up to four people. Try to book one of the two attic rooms with panoramic views. No phones or TVs are in the rooms.

MIDRANGE

Hotel Amsterdam Wiechmann (Map p91; ☎ 626 33 21; www.hotelwiechmann.nl; Prinsengracht 328; s/d from €85/120, 2-bed ste from €230; 🖳 ⑆) This family-run hotel occupies three houses. It has a marvellous canalside location, cosy but lovingly cared-for rooms furnished like an antiques shop with country quilts and chintz, and lobby knickknacks (such as a suit of armour) that have been there for some 50 years.

Truelove Antiek & Guesthouse (Map pp88-9; ☎ 320 25 00; www.truelove.be; Prinsenstraat 4; s/d/apt from €105/125/180; 🖳 ⑆) Run by the same owners as the antiques shop below (reception is the store counter), this friendly, snug and antique-filled guesthouse offers incredible value for money. Rates do not include breakfast, though each room contains a kettle, and breakfast options abound in the neighbourhood.

Western Canal Belt

BUDGET

Hotel Pax (Map p91; ☎ 624 97 35; Raadhuisstraat 37; s/d without bathroom from €30/35, d with bathroom from €45; 🛜) This budget choice in hotel-lined Raadhuisstraat is an eight-room hotel run by two friendly, funky brothers and has an artsy-student vibe. All rooms have a TV and each room is individually decorated. The larger rooms face a street with noisy trams, but the views of the Westerkerk and Keizersgracht more than make up for that.

Frederic's Rentabike & Houseboats (Map pp88-9; ☎ 624 5509; www.frederic.nl; Brouwersgracht 78; s/d from €50/100, apt from €90, houseboats from €115; 🛜) Frederic offers nicely outfitted houseboats on the Prinsengracht, Brouwersgracht and Bloemgracht that are bona fide floating holiday homes with all the mod cons. On land, the company also offers various rooms and apartments in central locations.

MIDRANGE

Budget Hotel Clemens (Map p91; ☎ 624 60 89; www.clemenshotel.nl; Raadhuisstraat 39; s/d without bathroom from €60/75, d/tr with bathroom €120/150; 🖥 🛜) Tidy, steep-staired Clemens gears itself to all budgets. Take your pick of the chic themed rooms (one with a sexy red-gold interior, another with delicate French antiques) or simpler, budget rooms. Breakfast costs €7.

Maes B&B (Map pp88-9; ☎ 427 51 65; www.bedandbreakfastamsterdam.com; Herenstraat 26hs; s €85-105, d €105-135, apt €115-285; 🖥 🛜) If you were designing a traditional home in the western canals, it would probably turn out a lot like this property: oriental carpets, wood floors and exposed brick. The kitchen (open all day for guests) is definitely *gezellig*. Rooms have TVs but no phones. There's a two- to three-night minumum stay.

Chic & Basic Amsterdam (Map pp88-9; ☎ 522 23 45; www.chicandbasic.com; Herengracht 13-19; s/d from €120/140; 🖥 🛜) Spread across three canal houses, the modern rooms here (all white with mood lighting options) merge minimalism with cosiness and flair. The ad-sized photos of skinny models might make you wish you hadn't wolfed down

those *frites*, but if you score a Herengracht-facing room all diet thoughts will disappear out the window and into the canal. The handful of basic (cheaper) rooms aren't nearly as good value. Breakfast costs €7.50.

Miauw Suites (Map p91; ☎ 717 34 29; www.miauw.com; Hartenstraat 36; r/ste €145/245; 🖥 🛜) Located above the same-named fashion shop, Miauw's spacious quarters are just what the doctor ordered for a weekend's shopping blitz in the Negen Straatjes area. The snug rooms mix stylish and vintage decor, and have widescreen TVs and DVD/CD players. The suites are more like one-bedroom flats, with a full living room and open kitchen. There's a two-night minimum stay.

TOP END

Hotel Pulitzer (Map p91; ☎ 523 52 35; www.luxurycollection.com/pulitzer; Prinsengracht 315-331; d from €320; 🛜 🖥 🛜) Occupying a row of 17th-century canal houses, Pulitzer combines big-hotel efficiency with boutique-hotel charm. Beautifully restored rooms feature mod cons galore, and there's a cigar bar, an art gallery, garden courtyards and a wonderful restaurant. Breakfast costs €29 and wi-fi is €19 per day.

Southern Canal Belt

BUDGET

Hotel Prinsenhof (Map pp92-3; ☎ 623 17 72; www.hotelprinsenhof.com; Prinsengracht 810; s/d without bathroom €49/69, s/d with bathroom €84/89; 🛜) For honest value, this 18th-century house features canal views and 'Captain Hook', an electric luggage hoist that gets around the no-lift issue. Staff are affable and the rooms spacious with antique and, well, not-antique furnishings. The attic quarters provide top views, and are most sought-after.

MIDRANGE

Hotel Freeland (Map pp92-3; ☎ 622 75 11; www.hotelfreeland.com; Marnixstraat 386; s without bathroom from €60, s/d with bathroom from €70/120; 🖥 🛜) Freeland has the Leidseplein scene twigged, because what it supplies – tidy rooms with themes (tulips, rose and sunflower and a few with Moroccan details) in an excellent location, some with balconies overlooking a canal, and unusually quiet – pretty much kills the competition. Plus you'll get a big tasty breakfast.

Hotel Amstelzicht (Map pp92-3; ☎ 623 66 93; www.hotelamstelzicht.nl; Amstel 104; s/d from €69/109; 🖥 🛜) The view out front is straight from a 17th-century painting, so make sure you get one of the rooms facing the Amstel River and the gabled houses beyond. From the blue-tiled lobby to the elegant decor, this hotel feels smooth and refined, and it's just a minute's walk from Rembrandtplein.

City Hotel (Map pp92-3; ☎ 627 23 23; www.city-hotel .nl; Utrechtsestraat 2; r €80-150; 🖳 🛜) Above the Old Bell pub, practically on Rembrandtplein, is this unexpectedly great choice: it's clean, neat, good value and well-run by a fine family. The rooms are decorated with crisp linen and each comes with a TV. Some share bathrooms. Breakfast costs €5.

Hotel Orlando (Map pp92-3; ☎ 638 69 15; www.hotel orlando.nl; Prinsengracht 1099; s/d from €95/115; 🍴 🖳) Oh Orlando, how do we love thee? Let us count the ways. One: five biggish, high-ceilinged, canalside rooms at smallish rates. Two: hospitable, gay-friendly hosts. Three: a hearty breakfast. Four: chic boutique style, with custom-made cabinetry and satin curtains. There's wired in-room internet access.

ourpick Seven Bridges (Map pp92-3; ☎ 623 13 29; Reguliersgracht 31; d €110-250; 🖳 🛜) Private, sophisticated and intimate, the Seven Bridges is one of the city's most exquisite little hotels on one of its loveliest canals. It has eight tastefully decorated rooms, all incorporating lush oriental rugs and elegant antiques. Room 5, with its private balcony, is the most coveted. Staff deliver breakfast to your room.

TOP END

Banks Mansion (Map pp92-3; ☎ 420 00 55; www.banks mansion.nl; Herengracht 519-525; d €200-450; 🍴 🖳 🛜) A plasma-screen TV, DVD player (free in-house films), plush beds and free gin, whisky and cognac fill the contemporary rooms. More complimentary tipples are available in the Frank Lloyd Wright–designed lobby. The first 50 minutes of wi-fi are free; after that you pay €14 per day.

Old South
MIDRANGE

Hotel Bema (Map pp92-3; ☎ 679 13 96; www.bemahotel .com; Concertgebouwplein 19b; s from €45, d with/without bathroom €85/65; 🖳 🛜) Climb the stairs to this seven-room hotel in an old movie theatre across from the Concertgebouw. Expect African-art decor, extra-big doubles and breakfast in bed, but no in-room phones.

Collector (Map pp92-3; ☎ 673 67 79; www.the-collector .nl; De Lairessestraat 46hs; r €80-115; 🖳 🛜) This spotless B&B, housed in a renovated 1914 building, is furnished with museum-style displays of clocks and Amsterdam School decor. Each room has a balcony and TV, and the owner provides organic fare to make your own breakfast (including eggs from his hens in the garden).

Hotel Aalders (Map pp92-3; ☎ 662 01 16; www.hotel aalders.nl; Jan Luijkenstraat 13-15; r from €99; 🖳 🛜) There are fancier hotels in town, but the Aalders is homey, family-owned and well situated on a quiet street near the Museumplein. The 28 rooms are spread among two row houses and come in varying sizes and styles (some with wood panelling and leaded-glass windows). In the morning, munch homemade pastries in the chandelier-adorned breakfast room.

Xaviera's Happy House (Map pp86-7; ☎ 673 39 34; www .xavierahollander.com; Stadionweg 17; d from €100; 🖳 🛜) This two-room B&B is run by the one and only Xaviera Hollander, author of *The Happy Hooker*. The interior contains plenty of racy allusions to her past life, in leather, shag and stain-proof formica, but chambers are uniformly luxurious, particularly the princely garden hut. There's a two-night minimum stay.

Hotel Fita (Map pp92-3; ☎ 679 09 76; www.hotelfita .com; Jan Luijkenstraat 37; s €100, d €130-160; 🖳 🛜) This tiny, family-owned hotel on a quiet street off Museumplein and PC Hooftstraat is one of the best in the Old South. It's got 15 handsome rooms with nicely appointed bathrooms, an English-style breakfast buffet and an elevator. Bonus: room rates include free phone calls to Europe and the USA.

Conscious Hotels Museum Square (Map pp92-3; ☎ 671 95 96; www.museumsquarehotel.nl; De Lairessestraat 7; r €100-179; 🛜) This is your place to go green. It starts with the lobby's living plant wall and the organic breakfast. Then come the modern rooms – beds made with 100% natural materials, desks constructed from recycled yoghurt containers and energy-saving plasma TVs. A second location at Overtoom 519 is due to open mid-2010. Wi-fi is free in the lobby; in-room it costs €10 per day.

TOP END

College Hotel (Map pp86-7; ☎ 571 15 11; www.collegehotel amsterdam.com; Roelof Hartstraat 1; r from €175; 🍴 🖳 🛜) Originally a 19th-century school, this boutique property has been updated with tremendous style, including flat-screen TVs, silk throw pillows and the occasional stained-glass window. Hospitality-school students now staff the hotel to earn their stripes. Continental breakfast costs €19.50, wi-fi €17 per day.

AMSTERDAM

GO GREEN

From rentable recycled bicycles to greenhouse dining to locally made beer, Amsterdam is getting in on the eco-action:

- Boerenmarkt (see boxed text, p134) – Farmers market with fresh cheese.
- Brouwerij 't IJ (p129) – Organic brewskis.
- Conscious Hotels Museum Square (p121) – A proper eco-hotel.
- De Kas (p127) – Meals from the greenhouse.
- Recycled Bicycles (p136) – The name says it all.

Vondelpark

BUDGET

Stayokay Vondelpark (Map pp92-3; ☎ 589 89 96; www .stayokay.com; Zandpad 5; dm €24-30, tw €74-90; 🖳 🛜) A blink away from the Vondelpark, this 535-bed hostel feels like a mini-UN (if the UN had a pool table). Part of the structure is housed in an old school, but it all feels pretty new, particularly the recently renovated rooms (think IKEA). All bedrooms have lockers, a shower, a toilet and well-spaced bunks. There's a two-night minimum stay at weekends.

MIDRANGE

Owl Hotel (Map pp92-3; ☎ 618 94 84; www.owl-hotel.nl; Roemer Visscherstraat 1; s/d from €80/105; 🖳 🛜) Some guests love this place so much that they send in owl figurines from all over the world. Staff are warm and welcoming, and rooms are dapper, bright and quiet. The included buffet breakfast is served in a serene, light-filled room overlooking a gorgeous garden. Wi-fi costs €10 per day.

Hotel de Filosoof (Map pp92-3; ☎ 683 30 13; www .hotelfilosoof.nl; Anna van den Vondelstraat 6; s/d/ste from €80/110/170) The 45 rooms are named after philosophers, ranging from Thoreau (with a mural of Walden Pond) to Nietzsche (lots of red, representing his book *Morning Red*). The decor can be lush or minimalist, depending on the room's honoree. Suites come with kitchenettes. Breakfast costs €15.

Hotel Piet Hein (Map pp92-3; ☎ 662 72 05; www .hotelpiethein.nl; Vossiusstraat 52-53; s/d €92/135; 🖳 🛜) Located close to the museums and looking at the Vondelpark's fine old arbour, this immaculate hotel offers a variety of contempo-

rary rooms (including snug single 'business' rooms), a sublime garden and a relaxing bar. Wi-fi costs €12 per day.

Hotel Zandbergen (Map pp92-3; ☎ 676 93 21; www .hotel-zandbergen.com; Willemsparkweg 205; s/d from €93/125; 🖳 🛜) The Zandbergen is a rare combination: peaceful and professional, but also personal. Staff go overboard for guests, and the rooms are absolutely faultless; those at the rear have balconies overlooking a quiet courtyard. The Vondelpark is just over the road, where the tram will get you to the centre in a jiffy.

TOP END

Hotel Roemer (Map pp92-3; ☎ 589 08 00; www.vondelhotels .com; Roemer Visscherstraat 8-10; d €155-255, ste €295-345; 🖳 🛜) All 23 rooms overlook either a quiet, leafy street or the stately back garden, and all have high ceilings, an abundance of natural light, flat-screen TVs, an iPod dock and a DVD player; most have spa baths, too. Breakfast costs €22.50; wi-fi is free in the lobby.

De Pijp

BUDGET

Bicycle Hotel (Map pp86-7; ☎ 679 34 52; www.bicyclehotel .com; Van Ostadestraat 123; d without bathroom €40-80, d with bathroom €70-115; 🖳 🛜) Run by Marjolein and Clemens, who love pedal-power, this place is great if you love the bed-and-bike thing. Casual, friendly and green-minded, has comfy rooms and serves a killer organic breakfast.

TOP END

Hotel Okura (Map pp86-7; ☎ 678 71 11; www.okura.nl; Ferdinand Bolstraat 333; s/d from €240/275; 🍴 🖳 🛜 🍸) This is the business-traveller's choice, with close proximity to the RAI exhibition centre, private in-room fax lines, wi-fi and professional staff. Plus, it's got the Netherlands's largest hotel pool, an amazing health club, Michelin-starred restaurants and panoramic city views. Wi-fi costs €22 per day.

Plantage, Oosterpark & Eastern Islands

BUDGET

Hotel Rembrandt (Map p95; ☎ 627 27 14; www .hotelrembrandt.nl; Plantage Middenlaan 17; s €73, d €95-115; 🖳 🛜) The Rembrandt shines: rooms are spotless and modern and most contain pop-art prints of Mr Rembrandt himself. Room 3 is particularly nice, with a balcony overlooking a small garden, plus a sauna. Breakfast (€7.50) is served in a wood-panelled room with chandeliers and 17th-century paintings.

MIDRANGE

Hotel Parklane (Map p95; ☎ 622 48 04; www.hotel-park lane.nl; Plantage Parklaan 16; s €78-99, d €115-170; 🖳 🛜) This one-time dressmaker's shop features 12 high-ceilinged rooms equipped with fridges; the baths are sparkling and modern with great water pressure (two rooms have spa baths); and the free well-sorted buffet breakfast will keep you going into the afternoon.

Lloyd Hotel (Map pp86-7; ☎ 561 36 36; www.lloyd hotel.com; Oostelijke Handelskade 34; r €95-450; 🖳 🛜) In 1921 the Lloyd was a hotel for migrants, and many of the original fixtures (tiles, cabinetry etc) still exist, now combined with triumphs of more contemporary Dutch design. This combination hotel, cultural centre and local gathering place boasts rooms that span one-star (facilities down the hall) to five-star (plush and huge). Breakfast costs €17.50.

Hotel Arena (Map p95; ☎ 850 24 00; www.hotelarena .nl; 's Gravesandestraat 51; d/ste from €109/209; 🖳 🛜) The Arena, next to lush Oosterpark, has been a chapel, an orphanage and a backpackers hostel. Now it's a chic, 116-room hotel with a stylish restaurant, cafe and nightclub. A recent makeover means minimalist rooms have a 'designer industrial' feel. Breakfast costs €18.50 and wi-fi is €10 per day.

Amstelveen & Around
MIDRANGE

Yotel (off Map pp86-7; ☎ 44 (0) 207 100 11 00; www.yotel.com; Schiphol Airport Plaza; r from €40 per 4hr; 🖳 🛜) Yotel's Japanese-style capsule hotel at Schiphol airport is a blessing for travellers who need to catch some shut-eye. The glam, 7 sq metre standard and twin rooms have bunks and fold-up desks; the premium rooms contain regular beds.

Qbic Hotel (Map pp86-7; ☎ 321 11 11; www.qbichotels .com; Strawinskylaan 241; r €69-159; 🖫 🖳 🛜) Located in the World Trade Centre office complex, this snazzy hotel pushes the design envelope with its sci-fi-esque, cube-shaped rooms, extra-long, queen-sized beds and shower-washrooms melded into single monolithic units (note: no toilet door). It's close to the to the RAI conference centre, and on the metro and tram lines. Breakfast costs €17.50.

EATING

Amsterdam's culinary scene has hundreds of restaurants and *eetcafés* (pubs serving meals) catering to all tastes.

Utrechtsestraat is a terrific all-round eat street, while Haarlemmerstraat has some of the latest hot spots. Zeedijk holds several Thai and Chinese options. West of Albert Cuypstraat there's a stash of exotic choices from Cambodian to Surinamese. Other happy hunting grounds include Spuistraat and any of the little streets lining and connecting the west canals, such as Berenstraat.

Note that many restaurants do not accept credit cards – even top-end places. Or if they do, they levy a 5% surcharge. Be sure your wallet is filled before dining out.

It never hurts to phone ahead and make a reservation for eateries in the upper price bracket (virtually everyone speaks English).

City Centre

Vleminckx (Map pp92-3; ☎ 624 60 75; Voetboogstraat 31; frites small/large €1.80/2.30, sauces €0.60-0.80; 🕙 11am-6pm Tue, Wed, Fri & Sat, to 7pm Thu, noon-6pm Sun & Mon) This hole-in-the-wall takeaway has drawn hordes for its monumental *frites* since 1887. The standard is smothered in mayonnaise, though you can ask for ketchup, peanut sauce or a variety of spicy toppings.

Rob Wigboldus Vishandel (Map pp88-9; ☎ 626 33 88; Zoutsteeg 6; sandwiches €2.50-4.50; 🕙 breakfast & lunch) A wee, three-table oasis in the midst of surrounding tourist tat, this fish shop in a tiny alley serves excellent herring sandwiches on a choice of crusty white or brown rolls.

'Skek (Map pp88-9; ☎ 427 05 51; Zeedijk 4-8; sandwiches €3-7, mains €12-14; 🕙 noon-1am Sun-Thu, noon-3am Fri & Sat; 🛜) Run by students for students (flashing your ID gets you one-third off), this friendly cafe-bar is an excellent place to get fat sandwiches on thick slices of multigrain bread and healthy main dishes with chicken, fish or pasta.

Gartine (Map pp88-9; ☎ 320 41 32; Taksteeg 7; mains €6-11, high tea €10-18; 🕙 8am-6pm Wed-Sun) Slow-food credentialed Gartine makes delectable breakfast pastries, sandwiches and salads from produce grown in its own garden. The sweet-and-savoury high tea is a scrumptious bonus.

Hofje van Wijs (Map pp88-9; ☎ 624 04 36; Zeedijk 43; mains €8.50-10.50; 🕙 noon-6pm Tue & Wed, noon-10.30pm Thu & Fri, 10am-10.30pm Sat, noon-7pm Sun) The 200-year-old coffee and tea vendor Wijs & Zonen (the Queen's purveyor) maintains this pretty courtyard cafe. In addition to cakes, it serves inexpensive Dutch stews plus beers and liqueurs.

Nam Kee (Map pp88-9; ☎ 624 34 70; Zeedijk 113-116; mains €8.50-18.50; 🕙 noon-10pm) It won't win any design awards, but Nam Kee is the most popular Chinese spot in town. There's a new, fancier location at Geldersekade 117 (Map pp88–9).

Lucius (Map pp88-9; ☎ 624 18 31; Spuistraat 247; mains €18.50-28, set menus €37.50; ❤ dinner) Simple, delicious and consistently full, this seafood place is known for fresh ingredients and for not overdoing the sauce and spice. The interior is all fish tanks and tiles, and service is thorough and efficient.

Hemelse Modder (Heavenly Mud; Map p95; ☎ 624 32 03; Oude Waal 9; mains €22.50-25.50; ❤ dinner Tue-Sun) It's a little hard to locate, but worth it. Celery-green walls and blond-wood tables are the backdrop for equally light and unpretentious food, which emphasises North Sea fish and farm-fresh produce.

d'Vijff Vlieghen (Map pp88-9; ☎ 530 40 60; Spuistraat 294-302; mains €24-33; ❤ dinner) The second you set foot in this dining complex of five 17th-century canal houses, you know you're in for a treat. Ask to be seated in the Rembrandt Room (with four original etchings) and join splurging business groups being treated to silver service and contemporary Dutch dishes.

Blauw aan de Wal (Map pp88-9; ☎ 330 22 57; Oudezijds Achterburgwal 99; mains from €27, 3-course menu €55; ❤ dinner Tue-Sat) Tucked away in a long, often graffiti-covered alley in the middle of the Red Light District, this charming 17th-century herb warehouse (complete with exposed brick and steel weights) is the setting for contemporary French- and Italian-inspired cooking. In summer, grab a table in the garden.

Jordaan

Festina Lente (Map p91; ☎ 638 14 12; Looiersgracht 40b; sandwiches €4-6, small plates €4-8; ❤ noon-1am Sun & Mon, 10.30am-1am Tue-Thu, 10.30am-3am Fri & Sat) This neighbourhood hangout is typical Jordaan *gezelligheid*, packed with regulars playing board games, reading poetry and snacking on small-portion Mediterranean dishes and big sandwiches.

De Vliegende Schotel (Map p91; ☎ 625 20 41; Nieuwe Leliestraat 162-168; mains €10-14.50; ❤ dinner) Service can be spotty at the 'Flying Saucer', but if you're prepared to take your time in the summer camp–chic dining room, you'll enjoy some of the city's favourite vegie gratins, lasagnes and Indian-inflected meals.

Koevoet (Map p91; ☎ 624 08 46; Lindenstraat 17; mains €12-23; ❤ dinner Tue-Sun) Koevoet's congenial Italian owners took over a former cafe on a quiet side street, left the *gezellig* decor untouched and started cooking up homemade pastas and seafood dishes.

SNACK TIME

Whatever the pretext – before drinking, after drinking, for sightseeing sustenance – be sure to try these classic local snacks:

■ Kroket from Van Dobben (opposite)

■ Fries with mayo from Vleminckx (p123)

■ Herring sandwich from Rob Wigboldus Vishandel (p123)

■ Aged gouda from De Kaaskamer (below)

■ Lamb roti from Roopram Roti (p127)

De Bolhoed (Map p91; ☎ 626 18 03; Prinsengracht 60-62; mains €13-15; ❤ lunch & dinner) The hippyish interior at Amsterdam's best-known vegetarian restaurant provides a nice setting for tucking into enormous, organic Mexican-, Asian- and Italian-inspired dishes; in warm weather, there's a verdant little canalside terrace.

Moeders (Map p91; ☎ 626 79 57; Rozengracht 251; mains €15-19, 3-course menus €26-30; ❤ dinner) Mum's the word at 'Mothers', a delightful hodge-podge of decor and food, including *stamppot* (potatoes mashed with kale, endive or sauerkraut), seafood, Moroccan dishes and an assortment of other lip-smacking traditional Dutch dishes.

Bordewijk (Map p91; ☎ 624 38 99; Noordermarkt 7; mains €20-31, set menus €39-57; ❤ dinner Tue-Sun) The interior here is so minimal that there's little to do but appreciate the spectacular French/Italian cooking. The chefs are not afraid to take risks (we once saw lamb's testicles on the menu), but the skilled staff take your wishes with aplomb. Locals love it.

Western Canal Belt

Wil Graanstra Friteshuis (Map p91; ☎ 624 40 71; Westermarkt 11; frites €2-3.75; ❤ 11am-6pm Mon-Sat) Wil's little stall near the Anne Frank Huis has been serving up freakishly golden crispy *frites* since 1956. Legions of Amsterdammers swear by them.

De Kaaskamer (Map p91; ☎ 623 34 83; Runstraat 7; sandwiches €4-7; ❤ noon-6pm Mon, 9am-6pm Tue-Fri, 9am-5pm Sat, noon-5pm Sun) This shop is stacked to the rafters with Dutch and organic cheeses, as well as olives, tapenades, salads and other picnic ingredients. Buy a hunk, or get the goods piled on a baguette as takeaway.

Hein (Map p91; ☎ 623 10 48; Berenstraat 20; mains €5-15; ❤ breakfast & lunch) Hein loves to cook, and it shows in her simple, stylish, sky-lit cafe. Media types, doing business over brunch, comment that she has a great touch with simple dishes: *croque monsieur* or *madame*, smoked salmon and fresh fruit salads.

Foodism (Map pp88-9; ☎ 427 51 03; Oude Leliestraat 8; mains €5-15; ☽ 11.30am-10pm Mon-Fri, to 6pm Sat & Sun) Foodism is a hip, colourful little joint run by a fun, relaxed crew. All-day breakfasts (€9.50), sandwiches such as chicken mango and salads make up the day menu; night-time sees patrons downing wild pasta dishes.

Buffet van Odette (Map pp88-9; ☎ 423 60 34; Herengracht 309; mains €5-15; ☽ 8.30am-5.30pm Mon & Wed-Fri, 10am-5.30pm Sat & Sun) Not a buffet but a sit-down cafe on the canal; Odette and Yvette show how good simple cooking can taste when you start with great ingredients and a dash of creativity. The soups, sandwiches, pastas and quiches are mostly organic.

Pancakes! (Map p91; ☎ 528 97 97; Berenstraat 38; mains €6-10; ☽ 10am-7pm) Just as many locals as tourists grace the blue-tiled tables at snug little Pancakes!, carving into all the usual options, plus daily creations such as ham, chicory and cheese or chicken curry pancakes.

Koh-I-Noor (Map p91; ☎ 623 31 33; Westermarkt 29; mains €12.50-20; ☽ dinner) The interior is gaudy but the Indian food is consistently good, running the gamut from mild to palate-searing for curries, tandoori and biryani dishes.

De Belhamel (Map pp88-9; ☎ 622 10 95; Brouwersgracht 60; mains €20-25; ☽ lunch & dinner) In warm weather the canalside tables at the head of the Herengracht are an aphrodisiac, and the sumptuous art nouveau interior provides the perfect backdrop for excellent, French- and Italian-inspired dishes such as silky roast beef.

Southern Canal Belt

FEBO (Map pp92-3; ☎ 620 86 15; Leidsestraat 94; items €1-2; ☽ 11am-3am Sun-Thu, to 4am Fri & Sat) Insert a few coins in the machine and live the legend at this fast-food icon. The *bami* (Indonesian noodle) rolls are scorching hot, the *frikadel* (fried meat dumplings) frightening and the *kaassoufflé* (fried cheese puffs) utterly unsoufflélike. But plucking a treat from the automat windows is a drunken Dutch tradition.

[ourpick] Van Dobben (Map pp92-3; ☎ 624 42 00; Korte Reguliersdwarsstraat 5; mains €2.50-7.50; ☽ 9.30am-1am Mon-Thu, to 2am Fri & Sat, 11am-8pm Sun) Open since the 1940s, the venerable Van Dobben has white tiled walls and white-coated counter men who specialise in snappy banter. Traditional

meaty Dutch fare is the forte: try the *pekelvlees* (something close to corned beef), or make it a *halfom*, if you're keen on that being mixed with liver. The *kroketten* (croquettes) are the best in town and compulsory after a late-night Rembrandtplein booze-up.

Maoz (Map pp92-3; ☎ 420 74 35; Muntplein 1; mains €3.70-7.40; ☽ 11am-1am Sun-Thu, to 3am Fri & Sat) Felafel, saviour of vegetarians the world over, is perfected at this minichain. Four other outlets pop up around town.

Pata Negra (Map pp92-3; ☎ 422 62 50; Utrechtsestraat 124; tapas €5-9; ☽ lunch & dinner) It's tapas and only tapas at this Spanish eatery. The alluringly tiled exterior is matched by a vibrant crowd inside, especially on weekends, downing sangria and all those small plates (the garlic-fried shrimp and grilled sardines are standouts).

Lo Stivale d'Oro (Map pp92-3; ☎ 638 73 07; Amstelstraat 49; mains €10-17.50; ☽ dinner, closed Tue) Loosen the belt for excellent pizzas and pastas at this trattoria's chummy tables. The Italian owner occasionally pulls out his guitar and strums for the crowd.

Piet de Leeuw (Map pp92-3; ☎ 623 71 81; Noorderstraat 11; mains €12.50-19; ☽ lunch Mon-Fri, dinner nightly) Dark and cosy Piet de Leeuw has been a steakhouse and hangout since the 1940s. Crowds descend for well-priced slabs of meat with toppings such as onions, mushrooms or bacon, served with salad and piping-hot *frites*.

Tujuh Maret (Map pp92-3; ☎ 427 98 65; Utrechtsestraat 73; mains €13.50-19; ☽ lunch Mon-Sat, dinner nightly) Tujuh Maret, next door to Tempo Doeloe (below), is just as good, but more casual. Grab a wicker chair and tuck into spicy Sulawesi-style dishes such as dried, fried beef or chicken in red-pepper sauce. *Rijsttafel* (array of spicy dishes served with rice) is laid out according to spice intensity; *makanan kecil* is a mini-*rijsttafel*.

Sluizer (Map pp92-3; ☎ 622 63 76; Utrechtsestraat 43-45; mains €15.50-25; ☽ 5-11pm) This Amsterdam institution, with a romantic, enclosed terrace, comprises two restaurants: a renowned house of fish at No 45 and a Parisian-style 'meat' establishment at No 43, although both menus are offered in either. Bouillabaisse and spare ribs are the respective house specialities.

Segugio (Map pp92-3; ☎ 330 15 03; Utrechtsestraat 96; pastas €17-20, mains €22-36; ☽ dinner Mon-Sat) This fashionably minimalist storefront is the sort of place other chefs go for a good Italian dinner. It's known for risotto and high-quality ingredients combined with a sure hand.

Tempo Doeloe (Map pp92-3; ☎ 625 67 18; Utrechtsestraat 75; mains €19.50-23.50; ☽ dinner Mon-Sat) One of the best Indonesian restaurants in the city, Tempo Doeloe's setting and service are pleasant and decorous without being overdone. The same applies to the *rijsttafel*: a ridiculously over-blown affair at many places, here it's a fine sampling of the country's flavours. Warning: dishes marked 'very hot' are like napalm.

La Rive (Map pp92-3; ☎ 520 32 64; Amstel Intercontinental Hotel, Professor Tulpplein 1; mains €48-55; ⏰ lunch Tue-Fri, dinner Tue-Sat) A Michelin star and a formal dining room with graciously spaced tables and views over the Amstel make La Rive the perfect venue for an out-to-impress lunch or dinner. The French menu changes frequently.

Old South & Vondelpark

De Peper (Map pp86-7; ☎ 412 29 54; Overtoom 301; meals €6-10; ⏰ 7-8.30pm Tue, Fri & Sun) The friendly, no-frills restaurant at the graffiti-covered OT301 squat serves cheap organic vegan meals. Same-day reservations are required; call after 4pm.

Hap Hmm (Map pp92-3; ☎ 618 18 84; Eerste Helmersstraat 33; mains €6.50-10; ⏰ 4.30-8pm Mon-Fri) Elsewhere €7 might buy you a bowl of soup, but at this wood-panelled neighbourhood place it might buy an entire dinner: simple Dutch cooking (meat + vegies + potatoes), served on stainless-steel dishes.

Lalibela (Map pp86-7; ☎ 683 83 32; Eerste Helmersstraat 249; mains €8.50-12.50; ⏰ dinner) This was the Netherlands' first Ethiopian restaurant, and it's still a good 'un. Drink Ethiopian beer from a half-gourd and eat your stews, egg and veg-etable dishes by hand with *endjera*, a spongy pancake.

La Falote (Map pp86-7; ☎ 622 54 54; Roelof Hartstraat 26; mains €13.50-19.50; ⏰ dinner Mon-Sat) Wee, checked-tablecloth La Falote is about Dutch home-style cooking, such as calf's liver, meat-balls with endives or stewed fish with beets and mustard sauce.

Sama Sebo (Map pp92-3; ☎ 662 81 46; Pieter Cornelisz Hooftstraat 27; rijsttafel per person €29.50; ⏰ lunch & dinner Mon-Sat) Another reliable old-timer, this Indonesian restaurant's got the ambience of a brown cafe. It's also got a wicked *rijsttafel* comprising 17 dishes (four to seven at lunch); order individual plates if that's too much.

De Pijp

Taart van m'n Tante (Map pp92-3; ☎ 776 46 00; Ferdinand Bolstraat 10; items €4-5; ⏰ 10am-6pm) This popular, uberkitsch parlour bakes apple pies, pecan pies, and tarts with lush ingredients such as truffles and marzipan with strawberry liqueur.

Albert Cuyp 67 (Map pp92-3; ☎ 671 13 96; Albert Cuypstraat 67; mains €5-10; ⏰ 1-10pm) If you're look-ing for stylish surrounds, turn away now. If, however, you're after quality examples of Surinamese food, take a seat. A colossal portion of *roti kip* (chicken curry, flaky roti bread, pota-toes, cabbage and egg) is a fine replenishment after a couple of hours at Albert Cuypmarkt.

De Burgermeester (Map pp92-3; ☎ 670 93 39; Albert Cuypstraat 48; burgers €6.50-8; ⏰ noon-11pm) This sleek little bistro makes the finest burgers in town, bar none. It uses only organic beef (or lamb, falafel or fish), in mouth-stretching portions that would pass as a main dish without a bun.

Cambodja City (Map pp92-3; ☎ 671 49 30; Albert Cuypstraat 58-60; mains €8-15.50; ⏰ dinner) The own-er's welcome is warm and friendly, and the flavours are from across Southeast Asia – *loem-pias* (spring rolls), Vietnamese noodle soups, Thai curries and Cambodian pancakes.

Bazar Amsterdam (Map pp92-3; ☎ 675 05 44; Albert Cuypstraat 182; mains €8-15; ⏰ 11am-midnight Mon-Thu, 11am-1am Fri, 9am-1am Sat, 9am-midnight Sun) In a glori-ous former Dutch Reformed Church, the light-filled, Middle Eastern-style decor matches the Middle Eastern-style food. Fish and chicken dishes please meat eaters; aubergine and por-tobello mushroom dishes gratify vegetarians. Breakfast and lunch are served all day.

De Waaghals (Map pp92-3; ☎ 679 96 09; Frans Halsstraat 29; mains €13-18.50; ⏰ 5-9.30pm Tue-Sun) The white-walled, vegetarian 'Dare-Devil' is stylish enough that even nonvegies might re-examine their dining priorities. The menu concentrates on one country each month, plus a few staples, such as a rich, mushroom-heavy aubergine stew.

Mamouche (Map pp92-3; ☎ 673 63 61; Quellijnstraat 104; mains €16.50-22.50; ⏰ dinner) Mamouche gets serious acclaim for sexy, modern Moroccan amid mini-malism. Exposed flooring, mottled walls and slat-beam ceilings complement the changing selection of couscous, lamb and fish dishes.

Plantage, Eastern Islands & Eastern Docklands

Koffiehuis van den Volksbond (Map p95; ⏰ 622 12 09; Kadijksplein 4; mains €12.50-17.50; ⏰ dinner) This laid-back place began life as a charitable coffee house for dockers, and it still has a fashionably grungy vibe. The ever-changing menu has huge plates of comfort food with ingredients such as mus-sels and *merguez* (a type of spicy sausage).

Fifteen (Map pp86-7; ☎ 0900 343 83 36; Jollemanhof 9; 4-course menu €46; ⏰ lunch & dinner Mon-Sat Sep-May, dinner only Tue-Sat Jun-Aug) 'Naked chef' Jamie Oliver has brought to Amsterdam a concept he began in London: take 15 young people from underprivileged backgrounds and train them for a year in the restaurant biz. Results: noble intention, sometimes spotty execution. The setting, however, is beyond question: Fifteen faces the IJ, and the busy, open-kitchen space is city-cool, with graffitied walls and exposed wood beams.

Oosterpark

Roopram Roti (Map pp86-7; ☎ 061 475 82 00; 1e Van Swindenstraat 4; mains €4-10; ☯ 2-9pm Tue-Sat, 3-9pm Sun) There's often a line out the door at this barebones Surinamese place, but don't worry, it moves fast. Place your order – lamb roti 'extra' (with egg) and a *barra* (lentil doughnut) at least – with the man at the bar, and don't forget the fiery hot sauce.

De Kas (Map pp86-7; ☎ 462 45 62; Kamerlingh Onneslaan 3, Frankendael Park; lunch menu €37.50, dinner menu €49.50; ☯ lunch Mon-Fri, dinner Mon-Sat) Admired by gourmets city-wide, De Kas has an organic attitude to match its chic glass greenhouse setting. It grows most of its own herbs and produce right there, and the result is incredibly pure flavours with innovative combinations. There's one set menu each day, based on whatever has been freshly harvested.

Western Islands

our pick Marius (Map pp86-7; ☎ 422 78 80; Barentszstraat 243; mains €13-28, set menu €45; ☯ dinner Tue-Sat) Foodies swoon over pocket-sized Marius. Chef Kees, an alumnus of California's Chez Panisse, shops daily at local markets, then creates his menu from what he finds. The result might be grilled prawns with fava bean purée, or beef rib with polenta and ratatouille. You can also choose from a few house-speciality standbys, such as bouillabaisse.

DRINKING

Atmospheric brown cafes (see p50) are Amsterdam's crowning glory. The city centre holds the mother lode of boozers. To drink with locals try the Jordaan.

City Centre

Doelen (Map pp88-9; ☎ 624 90 23; Kloveniersburgwal 125) On a busy crossroads between the Amstel and the Red Light District, this cafe dates to 1895 and looks it: carved wooden goat's head, leaded stained-glass lamps, sand on the floor.

During fine weather the tables spill across the street for picture-perfect canal views.

our pick Crea Café (Map pp88-9; ☎ 525 14 23; Turfdraagsterpad 17) Walking along Grimburgwal, you can't help but notice the prime cafe chairs across the canal. They're part of the University of Amsterdam's cultural centre, a laid-back spot that's superb for sipping well-priced beers while watching boats manoeuvre under the nearby bridge.

Hoppe (Map pp88-9; ☎ 420 44 20; Spuistraat 18) This gritty brown cafe has been luring drinkers for more than 300 years. Journalists, bums, socialites and raconteurs toss back brews amid the ancient wood panelling. Most months the energetic crowd spews out from the dark interior and onto the Spui.

Gollem (Map pp88-9; ☎ 626 66 45; Raamsteeg 4) All the brew-related paraphernalia is this miniscule space barely leaves room for the 200 beers and the connoisseurs who come to try them. The bartenders are happy to advise.

Proeflokaal Wijnand Fockink (Map pp88-9; ☎ 639 26 95; Pijlsteeg 31; ☯ 3-9pm) This wee tasting house (dating from 1679) serves scores of *jenevers* and liqueurs in an arcade behind Grand Hotel Krasnapolsky. Although there are no seats, it's an intimate place to knock back a taste or two with a friend. The barkeep will pour your drink to the brim, so do like the locals to prevent spillage: lean over it and sip without lifting.

Pilsener Club (Map pp88-9; ☎ 623 17 77; Begijnensteeg 4; ☯ Mon-Sat) Also known as Engelse Reet (English Arse), this brown cafe from 1893 is typical of the holes-in-the-wall around the Spui. Beer is served straight from the kegs via the 'shortest pipes in Amsterdam' (most places have vats in a cellar or side room with long hoses to the bar) – see if you can taste the difference.

In 't Aepjen (Map pp88-9; ☎ 626 84 01; Zeedijk 1) Candles burn even during the day at this bar based in a 15th-century canal house, which is one of two remaining wooden buildings in the city. The name allegedly comes from the bar's role in the 16th and 17th centuries as a crash pad for sailors from the Far East, who often carried *aapjes* (monkeys) with them.

Café de Jaren (Map pp92-3; ☎ 625 57 71; Nieuwe Doelenstraat 20) Watch the Amstel flow by from the balcony and waterside terraces of this soaring, bright, grand cafe. The great reading table has loads of foreign publications for whiling away hours over beers.

Café Cuba (Map pp88-9; ☎ 627 49 19; Nieuwmarkt 3) This place maintains fidelity to Fidel, Che and

'50s Cuba, with low lighting, indoor palms, faux faded elegance, rum posters, and cane chairs and tables. Try Papa Hemingway's favourite cocktail, the *caipirinha*, and the ubiquitous *mojito*. The outdoor seating is right on Nieuwmarkt.

Luxembourg (Map pp88-9; ☎ 620 62 64; Spui 24) Luxembourg occupies the best people-watching spot on the Spui. Our advice: grab a newspaper from the reading table, nab a sunny seat on the terrace and order the 'Royale' snack platter (bread, cured meats, Dutch cheese and deep-fried croquettes). Inside are parquetry floors, a marble bar and an art deco stained-glass skylight.

In De Wildman (Map pp88-9; ☎ 638 23 48; Kolksteeg 3) An oasis in the otherwise grim tourist ghetto south of Centraal Station, In De Wildman has seats outside on the quiet street and a good selection of beers (mostly from Belgium and Holland, but also the potent French 'Belzebuth' with 13% alcohol).

Kapitein Zeppo's (Map pp88-9; ☎ 624 20 57; Gebed Zonder End 5) This site, off Grimburgwal, has assumed many guises over the centuries: a cloister during the 15th, a horse-carriage storehouse in the 17th and a cigar factory in the 19th. These days it's festive, attractive and almost romantic, with a beautiful garden and Belgian brews.

Café de Sluyswacht (Map pp88-9; ☎ 625 76 11; Jodenbreestraat 1) Stoners beware: this tiny black building is built on foundations that lean dramatically. It was once a lock-keeper's house, and today the canalside terrace is one of the nicest spots we know to relax and down a beer (Dommelsch is the house speciality).

Jordaan

Café 't Smalle (Map p91; ☎ 623 96 17; Egelantiersgracht 12) There's no more convivial spot than this canalside terrace on a sunny day, and the 18th-century interior is perfect in winter. Proof of its powerful *gezelligheid* (cosy sense of wellbeing): it manages to remain a lively local bar even while newcomers discover it daily.

De Blaffende Vis (Map p91; ☎ 625 17 21; Westerstraat 118) Drinks at the affable, corner 'Barking Fish' are always accompanied by incessant people-watching. Tall windows open onto the sidewalk tables, ensuring the chatter flows both in and out. Staff dish up a some killer *bitterballen*.

De Pieper (Map pp92-3; ☎ 626 47 75; Prinsengracht 424) The interior of this 1665 brown cafe fea-

---

THINGS TO DO WHEN IT RAINS

It'll rain at some point during your stay – you can count on it – though it probably won't pour for long.

- Amsterdams Historisch Museum (p96) – Learn about your favourite city without waiting in a rain-soaked queue.
- Cafes (p127) – Loaf over a newspaper, drink and/or bite to eat.
- Centrale Bibliotheek (p84) – Check your email or read a book at the ubercool main library.
- Tropenmuseum (p108) – Learn about Dutch colonial activities, also sans soggy queue.
- Tuschinskitheater (p132) – Absorb the glorious architecture while watching a film.

---

tures stained-glass windows, antique Delft beer mugs hanging from the bar and a working, 19th-century Belgian beer pump. It's a sweet place for a nightcap.

Café de Jordaan (Map p91; ☎ 627 58 63; Elandsgracht 45) After midnight, merry and drunk crooners link arms and sing along to classic Dutch tunes in this local haunt. Earlier in the evening it's less vocal and a relaxed spot for a *bierjte* (small beer).

Het Papeneiland (Papists' Island; Map pp88-9; ☎ 624 19 89; Prinsengracht 2) This popular 1642 place features Delft-blue tiles and a central stove. The name goes back to the Reformation, when there was a clandestine Catholic church across the canal, allegedly linked to the other side by a tunnel that's still visible from the stairtop.

Western Canal Belt

Café de Vergulde Gaper (Golden Mortar Cafe; Map p91; ☎ 624 89 75; Prinsenstraat 30; 🛜) Decorated with old chemists' bottles and vintage posters, this former pharmacy has amiable staff and a terrace that catches the sun. It gets busy late in the afternoon, with all kinds of people meeting for after-work drinks and big plates of fried snacks or salads for dinner.

'T Arendsnest (Map pp88-9; ☎ 421 20 57; Herengracht 90) 'T Arendsnest, a restyled brown cafe, serves only Dutch beer – but with more than 300 varieties (many from small breweries) including 23 on tap, you'll need to move here to try them all.

Van Puffelen (Map p91; ☎ 624 62 70; Prinsengracht 377) This large cafe-restaurant, popular among cashed-up professionals and intellectual types, has lots of nooks and crannies for cosy drinks, and big, communal tables for sharing meals.

Vyne (Map p91; ☎ 344 6408; Prinsengracht 411; ☺ 6pm-midnight Mon-Thu, 5pm-1am Fri & Sat, 5-10pm Sun) The slickest wine bar in town employs knowledgeable staff who'll guide you in the right direction, no matter what your budget.

Southern Canal Belt

Café de Kroon (Map pp92-3; ☎ 625 20 11; Rembrandtplein 17) A popular venue for media events and movie-premiere parties, with its high ceilings, velvet chairs and the chance to wave at all the little people below on Rembrandtplein.

Eylders (Map pp92-3; ☎ 624 27 04; Korte Leidsedwarsstraat 47) During WWII, Eylders was a meeting place for artists who refused to toe the cultural line imposed by the Nazis, and the spirit lingers on. It's still an artists' cafe with poetry readings the third Sunday of every month (sometimes in English).

Café Americain (Map pp92-3; ☎ 556 32 32; Leidsekade 97) This art deco monument, opened in 1902, was a grand cafe before the concept even existed. There are huge stained-glass windows overlooking Leidseplein and a great terrace.

Café de Spuyt (Map pp92-3; ☎ 624 89 01; Korte Leidsedwarsstraat 86) Steps away from Leidseplein, the bar staff at this mellow cafe will happily guide you through the massive chalkboard beer menu, offering brewskis ranging from Belgian Trappist ales to American Sierra Nevada.

Old South & Vondelpark

Welling (Map pp92-3; ☎ 662 0155; Jan Willem Brouwersstraat 32; ☺ 4pm-1am Mon-Fri, from 3pm Sat & Sun) Tucked away behind the Concertgebouw, Welling is a relaxed spot to unwind with a newspaper, sip a frothy *biertje* and mingle with intellectuals and artists.

't Blauwe Theehuis (Map pp92-3; ☎ 662 02 54; Vondelpark 5) This spacey-looking teahouse from 1936 serves coffee, cake and alcohol in Vondelpark; it has a great terrace and balcony.

De Pijp

Bar Ça (Map pp92-3; ☎ 470 41 44; Marie Heinekenplein 30-31) Perhaps the hottest cafe in town, this 'Barcelona in Amsterdam' themed club has

brought real life to the area. Take it easy in the posh plush-red and dark wood interior, or spread out onto the terrace.

Plantage, Eastern Islands & Eastern Docklands

Brouwerij 't IJ (Map pp86-7; ☎ 622 83 25; Funenkade 7; ☺ 3-8pm, free tours 4pm Fri) The tasting room of Amsterdam's leading organic microbrewery has a cosy, down-and-dirty beer-hall feel. Bonus: most of the suds made here never leave the premises, so it's fresh *and* ecofriendly – and located at the foot of a big ol' windmill. See p108 for more information.

Star Ferry (Map pp86-7; ☎ 788 20 90; Piet Heinkade 1) The flash cafe at the Muziekgebouw aan 't IJ (p130) is hard to beat for boat-and-water views.

ENTERTAINMENT

Find out what's on in Thursday's papers, Saturday's *PS* section of *Het Parool* or the monthly *Time Out Amsterdam*.

Coffeeshops

'Cafe' means 'pub' throughout the Netherlands; 'coffeeshops' are where one procures pot. Ask at the bar for the list of goods on offer, usually packaged in small bags for €5 to €15. Note that new smoking regulations mean you can puff pot but not tobacco. Alcohol is not available in coffeeshops, either. Most do business from 10am to 1am Sunday to Thursday, and until 3am on weekends.

Amsterdam's coffeeshop scene will take a hit in coming years, as regulations go into effect restricting the number of venues in the Red Light District (see Put Out the Red Light, p99) and shops that are near schools. Fear not: several other shops, including many of those listed here, are in safe zones.

Abraxas (Map pp88-9; ☎ 626 57 63; Jonge Roelensteeg 12; ☎) The Abraxas management knows what stoners want: mellow music, comfy sofas, rooms with different energy levels and thick milkshakes. The considerate staff and laid-back clientele make this a great place for coffeeshop newbies, who can get stoned and send strange emails from the computers.

our pick Rokerij (Map pp92-3; ☎ 622 94 42; Lange Leidsedwarsstraat 41) Behind this black hole of an entrance you'll find Asian decor and candlelight for those tired of the Rastafarian vibe. Staff at this flagship branch have a reputation for friendliness, explaining why outlets have shot up like weed(s), but this is the cosiest location by far.

Yo-Yo (Map pp92-3; ☎ 664 71 73; 2e Jan van der Heijdenstraat 79) The large windows, minimalist furnishings and funky art might make you think you've stumbled upon an airy museum-cafe. But this female-run coffeeshop on a leafy residential corner of De Pijp is all about organic weed and quiet reflection.

Siberië (Map pp88-9; ☎ 623 59 09; Brouwersgracht 111; 🛜) Popular among locals, Siberië's loungey, canal-view ambience goes beyond marijuana – it's owners regularly schedule cultural events such as art exhibits, poetry slams, acoustic concerts, DJ nights and even horoscope readings.

Grey Area (Map pp88-9; ☎ 420 43 01; Oude Leliestraat 2; 🕙 noon-8pm) Owned by a couple of laid-back American guys, this tiny shop introduced the extra-sticky, flavoursome 'Double Bubble Gum' weed to the city's smokers. It also keeps up the wonderful American tradition of coffee refills (it's organic).

La Tertulia (Map p91; Prinsengracht 312; 🕙 11am-7pm Tue-Sat) A backpackers' favourite, this mother and daughter coffeeshop has a greenhouse feel. You can sit outside the Van Gogh-inspired murals, play some board games or take in those Jurassic-sized crystals by the counter.

Other options:

Bulldog (Map pp92-3; ☎ 627 19 08; Leidseplein 13-17; 🛜) Amsterdam's most famous coffeeshop chain, with multiple branches around town. At the time of writing this flagship location on the Leidseplein was under threat of closure due to its proximity to a school.

Greenhouse (Map pp88-9; ☎ 627 17 39; Oudezijds Voorburgwal 191) Undersea mosaics; psychedelic stained-glass windows; high-quality weed and hash.

Homegrown Fantasy (Map pp88-9; ☎ 627 56 83; Nieuwezijds Voorburgwal 87a; 🛜) Organic Dutch-grown product, 3m-long glass bongs, vaporisers, temporary art exhibits on the walls and famous space cakes attracts a good mixed crowd.

Live Music
CLASSICAL

Concertgebouw (Concert Bldg; Map pp92-3; ☎ 671 83 45; www.concertgebouw.nl; Concertgebouwplein 2-6; 🕙 ticket office 10am-8.15pm) Each year, this neo-Renaissance centre presents around 650 concerts attracting 840,000 visitors, making it the world's busiest concert hall (with reputedly the best acoustics). The venue holds free, half-hour 'lunch concerts' on Wednesdays at 12.30pm between September and June.

Muziekgebouw aan 't IJ (Map pp86-7; ☎ 788 20 00; www.muziekgebouw.nl; Piet Heinkade 1; 🕙 ticket office noon-7pm Mon-Sat) This magnificent, mod building plays host to everything from the Holland Symfonia (which typically backs the National Ballet) to the prestigious Metropole Orkest, which does smart arrangements of jazz and pop. Free lunchtime concerts are normally held in the main hall once a month on different weekdays from September to May – check the website for details. The jazzy Bimhuis (below) shares the building.

Muziektheater (Map pp92-3; ☎ 625 54 55; www .hetmuziektheater.nl; Waterlooplein 22; 🕙 closed Aug) The Stopera's swanky theatre is home to the Netherlands Opera, the National Ballet and the Netherlands Ballet Orchestra. There are free lunchtime concerts of 20th-century music on Tuesday from 12.30pm to 1pm between October and June.

Bethaniënklooster (Map pp88-9; ☎ 625 00 78; www .bethanienklooster.nl; Barndesteeg 6B; 🕙 closed Aug) This former monastery near Nieuwmarkt has a glorious ballroom, the perfect place to take in some exceptional chamber music.

JAZZ & BLUES

Bimhuis (Map pp86-7; ☎ 788 21 50; www.bimhuis.nl; Piet Heinkade 3; 🕙 closed Aug) The core of Amsterdam's influential jazz and improvisational music scene since 1973, the Bimhuis – located in the Muziekgebouw (left) – draws international jazz greats. The intimate auditorium has huge windows giving a view over the city, and a spiffy bar. There's an open jam session Tuesdays at 10.30pm from September to June – fun and free.

Maloe Melo (Map p91; ☎ 420 45 92; www.maloemelo .com; Lijnbaansgracht 163) Home to Amsterdam's blues scene, this dingy venue is rowdy and casual, and often adds bluegrass and soul to the calendar. If nothing appeals here, goth and new-wave Korsakoff (opposite) is next door.

Cotton Club (Map pp88-9; ☎ 626 61 92; www.cotton clubmusic.nl; Nieuwmarkt 5) Squish into this dark, bustling cafe every Saturday (4.30pm to 8pm) for free live, vibrant jazz. It's one of the oldest jazz clubs in town and attracts visitors and locals alike.

Bourbon Street Jazz & Blues Club (Map pp92-3; ☎ 623 34 40; www.bourbonstreet.nl; Leidsekruisstraat 6-8) Catch blues, funk, soul and rock'n'roll in this intimate venue, with friendly, everyone's-welcome open jam sessions on Tuesdays. Free entrance before 11pm.

ROCK & POP

Melkweg (Map pp92-3; Milky Way; ☎ 531 81 81; www.melk weg.nl; Lijnbaansgracht 234A) This former milk factory off Leidseplein has been a top venue since the 1970s, and surely must be Amsterdam's coolest club-gallery-cinema-cafe-concert hall. Its vibrant program of events is so full and varied that it's impossible not to find something you want to go to, from international DJ club nights to live Brazilian jazz.

Paradiso (Map pp92-3; ☎ 626 45 21; www.paradiso.nl; Weteringschans 6) This converted church has been the city's premier rock venue since the 1960s. Expect interesting dance music, anything from Finnish DJs spinning jazz to Afro new wave from New York and tech-hop from Detroit.

Korsakoff (Map p91; ☎ 625 78 54; www.korsakoff amsterdam.nl; Lijnbaansgracht 161) Still grungy after all these years, this hard-rock and alternative-music venue attracts a young clientele for lashings of punk, metal and goth.

Other venues (both well south of town):

Amsterdam ArenA (off Map pp86-7; ☎ 311 13 33; www .amsterdamarena.nl; Arena Blvd 1, Bijlmermeer) Stadium rock! Seats 52,000 for mega-acts such as the Rolling Stones.

Heineken Music Hall (off Map pp86-7; ☎ 0900 687 42 42; www.heineken-music-hall.nl; Arena Blvd 590, Bijlmermeer) Midsized venue praised for its quality acoustics and lighting.

Nightclubs

Most clubs close at 4am on weeknights and 5am on Friday and Saturday. The party doesn't really fire up until after midnight, or more like 1am or 2am on the weekends. Cover charges range from zero to €20. Melkweg and Paradiso (see above) also have awesome club nights.

Escape (Map pp92-3; ☎ 622 11 11; www.escape.nl; in Dutch; Rembrandtplein 11) A fixture of Amsterdam nightlife for two decades, this cavernous club is Amsterdam's slickest, with several dance floors, two smoking lounges, a video-screen-filled studio and an adjoining cafe. Dress to impress on weekends, or you may not get in.

Odeon (Map pp92-3; ☎ 521 85 55; www.odeonamsterdam .nl; in Dutch; Singel 460) This historic venue from the 1660s includes a classy restaurant, a swanky cocktail bar and a canalside terrace to give those ears a rest. Massive murals of models adorn the walls and club nights rarely rise above a €15 entry fee.

Sugar Factory (Map pp92-3; ☎ 626 50 06; www.sugar factory.nl; Lijnbaansgracht 238) A cool spot, an excellent location and a varied line-up are the hallmarks here. But this ain't your average club –

CHECK IT UIT

Not sure how to spend your evening? Head to the last-minute ticket desk at the **Uitburo** (Map pp92-3; ☎ 795 99 50; www.aub.nl; ☒ 10am-7.30pm Mon-Sat, noon-7.30pm Sun), in the corner of the Stadsschouwburg on the Leidseplein. Comedy, dance, concerts and even club nights are potentially available at a significant discount – and handily marked 'LNP' (language no problem) if the event doesn't hinge on understanding Dutch to have fun.

most nights start with music, cinema, or a dance or spoken-word performance, followed by late-night DJs and dancing.

Panama (Map pp86-7; ☎ 311 86 86; www.panama.nl; Oostelijke Handelskade 4) A glamorous restaurant-theatre-dance venue, most come for the club nights spinning Latin, Ibiza vibes, Cuban big bands and more.

Theatre & Comedy

Boom Chicago (Map pp92-3; ☎ 423 01 01; www.boom chicago.nl; Leidseplein 12) Performances of English-language stand-up and improv comedy year-round. See it over dinner and a few drinks. The 'Late Nite Improv' show (the second and third Friday of each month) is always a crowd-puller. Inspiration is drawn from Chicago's legendary Second City theatre.

Felix Meritis (Map p91; ☎ 623 13 11; www.felix .meritis.nl; Keizersgracht 324) This wonderful arts and culture space, established in 1787, puts on innovative, modern theatre, music and dance, as well as special talks on politics, art, literature and beyond.

Amsterdams Marionetten Theater (Map p95; ☎ 620 80 27; www.marionettentheater.nl; Nieuwe Jonkerstraat 8; adult/child from €15/7.50) Located in a former blacksmith's shop, the puppeteers put on a limited repertoire (mainly Mozart operas such as *The Magic Flute*), but the fairy-tale stage sets, period costumes and singing voices are absolutely enthralling. From June to August the theatre only performs for groups; at other times, check the website for a schedule.

Openluchttheater (Open-Air Theatre; Map pp92-3; ☎ 673 14 99; www.openluchttheater.nl; in Dutch; Vondelpark) From June to August Vondelpark hosts free concerts in its intimate open-air theatre, and it's a fantastic experience to share with others. Expect world music, dance, theatre and more.

Stadsschouwburg (Map pp92-3; ☎ 624 23 11; www .stadsschouwburgamsterdam.nl, in Dutch; Leidseplein 26) Amsterdam's most beautiful theatre was built in 1894 and refurbished in the 1990s. It features large-scale productions, operettas, dance and summer English-language productions and performances. Most major festivals also seem to have a presence here.

Koninklijk Theater Carré (Map p95; ☎ 0900 252 52 55; www.theatercarre.nl; Amstel 115-125) The largest theatre in town offers mainstream international shows, musicals, cabaret, opera, operetta, ballet and circuses.

Cinemas

What? Go to the movies on holiday? With Amsterdam's rainy weather and the city's abundance of gorgeous art-house cinemas, you may well find yourself at a flick. Screenings are usually in the original language with Dutch subtitles.

Het Ketelhuis (Map pp86-7; ☎ 684 00 90; www.ketelhuis .nl, in Dutch; Westergasfabriek, Haarlemmerweg 8-10) In the old gas works, the three screening rooms have a chic postindustrial vibe and comfy seats for art-house films.

Kriterion (Map p95; ☎ 623 17 08; www.kriterion.nl, in Dutch; Roeterstraat 170) Student-run since 1945, this theatre-cafe has a great array of premiers, theme parties, cult movies, classics and kids' flicks – all in a former diamond factory.

Movies (Map p91; ☎ 638 60 16; www.themovies.nl, in Dutch; Haarlemmerdijk 161) This *gezellig* art deco cinema (the oldest in Amsterdam, dating from 1912) features indie alongside mainstream flicks. Grab a pre-movie tipple at the cafe-bar.

Tuschinskitheater (Map pp92-3; ☎ 623 15 10, 0900 14 58; www.pathe.nl/tuschinski, in Dutch; Reguliersbreestraat 26-34) The cream of the crop: with its sumptuous interiors, the Tuschinski is a monument to art deco/Amsterdam School decor. It screens both mainstream blockbusters and art-house films.

Sport

FOOTBALL

Local club Ajax is the Netherlands' most famous team: they've won the European Cup four times and they launched Johan Cruyff to stellar heights in the '70s. The red-and-white stormers play in the **Amsterdam ArenA** (off Map pp86-7; ☎ 311 13 33; www.amsterdamarena.nl; Arena Blvd 1, Bijlmermeer) south of town. Matches usually take place on Saturday evening and Sunday afternoon during the season (early September to early June). The

ArenA conducts a one-hour guided **stadium tour** (☎ 311 13 36; adult/child €10.50/9.50; ✆ call for schedule) that includes a walk on the hallowed turf and entry to the Ajax museum.

KORFBAL

A cross between netball, volleyball and basketball, this sport elicits giggles from foreigners, but it has a lively local club scene. For information, contact the **Amsterdam Sport Council** (☎ 552 24 90), which can also provide information on other sports in town.

SHOPPING

During the Golden Age, Amsterdam was the world's warehouse, stuffed with riches from the far corners of the earth. Even if the Dutch empire has since crumbled, its capital remains a shopper's paradise.

The Damrak and the area around Leidseplein teem with tourist shops, while the busiest shopping streets are the midmarket Nieuwendijk and the more upmarket Kalverstraat and Leidsestraat, lined with department and clothing stores. The Old South's PC Hooftstraat is for fancy fashion brands such as Chanel, Louis Vuitton and Gucci. The Negen Straatjes (Nine Little Streets; p102), in the Western Canal Belt, offers the city's most satisfying browsing among its quirky, pint-sized boutiques. The narrow lanes of the Jordaan and the Haarlemerdijk are filled with tiny art galleries and young designer studios that double as shops. Antique and art buffs head for the Southern Canal Belt's Nieuwe Spiegelstraat.

Popular gifts include tulip bulbs, local cheeses such as gouda and bottles of *jenever*. Fantastic bargains are rare, but it's worth chasing photographic art, Dutch designer clothing and antiquarian books. For quality souvenirs, a Delft blue vase – or custom-made bong – are also in great supply.

Art & Antiques

Chiellerie (Map pp88-9; ☎ 620 94 48; Raamgracht 58; ✆ 2-6pm) Any artist can rent this gallery to mount an exhibit and keep all the profits; Amsterdam's younger artists make good use of the space.

Decorativa (Map pp92-3; ☎ 320 10 93; Nieuwe Spiegelstraat 9a; ✆ Tue-Sat) An amazing jumble of European antiques, collectables and weird vintage gifts.

EH Ariëns Kappers (Map pp92-3; ☎ 623 53 56; Nieuwe Spiegelstraat 32; ✆ Tue-Sat) Original prints, etchings, engravings, lithographs, 17th- to 19th-century maps and Japanese woodblock prints.

Jaski (Map pp92-3; ☎ 620 39 39; Nieuwe Spiegelstraat 27-29; ⌚ Tue-Sat) A large commercial gallery selling paintings, prints, ceramics and sculptures by famous CoBrA artists.

Books

For a list of bookshops, see p83; for book markets, see the boxed text, p134.

Boutiques

Eva Damave (Map p91; ☎ 627 73 25; 2e Lauriersdwarsstraat 51c; ⌚ Wed-Sat) Eva creates funky, one-off woollen sweaters and zip jackets with her signature front patchwork panels.

Hester van Eeghen (Map p91; ☎ 626 92 11; Hartenstraat 1; ⌚ Tue-Sat) Dramatic shoes for those who dare to dress their feet in bright colours, fur, suede and geometric patterns and prints. The designer's handbags (available down the street at Hartenstraat 37) are just as attention-grabbing.

Marlies Dekkers (Map p91; ☎ 421 19 00; Berenstraat 18) Dutch lingerie designer who's known for her subtle hints to bondage, detailed on exquisite undergarments. This shop itself is a bastion of decadence, with hand-painted wallpaper and a lounge area with fireplace.

Van Ravenstein (Map p91; ☎ 639 00 67; Keizersgracht 359; ⌚ Mon-Sat) Upmarket Dutch and Belgian designers such as Dries van Noten, Ann Demeulemeester and Viktor & Rolf.

SPRMRKT (Map p91; ☎ 330 56 01; Rozengracht 191-193; ⌚ Wed-Sat) Whether you want a supertight pair of Acne jeans, a vintage Thor Larson pod chair or the latest copy of *Butt* magazine, it's all here at this lofty industrial concept store, a major player in Amsterdam's fashion scene.

Young Designers United (Map pp92-3; ☎ 626 9191; Keizersgracht 447) A showcase for newbie Dutch designers, each of whom gets his/her own rack. The range is huge, from asymmetrical sheaths to flowy frocks, all fairly well priced.

Department Stores

Try the **Kalvertoren shopping centre** (Map pp92-3; Singel 457) and **Magna Plaza** (Map pp88-9; Nieuwezijds Voorburgwal 182) for upmarket fashion, gift and jewellery shops.

De Bijenkorf (Map pp88-9; ☎ 621 80 80; Dam 1) The city's most fashionable department store; quality clothing, toys, household accessories and books.

Hema (Map pp88-9; ☎ 638 99 63; Nieuwendijk 174) Once a Woolworths clone, Hema now attracts as many design aficionados as bargain hunters. It has wide-ranging stock, including good-value wine and deli foods.

Smart Shops

Remember that taking drugs out of the country is illegal.

Chills & Thrills (Map pp88-9; ☎ 638 00 15; Nieuwendijk 17; ⌚ 10am-10pm) Herbal trips, psychoactive cacti, novelty bongs and life-sized alien sculptures. It's usually packed with tourists.

Innerspace (Map pp88-9; ☎ 624 33 38; Spuistraat 108; ⌚ 11am-10pm) Known for good service and information, this large shop started as a supplier to big parties.

Kokopelli (Map pp88-9; ☎ 421 70 00; Warmoesstraat 12; ⌚ 11am-10pm) Large, beautiful space akin to a fashionable clothing or homewares store; sells coffee and juice in addition to truffles.

Speciality Shops

Diamonds have been an Amsterdam speciality since the 16th century. Ogle the bling after a tour at Gassan Diamonds (p100) or Coster Diamonds (p106).

Concerto (Map pp92-3; ☎ 623 52 28; Utrechtsestraat 52-60) This rambling shop has Amsterdam's best selection of new and secondhand CDs and records. It's often cheap, always interesting and has good listening facilities.

Condomerie het Gulden Vlies (Map pp88-9; ☎ 627 41 74; Warmoesstraat 141; ⌚ Mon-Sat) Hundreds of kooky condoms plus lubricants and saucy gifts.

Droog Design (Map pp88-9; ☎ 523 50 59; Staalstraat 7b; ⌚ noon-6pm Tue-Sat) The leading design firm has inventions such as the 85-lamp chandelier, the cow chair and curtains with dress patterns.

Himalaya (Map pp88-9; ☎ 626 08 99; Warmoesstraat 56; ⌚ Mon-Sat) A peaceful New Age oasis in the middle of the Red Light District, this is the place to stock up on crystals, ambient CDs and books on the healing arts. More good karma is available in the tea room.

Nukuhiva (Map pp88-9; ☎ 420 94 83; Haarlemerstraat 36) This ecoboutique stocks only ethical and fair-trade clothing and accessories by brands such as Veja (vegan shoes) and Dutch designer Kuyishi (organic denim).

Traditional Souvenirs

Galleria d'Arte Rinascimento (Map p91; ☎ 622 75 09; Prinsengracht 170) Royal Delftware, vases, platters,

AMSTERDAM MARKETS

Markets mean crowds: beware of pickpockets.

Albert Cuypmarkt (Map pp92-3; Albert Cuypstraat btwn Van Woustraat & Ferdinand Bolstraat; 10am-5pm Mon-Sat) Exotic goods as well as cheap basics from nations around the globe.

Antiques market Amstelveld (Map pp92-3; 9am-6pm last Fri of month in warmer months); Nieuwmarkt (Map pp88-9; 9am-5pm Sun May-Sep) There are many genuine articles here and lots of books and bric-a-brac. There's also the De Looier antiques market (see below).

Bloemenmarkt (Map pp92-3; Singel; 9am-5pm, closed Sun Dec-Feb) 'Floating' flower market that's actually on pilings. Traders can advise on import regulations.

Boerenmarkt (farmers market) Nieuwmarkt (Map pp88-9; 10am-3pm Sat); Noordermarkt (Map p91; 9am-4pm Sat) Pick up home-grown produce, organic food and picnic provisions.

Book market (Map pp88-9; Oudemanhuispoort; 11am-4pm Mon-Fri) In the old arcade between Oudezijds Achterburgwal and Kloveniersburgwal (blink and you'll miss either entrance), this is the place to find that 19th-century copy of *Das Kapital* or a semantic analysis of Icelandic sagas, and some newer books and art prints. Another book market takes place on the Spui (Map pp92–3; open 8am to 6pm Friday).

Dappermarkt (Map pp86-7; Dapperstraat btwn Mauritzkade & Witjenbacjstraat; 9am-5pm Mon-Sat) Similar to Albert Cuypmarkt but smaller and more ethnically diverse – just like the immigrant population residing in the surrounding neighbourhood.

De Looier antiques market (Map p91; ☎ 624 90 38; Elandsgracht 109; 11am-5pm Sat-Thu) Indoor stalls selling jewellery, furniture, art and collectibles.

Lindengracht market (Map p91; Lindengracht; 9am-4pm Sat) General market, very much a local affair.

Noordermarkt (Map p91; Noorderkerkstraat; 8am-1pm Mon, 9am-4pm Sat) This Jordaan market has a split personality: Monday is for antiques, fabrics and secondhand bric-a-brac, while Saturday sees a festive farmers market.

Plant market (Map pp92-3; Amstelveld; 3-6pm Mon Easter-Christmas) All sorts of plants, pots and vases.

Stamp & coin market (Map pp88-9; Nieuwezijds Voorburgwal 276; 10am-4pm Wed & Sat) This little streetside market sells stamps, coins and medals.

Waterlooplein flea market (Map pp88-9; Waterlooplein; 9am-5pm Mon-Sat) Amsterdam's most famous flea market is full of curios, secondhand clothing, music, electronic gear, hardware and cheap New Age gifts.

Westermarkt (Map p91; Westerstraat; 9am-1pm Mon) Cheapish clothes and textiles, some real bargains.

brooches, Christmas ornaments, 19th-century wall tiles and plaques.

't Klompenhuisje (Map pp88-9; ☎ 622 81 00; Nieuwe Hoogstraat 9a; Mon-Sat) Reasonably priced, finely crafted, traditional Dutch clogs.

Your Cup of T (Map p91; ☎ 420 71 53; Westerstraat 77; 10am-2pm Mon, 2-7pm Wed-Fri, noon-6pm Sat) Browse a million iron-on graphics and create your own souvenir T-shirt (fluorescent robots are a timeless option).

GETTING THERE & AWAY

Amsterdam is well connected to the rest of the world. If you're looking for cheap deals, advice or shared rides, you're in the right place.

Air

Most major airlines fly directly to **Schiphol** (off Map pp86-7; ☎ 0900 01 41; www.schiphol.nl), 18km southwest of the city centre. For information about getting to and from the Netherlands, see p294.

Bicycle

It's easy to get to and from Amsterdam by bike. National bike routes radiate in all directions. LF20 and LF23 go east to Muiden (p165) and beyond. LF7 goes north via ferry across the IJ and before you know it you're in the rural wilds of Waterland (p147). LF20 goes west to Haarlem (25km) and on to the coast while LF2 goes south to Gouda, Rotterdam and Belgium. For more options, see p70.

For further route planning in the region, visit **www.routecraft.nl**, which calculates the best bike paths; click on 'Bikeplanner' for (mostly) English.

Boat

Fast Flying Ferries (Map pp88-9; ☎ 639 22 47; www.connexxion.nl; adult/child return €8.50/5) runs a hydrofoil from pier 7 behind Centraal Station (hourly on the hour, half-hourly or more during peak times). The 25-minute trip drops you in Velsen,

3km short of IJmuiden (p146). For travellers to the UK and beyond, Scandinavian Seaways sails from IJmuiden to Newcastle (see p299).

Bus

For details of regional buses in the Netherlands, call the **transport information service** (☎ 0900 92 92, per min €0.70; www.9292ov.nl). Fares and travel durations are covered under towns in the regional chapters.

Amsterdam has good long-distance bus links with the rest of Europe and North Africa.

Eurolines (Map pp88-9; ☎ 560 87 88; www.eurolines .nl; Rokin 10) tickets can be bought at its office near the Dam, at most travel agencies and at NS Reisburo (Netherlands Railways Travel Bureau) in Centraal Station. Fares are consistently lower than those for the train, and departures are from the **bus station** (Map pp86-7; ☎ 694 56 31) next to Amstelstation (south of the city, but with an easy metro link to Centraal Station).

For further details on coach services, see p296.

Car & Motorcycle

Motorways link Amsterdam to Den Haag and Rotterdam in the south, and to Utrecht and Amersfoort in the southeast. Amsterdam is about 480km from Paris, 840km from Munich, 680km from Berlin and 730km from Copenhagen. The Hoek van Holland ferry port is 80km away; IJmuiden is just up the road along the Noordzeekanaal.

The Dutch automobile association, **ANWB** (Map pp92-3; ☎ 673 08 44; www.anwb.nl, in Dutch; Museumplein 5), provides information and services if you prove membership of your home association.

Train

Amsterdam's main train station is Centraal Station. See p297 for information about international trains. Although under construction

---

THE TRUTH ABOUT 'SHROOMS & TRUFFLES *As told to Caroline Sieg*

Smart shops have long been known for selling hallucinogenic 'magic' mushrooms. But in 2008, the government banned them after a high-profile incident in which a tourist died. Two hundred varieties of fungus then went on the forbidden list – though conspicuously missing was the magic truffle, or sclerotium, which smart shops had always sold alongside their 'shrooms, and which they continue to sell today.

So just what are these truffles? And how do they differ from what was outlawed? We sat down with Raoul Koning, manager at Kokopelli (p133), a smart shop in the city centre, to get the lowdown:

What is the difference between magic mushrooms and truffles? Truffles come from a different part of the plant, but they contain the same active ingredients as mushrooms.

Why were truffles excluded from the ban? Technically and scientifically, truffles are not mushrooms.

How does a truffle trip compare to a mushroom trip? It's a little more like a body high than a visual experience, though this varies according to where you are when you trip, as well as how you are feeling mentally and physically.

What do you recommend for beginners? A medium dose, roughly 7g to 10g (approximately €11.50).

Have you had a tough time selling truffles to customers, particularly when they come in wanting magic mushrooms? At first we did, but now that people know a little more about truffles they seem to be OK with it.

Do you ever refuse to sell truffles to someone? We don't sell to people under age 18, to anyone obviously drunk or who is taking other medication, such as antidepressants or antipsychotics. If we get the sense that someone is being bullied into taking a trip, we'll refuse the sale.

What is the best advice you can give to those seeking a pleasant trip? Ask lots of questions. If you aren't satisfied with the answers, or the salesperson won't give you the answers, go to another shop. Once you've purchased the truffles, have the experience in an outdoor space, ideally a park. Avoid bars and other enclosed spaces. Don't drink alcohol during your trip and don't mix truffles with other drugs. Take the trip with friends, or better yet, do it accompanied by a friend who is not taking the truffles.

for the next several years, it has lockers and other services.

Amsterdam is the terminus of the new high-speed line south to Rotterdam and Belgium. See p297 for details.

Destination	Price (€)	Duration (min)	Frequency (per hr)
Den Haag	10.10	50	4
Groningen	26.60	140	2
Maastricht	26.60	150	2
Rotterdam	13.30	65	5
Rotterdam (high-speed)	21	43	2
Schiphol Airport	3.80	20	6
Utrecht	6.70	30	5

GETTING AROUND
To/From the Airport

A taxi into Amsterdam from Schiphol airport takes 20 to 45 minutes and costs about €40. Trains to Centraal Station leave every 10 minutes or so, take 15 to 20 minutes, and cost €3.80/6.90 per single/return. Train-ticket counters and vending machines are in Schiphol Plaza's central court; buy your ticket before taking the escalator down to the platforms.

Another way to the airport is by **Schiphol Travel Taxi** (☎ 0900 88 76, per min €0.10; www.schiphol .nl). This minivan service takes up to eight people from anywhere in the country to the departure terminal, provided you book a day ahead. From central Amsterdam the fare is fixed at €21 per person, one way.

By car, take the A4 freeway to/from the A10 ring road around Amsterdam. A short stretch of A9 connects to the A4 close to Schiphol. The car-hire offices at the airport are in the right-hand corner of the complex, near the central exits of Schiphol Plaza.

PARKING

The airport's P1 and P2 short-term (under-cover) parking garages charge €2.10 per half-hour for the first three hours, then €3.20 per hour. Daily charges are €28.50 a day for the first three days, and €17.50 a day thereafter. The long-term (open-air) parking area is a fair distance from the terminal but is linked by a 24-hour shuttle bus. The charge is €55 for up to three days and €7.50 for each day thereafter – a reasonable alternative to parking in the city (see opposite).

Bicycle

Amsterdam is an urban cyclist's dream: flat, beautiful and crammed with 400km of dedicated bike paths. See p110 for tips on city riding; see p134 for suggestions of how to reach Amsterdam from other regions.

MacBike (below) produces themed cycling maps that take in architectural sights, windmills etc. Pied á Terre bookshop (p83) also carries cycling maps and guides.

HIRE

All the companies listed here require ID plus a credit-card imprint or a cash deposit with a passport. Many agencies require that you bring your passport as proof of ID. Prices below are for basic 'coaster-brake' bikes; gears and handbrakes, and especially insurance, usually cost more.

Bike City (Map p91; ☎ 626 37 21; www.bikecity .nl; Bloemgracht 68-70; per day/5 days €13.50/43.50) No advertising on the bikes, so you blend in better with the locals.

MacBike (☎ 620 09 85; www.macbike.nl; per day/week €9.50/30.80); Centraal Station (Map pp88-9); Mr Visserplein (Map p95; Mr Visserplein 2); Weteringschans (Map pp92-3; Weteringschans 2) Bikes come complete with an absolutely ENORMOUS logo. You *will* stand out.

Mike's Bike Tours (Map pp92-3; ☎ 622 79 70; www .mikesbiketours.com; Kerkstraat 134; per full day/ additional day €7/5)

Recycled Bicycles (Map pp88-9; ☎ 06 54 68 14 29; Spuistraat 84a; www.recycledbicycles.org; per day €5, plus €50 cash deposit) This owner collects used bike parts around town and assembles them into 'new' bikes you can rent for cheap.

Boat
FERRIES

Free ferries run to Amsterdam-Noord, departing from piers behind Centraal Station. The ride to Buiksloterweg is the most direct (five minutes) and runs 24 hours. Another boat runs to NDSM-werf (15 minutes) between 7am and midnight (1am on Saturday), and another goes to IJplein (6.30am to midnight). Bicycles are permitted.

CANAL BOAT, BUS & BIKE

The **Canal Bus** (Map pp92-3; ☎ 623 98 86; www .canal.nl; day pass per adult/child €20/10) does several circuits between Centraal Station and the Rijksmuseum, between 9.50am and 8.30pm. The day pass is valid until noon the next day. The same company rents canal bikes (paddle-

---

STAYING ON TRACK: AMSTERDAM'S NEW METRO LINE

It's only 9.7km long, but the new *Noord/Zuidlijn* (north–south metro line) is stretching into a problem of far greater size. Work began in 2003 and was originally targeted for completion in 2011, but the project deadline keeps getting pushed back (it's now post-2017) and the costs keep rising.

No wonder, given the massive task at hand. To build the metro's route between Amsterdam-Noord and the World Trade Centre in the south, engineers must tunnel under the IJ River and the centuries-old buildings of Amsterdam's city centre. The first part went OK, but when some of the historical monuments in the centre started to shift off their foundations, engineers halted construction.

Debate flared over what to do. Continue, even though the budget was running sky-high? Quit, and lose the millions of euros already spent? How much longer would residents tolerate the inconvenience of their main streets being torn to bits?

The city ultimately decided to proceed, and construction ramped back up in mid-2009. Engineers added additional support beams beneath the affected buildings. So far, so good.

---

boats) for €8 per person per hour (€7 if there are more than two people per canal bike). Docks are by Leidseplein and near the Anne Frank Huis. For canal boat tours, see p114.

Car & Motorcycle

Honestly, why on earth would you drive around Amsterdam when you can either bike it or take advantage of the superb public-transport system? Parking costs are steep – around €5/29/21 per hour/day/evening in most of the city centre. Nonpayers will find a yellow wheel clamp attached their car that costs €150 to remove. Try leaving your car at a park-and-ride near the edge of town. The airport lot is another alternative (see opposite).

Public Transport

Most public transport within the city is by tram; Amsterdam's buses and metro (subway) serve the outer reaches. The local transit authority is the **GVB** (Map pp88-9; ☎ 0900 80 11, per min €0.10; www.gvb .nl; Stationsplein 10; ☺ 7am-9pm Mon-Fri, 10am-6pm Sat & Sun), which has an information office across the tram tracks from Centraal Station's main entrance. Here you can get tickets, maps and the like. The website has lots of useful information, including details of how to reach key sights.

A newcomer to the GVB system is the handy Stop/Go bus (it looks like an airport shuttle bus), which runs from Waterlooplein to Centraal Station and the main library via Prinsengracht between 9am and 5.30pm; flag it down, as there are no fixed stops. It costs €1.

TICKETS & PASSES

Tickets on trams and buses are calculated by zone and are valid for one hour from the time they're stamped. Within the city centre you are in Zone 1. The single-trip fares for one hour in Zone 1 are €2.60. Long-stay visitors can invest in a *chipkaart* for €7.50, valid for five years; you can add up to €30 in credit at a time, and rides are cheaper.

GVB passes are valid in all zones, and fares for one/two/three days are €7/11.50/15.

Taxi

Amsterdam taxis are expensive, especially for short journeys. Flag fall is €3.50 and the rate is €1.98 per kilometre. Around Centraal Station, many drivers try to charge a flat fee of €10 to €15 for only a few miles. See if you can negotiate. If you must use a taxi, try **Taxicentrale Amsterdam** (☎ 677 77 77).

Noord Holland & Flevoland

Wrapping around Amsterdam like a crown, this region has some of the most iconic places in the country. West of the capital, elegant Haarlem is Noord Holland's crowning glory, a charming town of 17th-century grandeur. On its western outskirts are the wide, sandy beaches of Zandvoort and Bloemendaal, and the varied dunescape of Zuid-Kennemerland National Park.

Moving north, you'll get your fill of iconic windmills at intriguing Zaanse Schans. The Gouwzee Bay towns of Edam, Volendam and Marken hold a special place in Dutch culture for cheese, traditional customs, defiance of the sea, and tourism. Monnickendam, in the heart of the rural Waterland Region, is less frequented but has a treasury of 17th-century architecture. Not far north again, the Golden Age ports of Hoorn and Enkhuizen have engaging old centres; the latter is also home to the Zuiderzeemuseum, a not-to-be-missed open-air extravaganza that celebrates rural and historic Dutch life.

On the way to the Waddenzee island of Texel is Alkmaar, famous for its kitsch but oddly compelling traditional cheese auction. Texel itself is a gem, with long, fine beaches, busy little villages, sheep-swamped *polders* (strips of farmland separated by canals), and a forest or two.

To the east of Amsterdam, the leafy forests of Het Gooi are a refuge for urbanites; the towns of Muiden and Naarden have remarkable old fortresses worth a visit. Water sports and tender nature reserves are defining features of young Flevoland, pumped dry less than a half-century ago.

Excepting Texel, all of this region is easily reached by day trip from Amsterdam, or you can set you own pace and go explore.

HIGHLIGHTS

- Explore the world-class museums of **Haarlem** (p140) and its charming centre
- Go nuts for cheese in the pastoral climes of **Edam** (p150)
- Experience the hardy life of Noord Holland's seafaring towns before the Afsluitdijk at Enkhuizen's **Zuiderzeemuseum** (p157)
- Wander the high sand dunes, quiet forests and green pastures of **Texel** (p160)
- Cycle the dykes of the region crowned by cosy old **Marken** (p149)

NOORD HOLLAND & FLEVOLAND

NOORD HOLLAND

History

The peninsula now known as Noord Holland was part of Friesland until the 12th century, when storm floods created the Zuiderzee and isolated West Friesland. By this time the mercantile counts of Holland ruled the area – or thought they did. One of the early counts, Willem II, became king of the Holy Roman Empire in 1247 but perished in a raid against the West Frisians (his horse fell through the ice). His son, Count Floris V, succeeded in taming his defiant subjects 40 years later (see p159).

West Friesland was now owned by the county of Holland, a founding member of the Republic of Seven United Netherlands (1579). Northern Holland played a key role in the long struggle against Spanish domination, and the town of Alkmaar was the first to throw off the yoke. The era of prosperity known as the Golden Age ensued, and Noord Holland has its fair share of richly ornamented buildings from this period. The fishing and trading ports of Enkhuizen, Medemblik and Edam were at the centre of this boom.

Napoleon invaded Holland in 1795 and split it in two to break its economic power. Even after Holland came under the House of Orange in 1813, a divide remained and the provinces of Noord Holland and Zuid Holland were established in 1840.

Today Noord Holland's main business is agriculture including cheese, lots of cheese.

Getting There & Around

Noord Holland is well served by the national rail service, and where the train ends the bus networks take over.

Motorways run north–south from Haarlem to Alkmaar (the A9), and from Amsterdam to Den Oever (the A7), which continues on to Friesland via the 30km-long Afsluitdijk. From Enkhuizen there's another fast dyke road, the N302, running across the IJsselmeer to Lelystad in Flevoland. Bike trails lace the province in almost every direction, and you can cover the flat stretch from Amsterdam to Den Helder in two days at a very leisurely pace.

HAARLEM

☎ 023 / pop 149,000

This classic Dutch city of cobble-stone streets, historic buildings, grand churches, even grander museums, cosy bars, fine cafes and the odd canal is a sure-fire stop. It's a perfect day trip from Amsterdam, but as a place with so much on offer in such a compact area, you may find yourself turning the tables on the capital and using Haarlem as a base to explore the surrounds.

History

The name Haarlem derives from Haarloheim, meaning a wooded place on high, sandy soil. Its origins date back to the 10th century when the counts of Holland set up a toll post on the Spaarne River. Haarlem quickly became the most important inland port after Amsterdam, but suffered a major setback when the Spanish invaded in 1572. The city surrendered after a seven-month siege but worse was yet to come: upon capitulation virtually the entire population was slaughtered. After the Spanish were finally repelled by Willem van Oranje, Haarlem soared into the prosperity of the Golden Age, attracting painters and artists from throughout Europe.

Orientation

Grote Markt, the main square, is a 500m walk south of the bus and train stations. Walk in along Kruisstraat for an offbeat selection of shops. The centre has a large pedestrianised section. Grote Kerk van St Bavo, the central landmark, can be seen from anywhere in the city.

Information

GWK exchange office (⏲ 9am-7pm Mon-Fri, 9am-5pm Sat) In the train station.

Main post office (Gedempte Oude Gracht 2)

My Beautiful Laundrette (Botermarkt 20; ⏲ 8.30am-8.30pm) Takes last loads at 7pm.

Suny Telecom (Kruissweg 42; per 20min €1; ⏲ 10am-8pm) Has internet access and cheap calls.

Tourist office (☎ 0900 616 16 00; www.vvvhaarlem .nl; Verwulft 11; ⏲ 9.30am-5.30pm Mon-Fri, 10am-5pm Sat, 11am-3pm Sun Apr-Sep, 9.30am-5.30pm Mon-Fri, 10am-5pm Sat Oct-Mar) Located in a modern glass house in the middle of the road. Staff will reserve local accommodation for €5.

Sights & Activities

Large **Grote Markt**, with its flanks of restaurants and cafes and a clutch of historical buildings, is a good place to start an exploration of Haarlem. At the western end stands the florid, 14th-century **town hall**, which sprouted many extensions including a balcony where judgements from the high court were pronounced. The counts' hall contains 15th-century panel paintings and is normally open during office hours.

At the opposite end looms the **Grote Kerk van St Bavo** (☎ 553 20 40; www.bavo.nl; Oude Groenmarkt 23; adult/child €2/1.50; ⏰ 10am-4pm Mon-Sat), the Gothic cathedral with a towering 50m-high steeple. It contains some fine Renaissance artworks, but the star attraction is its stunning Müller organ – one of the most magnificent in the world, standing 30m high with about 5000 pipes. It was played by Handel and Mozart, the latter when he was just 10. Free organ recitals take place at 8.15pm Tuesday and Thursday, May to October.

In the centre of Grote Markt stand the 17th-century **Vleeshal**, a former meat market, and the **Verweyhal**, an old fish market; both serve as modern-art annexes of the Frans Hals Museum. On the square north of the Grote Kerk is a **statue of Laurens Coster**, whom Haarlemmers believe has a claim, along with Gutenberg, to be called the inventor of movable type.

Off Grote Houtstraat to the southwest stands the **Proveniershuis**, the former headquarters of St Joris Doelen (the Civic Guards of St George), which started life as a *hofje* (almshouse). This wonderful old building is one of Haarlem's prettiest (see the boxed text, p143). Around the corner to the west, down charming Korte Houtstraat, is the 17th-century **Nieuwe Kerk** (⏰ 10am-4pm Sun); the capricious tower by Lieven de Key is supported by a rather boxy design by Jacob van Campen.

Northeast of the Teylers Museum stands the striking **Bakenesserkerk** (cnr Vrouwestraat & Bakenesserstraat), a late-15th-century church with a lamp-lit tower of sandstone. The stone was employed here when the Grote Kerk proved too weak to support a heavy steeple – hence the wooden tower of the cathedral we see today. A private firm occupies it but you can still peek inside.

MUSEUMS

The **Frans Hals Museum** (☎ 511 57 75; www.frans halsmuseum.nl; Groot Heiligland 62; adult/child €7.50/free; ⏰ 11am-5pm Tue-Sat, noon-5pm Sun) is a must for anyone interested in the Dutch masters. Kept in an almshouse where Hals spent his final, impoverished years, the collection focuses on the 17th-century Haarlem School,

which is regarded as the pinnacle of Dutch mannerist art. Eight group portraits by Hals detailing the companies of the Civic Guard are the museum's pride and joy, revealing the painter's exceptional attention to mood and psychological tone. Don't miss his two paintings known collectively as the *Regents & the Regentesses of the Old Men's Almshouse* (1664). Among other treasures are ceiling-high illustrations of the human anatomy with biblical and mythological allusions. Five old masters stolen in 2002 were recovered in 2008 and are back on display.

It's shocking, but depending on your tastes, the **Teylers Museum** (☎ 531 90 10; www.teylersmuseum .eu; Spaarne 16; adult/child €7/2; ⏰ 10am-5pm Tue-Sat, noon-5pm Sun) may top Frans Hals. It's the oldest museum in the country (1778) and contains an array of whiz-bang inventions, such as an 18th-century electrostatic machine that conjures up visions of mad scientists. The eclectic collection also has paintings from the Dutch and French schools and numerous temporary exhibitions. The interiors are as good as the displays: the magnificent, sky-lighted Ovale Zaal (Oval Room) contains natural history specimens in elegant glass cases on two levels.

Also known as 'the hiding place', the **Corrie Ten Boom House** (☎ 531 08 23; www.corrietenboom .com; Barteljorisstraat; admission €2.50; ⏰ 10am-3.30pm Tue-Sat) is named for the matriarch of a family that lived in the house during WWII. Using a secret compartment in her bedroom, she hid hundreds of Jews and Dutch resistors until they could be spirited to safety. In 1944 the family was betrayed and sent to concentration camps where three died. Later, Corrie Ten Boom toured the world preaching peace.

On Grote Markt, the **Vleeshal** holds contemporary art exhibitions; the **Verweyhal** next door, in a fancy Renaissance building designed by Lieven de Key, houses the Frans Hals Museum's collection of modern art, including works by Dutch impressionists and the CoBrA movement. The museums are known collectively as **De Hallen** (Grote Markt 16; www.dehallenhaarlem.nl; adult/child €5/free; ⏰ 11am-5pm Mon-Sat, noon-5pm Sun).

Tours

Post Verkade Cruises (☎ 535 77 23; Spaarne 11a; adult/child €9.50/4.50; ⏰ noon-5pm Tue-Sun Apr-Sep) runs 50-minute canal boat tours in English.

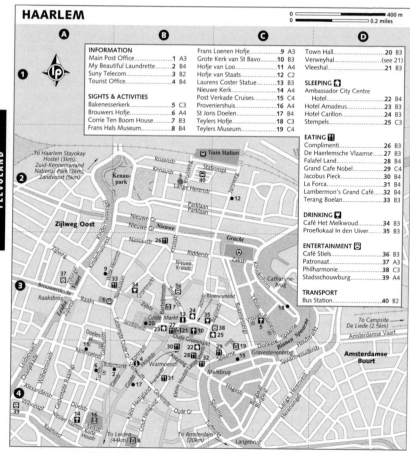

HAARLEM

0 — 400 m
0 — 0.2 miles

INFORMATION
Main Post Office...............1 A3
My Beautiful Laundrette.......2 B4
Suny Telecom................3 B2
Tourist Office..............4 B4

SIGHTS & ACTIVITIES
Bakenesserkerk...............5 C3
Brouwers Hofje...............6 A4
Corrie Ten Boom House.........7 B3
Frans Hals Museum............8 B4

Frans Loenen Hofje...........9 A3
Grote Kerk van St Bavo......10 B3
Hofje van Loo..............11 A4
Hofje van Staats..........12 C2
Laurens Coster Statue......13 B3
Nieuwe Kerk...............14 A4
Post Verkade Cruises.......15 C4
Provenershuis............16 A4
St Joris Doelen..........17 B4
Teylers Hofje..........18 C3
Teylers Museum.........19 C4

Town Hall.................20 B3
Verweyhal..............(see 21)
Vleeshal................21 B3

SLEEPING
Ambassador City Centre
  Hotel...................22 B4
Hotel Amadeus............23 B3
Hotel Carillon..........24 B3
Stempels...............25 C3

EATING
Complimenti..............26 B3
De Haerlemsche Vlaamse....27 B3
Falafel Land............28 B4
Grand Cafe Nobel........29 C4
Jacobus Pieck..........30 B4
La Forca..............31 B4
Lambermon's Grand Café....32 B4
Terang Boelan.........33 B3

DRINKING
Café Het Melkwoud.......34 B3
Proeflokaal In den Uiver...35 B3

ENTERTAINMENT
Café Stiels............36 B3
Patronaat.............37 A3
Philharmonie.........38 C3
Stadsschouwburg......39 A4

TRANSPORT
Bus Station...........40 B2

Sleeping

Campsite De Liede (☎ 533 86 66; Lieoever 68; camp sites €15) This leafy site 2.5km east of the old centre enjoys a lakeside location and rents canoes and paddle boats. Take bus 2 from the train station (direction: Spaarnwoude) and alight at Zoete Inval.

Haarlem Stayokay Hostel (☎ 537 37 93; www.stay okay.com; Jan Gijzenpad 3; dm from €25; 🖳) This 41-bed lakeside hostel has a 10pm silence rule but no curfew. The superclean rooms are basic, but the bar-cafe is full of character. Take bus 2 (direction: Haarlem Noord) from the train station (10 minutes).

Hotel Carillon (☎ 531 05 91; www.hotelcarillon.com; Grote Markt 27; s/d from €60/80; 🛜) Small but tidy white rooms in the shadow of the Grote Kerk

are the hallmark here. A few share bathrooms and cost from €40. Breakfast can be taken in wicker chairs on the sidewalk cafe.

Hotel Amadeus (☎ 532 45 30; www.amadeus-hotel .com; Grote Markt 10; r €60-90; 🖳 🛜) Amadeus enjoys a brilliant spot nestled in a row of old gabled houses on the main square. Rooms are one step up from spartan, but they're comfy and have a few mod cons, and there's a small cafe on the 1st floor. There's also free wi-fi.

Ambassador City Centre Hotel (☎ 512 53 00; www .acc-hotel.nl; Oude Groenmarkt 20; r/studios from €80/85; 🖳 🛜) More than 100 individual rooms spread over an entire block near the Grote Kerk; studios have kitchenettes. The hotel includes Joops Hotel, and the two function as one.

HAARLEM'S URBAN OASES

Collectively known as *hofjes* – leafy courtyards enclosed by rows of sweet little homes – Haarlem has a surprising number of these green spaces that served as monastery gardens in the Middle Ages. Eventually they took on broader roles as hospitals and inns, or as refuges for orphans, widows and the elderly. These private squares also give clues about Dutch social concerns and the origins of the modern welfare state.

Most *hofjes* date from the 15th to the 18th centuries and are open for viewing on weekends only, but you can usually take a discreet peek any time. Ask the tourist office for its walking-guide brochure, *Hofjeswandeling,* which includes the following:

■ **Brouwers Hofje** (Tuchthuisstraat 8) Lodging for members of the brewers' guild (1472).

■ **Frans Loenen Hofje** (Witte Herenstraat 24) Almshouses built from a merchant's estate (1607).

■ **Hofje van Loo** (Barrevoetestraat 7) A women's hospital donated by mayor Sijmon Pieterszoon van Loo (1489); one of the most visible in Haarlem.

■ **Hofje van Staats** (Jansweg 39) One of the town's biggest, donated by a Haarlem merchant to poor women of the Reformed Church (1733), and still houses single, elderly women.

■ **St Joris Doelen** (Grote Houtstraat 144) A *proveniershuis* given as a donation; almshouse, later a gentlemen's inn (1591).

■ **Teylers Hofje** (Koudenhorn 64) Unusually grand affair, built by Pieter Teyler van der Hulst, founder of the Teyler Museum (1787).

Stempels (☎ 512 39 10; www.stempelsinhaarlem.nl; Klokhuisplein 9; r €90-155; 🖳 🛜) Haarlem's most interesting lodging has 17 spacious rooms in a gorgeous old printing house on the east side of the Grote Kerk. Small luxuries abound including a computer in every room and collections of short stories on the bedside table. The on-site cafe may keep you from venturing far.

Eating

Haarlem has very good eating. There are lots of cafes and restaurants along Zijlstraat, Spaarne and especially Lange Veerstraat, but you can find gems throughout town.

De Haerlemsche Vlaamse (☎ 532 59 91; Spekstraat 3; frites €2) Practically on the doorstep of the Grote Kerk, this *frites* (French fries) joint, not much bigger than a telephone box, is a local institution. Line up for its crispy, golden fries made from fresh potatoes. Choose from one of a dozen sauces including three kinds of mayonnaise.

Complimenti (☎ 542 20 41; Nassaustraat 24; snacks from €3; 🕑 noon-6pm Wed-Fri, 10am-5pm Sat) Note the scent of garlic wafting over the street from this picknicker's heaven of a deli. Varieties of fresh Italian bread, pesto, cheese and more are arrayed in display cases. Try not to drool.

Jacobus Pieck (☎ 532 61 44; Warmoesstraat; mains from €10; 🕑 lunch & dinner Mon-Sat) Touches such as freshly squeezed OJ put this tidy bistro on

a higher plane. The menu bursts with fresh dishes, from salads and sandwiches at lunch to more complex pasta and seafood choices at dinner. Staff are welcoming; snag a sunny table on the back patio.

Lambermon's Grand Café (☎ 542 78 04; Korte Veerstraat 1; dishes €8-25) The 'grand' in the name is almost an understatement at this oh-so-chic corner hotspot in a beautiful former fashion store. Bottles of champagne are on ice for purchase by the glass; the all-male waiting staff even manages a bit of attitude coupled with élan.

La Forca (☎ 532 25 00; Frankestraat 17-19; mains €10-20; 🕑 dinner Tue-Sat) On a narrow quiet street, this trattoria (run by a charmer named Guiseppe) has tiled tables in a space as compact as the inside of a cannelloni. Perfect Tuscan and other Italian fare (the parmesan-crusted steak is amazing) draws gaggles of locals.

Also recommended:

Falafel Land (☎ 534 82 72; Lange Veerstraat 18; meals from €4; 🕑 noon-10pm) Luscious versions of the namesake chow; smile and get your picture in the window.

Grand Cafe Nobel (☎ 532 70 34; Spaarne 36; dishes €6-15) Good waterside views from a sprawling patio.

Terang Boelan (☎ 531 97 33; Zijlstraat 39; mains €8-15; 🕑 dinner) New and inviting, with fresh Indonesian fare.

Drinking

Haarlem's atmospheric cafes and bars are perfect spots to try Jopen beer, the local brew dating back to 1501. Koyt is dark, richly flavoured and has an alcohol content of 8.5%.

Proeflokaal In den Uiver (☎ 532 53 99; Riviervismarkt 13) This nautical-themed place has shipping knick-knacks and a schooner sailing right over the bar. There's jazz on Thursday and Sunday evenings. It's one of many atmospheric places overlooking the Grote Markt.

Café het Melkwoud (☎ 531 35 35; Zijlstraat 63; ☿ to 4am) A great place to nurse a beer (vast selection) with ecofriendly locals in ancient wooden surrounds behind ceiling-high windows.

Entertainment

NIGHTCLUBS

Café Stiels (☎ 531 69 40; www.stiels.nl; Smedestraat 21) For jazz and rhythm 'n' blues, bands play on the back stage almost every night of the week from 10pm onwards to as late as 4am weekends.

Patronaat (☎ 517 58 58; www.patronaat.nl; Zijlsingel 2) Haarlem's top music and dance club attracts bands with banging tunes. Events in this cavernous venue usually start around 9pm unless it's a midnight rave.

THEATRE

Philharmonie (☎ 512 12 12; www.theater-haarlem.nl; Lange Begijnestraat 11) Haarlem's venerable concert hall, which features music from every spectrum imaginable (except perhaps Death Metal, but with the Dutch, you never know).

Stadsschouwburg (☎ 512 12 12; Wilsonsplein 23) The city's municipal theatre and sister venue to the Philharmonie, the Stadsschouwburg reopened in 2008 after a lavish refurbishment.

Shopping

Monday is market day at Botermarkt and Grote Markt, and again on Saturday at Grote Markt. Friday also sees Botermarkt come alive to a local farmers market. On Wednesday it has a book market. Haarlem has many antiquarian and used bookshops. Ask for a map at the tourist office. Zijlstraat becomes less upmarket and more funky as you head west.

Getting There & Away

The city's stunning and restored art deco train station is served by frequent trains running between Amsterdam and Rotterdam. Lockers are up by track 3.

Destination	Fare (€)	Duration (min)	Frequency (per hr)
Alkmaar	5.70	30-50	4
Amsterdam	3.80	15	5-8
Den Haag	7.30	35-40	4-6
Rotterdam	10.50	50	4

Bus 300 links Haarlem train station and Schiphol airport (45 minutes, 10 times hourly) between 5am and midnight.

BICYCLE

Haarlem is linked to Amsterdam by national route LF20 over a distance of 25km. Given the heavy urbanisation in the area this is not exactly a pastoral ride. Just west you can link up with the much more bucolic LF1, which follows the coast north and south. There's a large **bicycle shop** (☎ 531 70 66) at the train station.

Getting Around

The **bus information kiosk** (☿ 7.30am-5.30pm Mon-Fri, 9.30am-4.30pm Sat) opposite the train station has plenty of schedules, as does the tourist office. Buses 2, 3, 4, 5 and 8 (and others) from the front of the train station stop at Zijlstraat, just east of Grote Markt (five minutes).

Taxis (☎ 515 15 15) are everywhere in Haarlem.

AROUND HAARLEM
Beaches

Just 5km west of Haarlem's peaceful outskirts lies **Zandvoort** (Map p139), a popular seaside resort. It's not pretty as beach towns go, and drab apartment blocks line the main drag, but its proximity to Amsterdam ensures a steady flow of pleasure-seekers.

About 3km north of Zandvoort is Haarlem's second beach, **Bloemendaal aan Zee** (Map p145), a much less developed spot with a handful of restaurants and cafes and uninterrupted beaches. It's frequented by those looking for a semblance of peace and quiet away from the hustle and bustle of its bigger neighbour to the south.

The closest accommodation to Bloemendaal is De Lakens (p146), but Zandvoort is littered with accommodation. Haarlem's tourist office (p140) can offer options.

Trains link Zandvoort to Amsterdam Centraal Station two times hourly (€5, 30 minutes) via Haarlem (€2.20, 10 minutes). Buses 81 and 84 go to Zandvoort bus station from Haarlem by way of Overveen (15 minutes, twice hourly).

Zuid-Kennemerland National Park

Some 3800 hectares of classic Dutch coastal dunes are being restored in this vast patch of nature in the midst of the busy Randstad. **De Zandwaaier** (☎ 023-541 11 23; www.npzk.nl; Zeeweg, Overveen; ⏰ 10am-5pm Tue-Sun Apr-Oct, noon-5pm Tue-Sun Nov-Mar), the park's visitors centre, has nature displays and is a good source of information, with a range of detailed walking and cycling maps including a great 35km-circuit. There are car parks at the Koevlak and Parnassia entrances, from where paths lead off into the reserve. Trails snake through hilltop copses of Corsican firs and valleys of low-lying thickets; at the western edge you come to a massive barrier of golden sand that's 1000 years old.

The dunes sprout an extra layer of colour in spring including desert orchids, the bright rosettes of the century weed and the white-blooming grass of Parnassus. Red foxes, fallow deer and many species of birds are native to the area. Bats slumber in the park's abandoned bunkers before appearing at dusk.

Among the main features, the **Vogelmeer** lake has a bird observation hut above the south shore. The artificial lake **'t Wed** teems with bathers in summer. Lookout points, with evocative names such as Hazenberg (Hare Mountain), are scattered throughout. At 50m, the **Kopje van Bloemendaal** is the highest dune in the country, just outside the eastern border of the park, with views of the sea and Amsterdam. Ticks in the dunes are known

ZUID-KENNEMERLAND NATIONAL PARK

to carry Lyme disease, so insect repellent is a good idea.

On a sombre note, the WWII cemetery **Erebegraafplaats Bloemendaal** (☎ 020-660 19 45; admission free; ☻ 9am-6pm Apr-Sep, 9am-5pm Oct-Mar) is the resting place of 372 members of the Dutch resistance. Its walled compound in the dunes is isolated from the rest of the park and accessible only via the main road.

Rough camping is a no-no, but **De Lakens** (☎ 023-541 15 70; www.kdc.nu; camp sites from €29, bungalows per week from €200; ☻ Mar-Oct) enjoys a sandy, grassy spot just a few metres from the beach and abutting a lake. There's a lovely kids playground, and its bungalows sleep four or more.

To reach the park, visitors centre and camping ground, take bus 81 or 84 from Haarlem train station or cycle/drive the N200 towards Bloemendaal aan Zee. The distance is less than 5km.

IJMUIDEN
☎ 0255 / pop 7000

Just 5km up the coast from Haarlem, at the mouth of the Noordzeekanaal (North Sea Canal) in the port town of IJmuiden, is the huge **North Sea locks**. The largest is the Zuidersluis (South Lock), some 400m long and 45m wide. Few people realise that IJmuiden is also the largest fishing port in Western Europe, home to the factory trawlers that plough the North Atlantic for weeks at a time. Unfortunately the view is marred by the steel mills north of the locks.

Getting There & Around

It's a thrill taking the **hydrofoil** (Fast Flying Ferry; ☎ 020-639 22 47; www.connexxion.nl; adult/child return €8.50/5; ☻ 7am-11pm Mon-Fri, 9am-11pm Sat & Sun) from behind Amsterdam Centraal Station (25 minutes, half-hourly) along the Noordzeekanaal to Velsen, 3km short of IJmuiden, where you catch Connexxion bus 74 or 82 into town. Take a bicycle (free) and pedal from Velsen along the dyke towards the locks and go across the 'small' and 'middle' locks to the big lock on the far side; along the way you'll find an information centre, **Noordzeekanaal in Zicht** (North Sea Canal in Pictures; ☎ 51 91 12; Noordersluisweg 120; ☻ 1-5pm Tue-Fri).

IJmuiden's Dennekoplaan, close to the locks and the beach, can be reached on buses 4 and 75 (40 minutes, four times hourly) from Haarlem.

If you travel by road along the Noordzeekanaal, you'll have the surreal experience of passing huge, ocean-going ships that float well above road level.

BEVERWIJK
☎ 0251

Every weekend up to 80,000 visitors flock to the town of Beverwijk to visit the covered **De Bazaar Beverwijk** (☎ 26 26 26; www.debazaar .nl; Montageweg 35; ☻ 8.30am-6pm Sat & Sun), one of Europe's largest ethnic markets. Piled high are Arabian foods and spices, Turkish rugs, garments and handcrafted ornaments.

The liveliest of the three biggest halls is the **Zwarte Markt** (Black Market; adult/child €2/free), an enormous flea market with a carnival attitude. You can haggle with one of the 3000-plus vendors or just bask in the market chatter, live music and exotic aromas. The admission price includes entry to the **Grand Bazaar**, where the booths are larger and more professional, while the **Oosterse Markt** is free.

Getting There & Away

Parking (€3, free before 9am) becomes a problem after 9.30am. From Amsterdam drive the A9 towards Alkmaar, exit at Beverwijk and follow signs to the bazaar; or take the train to Beverwijk (€5.30, 40 minutes, two times hourly) and then either catch bus 76 (six minutes) or walk 1km.

ZAANSE SCHANS
☎ 075

People come for an hour and stay for several at this open-air museum on the Zaan River, which is *the* place to see **windmills** operating. It's got a touristy element, but the six operating mills are completely authentic and are operated with enthusiasm and love. Visitors can explore the windmills at their leisure, seeing firsthand the vast moving parts that make these devices a combination of sailing ship and Rube Goldberg. As a bonus, the riverbank setting is lovely.

The six working windmills are the highlight. One mill sells fat jars of its freshly ground mustard, while the others turn out oils, meal and sawed planks. Most are open for inspection, and it's a treat to clamber about the creaking works while the mills shake in the North Sea breeze. The mill selling paint pigments will delight artists, as you get to see the actual materials that are used to produce Renaissance masterpieces being made into colourful powders. Ask to see the storeroom of ground pigments for sale.

The other buildings have been brought here from all over the country to re-create a 17th-century community. There is an early Albert Heijn market, a cheesemaker and a popular **clog factory** that turns out wooden shoes as if grinding keys (and which has a surprisingly interesting museum). The engaging pewter-smith will explain the story behind dozens of tiny figures while the soft metal sets in the moulds.

The impressive **Zaans Museum** (☎ 075-616 28 62; www.zaansmuseum.nl; adult/child €4.50/2.70; ☑ 10am-5pm) shows how the harnessing of wind and water was done.

Admission to the site is free, but some buildings charge a small admission. Hours tend to follow those of the museum, which also houses the information centre. Once you've finished poking about the village, take a **boat** (adult/child €3/1.50; ☑ 9am-6pm May-Sep) across the Zaan River. It runs on demand and the cheery volunteers will give you a walking guide of the old town of Zaandijk you can use for the 15-minute stroll to the train station.

Getting There & Away

From Amsterdam Centraal Station (€2.90, 17 minutes, four times hourly) take the stop train towards Alkmaar and get off at Koog Zaandijk – it's a well-signposted 1km walk to Zaanse Schans. You can ride national bike route LF7 to the site from Amsterdam Centraal Station. The 22km route meanders through farmlands and lakes once it escapes the big smoke.

ZAANDAM

☎ 075 / pop 26,000

A stone's throw from Zaanse Schans, Zaandam has played home to two famous residents: Russia's Peter the Great and Impressionist master Claude Monet. Claude stayed in a nice hotel while Peter preferred a rickety wooden shack, now a shrine and the main reason for visiting this commuter town.

The **Czaar Peterhuisje** (☎ 616 03 90; Krimp 23; adult/child €3/free; ☑ 1-5pm Tue-Sun Apr-Oct, 1-5pm Sat & Sun Nov-Mar) is the great abode where Peter spent a mere week of his life in 1697. The Russian ruler arrived incognito as sailor Peter Mikhailov to garner support for Western forces against the Turks. Despite the hush-hush, news spread and hordes of fans practically besieged the cabin to get a glimpse of his tsarness. Peter eventually slipped away to the wharves to learn shipbuilding and how to swear in Dutch, and became adept at both.

Many Russians came here on pilgrimage in the 19th century to scrawl their graffiti. So great was the PR value that Grand Duchess Anna Paulowna (wife of Dutch King Willem II) commissioned a brick shelter over the house, which finally emerged in Russian-orthodox style by the late 1800s. Napoleon stopped by and was apparently delighted.

Getting There & Away

To get here from Amsterdam Centraal, take the train toward Alkmaar and get off at Zaandam (€2.50, 12 minutes, eight hourly); from the station, follow the signs. By bike, follow the bike route south along the east bank of the river for 5km and then cross the bridge west into Zaandam.

WATERLAND REGION

☎ 075

Time moves slowly in this rural area that starts only 9km north of Amsterdam, which might as well be known as the Waterlogged Region. Fields of green are watched by herons standing motionless alongside watery furrows. Despite the proximity of the sea, you're most likely to smell cow dung from the many farms.

Broek in Waterland is a precious little burg in the heart of the Waterland Region. Some 17th- and 18th-century houses are painted a particular shade of grey, known as *Broeker grijs* after the landscapes painted here by Monet and other masters. The village church was burned by the Spanish in 1573 but restored with a pretty stained-glass window recalling the tragic event. On the lake's edge stands the so-called **Napoleonhuisje**, a white pagoda where the French emperor and the mayor met in 1811.

Near the town of Landsmeer, 6km west of Broek, lies the nature reserve and recreational area **Het Twiske**. This is where urbanites go for a calculated dose of nature: well-marked walking trails, playgrounds and artificial, but quite decent, beaches, especially for families. A full third of the area is water and there are several hides for bird-watchers on the lakeshores. The **visitors centre** (☎ 684 43 38; www.hettwiske.nl; Noorderlaak 1; ☑ 10am-4pm

THE WATERLAND TICKET

If you're planning to day trip around the Waterland Region, Monnickendam, Volendam and Marken by bus, consider purchasing a Waterland Ticket (€7). Available from Arriva bus drivers, it allows a day's unlimited travel in the area north of Amsterdam (covered by buses including 110, 111 and 115) and it's excellent value.

Tue-Fri, noon-4pm Sat & Sun) is next to the canoe rental shop.

Getting There & Away

The best way to experience the Waterland area is by bike; pick up a rental in Amsterdam (p136) and head north on the national bike route LF7 (for a suggested cycling itinerary, see p71). Otherwise pick up a Waterland Ticket (see the boxed text, above) and ride the buses.

MONNICKENDAM

☎ 0299 / pop 10,500

Monnickendam, which gained its name from the Benedictines, who built a dam here, is a sleepy town that can trace its roots back to 1356. It originally became prosperous by moving goods inland towards Alkmaar but after the fishing industry died, it reinvented itself as a yachting resort, and today the beautiful old trawlers mainly catch pleasure-seekers. History still pervades the narrow lanes around the shipyards and fish smokehouses that have been operating for hundreds of years. Noordeinde is the main street and is enlivened by the drama of old brick houses tilting at crazy angles as they sink into the soggy ground. Smoked eel (caught in the IJsselmeer) remains a local delicacy.

Sights

The town's trademark building is the 15th-century **Speeltoren**, an elegant, Italianate clock tower and former town hall. The tower's 17th-century carillon (glockenspiel) performs at 11am and noon on Saturday, when the four mechanical knights prance in the open wooden window twice before retiring.

Inside the clock tower you'll find the **Museum De Speeltoren** (☎ 65 22 03; Noordeinde 4; adult/child €1.50/0.50; ☒ 11am-4.30pm Sat, 1-4.30pm Sun May-Jul, 11am-4.30pm Tue-Sat, 1-4.30pm Sun Aug–mid-Sep), which displays various archaeological

finds uncovered during the building of the Afsluitdijk (see the boxed text, p169).

The Gothic **Grote Kerk** (☎ 65 06 00; De Zarken; admission free; ☒ 10am-4pm Tue-Sat, 2-4pm Sun & Mon Jun-Aug), on the southern outskirts of town, is notable for its triple nave, tower galleries and a dazzling oak choir screen dating from the 16th century. It's impossible not to focus on the enormous organ in the nave; restoration of the edifice is ongoing.

Other stars in the architecture department include the **Waag** (Weigh-house) on the central canal. Built in 1669, this focal point of local economic life was equipped in 1905 with grand Tuscan columns, a common trick of the day designed to make it look much older and more impressive. **In de Bonten Os** (Coloured Ox; Noordeinde 26) is the only house that's left in its original 17th-century state. In the days before proper glass, the curious vertical shutters at street level were made to let in air and light.

The old harbour along Haringburgwal is famous for its **fish smokehouses**, and you can poke your head inside for a glimpse of the process or have a taste. A bronze statue of a fisherman curing eels on a spit stands where the central canal meets the harbour.

Activities

As elsewhere on the IJsselmeer, large pleasure boats are the thing in Monnickendam. In July and August you can feel the spray in your face on day trips aboard an antique clipper. Reserve at **Holland Zeilcharters** (☎ 65 23 51; www.sailing.nl; Het Prooyen 4a; per person from €50, botter rental for up to 8 persons from €450).

The harbour bristles with splendid old *tjalken*, *botters* and *klippers*, historic boats available for hire (as are skippers if need be). The *botters* can be hired out for a group from around €450 per day. The sky's the limit at the top end, for example three-masted clippers for as long as you (and your wallet) see fit.

Smaller craft can be found at **Bootvloot** (☎ 06 5494 2657; www.bootvloot.nl; Hemmeland beach; ☒ 10am-5.30pm Apr-Oct) where two- to four-person sailboats cost €40/55 per half-day/day. It's a 500m walk through the leafy Hemmeland recreation area northeast of Monnickendam marina – just follow the sign 'Zeilbootverhuur'.

Right in town, **Café de Koperen Vis** (☎ 65 06 27; www.dekoperenvis.nl; Havennstraat 1) rents out small power boats for €150 per day.

Sleeping & Eating

Camping-Jachthaven Uitdam (☎ 020-403 14 33; www
.campinguitdam.nl; Zeedijk 2, Uitdam; camp sites/cabins/
bungalows €17/44/74; ☺ Mar-Oct) Tucked away
behind a dyke on the IJsselmeer, this well-
equipped site has mooring facilities, beach,
laundry, snack bar and bicycle rental. Both
the basic cabins and bungalows sleep up to
four; the latter has a kitchen. Take the dyke
road 5km southeast of Monnickendam or
jump aboard bus 111.

Posthoorn (☎ 65 45 98; www.posthoorn.eu; Noordeinde
43; r from €145; ☺) This beautifully restored boutique hotel dates back to 1697 but the owners
suspect it might be older. The 12 romantic
rooms fuse trad comforts with modern style:
bring on the pedestal sink. The restaurant
(mains from €15; open dinner Tuesday to
Saturday) uses local produce for solid mains
of meats and seafood. Book rooms and courtyard dining on weekends.

't Markerveerhuis (☎ 65 57 69; Brugstraat 6; mains
€10-15; ☺ lunch & dinner) Enjoy traditional Dutch
fare while joining the old salts pondering the
comings and goings in Monnickendam's harbour. Dutch folk music emanates from the
stage at weekends.

Getting There & Around

Arriva bus 111 (30 minutes, three to four times
an hour) links the centre of Monnickendam
to Amsterdam Centraal Station, harbour
side, as does bus 115 (twice hourly). Like
the paths throughout Waterland, good bike
routes abound, especially national route LF21,
which starts in Amsterdam and follows rural
dykes along the IJsselmeer.

Ber Koning (☎ 65 12 67; Noordeinde 12; per day €9;
☺ 10am-5pm Tue-Sat) rents out bicycles.

MARKEN
☎ 0299 / pop 500

Across Gouwzee Bay lies scenic Marken with
a small and determined population. It was
an isolated island in the Zuiderzee until 1957
when a causeway linked up with the mainland,
effectively turning it into a museum-piece
village. However, it still manages to exude a
fishing-village vibe, and the car-free centre
helps keep *some* of the hordes at bay.

The colourful Kerkbuurt is the most authentic area, with tarred or painted houses
raised on pilings to escape the Zuiderzee
floods. A row of eel-smoking houses here has
been converted to the **Marker Museum** (☎ 60 19

04; Kerkbuurt 44, Marken; adult/child €2.50/1.25; ☺ 10am-
5pm Mon-Sat, noon-4pm Sun Apr-Oct), which delves
into the island's history and includes the re-
created interior of a fisherman's home, with
a wealth of personal odds and ends. It sells a
walking tour brochure (€0.50), which will help
guide you around the stout wooden structures
that line the intricate pattern of lanes.

The **kerk** (Buurterstraat) is filled with ship models designed to attract God's good grace to
local seamen. The lighthouse at the east end
is a good 2km walk or ride.

our pick **Hof Van Marken** (☎ 60 13 00; www.hofvan
marken.nl; Buurt II 15, Marken; r €80-110) has big beds,
fluffy pillows and heavenly duvets that only a
hard heart could resist. The seven cosy rooms
have high-speed internet, and the restaurant
serves fresh and stylish takes on local produce
and seafood (mains €15 to €25; open lunch
Saturday and Sunday, dinner Wednesday to
Sunday). Be sure to book.

Getting There & Away
BICYCLE
The 8km ride along the dyke from
Monnickendam is perfect for pondering the
moody sea.

BUS
Arriva bus 111 links Marken with Amsterdam
(30 minutes, half-hourly) via Monnickendam
(12 minutes).

FERRY
Noordwest Rederij (☎ 035-582 26 22; www.rederijnoord
west.nl; adult/child return €12.50/10.50; ☺ Wed-Mon Jul &
Aug) links Monnickendam with Marken several
times daily (45 minutes).

The **Marken Express ferry** (adult/child return €7/4;
☺ 10.30am-6pm Mar-Sep) makes the 45-minute
crossing from Volendam to Marken every
half-hour. In Volendam the ferry leaves from
the docks at Havendijkje.

VOLENDAM
☎ 0299 / pop 20,700

Some 22km northeast of Amsterdam lies
Volendam, a former fishing port turned tourist trap. It's quaint all right, with its rows of
wooden houses and locals who don traditional
dress for church and festive events, but the
harbour is awash with souvenir shops and
cafes, and on weekends it's even hard to think
with all the people swarming about. Here the
ever-present regional smell of cow is replaced

by fried fish. You may want to limit your time here to enjoy more time in charming Marken (p149) or nearby Edam (below).

The **tourist office** (☎ 36 37 47; www.vvv-volendam .nl; Zeestraat 37; ⏰ 10am-5pm Mon-Sat year-round, 11am-4pm Sun Jun-Aug) has a brochure (€1.50) with a walking tour of Volendam.

Next door, the **Volendams Museum** (☎ 36 92 58; Zeestraat 41; adult/child €2.50/1.50; ⏰ 10am-5pm mid-Mar–Oct) is a must for cigar aficionados. Local culture is covered with traditional costumes, prints, paintings of harbour scenes and even a cramped ship's sleeping quarters, but this place is really devoted to lovers of cheap cigars: some 11 million bands are plastered on its walls. Both are off the N247; the tourist district is about 400m to the southeast.

Sleeping & Eating

Seafood is the undisputed king in Volendam, and the main street (and harbour) is lined with vendors offering smoked cod, eel, herring and tiny shrimp. But shop carefully as vendors are adept at making sandwiches look over-stuffed when the reality is all dough under the 'bursting' mound of seafood. This is a boon for bread-loving seagulls.

Hotel Spaander (☎ 36 35 95; www.spaander.com; Haven 15-19; r €105; 🛜 🖭) The town's best hotel has retained much of its atmosphere from the past, with traditional carved balconies and cushy rooms that have welcomed the likes of Picasso and Monet. The warren of public spaces linked by creaking wooden floors includes a grand dining room, which is the first word in local seafood (mains €22 to €35; open lunch and dinner).

Getting There & Around

Arriva bus 111 runs between Volendam and Amsterdam via Monnickendam (30 minutes). Bus 110 links Volendam with Amsterdam and Edam (12 minutes) every 30 minutes until 1.30am. National bike route LF21 passes right along the harbour; Monnickendam is 6km south.

EDAM

☎ 0299 / pop 7400

Once a renowned whaling port – in its 17th-century heyday it had 33 shipyards that built the fleet of legendary admiral Michiel de Ruijter – this scenic little town is another of Noord Holland's hidden gems. With its old shipping warehouses, quiet cobblestone streets, hand-operated drawbridges and picture-perfect canals, you'd be hard pressed not to enjoy a stroll around. And it's quite astounding that so many tourists prefer Volendam, only 2km away, unless Edam's cheese market is on, and then they're like flies to, well, cheese.

Information

Tourist office (☎ 31 51 25; www.vvv-edam.nl; Damplein 1; ⏰ 10am-3pm Mon-Sat Nov-Mar, 10am-5pm Mon-Sat Apr-Oct, 11am-3.30pm Sun Jul & Aug) Housed in the splendid 18th-century town hall. Pick up the good English-language booklet, *A Stroll Through Edam* (€2.50), for 90-minute self-guided tours.

Sights & Activities

In the 16th century Willem van Oranje bestowed on Edam the right to hold a **Kaasmarkt** (Cheese Market; ⏰ 10.30am-12.30pm Wed Jul–mid-Aug), which was the town's economic anchor right through to the 1920s. At its peak 250,000 rounds of cheese were sold here every year. On the western side of Kaasmarkt stands the old **Kaaswaag** (admission free; ⏰ 10am-5pm Apr-Sep), the cheese weigh-house, which has a display on the town's chief product. The cheese market is smaller than the one in Alkmaar but equally touristy.

Freely sample from an astonishing array of cheeses at the wonderful and barely commercial **Gestam** (☎ 37 15 30; Voorhaven 125; ⏰ 10am-4pm Wed & Fri), a warehouse for regional cheese producers.

The 15th-century **Grote Kerk** (admission free; ⏰ 1-5pm Apr-Sep) has an unfortunate past that stands witness to the vagaries of Dutch weather. The stained-glass windows bearing coats of arms and historical scenes were added after 1602, when the church burned to a crisp after a lightning strike. Its tower can be climbed (admission €2) for views of the surrounds. The taller **Speeltoren**, leaning slightly over Kleine Kerkstraat about 100m further south, is all that remains of the 15th-century Kleine Kerk.

The **Edams Museum** (☎ 37 24 31; Damplein 8; adult/child €3/free; ⏰ 10am-4.30pm Mon-Sat, 1.30-4.30pm Sun) has a basic collection of old furnishings, porcelain and silverware, spread over three cramped floors. It's best known for its floating cellar, a remarkable pantry that rises and falls with the river's swell to reduce stress on the structure above. The ornate brick structure is Edam's oldest, dating from 1530. Just over the unusual arched plaza across a canal, an annexe

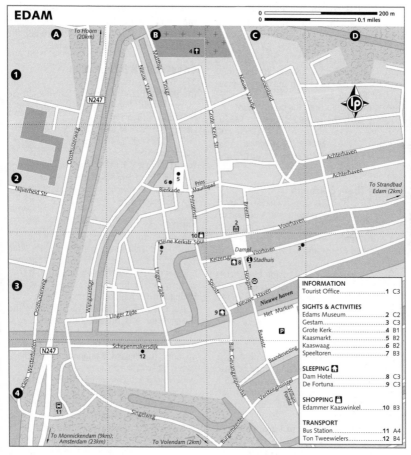

(Damplein 1) in the 1737 town hall above the VVV has exhibits that include some famous paintings, including *Tall Girl*.

Tours

The tourist office organises one-hour **boat tours** (tickets €4; ☉ departs noon & 2pm Wed Jul & Aug) aboard a *tuindersvlet* (small, open-topped boat) in summer, weather permitting. It also organises one-hour **walking** tours (tickets €4; ☉ departs 1pm Wed Jul & Aug). You can also rent a boat via the tourist office from about €450 per day.

Sleeping & Eating

In addition to the places reviewed here, the tourist office has a list of private accommodation and farmstays from €25 per person.

Strandbad Edam (☎ 37 19 94; www.campingstrandbad.nl; Zeevangszeedijk 7a; camp sites per person/tent €3.50/5; ☉ Apr-Sep) This sprawling seaside camping ground has a swimming beach, laundry and restaurant. It's usually overrun but remains a convenient base for boat trips into the IJsselmeer – the docks are right outside the camping ground.

De Fortuna (☎ 37 16 71; www.fortuna-edam.nl; Spuistraat 3; r €70-140; ☜) An Edam gem, this place might have stood as a model for an old Dutch painting. Its 24 cute rooms have bathrooms best described as cosy. The restaurant (mains €20; open lunch and dinner) serves classic Dutch dishes amid oil paintings, large bay windows and leather seats buffed shiny over the years. There are lush gardens and a waterside terrace.

Dam Hotel (☎ 37 17 66; www.damhotel.nl; Keizersgracht 1; r €100-175; 🔊) In the heart of the city, this boutique hotel is a perfect romantic retreat. Some of the 11 rooms are a little on the small side, but this is counterbalanced by huge beds and thoroughly modern bathrooms. Its restaurant (mains from €20; open lunch and dinner) serves modern French fare in elegant surroundings while the cafe spills onto the main square.

Along with the excellent Gestam (p150) there are several places to buy cheese and assemble picnics. **Edammer Kaaswinkel** (☎ 37 16 83; cnr Spui & Prinsenstraat) has a wide variety and there's a good adjoining deli.

Getting There & Around

Connexxion bus 110 stops twice an hour at the bus station and continues to Voldendam (five minutes), Monnickendam (25 minutes) and Amsterdam (40 minutes). Bus 114 travels to Hoorn (25 minutes, twice hourly) and Monnickendam (10 minutes).

Bicycles can be rented at **Ton Tweewielers** (☎ 37 19 22; Schepenmakersdijk 6; per day €7). Edam is on national bike route LF21; the many IJsselmeer dykes make for excellent riding.

ALKMAAR

☎ 072 / pop 93,500

If ever there was a cheese town, Alkmaar is it. Come Friday, its picturesque ringed centre is awash with tourists, all eager to catch a glimpse of the city's famous cheese market. However its charms may be best appreciated on nonmarket days.

The city is more than just a purveyor of curdled milk. It holds a special place in Dutch hearts as the first town, in 1573, to repel occupying Spanish troops; locals opened the locks

---

SCENIC DRIVE: DYKES & WINDMILLS

Midway between Edam and Alkmaar, the village of De Rijp on the N244 is at the south end of several good drives and rides along dykes that give an excellent feel for just how low the land is compared to the waterways coursing between the earthen walls. The Oostdijk–Westdijk road travels north 6km to the hamlet of Schermerhorn on the N243. Just west, another dyke road runs parallel and meanders past several windmills. Both are narrow and the domain of cyclists and sheep, so if you're in a car, go slow.

---

and flooded the area with sea water, forcing the perplexed invaders to retreat. The victory won the town weighing rights, which laid the foundation for its cheese market.

Orientation & Information

The town centre is focused on Waagplein, the main square where the famous cheese market is held. The pretty, canal-bound centre is 500m southeast of the train station.

Library (☎ 515 66 44; Gasthuisstraat 2; internet per hr €1.50; 🕙 9am-9pm Tue-Fri, 11am-5pm Sat) Has rows of internet terminals.

Tourist office (☎ 511 42 84; www.vvvalkmaar.nl; Waagplein 2; 🕙 1-5pm Mon, 10am-5pm Tue-Sat) In the Waaggebouw, the towering old weigh-house. Staff will book accommodation for €3.

Sights

Before beginning your exploration of the city, consider purchasing a copy of the *Walking Tour of the Town Among the Historic Buildings* booklet (€2.50) from the tourist office. It covers historical buildings such as the Renaissance **Stadhuis** (town hall) in extensive detail.

Built as a chapel in the 14th century, the **Waaggebouw** was pressed into service as a weigh-house two centuries later. This handsome building houses the tourist office and, upstairs, the **Hollands Kaasmuseum** (Dutch Cheese Museum; ☎ 511 42 84; adult/concession €3.50/1.50; 🕙 10am-4pm Mon-Sat Apr-Oct), a reverential display of cheesemaking utensils, photos and a curious stock of paintings by 16th-century female artists.

The **Stedelijk Museum** (Municipal Museum; ☎ 548 97 89; www.stedelijkmuseumalkmaar.nl; Canadaplein 1; adult/child €6/free; 🕙 10am-5pm Tue-Sun) is overlooked by many visitors who don't get past the cheese market. This is a shame because its collection of oil paintings by Dutch masters, including impressive life-sized portraits of Alkmaar nobles, is alone worth the entry fee. Other works show Alkmaar in post–Golden Age decline; sombre scenes of almswomen caring for the poor recall how the church's role grew as trade declined. The few modern works on display include Charley Toorop's odd oil painting of the Alkmaar cheese market; her cheese-bearers with grotesque features remain controversial.

The **Grote Kerk** (Kerkplein; adult/child €5/free; 🕙 10am-5pm Tue-Sun Jul & Aug) reminds us that Noord Hollanders are organ-lovers. The most famous here is the little 'Swallow Organ' (1511) in the north ambulatory. The

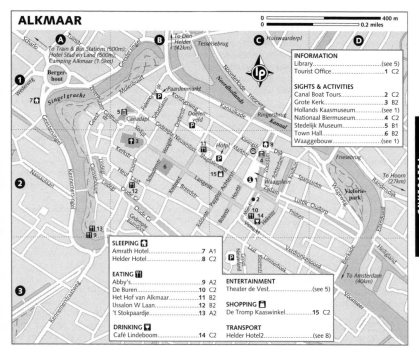

ALKMAAR

17th-century organ built by Jaco van Campen dominates the nave. Organ recitals take place from noon to 12.30pm and 1pm to 1.30pm and Wednesday evenings in July and August. Other times, you may be able to sneak a peek if the doors are open.

Housed in the attractive old De Boom brewery, the **Nationaal Biermuseum** (☎ 511 38 01; Houttil 1; adult/child €3.50/1.75; 1-4pm Mon-Sat) has a decent collection of beer-making equipment and wax dummies showing how the suds were made. The video of Dutch beer commercials since the 1950s will have you in stiches. Choose from 30 beers (eight on draught) in the friendly bar after your tour.

Tours
Canal boat tours (☎ 511 77 50; www.woltheus cruises.nl; adult/child €5.30/3.80; every 20min from 9.30am Apr-Oct) with multilingual commentary depart from Mient near the Waag and last 45 minutes.

Sleeping
The tourist office has a list of private rooms from about €25 per person.

Camping Alkmaar (☎ 511 69 24; www.campingalkmaar .nl; Bergerweg 201; camp sites €20-25, cabins €40) This site lies in a pleasant copse convenient to the ring road, 1km west of the train station. Tent sites are sheltered and wooden cabins sleep two people. Take bus 6 to Sportpark (10 minutes).

Hotel Stad en Land (☎ 512 39 11; www.stadenland .com; Stationsweg 92; r €65-90) Close to the train station, with basic yet comfy rooms, Stad en Land is a good choice for those making a short, overnight visit to Alkmaar. Of the four rooms those at the rear are the quietest and overlook a little pond.

Helder Hotel (☎ 520 25 00; www.hotelpakhuys.nl; Peperstraat 1; r €80-110;) A miniempire spread over several buildings right in the centre, the Helder has 17 rooms that while basic are quite comfortable and make the best of their historical surrounds. Some have canal views. There's also a wine shop and a vibrant cafe.

Amrath Hotel (☎ 518 61 86; www.amrathhotelalkmaar .nl; Geestersingel 15; r €90-130;) Only a short walk from the centre is this modern 84-room hotel. Its rooms are spacious and geared to business travellers and are of the typical anonymous three-star standard.

NOWHERE'S AS CHEESY AS HERE

Cheese is a big thing in the Netherlands; anyone who's breakfasted in a B&B or entered a super-market can tell you this. But in Noord Holland's Schiereiland, cheese is a very serious business.

Alkmaar's traditional **cheese market** (Waagplein; 10am-noon Fri Apr-early Sep) goes back to the 17th century. Every Friday morning around 30,000kg of waxed rounds of Gouda, Edam and Leiden *kaas* (cheese) are ceremoniously stacked on Waagplein, and soon the porters appear in their colourful hats, ready to spring into action. The dealers (looking official in white smocks) insert a hollow rod to extract a cheese sample and go into taste-test mode, sniffing and crumbling to check fat and moisture content. This is one of the few Dutch towns where the old cheese guilds still operate, and the porters' bright green, red and yellow hats denote which company they belong to. Once deals are struck the porters whisk the cheeses on wooden sledges to the old cheese scale in a stride reminiscent of someone hurrying to the toilet. It's primarily for show: nowadays the modern dairy combines have a lock on the cheese trade. Still, as living relics go it's a spectacle not to be missed, and it's fun to see so many people in a Wallace & Gromit state over cheese.

Ask at the tourist office for details on local cheese producers who give demonstrations and sell their wares. Or just go on a sampling binge at De Tromp Kaaswinkel (below).

Eating

Charming restaurants and bars surround the Waag and the quay named Bierkade. Koorstraat and Ritesvoort are away from the cheesy madness and have many excellent bistros and cafes.

ourpick IJssalon W Laan (511 56 85; Koorstraat 45; treats €1.20; noon-8pm) For more than six decades huge industrial mixers have created soft ice cream at this tiled gem. There's one flavour: a tongue-titillating vanilla.

De Buren (512 03 08; Mient 37; mains €6-20; lunch & dinner) This sprawling vintage cafe has outside tables that span the canal and wrap around to the old fish market. The menu is a fresh take on Dutch fare.

Abby's (511 11 11; Ritesevoort 60; meals €8-20) There's cool jazz inside and cool breezes outside on the terrace, which is shaded by an old windmill. Soups, salads and sandwiches please lunchtime diners.

Het Hof van Alkmaar (512 12 22; Hof van Sonoy 1; lunch €5-15, dinner mains €16-25; lunch & dinner Tue-Sun) Hof van Alkmaar occupies a former 15th-century nunnery with a rustic dining room overlooking the *hofje*. Cooking is global – expect satays, roasts and more. Lunchtime sandwiches are a treat.

't Stokpaardje (512 88 70; Vrouwenstraat 1; menus from €38; dinner Thu-Mon) One of Alkmaar's finest, this top-end restaurant is nestled on a tiny street off Ritesvoort. Local ingredients star on a changing line-up of set menus. The name means 'hobbyhorse', but none of the namesake graces the contemporary menu;

rather it may refer to the stamina you'll need to tackle the wine list.

Drinking & Entertainment

Alkmaar has a lively arts scene – pick up a copy of the monthly *Alkmaar Agenda* (free) from the tourist office to see what's on.

Café Lindeboom (512 17 43; Verdronkenoord 114) Over by the old fish market is this cosy bar where talkative locals live it up on the sunny canal terrace. Inside it's all old tiles and charm.

Theater De Vest (548 99 99; www.theaterdevest .nl; Canadaplein 2) The centre for Alkmaar's high-brow entertainment, De Vest runs the gamut from traditional plays and puppet shows to avant-garde dance. In summer Canadaplein turns into a stage for the performing arts festival Zomer op het plein (Summer on the square).

Shopping

Langestraat is the pedestrianised shopping street with mainstream stores. Laat has a more interesting and diverse collection.

ourpick De Tromp Kaaswinkel (511 34 22; Magdalenenstraat 11) There's not much else to buy in Alkmaar except cheese, and this place stocks an excellent range of Dutch and French varieties. Samples abound and purchases are hand-cut from huge rounds.

Getting There & Away

The train station has all services, including lockers and exchange. Trains to/from Alkmaar:

Destination	Fare (€)	Duration (min)	Frequency (per hr)
Amsterdam	6.70	30-40	4
Den Helder	7.20	35	2
Enkhuizen	7.20	50	2
Hoorn	4.50	25	2

There's also a **bicycle shop** (☎ 511 79 07) at the train station. Helder Hotel (p153) rents bikes (per day €10) and scooters (per day €50).

National route LF7 runs west 9km to link with the LF1 coastal route. It runs east 28km to join the LF21 which follows the IJsselmeer and links Edam and Hoorn.

Getting Around

Connexxion buses 2, 3 and 4 connect the train station to Kanaalkade (€1.50, five minutes). Cycling around town on cheese market days is very difficult due to the crowds, and bikes often 'disappear'.

BROEK OP LANGEDIJK
☎ 0226

Only in Holland! The vast water-logged area north of Alkmaar was once home to 15,000 tiny, yet productive, farms, each literally an island. Rather than tending to their crops by tractor or getting about by road, the farmers used rowboats. Most of the farms have been replaced by developments but in the town of Broek op Langedijk, about 8km northeast of Alkmaar, the **Museum Broeker Veiling** (Museum Broeker Auction; ☎ 31 38 07; www.broekerveiling.nl; Broek op Langedijk; adult/child €7/4.10; ☽ 10am-5pm Mon-Fri, 11am-5pm Sat & Sun, closed Mon Sep-Jun) preserves much of this fascinating era.

The centrepiece is a surprisingly vast auction house where farmers would arrive with their boatloads of produce and then wait – afloat – inside, until they could paddle through an auction room where wholesale grocery buyers would bid on the load of carrots, turnips, cabbage etc. Built in 1878, it sits on 1900 piles. Visitors can still tour the immense interior and re-created auctions where the winning bid gets a bag of apples rather than a boatload. It's great fun. A striking new museum building nearby promises to give even more context to this uniquely Dutch way of life.

The museum also runs 45-minute traditional tours around some of the 200 surviving island plots nearby. Combination tickets for museum and boat cost €11.20/6.20 per adult/child.

From Amsterdam, take the A9 to Alkmaar and N242 towards Heerhugowaard, exiting for Broek op Langedijk. By train, go to Alkmaar and change to bus 10 (20 minutes, twice hourly) and get off at Doofpot for a five-minute walk.

By bike, a 9km route from Alkmaar follows canals and goes through the tiny old village of Sint Pancras.

HOORN
☎ 0229 / pop 70,000

With a string of museums, a quiet affluent charm and a busy harbour, Hoorn attracts both weekend wanderers and skippers alike. It was once the capital of West Friesland and, thanks to the presence of the Dutch merchant fleet, a mighty trading city. As a member of the league of Seven Cities, it helped free the country from the Spanish who occupied the town in 1569.

Its most famous son, explorer Willem Schoutens, named South America's storm-lashed southern tip – Cape Horn – after his home town in 1616.

Orientation & Information

The old quarter begins about 1km southwest of the train station. From the station, walk south along broad Veemarkt to Gedempte Turfhaven, turn right and take the first left into Grote Noord, the pedestrianised shopping street. At the end is the scenic main square, Rode Steen, and the harbour area is a stone's throw further south, down Grote Havensteeg.

Library (Wisselstraat 8; internet per hr €3; ☽ 1-8.30pm Mon, Wed & Thu, 1-5pm Tue & Fri, 10am-1pm Sat) Has internet access.

Tourist office (☎ 072-511 42 84; www.vvvhoorn .nl; Veemarkt 44; ☽ 1-6pm Mon, 9.30am-6pm Tue-Fri, 9.30am-5pm Sat) Across from the train station with an ANWB office.

Sights & Activities

Hoorn's heyday as a shipping centre is long gone, but the imposing **statue of Jan Peterszoon Coen**, founder of the Dutch East India Company, still watches over the Rode Steen (Red Stone or Fortress), the square named for the blood that once flowed from the gallows. On the northeastern side of the square it's impossible to overlook the **Waag**, the 17th-century weigh-house that boasts a carved unicorn, the town symbol.

NOORD HOLLAND & FLEVOLAND

On the square also stands the former seat of the **Staten-College** (States' Council), the body that once governed seven towns in Noord Holland (Alkmaar, Hoorn, Enkhuizen, Medemblik, Edam, Monnickendam and Purmerend). Its wedding-cake facade bears the coat of arms of Oranje-Nassau, the Dutch-German royal dynasty that the Dutch named as rulers when Napoleon left Holland. It now houses the **Westfries Museum** (☎ 28 00 28; www.westfriesmuseum.nl; Rode Steen; adult/child €5/free; ☙ 11am-5pm Mon-Fri, 1-5pm Sat & Sun), an absorbing museum with a rich collection of historical paintings – so rich that it was the target of art theft in 2005. Some 20 paintings worth €10 million were stolen (and are still missing), but fortunately the four large group portraits of prominent *schutters* (civic guards) by Jan A Rotius (1624–66) were left in peace. The rear courtyard has a number of curious stone tablets from local facades.

Perhaps Hoorn's greatest joy is simply strolling the streets where 16th- and 20th-century buildings mix, the older ones leaning forward as if they are hard of hearing. The scenic harbour is lined by stately gabled houses, especially along Veermanskade. Overshadowing them all is the massive **Hoofdtoren** (1532), a defensive gate that now hosts a bar and restaurant. The tiny belfry was an afterthought.

Housed in two old cheese warehouses on a tiny in-town island that was mostly used for beer shipments, the **Museum of the 20th Century** (☎ 21 40 01; Bierkade 4; adult/child €4/2; ☙ 10am-5pm Tue-Fri, noon-5pm Sat & Sun) is devoted mainly to household goods and modern inventions. Among the eye-openers are a 1964 Philips mainframe computer – a clunky bookcase-sized unit with a whole 1KB of memory – and a 30-sq-metre scale *maquette* (model) of Hoorn in 1650.

The **Museum Stoomtram** (☎ 21 48 62; www.museumstoomtram.nl; adult/child one-way €12/9) isn't a museum in the traditional sense but rather a historical steam locomotive that puffs between Hoorn station and Medemblik (22km; one hour). You can combine the train and boat for a route called the 'Historic Triangle': first from Hoorn to Medemblik by the steam train and then by boat to Enkhuizen and finally on a regular NS train back to Hoorn. The steam train and boat portion costs €20/15 per adult/child. The schedule runs on weekends from March to November with more days during warmer months; see the website for details.

Sleeping

The tourist office has a list of B&Bs from around €25 per person.

Hotel de Keizerskroon (☎ 21 27 17; www.keizerskroonhoorn.nl; Breed 33; s/d from €70/90; ☜) Very much in the middle of things, this 25-room hotel-restaurant has rooms that have had a smart makeover. Its insulated windows afford a view of the bustling market streets below.

Hotel de Magneet (☎ 21 50 21; www.hoteldemagneet.nl; Kleine Oost 5D; s/d from €80/102; ☜) This family-run guesthouse lies in a quiet street just east of the old centre, and has a bar and restaurant. Rooms are large by Dutch standards, but are quite basic. The proximity to the coastal paths makes the hotel popular with cyclists.

Eating

Open-air markets are held on Wednesday (June to August) and Saturday (year round) along Breed.

Wormsbecher (☎ 21 44 08; Wijdebrugsteeg 2; snacks €3; ☙ 11am-6pm) Turquoise tiles front this classic fresh-fish shop, which is the perfect place to enjoy the locally loved smoked eel.

Vishandel Leen Parlevliet (snacks from €3, meals from €6; ☙ 10am-7pm) Next to the Hoofdtoren at the harbour, this small glass pod sells wonderful seafood rolls and bigger seafood meals.

De Waag Café-Restaurant (☎ 21 51 95; Rode Steen 8; mains €8-30) With pride of place on the main square in the stunning Waag building, this restaurant has always-popular outside tables and a bustling cafe. The restaurant is more formal and features top-notch takes on meaty Dutch staples.

Jozua's (☎ 21 31 15; West 52; mains €18-25; ☙ dinner Wed-Sun) Just southwest of the Rode Steen, this smart, modern restaurant excels at seafood, especially oysters. The frenetic pace of the open kitchen doesn't spill over to the intimate dining room.

De Hoornse Kogge (☎ 21 93 09; Nieuwendam 2; meals €25-40) The cafe tables lining the front have good views of harbour traffic chugging through the narrow entrance. Upstairs, the restaurant (dinner only) has a fine menu of modernised classics such as roasted pork, grilled fish and steaks.

Getting There & Around

Regular train services to/from Hoorn include the following:

Destination	Fare (€)	Duration (min)	Frequency (per hr)
Alkmaar	4.50	25	2
Amsterdam	7.30	40	2
Enkhuizen	3.70	22	2

See opposite for details of a heritage route to Medemblik and Enkhuizen run by Museum Stoomtram. The bus station is right outside Hoorn train station. Connexxion bus 135 goes twice hourly to Den Helder (one hour). Change buses at Den Oever for trips across the IJsselmeer towards Leeuwarden. Arriva bus 114 serves Edam (30 minutes, twice hourly).

Hire your bikes at the **bicycle shop** (☎ 21 70 96) just to the right as you exit Hoorn train station. National bike route LF21 runs 20km south to Edam and joins the LF15 for the 25km coastal run to Enkhuizen.

ENKHUIZEN
☎ 0228 / pop 18,200

Enkhuizen may be a small, quaint town in the present day but during the Golden Age its strategic harbour sheltered the Dutch merchant fleet. It slipped into relative obscurity in the late 17th century but now possesses one of the largest fleets on the IJsselmeer – of recreational vessels. For most travellers, however, Enkhuizen's biggest drawcard is the Zuiderzeemuseum, one of the country's finest.

Orientation

The train station is a terminus on the line to Amsterdam and stands on the southern edge of town. The yacht-filled Buitenhaven (Outer Harbour) and the narrower Oude Haven (Old Harbour) bisect the town east to west; canals ring the old centre. Dijk is the main cafe-and-restaurant strip, on the northern bank of Oude Haven. About 200m further north, the long, pedestrianised Westerstraat runs parallel and is lined with impressive historical buildings.

Information

Tourist office (☎ 31 31 64; www.vvvenkhuizen. nl; Tussen Twee Havens 1; 🕑 8am-5pm daily Jun-Aug, 8am-5pm Tue-Sat Sep-May) Just east of the train station; sells train and ferry tickets and a self-guided tour booklet in English (€1.50).

Sights & Activities
ZUIDERZEEMUSEUM

This captivating and amazing **museum** (☎ 35 11 11; www.zuiderzeemuseum.nl; adult/child €13/8, parking €5;

🕑 10am-5pm) consists of two parts: the open-air Buitenmuseum with more than 130 rebuilt and relocated dwellings and workshops, and an indoor Binnenmuseum, devoted to farming, fishing and shipping. The two parts lie about 300m from each other. To relieve congestion visitors are encouraged to leave their vehicles at a car park off the N302 at the south edge of town. A ferry (fare included in your ticket; every 15 minutes April to October) links the car park with the train station (look for the red and blue flags by the VVV) and the Buitenmuseum. Plan to spend a half-day for an unhurried visit to both sections.

The Buitenmuseum is worth the trip alone. Opened in 1983, it was carefully assembled from houses, farms and sheds trucked in from around the region to show Zuiderzee life as it was from 1880 to 1932. Every conceivable detail has been thought of, from the fence-top decorations and choice of shrubbery to the entire layout of villages, and the look and feel is certainly authentic. An illustrated guide (in English), included in the ticket price, is an essential companion on your tour of the entire museum.

Inhabitants wear traditional dress, and there are real shops such as a bakery, chemist and sweet shop. Workshops run demonstrations throughout the day. Though varying in character, the displays join seamlessly: lime kilns from Akersloot stand a few metres from Zuidende and its row of Monnickendam houses, originally built outside the dykes. Don't miss the **Urk quarter**, raised to simulate the island town before the Noordoostpolder was drained. For a special postmark, drop your letters at the old post office from Den Oever. The **Marker Haven** is a copy of the harbour built in 1830 on what was then the island of Marken. Note that while the grounds are open all year, there are activities here only from April to October.

Exit at the rear and walk 300m to reach the Binnenmuseum, which occupies a museum complex adjoining the **Peperhuis**, the former home and warehouse of a Dutch shipping merchant. The displays include a fine shipping hall: paintings, prints and other materials relating the rise and fall of the fishing industry, and the construction of the dykes. Here too are cultural artefacts, such as regional costumes, porcelain, silver and jewellery, that indicate the extent of Holland's riches at the time.

FROM THE STATION TO THE ZUIDERZEEMUSEUM

It is about a 2km walk from the train station to the Binnenmuseum along the waterfront. Along the way, between the Buitenhaven and the Oude Haven, the **Drommedaris** was built as a defence tower as part of the 16th-century town walls. Once a formidable prison, it now serves as an elevated meeting hall. Its clock-tower carillon still tinkles a playful tune on the hour.

Close by, the **Bottleship Museum** (☎ 31 85 83; Zuiderspui 1; adult/child €3/2; ☽ noon-5pm) has a surprisingly fascinating collection of ships in bottles carved by seamen through the ages. There are more than 1000 examples and a video shows the secret to their construction.

Follow Breedstraat north to the east end of Westerstraat where the 16th-century **Waag** (weigh-house) overlooks the old cheese market. Nearby is the classical **town hall**, modelled after the Amsterdam town hall that once stood on the Dam. You can peek through the windows at the lavish Gobelins and tapestries, but it's closed to the public.

OTHER SIGHTS

Moving east along Westerstraat you'll spy the remarkable **Westerkerk**, a 15th-century Gothic church with a removable wooden belfry. The ornate choir screen and imposing pulpit are worth a look. Opposite the church is the **Weeshuis**, a 17th-century orphanage with a sugary, curlicued portal.

The old harbour is chock-a-block with polished schooners, smacks and *tjalks* of a slower era, some of which are available for hire (p283). More modest skippers can hire kayaks, canoes and electric boats at **De Waterspiegel** (☎ 31 74 56; www.dewaterspiegel.com; Olifantsteiger 3; kayaks/canoes/electric boats per hr €5/7/15), mainly for use on the inner canals.

Sleeping

The tourist office has a list of private rooms from about €18.

Camping Enkhuizer Zand (☎ 31 72 89; www.camping enkhuizerzand.nl; Kooizandweg 4; camp sites from €15; ☽ Apr-Sep; ⛨) Next to the Zuiderzeemuseum, this popular site is a model of self-sufficiency with sandy beaches, tennis courts and a grocery store.

Hotel Garni RecuerDos (☎ 56 24 69; www.recuerdos .nl; Westerstraat 217; s/d €60/90; ☂) Owned by a warm and welcoming music-society patron, this stately manor house is the picture of calm,

with three immaculate rooms overlooking a manicured garden. Enjoy breakfast in the glassed-in conservatory.

Het Wapen van Enkhuizen (☎ 31 34 34; www .wapenvanenkhuizen.nl; Breedstraat 59; r €60-100) Close to the Zuiderzeemuseum and harbour is this small hotel, which is in the shadow of the town hall. Rooms are comfy, albeit with a dramatic striped motif; the best have bathtubs in the tiled bathrooms.

Stedemaagd Hotel (☎ 32 12 71; www.stedemaagd .nl; Spoorstraat 10-16; r from €80; ☂) A very appealing option 200m north of the train station along the waterfront. Rooms have vintage-style furniture in an art deco setting; bathrooms have Jacuzzis. The cafe downstairs is an excellent option for a pause whether you are staying here or not. It has a lovely terrace and long tables in the airy interior.

Eating

For a good cafe, try the Stedemaagd Hotel (above), which is on the waterfront.

Restaurant De Boei (☎ 31 42 80; Havenweg 5; mains around €20; ☽ lunch & dinner Mar-Oct) Occupying a peaceful corner near the harbour, De Boei is a place to head for excellent mussels and fine seafood. The menu always reflects what's fresh and it has a fine terrace on a balmy night.

Restaurant de Drie Haringhe (☎ 31 86 10; Dijk 28; mains €21-25; ☽ lunch Wed-Fri, dinner Wed-Sun) This upmarket locale excels in Dutch- and French-inspired cuisine, and has been receiving rave reviews for years. Comfortably ensconced in an old East India company warehouse, it has a lovely walled summer garden.

De Smederij (☎ 32 30 79; Breedstraat 158; meals from €30; ☽ dinner) Cute as a button, this cosy restaurant was actually once a forge. It has now been lavishly renovated although the interior still evokes its rough-edged past. Hearty Dutch standards are the perfect treat after you've spent the day pondering the past at the Zuiderzeemuseum.

Getting There & Away

For details on a fun and historical trip between Enkhuizen and Hoorn and Medemblik, see p156. The bus station behind Enkhuizen train station serves mainly local destinations.

BICYCLE

There is no bike shop in the station. Hoorn is 25km west along the coastal national routes LF15 and LF21.

DYKE ROAD

The N302 between Enkhuizen and Lelystad deserves a special mention because it runs along a 32km-long dyke, completed in 1976 as the first step of the reclamation of the Markerwaard (see boxed text, p169). As you get under way you'll pass below a high-tech causeway that connects Enkhuizen harbour with the IJsselmeer, with ships floating surreally over the motorway.

Sights are few along the route, apart from the boats bobbing on the IJsselmeer and a stone monument at the halfway mark in the form of a chain link symbolising the joining of West Friesland with Flevoland.

FERRY

The **Enkhuizen-Stavoren Ferry** (☎ 32 66 67; www .veerboot.nl; adult/child one-way €10/6.20; ⓨ mid-Apr–Oct) plies the IJsselmeer connecting Noord Holland with Freisland. The 90-minute trips depart once or twice daily from near the VVV, which sells tickets. Boats dock in Stavoren, which is on the train line to Leeuwarden via Sneek.

TRAIN

The Enkhuizen train station is an embarrassment. Services are nil, although you may be able to sweet talk the fine station cafe into storing your bags while you visit town. Buy train tickets from the coin machines or the VVV across the street. Regular train services to/from Enkhuizen:

Destination	Fare (€)	Duration (min)	Frequency (per hr)
Alkmaar	7.20	50	2
Amsterdam	9.80	60	2
Den Helder	11.10	90	2
Hoorn	3.70	22	2

For Alkmaar, change at Hoorn. For Den Helder connections mean a train change at both Hoorn and Heerhugowaard, which is inconvenient but the fastest option for public transport.

MEDEMBLIK

☎ 0227 / pop 7900

About 12km northwest of Enkhuizen lies Medemblik, the oldest port on the IJsselmeer, dating back to the 12th century and the Hanseatic League. It's not a pretty town but its busy harbour, old waterfront streets and medieval fortress are worth a few hours of your time.

Orientation & Information

The castle stands on the eastern side of town and is signposted from the harbour. The richly decorated facades on Kaasmarkt, Torenstraat, Nieuwstraat and along the Achterom canal are impressive. The old town is only 1km across and thus quickly absorbed.

Tourist office (☎ 54 28 52; www.vvv-medemblik.nl; Kaasmarkt 1; ⓨ 11am-4pm Mon-Sat Apr-Oct) A folksy all-in-one place, with a good stock of maps at the back of the local stationers, post office and tobacco store.

Sights & Activities

The pint-sized **Kasteel Radboud** (☎ 54 19 60; adult/child €5/3; ⓨ 11am-5pm Sat-Thu) at the head of the harbour is a more well-fortified mansion than the castle it once was. Built by Count Floris V in the 13th century to keep the feisty natives under his thumb, the fortress served as a prison before a 19th-century remodelling by Pierre Cuypers, the designer of Amsterdam's Rijksmuseum. The original floor plan has been preserved and the imposing **Ridderzaal** (Knights' Hall) still looks much as it did in the Middle Ages. The self-guided tour gives details of the castle's long history and the count's undoing.

Ever wondered what drove the industrial revolution? Part of the answer lies at the **Stoommachine Museum** (Steam Engine Museum; ☎ 54 47 32; Oosterdijk 4; adult/child €5.50/4.25; ⓨ 10am-5pm Tue-Sun mid-Feb–Oct), in the old pump station outside Medemblik. Thirty handsome old steam engines from Holland, England and Germany are fired up for demonstrations on various days; check the website for dates.

The **Museum Stoomtram** (p156) departs from the old train station for Hoorn.

Sleeping & Eating

You're best off making humble Medemblik a day trip.

Hotel Medemblik (☎ 54 38 44; www.hotelmedemblik .nl; Oosterhaven 1; r €70-130) Directly opposite the tourist office on one of the town's harbour canals is this shambling hotel with 26 rooms in various shapes and sizes. Remodelling is ongoing; in the meantime the terrace cafe is the best feature.

De Driemaster (☎ 54 30 20; Pekelharinghaven 49; mains €12-24; ⓨ lunch & dinner) Enjoy views of the harbour and IJsselmeer as you relish local fish while seated at the upstairs terrace. Watch large yachts drift under the drawbridge.

Getting There & Around

The NS train station is in Hoorn, from where bus 139 (twice hourly) makes the hour-long journey to Medemblik. Visit Enkhuizen via the Stoomtram boat (p156).

Ted de Lange (☎ 57 00 93; Vooreiland 1), on the eastern side of town, has a large selection of bicycles for hire. The national bike route LF21 runs south and east along dykes 21km to Enkhuizen.

DEN HELDER

☎ 0223

Before you reach Texel, the only attraction in the workmanlike naval town of Den Helder is the **Marine Museum** (☎ 65 75 34; Hoofdgracht 3; adult/child €6/3; ⏰ 10am-5pm Mon-Fri, noon-5pm Sat & Sun). It's housed in the vast former armoury of the Dutch Royal Navy. The display covers naval history mainly after 1815, the year the Netherlands became a kingdom. You can run rampant through several vessels moored on the docks outside, including an ironclad ram ship and a submarine left high and dry.

Driving through the town itself to/from the Texel ferry, the N250 passes a myriad of ships new and old that together form their own living maritime museum.

See p164 for information on trains to Den Helder and the ferry to Texel.

TEXEL

☎ 0222 / pop 13,700

Broad white beaches, lush nature reserves, forests and cute villages are the highlights of Texel, the largest and most visited of the Wadden Islands. About 3km north of the coast of Noord Holland, Texel (pronounced *tes*-sel) is 25km long and 9km wide. It actually consisted of two islands until 1835 when a spit of land to Eyerland Island was pumped dry.

Before the Noordzeekanaal opened in the 19th century, Texel was a main stop for ships en route to Asia, Africa and North America: the first trade mission to the East Indies began and ended here. It was also the scene of a spectacular maritime disaster: on Christmas day 1593, hurricane-force winds battered a merchant fleet moored off the coast and 44 vessels sank, drowning about a thousand seamen.

Texel relies chiefly on tourism, with the majority of visitors being either Dutch or German.

The local wool is highly prized and there are sheep everywhere, lazing, grazing or tippee-toeing along the dykes. It's the place to come if you want to find a beach – albeit a breezy beach – where you can wander for hours and not see a soul. Cyclists will be enchanted and there are just enough diversions – even a brewery – to keep you entertained for days on end.

Orientation

Ferries from the mainland dock at 't Horntje on the south side of the isle, from where buses head north to Texel's six main villages. Den Burg, 6km north of 't Horntje, is the island's modest capital and main shopping destination, while beachy De Koog, another 5km north again, is Texel's tourist heart with a distinctly tacky streak.

Cute Den Hoorn, only 5km northwest of the ferry terminal, is handy to tulip fields and windswept sand dunes. Oudeschild, 7km northeast of 't Horntje, has the best harbour facilities on the island, a fine museum and splendid fish restaurant. Oosterend, 6km northeast of Den Burg, is a quiet hamlet with distinctive architecture far from the water.

Tiny De Cocksdorp, at the northern end of the island, is a launch pad to the island of Vlieland (p235) and the rest of the Frisian Islands (see boxed text, p235). Beaches on the west coast are numbered by the kilometre from south to north.

Information

No one wants the local lifeblood – holiday-makers – to run short, so you'll find ATMs in every town. Den Burg has banks, bookshops, pharmacies and most other services.

Tourist office (☎ 31 47 41; www.texel.net; Emmalaan 66, Den Burg; ⏰ 9am-5.30pm Mon-Fri, 9am-5pm Sat) Signposted from the ferry terminal; on the southern fringe of town. Has free internet access, plenty of information, and staff can book accommodation for a fee.

Sights

DUINEN VAN TEXEL NATIONAL PARK

For many nature lovers this patchwork of varied dunescape running along the entire western coast of the island is the prime reason for visiting Texel. Salt fens and heath alternate with velvety, grass-covered dunes, and you'll find plants endemic to this habitat, such as the dainty marsh orchid or sea buckthorn, a ragged shrub with bright orange berries. Much of the area is bird sanctuary and accessible only

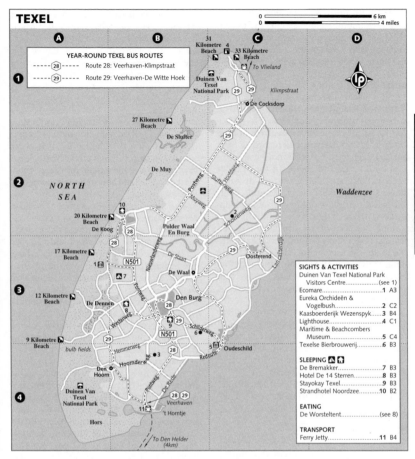

TEXEL

0 _____ 6 km
0 _____ 4 miles

YEAR-ROUND TEXEL BUS ROUTES
- - - 28 - - - Route 28: Veerhaven-Klimpstraat
- - - 29 - - - Route 29: Veerhaven-De Witte Hoek

31 Kilometre Beach
33 Kilometre Beach
To Vlieland
Duinen Van Texel National Park
Klimpstraat
De Cocksdorp

27 Kilometre Beach
De Slufter
De Muy
Postweg
Sluftermeer
Muyweg

N O R T H
S E A

Waddenzee

Schorrenweg
20 Kilometre Beach
De Koog
Polder Waal En Burg
17 Kilometre Beach
Nieuwlanderweg
De Staart
De Waal
Oosterend
Lancasterdijk

12 Kilometre Beach
De Dennen
Den Burg
Westerweg
Schilderweg
N501
Oudeschild
9 Kilometre Beach
bulb fields
Hemmerweg
Hoornderweg
Redoute

Den Hoorn
Pontweg
De Ruijt
Duinen Van Texel National Park
Veerhaven
't Horntje
Hors
To Den Helder (4km)

SIGHTS & ACTIVITIES
Duinen Van Texel National Park
  Visitors Centre.................(see 1)
Ecomare.................................1 A3
Eureka Orchideën &
  Vogelbush.........................2 C2
Kaasboerderij Wezenspyk.....3 B4
Lighthouse...........................4 C1
Maritime & Beachcombers
  Museum............................5 C4
Texelse Bierbrouwerij...........6 B3

SLEEPING
De Bremakker.......................7 B3
Hotel De 14 Sterren..............8 B3
Stayokay Texel.....................9 B3
Strandhotel Noordzee..........10 B2

EATING
De Worsteltent...................(see 8)

TRANSPORT
Ferry Jetty..........................11 B4

on foot. There is an excellent visitors centre located at Ecomare (right).

De Slufter became a brackish wetland after an attempt at land reclamation failed; when a storm breached the dykes in the early 1900s the area was allowed to flood and a unique ecosystem developed. To the south, **De Muy** is renowned for its colony of spoonbills that are monitored with great zeal by local naturalists.

Only a stone's throw from the windswept beach lies the dark, leafy forest of **De Dennen** between Den Hoorn and De Koog. Originally planted as a source of lumber, today it has an enchanting network of walking and cycling paths. In springtime the forest floor is carpeted with snowdrops that were first planted here in the 1930s.

ECOMARE
Initially created as a refuge for sick seals retrieved from the Waddenzee, **Ecomare** (☎ 31 77 41; www.ecomare.nl; Ruyslaan 92, De Koog; adult/child €9/6; ⏱ 9am-5pm) has expanded into a nature centre devoted to the preservation and understanding of Texel's wildlife. It has displays on Texel's development since the last ice age, islanders' interaction with the sea, large aquariums filled with fish from the Waddenzee and the North Sea (including sharks and sea skates), while outside there are marked nature trails.

The highlight for young and old, however, is the seals themselves. Their playful water ballet will delight all but the most jaded visitor. Try to catch feeding time at 11am or 3pm. Rescued birds are the other main tenants. The entire facility is impressive and despite the hype is definitely not a cheesy attraction. (Note that seals are rather delightfully called *zeehonden* in Dutch, which means 'sea dogs'.)

MUSEUMS
Local museums are a mixed bag, but the **Maritime & Beachcombers Museum** (☎ 31 49 56; Barentszstraat 21, Oudeschild; adult/child €6/4.50; ☉ 10am-5pm Tue-Sat, noon-5pm Sun) is a real winner. Its extraordinary variety of junk recovered from sunken ships and the shore is mind-boggling – and both tragic and comic. In the outdoor section there are demonstrations by rope-makers, fish-smokers and blacksmiths, while the indoor displays cover everything from underwater archaeology to windmill technology. Reede van Texel, which the museum translates accurately as Texel Roads, has nothing to do with asphalt but rather is a vast and amazingly detailed model of the shipping lanes and ports as they existed in the 17th century. Two hours will float away here just like a lost bottle at sea.

Texel's **lighthouse** (www.vuurtorentexel.nl; Vuurtorenweg 184, De Cocksdorp; admission €3) opened to visitors in 2009. Battered not just by storms but by war as well, this 45m crimson tower has views across the islands and shallow waters. The climb to the top is 153 steps.

Ecomare and the maritime museum are covered by the **CombiKaart** (adult/child €10.50/7.50) available from the tourist office.

OTHER SIGHTS
June is the time to see wild orchids on Texel, a rarity in the country; outside this month, dress lightly and head for the steamy **Eureka Orchideeën & Vogelbush** (☎ 31 83 64; www.eurekatexel .nl; Schorrenweg 20, Oosterend; ☉ 8.30am-6pm Mon-Fri, 8.30am-5pm Sat). Native orchid species can be viewed in all their tender, quivering glory alongside a menagerie of tropical birds in a large greenhouse. A large shop (silk orchids, oh dear) subsidises the free entrance.

The isle's brewery, the **Texelse Bierbrouwerij** (☎ 31 32 29; www.speciaalbier.nl; Schilderweg 214b, Oudeschild; tours adult/child €7/4) gives tours on an erratic schedule that may drive you to drink. Fortunately this former dairy has a terrace ideal for downing a few from the bar. The nine beers brewed here (try the bock) are widely available across Texel and are always worth ordering first.

Kaasboerderijk Wezenspyk (☎ 31 50 90; www .wezenspyk.nl; Hoondernweg 29), a small cheese farm between Den Hoorn and Den Burg, is the place to scoop up tasty rounds produced from the local cows, sheep and goats. Opening hours vary widely through the year so just drop by and see if you can cut the cheese.

Activities
Although summer can be balmy, don't count on it. One local exclaimed without a trace of irony: 'It's going to be hot! 20°C!' Winds and squalls can blow through off the North Sea all year, although at these times the island is at its most evocative and atmospheric. Goosebump fetishists rejoice!

The tourist office sells maps and booklets of **cycling routes** and **hiking trails** that criss-cross the island. There are several **horse-riding schools**, which operate between April and October. The well-marked 80km-long 'Texel Path' takes you through the dunes and over the mudflats before veering inland through the island's villages; the circular local routes along the way make for nice one- to three-hour hikes or bike trips. All the roads are suitable for bikes, and you can circumnavigate the island following the dykes in the east and the trails behind the dunes in the west.

Boat trips (leaving from Oudeschild) are conducted by shrimp trawlers such as the **Emmie TX 10** (☎ 31 36 39; www.garnalenvissen.nl; Oudeschild; adult/child €12/10; ☉ departs 10.30am & 2pm Mon-Sat). The two-hour trip around the island sails close to an endangered seal colony on the sandbanks. Some shrimp caught on the journey are prepared fresh for passengers. Other boats such as **Rival** (☎ 31 34 10; www.sportvissentexel .nl; anglers/observers €18/11) do outings for sports fishermen, complete with fishing equipment. If there's a late tide, some boats also go out at around 4.30pm.

Orion TX20 (☎ 0651 04 42 35, 31 36 39; www.robbentocht texel.nl; Oudeschild) explores the mudflats between Texel and Den Helder. Seal-spotting is usual. Prices vary and times depend on the tides.

Catamarans can be hired from **De Eilander** (☎ 0620 63 44 13; www.deeilander.nl; Paal 33, De Cocksdorp; catamaran hire per 5hr from €140; ☉ May-Oct) near the Vlieland boat dock. Five-hour sailing courses cost €145.

To gather your own beach treasure, board a horse-drawn wagon run by **Jutters Plezier** (☎ 31 62 25; www.juttersplezier.nl; De Cocksdorp; adult/child €10/6). The 1½-hour trips are really more

---

TEXEL'S BEACHES

Swimming, cycling, walking, boating, relaxing – Texel is an island to enjoy all these. Its pristine white beaches, lining the western shore in one unbroken ribbon, are numbered by the kilometre and marked with a *paal* (piling) from south to north.

The waters can be treacherous and lifeguards are on duty in summer from No 9 southeast of Den Hoorn to No 21 near De Koog. One told us they compete to see who has the fewest drownings (!).

No matter how crowded the island, with a little hiking you can always find a stretch of deserted sand. Among the notable beaches are the following:

- No 9 – Uncrowded, and popular with locals and nudists.
- No 12 – Uncrowded, with a sheltered cafe.
- No 17 – The party beach, where teens are on the make and there's always a groovy vibe.
- No 20 – Right in front of the tourist enclave of De Koog, and rather built up.
- No 27 – Another fairly isolated beach popular with nudists.
- No 31 – Near the lighthouse; no swimming due to treacherous rip tides but lots of wind sports.
- No 33 – Also no swimming, but lots of beach sports and occasional seal-spotting.

---

for the journey than the treasure, and end at the owner's private residence for a round of herbal schnapps. Tours (minimum 15 people) depart from the lighthouse – check with the tourist office for times.

Tessel Air (☎ 31 14 36; www.paracentrumtexel.nl; Texel Airport) offers pleasure flights over Texel from €38 per person (15-minute flight, minimum two people), and for a bit more cash they'll explore the other Wadden Islands. To really feel the wind in your face, try a tandem jump (€210 per jump); it includes all the thrill of free fall without the fear of screwing things up.

For nylon-attached adventure closer to ground, **Kite Surf School Texel** (☎ 0610 97 19 92; www.kitesurfschooltexel.nl; De Koog; lessons from €95) offers all manner of kite- and windsurfing lessons and rentals.

Festivals & Events

Lammetjes Wandeltrocht (Lamb Walking Route) Easter. Popular walk around the island, attracting plenty of mainland Dutch and other baaaaaad folk.

Ronde om Texel (www.roundtexel.com) Mid-June. The largest catamaran race in the world; spectators line the beaches for hours on end watching boats jive back and forth on the sea.

Sleeping & Eating

There are 46,000 beds on the island, but it's essential to book ahead, especially in July and August. De Koog has by far the most options, but hamlets such as Den Hoorn or De Cocksdorp are more peaceful and relaxing.

The tourist office has a list of B&Bs from around €25 per person per night; otherwise hit the VVV website (www.texel.net) or pick up a copy of *Texel Holiday Guide* and strike out on your own. Note that prices drop in the low season (October to April) when island life slips into a lower gear. Texel's 11 main camping grounds teem in summer; the tourist office can tell you which ones have vacancies. Many farms also offer rooms and camp sites.

With more than 27,000 sheep roaming the island, lamb naturally gets top billing on the menu, but seafood comes a close second. Asparagus season in the spring brings forth oodles of scrumptious local spears.

DEN BURG

Stayokay Texel (☎ 31 54 41; www.stayokay.com; Haffelderweg 28, Den Burg; dm €24-30, r €47-70) Texel's HI hostel has 240 beds in clean, colourful rooms, and has a cafe on-site. You can rent bikes; the beach is 6km away.

Hotel De 14 Sterren (☎ 32 26 81; www.14sterren .nl; Smitsweg 4, Den Burg; r €60-75) You couldn't wish for a nicer spot than this place, on the edge of De Dennen forest. Each of its 14 rooms is decorated in warm Mediterranean hues, and most have a terrace or balcony with garden views. The attached bistro, De Worsteltent (mains €15 to €25; open lunch and dinner), brings fine dining to a barnhouse.

Texel Yurts (☎ 32 21 00; www.texelyurts.nl; De Ruyterstraat 36, Den Burg; 2-person yurt per 3 nights €375) Feel the creak of the wind in your own fabric-sided yurt set in a shady clearing near town.

Taveerne De Twaalf Balcken (☎ 31 26 81; Weverstraat 20, Den Burg; mains €12-20; ☽ lunch & dinner) The 'Tavern of the 12 Beams' is a locals' haunt that specialises in lamb dishes and cosy ambience. The front section is dark and subdued – perfect for sipping away on one of the many Trappist beers on offer, while the rear conservatory is light and airy.

Freya (☎ 32 16 86; Gravenstraat 4, Den Burg; set menu €25; ☽ dinner Tue-Sat) This petite restaurant serves outstanding French and Dutch cuisine, so it's no surprise that reservations are a must. The hosts are warm and welcoming, and you're never sure what treats await on the blackboard.

Timmer (☎ 31 32 02; Hogerstraat 4; treats from €1) Don't leave town without a bag of the addictive handmade cookies from Timmer.

DE COCKSDORP

This village has a large grocery store and a few cafes along its tidy low-key streets.

't Anker (☎ 31 62 74; www.t-anker.texel.com; Kikkertstraat 24, De Cocksdorp; s/d €45/88) This small, family-run hotel is full of charm and cheer, and has basic yet comfy rooms set behind a stolid brick facade. Its lush garden is just an appetiser for the Roggesloot nature reserve close by.

DEN HOORN

Bij Jef (☎ 31 96 23; www.bijjef.nl; Herenstraat 34, Den Hoorn; s/d from €75/100; ☜) The nine simple, yet stylish, rooms here come with a bath tub, views of the countryside, and a sun-drenched balcony. However the real star is the sumptuous restaurant (menus from €55; open lunch and dinner) which has an ever-changing menu created from local produce, meats and seafood. Try for a garden table.

DE KOOG

The main drag of Dorpstraat, Texel's tourist haven, is lined with cheap chipperies, bistros of uncertain provenance and the island's only gaggle of boisterous bars.

De Bremakker (☎ 31 28 63; www.bremakker.nl; Templierweg 40; camp site €29, chalets per week from €285; ☽ Apr-Oct) This leafy and serene camping ground is situated between Den Burg and De Koog at the forest's edge, about 1km from the beach. There's a laundry and snack bar, plus sports facilities.

Hotel Ouwe Dijkstra Texel (☎ 31 79 06; www .hotelcafe-ouwedijkstra.nl; Nikadel 5; r €55-90; ☜) The

bargain of town, if you don't mind sleeping above a merry bar and a raucous nightclub. The 12 rooms share bathrooms but are spotless. Get one at the back away from the merriment.

Strandhotel Noordzee (☎ 31 73 65; www.noordzee .nu; Badweg 200; r per 3 nights from €400) This is the only hotel directly on Texel's sandy beaches. Its 10 rooms lack colour and flair, but they're suitably comfy, and several have sweeping balcony views of the North Sea.

Quinty's (☎ 31 74 72; Dorpsstraat 147; meals €8-30) The best dining on the strip; try a steak or something with shrimp. Small plates of little delights are a good companion to the long list of swanky cocktails.

OUDESCHILD

our pick Van Der Star (☎ 31 24 41; Heemskerckstraat 13, Oudeschild; meals €5-12, mains €5-8; ☽ 11am-9pm) The island's best fish is served at this seafood counter. The seafood soup is a garlicky delight while the many choices of smoked fish are simply sublime. An array of items fresh off the boats in the nearby harbour are available prepared in many ways. Seating is basic – go for a plastic chair on the terrace.

OOSTEREND

Rôtisserie Kerckeplein (☎ 31 89 50; Oesterstraat 6, Oosterend; mains €25-40; ☽ dinner Wed-Sun) This cosy restaurant has got cooking local lamb down to a fine art, with seven choices in this category alone. You can sit in the loft and wash it all down with a dark Texels Speciaalbier. In high season it serves lunch – enjoy on the small front terrace.

Getting There & Away

Trains from Amsterdam to Den Helder (€13, 75 minutes, twice hourly) are met by a bus that whisks you to the awaiting car ferry.

Teso (☎ 36 96 00; www.teso.nl; adult/child/car return €3/1.50/35) runs a service from Den Helder to 't Horntje. The crossing aboard the huge ferries takes 20 minutes and leaves at 30 minutes past the hour between 6.30am and 9.30pm; returning boats leave on the hour between 6am and 9pm. On some summer days there's a service every half-hour – check the timetable to be sure. If you're driving in high season, show up at the docks 15 to 30 minutes before departure as there'll be a queue.

For details on the ferry to car-free Vlieland, see p235.

Getting Around

Connexxion (☎ 0900 9292) operates two bus routes (28 and 29) on the island throughout the year, and supplements this with two more during summer months; day passes cost €5 from the bus driver. Bus 28 links 't Horntje with Den Burg (seven minutes) and De Koog (another 15 minutes) before returning via the Ecomare museum, while bus 29 starts at the ferry jetty and goes to Den Hoorn and Den Burg before snaking its way along the eastern shore to De Cocksdorp via Oudeschild and Oosterend. Summer-only bus 827 links De Koog with De Cocksdorp, while bus 26 is nearly a clone of 28. Buses tend to run hourly, roughly during daylight hours (which means 10pm in summer).

The welter of bicycle shops includes **Zegel** (☎ 31 21 50; Parkstraat 14, Den Burg), which charges €6.50/26 for touring bikes per day/week. Near the ferry terminal, **Verhuur Heijne** (☎ 31 95 88; Pontweg 2, 't Horntje) charges similar rates.

Taxi Botax (☎ 31 58 88; www.taxibotaxtexel.com) takes you between the ferry terminal and any destination on the island, including Den Burg (€10), De Koog (€19) and De Cocksdorp (€28). Book in advance.

AALSMEER

☎ 0297

This town is home to the world's biggest **flower auction** (☎ 39 39 39; www.vba-aalsmeer.nl; Legmeerdijk 131; adult/child €5/3; ☑ 7-11am Mon-Fri) and is run by a vast posy conglomerate named FloraHolland. Make sure you're in the viewing gallery before 9am to catch the best action as the flower-laden carts go to auction. Selling is conducted – surprise! – by Dutch auction, with a huge clock showing the starting price. From the starting bell, the hand keeps dropping until someone takes up the offer and a deal is struck. There's a self-guided audio tour that will let you peek into the auction rooms and see arrangers prepping the blooms for display.

The auction takes place in Europe's largest commercial complex (one million sq metres), and one look at the parking lot and truck fleets will tell you why so much space is necessary. Some 90 million flowers and two million plants change hands here every single day. More and more transactions are taking place online, so catch the action while it's still here. Monday is the busiest time, Thursday the quietest.

Take Connexxion bus 172 from Amsterdam Centraal Station to the Aalsmeer VBA stop (50 minutes, four times hourly).

MUIDEN

☎ 0294 / pop 3400

An ideal quick jaunt by bike from Amsterdam, Muiden is an unhurried historical town renowned for its red-brick castle, the Muiderslot. It's an idealised form of a castle and if you built it at the beach you'd be happy. Life otherwise focuses on the busy central lock that funnels scores of pleasure boats out into the vast IJsselmeer.

Sights

The town's draw is the **Muiderslot** (Muiden Castle; ☎ 25 62 62; www.muiderslot.nl; Herengracht 1; adult/child €11/6.25; ☑ 10am-4pm Mon-Fri, noon-5pm Sat & Sun Apr-Oct, noon-4pm Sat & Sun Nov-Mar), a fortress built in 1280 by the ambitious count Floris V, son of Willem II. The castle was one of the first in Holland to be equipped with round towers, a French innovation. The popular count was also a champion of the poor and a French sympathiser, two factors that were bound to spell trouble; Floris was imprisoned in 1296 and murdered while trying to flee.

In the 17th century historian PC Hooft entertained some of the century's greatest writers, artists and scientists here, a group famously known as the Muiderkring (Muiden Circle). Today it's the most visited castle in the country, with precious furnishings, weapons and Gobelin hangings designed to re-create Hooft's era. The interior can be seen only on guided tours; tours may be partly improvised in English. Reserve ahead if you want an English-only tour.

Off the coast lies a derelict fort on the island of **Pampus** (☎ 26 23 26; www.pampus.nl; adult/child ferry & guided tour €14/10; ☑ Apr-Oct). This massive 19th-century bunker was a key member of a ring of 42 fortresses built to defend Amsterdam. Rescued from disrepair by Unesco, the facility now receives preservation funds as a World Heritage site. Ferries to Pampus depart from Muiderslot port at 10.30am, 12.30pm and 2.30pm May through to September. It operates weekends only April and October.

Activities

You won't find a better area on the IJsselmeer for boating and windsurfing. The **Watersportcentrum Muiderberg** (☎ 0651 07 42 36;

www.wscmuiderberg.nl; (🕑 Apr–mid-Oct) rents small sailboats for two to four people (from €35 per day) as well as windsurfing boards and canoes (€5 to €10 per hour) in Muiderberg, 3.5km from Muiden. The shop isn't signposted, but seek out the harbourmaster and ask.

Eating & Drinking

Café Ome Ko (☎ 0294-26 13 30; cnr Herengracht & Naardenstraat; 🕑 8am-2am) In warm weather the clientele of this little bar with the big green-striped awnings turns the street outside into one big party. When there's no party on, the cafe is a perfect spot to watch the comings and goings through the busy lock right outside.

Getting There & Away

Connexxion bus 157 links Muiden with Amsterdam's Amstel station (20 minutes, twice hourly). Twice hourly bus 110 links the town with the train station at Weesp (15 minutes), Muiderberg (five minutes) and Naarden (15 minutes).

National bike route LF20 passes by Amsterdam's Leidseplein. Follow it east for 7km until it passes under the A10 and look for the start of the LF23 route. Cross the canal and follow the LF23 for 9km through parklands and over bridges southeast to Muiden.

HET GOOI

Along the slow-moving Vecht River southeast of Amsterdam lies Het Gooi, a shady woodland speckled with lakes and heath. In the 17th century this 'Garden of Amsterdam' was a popular retreat for wealthy merchants, and nature-hungry urbanites still flock to its leafy trails to hike and cycle today. The area's main centre is Hilversum, a one-time commuter town given a fresh start by the Dutch public-funded broadcast networks, which have their headquarters here. Naarden, on the Gooimeer to the north, has an intriguing fortress.

Naarden

☎ 035 / pop 17,000

Naarden would be just another satellite town to the capital if it wasn't for the remarkable fortress, Naarden-Vesting, on its northwest border. This military work of art is best seen from the air: a 12-pointed star, with arrowheads at each tip. This defence system, one of the best preserved in the country, was – like closing a barn door after the horse has bolted – built only after the Spanish massacred the

inhabitants in the 16th century. The bastions were staffed by the Dutch army until the 1920s, although its strategic importance had already paled before WWI. Today the walled town of Naarden-Vesting is an upmarket enclave with fine restaurants, galleries and antique shops.

INFORMATION

Tourist office (☎ 694 28 36; www.vvvnaarden .nl; Adriaan Dortsmanplein 1b; 🕑 10am-2pm Sat, also 10am-3pm Tue-Fri May–mid-Sep) In the old barracks; has an English-language self-guided walking tour of the town and accommodation information. There's good parking right outside.

SIGHTS & ACTIVITIES

Most of Naarden-Vesting's quaint little houses date from 1572, the year the Spaniards razed the place during their colonisation of Noord Holland. The bloodbath led by Don Frederick of Toledo is commemorated by a stone tablet on the building at Turfpoortstraat 7.

The **Vestingmuseum** (Fortress Museum; ☎ 694 54 59; Westwalstraat 6; adult/child €5.50/3; 🕑 10.30am-5pm Tue-Fri, noon-5pm Sat & Sun Mar-Oct, noon-5pm Sun Nov-Feb) brings context to this vast star-shaped fortress, which is thought to be the only one in Europe featuring a buffer of two walls and two moats. You can stroll around on the rolling battlements before descending into the casements for glimpses of a cramped soldier's life.

It's easy to spot the tall tower of the fort's central **Grote Kerk** (☎ 694 98 73; www.grotekerknaarden .nl; Markstraat 13; admission free; 🕑 10.30am-4.30pm Tue-Sat, 1.30-4.30pm Sun & Mon mid-Jun–Sep), a Gothic basilica with stunning 16th-century vault paintings of biblical scenes. You can climb the tower (265 steps) for a good view of the leafy Gooi and the Vecht River. Organ concerts (admission €5) are held throughout the year.

The 17th-century Czech educational reformer, Jan Amos Komensky (Comenius), is buried here in the Waalse Kapel. His life and work are related next door at the **Comenius Museum** (☎ 694 30 45; Kloosterstraat 33; adult/child €3.50/2.50; 🕑 noon-5pm Tue-Sun).

Enjoyable 45-minute **boat tours** (adult/child €6/4; 🕑 1-4pm Apr-Sep) around the moat depart from Nieuwe Haven.

SLEEPING & EATING

Sleeping inside the walls is more of a challenge than you'd think. Ask at the tourist office about B&Bs. However, top-notch eateries abound.

Jachthaven (☎ 695 60 50; www.thuishavens.nl; Onderwal 4; huts from €35) There's no camping ground or hostel close to Naarden, but you can book one of the basic *trekkershutten* (hikers huts) for up to four people at the yacht harbour. They're in a corner of the marina near a leafy recreation area, with hundreds of boats to view and a restaurant on-site. Take bus 110 to Jachthaven (five minutes).

Passionata (☎ 678 24 16; Marktstraat 31; snacks from €3; ☽ 10am-6pm Mon-Sat) This stylish Italian deli is the perfect source for picnic supplies you can then enjoy out on the town walls.

Fine (☎ 694 48 68; Marktstraat 66; mains €20-25) A cosy bar and restaurant, this fine choice features canalside dining and regular art exhibitions. The menu highlights local seafood, and mussels in season.

Promers (☎ 694 25 87; www.promers.nl; Dortsmanplein 3; mains €20-25; ☽ dinner Mon-Sat) Hidden deep in the town's walls, Promers surprises by opening up out the back to two intimate lavender-scented gardens. And that's not the only surprise: the open kitchen produces some truly stellar food on a changing menu of dishes created from locally sourced produce.

GETTING THERE & AWAY

There are direct trains between Amsterdam Centraal Station and Naarden-Bussum (€4.40, 25 minutes, twice hourly). From the station, bus 110 (five minutes, twice hourly) runs to the fortress, otherwise it's a pleasant 20-minute walk. Bus 110 continues on to Muiden (15 minutes) and finally Weesp (30 minutes).

National bike route LF23 passes right through Naarden-Vesting and is an ideal way to explore the extents of the star-shaped moat and nearby waters of the Gooimeer. The fort at Muiden is 11km northwest on the LF23.

Hilversum
☎ 035 / pop 84,500

Suburban Hilversum is best known to the Dutch as the national broadcasting centre. Its compact centre has a boffo attraction for 20th-century architecture buffs. Otherwise it's leafy, peaceful and skippable.

ORIENTATION & INFORMATION

The few attractions are in or near the pedestrianised centre, which is immediately west of the train station. Ringed by a street network

defined by the old city walls, the centre of Hilversum measures about 1.5km across and is easy to navigate.

Tourist office (☎ 629 28 10; www.vvvhilversum.nl; Kerkbrink 6; ☽ 10am-5pm Mon-Sat, 11am-5pm Sun) Signposted from the train station; in the heart of town. It has several excellent walking brochures in English.

SIGHTS & ACTIVITIES

Architecture buffs flock to Hilversum to see the legacy of Willem Dudok (1884–1974), the architect who shaped the city in the early 20th century. Nearly 100 buildings in Hilversum bear Dudok's stamp; the tourist office has a fine walking guide to his buildings. Most are easy to spot as they bear the unmistakable mark of Frank Lloyd Wright and the Prairie School, to which Dudok gave a Dutch modernist interpretation.

The pièce de résistance is the striking, modernist **Raadhuis** (Town Hall; Dudokpark 1; tours adult/child €5/3), 700m west of the train station and the epitome of Dudok's work. The fabulous interior, with its simple, elegant lines that recall both Wright and the Bauhaus movement, is a must for any architecture fan. The tower, restored in 1996, is stunning in its symmetry and inventive arrangement of horizontal and vertical brick. Inside is the **Dudok Dependence** (☎ 629 28 26; adult/child €2/free; ☽ noon-4.30pm Wed & Sun), which holds regular architecture exhibitions. Tours of the Raadhuis take place at 2pm on Sunday. At other times ask the guard to let you walk the halls.

Beeld en Geluid (Sound & Vision; ☎ 677 55 55; Sumatralaan 45, Media Park; adult/child €11/7.50; ☽ 10am-9pm Tue-Sun) tells the history of Dutch TV and radio going back to 1919. Housed in an arresting polychromatic building (think TV static), it takes a Disney approach to explaining the shows you may not have grown up with: it's aimed at a purely Dutch audience. It is just west of the Hilversum-Noord train station or 1.5km north of the town centre on bus 103.

EATING

Amid the cacophony of post-Dudok architectural squalor in the centre are numerous cafes where you can take a break.

Benk (☎ 623 33 61; Kerkbrink 2; meals €8-25) Occupying a sunny corner of the main square is this modern bistro. Benk's simple lunch offerings are a winner with locals, and its more complex dinner menu is a fine appetiser for the bar's cocktails. On sunny days, choose from two inviting terraces.

GETTING THERE & AROUND

Direct train services to/from Hilversum include the following:

Destination	Fare (€)	Duration (min)	Frequency (per hr)
Amsterdam	4.90	26	1
Naarden-Bussum	1.70	5-8	6
Utrecht	3.40	20	4

Bus 107 goes from the train station to the Raadhuis and Dudok Dependence (five minutes).

The train station rents bikes. Naarden-Vesting is 9km north along the bike paths along the N524.

Around Hilversum

In Laren, which is 5km northeast of Hilversum, the **Singer Museum** (☎ 539 39 39; www.singerlaren.nl; Oude Drift 1; adult/child €12/free; ☼ 11am-5pm Tue-Sun) houses a splendid changing collection of Dutch and foreign paintings, mostly modernist and Impressionist works from 1880 to 1950. Take bus 109 from Hilversum train station to Laren Kermisterrein (20 minutes, four hourly). It's a straight shot of the bike paths of the N525.

FLEVOLAND

Flevoland, the Netherlands' 12th and youngest province, is a masterpiece of Dutch hydro-engineering. In the early 1920s an ambitious scheme went ahead to reclaim more than 1400 sq km of land – an idea mooted as far back as the 17th century. The completion of the Afsluitdijk (see the boxed text, opposite) paved the way for the creation of Flevoland. Ringed dykes were erected, allowing water to be pumped out at a snail-like pace. Once part of Overijssel province, the Noordoostpolder was inaugurated in 1942, followed by the Eastern Flevoland (1957) and Southern Flevoland (1968). First residential rights were granted to workers who'd helped in reclamation and to farmers, especially those from Zeeland, who lost everything in the great flood of 1953.

The cities that sprang up bring to mind anything but the Golden Age. The main hubs – Almere, Lelystad and Emmeloord – are grindingly dull places, laid out in unrelieved grid

patterns. However, Lelystad has some good attractions and other highlights include the old fishing villages Urk and Schokland, and the bird-filled nature reserve of Oostvaardersplassen.

LELYSTAD

☎ 0320 / pop 74,000

With unattractive modern architecture dominating its disjointed sprawl, Lelystad, the capital of Flevoland province, is a good example of urban planning gone awry. The main reason for visiting this expanse of steel and concrete is its three museums, which will keep parents and their hangers-on entertained for hours.

Orientation

Most shops and restaurants are in the pedestrianised knot of streets opposite the station; the key museums are a short bus ride west on the IJsselmeer shore.

Sights

Lelystad's two big sights, the Batavia exhibit and Nieuw Land museum, are next to Bataviastad, a mock fort containing a huge outlet shopping centre 3km west of the train station. A combined ticket to both costs €12/6 per adult/child, and bus F (10 minutes, two to four hourly) connects the museums with the train station. Everything here is huge, even for the largest crowds. The parking system is infernal; it's accessed from the N302 as it heads across the IJsselmeer.

Bataviawerf (Batavia Yard; ☎ 26 14 09; Oostvaardersdijk 1-9; adult/child €9/4.50; ☼ 10am-5pm) is home to a replica of a 17th-century Dutch merchant frigate, the *Batavia,* which took 10 years to reconstruct. The original was a 17th-century *Titanic* – big, expensive and supposedly unsinkable. True to comparison, the *Batavia,* filled to the brim with cannon and goods for the colonies, went down in 1629 on its maiden voyage off the west coast of Australia. The replica, however, redeemed its predecessor in 2000 by sailing around the Pacific.

There's ample evidence of the era's wealth on the upper decks, where you'll see carved wooden likenesses of merchant seamen and a gold-leaf lantern above the captain's quarters. Little imagination is required, however, to grasp how punishing a sailor's life could be, especially for those who broke the rules: stealing a loaf of bread might merit a month's confinement in a cramped hole so constructed that it was impossible to either sit or stand upright.

KEEPING THE RELENTLESS SEA AT BAY

The Netherlands' coastline originally extended as far as the sandy beaches of Texel (p160) and its Frisian Island companions (p234). The relentless sea, however, never seemed to be in agreement with such borders, and by the end of the 13th century storms had washed sea water over flimsy land barriers and pushed it far inland. The end result was the creation of the Zuiderzee (literally South Sea).

The ruling Dutch had for centuries dreamed of draining the Zuiderzee to reclaim the huge tracts of valuable farmland. The seafaring folk of the villages lining the sea were of a different opinion, even though the shallow Zuiderzee constantly flooded their homes and businesses, and often took lives with it. A solution needed to be found, and the only way to tame the waves, it seems, was to block them off.

A huge dyke was proposed as early as the mid-17th century, but it wasn't until the late 19th century, when new engineering techniques were developed, that such a dyke could become reality. Engineer Cornelis Lely, who lent his name to Lelystad, was the first to sketch out a retaining barrier. A major flood in 1916 set the plan in motion, and construction began in 1927. Fishermen worried about their livelihood, and fears that the Wadden Islands would vanish in the rising seas were voiced, and while the former concerns were legitimate, the latter proved unfounded.

In 1932 the Zuiderzee was ceremoniously sealed off by the Afsluitdijk (Barrier Dyke), an impressive dam (30km long and 90m wide) that links the provinces of Noord Holland and Friesland. The water level remained relatively steady, but the fishing industry was effectively killed as the basin gradually filled with fresh water from the river IJssel – the IJsselmeer was born. However, vast tracts of land were created, and were soon turned into arable *polders* (strips of farmland separated by canals). A second barrier between Enkhuizen and Lelystad was completed in 1976 – creating the Markermeer – with the idea of ushering in the next phase of land reclamation, but the plan was shelved because of cost and environmental concerns.

For more information on this vast human endeavour, spend some time at Lelystad's Nieuw Land museum (below), which details the land reclamation.

The huge wooden skeleton alongside belongs to the *Seven Provinces*, a replica of Admiral Michiel de Ruijter's massive 17th-century flagship that's scheduled for completion in 2015. You can watch the craftsmen using old techniques for the re-creation. In a separate building on the northern perimeter, the Netherlands Institute for Maritime Archaeology displays the remains of a 2000-year-old Roman ship found near Utrecht.

Nearly half of the Netherlands was created by Brobdingnagian land reclamations. **Nieuw Land** (☎ 26 07 99; Oostvaardersdijk 1-13; adult/child €7/3.50; ☑ 10am-5pm Tue-Fri, 11.30am-5pm Sat & Sun, also 10am-5pm Mon Jul & Aug) has exhibits about *polder* reclamation aimed at kids, who can build model bridges or dams, and navigate ships through locks.

No expense has been spared for **Luchtvaart Themapark Aviodrome** (☎ 289 98 40; www.aviodrome.nl; Dakotaweg 11a; adult/child €16/14; ☑ 10am-5pm Tue-Sun). This huge museum has 70 historical aircraft on display, including a replica of the Wright Brother's 1902 Flyer, Baron von Richthofen's WWI triplane, a Spitfire and a huge KLM

747. You can also play air-traffic controller in a re-created flight tower or watch aviation films in the megacinema. It's at Lelystad Airport 4km east of town (bus 148 from the train station).

Sleeping & Eating

Lelystad is neither blessed with good hotels or great restaurants; visit the town on a day trip. The vast plaza by Nieuw Land has a few cafes.

Getting There & Away

Lelystad station is the terminus of trains coming from the south; services include Amsterdam (€8.80, 40 minutes, two hourly). From other places, change trains in Weesp. A new line linking Lelystad to Kampen and Zwolle is set to open in 2012.

Flevoland has poor regional bus services. Bus 150 goes from Lelystad station to Enkhuizen via the IJsselmeer dyke road N302 (35 minutes, every two hours). Bus 143 goes east to Kampen in Overijssel (one hour, every half-hour).

The national bike route LF20 starts near Muiden and then runs across the reclaimed *polder* 44km to Lelystad before veering off to the waterfront and the museums. From here it continues northeast to Urk.

OOSTVAARDERSPLASSEN NATURE RESERVE

Between Lelystad and Almere lies the marshy realm of Oostvaardersplassen, a 6000-hectare reserve of mostly swampy lake that developed virtually by accident. When Flevoland province opened in 1968 this area was earmarked for an industrial estate, but the planners dawdled and nature stepped in. A virgin landscape of reeds, willows and rough grasslands emerged.

Today it's a bird sanctuary of international repute with a formidable variety of species. Great white egrets, cormorants and spoonbills can be seen nesting, and lucky visitors may also catch a glimpse of endangered species such as the white-tailed eagle. Illustrated boards around the park help to identify what appears in your sights.

You'll also see quirky mammals such as the conic (a docile pony), the horned heck cattle, as well as red deer, all of which serve as lawn mowers on the meadows around the perimeter.

Entry into the marsh itself isn't allowed, but the next best thing is a visit to De Kluut observation hut on the northeastern edge of the reserve. The various hiking and bicycle paths begin here, including a 35km route around the entire lake. The Schollevaar observation post near a cormorant colony can only be visited with a park ranger.

The **visitors centre** (☎ 0320-25 45 85; Kitsweg 1; ◷ 10am-5pm Tue-Sun Apr-Oct, 10am-4pm Tue-Sun Nov-Mar) has hiking maps.

Getting There & Away

Public transport to the park is nonexistent. To get to the visitors centre by car from Amsterdam, drive the A6 north and take exit No 10 towards Lelystad on the N302 and take a left after 5km onto Buizardweg (also signposted 'Oostvaardersplassen'). By bike, the visitors centre is just off the LF20, 7km southwest of Lelystad.

URK

☎ 0527 / pop 18,100

This pious village was once a proud little island (not unlike Marken across the IJsselmeer), home to a sizeable fishing fleet and an important signal post for ships passing into the North Sea. In the 1940s Urk reluctantly

joined the mainland when the surrounding Noordoostpolder was pumped dry, and even today some locals pine for the isolation of island life, as tough as it obviously was.

Although now cut off from the North Sea, the town is still a centre of the seafood industry, a holdover from the days when its fleet sailed into the open Zuiderzee. Everything worth seeing sits on and near the knoll with the old town, otherwise Urk is surrounded by irksome modern housing developments.

You'll see dozens of historical fishing boats moored around the harbour, including the brown-sailed *botters* with gleaming wooden hulls and oversized leeboards. At the western end of town, take the coastal walk around the lighthouse for a pinch of local folklore. Just 70m off the shore lies the **Ommelebommelestien**, a slippery rock said to be the birthplace of all native Urkers. Legend also has it that, far from receiving the delivery by stork, dad had to take a rowboat to pick up his newborn.

The supports of the village church, **Kerkje aan de Zee** (Peter Salebienplein), are made entirely out of masts of VOC (Dutch East India Company) ships that brought back exotic goods from the East Indies. Inside are ship models and, at times, haunting recitals by the choir. Nearby you'll find the **Fishermen's Monument**, a lonely statue of a woman in a billowing dress gazing seaward where her loved ones were lost. Marble tablets around the perimeter list the Urk seafarers who never returned – name, age and ship's ID number – with new names still being added.

Just below the town's lighthouse is **Restaurant De Kaap** (☎ 68 15 09; www.dekaap-urk .nl; Wijk 5; mains €10-15), *the* place to sample Urk specialities, such as smoked gurnard, while taking in gorgeous views of the harbour and IJsselmeer. The interior is richly decorated with maritime ornaments.

Bus 141 runs between Urk and Zwolle several times an hour (1¼ hours). On Sunday there's only a handful of buses, starting in the late afternoon.

Urk is 34km northwest of Lelystad on the national bike route LF20. Zwolle in Overijssel is 50km southeast on the LF15, a scenic ride of dykes, rivers and Schokland.

SCHOKLAND

☎ 0527

A bleak variation on the island theme, the community of Schokland eked out an existence for hundreds of years on a long, narrow strip of land in the Zuiderzee. By the mid-19th century the clock had run out: fish prices plummeted and vicious storms were literally eroding the island away. The plucky locals hung on, despite the appalling living conditions, prompting Willem III to order their removal in 1859. Schokland was eventually swallowed up by the Noordoostpolder in the 20th century, just like Urk.

Now a Unesco World Heritage site, the **Schokland Museum** (☎ 25 13 96; www.schokland.nl; Middelbuurt 3; adult/child €4/3; ☼ 11am-5pm Tue-Sun Apr-Oct, daily Jul & Aug, Fri-Sun Nov-Mar) affords glimpses into this tortured past. The island's heritage is described in detail with a good historical slide presentation in English. Views from the lower path hint at just how big the waves were here,

at the prow-shaped barrier constructed from tall wooden pilings. Ironically, since the area was drained the foundations have begun to dry out. Schokland is sinking but, luckily, no longer into the sea.

Be sure to stop by the church, the **Waterstaatkerk**, built to replace the one virtually washed away in the storm of 1825. Here, as in so many Dutch fishing towns, a model ship hangs high above the congregation – the symbol of a union between sea and religious belief.

There's no public transportation to the museum; turn west off the N50 on the road at Ens and go another 2.5km. By bike, the LF15 from Urk 14km west passes right through and once here, you can follow a 10km route around the old island.

NOORD HOLLAND & FLEVOLAND

Utrecht

Don't underrate the petite province of Utrecht. Yes its famous namesake city and its throngs of students plus tree-lined canals and a medieval quarter hog the limelight. But this is no city-state. By bike you can explore scores of evocative castles and tiny towns in under a day.

The splendid Kasteel de Haar on Utrecht's doorstep is one of the country's most beautiful castles. Amersfoort oozes medieval character but also honours native son Piet Mondrian and his minimalist, angular palette plus the anti-way works of Armando. Then there's Oudewater in the southwest, synonymous with witchcraft (Monty Python fans will dig it) and a good bike ride from the capital. Palatial mansions in Doorn, where a defeated German Kaiser went into exile, and in Amerongen, seat of well-to-do aristocrats since the 13th century, make for another good day's ride across canals, farms and forests.

Back in Utrecht city, all those students at the ancient university support a plethora of edgy, fun bars and cafes. Those with calmer tastes can visit more than a dozen museums big and small. All will enjoy the many fine places to eat.

Yes, Utrecht has come some way since James Boswell whinged in 1763, 'I groaned with the idea of living all winter in so shocking a place'.

HIGHLIGHTS

- Look out towards Amsterdam, 50km north-west, from the top of Utrecht's **Domtoren** (p174)
- Find your own favourite spot along Utrecht's unique **bi-level canals** (p174)
- Feel the weight of history at the imposing **Kasteel de Haar** (p179)
- Discover the narrow canals and medieval confines at **Amersfoort** (p180)
- Find out if a witch weighs the same as gravy at **Oudewater** (p182)

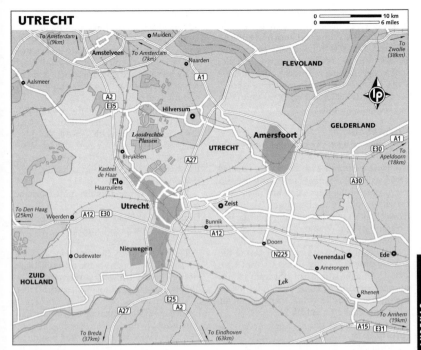

UTRECHT

0 _____ 10 km
0 _____ 6 miles

To Amsterdam (9km)

Muiden

Amstelveen

To Amsterdam (7km)

Naarden

Aalsmeer

A1

FLEVOLAND

To Zwolle (38km)

A2
E35

Hilversum

Loosdrechtse Plassen

GELDERLAND

Amersfoort

Breukelen

UTRECHT

A27

A1

E30

To Apeldoorn (18km)

Kasteel de Haar

Haarzuilens

A30

To Den Haag (25km)

Woerden

A12 E30

Utrecht

Zeist

Bunnik

A12

Oudewater

Nieuwegein

Doorn

N225

Veenendaal

Amerongen

Ede

ZUID HOLLAND

Lek

Rhenen

To Arnhem (19km)

E25

A27

A2

To Breda (37km)

To Eindhoven (63km)

A15 E31

UTRECHT

UTRECHT CITY

☎ 030 / pop 302,000

Utrecht is one of the Netherlands' oldest cities, with a compact, almost medieval centre set out around canals unique to the Netherlands. There's a lower level where warehouses were located in the 13th century, giving them a split-level character and meaning that diners and drinkers can nip off the street and enjoy a snack or a toot down at water level.

Of course a toot is what many people need after arriving in Utrecht, as the train station feeds into a vast enclosed mall, the Hoog Catharijne shopping centre, which goes on and on in all its unattractive glory until you are spat out at ground level in what seems to be a construction site. Wandering east you find the old town and suddenly you realise why you came.

Fortunately, the entire station region is undergoing the kind of rebuilding that will please anyone who thought the area needed to be blown up. Roads such as Catharijnebaan are being turned back into the canals they once were and the tatty, modern station is being replaced by something that will both inspire and relate to the old town. One down-

side: the project will last for a couple more decades (www.cu2030.nl).

Meanwhile, Utrecht's student population of 40,000 is the largest in the country, making the city one very vibrant place.

History

In Roman times the Rhine passed through present day Utrecht, then called Trajectum. In the following centuries the town had religious ties and was part of various empires. From the 11th century it was a centre of culture and learning while Amsterdam was still just a grubby fishing town to the west.

In 1579 several regions of today's Netherlands united under the Union of Utrecht (p25). The Protestant religion was made official but, in an early nod to tolerance, it was decreed that Catholics would not be persecuted. Utrecht's university was founded in 1636, the year after René Descartes, a local, wrote *Discourse on Method*.

In 1702 centuries of simmering animosity between the bishops of Utrecht and the Roman Catholic Church came to a head when the bishop was booted out of his job for failing to recognise the pope's infallibility. This caused a schism that resulted in the creation of the Old Catholics Church in Utrecht. The religion grew in popularity and peaked in 1889 when scores of disgruntled Catholics had a huge meeting in Utrecht. After that the Old Catholics lost following and there are only well under 10,000 members of the church in the Netherlands today.

Orientation

Two canals bisect Utrecht, the Oudegracht and the Nieuwegracht, the old and new canals from the 11th and 14th centuries. A third canal called the Singel surrounds the old core. Most of the interesting bits of the city lie within 500m of the Domtoren (Cathedral Tower), although the museum quarter is a pleasant stroll a couple of hundred metres further south.

The historic quarters are to the east of the train station (officially called Utrecht CS), but reaching the streets from the train station means traversing the Hoog Catharijne; follow the signs marked 'Centrum', then gasp for air when you finally get outside.

Information

Municipal library (☎ 286 18 00; Oudegracht 167; internet per hr €3; ☒ 1-9pm Mon, 11am-6pm Tue-Wed & Fri, 11am-9pm Thu, 10am-5pm Sat)
Selexyz Broese (☎ 233 52 00; Stadhuisbrug 5) Large bookshop.
Tourist office (☎ 0900 128 87 32; www.utrechtyour way.nl; Domplein 9; ☒ 10am-6pm Mon-Fri, 10am-5pm Sat, noon-5pm Sun)

Sights

Almost all sights within Utrecht's old town are within 10 minutes' walking distance of each other. In two to three hours you can easily cover the cathedral area and the main canals and have time left over for a museum visit.

DOMTOREN & AROUND

The **Domtoren** (Cathedral Tower; ☎ 233 30 36; www .domtoren.nl; Domplein; adult/child €7.50/4.50; ☒ tours 11am-4pm Mon-Sat, noon-4pm Sun) is 112m high, with 465 steps and 50 bells. It's a tough haul to the top but well worth the exertion, given that the tower gives unbeatable city views; on a clear day you can see Amsterdam. The guided tour, in Dutch and English, is detailed and gives privileged insight into this beautiful structure.

Finished in the 14th century, the cathedral and its tower are the most striking medieval landmarks in a city that once had 40 cathedrals. Appreciate the craft: it took almost 300 years to complete. In 1674 the North Sea winds reached hurricane force and blew down the cathedral's nave, leaving the tower and transept behind.

Back on terra firma, find the row of paving stones that mark the extents of the nave – across this extent is the **Domkerk** (Cathedral; ☎ 231 04 03; www.domkerk.nl; Achter de Dom 1; ☒ 10am-5pm Mon-Fri, 10am-3.30pm Sat May-Sep, from 11am Oct-Apr, 2-4pm Sun), the surviving chancel of the cathedral, with a few tombs within.

Behind the church is the most charming component of this ecclesiastical troika: the **Kloostergang**, a monastic garden and a peaceful refuge. A million pigeons and quite a few dope smokers can't be wrong.

The 19th-century buildings on the western side of Domplein are the **ceremonial buildings** of Utrecht University, surrounding the old church chapterhouse where the Treaty of Utrecht was signed in 1579. The Treaty formed a military alliance of the northern provinces.

Walk down Voetiusstraat from behind the cathedral to **Pieterskerk**, built in 1048 and the oldest Romanesque church in the Netherlands. Much damage was caused during the storm in 1674 and again during a dodgy 1965 restoration. Opening hours are sporadic, but try visiting on Friday or Saturday.

CANALS

Scene of many a wedding photo, the photogenic bend in the Oudegracht is illuminated by lamplight in the evening; hundreds sit at outside cafes here by day. South of this point is where the canal is at its most evocative, and the streets are quieter, stretching 1km to the southern tip of the old town.

A section of the Singel called the Stadsbuitengracht has its own turn as a lovely canal on the southeastern side of the old quarter, where it follows many parks built on the site of the old fortifications. Stroll down beside this canal and back north through Nieuwegracht, a peaceful stretch of plush canal houses and towering, grand old elms.

DICK BRUNA HUIS

One of Utrecht's favourite sons, Dick Bruna, is honoured at **Dick Bruna Huis** (☎ 236 23 62;

UTRECHT CITY

0 — 400 m
0 — 0.2 miles

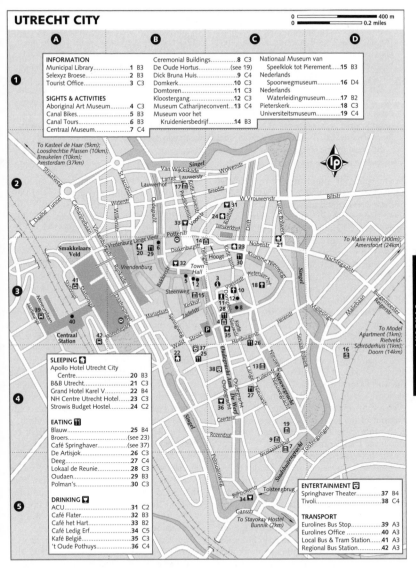

INFORMATION
Municipal Library.....................**1** B3
Selexyz Broese......................**2** B3
Tourist Office.......................**3** C3

SIGHTS & ACTIVITIES
Aboriginal Art Museum..........**4** C3
Canal Bikes...........................**5** B3
Canal Tours...........................**6** B3
Centraal Museum...................**7** C4

Ceremonial Buildings..............**8** C3
De Oude Hortus................(see 19)
Dick Bruna Huis.....................**9** C4
Domkerk.............................**10** C3
Domtoren............................**11** C3
Kloostergang.......................**12** C3
Museum Catharijneconvent...**13** C4
Museum voor het
   Kruideniersbedrijf..............**14** B3

Nationaal Museum van
   Speelklok tot Pierement.....**15** B3
Nederlands
   Spoorwegmuseum.............**16** D4
Nederlands
   Waterleidingmuseum.........**17** B2
Pieterskerk..........................**18** C3
Universiteitsmuseum.............**19** C4

SLEEPING
Apollo Hotel Utrecht City
   Centre.............................**20** B3
B&B Utrecht.........................**21** C3
Grand Hotel Karel V...............**22** B4
NH Centre Utrecht Hotel.......**23** C3
Strowis Budget Hostel...........**24** C2

EATING
Blauw.................................**25** B4
Broers.............................(see 23)
Café Springhaver................(see 37)
De Artisjok..........................**26** C4
Deeg.................................**27** C4
Lokaal de Reunie..................**28** C3
Oudaen..............................**29** B3
Polman's.............................**30** C3

DRINKING
ACU...................................**31** C2
Café Flater..........................**32** B3
Café het Hart.......................**33** B2
Café Ledig Erf......................**34** C5
Kafé België..........................**35** C3
't Oude Pothuys...................**36** C4

ENTERTAINMENT
Springhaver Theater.............**37** B4
Tivoli.................................**38** C4

TRANSPORT
Eurolines Bus Stop................**39** A3
Eurolines Office **40** A3
Local Bus & Tram Station.......**41** A3
Regional Bus Station.............**42** A3

UTRECHT

www.dickbrunahuis.nl; Nicolaaskerkhof 10; adult/child €9/4; 11am-5pm Tue-Sun). Bruna is the creator of beloved cartoon rabbit Miffy, and she naturally takes pride of place, along with an extensive overview of Bruna's career: from the book covers he designed for his family's publishing company to multimedia demonstrations of his technique and philosophy. Kids love this

place, as do adults who find their inner kid again. Admission here includes the Centraal Museum.

MUSEUM QUARTER
Utrecht likes its museums, with 14 of them, some quirkier than a bag of racoons – such as the one devoted to sewerage.

MIFFY & DICK

The illustrator Dick Bruna was born in Utrecht in 1927 and has lived there all his life. His most famous creation is of course Miffy, or Nijntje as she's known in the Netherlands, an adorable best-selling cartoon rabbit with dots for eyes and a cross for a mouth that's a clear inspiration for Japan's famous Hello Kitty character.

But there's much more to Dick Bruna than Miffy (wonderful as she is). Our man from Utrecht has written and illustrated more than 120 children's books and designed more than 2000 book covers, as well as hundreds of other books, posters, postcards and prints. Today Bruna still rises to go to work early every day at his Utrecht studio and is still every bit as obsessive in his search for perfect design. As he says, 'I'll never do 3-D illustration. I haven't simplified 2-D enough'.

His most recent Miffy book is 2007's *Queen Miffy*.

The pick of the litter is the **Museum Catharijneconvent** (☎ 231 72 96; www.catharijne convent.nl; Nieuwegracht 63; adult/child €10/6; ⏰ 10am-5pm Tue-Fri, 11am-5pm Sat & Sun), with the finest collection of medieval religious art in the Netherlands – virtually the history of Christianity, in fact – housed in a Gothic former convent and a 18th-century canalside house. Marvel at the many beautiful illuminated manuscripts, carvings and robes and then contemplate it all in the old cloisters.

The **Centraal Museum** (☎ 236 23 62; www.centraal museum.nl; Nicolaaskerkhof 10; adult/child €9/4; ⏰ 11am-5pm Tue-Sun) has a wide-ranging collection. It displays applied arts dating back to the 17th century, as well as paintings by some of the Utrecht School artists and a bit of De Stijl to boot – including the world's most extensive Gerrit Rietveld collection, a wet dream for all minimalists. There's even a 12th-century Viking longboat that was dug out of the local mud, plus a sumptuous 17th-century dollhouse. Admission here includes the Dick Bruna House.

The **Universiteitsmuseum** (☎ 253 80 08; www .museum.uu.nl; Lange Nieuwstraat 106; adult/child €7/3.50; ⏰ 11am-5pm Tue-Sun) is a mixed bag – and that's the 'toof'! There's a re-created late-19th-century classroom, historic dentistry tools ('Is it safe?') and way too many models of medical maladies. You can find refuge out the back in **De Oude Hortus**, the old botanical garden, along with all the other dentophobes, who'll be quivering amid venerable trees and plants collected by the Dutch during their world exploits. The garden is an oasis of calm, sheltering numerous rare flowers and plants such as the ancient *Gingko biloba* tree.

The **Nederlands Spoorwegmuseum** (Dutch Railway Museum; ☎ 230 62 06; www.spoorwegmuseum .nl; Maliebaanstation; adult/child €14.50/11.50; ⏰ 10am-5pm Tue-Sun) features historic trains and thematic displays in an old station building; a high-speed minitrain takes kids around the grounds. To get there, take bus 3 from Centraal Station to Maliebaan and walk southeast for about five minutes.

SMALL MUSEUMS
A bit of a surprise in Utrecht, the **Aboriginal Art Museum** (☎ 238 01 00; www.aamu.nl; Oudegracht 176; adult/child €8/5; ⏰ 10am-5pm Tue-Fri, 11am-5pm Sat & Sun), devoted to contemporary Australian Aboriginal art, is sure to delight those bored with Rembrandt and Van Gogh.

The **Museum voor het Kruideniersbedrijf** (Grocery Museum; ☎ 231 66 28; Hoogt 6; admission free; ⏰ 12.30-4.30pm Tue-Sat), a charming replica of an old grocery store, isn't a museum per se. It's more like a sweetshop with lovely ladies in old-fashioned aprons selling sweets and tea in decorative containers. Pick up a block of white liquorice candy to add to hot milk – an old Dutch tradition.

The **Nationaal Museum van Speelklok tot Pierement** (National Museum from Musical Clock to Street Organ; ☎ 231 27 89; www.museumspeelklok.nl; Steenweg 6; adult/child €8/4.50; ⏰ 10am-5pm Tue-Sun) has a colourful collection of musical machines from the 18th century onwards. Hourly tours demonstrate these with gusto. The newly opened restoration workshop lets you see how these mechanical marvels work.

Spread throughout the various levels of a soaring brick water tower built in 1896, the **Nederlands Waterleidingmuseum** (Sewer Museum; ☎ 248 72 11; www.waterleidingmuseum.nl; Lauwerhof 29; adult/child €2/1; ⏰ 1.30-5pm Tue-Fri & Sun, 11am-4pm Sat) takes a good, hard look at what happens to water before and after humans use it.

RIETVELD-SCHRÖDERHUIS
Just out of the city, the **Rietveld-Schröderhuis** (☎ 236 23 10; www.rietveldschroderhuis.nl; Prins Hendriklaan

50; adult/child €16/8) is a Unesco-protected landmark built in 1924 by Utrecht architect Gerrit Rietveld. Inside and out, the entire structure conforms to the principles of De Stijl architecture (see p60) – as form really does follow function here. Only six colours are used: red, blue, yellow, white, grey and black. Visits *must* be booked in advance through the website, by phone or through the Centraal Museum. Visits here are included in the museum admission, but the guided tour (adult/child €16/11, which includes a shuttle from Centraal Museum) is best.

A second building, a **model apartment** (Erasmuslaan 9) from 1931, is behind the main house and also open to the public. It's included in the admission to Rietveld-Schröderhuis.

Activities

Canal Tours (☎ 272 01 11; adult/child €9/6; ☺ 11am-5pm) are a fine way to see the old town and the old water-level warehouses. The landing is on Oudegracht just south of Lange Viestraat. You can also rent **canal bikes** (paddleboats; per person per hr €8) from in front of the municipal library.

Festivals & Events

Holland Festival Oude Muziek (Holland Festival of Ancient Music; www.oudemuziek.nl) Held in late August, this festival celebrates music from the Middle Ages through to the baroque period.

Nederlands Film Festival (NFF; www.filmfestival .nl) The Dutch film industry may be tiny, but its output is generally good. Find out for yourself at the NFF in late September, culminating in the awarding of the coveted Golden Calf.

Sleeping

BUDGET

Strowis Budget Hostel (☎ 238 02 80; Boothstraat 8; www .strowis.nl; dm from €15, r €58; ☐) This 17th-century building is near the town centre and has been lovingly restored and converted into a hostel (four- to 14-bed rooms). It's open 24 hours a day, has a cosy bar and is run by a bunch of ex-hippies. It rents bikes.

our pick **B&B Utrecht** (☎ 06 5043 4884; www .hostelutrecht.nl; Lucas Bolwerk 4; dm from €19, r from €55; ☐) Straddling the border between hostel and hotel, this spotless inn in an elegant old building has an internal Ikea vibe. Breakfast and internet access (in a computer room with scanners, printers etc) are free as is use of a huge range of musical instruments.

Stayokay Hostel Bunnik (☎ 656 12 77; www.stay okay.com; Rhijnauwenselaan 14; dm from €22, r from €44; ☺ Mar-Oct) This charming old mansion overlooks a canal on the fringes of a nature reserve, 5km east of the city centre in Bunnik. There are three dining halls, a traditional bar and a lovely terrace. It is right on national bike path LF4 or take bus 40, 41 or 43 from CS.

MIDRANGE

Apollo Hotel Utrecht City Centre (☎ 233 12 32; www .apollohotelresorts.com; Vredenburg 14; r €80-150; ☺) A low-key business hotel, the Apollo has 90 spacious, comfortable rooms. Those in the back are dead quiet, those in the front have views of the town centre reconstruction. Those enormous red lips hovering over you are not a dream but a print above the headboard.

NH Centre Utrecht Hotel (☎ 231 31 69; www.nh -hotels.com; Janskerkhof 10; r €100-150; ☒ ☐ ☺) Trad style trumps modernity at this atmospheric old hotel (1870). The rooms (with minibars, trouser press etc) are comfortable, with good church views and modern, stylish decor.

Malie Hotel (☎ 231 64 24; www.maliehotel.nl; Maliestraat 2; r from €110; ☒ ☐ ☺) Tucked away in a beautiful tree-lined avenue, this elegant and comfortable 19th-century house offers large rooms and old-world charm. There's a nice garden out the back, and the hotel is away from the city centre for a bit of peace and quiet.

TOP END

Grand Hotel Karel V (☎ 233 75 55; Geertebolwerk 1, off Walsteeg; www.karelv.nl; r €130-275; ☒ ☐) The lushest accommodation in Utrecht can be found in this former knights' gathering hall from the 14th century. The service and decor are understated. The 117 rooms are split between the old manor and a new wing. Taking tea in the walled garden is sublime.

Eating

Do as the discerning locals do: avoid the cluster of wharf-side restaurants on the Oudegracht in the dead centre of the old town near the town hall. It's a pretty spot better known for its views than culinary delights. Utrecht's best restaurants lie elsewhere.

RESTAURANTS

Oudaen (☎ 231 18 64; www.oudaen.nl; Oudegracht 99; mains €8-22) The best choice on this busy stretch of the canal. Set in a restored 14th-century banquet hall, it has a varied menu of salads,

UTRECHT

steaks and seafood. Best of all, it brews its own beer, which you can enjoy under the high ceilings or outside on the canal.

Polman's (☎ 231 33 68; cnr Jansdam & Keistraat; mains €12-25) Diners at this grand cafe are welcomed in an elegant former ballroom with ceiling frescoes and extravagant floral displays. French and Italian flavours dominate the menu *and* the extensive wine list.

ourpick Blauw (☎ 234 24 63; Springweg 64; set menu from €20; ☽ dinner) Blauw is *the* place for stylish Indonesian food in Utrecht. Young and old alike enjoy superb *rijsttafels* (array of spicy dishes served with rice) amid the red decor that mixes vintage art with hip minimalism.

De Artisjok (☎ 231 74 94; Nieuwegracht 33; mains €20; ☽ dinner) As surprising as the pastel colours inside the flower of its namesake artichoke, this bistro has fresh and inventive fare featuring organic ingredients grown locally. It's on a leafy and quiet stretch of the Nieuwgracht.

Deeg (☎ 233 11 04; Lange Nieuwstraat 71; menus from €32; ☽ dinner) A charming corner location in the museum quarter is but the first draw at this casual bistro, which has nightly set menus that change regularly. Fresh local produce gets a Mediterranean accent and many items – such as the cheeses – are organic.

CAFES

Café Springhaver (☎ 231 37 89; www.springhaver.nl; Springweg 50-52; mains €12-14) The cafe next to the theatre (right) is a fine place for a drink, snack or meal even if you aren't debating the merits of a film. It's a little spot of charm on this sinuous old street away from the bustle.

Lokaal de Reunie (☎ 231 01 00; www.lokaaldereunie .nl; 't Wed 3A; mains €12-30) One of many atmospheric cafes near the cathedral tower, Lokaal de Reunie is distinguished by its attractive, airy interior.

Broers (☎ 234 34 06; www.stadscafe-broers.nl; Janskerkhof 9; mains €14-23) This place is a stylish, modern version of a brown cafe, with good views. It serves basic dishes such as pasta and steak, and there's live music some nights.

Drinking

ourpick ACU (☎ 231 45 90; www.acu.nl; Voorstraat 71) Billing itself as a 'political cultural centre', ACU is a classic student dive. It combines bar, disco, lecture hall and more. Argue about whether Trotsky was too conservative while downing organic vegan food. Note: 'Racism, sexism, homophobia are not tolerated'.

Café Flater (☎ 232 17 28; Oudegracht 140) On a curvaceous part of the main canal, Flater is first among many neighbouring bars, busy when others are quiet.

Café het Hart (☎ 231 97 18; www.hethart.com; Voorstraat 10) This is the apex of the A-list of the Utrecht bar scene, with bleeding-edge beats plus stacks of magazines and board games.

Café Ledig Erf (☎ 231 75 77; Tolsteegbrug 3) This classy pub overlooks a confluence of canals (and other cafes) at the southern tip of town. The terrace vies with the beer list in offering the most joy. The autumn bock beer fest is a winner.

Kafé België (☎ 231 26 66; Oudegracht 196) This lively bar is an absolute must for beer-lovers. It has 20 Benelux brews on tap and cheap food for absorption. There's a couple of nice tables out the front.

't Oude Pothuys (☎ 231 89 70; Oudegracht 279) Small and dark, this basement pub has nightly music – jam sessions with locals trying their hand at rock and jazz. Enjoy drinks on the totally refurbished canalside pier.

Entertainment

Tivoli (☎ 231 14 91; www.tivoli.nl; Oudegracht 245) This former monastery, now a cavernous dance hall with medieval chandeliers, is a fixture on Utrecht's student-oriented music scene. There's everything from big band jazz to new Brit bands such as Rolo Tomassi.

Springhaver Theater (☎ 231 37 89; www.springhaver .nl; Springweg 50-52) This art deco complex houses intimate cinemas that screen art-house and independent films.

Shopping

We've said enough about the horrors of the Hoog Catherine Shopping Centre. Between here and the town hall are pedestrian streets with lots of chains and mainstream shops. For more interesting choices, wander down Voorstraat and Oudegracht. Huge markets take place on Vredenburg on Wednesday, Friday and Saturday. Most unusual, however, is the Saturday fabric market on Breedstraat.

Getting There & Away

Utrecht is a travel hub: bike routes, train lines and motorways converge on the city from all directions.

BICYCLE

National bike route LF9 runs north through farmlands for 23km to a junction with LF23, which covers both Muiden (p165) and Flevoland. To the south it runs through rich farmlands towards Breda. Marathon route LF7 passes through Utrecht on its 350km route from Alkmaar to Maastricht; Amsterdam is about 50km northwest. LF4 runs east 80km to Arnhem.

BUS

Eurolines (☎ 296 90 90; www.eurolines.nl; Stationplein 57; ☒ 9.30am-5.30pm Mon-Fri, 10am-4pm Sat & Sun) has a ticket office opposite the tram station. Buses stop on the west side of the train station on Jarbeursplein.

TRAIN

As part of the rebuilding/resurrection of the quarter by the train station, the entire complex will be replaced by 2013, so expect a fair bit of chaos. Lockers, the bike shop and all other services will be moving about. Meanwhile Utrecht CS is the national hub for Dutch rail services, so you'll probably change trains here at some point.

Destination	Price (€)	Duration (min)	Frequency (per hr)
Amsterdam	6.70	30	4
Den Helder	17.60	105	2
Groningen	24.80	115	2
Maastricht	23.50	120	2
Rotterdam	9.10	40	4

Getting Around

Local buses and trams leave from underneath the passage linking CS to Hoog Catharijne. Regional buses leave from the adjoining area to the south, although this may shift as construction continues.

AROUND UTRECHT CITY
Loosdrechtse Plassen

The town of Breukelen is 10km northwest of Utrecht. Although the town in itself is unremarkable, it was actually the namesake for the New York district of Brooklyn. Breukelen is also the gateway to the **Loosdrechtse Plassen**, a large series of lakes formed from the flooded digs of peat harvesters.

There are all manner of bike paths around the waters and quite a bit of interesting scenery. Parts of the lakes are somewhat desolate, while others are surrounded by lovely homes on small islands joined to the road by little bridges.

The best way to visit is by bike from Utrecht; it's 15km northwest by national route LF7. Follow the signs to Breukelen. Otherwise, it's just a short run by train to Breukelen from Utrecht CS (€2.80, 13 minutes, four per hour).

Kasteel de Haar

Feast your senses on one of the most imposing castles in the country, **Kasteel de Haar** (☎ 030-677 85 15; www.kasteeldehaar.nl; Kasteellaan 1; tour adult/child €8/5; ☒ park 10am-5pm, tours 11am-4pm Tue-Sun), which was restored in a fit of nostalgia little more than a century ago, long after its Gothic turrets ceased to have any defensive purpose. But architect PJ Cuypers (of Rijksmuseum fame) misjudged the weight on the centuries-old foundations; big cracks can be seen above moat level.

What you see now is a spiffed-up version of the fortress as it was believed to look around 1500, but (understandably) equipped with all the creature comforts available in the late 19th century, such as electric lighting and running water. The project was so extensive that the church and the nearby hamlet of **Haarzuilens** became involved. The castle's owner, Baron Etienne van Zuylen, spared little expense and had the entire village moved so there'd be adequate space for the park and hunting grounds.

The castle is surrounded by a large English landscaped garden with broad paths, canal-like stretches of pond and statues throughout. The French baroque garden near the entrance bears the stamp of Héléne de Rothschild, the baron's wife and heir of the renowned Rothschild banking family – it was her fortune that paid for the 19th-century restoration. You can just wander the grounds (adult/child €3/2).

To get here from Utrecht, take the A2 north to exit 6 (Maarssen) and drive 2km east to Haarzuilens. Alternatively, take bus 127 (hourly) from Utrecht CS towards Breukelen and get off at Castle or Brink, from where it's a 15-minute walk. The castle is right on national bike route LF4, 15km west of Utrecht.

AMERSFOORT
☎ 033 / pop 143,300

Beer, wool and tobacco made Amersfoort an exceedingly rich town from the 16th century onwards. Well-heeled with a touch of the provincial, the town has many striking merchants' homes that have been lovingly restored. And the egg-shaped old town offers quiet, wonderfully

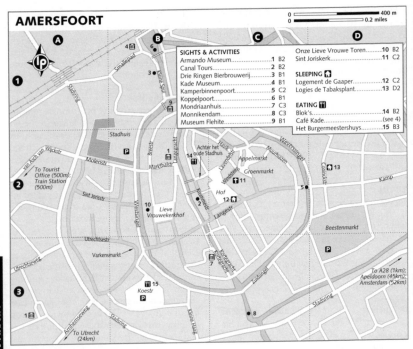

AMERSFOORT

SIGHTS & ACTIVITIES		Onze Lieve Vrouwe Toren.........**10** B2
Armando Museum......................**1** B2		Sint Joriskerk.............................**11** C2
Canal Tours..............................**2** B2		
Drie Ringen Bierbrouwerij........**3** B1		SLEEPING
Kade Museum...........................**4** B1		Logement de Gaaper.................**12** C2
Kamperbinnenpoort..................**5** C2		Logies de Tabaksplant..............**13** D2
Koppelpoort.............................**6** B1		
Mondriaanhuis.........................**7** C3		EATING
Monnikendam..........................**8** C3		Blok's.......................................**14** B2
Museum Flehite........................**9** B1		Café Kade................................(see **4**)
		Het Burgermeestershuys...........**15** B3

evocative strolls along canals and narrow alleys that still ooze medieval atmosphere.

Amersfoort makes for a good break on a train journey to/from Friesland or Groningen. You can have an interesting stroll of an hour and then get a good meal.

Information

Tourist office (☎ 0900 112 23 64; www.amersfoort yourway.nl; Stationsplein 9-11; 9.30am-5.30pm Mon-Fri, also 10am-4pm Sat Jun-Aug) Excellent cycling maps.

Sights & Activities

Much of Amersfoort's appeal comes from wandering the old centre, which has attractive little canals and more than 300 pre-18th-century buildings.

MUSEUMS

Kade Museum (☎ 422 50 30; www.kunsthalkade.nl; Smallepad 3; adult/child €7/3.50; 11am-5pm Tue-Fri, noon-5pm Sat & Sun) All angles, this bold museum has all manner of modern art, sculpture and installations. The cafe is excellent (see opposite).

Mondriaanhuis (☎ 462 01 80; Kortegracht 11; www .mondriaanhuis.nl; admission €5; 10am-5pm Tue-Fri, noon-

5pm Sat & Sun) The famous De Stijl artist Piet Mondrian was born in Amersfoort. This small but absorbing museum, in the house where he was born, honours his life and work with a detailed retrospective of prints, reproductions and some originals. His iconic colours dominate the complex.

Armando Museum (☎ 461 40 88; www.armando museum.nl; Zonnehof 8; adult/child €3.50/free; 11am-5pm Tue-Fri, Sat & Sun noon-5pm) The painter, writer, violinist, and documentary filmmaker Armando was one of the major artists to emerge from the postwar era in the Netherlands. His work is strongly antiwar, derived from his experiences growing up in Amersfoort during WWII. The utilitarian surrounds of the building suitably highlight his paintings, drawings, sculptures, writings and films.

OLD TOWN

Zuidsingel is a fine place to start: the inner ring on the north side of town along **Muurhuizen** is quaint and good for walks. **Langestraat** is the mainstream shopping strip but **Krommestraat** is the street for interesting and offbeat choices.

Onze Lieve Vrouwe Toren (Lieve Vrouwekerkhof; adult/child €4/3; 11am-5pm Tue-Sun Jul & Aug) is the surviving 15th-century Gothic tower (346 steps, fine views) of the church that used to stand on this spot. Like so many of the Netherlands' churches, it was destroyed by tragedy – in this case a gunpowder explosion in 1787. The square in front, **Lieve Vrouwekerkhof**, is Amersfoort's most charming spot. A flower market is held here on Friday morning.

Amersfoort's surviving old church is **Sint Joriskerk** (Hof 1; admission €1; 1-4.30pm Mon-Sat). It was rebuilt in a sort of Gothic-cum-aircraft-hangar style in the 16th century after the original Romanesque church burnt down (obviously, insuring Dutch churches has never been a lucrative proposition).

The collections at the **Museum Flehite** (461 99 87; Westsingel 50; adult/child €6/free; 11am-6pm Tue-Fri, 11am-5pm Sat & Sun) cover local geology, history and decorative arts. The building is attractively set at a junction of canals, and you enter the museum courtyard over a bridge. It has a fantastic free map showing historical highlights around town.

The town has three surviving gateways, either to the city roads or over the canals. The **Koppelpoort** guards the north and was built in the 15th century, the **Kamperbinnenpoort** is at the eastern side and dates from the 13th century, while the picturesque **Monnikendam** to the southeast was built in 1430.

Possibly the most fun you will have in Amersfoort is touring **Drie Ringen Bierbrouwerij** (465 65 75; Kleine Spui 18; 1-7pm Fri-Sun). You can wander enjoyably around this much-heralded microbrewery and try one of the five beers on tap.

Tours

Canal Tours (465 46 36; www.amersfoort-rondvaarten .nl; Krommestraat 5; adult/child from €4/3; May-Oct) sail around the old canals on four different routes through the day.

Sleeping

Logies de Tabaksplant (472 97 97; www.tabaks plant.nl; Coninckstraat 15; r €60-140;) This small hotel is just beyond the old town gate of Kamperbinnenpoort. The 24 rooms are very smart, cheery and full of good vibes. The owner of a tobacco plantation built this heritage-listed 17th-century building.

Logement de Gaaper (453 17 95; www.degaaper.nl; Hof 39; r €70-120) Home to a pharmacy in the 19th century, this stylish hotel occupies a prime spot on the main square, and most of the 18 rooms have great views of Sint Joriskerk. Some of the original structure is visible inside the hotel. The ground-floor cafe is excellent.

Eating & Drinking

Both Hof and Lieve Vrouwekerkhof groan or – depending on the time of day – shriek with cafes and pubs.

Café Kade (06 2393 8386; Smallpad 3; meals from €5; lunch Tue-Sun) The fab cafe in the cutting-edge museum has a fine terrace with views of passing trains, a canal and the Koppelpoort.

Het Burgermeestershuys (461 80 00; Koestraat 9; meals €10-30; lunch & dinner) Enjoy traditional Dutch fare (roasts, seafood, stews and more) inside a perfectly mannered historic building or at a slew of tables outside.

Blok's (461 02 22; Krommestraat 49; meals €20-40; dinner Wed-Mon) On a street with many good choices, Blok's has a kitchen with a big window onto the street. Watch as all manner of contemporary, fresh creations stream forth to the stylish dining room.

Getting There & Around

Amersfoort's train station is an easy 500m walk west of the centre. It has lockers and currency exchange services. Sample train fares and schedules:

Destination	Price (€)	Duration (min)	Frequency (per hr)
Amsterdam	7.60	35	4
Deventer	9.40	37	3
Utrecht	4.10	19	6

There's a bicycle shop at the train station. Utrecht is 23km southwest on a beautiful ride through forests and farms on national bike route LF9. It also runs north 23km to meet LF23, and both continue into Flevoland.

DOORN

 0343 / pop 10,399

Around 20km southeast of Utrecht lies Doorn, a wealthy little burg with a claim to an oddment in 20th-century Dutch history: **Huis Doorn** (42 10 20; www.huisdoorn.nl; Langbroekerweg 10; adult/child €7.50/free; 10am-5pm Tue-Sat, 1-5pm Sun 15 May-15 Sep, 1-5pm Tue-Sun 16 Sep-14 May), a 14th-century castle that was turned into a sort of indefensible mansion during the 1700s. It had numerous owners during its time, but none of them

---

WITCHERY

During the horrific witch-hunts of the 16th century, close to a million women all over Europe were executed – burnt, drowned or otherwise tortured to death – on suspicion of being witches. Weighing was one of the more common methods of determining witchery, as popular belief held that any woman who was too light for the size of her frame was obviously a witch (because hags like that have no soul). A woman who weighed the 'proper' amount was too heavy to ride a broom and thus was not a witch. (Fans of the movie *Monty Python and the Holy Grail* will be familiar with the procedure.) Women who passed the weight test were given a certificate, good for life, proclaiming them to be human.

Women under suspicion were also required to walk over burning coals (if their feet didn't blister, they were witches) or were dropped into the lake – if you sank you were human, if you floated you were a witch. Needless to say, all of this was grossly unfair: if you managed to make it over the coals, your feet would be charred to the stumps. If you sank, you drowned. You win, you lose.

Oudewater emerges with some honour here. No one was ever proved to be a witch in the town and this is held up as a symbol of the honesty of the locals, as they refused to take bribes to rig the weights. It's also seen as the first stirrings of people power and a turn against the church, which was behind the witch-hunts.

---

was more infamous than Kaiser Wilhelm II of Germany, who inhabited Huis Doorn in exile from 1920 until his death in 1941.

There's a fine collection of German art that it seems the Kaiser brought with him from various German palaces. Afterwards, stroll the grounds and ponder the fate of the Kaiser, who had been allowed into exile by the Dutch as long as he remained under 'house arrest' (some house, eh?). Events throughout the year recall his highness: at Christmas you can drop by for *gluhwein* (mulled wine) and *lebkuchen* (spiced biscuits).

Bus 50 from Utrecht CS makes the 20km journey to Doorn (50 minutes) every 30 minutes. The castle is right near the bus stop. On national bike route LF4, ride 24km southeast from Utrecht.

AMERONGEN
☎ 0343 / pop 5200

The countryside around the small town of Amerongen on the Nederrijn river is dotted with old wooden tobacco-drying sheds. It's also home to **Kasteel Amerongen** (☎ 45 42 12; www .kasteelamerongen.nl; Drostestraat 20; 🕙 10.30am-4.30pm Tue-Fri, 1-4.30pm Sat & Sun Apr-Oct), a fortified castle built in the 13th century that took on its present twee appearance in the late 1600s; it was originally owned by Europe's old aristocracy. It's 38km southwest from Utrecht on national bike route LF4. Combine it with Doorn (p181).

OUDEWATER
☎ 0348 / pop 10,100

There's one real reason to visit the sweet little town of Oudewater in the province's southwest: witchcraft. Until the 17th century the **Heksenwaag** (Witches' Weigh-House; ☎ 56 34 00; www .hekenswag.nl; Leeuweringerstraat 2; adult/child €1.50/0.75; 🕙 11am-5pm Tue-Sun Apr-Oct) in the town centre was thought to have the most accurate scales in the land; women came from all over the place to be weighed here, on suspicion of being witches (see the boxed text, above).

The house has a modest display of witchcraft history in the loft upstairs, and at the end of your visit you'll be invited to step onto the old scale. If you feel light on your feet it's because your *certificaet van weginghe* (weight certificate) makes your weight shrink – an old Dutch pound is 10% heavier than today's unit.

Two doors away, the tourist office also has a **witch museum** (adult/child €4.75/2; 🕙 10am-4pm Mon-Sat Apr-Sep, also 11am-3pm Sun Jul & Aug). Several bewitching cafes line the tiny canal here.

Oudewater is on the route of bus 180, which runs in either direction between Gouda (33 minutes) and Utrecht CS (53 minutes) every half-hour. The town is 10km by a cycling route across canal-laced fields south of Woerden and national route LF4, which is 26km from Utrecht and 11km further southwest from Kasteel de Haar (p179).

Zuid Holland & Zeeland

Think Holland and you're thinking about these two provinces where tulips, cheese, plucky tall Dutch people standing up to the sea, Vermeer and tulips avoid cliché simply by their omnipresence.

The Keukenhof gardens are a place of pilgrimage for lovers of tulips. Not much further west, the beaches are great for biking and hiking, with trails and paths everywhere along the coast.

Zuid Holland's major cities are the biggest attractions: there's Leiden, with its university culture and old town (and proximity to the bulb fields); Den Haag, with its museums, stately air, fun shopping and kitsch beach; charming, beautiful Delft, the home of Jan Vermeer; and mighty Rotterdam, blessed with an edgy urban vibe, surprising cultural scene and striking architecture.

Several smaller places are also worth your time: Gouda is a perfect old canal town, while Dordrecht has its own surprises amid canals and charm. Just east and south of Dordrecht is Biesbosch National Park, a sprawling natural area along the border with Noord Brabant.

Further south, Zeeland (Sea Land) is the dyke-protected province that people often associate with the Netherlands when they're not thinking of tulips, cheese and windmills. Middelburg is the main town, with a serenity belying its proximity to the tragedies that spawned the Delta Project.

Cycling in this flat, mostly near- and sub-sea-level region is unparalleled. Ferries offer chances to get out on the water and short distances between towns, especially in Zuid Holland, mean that you can pick a town you fancy as a base and see the rest via quick and frequent trains.

ZUID HOLLAND & ZEELAND

HIGHLIGHTS

- Realise that Holland's second city should be its first in **Rotterdam** (p203)
- Pop off for posies at **Keukenhof Gardens** (p189)
- Get your Art 101 in splendid form at Den Haag's **Mauritshuis** (p191)
- Look for girls wearing pearl earrings in old-world **Delft** (p199)
- Go for a spin in **Kinderdijk** (p215)

Keukenhof Gardens ★
Den Haag ★
★ Delft
★ Rotterdam
★ Kinderdijk

ZUID HOLLAND

Along with Noord (North) Holland and Utrecht, Zuid Holland is part of the Randstad, the economic and population heart of the Netherlands. Two of the nation's most important cities are here: Den Haag, the seat of the royal family and the government; and Rotterdam, Europe's busiest port. You could easily make a trip just exploring these classic Dutch destinations.

LEIDEN

☎ 071 / pop 116,800

Lovely Leiden is a refreshing, vibrant town, patterned with canals and attractive old buildings. It also has a few claims to fame:

it's Rembrandt's birthplace, and it's home to the Netherlands' oldest university (and 20,000 students), the alma mater of René Descartes.

The university was a gift from Willem the Silent for withstanding two Spanish sieges in 1574. It was a terrible time, ending when the Sea Beggars arrived and repelled the invaders. According to lore, the retreating Spanish legged it so quickly, they abandoned a kettle of *hutspot* (hotchpotch) – today it's still a staple of Dutch menus in restaurants, and in homes.

Decades later, Protestants fleeing persecution elsewhere in the Low Countries, France and England arrived in Leiden to a somewhat warmer welcome. Most notable was the group led by John Robinson, who would sail to America and into history as the pilgrims aboard the *Mayflower*.

Wealth from the linen industry buttressed Leiden's growing prosperity, and during the 17th century the town produced several brilliant artists, most famously Rembrandt van Rijn – better known by his first name alone. Rembrandt was born in Leiden in 1606, and remained here for 26 years before achieving fame in Amsterdam.

Orientation

Old Leiden is a compact town. From Centraal Station a five-minute walk brings you to Beestenmarkt. Haarlemmerstraat and Breestraat are the town's pedestrian arteries, and most sights are within five minutes' walk of one of them. The town is bisected by many waterways, the most notable being the Oude Rijn and the Nieuwe Rijn, which meet at Hoogstraat to form a canal simply called the Rijn.

Information

Stationsweg has numerous banks and ATMs.

BOOKSHOPS

Joho (☎ 516 12 77; www.joho.nl; Stationsweg 2d) Has travel books, maps, travel gear and supplies.
Mayflower Bookshop (☎ 513 84 97; Hogewoerd 107) Compact selection of new and used classics and fine fiction.

INTERNET ACCESS

Centrale Bibliotheek (Central Library; ☎ 514 99 43; Nieuwstraat; internet per hr €3; ⊗ 10am-6pm)
Oruc Telecom (Steenstraat; internet per hr €2) Cheap calls.

LAUNDRY

Wasserette Splash (☎ 513 72 99; Noordeinde 11; ⊗ 8.30am-7pm Mon-Sat) Loads from €8.

TOURIST INFORMATION

Tourist office (☎ 0900 222 23 33; www.vvvleiden.nl; Stationsweg 41; ⊗ 8am-6pm Mon-Fri, 10am-4pm Sat, 11am-3pm Sun) Across from the train station, this office has good maps and historic info.

Sights

Leiden is right up there with the great historic cities of the Netherlands. As you get further south from its striking Centraal Station, the city's traditional character unfolds, especially around the Pieterskerk and south. A five-

minute walk takes you into Leiden's district of historic waterways.

OLD LEIDEN

De Burcht (admission free; ⊗ sunrise-sunset), an 11th-century citadel on an artificial hill, lost its protective functions as the city grew around it. Now it's a park with lovely places to view the steeples and rooftops, with a wonderful cafe at its base.

Just south, the huge pile of bricks is the 15th-century **St Pancraskerk** (Nieuwstraat), an agglomeration of styles. To the west follow the huge steeple to **Pieterskerk** (⊗ 1-4pm), which is often under restoration (a good thing as it's been prone to collapse since it was built in the 14th century). The precinct here is as old Leiden as you'll get and includes the gabled old **Latin School** (Schoolstraat), which – before it became a commercial building – was graced by a pupil named Rembrandt from 1616 to 1620. Across the plaza, look for the **Gravensteen**, which dates to the 13th century and was once a prison. The gallery facing the plaza was where judges watched executions.

Back north, the **Marekerk** (Lange Mare) dates to 1639 and has a beautiful eight-sided wooden interior. Try to sneak a peak during Sunday services.

MUSEUMS

Get your Rembrandt fix at the 17th-century **Lakenhal** (Cloth Hall; ☎ 516 53 60; www.lakenhal.nl; Oude Singel 28-32; adult/child €4/free; ⊗ 10am-5pm Tue-Fri, noon-5pm Sat & Sun), which houses the Municipal Museum, with an assortment of works by Old Masters, as well as period rooms and temporary exhibits. The 1st floor has been restored to the way it would have looked when Leiden was at the peak of its prosperity.

The **Rijksmuseum van Oudheden** (National Museum of Antiquities; ☎ 516 31 63; www.rmo.nl; Rapenburg 28; adult/under 18yr €8.50/5.50; ⊗ 10am-5pm Tue-Sun) has a hieroglyphics collection and 94 human and animal mummies. The entrance hall contains the Temple of Taffeh, a gift from Egypt in 1969 for Dutch help in saving ancient monuments when the Aswan High Dam was built.

Cultural achievements by civilisations worldwide are on show at the **Museum Volkenkunde** (National Museum of Ethnology; ☎ 516 88 00; www.volkenkunde.nl; Steenstraat 1; adult/child €7.50/4; ⊗ 10am-5pm Tue-Sun). More than 200,000 artefacts span China, South America and Africa, much like Amsterdam's Tropenmuseum

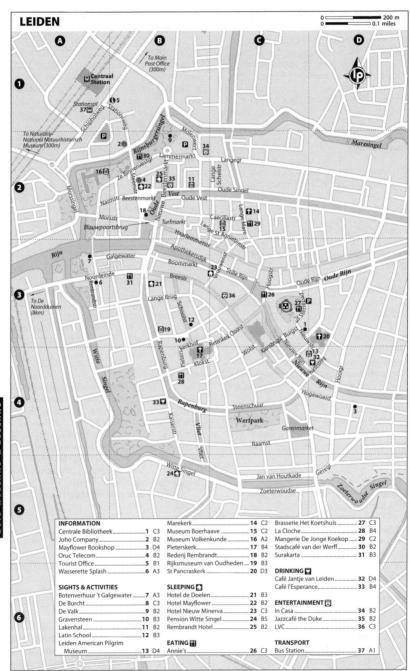

LEIDEN

PILGRIMS' PROGRESS

In 1608 a group of Calvinist Protestants split from the Anglican church and left persecution in Nottinghamshire, England, for a journey that would span decades and thousands of miles. Travelling first to Amsterdam under the leadership of John Robinson, they encountered theological clashes with local Dutch Protestants.

In Leiden they found a more liberal atmosphere, thanks to the university and some like-minded Calvinists who already lived there. They also found company with refugees who had escaped from persecution elsewhere. However, the group's past was to catch up with them. In 1618 James I of England announced he would assume control over the Calvinists living in Leiden. In addition, the local Dutch were becoming less tolerant of religious splinter groups.

The first group of English left Leiden in 1620 for Delfshaven in what is now Rotterdam, where they bought the *Speedwell* with the intention of sailing to the New World. Unfortunately, the leaky *Speedwell* didn't live up to its name; after several attempts to cross the Atlantic, the group gave up and, against their better judgement, sailed into Southampton in England. After repairs to their ship and a thwarted attempt to restart their journey, the group joined the much more seaworthy *Mayflower* in Dartmouth and sailed, as it were, into history as the Pilgrims.

This legendary voyage was actually just one of many involving the Leiden group. It wasn't until 1630 that most had made their way to the American colonies founded in what is today New England. Some 1000 people made the voyages, including a number of Dutch who were considered oddballs for their unusual beliefs.

In Leiden today, traces of the Pilgrims are elusive. The best place to start is the tiny **Leiden American Pilgrim Museum** (☎ 512 24 13; Beschuitsteeg 9; admission €3; ⏰ 1-5pm Wed-Sat), a fascinating restoration of a house occupied around 1610 by the soon-to-be Pilgrims. The house itself dates from 1375, but the furnishings are from the Pilgrims' period. Note the tiles on the floor, originals from the 14th century. Pick up a walking-tour brochure, which helps you explore the surviving parts of 17th-century Leiden.

(p108). There's a rich Indonesian collection; watch for performances by the museum's gamelan troupe.

Leiden's landmark windmill museum, **De Valk** (The Falcon; ☎ 516 53 53; 2e Binnenvestgracht 1; adult/child €3/2; ⏰ 10am-5pm Tue-Sat, 1-5pm Sun), has been carefully restored, and many consider it the best example of its kind. Its arms are free to turn 'whenever possible' and can still grind the grain.

Leiden University was an early centre for Dutch medical research. You can see the often-grisly results (five centuries of pickled organs, surgical tools and skeletons) at the **Museum Boerhaave** (☎ 521 42 24; www.museum boerhaave.nl; Lange St Agnietenstraat 10; adult/concession €6/3; ⏰ 10am-5pm Tue-Sat, noon-5pm Sun).

A stuffed elephant greets you at **Naturalis – Nationaal Natuurhistorisch Museum** (National Museum of Natural History; ☎ 568 76 00; www.naturalis.nl; Darwinweg 2; adult/child €11/7; ⏰ 10am-5pm Tue-Fri, to 6pm Sat & Sun), a large, well-funded collection of all the usual dead critters and, notably, the million-year-old Java Man discovered by Dutch anthropologist Eugene Dubois in 1891. It's 300m west of the town centre.

Activities
Rent a canoe or kayak from **Botenverhuur 't Galgewater** (☎ 514 97 90; www.galgewater.nl; per hr from €5; ⏰ 11am-7pm mid-Apr–Sep) and explore the canals. Two hours with a motorboat costs €80.

Tours
There are leisurely one-hour canal boat tours of the channel around the old town centre with **Rederij Rembrandt** (☎ 513 49 38; www .rederij-rembrandt.nl; Beestenmarkt; adult/child €6/4; ⏰ sailing times 11am-4pm Mar-Oct) with commentary (English available).

There are longer, three-hour cruises of the waterways and lakes around Leiden. Ask the tourist office for details.

Festivals & Events
Leiden grinds to a halt in early October for **Leidens Ontzet**, commemorating the day the Spanish-caused starvation ended in 1574. The revelry is undiminished even four centuries later, and there is much eating of the ceremonial *hutspot*, herring and white bread. But more than anything, consumption focuses on beer sandwiches (hold the bread) and a

ZUID HOLLAND & ZEELAND

drunken time is had by all – especially the night before.

Sleeping
BUDGET

De Noordduinen (☎ 402 52 95; www.noordduinen.nl; Campingweg 1, Katwijk aan Zee; camp sites from €30; ⊗ Apr-Oct; ☎) The closest camping ground, 8km to the west, it enjoys a beachy setting. Take bus 37 (20 minutes, two per hour).

MIDRANGE

Pension Witte Singel (☎ 512 45 92; www.pension -ws.demon.nl; Witte Singel 80; r €50-100; 💻 ☎) Seven bright rooms (some sharing bathrooms) with large windows overlookin agreeable scenery: the perfectly peaceful Singel canal at the front and a typically Dutch garden out the back.

Hotel Mayflower (☎ 514 26 41; www.hotelmayflower .nl; Beestenmarkt 2; s/d from €75/95) These large rooms are bright but are something of a throwback to another era of lodging – say the 1980s. But the hotel is well located and a short walk from the station. Apartments are also available.

ourpick **Hotel Nieuw Minerva** (☎ 512 63 58; www.nieuwminerva.nl; Boommarkt 23; r €80-150; 💻 ☎) Located in six 16th-century canalside houses, this central hotel has a mix of 40 regular and themed rooms, including a room with a bed in which King Lodewijk Bonaparte (aka Louis Bonaparte) slept.

Hotel de Doelen (☎ 512 05 27; www.dedoelen.com; Rapenburg 2; s/d from €85/105; 💻 ☎) It has a slightly faded air of classical elegance; some canalside rooms in this regal building are larger and better appointed than others.

Rembrandt Hotel (☎ 514 42 33; www.rembrandthotel .nl; Nieuw Beestenmarkt 10; r €90-120; 💻) Light pouring in the windows makes the white decor of the 20 rooms that much brighter at this historic but well-cared-for inn. Rooms have high-speed internet and work desks.

Eating

Annie's (☎ 512 57 37; Hoogstraat 1a; mains from €8; ⊗ 11am-1am) At the confluence of canals and pedestrian zones, Annie's has a prime water-level location with dozens of tables on a floating pontoon. This classy cafe is good for a drink or a casual meal.

Brasserie Het Koetshuis (☎ 512 16 88; Burgsteeg 13; meals from €8) Right in the shadow of De Burcht, you can sit on the large terrace and ponder the ramparts or huddle inside at a long table in what was once stables. Cafe classics dominate

the long and varied menu. It's a good place just for a drink through the day and evening.

Stadscafé van der Werff (☎ 512 61 20; Stationsweg 7-9; meals €9-15; ⊗ lunch) Bright, with large windows and the usual cafe menu. The terrace is a wonderful place on a sunny day.

Surakarta (☎ 512 35 24; Noordeinde 51-53; mains from €12; ⊗ dinner; 🍴) Javanese art lines the walls at this neighbourhood Indonesian place, which does a busy takeaway service in addition to its elegant *rijsttafel* (array of spicy dishes served with white rice) service. Several other ethnic places are nearby.

ourpick **Mangerie De Jonge Koekop** (☎ 514 19 37; Lange Mare 60; meals from €32; ⊗ dinner Mon-Sat) Always popular, this bistro has fresh and inventive fare. Dine under the stars at outside tables in summer. Look for the sculpted cow's head on the front, which is as narrow as the first stalk of spring asparagus.

La Cloche (☎ 512 30 53; Kloksteeg 3; meals from €40; ⊗ dinner Mon-Sat) A stalwart of the Pieterskerk district, the years have not dimmed the passion for fine dining at this very inviting Frenchified restaurant. In fact the flowers just seem to get fresher and more numerous. The inside is all elegance: brass and chandeliers.

Drinking

Café l'Esperance (☎ 512 16 00; Kaiserstraat 1) Long, dark and handsome, all decked out in nostalgic wood panelling *and* overlooking an evocative bend in the canal. Tables abound outside in summer.

Café Jantje van Leiden (☎ 514 04 18; Hartesteeg 2) As narrow a brown cafe as you'll find. Take your glass of beer and plop down on a bench out the front.

Entertainment
LIVE MUSIC

In Casa (☎ 512 49 38; www.danssalonincasa.nl; Lammermarkt 100; ⊗ from 11pm Thu-Sat) This place is huge and, from the outside, looks as though it has no atmosphere – but appearances can be deceiving. It has live music, a dance floor, comedy and a variety of other events.

Jazzcafé the Duke (☎ 566 15 85; www.jazzcafetheduke .nl; Oude Singel 2) 'If we don't have it, you don't need it' is its motto, and amid this cool-cat interior of yellowing, vintage jazz posters, the fine live jazz never makes you doubt it.

LVC (☎ 514 64 49; www.lvc.nl; Breestraat 66; ⊗ from 11pm Fri & Sat) Huge pulsing venue with everything from disco to rave.

Shopping

Haarlemmerstraat has all the mainstream chain stores. Big department stores spill across to Breestraat. Look for more interesting shops on side streets such as Vrouwenstraat and in the lanes around Pieterskerk.

Getting There & Away

BICYCLE

The bicycle shop in Centraal Station is on the west side. Head west from the station on bike paths along Geversstraat and then via Rijnsburg for 10km to the beach at Katwijk. There you can pick up national route LF1, which connects with the LF20 for the 34km ride north to Haarlem. Head south on the LF1 20km along the shore to Scheveningen and Den Haag.

BUS

Regional and local buses leave from the bus station directly in front of Centraal Station.

TRAIN

Centraal Station is bold and modern. It has full services ad many shops; lockers are up near platform No 1. Sample fares and schedules:

Destination	Price (€)	Duration (min)	Frequency (per hr)
Amsterdam	8	34	6
Den Haag	3.20	10	6
Schiphol Airport	5.30	15	6

Getting Around

Leiden is compact and you'll have a hard time walking for more than 20 minutes in any one direction.

AROUND LEIDEN
Keukenhof Gardens

Covering some 32 hectares, the **Keukenhof** (www.keukenhof.nl; adult/under 11yr €13.50/6.50; ☒ 8am-7.30pm mid-Mar–mid-May, last entry 6pm) is the world's largest bulb-flower garden, attracting nearly 800,000 visitors during a mere eight weeks every year.

The gardens stretch on and on, and there are greenhouses full of more delicate varieties of flowers besides the ephemeral tulips. You'll forgive the presence of thousands of other tourists – little can detract from the rainbow of natural beauty. Wandering about can easily take half a day. From the edges of the gardens,

you can see the stark beauty of the commercial bulb fields stretching in all directions.

Opening dates vary slightly from year to year, so check before setting out. Connexxion bus 54 travels from Leiden Centraal Station to Keukenhof (25 minutes, four times per hour). A combo ticket for the bus and the gardens costs adult/child €20/11. All tickets can be purchased online, which helps avoid huge queues. The gardens are 4km inland from the coastal national bike route LF1. You'll need a map.

See p165 for details on the Aalsmeer Flower Auction, the largest of its type in the world.

Lisse

Located just 1km east of Keukenhof, the **tourist office** (☎ 0252-41 42 62; Grachtweg 53a; ☒ noon-5pm Mon, 9am-5pm Tue-Fri, 9am-4pm Sat) in the village of Lisse can give you many options for bulb-field touring. Also in town, the small **Museum de Zwarte Tulp** (Museum of the Black Tulip; ☎ 0252-41 79 00; www.museumdezwartetulp.nl; Grachtweg 2a; adult/child €3/2; ☒ 1-5pm Tue-Sun) displays everything you might want to know about bulbs, including why there's no such thing as a black tulip, a mythical posy that helped drive Tulipmania in 1636 (see the boxed text, p26).

DEN HAAG (THE HAGUE)
☎ 070 / pop 486,000

Den Haag today is a stately, regal place filled with palatial embassies and mansions, green boulevards and parks, a brilliant culinary scene, a clutch of fine museums and a sybaritic cafe culture. It's the kind of place where the musky aftershave of suave men wearing pink cravats mingles with the frilly scents of sachets sold in pricey boutiques. More elemental, the seaside suburb of Scheveningen boasts lively kitsch and a long stretch of beach.

Den Haag, officially known as 's-Gravenhage (the Count's Hedge), is the Dutch seat of government and home to the royal family. Prior to 1806, Den Haag was the Dutch capital. However, that year, Louis Bonaparte installed his government in Amsterdam. Eight years later, when the French had been ousted, the government returned to Den Haag, but the title of capital remained with Amsterdam.

In the 20th century Den Haag became the home of several international legal entities, including the UN's International Court of Justice, which regularly holds trials that put Den Haag in the headlines.

ZUID HOLLAND & ZEELAND

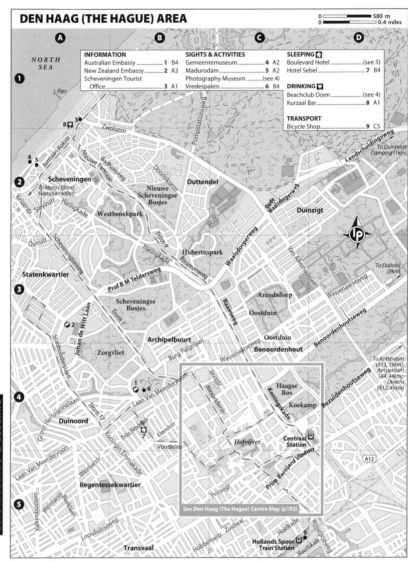

DEN HAAG (THE HAGUE) AREA

0 ————— 580 m
0 ————— 0.4 miles

INFORMATION
Australian Embassy **1** B4
New Zealand Embassy **2** A3
Scheveningen Tourist
Office **3** A1

SIGHTS & ACTIVITIES
Gemeentemuseum **4** A2
Madurodam **5** A2
Photography Museum ......(see 4)
Vredespaleis **6** B4

SLEEPING
Boulevard Hotel ....(see 5)
Hotel Sebel **7** B4

DRINKING
Beachclub Doen ....(see 4)
Kurzaal Bar **8** A1

TRANSPORT
Bicycle Shop **9** C5

Orientation

Den Haag is spread over a fairly large area. Centraal Station (CS) is near the heart of town; Hollands Spoor station (HS), on the main line from Amsterdam to Rotterdam and destinations further south, is 1km south of the town centre. Most streets heading west reach Scheveningen, 4km away, but it's more pleasantly approached at the end of a 15- to 20-minute bike ride that will take you past the lush homes of some of Den Haag's most well-heeled residents.

Den Haag has no true city centre; instead you'll find there are several areas of concentration, including the Binnenhof and the nearby Kerkplein.

Information

BOOKSHOPS

Stanley & Livingstone (Map p192; ☎ 365 73 06; Schoolstraat 21) An excellent travel bookshop.

Van Stockum (Map p192; ☎ 365 68 08; www.vanstock um.nl; Venestraat 11) Travel books and magazines.

INTERNET ACCESS

Many cafes have free wi-fi.

Kado Internet (Map p192; Spui 165; per hr €3)

Koninklijke Bibliotheek (Royal Library; Map p192; ☎ 314 09 11; Prins Willem-Alexanderhof 5; per hr €3; ⏰ 9am-6pm Mon & Wed-Fri, 9am-8pm Tue, 9am-1pm Sat) Free wi-fi.

POST

Post office (Map p192; ☎ 365 38 43; Kerkplein 6; ⏰ 9am-6pm Mon-Wed & Fri, 9am-8pm Thu, 9am-4pm Sat)

TOURIST INFORMATION

Scheveningen Tourist Office (Map p190; ☎ 0900 3403 405; www.scheveningen.nl; Gevers Deynootweg 1134; ⏰ 9am-5.30pm Mon-Fri, 10am-5pm Sat, 11am-4pm Sun)

Tourist office (Map p192; ☎ 0900 340 35 05; www .denhaag.com; Hofweg 1; ⏰ 10am-6pm Mon-Fri, to 5pm Sat, noon-5pm Sun) Adjoins a large cafe.

Dangers & Annoyances

The area south of the town centre (the Schilderswijk) near HS can seem far removed from its urbane counterpart to the north. Watch out for pickpockets.

Sights & Activities

Den Haag has no true core, rather a scattering of districts. All are easily reached by trams or bike.

MAURITSHUIS

For a painless introduction to Dutch and Flemish Art 101, visit the **Mauritshuis** (Map p192; ☎ 302 34 56; www.mauritshuis.nl; Korte Vijverberg 8; adult/child €12/free; ⏰ 10am-5pm Tue-Sat, 11am-5pm Sun), a small museum in a jewel-box of an old palace. Highlights include the Dutch *Mona Lisa*: Vermeer's *Girl with a Pearl Earring*. Rembrandts include a wistful self-portrait from the year of his death, 1669, and *The Anatomy Lesson of Dr Nicolaes Tulp*.

The building was constructed as a mansion in 1640 in classical style; all its dimensions are roughly the same (25m), and the detailing shows exquisite care. In 1822 it was made the home of the royal collection. The collection is

displayed in 16 rooms on two floors – almost every piece is a masterpiece.

Even if you're just passing Den Haag on the train, it's well worth hopping off to visit.

BINNENHOF

Adjoining the Mauritshuis, the Binnenhof (Inner Court; Map p192) is surrounded by parliamentary buildings that have long been at the heart of Dutch politics, though parliament now meets in a modern building on the south side.

The central courtyard looks sterile today but was once used for executions. A highlight of the complex is the 13th-century **Ridderzaal** (Knights' Hall). The Gothic dining hall has been carefully restored.

The North Wing is still home to the Upper Chamber of the Dutch Parliament, in 17th-century splendour. The Lower Chamber used to meet in the ballroom, in the 19th-century wing. It all looks a bit twee and you can see why the politicians were anxious to decamp to the sleek new extension nearby.

The best way to see the Binnenhof's buildings is on a one-hour tour, which leaves from the **visitors centre** (☎ 364 61 44; ⏰ 10am-4pm Mon-Sat). Here you can see a model showing the hotchpotch of buildings that make up the Binnenhof, and you can learn about the turbulent past of the Low Countries, where invaders have flooded in more often than the waters.

After your walk, stroll around the Hofvijver, where the reflections of the Binnenhof and the Mauritshuis have inspired countless snapshots.

DEN HAAG: OLD & NEW

Across the Hofvijver from the Binnenhof, the **Gevangenpoort** (Prison Gate; Map p192; ☎ 346 08 61; www.gevangenpoort.nl; Buitenhof 33) is a surviving remnant of the 13th-century city fortifications. It usually has hourly tours showing how justice was dispensed back then, but is under renovation throughout 2010.

Next door, the **Galerij Prins Willem V** (Map p192; ☎ 362 44 44; www.mauritshuis.nl; Buitenhof 35) was the first public museum in the Netherlands when it opened in 1773. Paintings are hung in the manner popular in the 18th century. The gallery is also part of the Gevangenpoort renovations.

The **Grote Kerk** (Map p192; ☎ 302 86 30; Rond de Grote Kerk 12), dating from 1450, has a fine

DEN HAAG (THE HAGUE) CENTRE

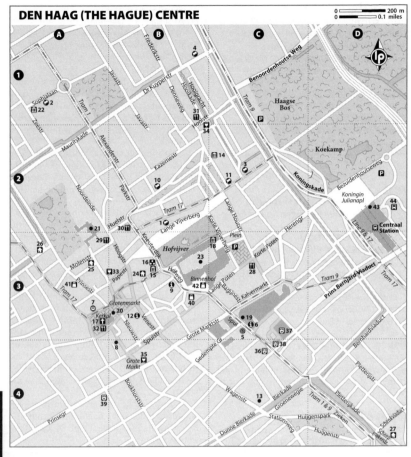

pulpit that was constructed 100 years later. The neighbouring 1565 **old town hall** (*oude raadhuis*; Map p192) is a splendid example of Dutch Renaissance architecture.

The huge **new town hall** (Map p192; Spui 170) is the hotly debated work by US architect Richard Meier. The 'official' nickname of the building is the 'white swan', but locals prefer the 'ice palace'. Even better are the local nicknames for two government buildings nearby; if allowed, take the elevator to the town hall's 11th floor and look at the complex that has two pointed towers at one end and a dome-topped round tower at the other. The local moniker is 'the tits and penis'.

Names are more polite for the king's and queen's official quarters at **Paleis Noordeinde** (Map p192). The Renaissance formality of the structure bespeaks regal digs. It's not open to the public, and the strong gates ensure security in case the populace revolts for having their taxes spent on anatomically suggestive buildings.

ESCHER IN HET PALEIS MUSEUM

The Lange Voorhout Palace was once Queen Emma's residence. Now it's home to the work of Dutch graphic artist MC Escher. **Escher in het Paleis Museum** (Map p192; ☎ 338 11 20; www.escherin hetpaleis.nl; Lange Voorhout; adult/child €7.50/5; ⊗ 11am-5pm Tue-Sun) is a permanent exhibition featuring notes, letters, drafts, photos and fully mature works covering Escher's entire career, from his early realism to the later phantasmagoria. There are some imaginative displays, including a virtual reality reconstruction of Escher's impossible buildings.

GEMEENTEMUSEUM

Admirers of De Stijl, and in particular of Piet Mondrian, mustn't miss the Berlage-designed **Gemeentemuseum** (Municipal Museum; Map p190; ☎ 338 11 20; www.gemeentemuseum.nl; Stadhouderslaan 41; adult/under 18yr €9/free; ⊗ 11am-5pm Tue-Sun). It houses a large collection of works by neoplasticist artists and others from the late 19th century, as well as extensive exhibits of applied arts, costumes and musical instruments.

Mondrian's unfinished *Victory Boogie Woogie* takes pride of place (as it should: the museum paid €30 million for it), and there are also a few Picassos and other works by some of the better-known names of the 20th century. Take tram 17 from CS and HS.

PHOTOGRAPHY MUSEUM

Adjoining the Gemeentemuseum, the **Photography Museum** (Foto-Museum Den Haag; Map p190; ☎ 338 11 44; www.fotomuseumdenhaag.nl; Stadhouderslaan 43; adult/child €5/free; ⊗ noon-6pm Tue-Sun) has several major exhibitions a year.

PANORAMA MESDAG

Just past the north end of Noordeinde, the **Panorama Mesdag** (Map p192; ☎ 364 45 44; www .panorama-mesdag.nl; Zeestraat 65; adult/under 13yr €5/2.50; ⊗ 10am-5pm Mon-Sat, noon-5pm Sun) contains the *Panorama* (1881), a huge 360-degree painting of Scheveningen that was painted by Hendrik Willem Mesdag. The panorama is viewed from a constructed dune, with real sand and beach chairs; birdsong and wave sounds are piped through. Masterful achievement aside, you could just head 4km west to the real thing.

VREDESPALEIS

The UN International Court of Justice is housed in the **Vredespaleis** (Peace Palace; Map p190; ☎ 302 41 37; Carnegieplein 2; tours adult/child €5/3; ⊗ 10am-3pm Mon-Fri). The grand building was donated by American steel maker Andrew Carnegie for use by the International Court of Arbitration, an early international body whose goal was the prevention of war. Sadly, WWI broke out one year after it opened in 1913.

There are hourly guided tours, but if the courts are in session these tours may be cancelled – check first. You need to book ahead (security is strict). Take tram 1 from HS.

MADURODAM

Complete with 1:25 scale versions of Schiphol, Amsterdam, windmills and tulips, Rotterdam harbour and the Delta dykes, **Madurodam** (Map p190; ☎ 355 39 00; www.madurodam.nl; George Maduroplein 1; adult/child under 11yr €12.50/9; ⊗ 9am-8pm) is a miniaturised Netherlands. It's an enlightening example of the Dutch tendency to put their world under a microscope.

Take tram 9 from CS and HS.

SCHEVENINGEN

The long beach at **Scheveningen** (Map p190; www .scheveningen.nl), pronounced – if possible – as s'CHay-fuh-ninger, attracts nine million visitors per year. It's horribly developed: architects who lost hospital commissions have designed all manner of modern nightmares overlooking the strand. Scads of cafes elbow each other for space on tiers of promenades

---

ESCAPE TO THE DUNES

Open sand, endless beach, hillocks of dunes, the sounds of seagulls and shore; all this is easily accessible from Den Haag and Scheveningen.

To the south, a mere 1km past the harbour puts you in the heart of nature. From here you can continue along the coast for pretty much as long as you've got the fortitude, with only the odd simple beach cafe for relief. Take tram 12 from Hollands Spoor station (HS) to the end of the line right in the heart of the dunes.

Heading north, follow the beach past the end of tram lines 1 and 9. Here the dunes are pristine and the further you walk or cycle, the greater the rewards. You'll also pass a series of WWII bunkers, part of the Nazi Atlantic Wall defence system and an eerie reminder of the Netherlands' place in European history.

National bike route LF1 follows the coast throughout the region. Tellingly, it only diverts inland near Scheveningen when it passes through parks to avoid the chaos.

---

by the beach, their themes taken from resorts with more reliable weather worldwide. It's tacky, but you might just find pleasure in the carnival atmosphere. Better yet, you can escape to wide-open beaches and nature with just a bit of effort, especially to the south where the hype tapers off as you pass the harbour. See above for details.

Tours

The tourist office offers excellent walking and cycling guides (€2) in English with a variety of themes, including 'The Royal Kilometres'.

De Ooievaart (Map p190; www.ooievaart.nl; adult/3-12yr €10/6; ☼ departures 10.30am-4.30pm Fri & Sat May-Sep) offers boat tours over various 1½-hour routes, taking in Den Haag's most interesting sights at canal level. Check for sailings in spring and fall.

Festivals & Events

Parkpop (www.parkpop.nl) in late June draws some 350,000 pop music fans to town for free concerts by big names in Zuiderpark.

Sleeping

BUDGET

Duinhorst (off Map p190; ☎ 324 22 70; www.duinhorst.nl; Buurtweg 135; camp sites from €13; ☼ Apr-Sep) To get to this camping ground take bus 28 from HS or bus 22 from CS to the end of the line at Oude Waalsdorperweg and then walk about 1km west, or take a taxi.

Stayokay Den Haag (Map p192; ☎ 315 78 88; www.stayokay.com/denhaag; Scheepmakerstraat 27; dm from €23; ▯) This branch of the Stayokay hostel chain has all the usual facilities, including a bar, a

restaurant, internet and games. It's around 15 minutes' walk from HS station.

MIDRANGE

Hotel 't Centrum (Map p192; ☎ 346 36 57; www.hotelhetcentrum.nl; Veenkade 5-6; r €50-120; ☏) The 21 rooms here are the best deal close to the centre. Things are basic white but spotless and comfortable; some rooms share bathrooms. Apartments have basic cooking facilities and there's a small cafe. Book ahead.

Boulevard Hotel (Map p190; ☎ 354 00 67; www.boulevardhotel.nl; Seinpostduin 1, Scheveningen; r €85-140; ☏) A classic old beach hotel that's more attractive than its modern neighbours, the Boulevard is unpretentious. Rooms are seashore simple, but you can take your breakfast in the conservatory or patio with views down to the surf.

Corona Hotel (Map p192; ☎ 363 79 30; www.corona.nl; Buitenhof 39-42; r from €90; ▯ ☏) This pleasant hotel is across from the Binnenhof and has all the usual business facilities and amenities. Rooms span a range of styles out of the corporate catalogue.

Hotel Sebel (Map p190; ☎ 385 92 00; Prins Hendrikplein 20; r €80-150; ☏) This 33-room boutique hotel is in a proud art nouveau corner building. Everything has been tastefully updated and the lobby is downright minimalist. The cheapest rooms let you touch the walls – all at once. It's on tram line 17 from CS and HS.

TOP END

Het Paleis Hotel (Map p192; ☎ 362 46 21; www.paleishotel.nl; Molenstraat 26; r from €200; ▨ ▯ ☏) Near the Noordeinde palace, its location alone is atmospheric, but the antique trimmings in the room match it superbly. The 20 rooms are traditionally luxurious with thick drapes and carpet that will swallow your toes.

Eating

Den Haag's gastronomic scene is very good, with quality matched by the variety you'd expect in an international city. The cobbled streets and canals off Denneweg are a excellent place to stroll hungry.

Coffee @ Company (Map p192; ☎ 362 41 12; Noordeinde 54; treats from €2; ☺ 10am-7pm; ☎) One of the slicker of several funky coffee joints off Molenstraat. Free wi-fi.

Zebedeüs (Map p192; ☎ 346 83 93; Rond de Grote Kerk 8; meals from €7; ☺ 11am-7pm) Built right into the walls of the Grote Kerk, this bright cafe is a day-tripper's dream, with huge, fresh sandwiches served all day. Grab one of the many tree-shaded tables outside or relax with a coffee and a newspaper at the big tables within.

Cloos (Map p192; ☎ 363 97 86; Plein 12a; mains from €8) One of a gaggle of swank cafes on the vast Plein. Rest your gentrified butt on the comfy wicker chairs and watch the pigeons bedevil the solemn statue of Willem Den Eerste, hero of the Spanish war. No telling what the famous nationalist would have thought about Cloos' Italian menu.

ourpick Les Ombrellas (Map p192; ☎ 365 87 89; Hooistraat 4; mains €15-30; ☺ lunch Mon-Fri, dinner Mon-Sat) At a confluence of canals in one of the city's most charming districts, this long-running favourite sets up tables across the shady plaza. The tank with live crabs tells you that this is seafood country and the very long menu abounds with choice.

Garoeda (Map p192; ☎ 346 53 19; Kneuterdijk 18a; meals €15-30) Since 1949, this elegant restaurant has been serving spicy and fresh Indonesian fare from its airy corner location. Most people opt for one of seven variations of *rijsttafel*, the panoply of dishes that let you savour foods from across the archipelago.

Mero (off Map p190; ☎ 352 36 00; Vissershavenweg 61, Scheveningen; mains €20-30; ☺ lunch Tue-Fri, dinner Tue-Sat) Industrial chic is the style at this harbourside brasserie serving the best fish in the area. The bold crustacean art on the walls is matched by the bold flavours on the plate. Near tram 11.

Drinking

Beachclub Doen (Map p190; Strandweg 9, Scheveningen; ☺ May-Sep) A vision of white, Doen is one of the least tacky of the plethora of beach bars lining the sands. Palm trees shivering in the North

Sea breeze add atmosphere to sofas, loungers and other good chillin' and drinkin' spots.

Café De Oude Mol (Map p192; ☎ 345 16 23; Oude Molstraat 61; snacks from €3) Some of the *oude* (old) *National Geographics* piled in the window actually predate the crusty yet genial characters arrayed around the bar. Pass through the ivy-covered door and you'll find Den Haag without the pretence.

Cafe Hathor (Map p192; ☎ 346 40 81; Maliestraat 22; meals from €10; ☺ 11am-1am Mon-Sat) Sit out on a barge/annexe behind this quaint little boozer hard on a canal. It's always merry and you can get a burger to wash down your pints.

ourpick De Zwarte Ruiter (The Black Rider; Map p192; ☎ 364 95 49; Grote Markt 27; snacks from €4) The Rider faces off with the competing Boterwaag across the Markt like rival Kings of Cool. We call this one the winner, with its terrace and art deco mezzanine – light-filled, split-level and cavernous – and boisterous crowds of commoners, diplomats and, no doubt, the odd international jewel thief.

Entertainment

Paard van Troje (Map p192; ☎ 750 34 34; www.paard.nl; Prinsegracht 12) This emporium has club nights and live music, as well as a cafe. The program's eclectic: everything from booty-shaking DJs to cutting-edge State-X New Forms.

Nederlands Dans Theater (Map p192; ☎ 880 01 00; www.ndt.nl; Schedeldoekshaven 60) This world-famous dance company has two main components: NDT1, the main troupe of 32 dancers, and NDT2, a small group of 12 dancers under 21.

Other options:
Cinematheek Haags Filmhuis (Map p192; ☎ 365 60 30; www.filmhuisdenhaag.nl; Spui 191) Screens foreign and indie movies.
Dr Anton Philipszaal (Map p192; ☎ 360 98 10; www .dapz.ldt.nl; Spui 150) Home to the Residentie Orkest, Den Haag's classical symphony orchestra.

Shopping

Den Haag is brilliant for shopping, with several good districts for browsing.

Grote Marktstraat is, fittingly enough, where you'll find all the major department stores and chains. Going north things get much more interesting. **De Passage** (Map p192; www.depassage.nl), off Hofweg ad Spuistraat, is a 19th-century covered arcade built to give locals an option for luxury goods from Paris.

Hoogstraat, Noordeinde and Heulstraat are all good for interesting and eclectic shops and galleries. But the real treats are along Prinsestraat, where **Pussy Deluxe Store** (Map p192; ☎ 365 47 47; Prinsestraat 88) has a boffo selection of upmarket women's undies.

Denneweg is another fine area for retail therapy, with some fine antique galleries and shops. Wander north over a canal and the street becomes Frederikstraat, with some excellent delis and bakeries.

Den Haag has many markets. One of the best is the **Traditional Market** (Map p192; Hofweg; ⊙ 10am-6pm Wed), which has all manner of foodstuffs and household items, many organic and/or green.

Getting There & Away
BICYCLE
The **bicycle shop** (Map p192; ☎ 385 32 35) in CS is under the terminal. The HS **bicycle shop** (Map p190; ☎ 389 08 30) is at the southern end of that station. Both shops rent out bikes. The coastal national bike route LF1 runs just inland of Scheveningen. Leiden can be reached by going 20 miles north and heading inland. LF11 runs southeast 11km to Delft.

BUS
Eurolines long-distance buses and regional buses depart from the Eurolines bus station (Map p192) above the tracks at CS.

TRAIN
Den Haag has two main train stations. CS (or Centraal Station) – a terminus – is close to the centre. It is a hub for local trams and buses. HS is about 1km south of the centre and is on the main railway line between Amsterdam and Rotterdam. Both have lockers and a full array of services.

Den Haag is meant to have high-speed Fyra rail services via Rotterdam, once that service starts running. Current sample train services:

Destination	Price (€)	Duration (min)	Frequency (per hr)
Amsterdam	10	50	4
Leiden	3.20	15	4
Rotterdam	4.30	25	4
Schiphol	7.30	30	4
Utrecht	9.70	40	4

Getting Around
Most tram routes converge on CS, at the tram and bus station above the tracks and on the western side. A number of routes also serve HS, including the jack-of-all-trades tram 1, which starts in Scheveningen and runs all the way to Delft, passing through the centre of Den Haag along the way. Trams 1, 9 and 11 link Scheveningen with Den Haag. The last tram runs in either direction at about 1.30am.

Tram and bus operator **HTM** (www.htm.net) sells a highly useful day pass for €6.40, but you can only buy it from windows with often-long lines in CS and HS. There are no ticket machines.

Call **ATC Taxi** (☎ 317 88 77) for a cab.

GOUDA
☎ 0182 / pop 70,800
Gouda's association with cheesy comestibles has made it famous – the town's namesake fermented curd is among the Netherlands' best-known exports. But Gouda, the town, has a bit more to it than that.

Gouda enjoyed economic success and decline in the same manner as the rest of Holland from the 16th century onwards. Its cheese has brought recent wealth, as has the country's largest candle factory, which stays busy supplying all those Dutch brown cafes. The acclaimed 16th-century stained-glass windows in its church are a highlight.

Gouda makes a fine day trip, easily accessible from any city in Zuid Holland. The compact centre is entirely ringed by canals and is a mere five minutes' walk from the station. The large central square, the Markt, is the focus of the town.

Information
Gouda is in the middle of a region tourist authorities have dubbed the 'Groene Hart' (Green Heart) for its many farms laced with canals and dotted with tidy small Dutch towns. There's a useful regional website, www .vvvhetgroenehart.nl, with touring info.
Tourist office (☎ 0900 4683 2888; www.vvvgouda .nl; Markt 27; ⊙ 1-5.30pm Mon, 9.30am-5.30pm Tue-Fri, 10am-4pm Sat year-round, also noon-4pm Sun Jul & Aug)

Sights
Most of the notable sights are within 10 minutes' walk of the trapezoidal Markt, but wander off down little side streets such as Achter de Kerk and Lage Gouwe, which pass quiet canals and seem untouched by the centuries. Or try the Lange Tiendeweg and Zeugstraat with its tiny canal and even tinier bridges.

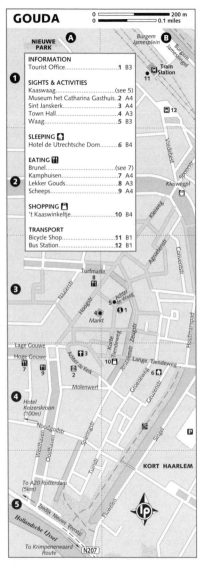

provide a fine counterpoint to the carefully maintained stonework.

On the north side of the Markt, you can't miss the **Waag**, a former cheese-weighing house built in 1668. If you have any doubt about its use, check out the reliefs carved into the side showing the cheese being weighed. It houses the **Kaaswaag** (☎ 52 99 96; adult/child €3.50/3; ☺ 1-5pm Tue-Sun Apr-Oct), a museum that follows the history of the cheese trade in the Netherlands, especially its history in Gouda. For more about the local curds, see p48. There is also a cool model of the Markt c 1990.

A traditional **cheese market** (www.goudakaas .nl; ☺ 10am-12.30pm Thu late-Jun–Aug) on the Markt draws plenty of tourists and there are dozens of stalls selling dairy goods and souvenirs. A few locals dress up in costume and pose for countless photos.

SINT JANSKERK & AROUND

Just to the south of the Markt is **Sint Janskerk** (☎ 51 26 84; www.sintjan.com; Achter de Kerk; adult/child €3/2; ☺ 10am-5pm Mon-Sat Mar-Oct, 10am-4pm Mon-Sat Nov-Feb, also 10am-5pm Sun year-round). The church itself had chequered beginnings: it burned down with ungodly regularity every 100 years or so from 1361 until the mid-16th century, when what you see today was completed. At 123m it is the longest church in the country.

Architecturally, Sint Janskerk is an attractive late-Gothic church in need of a better steeple, but its huge windows set it apart, especially those created by Dirck Crabeth, his brother Wouter, and Lambert van Noort from around 1550 to 1570. Their works, which are numbered, include highlights such as window No 6 (John the Baptist; the folks on either side paid for the window) and No 22 (Jesus purifies the temple; note the look on the face of the moneychanger).

To the immediate southwest of the church, near a small canal, the **Museum het Catharina Gasthuis** (☎ 58 84 40; Achter de Kerk 14; adult/child €5/free; ☺ 10am-5pm Wed-Fri, noon-5pm Sat & Sun), housed in an old hospital, covers Gouda's history and has a few artworks. In the basement there's a ghoulish section on local torture in the Middle Ages, including devices for the condemned (men were hanged but women were strangled to avoid people looking up their skirts).

Activities

There's a good circle ride through, well, the heart of the Groene Hart. It begins just

MARKT

The central Markt is one of the largest such squares in the Netherlands. Right in the middle is the mid-15th-century **town hall**. Constructed from shimmering sandstone, this regal Gothic structure bespeaks the wealth Gouda enjoyed from the cloth trade when it was built. The red-and-white shutters south of the centre and runs 42km through the canal-laced farmlands south of Gouda. Called the Krimpenerwaard Route after the region it covers, the route includes stops at dairies where cheese is made. Get the brochure from the tourist office, which can also help with the detailed maps needed for the ride.

Tours

Ask at the tourist office if there are any boat tours on. Schedules are erratic at best.

Sleeping

Given that Gouda is such a natural day trip, you might not think of staying here, but you may just appreciate its charms after dark. The tourist office has a list of a few private rooms it will book for a small fee.

Hotel Keizerskroon (☎ 52 80 96; www.hotelkeizers kroon.nl; Keizerstraat 11-13; r €50-100; 🛜) Centrally located, cosy, comfortable, warm and welcoming. The cheapest rooms share baths; you can rent bikes. Take your included breakfast in the restaurant at ground level.

Hotel de Utrechtsche Dom (☎ 52 88 33; www .hotelgouda.nl; Geuzenstraat 6; r €60-80; 🛜) Neat, clean and on a quiet street, this is a lovely, low-key place to stay, with good amenities. The complex has been an inn for more than 300 years, although the stables get little use from coachmen these days.

Eating & Drinking

Lekker Gouds (☎ 52 92 16; Hoogstraat; snacks from €3; 🕑 10am-6pm) An appealing deli right off the Markt, it's run by a longtime local cafe owner. There's a vast array of cheeses – try your old gouda here, or create a picnic.

ourpick Kamphuisen (☎ 51 41 63; Hoge Gouwe 19; mains €16-20; 🕑 5pm-midnight Tue-Sun, kitchen till 10pm) As brown a cafe as you'll find: a blackboard of drinks overlooks ancient wooden tables and light fixtures. Outside, there are tables under the eaves of the old fish market. The bar menu is ambitious: lamb, steak, fish and more. Book for dinner.

Scheeps (☎ 51 75 72; www.restaurantscheeps .nl; Westhaven 4; mains €17-30; 🕑 lunch & dinner) The flawless cream facade and potted olive trees suggest this place is special, and it is. The dining room is lined with art and features a contemporary menu of seasonal items prepared with a Mediterranean flair. Nice garden out the back, too.

Brunel (☎ 51 89 79; www.restaurantbrunel.nl; Hoge Grouwe 23; menus from €33; 🕑 dinner Tue-Sat) Classic top-end Dutch fare with a few twists: the mustard soup comes with fresh local shrimp, the roasted fish is served with a fine risotto of local vegetables and the white chocolate mousse? It's simply to die for. In summer, dine along the canal in the old colonnaded fish market.

Shopping

Kleiweg on the way from the train station has the usual chains. Better are the idiosyncratic shops in and around Jeruzalemstraat and Zeugstraat. Did we mention you can buy cheese?

't Kaaswinkeltje (☎ 51 42 69; www.kaaswinkeltje .com; Lange Tiendeweg 30) A cheese shop filled with fabulous smells and it's here that you can sample some of the aged Goudas that the Dutch wisely keep for themselves. The older the cheese, the sharper the flavour, and some of the very old Goudas have a Parmesan-like texture and a rich, smoky taste. With a little mustard smeared on, a hunk of this cheese is great with beer.

Lekker Gouds (left) is also a good cheesy stop.

Getting There & Around

Gouda's train station is close to the city centre and all you'll need are your feet for local transport. The lockers are near track 8. Sample fares and schedules:

Destination	Price (€)	Duration (min)	Frequency (per hr)
Amsterdam	10	60	2
Den Haag	5.10	20	4
Rotterdam	4.50	19	6
Utrecht	5.70	20	6

The bus station is immediately to the left as you exit the train station on the Centrum side. The one bus of interest here is bus 180 to Oudewater (p182) and on to Utrecht.

There are large car parks for your car or motorcycle on the town's periphery. Gouda is near the A12 motorway between Den Haag and Utrecht and the A20 to Rotterdam.

The **bicycle shop** (☎ 51 97 51) is in the train station on the far side from the centre. National bike route LF2, which links Amsterdam and Rotterdam, runs right through the Markt. Follow its twisting route 12km north along dramatic dykes across several large bodies of water to the village of Bodegraven, where you

can join the LF4 for the farm-filled 38km run
west to Den Haag.

DELFT
☎ 015 / pop 96,600

Ah, lovely Delft: compact, charming, relaxed.
It's a very popular tourist destination – day-
trippers (and lovers of beauty and refinement)
clamour to stroll Delft's narrow, canal-lined
streets, gazing at the remarkable old buildings and meditating on the life and career of
Golden Age painter Johannes Vermeer. The
artist was born in Delft and lived here – *View
of Delft*, one of his best-loved works, is an
enigmatic, idealised vision of the town (see
the boxed text, p201). Delft is also famous for
its 'delftware', the distinctive blue-and-white
pottery originally duplicated from Chinese
porcelain by 17th-century artisans.

Delft was founded around 1100 and grew
rich from weaving and trade in the 13th and
14th centuries. In the 15th century a canal
was dug to the Maas River, and the small port
there, Delfshaven, was eventually absorbed
by Rotterdam.

Orientation
The train station and neighbouring bus sta-
tion are a 10-minute stroll south of the central
Markt.

Information
If you need a post office, go to Rotterdam –
seriously.

Boekhandel Huyser (☎ 212 38 20; Choorstraat 1)
Good travel section and lots of English-language books.
Tourist office (☎ 0900 515 15 55; www.delft.nl; Hip-
polytusbuurt 4; ⌚ 11am-4pm Mon, 10am-4pm Tue-Fri,
10am-5pm Sat, 10am-4pm Sun) Free internet access and
excellent walking-tour brochures.

Sights & Activities
Delft is best seen on foot: almost all the interesting sights lie within a 1km radius of the Markt.
Much of the town dates from the 17th century
and is remarkably well preserved. Before you
leave the crowded Markt, note the **town hall**,
with its unusual combination of Renaissance
construction surrounding a 13th-century tower.
Behind it, the **Waag** is a 1644 weigh-house.

East of here, **Beestenmarkt** is a large open
space surrounded by fine buildings. Further
east, **Oostpoort** is the sole surviving piece of the
town's walls. **Koornmarkt**, leading south from
the Waag, is a quiet, tree-lined canal. Look for

the opulent facade of the **Gemeenlandshuis van
Delfland** on Oude Delft across the canal from
the Oude Kerk. It dates from 1505.

Sort of a high-brow theme park, the **Vermeer
Centre Delft** (☎ 213 85 88; Voldersgracht 21; adult/child
€6/4; ⌚ 10am-5pm) explores the artist's life and
works in detail, but actually has none of his
paintings. Displays go into great detail about
each of his paintings and place the subjects in
their historical context.

CHURCHES
The 14th-century **Nieuwe Kerk** (☎ 212 30 25; www
.nieuwekerk-delft.nl; Markt; adult/child €3.20/1.60; ⌚ 9am-
6pm Apr-Oct, 11am-4pm Nov-Mar, closed Sun) houses
the crypt of the Dutch royal family and the
mausoleum of Willem the Silent. There are
exhibitions about the House of Orange and
the church.

The fee includes entrance to the Gothic
Oude Kerk (☎ 212 30 15; www.oudekerk-delft.nl; Heilige
Geestkerkhof; ⌚ 9am-6pm Apr-Oct, 11am-4pm Nov-Mar,
closed Sun) – and vice versa. The latter, 800
years old, is a surreal sight: its tower leans
2m from the vertical. One of the tombs inside
is Vermeer's.

MUSEUMS
Opposite the Oude Kerk is the **Municipal Museum
het Prinsenhof** (☎ 260 23 58; www.gemeentemusea-delft
.nl; St Agathaplein 1; adult/child €7.50/free; ⌚ 11am-5pm
Tue-Sun), a former convent where Willem the
Silent was assassinated in 1584 (the bullet
hole in the wall is covered in Perspex to protect it from inquisitive visitors). The museum
displays various objects telling the story of
the Eighty Years War with Spain, as well as
17th-century paintings.

The **Museum Nusantara** (☎ 260 23 58; www
.nusantara-delft.nl; St Agathaplein 4; adult/child €3.50/free;
⌚ 10am-5pm Tue-Sat, 1-5pm Sun) shines a light on
the Netherlands' colonial past. There's a collection of furniture and other lifestyle artefacts
from 17th-century Batavia (now Jakarta), as
well as a 'colonial department' detailing the
beginnings of Dutch rule in Indonesia.

The **Legermuseum** (☎ 215 05 00; www.leger
museum.nl; Korte Geer 1; adult/child €7.50/3; ⌚ 10am-5pm
Mon-Fri, noon-5pm Sat & Sun) has a collection of old
Dutch military hardware displayed in a restored 17th-century arsenal. There are also
exhibits on the modern Dutch army, including the controversial and disastrous role it
played as part of the Bosnian peacekeeping
force during the 1990s.

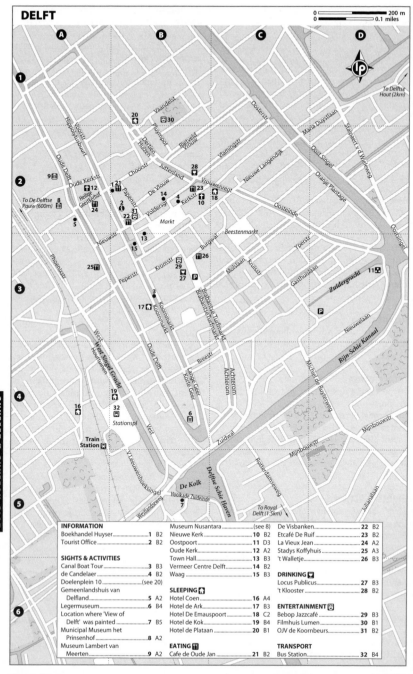

DELFT

INFORMATION		
Boekhandel Huyser	**1**	B2
Tourist Office	**2**	B2

SIGHTS & ACTIVITIES		
Canal Boat Tour	**3**	B3
de Candelaer	**4**	B2
Doelenplein 10	(see 20)	
Gemeenlandshuis van		
Delfland	**5**	A2
Legermuseum	**6**	B4
Location where 'View of		
Delft' was painted	**7**	B5
Municipal Museum het		
Prinsenhof	**8**	A2
Museum Lambert van		
Meerten	**9**	A2

Museum Nusantara	(see 8)	
Nieuwe Kerk	**10**	B2
Oostpoort	**11**	D3
Oude Kerk	**12**	A2
Town Hall	**13**	B3
Vermeer Centre Delft	**14**	B2
Waag	**15**	B3

SLEEPING		
Hotel Coen	**16**	A4
Hotel de Ark	**17**	B3
Hotel De Emauspoort	**18**	C2
Hotel de Kok	**19**	B4
Hotel de Plataan	**20**	B1

EATING		
Cafe de Oude Jan	**21**	B2

De Visbanken	**22**	B2
Etcafé De Ruif	**23**	B2
La Vieux Jean	**24**	A2
Stadys Koffyhuis	**25**	A3
't Walletje	**26**	B3

DRINKING		
Locus Publicus	**27**	B3
't Klooster	**28**	B2

ENTERTAINMENT		
Bebop Jazzcafé	**29**	B3
Filmhuis Lumen	**30**	B1
OJV de Koornbeurs	**31**	B2

TRANSPORT		
Bus Station	**32**	B4

VERMEER'S DELFT

Johannes Vermeer, one of the greatest of the Dutch old masters, lived his entire life in Delft (1632–75), fathering 11 children and leaving behind just 35 incredible paintings (the authenticity of two more is debated). Vermeer's works have rich and meticulous colouring and he captures light as few other painters have ever managed to. His scenes come from everyday life in Delft, his interiors capturing simple things such as the famous *Girl with a Pearl Earring,* giving a pho-tographic quality to his compositions.

Vermeer's best-known exterior work, *View of Delft,* brilliantly captures the play of light and shadow of a partly cloudy day. Visit the location where he painted it, across the canal at Hooikade, southeast of the train station. Unfortunately, none of Vermeer's works remain in Delft, although the Vermeer Centre Delft (p199) is a fine resource and the tourist office has a good walking tour brochure. The two works mentioned above can be seen at the Mauritshuis in Den Haag (p191), while arguably his most famous painting, *The Milkmaid,* resides in Amsterdam's Rijksmuseum (p105).

Vermeer's life is something of an enigma. What little is known about him is not flattering. His wife wrote this after he died:

…as a result and owing to the great burden of his children, having no means of his own, he had lapsed into such decay and decadence, which he had so taken to heart that, as if he had fallen into a frenzy, in a day or day and a half had gone from being healthy to being dead.

His fame grows by the year, however. The 2003 film *Girl with a Pearl Earring* (based on Tracy Chevalier's novel) speculated on his relationship with the eponymous girl. The following year, a work long thought to be a forgery was finally confirmed as authentic – *Young Woman Seated at the Virginals* was the first Vermeer to be auctioned in more than 80 years, selling to an anony-mous buyer for €24 million.

The excellent website www.essentialvermeer.com has exhaustive details on the painter and his works.

DELFTWARE

The town's ubiquitous blue-and-white china is almost a cliché. Given that the process was first developed in China, it's ironic that the mass of fake delftware sold in tourist shops also comes from China. The real stuff is produced in fairly small quantities at four factories in and around Delft. There are three places where you can actually see the artists at work.

The most central and modest outfit is **de Candelaer** (☎ 213 18 48; www.candelaer.nl; Kerkstraat 13; ☻ 9am-5.30pm Mon-Fri, 9am-5pm Sat year-round, also 9am-5pm Sun Mar-May), just off the Markt. It has five artists, a few of whom work most days. When it's quiet they'll give you a detailed tour of the manufacturing process.

The other two locations, outside the town centre, are basically factories. **De Delftse Pauw** (The Delft Peacock; ☎ 212 49 20; www.delftsepauw.com; Delftweg 133; ☻ 9am-4.30pm Apr-Oct, 9am-4.30pm Mon-Fri, 11am-1pm Sat Nov-Mar) is the smaller of the two, employing 35 painters who work mainly from home. It has daily tours, but you won't see the painters on weekends. Take tram 1 to Vrijenbanselaan.

Royal Delft (☎ 251 20 30; www.royaldelft.com; Rotterdamseweg 196; ☻ 9am-5pm Apr-Oct, closed Sun Nov-Mar) is the only original factory operating since the 1650s. Bus 129 from the train station stops nearby at Jaffalaan, or it's a 15-minute walk from the train station.

The **Museum Lambert van Meerten** (☎ 260 23 58; Oude Delft 199; adult/child €3.50/1.50; ☻ 10am-5pm Tue-Sat, 1-5pm Sun) has a fine collection of porcelain tiles and delftware dating back to the 16th century, all displayed in a 19th-century mansion.

Tours

See Delft on a 45-minute **canal boat tour** (☎ 212 63 85; www.rondvaartdelft.nl; adult/child under 12 €6/3; ☻ 11am-5pm Apr-Oct) departing from Koornmarkt 113.

Sleeping

Note that in summer Delft's accommodation is heavily booked. Reserve well ahead, or visit the town as a day trip. Conversely, Delft's small size and the proximity of the train sta-tion makes it a great base for exploring the rest of Zuid Holland. Rates at many places shoot up on weekends in summer.

BUDGET

Delftse Hout (☎ 213 00 40; www.delftsehout.nl; Korftlaan 5; camp sites €24-28; 🖳 🛜) This well-equipped camping ground is just northeast of town. Take bus 80 or 82 from the bus station or use the camping ground's shuttle. It has 160 sites and is a 15-minute walk from the Markt.

MIDRANGE

Hotel de Kok (☎ 212 21 25; www.hoteldekok.nl; Houttuinen 15; r €70-125; 🛜) The 30 rooms here are simple but very conveniently located near the train station. There's a sweet garden terrace.

Hotel Coen (☎ 214 59 14; www.hotelcoen.nl; Coenderstraat 47; r from €75; 🖳 🛜) Just behind the train station, this family-run hotel has 55 beds in a variety of rooms, from budget singles as thin as your wallet to grander doubles.

Hotel De Emauspoort (☎ 219 02 19; www.emaus poort.nl; Vrouwenregt 9-11; s/d from €90/100, s/d caravan €75/85; 🛜) Comfy, old-style rooms, plus two attentively restored gypsy caravans out the back. The family's bakery-confectionery store next door provides the breakfast treats.

Hotel de Plataan (☎ 212 60 46; www.hoteldeplataan .nl; Doelenplein 10; s/d from €100/130; 🛜) Delft's finest accommodation is on a delightful square. Standard rooms are small but elegant and have fridges. Then there are the wonderfully opulent theme rooms, including the 'Garden of Eden'; the 'Amber', based on Eastern stylings; or the jaw-dropping 'Tamarinde', themed after a desert island.

Hotel de Ark (☎ 215 79 99; www.deark.nl; Koornmarkt 65; r €115-160; 🖳 🛜) Four 17th-century canal-side houses have been turned into this gracious and luxurious small hotel. Rooms are reached by elevator and have vintage beauty that isn't stuffy. Out the back there's a small garden; nearby are apartments for longer stays.

Eating

RESTAURANTS

De Visbanken (☎ 361 20 14; Camaretten 2; snacks from €3; 🕙 10am-6pm) People have been selling fish on this spot since 1342. The present vendors line the display cases in the old open-air pavilion with all manner of things fishy. Enjoy marinated and smoked treats or go for something fried.

Stadys Koffyhuis (☎ 212 46 25; www.stads -koffyhuis.nl; Oude Delft 133; mains €7-10) Savour Delft from seats on a terrace barge moored out the front. Savour drinks, sandwiches and pancakes while admiring possibly the best view in Delft – the Oude Kerk, just ahead at the end of the canal.

ourpick 't Walletje (☎ 214 04 23; Burgwal 7; mains €7-12) Tables front this small bistro on a pedestrian street near the town centre. Lunch has good smoothies, sandwiches and salads. At night three-course specials (€20) are artfully prepared and feature nice accents such as pesto side dishes with seafood and steaks.

Eetcafé De Ruif (☎ 214 22 06; Kerkstraat 22; mains €12-18; 🕙 lunch & dinner) Wonderfully rustic, with a low ceiling and canal views from a rear terrace. Try the much-loved local Stellendam prawns. At night it's a popular place for a glass of this or that, with or without prawns.

La Vieux Jean (☎ 213 04 33; www.levieuxjean.nl; Heilige Geestkerkhof 3; menus from €35; 🕙 lunch Tue-Fri, dinner Tue-Sat) Brilliant displays of flowers grace the front window of the fine French bistro, which serves a delicious steak *frites* (French fries) and other classic fare. It's as thin as a shaving of truffle and seating is limited. Book.

CAFES

Cafe de Oude Jan (☎ 214 53 63; Heilige Geestkerkhof 4; 🕙 10am-6am) A late, late option dating back 100 years (lovely copper beer taps), by day this cafe has fine tables on a tiny square just a bit away from the mobs of the Markt.

Drinking

Locus Publicus (☎ 213 46 32; Brabantse Turfmarkt 67) Glowing from within, this beer cafe has more than 200 beers. It's charming and filled with cheery locals who've found their new candy store.

't Klooster (☎ 212 10 13; Vlamingstraat 2) More than 120 regional beers by the bottle and six Belgian brews on tap. Nice, airy and convivial.

Entertainment

Low-key Kromstraat has coffeeshops and boozers.

Bebop Jazzcafé (☎ 213 52 10; Kromstraat 33) Dark and small, with moody music and a great selection of beers.

OJV de Koornbeurs (☎ 212 47 42; www.koornbeurs .nl; Voldersgracht 1) An underground dance floor with alternative tunes. It's a 21st-century meet market in a 14th-century meat market.

Filmhuis Lumen (☎ 214 02 26; www.filmhuis-lumen .nl; Doelenplein 5) Screens alternative films.

Shopping

Given the popularity of Delftware, many visitors leave town treating their bags much more gently than when they arrived (although the factory shops will ship). Otherwise Delft has a limited retail district around Brabantse Turfmarkt. Markets are held on the Markt on Thursday, Saturday and Sunday. In summer there's a flea market held along the canals.

Getting There & Around

BICYCLE

The bicycle shop is immediately south of the train station. National bike route LF11 goes right through town: Den Haag is 11km northwest (after about 8km you pass a windmill) and Rotterdam is 28km southeast on a meandering route that enters Rotterdam from the west at pretty Delftshaven.

TRAIN

Sample train service fares and schedules:

Destination	Price (€)	Duration (min)	Frequency (per hr)
Amsterdam	11.60	60	2
Den Haag	2.50	12	4
Rotterdam	3.20	12	4

Note the train station does not have lockers, so day-trippers will want to store bags at either Den Haag station or in Rotterdam.

Den Haag is also linked to Delft by tram 1, which takes 30 minutes.

ROTTERDAM

☎ 010 / pop 588,000

Rotterdam bursts with energy. Vibrant nightlife, a diverse, multi-ethnic community, an intensely interesting maritime tradition and a wealth of top-class museums all make it a must-see part of any visit to Holland, especially if you are passing by on the new high-speed trains.

The Netherlands' 'second city', Rotterdam was bombed flat during WWII and spent the following decades rebuilding. You won't find the classic Dutch medieval centre here – it was swept away along with the other rubble and detritus of war. In its place is an architectural aesthetic that's unique in Europe, a progressive perpetual-motion approach to architecture that's clearly a result of the city's postwar, postmodern 'anything goes' philosophy. (A fine example of this is the Paul McCarthy statue titled 'Santa with Butt Plug', Map p206, that the city placed in the main shopping district.)

History

Rotterdam's history as a major port (it's Europe's busiest) dates to the 16th century. In 1572, Spaniards being pursued by the rebel Sea Beggars were given shelter in the harbour. They rewarded this generosity by pillaging the town. Needless to say, Rotterdam soon joined the revolution and became a major port during this time.

With its location astride the major southern rivers, Rotterdam is ideally suited to service trading ships. Cargo from abroad can be easily transferred inland and to the rest of Europe. Large canals first constructed in the 1800s and improved ever since link the port with the Rhine River and other major waterways.

On 14 May 1940 the invading Germans issued an ultimatum to the Dutch government: surrender or cities such as Rotterdam will be destroyed. The government capitulated; however, the bombers were already airborne and the raid was carried out anyway.

Orientation

Rotterdam, split by the Nieuwe Maas shipping channel, is crossed by a series of tunnels and bridges, notably the Erasmusbrug. The centre is on the northern side of the water, and new neighbourhoods are rising to the south. Centraal Station (CS) will be a vast building site for the next few years as a striking new station (www.rotterdamcentraal.nl) rises along with new subways and underground parking. In the meantime, a 15-minute walk along the canal-like ponds leads to the waterfront. The commercial centre is to the east and most museums are to the west. The historic neighbourhood of Delfshaven is a further 3km west.

Information

BOOKSHOPS

Selexyz & Donner (Map p206; ☎ 413 20 70; Lijnbaan 150; ⏰ 9.30am-6pm Mon-Sat, noon-5pm Sun) The largest bookshop in the country has a delightful rooftop cafe.

DISCOUNT CARD

The Rotterdam Welcome Card offers discounts for sights, hotels and restaurants; it's €5. Buy it from the tourist office.

INTERNET ACCESS

The library and tourist offices have free internet access. Many cafes have free wi-fi.

LIBRARIES

Centrale Bibliotheek (Map p204; ☎ 281 61 14; Hoogstraat 110; ۞ 1-8pm Mon, 10am-8pm Tue-Fri, 10am-5pm Sat) An attraction in itself, with a cafe, an indoor life-sized chessboard and 30 minutes of free internet access each day.

MEDICAL SERVICES

For a doctor, call ☎ 420 11 00.
Erasmus MC (Map p204; ☎ 463 92 22; 's-Gravendijkwal 320) Major teaching hospital.

POST

Post office (Map p206; ☎ 454 22 44; 20 Weena Zuid; ۞ 9am-6pm Mon-Fri, 9.30am-3pm Sat)

TOURIST INFORMATION

Delfshaven Info (Map p204; Voorstraat; ۞ 11am-4pm Tue-Sun May-Sep) Provides tourist information for the Delfshaven area.

Tourist office (☎ 14 010; www.rotterdam.info) City (Map p206; Coolsingel 197; ۞ 9am-6pm Mon-Fri, to 5pm Sat & Sun); Groothandelsgebouw (Map p206; Weena; ۞ 9am-5.30pm Mon-Sat, 10am-5pm Sun) Free internet; pick up the essential *R Zine*. The main (city) branch is located in the City Information Centre, with a good display on architecture since the war and a huge town model. A second location is near the train station in the landmark Groothandelsgebouw.
Use-It (Map p206; ☎ 240 91 58; www.use-it.nl; Schaatsbaan 41-45; ۞ 9am-6pm Tue-Sun mid-May–mid-Sep, to 5pm Tue-Sat mid-Sep–mid-May) Offbeat independent tourist organisation all but lost amid the station construction. Has free wi-fi, books cheap accommodation

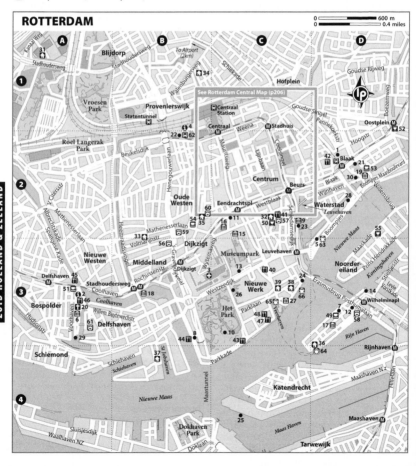

See Rotterdam Central Map (p206)

and publishes the invaluable *Simply the Best* local guide. Free lockers.

Dangers & Annoyances

Note that the area about 1km west of CS is the scene of many hard-drug deals and accompanying dubious behaviour.

Bike theft, as in any European city with a significant junkie population, is rampant.

Sights & Activities

Rotterdam is easy to navigate, with so many memorable buildings and landmarks with which to orientate yourself. The city centre is also a lot smaller than it seems for such a bustling metropolis – you might never need to use the efficient public transport system. The best way to see the city is by bike, though the trams make for good sightseeing.

MUSEUM BOIJMANS VAN BEUNINGEN

Among Europe's very finest museums, the **Museum Boijmans van Beuningen** (Map p204; ☎ 441 94 00; www.boijmans.nl; Museumpark 18-20; adult/child €9/free, Wed free; 11am-5pm Tue-Sun) has a permanent collection spanning all eras of Dutch and European art, including superb old masters. Among the highlights are *The Marriage at Cana* by Hieronymus Bosch, the *Three Maries at the Open Sepulchre* by Van Eyck, the minutely detailed *Tower of Babel* by Pieter Brueghel the Elder, and *Portrait of Titus* and *Man in a Red Cap* by Rembrandt. Renaissance Italy is well represented; look for *The Wise and Foolish Virgins* by Tintoretto and *Satyr and Nymph* by Titian.

Paintings and sculpture since the mid-19th century are another strength. There are many Monets and other French Impressionists; Van Gogh and Gauguin are given space; and there are statues by Degas. The museum rightly prides itself on its collection by a group it calls 'the other surrealists', including Marcel Duchamp, René Magritte and Man Ray. Salvador Dalí gained a special room in the recent expansion and the collection is one of the largest of his work outside Spain and France. All in all, the surrealist wing is utterly absorbing, with ephemera and paraphernalia rubbing against famous works.

Modern modes are not forgotten, and the whole place is nothing if not eclectic: a nude or an old master might be nestled next to a '70s bubble TV – some kind of installation – or a vibrating table.

There's also a good cafe and a pleasant sculpture garden (featuring Claes Oldenburg's famous *Bent Screw*, among others).

INFORMATION

Centrale Bibliotheek	1	D2
Delfshaven Info	2	A3
Erasmus MC	3	B3
Use-It	4	B1

SIGHTS & ACTIVITIES

Blaak Market	(see 42)	
Boompjestorens	5	D3
De Dubbelde Palmboom	6	A3
De Rotterdam	7	D3
Euromast	8	B3
Haven Museum	9	C2
Het Park	10	C3
Huis Sonneveld	11	C2
KPN Telecom Headquarters	12	D3
Kunsthal	13	C3
MaasToren	14	D3
Museum Boijmans van Beuningen	15	C2
Nederlands Architectuur Instituut	16	C2
Nederlands Fotomuseum	17	D3
Oorlogs Verzets Museum	18	B3
Openlucht Binnenvaart Museum	19	D2
Oude Haven	(see 21)	
Oude Kerk	20	A3
Overblaak Development	21	D2
RailZ Miniworld	22	B2
Rotterdam Walk of Fame	23	C2
Show Cube	(see 21)	
Spido	24	C3
SS Rotterdam	25	C4
Tuin Schoonoord	26	C3
Wereldmuseum	27	C3
Willemswerf	28	D2
Windmill	29	A3
Witte Huis	30	D2

SLEEPING

City Camping Rotterdam	31	A1
Home Hotel	32	C2
Hotel Amar	33	B2
Hotel Bazar	(see 41)	
Hotel Bienvenue	34	B1
Hotel Breitner	35	B2
Hotel New York	36	D3
Hotel Stroom	37	B4
Maritime Hotel Rotterdam	38	C3
Room Rotterdam	39	C3
Sleep-in Mafkees	(see 4)	
Stayokay Rotterdam	(see 21)	

EATING

Abacanto	40	C3
Bazar	41	C2
Blaak Market	42	D2
De Ballentent	43	C3
De Pannenkoekenboot	44	B3
Het Eethuisje	45	A3
Stadsbrouwerij De Pelgrim	46	A3
Zee Zout	47	C3
Zinc	48	C3

DRINKING

Café Rotterdam	49	D3
C'est La Vie	50	C2
De Ballentent	(see 43)	
De Oude Sluis	51	A3
Locus Publicus	52	D1
Weimar	53	D2
Westerpaviljoen	54	B2
Willemsbrug	55	D2

ENTERTAINMENT

Dizzy	56	B3
Gay Palace	57	C2
Luxor Theater	58	D3
Nemo	59	B2
Pluto	60	B2
Worm	61	A3

TRANSPORT

Long-Distance Bus Stops	62	B2
Rebus	63	D3
Water Taxi Stop	64	D4
Water Taxi Stop	65	C3
Waterbus dock	66	C3

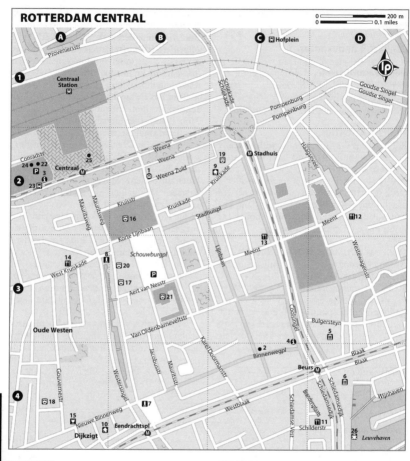

ROTTERDAM CENTRAL

KUNSTHAL

At the southern end of Museumpark, the **Kunsthal** (Map p204; ☎ 440 03 00; www.kunsthal.nl; Westzeedijk 341; adult/child €7.50/2; ☿ 10am-5pm Tue-Sat, 11am-5pm Sun) hosts around 20 temporary exhibitions (including art and design) each year. As the publicity says, everything from 'elitist to popular' gets an airing.

EUROMAST

At 185m, a shimmy up the **Euromast** (Map p204; ☎ 436 48 11; www.euromast.com; Parkhaven 20; adult/child €8.30/5.40; ☿ 10am-11pm) offers unparalleled 360-degree views of Rotterdam. There are all manner of extra diversions here and a bevy of combo tickets with other attractions around town.

HET PARK

You can escape the madness of the city surprisingly easy among the lakes of **Het Park** (Map p204). In summer locals love to barbeque here on the grassy expanses. Just east is **Tuin Schoonoord** (Map p204; Kievitslaan; ☿ 8.30am-4.30pm Mon-Fri, from 11am Sat & Sun), a hidden re-creation of an idealised Dutch wilderness that seems to have been taken right from a Renaissance painting.

DELFSHAVEN

One of Rotterdam's best districts for strolling, quaint Delfshaven (it survived the war) was once the official seaport for the city of Delft. A reconstructed 18th-century **windmill** (Map p204) overlooks the water at Voorhaven 210.

One of the area's claims to fame is that it was where the Pilgrims tried leaving for America aboard the leaky *Speedwell* (see the boxed text, p187). The **Oude Kerk** (Map p204) on Voorhaven is where the Pilgrims prayed for the last time before leaving on 22 July 1620.

Just south, **De Dubbelde Palmboom** (Map p204; ☎ 476 15 33; www.hmr.rotterdam.nl; Voorhaven 12; adult/child €3/free; ☑ 11am-5pm Tue-Sun) is a history museum housing an excellent collection of items relating to Rotterdam's history as a port. Displays are spread throughout the 1826 warehouse, and many have a sociological bent.

Delfshaven Info (p204) has a good walking-tour brochure and other excellent free publications on the neighbourhood. Just west on Schiedamseweg are all manner of ethnic groceries and eateries; Delftshaven is wonderfully un-twee. It is best reached by taking tram 4, 6 or 9.

ARCHITECTURE

Rotterdam is one vast open-air museum of modern architecture. The much-loved, 800m-long, 1996 **Erasmusbrug**, designed by Ben van Berkel, is a city icon. With its spread-eagled struts, it's nicknamed 'The Swan'.

To the south of Erasmusbrug is **KPN Telecom headquarters** (Map p204), built in 2000 and designed by Renzo Piano, who also designed Paris' Pompidou Centre. The building leans at a sharp angle, seemingly resting on a long pole. Nearby are two other notables among many: the tallest building in the Netherlands, the new **MaasToren** (Map p204; 165m) and **De Rotterdam** (Map p204), which broke ground on the waterfront in 2009 and will be the largest building in the country.

Retrace your steps across the river and walk northeast alongside the water on Boompjes, where you'll see the three distinctive **Boompjestorens** (Map p204) – apartment blocks built in 1988. Continue along the water until you see the striking 1998 **Willemswerf** (Map p204), the headquarters of the huge Nedlloyd shipping company. Note the dramatic lines casting shadows on its sleek, white surface.

Another 100m will bring you to Rotterdam's other signature bridge, the **Willemsbrug** (1981), which makes a bold statement with its red pylons. Turn north at Oude Haven on Geldersekade. The regal 12-storey building on the corner is the 1897 **Witte Huis** (White House; Map p204), a rare survivor of the prewar period, giving an idea of the wealth Rotterdam achieved thanks to the shipping industry.

The **Overblaak development** (Map p204), designed by Piet Blom and built from 1978 to 1984, is near Blaak metro station. Marked by its pencil-shaped tower and upended, cube-shaped apartments, it seems plucked straight from the novels of JG Ballard. One apartment, the fittingly named **Show Cube** (Kijk-Kubus; Map p204; ☎ 414 22 85; www.cubehouse.nl; adult/child €2.50/1.50; ☑ 11am-5pm), is open to the public. Look for the tiny chess museum in the cube complex, with all kinds of chess pieces on display – everything from ancient Hindu examples to likenesses of Jabba the Hut.

The **Nederlands Architectuur Instituut** (NAI; Map p204; ☎ 440 12 00; www.nai.nl; Museumpark 25; adult/child €8/free; ☑ 10am-5pm Tue-Sat, 11am-5pm Sun), with one side surrounded by a dirty green moat and the other comprising a sweeping flow of brick along Rochussenstraat, is striking. However, exhibits change regularly; there is nothing permanent on Dutch architecture so its value as a stop depends on what is on.

Included in the admission price is a ticket to **Huis Sonneveld** (Map p204; Jongkindstraat25), designed by Brinkman and Van der Vlugt and an outstanding example of the Dutch New Building architectural strain (also known as Dutch functionalism). This 1933 villa has been lovingly restored, with furniture, wallpaper and fixtures present and correct – it is an astonishing experience, almost like virtual reality.

OTHER SIGHTS

Maritiem Museum Rotterdam (Map p206; ☎ 413 26 80; www.maritiemmuseum.nl; Leuvehaven 1; adult/child €5/3; ☒ 10am-5pm Tue-Sat, 11am-5pm Sun year-round, also 10am-5pm Mon Jul & Aug) is a comprehensive museum that looks at the Netherlands' rich maritime traditions. There's an array of models that any youngster would love to take into the tub, plus interesting and explanatory displays.

Just south, the **Haven Museum** (Map p204; ☎ 404 80 72; Leuvehaven 50; admission free; ☒ visitors centre 10am-5pm Tue-Sun) comprises all manner of old and historic ships moored in the basin. You can always wander the quays; when the visitor centre is open you can learn more about what's tied up.

Just outside on Schiedamsedijk, the **Rotterdam Walk of Fame** (Map p204) features handprints from C-grade luminaries who've been to town (Joan Collins) plus the odd A-lister (Dizzy Gillespie).

The **Oude Haven** area, near the Overblaak development and the Blaak train, metro and tram station, preserves the oldest part of the harbour, some of which dates from the 14th century. It's a decent place for a stroll, especially if you check out the **Openlucht Binnenvaart Museum** (Map p204; ☎ 411 88 67; Koningsdam 1; admission free; ☒ varies), which has a collection of historic inland waterway boats that fills much of the basin. Restorations are ongoing; sit on a shady wall and watch.

The city's history is preserved at one of the centre's few surviving 17th-century buildings, now the **Historisch Museum het Schielandhuis** (Map p206; ☎ 217 67 67; www.hmr.rotterdam.nl; Korte Hoogstraat 31; adult/child €3/1.50; ☒ 10am-5pm Tue-Fri, 11am-5pm Sat & Sun). Exhibits focus on everyday life through the ages, such as the (purportedly) oldest surviving wooden shoe. Its sister museum is the De Dubbelde Palmboom in Delfshaven (p206).

The **Wereldmuseum** (World Museum; Map p204; ☎ 270 71 72; www.wereldmuseum.nl; Willemskade

25) celebrates multiculturalism, focusing on rituals, stories and sacred objects. Closed for several years of renovations, it should reopen by this book's publication. Major exhibits will change regularly.

The Dutch love of the world in miniature is celebrated at **RailZ Miniworld** (Map p204; ☎ 240 05 01; Weena 745; adult/child €9.25/6; ☒ noon-5pm Wed & Thu, from 10am Fri-Sun), a ginormous 500 sq metre model railroad re-creating Rotterdam and the Randstad.

A much darker theme is found at the **Oorlogs Verzets Museum** (War & Resistance Museum; Map p204; ☎ 484 89 31; www.ovmrotterdam.nl; Coolhaven 375; adult/child €3/1.50; ☒ 10am-5pm Tue-Fri, noon-5pm Sun), where the sounds of German bombers greet you for exhibits that fittingly are sheltered under a bridge. Displays recount life in Rotterdam during WWII; the fear in the faces of people fleeing the bombing in a 1940 photo is raw.

Unbroken Resistance (Map p206) is the name of a statue at the start of the Westersingel. It recalls the war and shows an enigmatic man, unbowed and calmly searching the skies. Many more statues line the water as you walk south.

Down on the waterfront across the Maas, the **Nederlands Fotomuseum** (Map p204; ☎ 213 20 11; www.nederlandsfotomuseum.nl; Wilhelminakade 332; adult/child €6/free; ☒ 10am-5pm Tue-Fri, 11am-5pm Sat & Sun) mainly has large, special exhibitions, so like NAI the value of a visit depends on what's on (if it's Hans van der Meer, go!). Bits of the permanent collection (which is magnificent but hidden) can be accessed by various form-over-function gizmos. Take tram 20, 23 or 25 or the water taxi.

Walking Tour

Start at the **Haven Museum** (**1**; left) and the **Maritiem Museum Rotterdam** (**2**; left) for a maritime history lesson, before making your way over the pedestrian bridge, along Wijnhaven and past the **Witte Huis** (**3**; p207) to **Oude Haven** (**4**; left) for real-world aquatic nostalgia.

Follow the walkways clockwise around the water and view the vessels on display at the **Openlucht Binnenvaart Museum** (**5**; left), then cross the **Willemsbrug** (**6**; p207), drinking in the superb views over the river, before emerging on the other side in **Noordereiland (7)**, a residential island that has been styled as the MS *Noordereiland*, a 'ship on the Maas', by artist Joe Cillen, with its 3000 'sailors' (residents). To the left is **De Brug (8)**, an apartment block

ROTTERDAM WALKING TOUR

WALK FACTS

Start Haven Museum
Finish De Ballentent
Duration Three hours

with Cillen-constructed port and starboard lights on the roof (green and red).

Walk towards Noordereiland's eastern tip, where you'll find the ship's **engine room (9)** – an alleyway behind the Aldi supermarket that's been decorated with mechanical sculptures by local artists and kids. Backtrack and walk west along Maaskade, admiring more watery views before stopping in at the maritime-themed pub also named **Willemsbrug (10;** p212). Here you can have a beer and a sea-dog singalong with the feisty locals.

Emerging from the cigar smoke, walk through the 'ship's' **cargo holds (11)**, actually the streets and alleys bisecting the island, before making your way across the Koninginnebrug. Look to the left as you cross the water: **De Hef (12)** is a magnificent railway bridge from the 1920s that's been preserved as a National Monument, its drawbridge permanently raised high in the air.

Walk west along Stieltjesstraat and pass the country's tallest building, the **MaasToren (13;** p207), before crossing busy roads and walking down to the old port area of Wilhelminakade, an area undergoing huge change with new development such as **De Rotterdam (14;** p207) overshadowing **old shipping warehouses (15)**

such as this one with 'Celebes, Borneo, Java, Sumatra' carved into its facade. Pause at the art deco **Café Rotterdam (16;** p212) for refreshment and great views of the water and the iconic **Erasmusbrug (17;** p207).

At the southeast tip of the peninsula, take in the grand old maritime hotel, the **Hotel New York (18;** p211), from where generations of people sailed to America. Board the scheduled **water taxi (19;** p214) and enjoy a quick run across the Nieuwe Maas to **Veerhaven (20)**. Walk through this gentrified neighbourhood with its many old maritime offices and then meander around the lakes of **Het Park (21;** p206) before settling in for a fine meal among sailors at **De Ballentent (22;** p211), which has views of the grand old liner, the *SS Rotterdam* (Map p206), permanently moored across the water and now used as a hotel.

Tours

There are harbour tours offered daily by **Spido** (Map p204; ☎ 275 99 88; www.spido.nl; Willemsplein 85; adult/child €9.50/6; ☼ 9.30am-5pm Jun-Sep, 11am-3.30pm Apr, May & Oct, to 2pm Thu-Sun Nov-Mar). Departures are from the pier at Leuvehoofd near the Erasmusbrug, the Leuvehaven metro stop and tram 7 terminus. Longer trips are possible in the high season.

You can also bob around the harbour on various themed dining boats, including one serving pancakes (see p212).

Rotterdam ArchiGuides (☎ 433 22 31; www.rotterdam -archiguides.nl; tours €10) takes groups on two-hour walking tours of Rotterdam's striking architecture, usually on summer weekends. Confirm times and departure point with the tourist office.

Ride a historic tram throughout the city on **Line 10** (☎ 06 5351 3630; www.lijn10.nl; adult/child €5/2.50; ☼ departures 10.30am-3.30pm Tue-Sun mid-Jul–early Sep) Staff are charming and there's an excellent guidebook in English. It's a great way to see some of the far reaches out of the centre. Trams depart from near the Spido dock on Willemsplein, at the terminus of tram 7 from the train station (also a scenic ride).

Festivals & Events

Rotterdam has festivals and events big and small all summer long.

JANUARY–FEBRUARY

International Film Festival Rotterdam (www.film festivalrotterdam.com) Late January. A top-notch selection of independent and experimental films.

JUNE
Poetry International Festival (www.poetry.nl) Mid-June. Hosting top-notch poets, don't ya know it, from all over the world.

JULY
North Sea Jazz Festival (www.northseajazz.nl) Mid-July. One of the world's most-respected jazz events. Rooms throughout the region are at a premium as thousands of fans descend on the city. A lot of the acts organise unofficial jams outside the festival dates, a kind of prefestival festival.
Zomer Carnaval (Summer Carnival; www.zomercarnaval .nl) Last weekend of July. A carnival-like tropical bash with music, parades, dancing and parties.

AUGUST
Dance Parade (www.fitforfreedanceparade.nl) Early August. Turns the centre into one big open-air club with areas for techno, hip-hop, big beat etc. Floats on the backs of trucks drive through town, catering to a crowd of around 350,000 people.

SEPTEMBER
Wereld Havendagen (World Harbour Festival; www .wereldhavendagen.nl) Early September. Celebrates the role of the harbour, which directly or indirectly employs more than 300,000 people. There are lots of open houses, ship tours and fireworks.

Sleeping

Rotterdam has a good array of lodging, from scads of hostels to hotels grand and modest, many with views of the water.

The tourist office makes room reservations, as does Use-It (p204), the latter with discounts.

BUDGET
Room Rotterdam (Map p204; ☎ 282 72 77; www.roomrot terdam.nl; Van Vollenhovenstraat 62; dm from €16; 🖳 🛜) A popular hostel with 16 dorm rooms, each with two to 10 beds. Each has its own decor, ranging from 'Dutch Delight' to 'Love'. It's a lively, young place and rocks much of the night.

Stayokay Rotterdam (Map p204; ☎ 436 57 63; www .stayokay.com/rotterdam; Overblaak 85-87; dm €17-25, r from €65; 🖳 🛜) Those odd angles you see at this hostel may not be to do with what you just smoked; this hostel is now in fancy new digs within the landmark Overblaak development (p207). There are 245 beds in oddly shaped rooms that sleep two to eight. Some have air-con and those on the top floor have cool views.

Hotel Amar (Map p204; ☎ 425 57 95; www.amarhotel .nl; Mathenesserlaan 316; r €50-80; 🖳) This friendly, 24-room place is in a leafy neighbourhood close to Delfshaven, the Museumplein and good nightlife. Rooms are simple but comfy, and the ones at the back overlook a large and peaceful garden. Most share bathrooms.

Other options:

City Camping Rotterdam (Map p204; ☎ 415 34 40; www.stadscamping-rotterdam.nl; Kanaalweg 84; camp sites per person/tent €4.95/3.90, 2-person cabins €30) A 20-minute walk northwest from CS towards the A13-A20 interchange, or take bus 33 (direction: Airport).

Sleep-in Mafkees (Map p204; ☎ 240 91 58; www .use-it.nl; Schaatsbaan 41-45; dm €10; 🌣 Jul & Aug; 🖳 🛜) Run by Use-It and right above its offices near the train station, these are the cheapest beds in town. One room sleeps 122, another is women only and sleeps 34.

MIDRANGE
ourpick **Maritime Hotel Rotterdam** (Map p204; ☎ 411 92 60; www.maritimehotel.nl; Willemskade 13; r €35-130; 🖳 🛜) Popular with shore-leave-seeking seamen and travellers who appreciate the fine value here. The modern facility offers attentive service, a big breakfast buffet, a cheap bar with pool table and oodles of models and posters featuring modern ships. The 135 rooms are small and the cheapest share bathrooms, but spend a little extra and you can enjoy the best waterfront views in town.

Hotel Bazar (Map p204; ☎ 206 51 51; www.hotelbazar .nl; Witte de Withstraat 16; r €65-125; 🛜) Bazar is deservedly popular for its 27 Middle Eastern–, African– and South American–themed rooms: lush, brocaded curtains, exotically tiled bathrooms and more. Top-floor rooms have balconies and views. Breakfast is spectacular: Turkish bread, international cheeses, yoghurt, pancakes and coffee. The ground-floor bar and restaurant (opposite) is justifiably popular.

Home Hotel (Map p204; ☎ 411 21 21, 414 21 50; www .homehotel.nl; Witte de Withstraat 38; r from €80) More than 85 studio apartments are available for rent in various buildings in one of Rotterdam's most appealing neighbourhoods. Some have wi-fi and others don't, but all have cooking facilities. Rates fall for multiple nights and many people stay by the week or month.

Grand Hotel Central (Map p206; ☎ 414 07 44; www.grandhotelcentral.nl; Kruiskade 12; s/d €80/95; 🛜) Memories of the kitsch this hotel was once known for have literally been whitewashed. The decor is now a restful combo of white, blue and slate. However, the public spaces retain their old grandeur (1917) with lots of rich wood and over-stuffed chairs.

Hotel Emma (Map p206; ☎ 436 55 33; www.hotelemma
.nl; Nieuwe Binnenweg 6; r €90-150; 🖥 🛜) Recently
refurbished, the Emma is a modern place with
24 rooms close to the city centre. Touches
include posh bathrooms and double-glazed
windows. The decor is bright and simple.

Other options:

Hotel Bienvenue (Map p204; ☎ 466 93 94; www
.hotelbienvenue.nl; Spoorsingel 24b; r €55-85; 🖥 🛜) In
a quiet though central area; basic rooms with Ikea accents.

Hotel Breitner (Map p204; ☎ 436 02 62; www.hotel
breitner.nl; Breitnerstraat 23; s/d from €80/100; 🖥 🛜)
Near Museumpark; modest except for the leopard-print
bedspreads in some rooms.

TOP END

Hotel New York (Map p204; ☎ 439 05 00; www.hotel
newyork.nl; Koninginnenhoofd 1; r €100-250; 🛜) The
city's favourite hotel is housed in the former
headquarters of the Holland-America passen-
ger-ship line, and has excellent service and
facilities. It's noted for its views, cafe and water
taxi that takes guests across the Nieuwe Maas to
the city centre. The art nouveau rooms – with
many original and painstakingly restored decorative items and fittings – are divine and come
in various styles, from standard to rooms in
the old boardrooms complete with fireplaces.
Watch for deals as low as €100 a night.

Hotel Stroom (Map p204; ☎ 221 40 60; www.stroom
rotterdam.nl; Lloydstraat 1; r €150-350; 🛜) Stroom is
so modern and alternative it hurts. Housed in
a converted power station, its designer studios
come in a range of configurations, such as
the 'videstudio' option, a jaw-dropping split-
level abode under a glass roof with an open
bathroom.

Eating

Rotterdam is an excellent place for dining. Good places abound, especially in and
around Veerhaven, Witte de Single, Nieuwe
Binnenweg and Oude Haven. The city's (always growing) multicultural population keeps
choices exciting.

Blaak Market (Map p204; 🕙 8am-5pm Tue & Sat) is
the city's best and sprawls across its namesake square across from the cube houses. A
striking new indoor market is set to open
here by 2011.

RESTAURANTS

Bazar (Map p204; ☎ 206 51 51; Witte de Withstraat 16;
mains €4-15) On the ground floor of the inventive
Hotel Bazar, this eatery comes up with crea-

tive Middle Eastern fusion fare that compliments the stylised decor. Dolmades haven't
tasted this good any place west of Istanbul.
The outside tables are *the* neighbourhood
meeting spot day and night.

De Ballentent (Map p204; ☎ 436 04 62;
www.deballentent.nl; Parkkade 1; meals from €5; 🕙 9am-
11pm) Rotterdam's best waterfront pub-cafe
is also a great spot for a meal. Dine on one of
two terraces or inside. Mussels, schnitzels and
more line the menu but the real speciality here
are *bals*, huge homemade meatloafy meatballs.
The plain ones are tremendous, but go for
the house style with a piquant sauce of fresh
peppers, mushrooms and more.

Dudok (Map p206; ☎ 433 31 02; Meent 88; dishes €6-
20) There are always crowds at this sprawling
brasserie near the city centre. Inside it's all
high ceilings and walls of glass. Outside, you
have your pick of an array of tables lining the
street. Meals range from breakfasts to snacks
to cafe fare such as soup and pasta. The name
comes from noted architect WM Dudok who
designed these former insurance offices.

Stadsbrouwerij De Pelgrim (Map p204; ☎ 477 11
89; Aelbrechtkolk 12, Delfshaven; mains €7-20; 🕙 lunch &
dinner Wed-Sun) It's named for the religious folk
who passed through on their way to America,
and you can take your own voyage through
the various beers brewed in the vintage surrounds. Meals range from casual lunches to
more ambitious multicourse dinners.

Abacanto (Map p204; ☎ 225 01 01; Van Vollenstraat 15;
mains €10-25; 🕙 lunch & dinner) Classic Italian fare,
including pizza. You can dine under the glass
here in the Westelijk Handelsterren, a converted warehouse complex that now houses
numerous stylish restaurants, cafes and bars.

Zinc (Map p204; ☎ 436 65 79; Calandstraat 12a; set
menus €25; 🕙 dinner Tue-Sun) A cosy, chic French/
Mediterranean bistro revered for using only
organic produce from small farms, a rarity in
the factory-farm-laden Netherlands. The busy
little kitchen overlooks the street and outside
tables. Famous mashed potatoes.

Zee Zout (Map p204; ☎ 436 50 49; Westerkade 11b;
meals from €45; 🕙 lunch Tue-Fri, dinner Tue-Sat) The
name means sea salt and that's all you need
to know. Well, actually, details such as the
superbly prepared fresh fish, wrap-around
windows, outside seating with waterfront
views and polished service are also key.
Other choices:

Het Eethuisje (Map p204; ☎ 425 49 17; Mathenesser-
dijk 436, Delfshaven; mains €8-10; 🕙 dinner Mon-Sat)

Traditional meaty, filling Dutch food is served from this little storefront near a canal. Utterly tourist free.

De Pannenkoekenboot (Map p204; ☎ 436 72 95; www.pannenkoekenboot.nl; Parkhaven; adult/child from €15/10; ☻ varies Apr-Oct) All-you-eat pancakes in a variety of flavours served aboard a boat touring the harbour. Departs across from Euromast. Other themed chow boats include Chinese and tapas.

QUICK EATS

Bagels & Beans (Map p206; ☎ 217 52 87; Lijnbaan 150; snacks from €3; ☻ 9.30am-6pm Mon-Sat, noon-5pm Sun) On the 4th floor of the Selexyz & Donner bookshop; excellent coffees and a huge terrace with views and sun loungers.

Bagel Bakery (Map p206; ☎ 412 15 60; Schilderstraat 57; meals from €4; ☻ breakfast & lunch Tue-Sun, dinner Thu-Sat) Excellent bagel sandwiches to takeaway. Dine in (or under the trees out the front) and enjoy excellent breakfasts, fresh lunches and inventive dinners. Lots of vegie options.

Maoz (Map p206; ☎ 428 32 83; Coolsingel 87; meals from €4; ☻ lunch) Felafel pita-bread sandwiches that can be refilled as much as you like with salad toppings and sauces. Popular all over the country.

Toko Konfa (Map p206; ☎ 433 13 78; West Kruiskade 59b; meals from €4; ☻ 9am-6pm Mon-Sat) On Rotterdam's Asian strip amid groceries and markets, enjoy all manner of fresh and cooked dishes ready to go.

Drinking
CAFES

In the city centre, Karel Doormanstraat is lined with shady cafes. But the real gaggle is at Oude Haven, which has dozens of places along the water.

Westerpaviljoen (Map p204; ☎ 436 26 45; Nieuwe Binnenweg 136; meals €6-16) A huge buzzy cafe with a very popular terrace, it's the perfect spot for a respite in this prime shopping district. Breakfast is served until 3pm and the long menu has many vegie options and even some Mediterranean flair.

Weimar (Map p204; ☎ 704 76 00; Haringvliet 637; meals from €8) Named for the Hotel Weimer that stood here and was blasted to rubble in 1940, this is one of scores of waterside cafes in Oude Haven. Have a wander and pick one or several, depending on your mood. The Weimar is one of the more gracious.

Café Rotterdam (Map p204; ☎ 290 84 42; Wilhelminakade 699; mains from €10) In a soaring, light-filled space in the old ship passenger terminal,

the real draw here is the huge terrace with its views of the water and the Rotterdam skyline.

De Oude Sluis (Map p204; ☎ 477 30 68; Havenstraat 7, Delftshaven) The view up the canal from the tables outside goes right out to Delftshaven's windmill at this ideal brown cafe. Inside you'll find peanut shells littering the floor; the perfect accompaniment/inducement for beer.

BARS & PUBS

C'est La Vie (Map p204; ☎ 411 16 57; Zwarte Paardenstraat 91A) Swanky gay bar near a lot of gay nightlife. Think gold leaf, chandeliers and leather (on the chairs if not the patrons).

De Ballentent (Map p204; ☎ 436 04 62; www .deballentent.nl; Parkkade 1; meals from €5; ☻ 9am-11pm) Rotterdam's best waterfront pub-cafe was officially recognised as such so many times that the group responsible for the honour finally stopped holding a competition. Waiters and customers alike enjoy a good laugh. Fine food (p211).

Locus Publicus (Map p204; ☎ 433 17 61; www.locus -publicus.com; Oostzeedijk 364) With more than 200 beers on its menu (including 12 always on tap), this is an outstanding specialist beer cafe.

Stalles (Map p206; ☎ 436 16 55; Nieuwe Binnenweg 11a) A highlight among the many good shops, cafes and bars here. Gets very busy after work and stays hopping through the evening.

Willemsbrug (Map p204; ☎ 413 58 68; Maaskade 95) This old-time, maritime-themed pub attracts salty sea dogs from the island. However, it's all bark and no bite. There's an underlying genial charm that finds full throat when impromptu singing spreads like a fire on the poop deck.

Entertainment
NIGHTCLUBS

Bootleg DJ Cafe (Map p206; ☎ 484 06 94; www.bootleg djcafe.com; Mauritsweg 33) A fab place for electronic music, Bootleg is where DJs go on their rare nights off. Techno, electro, breaks and more. Not huge but oh-so-cool.

Gay Palace (Map p204; ☎ 414 14 86; www.gay -palace.nl; Schiedamsesingel 139) And here we have Rotterdam's only weekly gay nightclub, with four floors of throbbing gay action – with different scenes on each floor – to work you into a lather and get you sweaty.

off_corso (Map p206; ☎ 411 38 97; www.off-corso .nl; Kruiskade 22) This is where it's at: bleeding-edge local and international DJs mashing up a high-fibre electronic diet of bleeps 'n' beats.

ZUID HOLLAND & ZEELAND

Art displays provide diversions at this proto-typical Rotterdam club.

Worm (Map p204; ☎ 476 78 32; www.wormweb.nl; Achterhaven 148) Off in a corner of Delfshaven is the ideal Dutch venue: parties are chaotic with a try-anything, do-anything vibe. Media mash-ups, performance art and experimental music are some of the more mundane events. The free magazine gives a peak inside.

LIVE MUSIC

De Unie (Map p206; ☎ 404 97 86; www.deunie.nu; Mauritsweg 35) Truly cultural, this venue is a vision in white, which provides a blank slate for events from cabaret to forums about taxation and the middle class to acoustic folk. It's safe to say that the high-brow debates here continue right out to the tables out the front.

Dizzy (Map p204; ☎ 477 30 14; www.dizzy.nl; 's-Gravendijkwal 127) Live concerts Monday and Tuesday nights and Sunday afternoons. The evening performances are scorching: everything from hot jazz to fast and funky Brazilian and salsa. There's regular jazz jam sessions.

De Doelen (Map p206; ☎ 217 17 17; www.dedoelen.nl; Schouwburgplein 50) Home venue of the renowned Rotterdam Philharmonic Orchestra, a sumptuous concert centre that dates from 1935 and seats 1300.

COFFEESHOPS

There's a huge number of coffeeshops in Rotterdam, probably the highest concentration outside the capital. The following are friendly and, well, mellow.

Nemo (Map p204; ☎ 495 99 11; www.coffeeshop-nemo .nl; Nieuwe Binnenweg 181) Disney would not approve of the logo at this slick yet cheery shop. Browse the 15 kinds of weed on offer before you visit.

Pluto (Map p204; ☎ 436 67 68; www.pluto.nl; Nieuwe Binnenweg 54) Space, not the Disney dog, is the inspiration at this head shop, which sells every kind of pot accessory and goods to fill them.

THEATRE

Schouwburg (Map p206; ☎ 411 81 10; www.schouwburg .rotterdam.nl; Schouwburgplein 25) The main cultural centre, the Schouwburg has a changing calendar of dance, theatre and drama. Note the intriguing light fixtures with red necks out the front.

Luxor Theater (Map p204; ☎ 484 33 33; www .luxortheater.nl; Posthumalaan 1) A major performance venue (and architectural showpiece), the Luxor features musicals, theatre, classical music etc.

CINEMA

Rotterdam hosts the annual International Film Festival (p209), which has been described as the 'European Sundance'.

Lantaren/Venster (Map p206; ☎ 277 22 66; www .lantaren-venster.nl; Gouvernestraat 133) Great central art-house alternative that spices up the screen with live jazz and house.

Pathé Cinemas (Map p206; ☎ www.pathe.nl; Schouwburgplein 101) Multiplex with the usual Hollywood selection.

Shopping

An afternoon strolling the length of Nieuwe Binnenweg yields a captivating mix of stylish cafes, coffeeshops and shops selling used CDs, vintage clothing and plastic/fluorescent club wear. The odd local designer hoping for more adds spice.

Lijnbaan and side streets stretching to Coolsingel and Mauritsweg are lined with mainstream stores, chains and the big department stores. Every other bag says C&A or H&M. Dart further south to Witte de Withstraat for boutiques, galleries and general funkiness.

You can literally buy the salt of the earth at the ethnic groceries on West Kruiskade, which has a welter of ethnic groceries and stores. Buy anything you can imagine at the huge market at Blaak (p211).

Rotterdam has gone for Sunday shopping in a big way. Most stores in the centre are open noon to 5pm.

Getting There & Away

AIR

Rotterdam Airport (code RTM; ☎ 446 34 44; www .rotterdam-airport.nl) has limited service. But if you can get a deal, it's a low-key, hassle-free ingress to the country. The main airlines using the airport:

Transavia (www.transavia.com) Mediterranean destinations plus London Luton.

VLM (www.flyvlm.com) London City Airport, Manchester and Hamburg.

BICYCLE

Two important national bike routes converge just east of Het Park. LF2 runs north through Gouda to Amsterdam and south through Dordrecht to Belgium. LF11 runs from Den Haag through Rotterdam and on to Breda. Although the city seems large, 15 minutes of fast pedalling will have you out in the country.

BOAT

The **Waterbus** (Map p204; ☎ 0900 899 89 98; www
.waterbus.nl; day pass adult/child €11/6.75) is a fast ferry
service linking Rotterdam with Dordrecht via
Kinderdijk and is an enjoyable option for day
trips, or in place of the train. Boats leave from
Willemskade every 30 minutes.

BUS

Rotterdam is a hub for Eurolines bus services
to the rest of Europe. See p297 for details. The
Eurolines office (Map p206; ☎ 412 44 44; Conradstraat
16; ☺ 9.30am-5.30pm Mon-Fri, 10am-4pm Sat) is in the
Groothandelsgebouw by Centraal Station.
Long-distance buses stop nearby.

CAR & MOTORCYCLE

Rotterdam is well linked by motorways to the
rest of the Netherlands and Belgium. Car-
rental firms at the airport:
Avis (☎ 433 22 33)
Europcar (☎ 437 18 26)
Hertz (☎ 415 82 39)

TRAIN

Rotterdam Centraal Station (CS) is a major
hub. Regular rail lines radiate out in all directions. In addition it is a stop on the high-speed
line from Amsterdam south to Belgium used
by Thalys and Fyra fast trains (see the boxed
text, p298).

Sample fares and schedules:

Destination	Price (€)	Duration (min)	Frequency (per hr)
Amsterdam (regular)	13.30	65	5
Amsterdam (high-speed)	21	43	2
Breda	8.30	32	3
Schiphol	10.70	47	3
Utrecht	9.10	40	4

Until at least 2013 the trip won't be the adventure; however, the station will be. The entire
CS area is being massively rebuilt. Until at
least 2011 CS services are in what's literally
a pile of containers near a temporary tunnel
to the tracks. Ticketing is on the 2nd floor,
the lockers are by track 1 etc. All should be
forgotten, however, when the new station
opens (www.rotterdamcentraal.nl). In keeping with local culture it will be an architectural
stunner with a broad metallic roof arrowing
towards the huge new plaza running south
along Westersingel.

Getting Around

TO/FROM THE AIRPORT

Bus 33 makes the 20-minute run from the
airport to CS every 15 minutes throughout
the day. A taxi takes 10 minutes to get to the
centre and costs around €22.

BICYCLE

The bicycle shop (Map p206) at CS is in the
backside of the Groothandelsgebouw during
construction. Use-It (p204) rents bikes for
€6 per day.

CAR & MOTORCYCLE

Rotterdam has numerous places to park, including along the streets. Look for the blue P
signs for large and enclosed garages.

PUBLIC TRANSPORT

Rotterdam's trams, buses and metro
are provided by **RET** (☎ 447 69 11; www.ret
.nl). Most converge near CS in front of the
Groothandelsgebouw during construction.
The **information booth** (☺ 6am-11pm Mon-Fri, 8am-
11pm Sat & Sun) sells tickets and is somewhere
in front of CS during construction (it's in a
movable hut). There are other information
booths in the major metro stations.

The system has converted to the OV-chipkaart (p304), which can be used as a day
pass for varying durations: 1/2/3 days costs
€6/9/12. A two-hour single use OV-chipkaart
costs €3.50. A single-ride ticket purchased
from a bus driver or tram conductor costs
€2.40. Ticket inspections are common.

Trams are the best way to get around the
city. They go virtually everywhere and you get
to sightsee along the way. The metro (subway)
is geared more for trips to the suburbs.

TAXI

For a taxi, call the **Rotterdamse Taxi Centrale**
(☎ 462 60 60).

WATER TAXI

Fast black and yellow **water taxis** (☎ 403 03 03;
www.watertaxirotterdam.nl) are the Ferraris of the
Nieuwe Maas and cost about €30 per 15 minutes. But you can get a taste of this service for a
fraction of the cost on two handy fixed routes
between the Hotel New York and Veerhaven
(€3) and Leuvehaven (€3.60). They run two
to four times per hour from 11am to 9pm
Monday to Thursday and 9am to midnight
Friday to Sunday.

AROUND ROTTERDAM
Kinderdijk

The **Kinderdijk** (Child's Dyke; www.kinderdijk.nl) is a great spot to see windmills out in the countryside. Declared a Unesco World Heritage site in 1997, it has 19 windmills strung out on both sides of canals, which you can wander by foot or bike.

This spot has been a focus of Dutch efforts to claim land from the water for centuries. Indeed the name Kinderdijk is said to derive from the horrible St Elizabeth's Day Flood of 1421 when a storm and flood washed a baby in a crib with a cat up onto the dyke. Stories aside, it is a starkly beautiful area, with the windmills rising above the empty marshes and waterways like so many sentinels.

Several of the most important types of windmill are here, including hollow post mills and rotating cap mills (see below). The latter are among the highest in the country as they were built to better catch the wind. The mills are kept in operating condition and date from the 18th century. In summer tall reeds line the canals, lily pads float on the water and bird calls break the silence. If you venture past the first couple of mills, you leave 90% of the day-trippers behind.

A visit to Kinderdijk is an ideal day trip. A small cafe near the entrance, **De Molenhoek** (www.kantinedemolenhoek.nl; 9.30am-6pm Apr-Sep), rents bikes (per hour €2.50), which are the best way to explore the basic 7km round-trip on the main paths. One of the mills functions as a **visitors centre** (☎ 078-613 28 00; admission €3.50; 9.30am-5.30pm mid-Mar–mid-Oct). On most days the windmill operates, which is good as most of the others don't. The exception is Saturdays in July and August from 2pm to 5pm when most are in operation, an unforgettable sight that was once common but is now impossible to find anywhere else.

You can wander the canals of Kinderdijk year-round. It's close to Rotterdam (16km) or

---

BLOWING IN THE WIND

Long before they appeared in a billion snapshots, the earliest known windmills appeared in the 13th century, simply built around a tree trunk. The next leap in technology came 100 years later, when a series of gears ensured the mill could be used for all manner of activities, the most important of which was pumping water. Hundreds of these windmills were soon built on dykes throughout Holland and the mass drainage of land began.

The next major advancement in Dutch windmill technology came in the 16th century with the invention of the rotating cap mill. Rather than having to turn the huge body of the mill to face the wind, the operators could rotate just the tip, which contained the hub of the sails. This made it possible for mills to be operated by just one person.

In addition to pumping water, mills were used for many other industrial purposes, such as sawing wood, making clay for pottery and, most importantly for art lovers, crushing the pigments used by painters.

By the mid-19th century there were more than 10,000 windmills operating in all parts of the Netherlands. But the invention of the steam engine soon made them obsolete. By the end of the 20th century there were only 950 operable windmills left, but this number has stabilised and there is great interest in preserving the survivors. The Dutch government runs a three-year school for prospective windmill operators, who must be licenced.

Running one of the mills on a windy day is as complex as being the skipper of a large sailing ship, and anyone who's been inside a mill and listened to the massive timbers creaking will be aware of the similarities. The greatest hazard is a runaway, when the sails begin turning so fast that they can't be slowed down. This frequently ends in catastrophe as the mill remorselessly tears itself apart.

It's sad to see abandoned mills stripped of sails and standing forlorn and denuded, especially since these days you're more likely to see turbine-powered wind farms in the Dutch countryside than rows of windmills. However, there are opportunities to see healthy examples throughout the country.

To see oodles of windmills in a classic *polder* setting (with strips of farmland separated by canals), visit Kinderdijk (above) near Rotterdam. To see mills operating and learn how they work, head to Zaanse Schans (p146) near Amsterdam.

Just about every operable windmill in the nation is open to visitors on National Mill Day, usually on the second Saturday of May. Look for windmills flying little blue flags.

Dordrecht (11km) on national bike routes LF2 and LF11. The most enjoyable way to visit is by the Waterbus fast ferry (p214). From either Rotterdam or Dordrecht it takes about an hour and costs €4, with a transfer to a small ferry at Ridderkerk. The connection runs every half-hour but the Kinderdijk ferry takes a long lunch break (10am until noon). Bikes are carried for free; the ferry dock is 1km from the first mill.

Rebus (Map p204; ☎ 218 31 31; www.rebus-info.nl; adult/child €13.50/11; ☼ 10.45am & 2.15pm Tue-Sun Apr-Sep) runs three-hour boat tours from Rotterdam that allow a fairly quick visit to the mills.

By train from Rotterdam CS, get off at Rotterdam Lombardijen station, then catch the hourly bus 90 (one hour).

DORDRECHT
☎ 078 / pop 119,000

Under-appreciated Dordrecht, with its lovely canals and busy port, sits at the confluence of the Oude Maas River and several tributaries and channels. This strategic trading position (precipitating a boom in the wine trade), along with the fact that it is the oldest Dutch city (having been granted a town charter in 1220), ensured that Dordrecht was one of the most powerful Dutch regions until the mid- to late 16th century. Accordingly, in 1572, it was here that town leaders from all over Holland met to declare independence from Spain.

Dordrecht and its evocative historical centre is a good stop on busy train lines or is a fun day trip by fast ferry from Rotterdam.

Orientation

The train station is a good 700m walk from the centre, a journey that passes through some less interesting, newer areas. The ferry stop is in the old town where most of the sights are on or near the three old canals – the Nieuwehaven, the Wolwevershaven and the Wijnhaven.

Information

The vast **tourist office** (Intree Dordrecht; ☎ 632 24 40; www.vvvdordrecht.nl; Spuiboulevard 99; ☼ noon-5.30pm Mon, 9am-5.30pm Tue-Fri, 10am-5pm Sat) is midway between the train station and old town (of which it has a fascinating model).

Sights & Activities

See Dordrecht on foot: it's eminently suited to it. Begin at the **Visbrug**, the bridge over Wijnhaven that gives fine views of the dignified **town hall**. At the northern end of Visbrug,

turn right onto Groenmarkt. As you walk northeast you'll pass the oldest houses in town, many from the early 1600s.

At the next square, Scheffersplein, cross diagonally to Voorstraat, the main retail street. The canal runs under this area, which is home to numerous markets.

The **Augustinerkerk**, an old church with a facade dating from 1773, is a little further along on the right. Just past it, watch carefully for a passage leading to **Het Hof** (☼ 1-5pm Tue-Sun), where the setting alone – especially at night – is moody and evocative. It was here that the states of Holland and Zeeland met in 1572.

Back on Voorstraat, continue north to the next bridge over the canal: Nieuwbrug. Cross over to Wijnstraat and turn right, continuing north. Many of the lopsided houses along here date from the peak of the wine trade, when the nearby canals were filled with boats bearing the fruits of the fermented grape.

The street ends at an attractive bridge. Pass along the west or left side of the canal to the river – and the **Groothoofdspoort**, once the main gate into town. Here there's a small square with fine **riverfront views** of the busy confluence of waterways and a few cafes with leafy seating.

Circling to the south you'll see the Kuipershaven, the street along the Wolwevershaven, another old canal lined with restored wine warehouses and filled with many historic boats. On warm days boys complete the timeless tableau by plunging into the waters. At the tiny drawbridge, cross over to the north side of the Nieuwehaven. On the right, watch for the small **Museum 1940-1945** (☎ 613 01 72; www.dordrechtmuseum19401945.nl; Nieuwehaven 28; adult/child €2/1; ☼ 10am-5pm Tue, Wed, Fri & Sat, 1-5pm Sun). It has a collection of materials from WWII and shows the privations of the region during the war.

Just south, the **Museum Simon van Gijn** (☎ 613 37 93; www.dordrechtmuseum.nl; Nieuwehaven 29; adult/child €6/3.50; ☼ 11am-5pm Tue-Sun) depicts the life of an 18th-century patrician, with vintage knick-knacks, furnishings and tapestries.

Continue southwest to the Engelenburgerbrug over the Nieuwehaven's access to the Oude Maas. Take an immediate right onto narrow Engelenburgerkade. At No 18, **Beverschaep** (Beaver & Sheep House) is a 1658 structure that takes its name from the animals supporting a coat of arms over the door.

At the end of the street is **Blauwpoort**, an old trading gate from 1652.

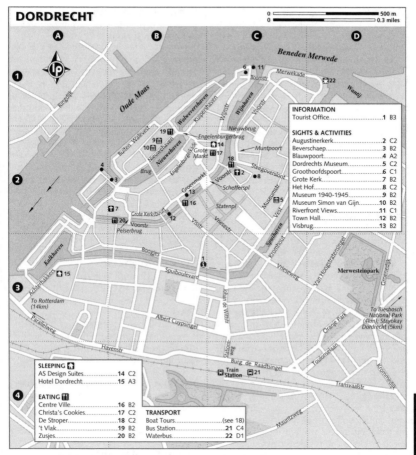

DORDRECHT

INFORMATION	
Tourist Office.............................**1** B3	

SIGHTS & ACTIVITIES	
Augustinerkerk...........................**2** C2	
Beverschaep...............................**3** B2	
Blauwpoort.................................**4** A2	
Dordrechts Museum.....................**5** C2	
Groothoofdspoort........................**6** C1	
Grote Kerk.................................**7** C2	
Het Hof......................................**8** C2	
Museum 1940-1945.....................**9** B2	
Museum Simon van Gijn...........**10** B2	
Riverfront Views.......................**11** C1	
Town Hall.................................**12** B2	
Visbrug.....................................**13** B2	

SLEEPING 🛏	
AS Design Suites...................**14** C2	
Hotel Dordrecht....................**15** A3	

EATING 🍴	
Centre Ville..........................**16** B2	
Christa's Cookies..................**17** B2	
De Stroper............................**18** C2	
't Vlak.................................**19** B2	
Zusjes..................................**20** B2	

TRANSPORT	
Boat Tours.........................(see 18)	
Bus Station.........................**21** C4	
Waterbus............................**22** D1	

GROTE KERK

The massive tower of the 14th- to 15th-century **Grote Kerk** (☎ 614 46 60; www.grotekerk-dordrecht.nl; Langegeldersekade 2; church admission free, tower adult/child €1/0.50; ☷ 10.30am-4.30pm Apr-Oct, 1-4pm Sat & Sun Nov-Mar) was originally meant to have been much higher, but it took on a lean during its 150-year-plus construction. You can climb to the top – 275 steps – to enjoy excellent views of the town. Inside, the choir stalls are finely carved and there are stained-glass windows depicting local historical scenes.

DORDRECHTS MUSEUM

Away from the old town, the **Dordrechts Museum** (☎ 648 21 48; www.dordrechtsmuseum.nl; Museumstraat 40) has works by local artists. Most noteworthy

are pieces by Jan van Goyen (1596–1656) and Albert Cuyp (1620–91). Van Goyen was one of the first Dutch painters to capture the interplay of light on landscapes – look for his *View of Dordrecht* – while Cuyp, who lived in Dordrecht his entire life, is known for his many works painted in and around his hometown. These included, in his early career, landscapes featuring, inevitably, the town mascot: sheep. The museum is set to open by this book's publication after a vast reconstruction.

Tours

The excellent restaurant De Stroper (p218) runs **boat tours** (adult/child €6/5; ☷ departures 2-5pm Apr-May & Sep-Oct, 11am-5pm Jun-Aug) that are a fine way to see Dordrecht's many delights.

Sleeping

Stayokay Dordrecht, on the edge of Biesbosch National Park, is a combined youth hostel, camping ground and hotel (see opposite).

Hotel Dordrecht (☎ 613 60 11; www.hoteldordrecht .nl; Achterhakkers 72; r €100-160; 🔀) A lovely option with excellent, spacious rooms that feature four-poster beds with curtains. Some rooms have private balconies. There's parking and a garden terrace.

AS Design Suites (☎ 614 57 39; www.as-designsuites .nl; Wijnstraat 241; r from €135; 🔀 🛜) In the heart of town above a cafe, this B&B has three stylish suites with many luxuries and king-sized beds. The 'Sweetest Suite' has a skylight so you can see stars while in bed.

Eating & Drinking

Dordrecht has some excellent eating. Scheffersplein, a large central square built over a canal, has many fine cafes.

our pick Christa's Cookies (☎ 843 75 89; 'S-Heer Boeijnstraat 2; treats from €1; ⏰ 10.30am-6pm Wed-Sat) Fantastic organic bakery where the owner is as sweet as her delectable cookies.

Zusjes (☎ 635 11 06; Voorstraat 431; meals from €4; ⏰ 10am-5pm Tue-Sat) A gem of a little lunchroom run by namesake sisters where all the dishes are vegie and most of the produce is local and organic. Try a grilled eggplant and pesto baguette with a pot of fine tea or kick back with a fairtrade coffee.

't Vlak (☎ 613 10 88; Vlak 11; dishes from €5; ⏰ 4pm-midnight) A fun and friendly tapas bar, where you can sit under trees canalside and gaze over two old canals while drinking in both excellent riojas and timeless views.

Centre Ville (☎ 631 15 75; Voorstraat 347; meals from €6) As the name implies, this bustling 1902 cafe is right in the heart of town in the busy Voorstraat shopping strip. Huge windows on three sides let in light.

De Stroper (☎ 613 00 94; www.destroper.com; Wijnbrug 1; menus €25-50; ⏰ lunch Mon-Fri, dinner daily) Gaze out on the canal or in summer dine on a floating platform at this superb fish restaurant. The menus change daily; the six-course option at dinner is a culinary tour de force.

Shopping

Voorstraat is the street for shopping. To the north it has interesting galleries and boutiques, in and around Visbrug is a fascinating stretch of ethnic grocery stores, and as it curves to the west there are lots of new and creative shops.

Getting There & Away

Buses leave from the area to your right as you exit the train station.

BICYCLE

The bike shop is in a sparkling new building to the left as you exit the train station. National routes LF2 and LF11 run north 27km to Rotterdam along pleasant countryside that includes Kinderdijk. South, LF11 runs 43km to Breda. Biesbosch National Park (below) is just a 10km ride east by a number of good routes.

BOAT

The **Waterbus** (☎ 0900 899 8998; www.waterbus.nl; day pass adult/child €11/6.75) is a fast ferry service linking Dordrecht with Rotterdam via Kinderdijk and is an enjoyable alternative to the train. The boat leaves from Merwekade every 30 minutes and takes one hour to Rotterdam (€4.20).

CAR & MOTORCYCLE

The busy E19 south to Belgium and north to Rotterdam and beyond passes close to town.

TRAIN

The train station has currency exchange and lockers and is right on the old main line from Rotterdam south towards Belgium. Sample fares and schedules:

Destination	Price (€)	Duration (min)	Frequency (per hr)
Amsterdam	15.90	72-90	4
Breda	5.40	18	3
Rotterdam	4	14	6

BIESBOSCH NATIONAL PARK

Covering 7100 hectares, Biesbosch National Park encompasses an area on both banks of the Nieuwe Merwede River, east and south of Dordrecht. It's so big that it sprawls across a provincial border; there's a region known as the Brabantse Biesbosch, further east, while the part in this province is the Hollandse Biesbosch. Before 1421 the area was *polder* land (strips of farmland separated by canals) and had a population of more than 100,000 living in more than 70 villages. However, the huge storm on St Elizabeth's Day (18 November) that year breached the dykes and floodwaters destroyed all the villages – virtually everyone lost their life.

However, out of this calamity grew both new life and a new lifestyle. The floods created several channels in their wake, including what is today called the Nieuwe Merwede. Linked to the sea, these areas were subject to twice-daily high tides, leading to the growth of tide-loving reed plants, which the descendants of the flood's survivors took to cultivating.

Fast forward to 1970 when the Delta Project (see the boxed text, p224) shut off the tides to the area. The reeds, which had been growing wild during the decades since the collapse of the reed markets, began to die, focusing attention on what is one of the largest expanses of natural space left in the Netherlands.

The park is home to beavers (reintroduced to the Brabant area of the park in 1988) and voles, along with scores of birds. There's an observation point right near the visitors centre where you can see some that have been fenced off in their own little pond.

Information

The **visitors centre** (☎ 630 53 53; www.biesbosch .org; Baanhoekweg 53; ⊙ 9am-5pm Tue-Sun year-round, also 9-5pm Mon May-Aug) is some 7km east of the Dordrecht train station by road. There are displays about the park's ecology, and you can rent kayaks and canoes (per half-hour from €5) to explore the park and its many channels and streams. There are also numerous trails through the marshlands and along the river.

The visitors centre is also the boarding place for a variety of boat tours of the Biesbosch. The longer cruises are better value, though, because they go to more places, including the **Biesboschmuseum** (☎ 0183-504 009; Hilweg 2; adult/child €3/2.10; ⊙ 10am-5pm Tue-Sun Apr-Oct) on the southern shore of the Nieuwe Merwede.

Sleeping

Stayokay Dordrecht (☎ 621 21 67; www.stayokay .com/dordrecht; Baanhoekweg 25; dm from €25, r from €47) This place includes a hostel, camping ground and hotel. The hotel, which has a bar and restaurant and rents bicycles, is in a modern building right next to the park and is 2km west of the visitors centre. Book in advance, especially at weekends.

Getting There & Away

The Stayokay and the park are within an easy 10km ride on bike routes going east from the Dordrecht train station. Otherwise, bus 5 (every 30 minutes) travels to within 2km of Stayokay and 3km of the park.

The **Waterbus** (☎ 0900 899 89 98; www.waterbus.nl; day pass adult/child €11/6.75) has an hourly boat from the Merwekade dock in Dordrecht to a dock 500m north of the visitors centre (adult/child €2/1.40).

SLOT LOEVESTEIN

Near the tiny, beautiful little walled town of Woudrichem you'll find the 14th-century castle, **Slot Loevestein** (☎ 0183-447 171; www.slot loevestein.nl; Loevestein 1; adult/child €8/6.50; ⊙ 10am-5pm Tue-Fri, 1-5pm Sat-Mon May-Sep, 1-5pm Sat & Sun Oct-Apr). The ancient keep is wonderfully evocative, perhaps more so for the difficulty involved in getting there. It's been a prison, residence and toll castle, though more recently it has hosted a varied calendar of cultural events (check the website). It's best accessed by the ferry (www.veerdienstgorinchem.nl) from nearby Woudrichem or Gorinchem, where there is a train station. National bike route LF12 passes through between Dordrecht and Den Bosch.

ZEELAND

The province of Zeeland consists of three slivers of land that nestle in the middle of a vast delta through which many of Europe's rivers drain. As you survey the calm, flat landscape, consider that for centuries the plucky Zeelanders have been battling the North Sea waters, and not always with success. In fact the region has suffered two massive waterborne tragedies.

In 1421 the St Elizabeth's Day flood killed more than 100,000, irrevocably altering the landscape – and some say the disposition – of the Netherlands and its people.

In 1953, yet another flood laid waste to 2000 lives and 800km of dykes, leaving 500,000 homeless and leading to the Delta Project, an enormous nearly 45-year construction program that aims to finally ensure the security of these lands. It ranks among the world's greatest engineering feats (see the boxed text, p224).

Middelburg is the somnolent historic capital, while the coast along the North Sea is lined with beaches beyond the ever-present dykes. Many people venture to this place of tenuous land and omnipresent water just to see the sheer size of the Delta Project's dykes and barriers.

Getting There & Away

In Zeeland, Middelburg is easily reached by train, but for most other towns you'll need to rely on the bus network. The most important include Connexxion bus 395, which makes a one-hour journey every hour between Rotterdam's Zuidplein metro station and Zierikzee, where you can transfer to buses for the rest of Zeeland.

National bike route LF1, which follows the entire North Sea coast of the Netherlands, is a vital link in Zeeland, as is LF13, which runs from Breda in the east to Middelburg and on to the coast (and LF1). However, it is also easy to explore on your own as the vast dyke-webbed farmlands make for easy, mellow riding. Regional bike routes are also numbered and maps are widely available.

MIDDELBURG
☎ 0118 / pop 47,600

Pleasant and prosperous Middelburg, Zeeland's sedate capital, is a perfect base for exploring the region and for getting to know the stolid, obliging Zeelanders.

Although Germany destroyed much of the town's historic centre in 1940, many parts have been rebuilt and you can still get a solid feel for what life must have been like hundreds of years ago. The fortifications built by the Sea Beggars in 1595 can still be traced in the pattern of the main canals encircling the old town.

As the main town of the Walcheren peninsula, Middelburg is fairly removed from the rest of the Netherlands – crowds are seldom a problem.

Orientation & Information
The train station for Middelburg is a five-minute walk from the centre, across two canals. The Markt is the focus of commercial life, but Middelburg's history is concentrated on the medieval Abdij (Abbey).

There's no official VVV tourist office, but there is a **tourist shop** (☎ 67 43 00; www.touristshop .nl; Markt 65C; ✆ 9.30am-5.30pm Mon-Sat), which sells tours.

De Drvkkery (☎ 88 68 86; www.de-drvkkery.nl; Markt 51; internet per hr €4) is one of the country's best bookshops. It has an excellent magazine selection, a cafe, internet access, art and photography displays on the walls – and oodles of books, including a huge travel section.

Sights & Activities
This pretty, airy little town is eminently suitable for walking, with cobblestones and snak-

ing alleyways leading in and away from the town square, which hosts a famous market on Thursdays.

ABDIJ
This huge abbey complex dates from the 12th century and houses the regional government as well as three churches. It features a vast inner courtyard.

The three churches are all in a cluster and reached through one tiny entrance (no ostentations for the Zeelanders!). The **Wandelkerk** (☎ 61 35 96; admission free; ✆ 10.30am-5pm Mon-Fri, 1.30-5pm Sat & Sun mid-Apr–Oct) dates from the 1600s and holds the tombs of Jan and Cornelis Evertsen, admirals and brothers killed fighting the English in 1666. It encompasses Lange Jan ('Long John'; it has its own locally brewed beer named after it), the 91m **tower** (207 steps; admission €4; ✆ 10am-5pm).

The other two churches are reached through the Wandelkerk. Just east, the **Koorkerk** has parts that date from the 1300s. Just west is **Nieuwe Kerk**, which has a famous organ and dates from the 16th century. All surround a gem of a cloisters with a tiny herb garden.

The **Zeeuws Museum** (☎ 65 30 00; www.zeeuws museum.nl; Abdij; adult/child €8/free; ✆ 10am-5pm Tue-Sun) is housed in the former monks' dormitories, and was given a recent massive revamp. Its collection is excellent, especially the traditional garb, which must have been an expensive burden for people barely eking out a living farming.

TOWN HALL
Dominating the Markt, the **town hall** (☎ 67 54 52; adult/child €4.25/3.75; ✆ tours 11.30am & 3.15pm) grabs the eye. It's ornately beautiful, and a pastiche of styles: the Gothic side facing the Markt is from the 1400s; the more-classical portion on Lange Noordstraat is from the 1600s.

Inside there are several sumptuous ceremonial rooms that boast treasures such as the ubiquitous Belgian tapestries. Visits to the building are by 40-minute guided tour organised by the tourist shop.

OTHER SIGHTS
The area around **Damplein** (east of the Abdij) preserves many 18th-century houses, some of which have recently been turned into interesting shops and cafes.

There is a fairly large old **Jewish Cemetery** on the Walensingel. It has the all-too-common

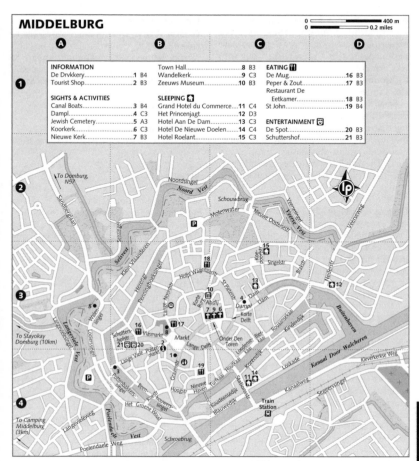

MIDDELBURG

0 ———— 400 m
0 ———— 0.2 miles

INFORMATION		
De Drvkkery	**1**	B4
Tourist Shop	**2**	B3

SIGHTS & ACTIVITIES		
Canal Boats	**3**	B4
Dampl	**4**	C3
Jewish Cemetery	**5**	A3
Koorkerk	**6**	C3
Nieuwe Kerk	**7**	B3

Town Hall	**8**	B3
Wandelkerk	**9**	C3
Zeeuws Museum	**10**	B3

SLEEPING		
Grand Hotel du Commerce	**11**	C4
Het Princenjagt	**12**	D3
Hotel Aan De Dam	**13**	C3
Hotel De Nieuwe Doelen	**14**	C4
Hotel Roelant	**15**	C3

EATING		
De Mug	**16**	B3
Peper & Zout	**17**	B3
Restaurant De Eetkamer	**18**	B3
St John	**19**	B4

ENTERTAINMENT		
De Spot	**20**	B3
Schuttershof	**21**	B3

stark memorial to the many Middelburg Jews taken away to their deaths by the Nazis.

Tours

Canal Boats (☎ 64 32 72; www.rondvaartmiddelburg .nl; Achter de Houttuinen 39; adult/child €6/3.25; ⏱ Apr-Oct) has 40-minute tours along the southern canal.

Festivals & Events

The **Ringrijdendagen** (Ring riding days) are held on two separate days, the first in July around the Abbey square, the second in August at the Molenwater. 'Ring riders' charge about on horseback in fancy dress carrying big sticks towards a target, with the aim of trying to tilt it.

Sleeping

Hotel Roelant (☎ 62 76 59; www.familiehotelroelant.nl; Koepoortstraat 10; s/d from €60/100; 🖳) Dating from 1530, this building has basic, comfortable rooms with bathroom. It's a small, family-run establishment, a pleasant walk away from the centre on a beautiful old cobbled street. There's a nice garden; rooms have high-speed internet access.

Het Princenjagt (☎ 61 34 16; www.hotelhetprin cenjagt.nl; Nederstraat 2; r from €75) This eight-room B&B has a kitchen for guests to use and a jaunty location by the marina. Touches include a little toaster on each table at breakfast and nice chairs for slouching in the rooms.

ourpick Hotel Aan De Dam (☎ 64 37 73; www .hotelaandedam.nl; Dam 31; r €75-140; 🛜) An opulent 1652 mansion has been converted into Middelburg's most appealing hotel. The seven rooms are mostly very large and have period decor that's been tricked out with modern conveniences – such as luxurious bathrooms as opposed to pots. It overlooks a canal and small park.

Grand Hotel du Commerce (☎ 63 60 51; www.hotel ducommerce.nl; Loskade 1; r from €80; 💻) In a building that would look at home on the Cannes beachfront, this hotel has gaudy red awnings juxtaposed against whitewashed, sun-bleached walls. The sum is less than the parts, however, but it is a comfortable, convenient option. And it rents bikes.

Other options:

Camping Middelburg (☎ 62 53 95; www.camping middelburg.nl; Koninginnelaan 55; camp sites from €12) Three kilometres from the train station – take bus 56 or 58 and tell the driver where you want to get off.

Hotel De Nieuwe Doelen (☎ 61 21 21; www .hoteldenieuwedoelen.nl; Loskade 3-7; s/d from €75/115; 🛜) This is an older-style hotel with 35 rooms and an enclosed garden.

Eating & Drinking

You'll almost be eating out of a vending machine on Sunday nights; at other times you'll do very well.

St John (☎ 62 89 95; St Jaanstraat 40; snacks from €2; 🕑 8.30am-6pm Mon-Sat) A perfect, creaky little old spot for a coffee. Woodsy inside and shady outside on the lovely square near the old fish market.

Peper & Zout (Pepper & Salt; ☎ 62 70 58; www.peperen zout.com; Lange Noordstraat 8; mains €12-25; 🕑 lunch Mon-Fri, dinner daily, closed Wed) The cute fishy tiles outside tell you what's on the menu inside. Excellent seafood that changes by the season is the draw here, as is the cheery owner.

De Mug (The Mosquito; ☎ 61 48 51; www.demug.nl; Vlasmarkt 54-56; mains €16-21; 🕑 dinner Tue-Sat) Don't be fooled by the Heineken signs; the beer list is long and boasts many rare Trappist varieties. Also try the Mug Bitter, heavy on the hops. The menu goes well with the brews: hearty seafood and meat plus more simple fare for snacking.

Restaurant De Eetkamer (☎ 63 56 76; Wagenaarstraat 13-15; meals €35-70; 🕑 lunch & dinner Tue-Sat) So prim and tidy out the front that you just have to step in. Produce is sourced locally and the menu changes with the seasons. Meats are house-cured and this attention to detail continues throughout your meal.

Entertainment

De Spot (☎ 63 32 29; www.despotmiddelburg.nl; Beddewijkstraat 15; 🕑 10pm-4am Fri & Sat) A wide-ranging venue with everything from jazz to rock to rap. Enter through an ancient arch.

Schuttershof (☎ 61 34 82; www.schuttershoftheater.nl; Schuttershofstraat 1) The Schuttershof is a cinema that sometimes has live music.

Getting There & Around

Regional buses stop along Kanaalweg in front of the train station.

BICYCLE

The train station has a bike shop (to the left as you exit). National bike route LF1 passes right through town; it crosses the many delta barriers to the north. Head east on LF13 to Breda (140km) via the fertile countryside and detour to charming villages such as Goes (36km).

TRAIN

Middelburg is near the end of the train line in Zeeland, and the austere train station has that end-of-line feel. Services are limited: store your bags (€5) at the bicycle shop. Sample fares and schedules:

Destination	Price (€)	Duration (min)	Frequency (per hr)
Amsterdam	26.30	150	1
Roosendaal	11	45	2
Rotterdam	18.40	60	1

AROUND MIDDELBURG

The Walcheren peninsula is a very enjoyable place for bicycling: combine journeys to old towns with time at the beach.

Veere

☎ 0118 / pop 1550

Veere is a former fishing village that found a new catch – tourists – when its access to the sea on the Veerse Meer (Veere Lake) was closed as part of the Delta Project. The town now boasts a busy yacht harbour. Much of Veere dates from the early 16th century – thus, it's a lovely place to stroll around.

The **tourist office** (☎ 0900 202 02 80; Oudestraat 28; 🕑 10am-4.30pm Mon-Sat Jul & Aug, 1.30-4.30pm Mon-Sat Sep-Jun) is in a small building near the Grote Kerk. Staff can advise on boat rentals and bike routes. It has internet access (per 30 minutes €1) and free wi-fi.

SIGHTS & ACTIVITIES

Here, you'll feel like you're in a Vermeer painting: rich Gothic houses abound, a testament to the wealth brought in by the wool trade with the Scots, and at the waterfront, the **Campveerse Toren** was part of the old fortifications. Look for the indications on the side showing the levels of various floods.

The **town hall** on the Markt dates from 1474, but was mostly completed in 1599. Its tower is still stuffed with bells – 48 at last count.

At the south end of town is the 16th-century **Grote Kerk**, another edifice that never matched its designer's intentions – its stump of a steeple (42m) looms ominously.

SLEEPING & EATING

Hotel 't Waepen van Veere (☎ 50 12 31; www .waepenvanveere.nl; Markt 23-27; r €100-140; ☎) On the central square and with a fine outdoor cafe, the 16 rooms here are comfy and stylish. It also has an elegant restaurant (mains €16 to €26).

Hotel de Campveerse Toren (☎ 50 12 91; www .campveersetoren.nl; Kade 2; r €100-185; ☎) Veere's other hotel is a smart place in an historic, castle-shaped building right on the waterfront. It offers 12 delightful rooms and particularly fabulous views. Food in the elegant restaurant (mains from €20) and cafe is as posh as the rooms.

GETTING THERE & AWAY

Veere is an easy bike ride from Middelburg on national route LF1 (8km). Otherwise, bus 54 makes the 12-minute run every hour (every two hours on Sunday).

Domburg
☎ 0118 / pop 1300

Although Domburg is a low-key seaside town by Dutch standards (meaning 'not very tacky'), it's still jammed in summer. The **beach** is the main event. To escape the urban crowds, head south along the tall dunes. Keep going past the golf course for a good 4km.

The **tourist office** (☎ 58 13 42; www.vvvwnb.nl; Schuitvlotstraat 32; ☒ 10am-6pm Mon-Sat, 2-4pm Sun) is near the entrance to town on Roosjesweg. The staff are experts at ferreting out accommodation.

The tourist office can steer you to one of many bike rental shops and provides maps of the popular 35km Mantelingen bicycle route,

which begins and ends at Domburg. It takes in beaches, countryside and atmospheric little villages such as Veere.

SLEEPING & EATING

The tourist office has myriad accommodation options, including holiday apartments.

Camping Hof Domburg (☎ 58 82 00; www.room potparken.nl; Schelpweg 7; camp sites from €16, cabins from €60; ☒ year-round; ☒ ☎) Located west of the town centre; like a miniresort with oodles of options.

Stayokay Domburg (☎ 58 12 54; www.stayokay .com/domburg; Duinvlietweg 8; dm from €26, r from €75; ☒ Apr-Oct) A hostel notable for its location in a real castle, complete with moat, 2km east of Domburg and 1km from the beach. Reserve in advance, as it's very popular. Bus 52 from Middelburg stops along the N287 near the entrance.

GETTING THERE & AWAY

Bus 52 links Domburg to Middelburg directly every hour, while bus 53 goes via the southern beaches.

The area is laced with ideal bike paths along dykes and through the green countryside. Get a map and start exploring. Middelburg is about 13km via various routes.

WATERLAND NEELTJE JANS

Travelling the N57, you are on the frontlines of the Dutch war with the sea as you traverse the massive developments of the Delta Project: a succession of huge dykes and dams designed to avoid a repeat of the many floods. Possibly the most impressive stretch is between Noord Beveland and Schouwen-Duiveland, to the north. The long causeway built atop the massive movable inlets is designed to allow the sea tides in and out of the Oosterschelde. This storm-surge barrier, more than 3km long and spanning three inlets and two artificial islands, took 10 years to build, beginning in 1976.

At about the midway point (Haringsvliet), the former visitors centre for the project has morphed into a theme park, complete with a busty mermaid mascot. **Waterland Neeltje Jans** (☎ 111-655 655; www.neeltjejans.nl; admission Nov-Mar €14, April-Oct €20; ☒ 10am-5.30pm), located by the main surge barrier, is an ever-growing complex surrounding the former visitors centre for the barrier. You can still see absorbing exhibits about floods, dams and plucky Dutch courage

---

THE DELTA PROJECT

Begun in 1958, the Delta Project consumed billions of guilders, millions of labour hours and untold volumes of concrete and rock before it was completed in 1996. The goal was to avoid a repeat of the catastrophic floods of 1953, when a huge storm surge rushed up the Delta estuaries of Zeeland and broke through inland dykes. This caused a serial failure of dykes throughout the region, and much of the province was flooded.

The original idea was to block up the estuaries and create one vast freshwater network. But by the 1960s this kind of sweeping transformation was unacceptable to the Dutch public, who had become more environmentally aware. So the Oosterschelde was left open to the sea tides, and 3km of movable barriers were constructed that could be lowered ahead of a possible storm surge. The barriers, between Noord Beveland and Schouwen-Duiveland, are the most dramatic part of the Delta Project and the focus of Waterland Neeltje Jans (p223), which details the enormous efforts to complete the barrier.

The project raised and strengthened the region's dykes and added a movable barrier at Rotterdam harbour, the last part to be completed. Public opinion later shifted, but large areas of water had already been dammed and made into freshwater lakes. At Veerse Meer (p222) the fishing industry has vanished and been replaced by tourists and sailboats.

The impact of the Delta Project is still being felt. At Biesbosch National Park (p218) the reduction of tides is killing reeds that have grown for centuries. But those who recall the 1953 floods will trade some reeds for their farms any day.

Although the entire, enormous project was finally completed in 1997, work has already begun to strengthen and heighten portions to deal with rising water levels due to climate change.

---

in battling the sea, but now the complex also includes seals, a water park, fake beach and the worrisomely named thrill ride: the Moby Dick. For a big blow, try the hurricane simulator.

It's all a bit overblown and rather expensive if you just want to learn a little about the storm barrier. A boat trip takes you out onto the Oosterschelde for a panoramic view of the barriers and beyond.

The island on which Waterland is located has a long beach at the southern end, which is hugely popular with windsurfers. The entire region has coastal sections that are part of the **National Park Oosterschelde** (www.npoosterschelde.nl; admission free; ☑ 10am-5pm); there's a small information booth in the building across the N57 from Waterland.

Bus 133 follows the N57 and stops at Waterland on its run from Middelburg train station (30 minutes, every 30 to 120 minutes) north to Renesse.

SCHOUWEN-DUIVELAND

The middle 'finger' of the Delta, Schouwen-Duiveland, is a compact island of dunes. Beaches and holiday developments can be found southwest from the village of Renesse. Buses hub at Zierikzee; from here you can catch bus 128 and 134 to Renesse in the west

and transfer again to bus 133 for the ride over the Delta Works to Middelburg.

Bikes are the best mode of transit here. Routes abound, including national route LF1 which runs north and south along the coast and over the various parts of the Delta Project.

Zierikzee
☎ 0111 / pop 10,500
Zierikzee grew wealthy in the 14th century from trade with the Hanseatic League, but things took a turn for the worse in 1576 when a bunch of Spaniards waded over from the mainland at low tide and captured the town, precipitating a long economic decline. There's good strolling along the long waterfront.

The **tourist office** (☎ 41 24 50; www.vvvschouwenduiveland.nl; Nieuwe Haven 7; ☑ 10am-4pm Mon-Sat) has an internet kiosk and can supply you with a list of local rooms for overnight stays, plus cycling maps.

SIGHTS & ACTIVITIES
The **Maritiem Museum** (☎ 45 44 64; Mol 25; adult/child €2/1; ☑ 10am-5pm Mon-Sat, noon-5pm Sun) is just off Havenpark. It is in the 's-Gravensteen, a sturdy 16th-century prison that still has its bars. Besides the displays on local seafaring, there's a fine garden in the back.

The **town hall** (☎ 45 44 64; Meelstraat 6-8; adult/child €2/1; ☽ 10am-5pm Mon-Sat, noon-5pm Sun) has a unique 16th-century wooden tower topped with a statue of Neptune.

At Oude Haven, at the east end of town, the **Noordhavenpoort** and the **Zuidhavenpoort** are old city gates from the 16th and 14th centuries respectively.

GETTING THERE & AWAY

The bus stop is north of the town centre, a five-minute walk across the canal along Grachtweg. Bus 132 makes the 30-minute run to Goes at least every 30 minutes. Connexxion bus 395 runs to Rotterdam's Zuidplein metro station (the one-hour ride leaves at least every hour).

Westerschouwen

☎ 0111 / pop 18,000

Sheltered by tall dunes, this village at the west end of Schouwen-Duiveland adjoins a vast park set among the sands and woods. There are hiking and biking trails for outdoors enthusiasts and, although busy in summer, you can easily find solitude in some of the more remote parts of the park.

The **tourist office** (☎ 65 15 13; Noordstraat 45a; ☽ 9am-5pm Mon-Fri, 9am-2pm Sat), in the neighbouring town of Haamstede, can help with accommodation.

Bus 133 from Middelburg and Waterland connects at Renesse in the north for other buses to Zierikzee

ZEEUWS-VLAANDEREN

Running along the Belgian border south of the Westerschelde, Zeeuws-Vlaanderen is an unremarkable place with farms and a few chemical plants.

The many small villages, such as IJzendijk, all have their 'holy trinity' of the Dutch skyline: a church steeple, town hall tower and windmill.

No part of Zeeuws-Vlaanderen joins the rest of the Netherlands by land. The **Vlissingen-Breskens ferry** (www.veolia-transport.nl) is a link for the Belgian channel ferry ports and takes 30 minutes (adult/child €3/1.70, bikes €1, every 30 minutes).

Foot passengers can travel to Brugge in Belgium by Veolia bus 42 from Breskens (75 minutes, hourly). From the port in Vlissingen, catch a bus or train to points beyond, such as Middelburg.

Friesland (Fryslân)

At first Friesland seems typically Dutch: it's flat, it's green and there are plenty of cows (the namesake Frisian black-and-white jobbies here). But explore a bit and you'll find differences. Around the aquatic sports town of Sneek, you'll wonder what's this 'Snit' all about? Well, Snit is Frisian for Sneek. The province has its own language, and while you won't encounter it widely, you will find it on road signs and other signage.

Language is just one thing that sets Frisians apart. Even by Dutch standards, they're a very self-reliant bunch. Here they didn't just have to build dykes to protect their land, they had to build the land as well. North Friesland segues into the Waddenzee in such a subtle way that in the old days you could never be sure when you were on watery mud or muddy water. A mix of holiday homes, farms, mud and beaches, the islands and sea were recognised by Unesco in 2009.

Self-reliant and stoic, the Frisians were integrated further into Dutch society in 1932 when the Afsluitdijk opened, closing the Zuiderzee. This provided better transport links to Amsterdam and the south but it also proved devastating for small fishing villages, which the found themselves living on a lake. Only now are places like Hindeloopen finding sure footing as tourist destinations.

At the centre is Leeuwarden, the provincial capital and the sort of beguiling old Dutch town where you soon have a favourite cafe and you've lost track of the days.

HIGHLIGHTS

- Explore the excellent museums and shady back streets of **Leeuwarden** (p228)
- Take to the water around **Sneek** (p231 – whether it be fresh, salty, in it, or on it
- Kick back in **Hindeloopen** (p233), a coastal town almost forgotten by time
- Combine a cycling trip through sand dunes and farmland on **Terschelling** (p236) and **Ameland** (p237)
- Find your little piece of island solitude on **Vlieland** (p235) and **Schiermonnikoog** (p237), which has a fine national park

FRIESLAND

History

Having dredged their home out of the Waddenzee armload by armload, the Frisians are no strangers to struggling with their natural environment.

Farming, fishing and nautical know-how (the building, repair and maintenance of ships) have been the area's principal activities for centuries, and in the prerepublic era made Friesland one of the wealthiest regions in the Netherlands. The Frisians became integrated further into Dutch society – not entirely willingly – in 1932 when the Afsluitdijk (Barrier Dyke; see boxed text, p169) opened, closing the Zuiderzee. This provided better links to Amsterdam and the south but was devastating for small fishing villages, who suddenly found

themselves sitting beside a lake. Fortunately adversity brought a solution: rebrand the region as a holiday sailing mecca, which brings more and more people each summer.

Language

Frisians speak Frisian, which is actually closer (in some ways) to German and Old English than Dutch; there's an old saying that goes 'As milk is to cheese, are English and Frise'. The majority of Frisians are, however, perfectly conversant in mainstream Dutch.

Most people who have lived in the region for a significant time will speak some Frisian, although you're more likely to hear Frisian coming from the mouths of older residents than younger people's. Don't worry if you can't make head nor tail of it – even the Dutch have difficulty deciphering Frisian. You'll usually see written examples, such as street signs. You might, for example, see the word 'Snits', which is the Frisian version of Sneek, the region's second city.

A ruling in 2002 officially altered the spelling of the province's name from the Dutch 'Friesland' to 'Fryslân', the local version of the name.

Getting There & Around

The capital, Leeuwarden, is easily reached by train from the south, from where trains can be caught to the coastal towns of the southwest, the port of Harlingen in the west, and Groningen in the east. The rest of the province requires more patience, but can be reached by bus; various day passes are available on buses and cover the entire region.

Cycle paths crisscross Friesland. National bike route LF3 bisects the province north and south through Leeuwarden, LF10 cuts across Waddenzee on the Afsluitdijk (30km) from Noord Holland and takes in the north Frisian coast and all the ferry ports while LF22 covers the southern coast before heading inland towards Zwolle (p255).

By car is also a good way to explore the entire province; the quickest route from Amsterdam is over the Afsluitdijk.

LEEUWARDEN (LJOUWERT)

☎ 058 / pop 93,500

While most tourists to Friesland head directly for the islands, don't pass Leeuwarden without making a stop in the province's capital. This laid-back, pretty town is worth a visit, if only to explore its superb trinity of museums. Spending the night here will also allow time to wander its peaceful old streets, and sample some northern hospitality, something easily found in its many bars and cafes. You might even spy a trace of its somewhat-favourite daughter Mata Hari.

Orientation

The old town is compact and easily traversed on foot. Much of the commercial life is on or near the network of canals that wind through the centre.

Information

Leeuwarden is dotted with ATMs; for those arriving by train and needing cash, there's a couple located to the right as you exit the station.

GSM Clinic (☎ 212 49 30; Berlikumermarkt 21; internet per hr €2; ⏰ 1-10pm) Good for cheap calls and SIM cards.

Tourist office (☎ 234 75 50; www.vvvleeuwarden.nl; Sophialaan 4; ⏰ noon-5.30pm Mon, 9.30am-5.30pm Tue-Fri, 10am-3pm Sat) Stocks loads of information on the province, has free internet access, and books accommodation for a fee of €2 per person.

Van der Velde (☎ 213 23 60; Nieuwestad NZ 57) Bookshop with a smallish but decent selection of English-language and travel books.

Sights

Most of Leeuwarden's sights are concentrated within a leisurely 10-minute walk of Nieuwestad, predominantly on the northern side (Nieuwestad NZ) of the water. However the big news is that Zaailand, the huge central square otherwise known as Wilhelminaplein is being entirely redeveloped (www.nieuwzaailand.nl). From 2012 it will be the cultural centre of town.

FRIES MUSEUM

This **museum** (☎ 255 55 00; www.friesmuseum.nl; Turfmarkt 11; adult/child €6/free; ⏰ 11am-5pm Tue-Sun), Leeuwarden's biggest, is wonderful and concentrates on the history of Friesland from the time when locals began the necessary task of mud-stacking. Currently spread over several historic buildings, the Kanselarij, a 16th-century courthouse, and the Eysinghaus, a mansion from the late 1700s, it's a place to spend a couple of hours.

The huge collection of silver items – long a local speciality – is spectacular, as are the 19th-century period pieces. There is also a section on the efforts by locals to resist the Nazis and a sorrowful examination of the life of Mata Hari (see the boxed text, p230). Temporary exhibits feature cutting edge works by young artists. In 2012 the museum will move to a stunner of a new building on Zaailand.

PRINCESSEHOF MUSEUM

Pottery lovers will adore the **Princessehof Museum** (☎ 294 89 58; www.princessehof.nl; Grote Kerkstraat 11; adult/child €8/free; ⏰ 11am-5pm Tue-Sun), the official museum for ceramics in the Netherlands. Here you'll find the largest collection of tiles on the planet, an unparalleled selection of Delftware, and works from around the globe – its Japanese, Chinese and Vietnamese sections are world class. It's all suitably housed in a 17th-century mansion.

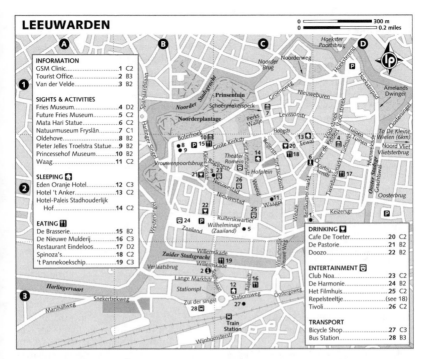

LEEUWARDEN

0   300 m
0   0.2 miles

NATUURMUSEUM FRYSLÂN

Even the most brow-beaten parent should let their lovely angels run rampant in the **Natuurmuseum Fryslân** (☎ 233 22 44; www.natuur museumfryslan.nl; Schoenmakersperk 2; adult/child €5/4; ☼ 11am-5pm Tue-Sun), Leeuwarden's revamped children's museum. This well-planned, interactive museum is an engaging experience for all ages, concentrating on Friesland's flora and fauna. Highlights include spooky Captain Severein's collection of curiosities and a virtual bird-flight simulation (strap yourself into the hang-glider harness and away you go), but nothing tops the basement; here you can take in 'Friesland onder Water', an exploration of the bottom of a canal from a fish's perspective.

The museum's cafe, which occupies the inner courtyard, is topped by a glass roof, making it cheery refuge on a cold day.

OTHER ATTRACTIONS

Just past the west end of Bagijnestraat, the off-balance **Oldehove** (adult/child €2/1; ☼ 2-5pm Tue-Sat May-Sep) dominates its unfortunate spot on the Oldehoofsterkerkhof parking lot. Things

went wrong shortly after the tower was started in 1529 and it started to lean severely when it was only 40m high. While by no means a Leaning Tower of Pisa, it must still be quite worrying for the neighbours. Compare the tilt to the very erect neighbouring **statue of Pieter Jelles Troelstra**, a Dutch socialist who called for revolution after WWI.

The petite **Waag** dominates Waagplein, and is now surrounded by stores. It was the weigh-house for butter and other goods from 1598 to 1884. The pedestrian zone includes the evocative old street **Weerd**.

Sleeping

Leeuwarden isn't swamped with accommodation options, but there's variety enough to suit everyone's tastes. For B&Bs at around €25 per person, try the tourist office.

De Kleine Wielen (☎ 0511-43 16 60; www.dekleine wielen.nl; De Groene Ster 14; camp sites from €15, cabins from €50) Centred on a small lake some 6km east of the city off the N355, De Kleine Wielen is a pleasant, green camping ground suitable for families and nature lovers. Bus 10 and 51 pass close to the camp; ask the driver to let

---

MATA HARI

Had she been born a few decades later, Leeuwarden's own Gertrud Margarete Zelle probably would have hosted a TV chat show. Instead, the irrepressible Margarete ended up a martyr to salacious legend.

Margarete was born in 1876. Her wealthy family fell apart in her teens, so she married and moved to Indonesia. By 1902 the marriage was on the rocks and they were back in Leeuwarden. She left her husband and child and moved to Paris, where she changed her name to Mata Hari (Malaysian for 'sun') and began a career as a dancer, achieving fame with her erotic, naked act.

Her affairs and dalliances were legendary. She favoured rich men-in-uniform, and when WWI broke out she had high-ranking lovers on both sides. Things inevitably became tricky; French officers persuaded her to spy on her German lovers, and German officers managed to do the same. This web of intrigue was not helped by her keen imagination, and mistrust began to rise from both sides.

In 1917, at age 40, she was arrested by the French for spying. There was a dubious trial, during which none of her former 'pals' offered any assistance – probably out of embarrassment – and later that year she was sentenced to death and shot.

Today Margarete/Mata Hari is still – in a manner of speaking – alive and well in Leeuwarden. Her statue as a sultry dancer can be found on a bridge over the canal close to her birthplace at Over de Kelders 33, and the Fries Museum has a large and detailed exhibit on her life. The residence where Margarete spent much of her childhood, Grote Kerkstraat 212, currently lies empty awaiting its next incarnation.

---

you off at De Skieppepoel, from where it's a five-minute walk south. A bike ride to here is a breeze.

Hotel 't Anker (☎ 212 52 16; www.hotelhetanker.nl; Eewal 73; r €30-70; 🛜) This simple hotel is a fine bet for those just looking for a bed and a clean room in an ideally located spot. It's surprisingly quiet as well, considering the ground floor contains a lively bar, and a string of restaurants and bars line the street.

Eden Oranje Hotel (☎ 212 62 41; www.edenhotelgroup.nl; Stationsweg 4; r €60-150; 🛁 🖥 🛜) Directly opposite the train station, this business hotel has grand common spaces and comfy, large rooms with a flash of style (ones in the far rear are leafy and quiet). Frequent discounts are amazing, given the quality here.

Hotel-Paleis Stadhouderlijk Hof (☎ 216 21 80; www.stadhouderlijkhof.nl; Hofplein 29; r €95-200; 🛁 🛜) The plain pink facade of the Stadhouderlijk belies the plush interior of this one-time royal home. Inside, the red-carpeted stairwells lead to 24 basic rooms, which have a semblance of elegance. The yellow water in the fountain out front is troubling.

Eating

our pick Spinoza's (☎ 212 93 93; Eewal 50-52; mains €10-17; 🕒 lunch & dinner) This large eatery is great in summer when you can enjoy the tables out front or the private courtyard. In winter, huddle up in the candle-lit interior. The menu features regional specialities (soups and stews are big) and plenty of vegetarian options.

't Pannekoekschip (☎ 212 09 03; Willemskade 69; meals from €6; 🕒 noon-5pm Wed-Sun) Sure it's hokey! But no kid of any age can resist heading below decks on this old two-masted sailing ship for any of 90 kinds of pancakes.

De Nieuwe Mulderij (☎ 213 48 02; Baljeestraat 19; menus from €32; 🕒 lunch Tue-Fri, dinner Tue-Sat) Away from the old town, this gem of a bistro has creative and fresh fare with produce sourced locally. Menus comprise two to five courses and change weekly.

De Brasserie (☎ 215 13 80; Grote Kerkstraat 7; meals from €6; 🕒 10am-8pm) A sprawling cafe popular with locals lounging and shoppers not shopping, it has a classic menu and absolutely fab coffees and teas. Knock back a few brews and head next door to the ceramics museum to do your bull act in the china exhibit.

Restaurant Eindeloos (☎ 213 08 35; www.restauranteindeloos.nl; Korfmakersstraat 17; menus from €42; 🕒 dinner Wed-Sat) Menus change constantly at this perfect little restaurant with a precision to the decor of white and black that matches the efforts in the kitchen. Local produce, seafood and lamb usually figure in the line-up.

Drinking

A concentration of bars, clubs and cof-feeshops can be found around Doelesteeg, Kleine Hoogstraat and Grote Hoogstraat. Ruiterskwartier is lined with bars catering to young folks on lively nights out.

Café De Toeter (☎ 215 79 76; Kleine Hoogstraat 2) A fine place to chill out on faux wicker chairs under a huge tree.

De Pastorie (☎ 213 32 14; Kleine Kerkstraat 9) A merry little brown cafe typical of a slew of places tucked away on the narrow streets north of Nieustad.

Doozo (☎ 213 60 69; Ruiterskwartier 93) Part club and part sushi bar, there's lots of sofas for lounging about and sucking down raw eel amidst the local beautiful folk.

Entertainment

Club Noa (www.club-noa.nl; Nieuwstad 63-65; ⏰ 11pm-5am Fri & Sat) Big, bold, brash club attracting pretty young things with its sexy red interior, *Saturday Night Fever* dance floor and thumping music.

De Harmonie (☎ 233 02 33; www.harmonie.nl; Ruiterskwartier 4) The local home to theatre per-formances, both mainstream and fringe. Last minute tickets are half price.

Repelsteeltje (☎ 216 48 22; Grote Hoogstraat 44) A mellow coffeeshop that's a gateway to the entire concept. Repelsteeltje has the look and feel of a normal coffee house, a chatty owner, regular DJs and a distinct absence of pot-caused paranoia.

Tivoli (☎ 212 38 87; www.filmhuisleeuwarden.nl; Nieuwstad 38-42) unspools an interesting line-up of art-house and festival films, as does **Het Filmhuis** (☎ 212 50 60; www.filminfriesland.nl; Ruiterskwartier 4).

Getting There & Around

Leeuwarden is at the end of the main train line from the south (trains often split at Meppel, so don't end up in the half going to Groningen); it's also the hub for local services in Friesland. Lockers can be found on plat-form No 8 and the station has full services. Fares and schedules:

Destination	Fare (€)	Duration (min)	Frequency (per hr)
Groningen	8.80	36	3
Utrecht	23.90	120	1
Zwolle	14.50	60	2

Buses are to the left as you exit the train station.

The **bicycle shop** (☎ 213 98 00) is to the right as you exit the train station. Leeuwarden is about 110km north of Kampen (near Zwolle; p255) on the dairy cow–lined national bike route LF3. Otherwise the region is laced with bike routes atop dykes and past lakes and farms.

AROUND LEEUWARDEN

The N357, which connects Leeuwarden with the Ameland ferry port at Holwerd, 23km north, passes some of the oldest settled parts of Friesland – an excellent route for touring. On bikes, national route LF3 covers the route in 28km.

At Ferwerd, 6km southwest of Holwerd, watch for a road northeast to **Hogebeintum**, which is 3km off the N357. You'll soon see the highest *terp* (mud mound) in Friesland with a lovely old church perched on top. There are some good displays explaining the ongoing archaeological digs. It's 10km ride southwest of Holwerd on the coastal LF10.

SNEEK (SNITS)

☎ 0515 / pop 33,300

'All Frisians know how to sail, and all Frisians know how to sail', so the saying goes. This is certainly true of the residents of Sneek, but then again, they have no choice in the mat-ter: Frisian lakes and rivers are linked to the IJsselmeer and decorate the land not unlike the spots on the local dairy cows. If you've got a hankering to get out under sail, this is the place.

Information

Post office (Martiniplein 15A) In the heart of town.

Tourist office (☎ 41 40 96; www.vvvsneek.nl; Markt-straat 18; ⏰ 9.30am-6pm Mon-Fri, 9.30am-5pm Sat) Has long lists of boat rental and charter firms, sailing schools and more, and shares its office with the ANWB.

Sights & Activities

You won't find many conventional sights here in Sneek, given its overwhelming bias towards the water. The **Waterpoort** dates from 1613 and is the former gateway to the old port. Its twin towers are local landmarks. Across from the tourist office, the **town hall** (Marktstraat 15) is an excellent example of the breed. The town's best museum, the **Fries Scheepvaart Museum** (☎ 41 40 57; www.friesscheepvaartmuseum.nl; Kleinzand 14; adult/child €3/1; ⏰ 10am-5pm Mon-Sat, noon-5pm Sun), is a maritime museum focusing on local seafaring life.

SNEEK'S WATER-SPORTS BOUNTY

Sneek is surrounded by water, and any activity associated with it – particularly if it involves wind, of which there is hardly ever a shortage – is big.

Several sailing and windsurfing schools, where you can learn from scratch or top up existing skills, operate in the area. One of the largest is **Zeilschool de Friese Meren** (☎ 0515-41 21 41; www.zfm.nl; Eeltjebaasweg 7), which has a range of courses (a basic weekend sailing course costs €185). The tourist office has a long list of various operators and services available.

If you'd just prefer to watch sleek ships skip across the water, then sail into town in early August to catch **Sneekweek** (www.sneekweek.nl), the largest sailing event on Europe's inland waters. You'll be treated to plenty of racing activity and lots of frivolity.

During the summer months there are **boat cruises** on the local waters. The schedules change by whim, weather and number of operators each season. Most leave from the Oosterkade, at the end of Kleinzand, so either wander over or inquire at the tourist office.

Sleeping & Eating

The tourist office has lists of local rooms from around €20 to €25 per person.

De Wijnberg (☎ 41 24 21; www.hoteldewijnberg.nl; Marktstraat 23; s/d €54/74) Opposite the tourist office is this standard hotel with 23 plain rooms with either bathtubs or showers. The restaurant-pub on the ground floor is often lively and convivial.

Sneek aan Zee (☎ 41 27 56; Oosterdijk 10; mains from €14; 🕑 lunch & dinner Mon-Sat) Seafood, seafood, seafood. That's what's both fresh and on the menu at this popular new spot.

Other choices:

De Domp Camping (☎ 41 25 59; www.dedomp.nl; Domp 4; camp sites €14) This lush camping ground is about a 20-minute walk from town; follow the signs for the *zwembad* (public swimming pool). Sites for hikers/bikers are well away from vehicles.

Stayokay Sneek (☎ 41 21 32; www.stayokay.com/sneek; Oude Oppenhuizerweg 17; dm from €24, r from €80; 🖳) Typically modern and slick hostel with private rooms. A five-minute walk from town.

Getting There & Around

From the decommissioned train station, which now sports a huge **model train museum** (www.modelspoormuseum.nl), the centre of town is a five-minute walk along Stationstraat. Trains to/from Leeuwarden cost €4.30 (22 minutes, two per hour).

Rijwielhandel Twa Tsjillen (☎ 41 38 78; Wijde Noorderhorne 8; per day from €7), 400m to the northeast of the station, rents bikes. You'll find that the area's cycling options are almost as bounteous as the fertile fields as you wend your way along the many small lanes in the countryside between Sneek and Leeuwarden (about 32km).

HARLINGEN (HARNS)

☎ 0517 / pop 15,700

Of all the old Frisian ports, only Harlingen has kept its link to the sea. It still plays an important role for shipping in the area, and is the base for ferries to Terschelling and Vlieland.

Harlingen has also managed to retain a semblance of its architectural history; much of the attractive centre is a preserved zone of pretty 16th- and 18th-century buildings that make for a good hour of strolling as you wait for your sailing.

Information

Large maps are posted around town. The website www.harlingen-friesland.nl has full details of local attractions, lodging and more.

Sights & Activities

Harlingen is best enjoyed on foot. Stroll along the canals, many with drawbridges that rise with rhythmatic regularity – especially yacht-filled Noorderhaven and Zuiderhaven. Voorstraat has shops, attractions and cafes.

The **Gemeentemuseum het Hannemahuis** (☎ 41 36 58; Voorstraat 56; adult/child €3.50/1.50; 🕑 11am-5pm Tue-Fri, 1.30-5pm Sat & Sun) is housed in an 18th-century building and includes material on Harlingen's past as a whaling town. Along with farming, whaling was one of the industries that made Friesland one of the most prosperous regions in the Netherlands in the 1700s. Hence the celebration of flensing and flensers – the process of stripping blubber from a whale's carcass, and the lucky chaps who got to do it. Much improved since a 2008 revamp, it also has a *jenever* (Dutch gin) exhibit.

Sleeping & Eating

Zeezicht Harlingen (☎ 41 25 36; www.hotelzeezicht.nl; Zuiderhaven 1; r €65-100; 🛜) Zeezicht (it means 'sea view' not 'sea sick') lives up to its name. The 24 rooms are in great order; you can watch the comings and goings of boats from bed, terrace or cafe.

De Tjotter (☎ 41 46 91; www.detjotter.nl; St Jacobsrtraat 1-3; meals from €30; 🕑 noon-10pm) Back along Noorderhaven, this fishy empire has a fine restaurant that buys its fare right from the boats. Specials are listed on a board – and the web. The casual cafe out front is just the place to ponder passing boats and make trenchant comments about the skills of the skippers.

Getting There & Away

Harlingen is connected to Leeuwarden (€4.80, 23 minutes) by two trains hourly. There is a harbour station right near the ferries (Harlingen Haven) but it is being reconstructed through 2010. In the meantime passengers use Harlingen station and shuttle by bus to the ferry dock. If the new station has any services like lockers it will be a bonus. For ferry details to Vlieland and Terschelling, see p235 and p236 respectively.

There is no ideal bike route between Harlingen and Leeuwarden; you'll have to meander over back roads (about 30km via Franeker). The ferry port is on national bike router LF10, which runs 8km south on the coast to the Afsluitdijk and the crossing to Noord Holland. Going northeast, LF10 passes all the ferry ports.

FRANEKER (FRJENTSJER)

☎ 0517 / pop 21,000

About 6km east of Harlingen, the quaint town of Franeker was once a big player in education, until Napoleon closed its university down in 1810. Today its well-preserved centre makes for a nice meander, but Franeker's highlight is its planetarium.

The **Eise Eisinga Planetarium** (☎ 39 30 70; www .planetarium-friesland.nl; Eise Eisingastraat 3; adult/child €4.50/3.75; 🕑 10am-5pm Tue-Sat, 1-5pm Sun year-round, 1-5pm Mon Apr-Oct) is the world's oldest working planetarium. The namesake owner was a tradesman with a serious sideline in cosmic mathematics and astrology, who clearly could have been a 'somebody' in the astronomical world. Beginning in 1774, he built the planetarium himself to show how the heavens actually worked. It's startling to contemplate how

Eisinga could have devised a mechanical timing system built to a viewable working scale that could encompass and illustrate so many different variables of time and motion. There's an artful cafe right next door and the ornate 1591 Stadhuis is right across the canal.

The Harlingen–Leeuwarden train stops in Franeker (from Leeuwarden €3.50, 16 minutes, two hourly), 500m from the centre. The town is a good reward for cycling the area's little lanes.

HINDELOOPEN (HYLPEN)

☎ 0514 / pop 900

Huddled up against the banks of the IJsselmeer, Hindeloopen, a cloistered fishing town among the farms, has been set apart from Friesland for centuries. Today as you approach across the fields of corn and groups of sheep that cover the flat Frisian countryside, the sudden appearance of a forest of yacht masts marks Hindeloopen in the distance.

With its narrow streets, tiny canals, little bridges, long waterfront and lack of traffic, Hindeloopen makes for an atmospheric afternoon escape. In extraordinarily cold winters it is one of the key towns on the route of the Elfstedentocht (see boxed text, p234) and has a quaint, yet reverent, museum devoted to the race.

Other coastal towns in the area worth a peek, if you have time, are pretty Makkum and busy Workum; both towns are north of Hindeloopen.

Information

The staff at the **tourist office** (☎ 52 25 50; www.vvvhin deloopen.nl; Nieuwstad 26; 🕑 10am-5pm Mon-Sat) can help with accommodation. For banks and shops, you'll have to go 4km north to Workum.

Sights & Activities

Hindeloopen is best experienced at a slow pace. If, however, you need a diversion, head for the **Het Eerste Friese Schaatsmuseum** (☎ 52 16 83; www.schaatsmuseum.nl; Kleine Weide 1-3; adult/child €2.50/1.50; 🕑 10am-6pm Mon-Sat, 1-5pm Sun), which focuses on the Elfstedentocht, and ice skating in general. Its displays about skating through the centuries are quite enthralling, as is the history of the Elfstedentocht. The shop seems to have every ice-skating book ever published.

Museum Hindeloopen (☎ 52 15 08; Tuinen 18; adult/child €3/2; 🕑 11am-5pm Mon-Fri, 1.30-5pm Sat & Sun Apr-Oct) has displays about the traditional lifestyles practised locally until quite recently. It has a good walking-tour flyer and other local info.

Sleeping & Eating

Camping Hindeloopen (☎ 52 14 52; www.camping hindeloopen.nl; Westerdijk 9; camp sites from €22) To the south of the town, behind the protective dyke, is this large camping ground, with beach access, windsurfing school, and restaurant on site.

De Stadsboerderij (☎ 52 12 78; www.destads boerderij.nl; Nieuwe Weide 9; s/d €46/72) With comfy rooms in a leafy, quiet corner of town, De Stadsboerderij offers a peaceful night's sleep. There's also a restaurant-pub next door, with photos of boats sailing the IJsselmeer at uncomfortable angles.

There's a sprinkling of restaurants and fish stands overlooking the town's harbour. A good place to while away the hours is the terrace at **Café-Restaurant de Hinde** (☎ 52 38 68; Tuinensteeg 5; meals from €7; ☺ 11am-9pm).

Getting There & Away

The train stop is a lovely tree-lined 2km walk from town. There is an hourly service to Leeuwarden (€7.20, 40 minutes) via Sneek (€4, 18 minutes). By bike, it's about 30km via country lanes from Sneek to Hindeloopen, which is also on the coastal national bike route LF22. Harlingen is about 32km north.

FRISIAN ISLANDS

Friesland's four islands – Vlieland, Terschelling, Ameland and Schiermonnikoog – are collectively known as the Frisian Islands.

Despite the fact that they're basically raised banks of sand and mud (with plenty of introduced pine forests to stabilise them) amid the mudflats of the Waddenzee, they are popular with Dutch and German holidaymakers in search of a rural beach retreat in the warmer months. (Noord Holland's Texel completes the island chain; see p160.)

In 2009, much of the Waddenzee off both the coasts of the Netherlands and Germany was named a Unesco World Heritage site. Although the built-up portions of the islands were not included, the designation does include the windy, natural expanse of Schiermonnikoog's national park.

Each of the islands has been developed for tourism, and the number of hotels, B&B rooms and cottages for rent is staggering, considering the size of the islands. Despite the development, all have large open spaces where you can get close to the sea grasses or the water itself. Any one of the islands makes an interesting trip on its own and there are copious bicycle-rental options near the ferry ports. Paths suitable for hiking and biking circle each of the islands and, away from the built-up areas, you're rewarded with long sandy beaches on the seaward sides. Throughout the Waddenzee, you'll see opportunities to go *wadlopen* (mudflat-walking). See the boxed text, p246 for details.

In summer the islands are very crowded, so don't just show up and expect to find a room; populations routinely multiply by 10 on warm weekends.

A DAY AT THE RACES

Skating and the Dutch culture are interwoven and no event better symbolises this than the **Elfstedentocht** (Eleven Cities Race; www.elfstedentocht.nl). Begun officially in 1909, although it had been held for hundreds of years before that, the race is 200km long, starts and finishes in Leeuwarden, and passes through 10 Frisian towns (11 including Leeuwarden): Sneek, IJlst, Sloten, Stavoren, Hindeloopen, Workum, Bolsward, Harlingen, Franeker and Dokkum. The record time for completing the race is six hours and 47 minutes, set in 1985 (Evert van Benthem won again in 1986, making him a living legend).

While it is a marathon, what makes the race a truly special event is that it can only be held in years when it's cold enough for all the canals to freeze totally; this has only happened 15 times since 1909. The last time was in 1997. So how do you schedule such an event? You don't.

Instead, there is a huge Elfstedentocht committee that waits for the mercury to plummet. When it looks as though the canals will be properly frozen, 48 hours' notice is given. All work effectively ends throughout the province as armies of volunteers make preparations for the race, and the thousands of competitors get ready.

On the third day, the race begins at 5.30am. The next few hours are a holiday for the rest of the Netherlands as well, as the population gathers around TVs to watch the live coverage.

ISLAND-HOPPING

With a little planning, good weather karma (storms cause ferry cancellations) and some plain old pluck, you can travel between all five islands on the Waddenzee: Texel and the four Frisians. Going east, here's how to do it (after confirming all times):

■ **Texel–Vlieland** From the long beach north of De Cocksdorp, catch a boat with **De Vriendschap** (☎ 0222-316 451; www.waddenveer.nl). After a 30-minute trip (adult/child/bicycle one-way €14.50/8.50/7.50, departs 10.45am) over the very shallow waters, you are met by a truck, which takes you across the military reservation to Bomenland. Here you take a bus or cycle to Oost-Vlieland.

■ **Vlieland–Terschelling** Fast ferries are run by **Rederij Doeksen** (☎ 0900 363 57 36; www.rederij -doeksen.nl) usually once per day (adult/child/bicycle one-way €8/4/12).

■ **Terschelling–Ameland** Options here are more adventurous. **Robbenboot** (☎ 0519-720 550; www.robbenboot.nl) runs a boat (adult/child/bicycle one-way €28/18/5, 3½ hours) about once a week in summer. **Eiland Hopper** (☎ 06-479 80 324; www.eilandhopper.nl) sails about every two weeks in summer (adult/child/bicycle one-way €59/39/29).

■ **Ameland–Schiermonnikoog** About once a week in summer **Robbenboot** (☎ 0519-720 550; www.robbenboot.nl) runs a boat (adult/child/bicycle one-way €28/18/5, three hours) .

Getting There & Away

Frequent ferries link the islands with the mainland and bikes are carried free. Texel in Noord Holland is the only one of the Wadden Islands to allow people to bring cars. However all the Frisian Islands have decent bus service as well as huge bike rental shops near the ferry docks. Always confirm ferry schedules in advance.

Island hopping is a real adventure. See boxed text, above for details.

Vlieland

☎ 0562 / pop 1150

Historically the most isolated of the islands, Vlieland (4022 hectares) is still ignored by most tourists today. It's a windswept and wild place, with much of its western end at the mercy of sand and sea, but this is part of its charm. The sole town, Oost-Vlieland, is small, and only residents are allowed to bring cars across on the ferry.

Much of the west end of the islands is nothing but sand and is used by the military. There are just a couple of lonely tracks across it.

INFORMATION

The **tourist office** (☎ 45 11 11; www.vlieland.net; Havenweg 10; internet per hr €6; ⏰ 9am-5pm Mon-Fri, 1hr after each ferry arrival Sat & Sun) is opposite the ferry dock.

SIGHTS & ACTIVITIES

There's not much in the way of human-made attractions on Vlieland, and that's exactly the point: nature is the attraction. Most of the 72

sq km of island lies waiting to be explored by bike or on foot, although its 18km of beaches aren't as much fun to cycle as the untamed interior. Depending on how fit you consider yourself, cycling around Vlieland can be gentle or moderately gruelling; there are many unsealed tracks that confident 'off-roaders' can opt to tackle. You can rent sea kayaks to venture out on the usually sedate waters.

For nature hikes and bird-watching walks, consult the tourist office.

SLEEPING & EATING

Vlieland has several cafes and restaurants, all with a basic sort of steak-seafood-bit-of-pasta menu. Sleeping options are legion, although over the summer months, and on sunny weekends, be sure to book ahead.

Camping Stortemelk (☎ 45 12 25; www.stortemelk.nl; Kampweg 1; camp sites from €20, cabins from €80) Stortemelk is a typically beachy camp site, with little wind protection but close proximity to sandy beaches. There's a small restaurant, playground and shop on site and you can rent a tent.

Hotelletje de Veerman (☎ 45 13 78; www.hotelletje deveerman.nl; Dorpsstraat 173, Oost-Vlieland; r €50-100) Veerman has 12 simple rooms that are a short walk from the ferry. Nothing is so fancy you won't want to get sand on it, and there are also six apartments in the village.

GETTING THERE & AROUND

Rederij Doeksen (☎ 0900 363 57 36; www.rederij -doeksen.nl) runs regular ferries from Harlingen to Vlieland (adult/child return €22/11, bicycle €12) that take approximately 90 minutes. Departures are typically at 8.45am, 2.15pm and 7pm. A fast service (€28/17) takes 45 minutes direct and 90 minutes via Terschelling, and also operates from Harlingen. Schedules change often.

Ferries sail to nearby Texel over the summer months. See the boxed text, p235 for details.

You can cycle (bike hire around €6) around the island, and there is also a little bus that wanders the few roads of Oost-Vlieland.

Terschelling
☎ 0562 / pop 4800

Terschelling (11,575 hectares) is the largest of the Frisian Islands; it's also the most visited and commercial. Its small villages, of which West-Terschelling is the largest, are strung out along the southern edge of the island, while its northern coast is all sand dunes and white beaches. The eastern end of the island is a wild and isolated place, and perfect for escaping the crowds. Overall there are 250km of walking and cycling trails, many sandy.

The smaller villages of Hoorn and Oosterend are east of West-Terschelling, much less commercial and closer to the very pretty natural parts of the island.

INFORMATION
The **tourist office** (☎ 44 30 00; www.vvv-terschelling .nl; Willem Barentszkade 19A, West-Terschelling; internet per hr €6; ⊙ 9.30am-5.30pm Mon-Fri, 10am-3pm Sat) has a great range of maps for cycling or walking. All manner of rooms can be booked for under €10. The ferry port is just over the road.

SIGHTS & ACTIVITIES
De Boschplaat, a huge car-free natural reserve at the eastern end of the island, is the highlight. It is the only EU-designated European Natural Monument in the Netherlands.

The **Terschelling Museum 't Behouden Huys** (☎ 44 23 89; www.behouden-huys.nl; Commandeurstraat 30-32; adult/child €3/2; ⊙ 10am-5pm Mon-Fri, 1-5pm Sat Apr-Oct, 1-5pm Sun mid-Jun–Sep, closed Oct-Mar) covers the island's maritime past.

FESTIVALS & EVENTS
The annual **Oerol** (www.oerol.nl) outdoor performance festival on Terschelling is revered nationwide as a perfect excuse for going to sea. It started years ago with farmers letting their cows run loose one day each year (hence

the name *oerol*, which means 'everywhere' or 'all over') – these days, *everybody* gets into the spirit of things. It's a wild, arty party, piercing the otherwise unflappable northern facade for 10 days in the latter half of June.

SLEEPING & EATING
Camping de Duinkant (☎ 44 89 17; www.duinkant.nl; camp sites from €12) This basic camping ground at the eastern end of the main road is just a farmer's field, with no cooking facilities. It is, however, lovely and remote, with nothing but green pastures, cows and sand dunes as neighbours.

Stayokay Terschelling (☎ 44 23 38; www.stayokay .com/terschelling; Burg van Heusdenweg 39, West-Terschelling; dm from €28; ⊙ Apr-Oct) Just outside West-Terschelling's borders, this typically well-run Stayokay hostel has a laundry, rents bikes, and has a small restaurant and kids playground.

Hotel Eeetcafé 't Wapen van Terschelling (☎ 44 88 01; www.twapenvanterschelling.nl; Oosterburen 25; r €63-90) A delightful village cafe with the best beer list on the island. There are also very simple rooms, of which the cheapest share bathrooms while the better ones have balconies.

Also recommended:

H2O Hostel (☎ 44 82 52; www.h2ohostel.nl; Dorpstraat 104, Hoorn; s/d from €32/64) Set in a modern barn amid a farm and riding school. Very clean two-bed rooms.

De Heeren Van Der Schelling (☎ 44 87 80; Oosterend; mains €11-22; ⊙ lunch & dinner Thu-Mon) Owner Arno van Veen State is one of the Dutch promoters of the Slow Food movement; his lovely stone restaurant has a changing menu created from local produce, lamb and seafood. Book.

GETTING THERE & AROUND
Rederij Doeksen (☎ 0900 363 57 36; www.rederij -doeksen.nl) runs regular ferries from Harlingen to Terschelling (adult/child return €22/11, bicycle €12) and take approximately two hours. Departures are several times daily aboard very large boats. A fast service (adult/child return €28/17) takes 45 minutes direct and usually goes three times daily. Note that these ferries have little deck space compared to the large ones. Schedules change often.

Ferries sail to nearby Vlieland over the summer months. See boxed text, p235 for details.

Hourly buses (day ticket €6) run the length of the main road; bicycles can be hired for as little as €7, and some bicycle rental places will also deliver bikes to the ferry, and transport your luggage to your accommodation.

Ameland

☎ 0519 / pop 3600

If the Frisian Islands were given personalities, Ameland (8500 hectares) would be the person sitting on the fence. Its four peaceful villages – Buren, Nes, Ballum and Hollum – are less developed than those on Terschelling and Texel, but they provide enough social structure for the majority of tourists. Its large swaths of untouched natural splendour offer places to escape the crowds, but Mother Nature doesn't rule the roost as on Schiermonnikoog or Vlieland.

All in all, Ameland is an island for those looking for an idyll that's 'just right'.

INFORMATION

The island's main **tourist office** (☎ 54 65 46; www.vvv-ameland.nl; Bureweg 2, Nes; ☒ 9am-5pm Mon-Fri, 10am-3.30pm Sat) is seven minutes' walk, or one bus stop, from the ferry terminal. It has plenty of information on the island, including an excellent map and internet access (€3 per hour). It books rooms by phone and the internet.

SIGHTS & ACTIVITIES

At only 85 sq km in size, Ameland is easily tackled by pedal power. **Bicycle paths** cover the entire island, and include a 27km bicycle path that runs almost the entire length of the northern shore just south of protective sand dunes. The eastern third of the island is given over to a combination of wetlands and dunes, with not a settlement in sight; it's by far the best place to take time out for yourself.

Of the villages, the 18th-century former whaling port of **Nes** is the prettiest and most carefully preserved (although all are interesting for a brief stroll), its streets lined with tidy little brick houses. **Hollum**, the most western village, has windswept dunes within easy walk, and is in sight of a famous red and white **lighthouse** (adult/child €5/2.50; ☒ 10am-5pm & 7-9pm Tue-Sat, 1-5pm & 7-9pm Sun) with expansive views.

SLEEPING & EATING

All four villages have accommodation options, although Nes is the most convenient, being a hop, skip and a jump from the ferry port.

Camping Duinoord (☎ 54 20 70; www.campingduinoord.eu; Jan van Eijckweg 4; camp sites from €20, cabins from €75; ☎) This camping ground is only 2km north of Nes, right near the beach. It's exposed to the wind; shops, services and restaurants are close by.

Stayokay Ameland (☎ 55 53 53; www.stayokay.com/ameland; Oranjeweg 59; dm/r from €26/70) This Stayokay establishment is 200m west of the lighthouse outside Hollum. The atmosphere is decidedly summer-camp, dorm rooms are basic (four or six beds) but in great condition, and sand dunes are literally outside the doorstep. Meals, pack lunches and bicycles are available.

Hotel de Klok (☎ 54 21 81; www.hoteldeklok.nl; Hoofdweg 11, Buren; r from €80; ☎) Right in the village, Hotel de Klok has a popular and sunny cafe. Rooms are comfy, and best of all the building is attractively traditional as opposed to so many that combine 'modern' and 'ugly' in their descriptions.

GETTING THERE & AROUND

Wagenborg (☎ 54 61 11; www.wpd.nl; adult/child return €13/7, bicycle €8) operates ferries between Nes and the large ferry port at Holwerd on the mainland. The latter has a large parking area for people who sensibly forgo taking cars to the island. The ferries run almost every two hours (45 minutes) all year from 7.30am to 7.30pm, hourly on Friday and Saturday from June to August.

To reach the Holwerd ferry terminal from Leeuwarden, take Connexxion bus 66 (40 minutes, hourly). For details on reaching the port by bike, see p231.

Taxis and a small network of public buses that serve the island's four towns meet the ferries. Like other islands, bus day passes cost €5. Bicycles can be rented all over the island.

Schiermonnikoog

☎ 0519 / pop 1000

The smallest and most serene of the Frisian Islands, Schiermonnikoog (7200 hectares) is the place to get away from it all; the feeling of sheer isolation as you move through Schiermonnikoog's 40 sq km, or along the 18km of beaches, can be intoxicating. Its name means 'grey monk island', a reference to the 15th-century clerics who once lived here; however all traces of these folk are gone and the island is mostly wild. The Dutch government made Schiermonnikoog a national park in 1989.

The island's sole town, Schiermonnikoog (sound familiar?), is quiet, even when crowded. Nonresidents are not allowed to bring cars onto the island.

INFORMATION

The **tourist office** (☎ 53 12 33; www.vvvschiermonnikoog.nl; Reeweg 5; internet per hr €3; ☒ 9am-1pm & 2-6pm

Mon-Fri, to 4pm Sat May-Oct) is in the middle of town and has internet access (per hour €4). A good grocery store, an ATM, a pharmacy, a bicycle-repair shop and other services are in a tight little knot in town.

SIGHTS & ACTIVITIES

The sights and activities on the island revolve around one thing – the great outdoors. The best idea is to grab a map, rent a bike, pack a picnic, and head off in any direction that takes your fancy. Even when the ferry is packed on the way over, the endless beach absorbs like a sponge and you'll soon hardly see a soul.

It's easy to lose yourself (but not get lost) on the many trails. Near town there is a moving little cemetery filled with the young men whose damaged planes crashed here during WWII. Elsewhere, when the wind rustles through the trees and not another person is in sight, you could be just about anywhere.

The national park's **visitors centre** (☎ 53 16 41; www.nationaalpark.nl/schiermonnikoog; Torenstreek 20; ☒ 10.30am-5.30pm Mon-Sat Apr-Oct, 1.30-5.30pm Sat Nov-Mar) is in an old power station in town. It reveals the natural features of the island and is more than happy to share details of Unesco's recognition of the Waddenzee, including the park.

The island is the most popular destination for *wadlopers* ('mud-walkers') from the mainland (see the boxed text, p246).

SLEEPING & EATING

Schiermonnikoog has very few hotels and B&Bs, but plenty of bungalows and apartments; cafes line the few streets of downtown Schiermonnikoog. Camping is not allowed in the national park.

Seedune (☎ 53 13 98; www.schiermonnikoog.net/seed une; Seeduneweg 1; camp sites from €17) North of town, this huge camping ground (room for 800 tents) is, as expected, sandy, windswept and isolated, which for many will be absolutely perfect.

Hotel Pension van der Werff (☎ 53 13 06; www .hotelvanderwerff.nl; Langestreek 70; r €70-120) Parts of this grand hotel date back 200 years. Rooms are modern, comfortable and some have balconies. The cafe out front is *the* spot for a long breakfast.

GETTING THERE & AWAY

Wagenborg (☎ 0900 455 44 55; www.wpd.nl; adult/child return €13/7, bicycles €7.45) runs large ferries between Schiermonnikoog and the port of Lauwersoog in Groningen province. At least three ferries daily make the 45-minute voyage; the first sails at 6.30am, the last at 5.30pm. Hotel and public buses (€2.50 return) meet all incoming ferries, which arrive at the island's port, for the 3km run into the town of Schiermonnikoog. There is a huge bicycle-rental facility at the port.

Arriva bus 163 and Connexxion bus 50 make the one-hour run to Lauwersoog five times daily from Groningen (p245) and Leeuwarden respectively.

Groningen & Drenthe

The provinces of Groningen and Drenthe are far from the tourist trails. Many travellers don't venture this far north, and if they happen to, they choose the islands of Friesland for entertainment instead. But in so doing they're missing out on the Netherlands' rural heart, a place where traditions are kept alive, and relics of prehistoric residents dot the landscape.

Groningen may be the smaller of the two provinces, but it has the obvious attractions. Its namesake capital is a buzzing, youthful city (thanks to its substantial student population). Museums, restaurants, bars, theatres, canals, festivals – you name it, the city has it. It's the centre of culture and entertainment in the north and makes a very good base for further exploration – or for just getting lost in a few of its fine cafes.

The rest of Groningen province – a rural landscape dotted with ancient churches – is sleepy by contrast. In Pieterburen, even the hardest of hearts will empty their wallets in support of the Zeehondencreche, a refuge for sick seals. The town is also the base for the strangely intriguing pastime of *wadlopen* (mudflat-walking). Bourtange, on the eastern border to Germany, makes the shortlist for 'Best Fortified Town in Europe'; its hefty defences are just as forbidding now as they were in the 16th century.

Drenthe is an agricultural province, no question. Paddocks are separated by pockets of woodlands, creating a peaceful environment meant for slow exploration of its national parks and quiet contemplation of its dark chapter at Kamp Westerbork. Its biggest draw is its *hunebedden*, prehistoric rock masses purportedly used as burial chambers; but the likes of Orvelte, a village with one foot firmly planted in the 19th century, will also interest many travellers.

HIGHLIGHTS

- Experience northern culture at its best in the museums, cafes, bars and clubs of vibrant **Groningen** (p240)

- Join a *wadlopen* (mudflat-walking) excursion and stomp out a muddy trail on the **Wadden mudflats** (see the boxed text, p246)

- Walk the fortified ramparts of 16th-century **Bourtange** (p247)

- Wonder at the **hunebedden** (see boxed text, p249), mighty stone constructions left behind by ancestors long since gone

- Wander or cycle the beautiful boggy marshes of **Dwingerveld National Park** (p248)

GRONINGEN & DRENTHE

GRONINGEN

Following the style of Utrecht, Groningen is a small province named after its primary city. Beyond the buzzing town itself, farmland dominates the landscape in every direction, but among the *polders* (strips of farmland separated by canals), cows and sheep are a few other attractions worth seeking out. If it just so happens that mud, mud and more mud is your thing, then the northern coast will appeal, though the scenery is best near the German border around the fortified town of Bourtange. The regional tourism website, www.toerisme.groningen.nl, can be quite useful.

GRONINGEN CITY
☎ 050 / pop 184,300

Looking at a map of the Netherlands, Groningen seems a long way from anywhere (we're talking Dutch distances here, not Saharan), but looks can be deceiving.

This vibrant, youthful city is very much part of the comings and goings of the country, and has all you'd expect of a progressive metropolis. Its student population (which has been around since 1614 when the university opened) of 20,000 ensures a healthy, hedonistic nightlife exists alongside the museums and other culture its more mature, established residents (think professors) demand. And like everywhere in this waterlogged country, you'll find gabled houses reflected in still canals.

Orientation

The old centre, which can be crossed on foot in 15 minutes, is nicely compact and entirely ringed by canals. The train station is just across from the Groninger Museum, and around a 10-minute walk from Grote Markt, the main town square. Virulent anticar policies dating from the 1970s mean that the centre is free of traffic. There's a seedy red light district at the east end of Nieuwstad.

Information

See p245 for bookshops.

INTERNET ACCESS

Many cafes have wi-fi and the tourist office has a free computer terminal to use.

Library (☎ 368 36 83; Oude Boteringestraat 18; per hr €2; ☷ 1-6pm Mon, 10am-6pm Tue, Wed & Fri, 10am-8pm Thu, 11am-4pm Sat year-round, 1-5pm Sun Sep-Apr) Main city library with internet access.

LAUNDRY

Handy Wash (☎ 318 75 87; Schuitendiep 58; wash & dry €7; ☷ 7.30am-8pm) Small laundry in a row of cafes and bars; perfect for dropping off the washing and grabbing something starchy next door.

MEDICAL SERVICES

UMCG (☎ 361 61 61; Hanzeplein 1) Teaching hospital with the added bonus of an anatomy museum.

MONEY

GWK (☷ 8am-7pm) Currency exchange; in the train station.

POST

Post office (☎ 313 63 75; Munnekeholm 1)

TOURIST INFORMATION

Tourist office (☎ 0900 202 30 50; www.vvvgroningen .nl; Grote Markt 25; ☷ 9am-6pm Mon-Fri, 10am-5pm Sat year-round, 11am-3pm Sun Jul & Aug) Offers advice and sells tickets, tours and excellent walking-tour maps in English (€1.50). Also has free internet.

Sights & Activities

GRONINGER MUSEUM

Arriving by train it's impossible to miss the **Groninger Museum** (☎ 366 65 55; www.groninger -museum.nl; Museumeiland 1; adult/child €10/3; ☷ 10am-5pm Tue-Thu, Sat & Sun, to 10pm Fri). Occupying three islands in the middle of the canal in front of the station, the museum is, at the very least, a striking structure that will draw an opin-

ion from any observer. Opinions vary wildly, however, from a breathtaking venture in form and design, to 'WTF?'

This colourful, oddly shaped museum was the brainchild of architect Alessandro Mendini, who invited three 'guest architects' to each tackle a section. This explains why, to many, the museum has little consistency and appears thrown together at a whim. Inside, things are quite different; bright, pastel colours add life to the large, square exhibition rooms, and natural light seeps in from all angles.

The large spaces below the waterline were originally intended as a permanent exhibition house for historical pieces, modern applied arts and other regional artworks. The architects proclaimed it would 'remain dry for 200 years'. In 1998 the entire lower level flooded and precious works were rushed above the water to the bronze tower where they remain. The flood-prone space is now filled with temporary exhibitions, which, like the curatorial direction, are a wonderfully eclectic mix.

NOORDELIJK SCHEEPVAARTMUSEUM

Well worth an hour or two, the **Noordelijk Scheepvaartmuseum** (Northern Shipping Museum; ☎ 312 22 02; www.noordelijkscheepvaartmuseum.nl; Brugstraat 24-26; adult/child €4/2.50; ☷ 10am-5pm Tue-Sat, 1-5pm Sun) is well funded and well organised. The museum is laid out over several floors of buildings that once comprised a 16th-century distillery. Just getting through the labyrinth of 18 rooms is an adventure in itself and guarantees an excellent workout.

Highlights of the museum include an intricately carved replica of the church at Paramaribo – the capital of former Dutch colony Surinam – in a bottle (Room 3), showing just how much time sailors had to kill on long voyages, and detailed models demonstrating just how the many local shipyards operated throughout the centuries (Room 8). After Room 8, there are three rooms devoted to the **Niemeyer Tabaksmuseum** (Niemeyer Tobacco Museum), which is dedicated to the smoking habits of the Dutch through the ages. Some of the dummies aren't just toking on tobacco.

OTHER SIGHTS

The **Grote Markt** is a big, cafe-ringed square with some 1950s duds that ruin the scene. Amid the yuck, the **town hall**, which dates from 1810, is

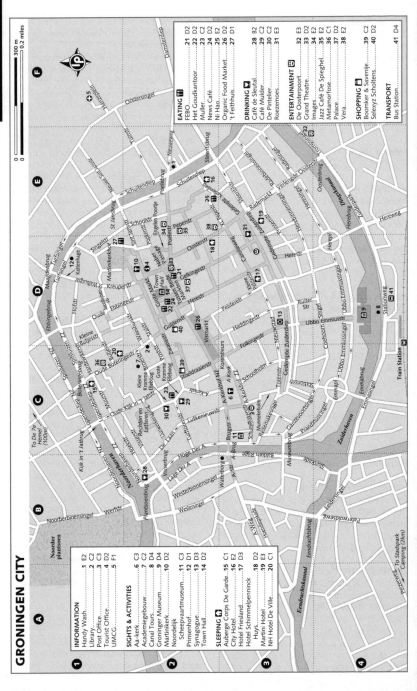

a star, but the 16th-century **Martinikerk** (☎ 311 12 77; Grote Markt; admission €1; ☺ 11am-5pm Mon-Sat mid-April–mid-Nov), at the northern corner of the Grote Markt, steals the show. Its tower, the **Martinitoren** (admission token from VVV €3; ☺ 11am-5pm Mon-Sat mid-April–mid-Nov), is 96m tall and is considered to have one of the most finely balanced profiles in the country. A climb to the top yields stellar views.

Just southwest of the Grote Markt, **Vismarkt** is a more intimate and attractive square, and not far south of Vismarkt is one of the few working **synagogues** (☎ 312 31 51; Folkingestraat 60; adult/child €4/free; ☺ 1.30-5.30pm Tue-Fri & Sun) left in the country. It began life a century ago as a mosque (the light arches and minarets are dead giveaways) but now houses a school and temporary exhibition space; its beautifully restored wooden ceiling is one of the interior's highlights.

Aa-kerk on A-Kerkhof has parts dating to the 15th century and was a seaman's church, as this was the old harbour area. From most parts of town it is hard to miss the **Academiegebouw**, the main building of the university. Its richly decorated exterior was completed in 1909. Around the corner on **Oude Boteringestraat** are a number of appealing buildings dating from the 17th and 18th centuries.

If you're exploring the northeastern corner of the city, take a breather at the serene **gardens** (Turfsingel; admission free; ☺ 10am-dusk) of **Prinsenhof**, a 16th-century mansion. The **Noorder plantsoen** is a fine park.

Tours

Bike Tours (☎ 301 18 81; www.fietsstadgroningen .nl; tours €15; ☺ 3pm Fri, 10.30am Sat) Take a 2½-hour tour of the city. Prices include bikes; book online ahead of time to arrange a meeting place.

Canal tours (☎ 312 83 79; www.rondvaartbedrijfkool .nl; adult/child €9/6) Tours of the city's largest canals take approximately one hour and leave from out the front of the train station anywhere between one and six times daily, depending on the season.

Festivals & Events

Eurosonic Noorderslag (www.eurosonic.nl) A series of concerts by up-and-coming (they hope) bands. Mid-January.
Noorderzon (www.noorderzon.nl) Eleven-day arts festival featuring everything from theatre and music to children's entertainers and electronic installations. Huge fun. Mid-August.
Bommen Berend Celebration of the day the city repelled the invading troops of the Bishop of Munster (28 August). Fireworks, drinking.

Studenten Cabaret Festival (www.gscf.nl) Draws performers from around Europe. Late October.
Sint Maarten Locally grown sugar beets are carved by kids, not unlike what their US counterparts do to pumpkins for Halloween. Then they go door-to-door singing about the saint and getting sweets. Held on 11 November.

Sleeping

The tourist office will book accommodation and carries a list of B&Bs and *pensions* starting at €25 per person.

BUDGET

Stadspark Camping (☎ 525 16 24; www.stadscampings .nl; Campinglaan 6; camp sites from €16; ☺ mid-Mar–mid-Oct) Stadspark is a spacious, green camping ground surrounded by a huge park, yet is within easy shot of the city. Facilities include a shop, restaurant and playground for the kids. From the train station, take bus 4 (direction: Hoogkerk) about 3km west to the Stadspark stop.

Hotel Friesland (☎ 312 13 07; www.hotelfriesland .nl; Kleine Pelsterstraat 4; s/d €40/65) The Friesland is bare bones (or given the neighbourhood, bareback?), but it's central and the prices are unbeatable. Service is friendly and amenable, and the 17 rooms are adequate. Bathrooms are down the hall.

MIDRANGE

Martini Hotel (☎ 312 99 19; www.martinihotel.nl; Gedempte Zuiderdiep 8; r €80-110; ☐ ☎) Parts of the Martini date to 1871, a time when people were smaller and rooms were too. But most of the hotel is housed in modern wings lurking back from the street. The decor is cheery and there's plenty of modern elbow room.

our pick Hotel Schimmelpenninck Huys (☎ 318 95 02; www.schimmelpenninckhuys.nl; Oosterstraat 53; r €80-170) The Schimmelpenninck is Groningen's *grande dame*, and like a dowager of a certain age, it sprawls in several directions; in this case to three sides of its block. Antique-filled common areas lead to a serene courtyard and bistro, while the rest of the building is filled with rooms ranging from simple, stylish standard doubles to suites with antique pieces and chandeliers.

City Hotel (☎ 588 65 65; www.edenhotelgroup. com; Gedempte Kattendiep 25; r €85-160; ☒ ☐ ☎) Windows like slits aren't conducive to light (and some of the 93 rooms are cavelike) but bonuses such as a great location, rooftop deck, free coffee and tea on every floor, and in-house scooter rental compensate.

Other choices:

NH Hotel De Ville (☎ 318 12 22; www.nh-hotels.com; Oude Boteringestraat 43-45; r €85-200; 🖳 🛜) Two 18th-century houses and a recent addition have 65 luxurious rooms. Enjoy the fireplace and courtyard.

Auberge Corps De Garde (☎ 314 54 37; www .corpsdegarde.nl; Oude Boteringestraat 72-74; r €90-120; 🛜) Originally the town guard's quarters, the 17th-century building sports carved animal heads above the door (woodchucks?). The rooms are OK.

Eating

Groningen may be a student city, but it has many a fine restaurant.

News Café (☎ 311 18 44; Waagplein 5; meals from €8; 🛜) Almost stylish to a fault, News Café redeems itself with a cheery staff and a long menu of tasty big and small bites. The soundtrack is smooth and it's the best of the Grote Markt lot.

't Feithhuis (☎ 313 53 35; www.restaurant-feithhuis.nl; Martinikerkhof 10; mains €8-16) In a leafy pedestrian quarter just off the Grote Markt, this stylish grand cafe has a wide terrace outside and a stark, woodsy interior. The walls are lined with posters, and floral arrangements abound. Food ranges from bagels to complex sandwiches and Mediterranean-flavoured mains.

Het Goudkantoor (Gold Office; ☎ 589 18 88; Waagplein 1; mains €12-20) The architecture of this restored historical cafe is amazing. Dating from 1635, the 'Gold Office' features a gold-tinted exterior and graceful interior, complete with striking paintings. The menu is, not surprisingly, traditional (eg steak with mustard).

De 7e Hemel (7th Heaven; ☎ 314 51 41; Zuiderkerkstraat 7; mains €15-18; 🕏 dinner Tue-Sat) Details matter at De 7e Hemel: it even goes so far as to import Scottish mineral water direct from the Glens because of its purity. The menu, which combines vegan, fish and meat dishes, changes seasonally. Cherubs, chandeliers and calming yellow shades all help to create a cosy, romantic air. It's just north of the centre.

Ni Hao (☎ 318 14 00; Gedempte Kattendiep 122; buffet from €18; 🕏 5-10pm) About eight cuts above your average Chinese buffet, the locally renowned Ni Hao serves up a vast range of dishes plus stir-fries and grills to your order. It's like an Asian culinary playground.

ourpick Muller (☎ 318 32 08; www.restaurantmuller .nl; Grote Kromme Elleboog 13; menus from €60; 🕏 dinner Tue-Sat) You can enjoy the show here for free by watching the artistry in the kitchen from the windows on the street. But really why settle for half? Menus change regularly and include

delights such as lobster, scallops, lamb and much more. One of the region's best.

The **organic food market** (Vismarkt; 🕏 Tue) is a regional favourite. For those needing a late-night taste of Amsterdam, the bright lights and silvery slots of a **FEBO** (☎ 313 31 02; Grote Markt 34; sustenance from €1; 🕏 10am-4.30am) beckon near the bars of Poelestraat.

Drinking

Groningen's student bar-hopping nightlife is centred on Poelestraat and its adjoining streets.

Café Mulder (☎ 314 14 69; Grote Kromme Elleboog 22) Artists, writers and musicians highlight a slightly older crowd that debates the events of the day at this classy pub. The interior is both rich and intimate.

De Pintelier (☎ 318 51 00; Kleine Kromme Elleboog 9) Step back to the 1920s at this cosy bar where the selection of beer and *jenever* (Dutch gin) reads like an encyclopaedia. Its long wooden bar and thicket of candle-lit tables are timeless. Take in the breeze in the shot-glass-sized courtyard.

Café de Sleutal (☎ 318 14 54; Noorderhaven 72) In a 17th-century brewery (note the keg hanging outside) in an old brewing district, this vintage cafe has a local following for its €10 meals and cosy canalside vibe.

Roezemoes (☎ 314 03 82; Gedempte Zuiderdiep 15) You can tell this gem of a brown cafe has been around a while; the bullet holes from the 1672 invasion attempt are a dead giveaway. Come evening, expect to find late-night drinking and the occasional blues band.

Entertainment

To find out what's going on around town, check out some of the posters that appear everywhere, or pick up a copy of either the simple and informative *Uit-Loper* (weekly) or meatier *Uit Magazine* (monthly); both are free and in Dutch.

NIGHTCLUBS

Clubs open and close regularly in Groningen, but those listed here are mainstayers.

Vera (☎ 313 46 81; www.vera-groningen.nl; Oosterstraat 44; 🕏 Thu-Sat) The club to see the next big rock act at; U2 played to 30-odd people in the early 1980s here, and Nirvana later gave a performance to a crowd of about 60 people before going supernova. Maybe less is more?

Palace (☎ 313 91 00; www.thepalace.nl; Gelkingestraat 1; 🕏 Thu-Sat) Standard club attracting a predominantly young crowd with an array of music styles, and a huge dance floor.

COFFEESHOPS
Metamorfose (☎ 314 44 60; Oude Boteringestraat 53) Lots of chairs in a large space that's more suburban rumpus room than cool hang-out for smokin' and chillin'. Need we say it: mellow.

LIVE MUSIC
De Oosterpoort (☎ 368 03 68; www.de-oosterpoort .nl; Trompsingel) De Oosterpoort is *the* place in Groningen to catch many of the large musical acts passing through town. Jazz and classical concerts are the mainstay of its monthly program.

Jazz Café De Spieghel (☎ 312 63 00; www.jazz cafedespieghel.nl; Peperstraat 11; ☻ music from 10.30pm) A perennial favourite – this lively brown cafe features nightly live jazz music, a smooth sultry atmosphere, and a great bar.

THEATRE & CINEMA
Grand Theatre (☎ 314 46 44; www.grand-theatre.nl; Grote Markt 35) This is the city's premiere theatre and offers a thought-provoking array of musical and theatrical performances.

Images (☎ 312 04 33; www.liga68.nl; Poelestraat 30; tickets €8) Offbeat films, festival titles and classics shown on three screens plus a fine cafe give Images a good highlights reel.

Shopping
Large markets are held on Grote Markt and Vismarkt Tuesday, Friday and Saturday. Galleries abound on the west side, especially on Visserstraat, Oude Kijk in 't Jatstraat and Lopendediep NZ.

Being an academic town, Groningen has many fine bookshops. **Selexyz Scholtens** (☎ 317 25 00; Guldenstraat 20) has a large selection of English novels and travel titles. **Boomker & Savenije** (☎ 312 67 49; Zwanestraat 41-43) is an academic store with titles that you don't want to a) drop on your toe, and b) read while operating heavy equipment.

Getting There & Away
The regional bus station is to the right as you exit the train station; the **Arriva bus office** (☻ 7am-11pm) is found opposite the train information office.

BICYCLE
Riding in Groningen province means a lot of back roads meandering; however there are some key national routes. LF9 runs south to Utrecht (about 200km) and beyond. It has been designed to follow what would be the Dutch coastline if there were no dykes. LF14 heads 48km northwest to Lauwersoog, where you can get the ferry to Schiermonnikoog.

TRAIN
The grand 1896 train station, restored to its original glory, is worth seeing even if you're not catching a train. Lockers can be found on platform 2b and there is a good range of services. It doesn't feel like the end of the main line from the south but it is (trains often split at Meppel, so don't end up in the half going to Leeuwarden); it's also the hub for local services in the province.

Sample train fares and schedules:

Destination	Fare (€)	Duration (min)	Frequency (per hr)
Leeuwarden	8.80	36	3
Utrecht	24.80	120	1
Zwolle	15.90	69	3

Getting Around
Groningen is easily tackled on foot or by bicycle, but if you plan to use the buses, one-day passes (€1) are available from drivers after 9am. Bus 6 connects Grote Markt to the train station.

AROUND GRONINGEN CITY
Wandering the verdant countryside around Groningen by bike is rewarding and there are numerous little delights to give you good reason.

Museum De Buitenplaats
In the little town of Eelde, 5km south of Groningen, is this charming **museum** (☎ 050-309 58 18; www.museumdebuitenplaats.nl; Hoofdweg 76; adult/child €7/free; ☻ 11am-5pm Tue-Sun) devoted to figurative art from around Europe. The main organic structure, which blends into its natural surroundings, features paintings from some of the Netherlands' more progressive 20th-century artists, such as Wout Muller, Henk Helmantel, Herman Gordijn and Matthijs Röling. Its manicured gardens are peppered with sculptures and there's also a sun-bathed cafe. Poetry readings, storytelling and musical concerts are featured over the summer months on the museum's open-air stage.

POUNDING MUD

Some pay dearly for mud treatments and organised walks; Groningen and Friesland have an activity that combines both. When the tide retreats across the Unesco-recognised mudflats off the north coast of the Waddenzee, locals and visitors alike attack it with abandon, marching, and inevitably sinking, into the sloppy mess. Known as *wadlopen* (mudflat-walking) it's an exercise in minimalism, forcing you to concentrate on the little things while you march towards the featureless horizon.

The mud stretches all the way to the Frisian Islands offshore, and treks across to the islands are quite popular. Because of the treacherous tides, and the fact that some walkers can become muddled and lose their way, *wadlopen* can only be undertaken on a guided tour. Those who enjoy *wadlopen* say that it is strenuous but enlivening; the unchanging vista of mud and sky has an almost meditative quality, the call of birds and the chance to focus on little details, such as small crabs and cockles underfoot, puts one in touch with nature's finer points.

The centre for *wadlopen* is the tiny village of Pieterburen, 22km north of Groningen, where several groups of trained guides are based; **Stichting Wadloopcentrum** (☎ 0595-52 83 00; www.wadlopen.org; Hoofdstraat 105) and **Dijkstra's Wadlooptochten** (☎ 0595-52 83 45; www.wadloop-dijkstra.nl; Hoofdstraat 118) are two of the better known. Guided walks, which take place between May and October, range from a short 5km jaunt across the mudflats (€11, 2½ hours) to a gruelling yet exhilarating 20km pound to Schiermonnikoog (€33, five hours); the latter (p237), with its national park, is the most popular destination. The ferry ride back from the islands is not included in the price; it's essential to book around a month in advance. You'll be told what clothes to bring depending on the time of year.

See below for transport details to Pieterburen.

From Groningen, take bus 52 (28 minutes, every half-hour). And there's a good bike route on the west side of Paterswolder Meer.

Zeehondencreche Pieterburen

Back in 1972 Lenie 't Hart, a resident of the small Groningen coastal town of Pieterburen, began caring for seals in her backyard. Pollution and tourism were taking their toll on the local seal colonies, and it was her way of doing something about it. Her efforts over the years have resulted in the **Zeehondencreche** (Seal Creche; ☎ 0595-52 65 26; www.zeehondencreche.nl; Hoofdstraat 94a; admission €4.50; ⏰ 9am-6pm), a centre devoted to the rescue and rehabilitation of sick seals.

The centre normally houses 20 to 30 seals, which can be seen lounging and swimming in various pools. The most popular times to visit are the 11am and 4pm feeding times. More than 200 have been released back into the wild.

To get to Pieterburen, on weekdays take the train from Groningen to Winsum (€3.40, 14 minutes, hourly), then Arriva bus 68 to Pieterburen (20 minutes, every two hours). On weekends bus 68 runs hourly.

Menkemaborg

Some 25km northeast of Groningen in the small farming town of Uithuizen is one of the Netherlands' most authentic manor houses,

Menkemaborg (☎ 0595-43 19 70; www.menkemaborg .nl; Menkemaweg 2; adult/child €6/free; ⏰ 10am-5pm Tue-Sun Mar-Dec, 10am-5pm Mon Jun-Sep). Originally a fortified castle dating back to the 14th century, Menkemaborg received its present gentrified appearance – a moated estate of three houses surrounded by immaculate gardens – early in the 18th century, and it has barely been altered since. Inside, the rooms retain all the pomp and ceremony of 18th-century aristocratic life, complete with carved-oak mantelpieces, stately beds and fine china.

Hourly trains run between Uithuizen and Groningen (€5.70, 34 minutes). The train station is a 1km walk west of Menkemaborg. National bike route LF10 passes right through.

Rural Churches

Stoic churches centuries old dot the flat countryside northeast from Groningen to the coast. They are lasting testament to the pious and hardscrabble people who eked out lives in the muddy, sandy soil.

Reaching these can be difficult by bus and train, but they make for excellent touring by bike as you can use the distant steeples like points on a compass for navigating the tiny back roads and dykes (also get a map from the Groningen tourist office). Doors may be open – or not.

A few favourites:

Zeerijp A large church with a high bell tower and an unusual fake brick motif inside. A 3km walk northeast from the Loppersum train station.

Kreward Surrounded by a tiny moat with ducks, this picture-perfect 16th-century church sits primly on a *terp* (mud mound). It's near the coast and the N33.

Bierum This 13th-century church's leaning tower was saved by adding a huge flying buttress in the 1800s. The town of Bierum is 24km northeast of Groningen and near the N33 and coast. It's on the LF10 national bike route.

BOURTANGE
☎ 0599 / pop 1200

Bourtange, a tiny town near the German border, is home to one of the best-preserved fortifications in the country. While rather small and best seen from the air, it is nonetheless a sight to behold, with its flooded moats, stolid defences and quaint houses protected from all sides. The region around Bourtange is also worth exploring; off the beaten path, it consists of pretty countryside and tree-shaded canals, ideal for tackling by bike.

Sights

Built in the late 1500s, Bourtange represents the pinnacle of the arms and fortification of the time. Behind its walls and moats, it could withstand months of siege by an invading army.

In 1964 the regional government restored the battlements and the town itself to its 1742 appearance, when the fortifications around the citadel had reached their maximum size. It took three decades, during which time roads were moved and buildings demolished or reconstructed. Archaeologists generally had a party.

The results are impressive and Bourtange is stunningly pretty. The star-shaped rings of walls and canals have been completely rebuilt and the village has been returned to a glossier version of its 18th-century self. It's a cliché, but a visit to Bourtange is truly a step into the past, to a time when rogue armies wandered the lands, and villagers hid behind defences designed to keep them at bay.

From the parking area and tourist office, you pass through two gates and across three drawbridges over the moats before you reach the old town proper. From the town's central square, the Marktplein, cobblestone streets lead off in all directions; the pentagram-shaped inner fortification can be crossed in a matter of minutes by foot. The town's **tourist office** (☎ 35 46 00; www.bourtange.nl; William Lodewijkstraat 33;

☼ 10am-5pm Mar-Oct, noon-5pm Sat & Sun Nov-Feb) sells a handy English-language booklet. The **museum** (adult/child €5.50/3.50; ☼ 10am-5pm Mar-Oct, noon-5pm Sat & Sun Nov-Feb) has detailed displays showing the reconstruction and restoration. Aerial photographs show the remarkable changes between 1965 and 2004.

Inside the walls at the core of the fortification (which you can wander around freely at any time), brick houses make good use of what little space the five bastions afford. **Marktplein** is a good spot to start exploring, with its cafes, small craft shops and tree-shaded benches.

Of the old buildings, six have been turned into exhibits that are part of the museum admission. Two – the **Captain's Lodge** and **De Dagen van Roam** – cover the life and times of the militia stationed at Bourtange in the 17th and 18th centuries, while the **Museum de Baracquen** displays artefacts and curios uncovered during the fort's reconstruction. **De Poort** has an excellent model of Bourtange, and the town's **synagogue**, built in 1842, explains the life and times of its Jewish population, and includes a plaque listing the 42 locals taken away to their deaths by the Nazis.

However, the best thing to do is wander up and down its defensive walls. More often than not you'll have whole stretches to yourself.

Sleeping & Eating

It's possible to stay within the walls, in the original soldiers' (€72) or captains' (€82) quarters. Bookings are taken at the tourist office. Rooms are tidy, with polished wooden floors, and breakfast is included.

The two atmospheric cafes on Marktplein are the only places to eat within the old town.

Getting There & Away

Bourtange is not easy to get to without your own wheels. From Groningen, take the hourly train east to Winschoten (€5.70, 33 minutes), then Arriva bus 14 south to Vlagtwedde (25 minutes, at least one every hour) and transfer to Arriva bus 72 for Bourtange (12 minutes, 10 daily). With waiting time and transfers, count on the trip taking about two hours – bus 72 only runs before 9am and after 1pm.

If touring by bike, you can combine Bourtange with visits to the rural churches east of Groningen and the *hunebedden* (see the boxed text, p249) in Drenthe, some 30km to the west for a multiday ride. The area is laced with bike paths across farmlands but a cycling map is essential.

DRENTHE

If ever there was a forgotten corner of the Netherlands, this is it. With no sea access or major city to call its own (charm-starved Emmen is its largest) and few five-star attractions, Drenthe is as Vincent van Gogh described in 1833: 'Here is peace.' Of course, he later went mad.

But peace (and war) are exactly why this small backwater deserves some of your time, simply to experience something different in a land where one pretty town follows another and there's a growing collection of national parks. Plus you get to explore the mysterious *hunebedden* (see the boxed text, opposite) and follow the legacy of Anne Frank.

ASSEN

☎ 0592 / pop 66,400

With a close proximity to Groningen, Drenthe's capital, Assen, brings up the rear in terms of appeal. The **tourist office** (☎ 24 37 88; www.vvvdrenthe .nl; Marktstraat 8; ☺ 1-6pm Mon, 9am-6pm Tue-Fri, 9am-5pm Sat) is a good source of bike maps for the region and info on the national parks.

The **Drents Museum** (☎ 37 77 73; www.drents museum.nl; Brink 1; adult/child €6/3; ☺ 11am-5pm Tue-Sun), near the centre, has *hunebedden* artefacts and various artworks and furnishings from Drenthe's history.

The tourist office and museum are 500m from the station by way of Stationsstraat. Frequent trains connect Assen with both Groningen (€5.10, 18 minutes) and Zwolle (€12.30, 50 minutes).

Buses depart from the area to the left as you exit the train station. The **bicycle shop** (☎ 31 04 24) is right next door. National bike route LF14 runs south 34km from Groningen and on to Emmen (about 40km southeast).

KAMP WESTERBORK

More than 107,000 Jews were deported from the Netherlands by the Nazis in WWII. Almost all died in the concentration and death camps of Central and Eastern Europe and almost all began their fateful journey here, a rural forest about 10km south of Assen, near the tiny village of Hooghalen.

Kamp Westerbork (☎ 0593-59 26 00; www.kampwester bork.nl; Oosthalen 8, Hooghalen; adult/child €5/2.50; ☺ 10am-5pm Mon-Fri year-round, 1-5pm Sat & Sun Sep-Jun, 11am-5pm Sat & Sun Jul & Aug), ironically, was built by the Dutch government in 1939 to house German Jews fleeing the Nazis. When the Germans invaded in May 1940, they found Westerbork ideal for their own ends. Beginning in 1942 it became a transit point for those being sent to the death camps, including Anne Frank.

A visit to the camp starts with the excellent museum at the car park. Displays trace the holocaust in the Netherlands and there is a moving timeline covering Anne Frank, her diary and her ultimate death at Bergen-Belsen in Germany in 1945. The bookshop has many excellent brochures and books.

The actual camp is a 2km walk through a forest from the museum (or a €2 bus ride that gets overcrowded in summer). There is little to see here today from the 1940s as the Dutch government rather incredibly used it as a refuge camp after the war, first for surviving Jews and later for immigrants such as the South Mollucans. However, displays show the location of Nazi-era features such as the punishment building and the workshops where internees worked as virtual slaves.

Monuments include a series of stones showing where Dutch Jews and Roma died (Auschwitz-Birkenau 60,330…).

Despite the name, the camp is 7km north of Westerbork town. By train, use the station at Beilen (one stop south of Assen, €3.40, 10 minutes, every half-hour). From here a *treintaxi* (special taxi for train passengers; see p305) to the site, which you summon at the station, costs €4.60 and takes 10 minutes. By bike, use any of the many rural bike paths; the museum is 7km south of Assen.

NATIONAL PARKS

Various national parks have been created amid the farmlands and natural areas of Drenthe. **Drentsche Aa National Landscape** (☎ 0592-36 58 64; www.drentscheaa.nl) takes in a varied 10,000 hectare landscape of ancient farms, fields of wildflowers, *hunebedden* and evocative country roads. It's mostly undeveloped but the park map, available from tourist offices, is a good guide. Cycling through this bell-shaped area just northwest of Assen is sublime. National bike route LF14 goes right down the middle.

Dwingerveld National Park (☎ 0592-36 57 31; www .nationaalpark-dwingelderveld.nl) preserves 3700 hectares of the largest wet heathland in Europe. More than 60km of hiking paths and 40km of cycling paths wander amid the bogs, meadows and forest. It's a starkly beautiful place

HUNEBEDDEN

People have been enjoying the quiet in Drenthe since as early as 3000 BC, when prehistoric tribes lived here amid the bogs and peat. These early residents began cultivating the land, a pastime still enjoyed by many in the province, and created what is arguably the most interesting aspect of Drenthe today, the *hunebedden*.

Hunebedden, which predate Stonehenge, are prehistoric burial chambers constructed with huge grey stones, some of which weigh up to 25,000kg. It is thought the stones arrived in the Netherlands via glaciers from Sweden some 200,000 years ago, but no one can be certain of the fact. Little is also known about the builders of the *hunebedden*, except that they took burying their dead very seriously, burying people, along with their personal items and tools, under the monolithic stones. Theories as to how the chambers were constructed have been bantered about by the scientific community, but once again, a definitive answer is yet to be found. A total of 54 of these impressive groupings of sombre grey stones can be seen in Drenthe and Groningen.

The impressive **Hunebedden Centrum** (☎ 0599-23 63 74; www.hunebedcentrum.nl; Bronnegerstraat 12; adult/child €5.75/3; ☯ 10am-5pm Mon-Fri, 11am-5pm Sat & Sun) in Borger, a little town 17km northwest of Emmen, is the centre for the *hunebedden*, and the logical place to start a tour. The website www.hunebedden.nl is also a good source of info.

The centre has many displays relating to the stones as well as excavated artefacts, and the largest *hunebed* is located just outside its doors. Maps of all the sites are also available; most are clumped around the villages of Klijndijk, Odoorn, Annen and Midlaren, which are strung out along the N34, a picturesque road linking Emmen and Groningen.

It's best to explore the *hunebedden* with your own transport; pick up a map from the Assen tourist office or Hunebedden Centrum and look out for the large brown signs showing a pile of rocks while driving or cycling. Borger is 25km southeast of Assen on national bike route LF14.

and very popular on summer weekends. Of the several in the area, the best **visitor centre** (☎ 0521-59 66 00; ☯ 10am-5pm daily, until 4.30pm Nov-Mar) is in tiny Lhee, 6km west of the A28 on the N855. Get maps here. The park is a 15km ride south of Kamp Westerbork, or 3km from the train station at Beilen.

ORVELTE
☎ 0593

A foundation governs the tiny village of Orvelte, 17km south of Assen. Its goal – to preserve the feel of a 19th-century Drenthe community – is alive and well here, and visitors are welcome to join them in the past for a day, between Easter and the end of October.

No cars are permitted (aside from those of the residents) and owners cannot alter the old buildings in uncharacteristic ways. Residents mainly engage in traditional activities; there's the butcher, the baker…you get the idea. During summer, there are lovely vegetable and flower gardens growing near every house.

The **tourist office** (☎ 32 23 35; www.orvelte.eu; ☯ 10.30am-5pm Tue-Sun Easter-Jun, Sep & Oct, 10.30am-5pm daily Jul & Aug, closed Nov-Easter) has brochures and maps of the village, and can inform you about what's on when. It can also arrange B&B accommodation in one of the traditional houses (from €25 per person).

Beilen is a stop on the Zwolle–Assen–Groningen train line (at least two trains per hour); change to Arriva bus 22 (16 minutes, hourly Monday to Friday, less frequent weekends) for Orvelte. Bike routes converge on Westerbork, just 3km west.

EMMEN
☎ 0591 / pop 109,400

A modern city of industry, Emmen is a common point of entry driving from Germany on the A37. The **tourist office** (☎ 64 17 92; www.drenthe .nl; Hoofdstraat 22; ☯ 1-5.30pm Mon, 9.30am-5.30pm Tue-Fri, 10am-4pm Sat) right in the centre has a good range of bike maps for exploring the *hunebedden*.

Overijssel & Gelderland

Although the 'forgotten' provinces of Overijssel and Gelderland can't boast blockbuster cities like Amsterdam, Rotterdam or Maastricht, they make up for it with reserves of natural beauty – forest, rivers, lakes, national parks – and abundant history. That's not to say that there aren't major attractions: Hoge Veluwe National Park, containing the Kröller-Müller Museum (with probably the world's finest Van Gogh collection), should be near the top of any Dutch itinerary.

Generally, though, the region's pleasures are small and concentrated, adding up to a compelling whole. If you're looking to escape the Randstad's hectic urban sprawl, then take some time out here. Just riding the myriad bike routes among the lush, watery scenery will cleanse the soul. Weerribben National Park sprawls across wetlands rife with otters, beavers, birds and eels. Rent a canoe and make some new friends.

Zwolle, Deventer and Kampen, in Overijssel, are centuries-old towns, filled with atmospheric historical buildings that recall a time in history when they were key members of the Hanseatic League. Each has cafes that will entice you to linger.

Nijmegen, in Gelderland, is underrated. But with its waterfront vibe, mass of students and an annual march that now takes the form of a weeklong party, it's full of bounce. On the other side of history, it was here and near Arnhem that attempts to liberate the occupied Netherlands went horribly awry for the Allies in 1944; there are many WWII memorials and locations to contemplate.

HIGHLIGHTS

- Lose yourself in bucolic **Hoge Veluwe National Park** (p264)

- Find your favourite masterpiece at the **Kröller-Müller Museum** (p265)

- Spook yourself in the otherworldly ambience of the **Weerribben** (opposite), Overijssel's strange wetlands

- Discover hidden treasures along the backstreets of Hanseatic **Deventer** (p253)

- Consider the costs of war at Gelderland's **war cemeteries and memorials** (p264) at Oosterbeek and Groesbeek

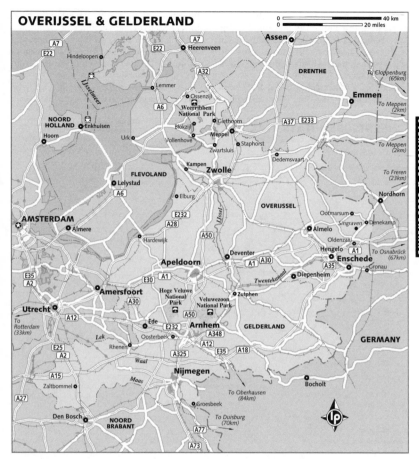

OVERIJSSEL & GELDERLAND

OVERIJSSEL

Overijssel means 'beyond the IJssel', after the river forming much of the province's western border. The province is hilly in the east near Germany and flat and soggy in the west along the former coastline, now landlocked by Flevoland's Noordoostpolder.

You might like to anchor yourself in Deventer to explore Overijssel, though Zwolle also has its charms. Giethoorn in the north is pretty too, but beware of swollen summer crowds.

WEERRIBBEN NATIONAL PARK

A serene and occasionally eerie landscape of watery striations, **Weerribben National Park** is

3500 hectares of marshy land. This entire area was worked by peat and reed harvesters, back-breaking, muddy jobs. The long, water-filled stripes across the landscape are the result of peat removal: as one line of peat was dug, it was laid on the adjoining land to dry.

Reed harvesting was no easier, and still goes on; you can see huge piles at many points in the park. Generations of harvesters lived out here with little contact with the outside world. Even now, their descendants live on some of the farms in the surrounding countryside in Ossenzijl and Blokzijl. Weerribben is also an amazing natural landscape and an important stop for migratory birds in Europe.

As you ride along one of the isolated bike paths or row the channels, you might get the sense you're on another planet. A chief factor in creating this illusion is the sound of the Weerribben: as you move through the sea of reeds, you'll hear the calls, clucks, coos and splashes of numerous birds, fish, frogs, otters, beavers and eels.

The park's **visitors centre** (☎ 0561-47 72 72; www .staatsbosbeheer.nl; ☒ 10am-5pm) is in Ossenzijl, a tiny village on the northern edge of the park. Pick up scads of maps of different cycling and walking routes. There's a small cafe here and vendors hire out bikes (€7 per day), canoes (from €15 per two hours) and kayaks (from €12 for two hours).

To reach the visitors centre in Ossenzijl, take Connexxion bus 276 from Steenwijk

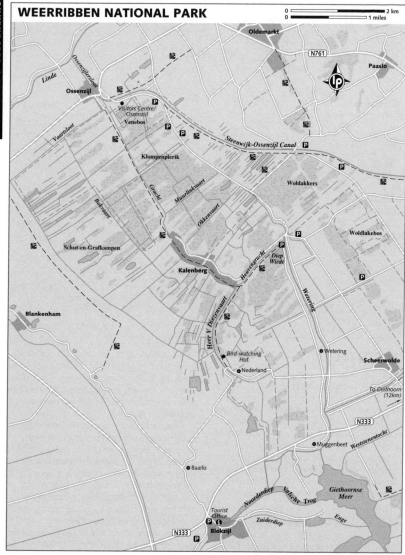

WEERRIBBEN NATIONAL PARK

(hourly, 25 minutes), a stop on the train line from Leeuwarden to Zwolle. National bike routes LF3 and LF22 bisect the park and go right past the visitors centre. The former continues north towards Friesland and Leeuwarden. LCF3 follows a scenic and circuitous path south 60km to Zwolle.

DEVENTER

☎ 0570 / pop 97,900

Deventer surprises. On a beautiful August night you can wander alone among the Hanseatic ghosts along the twisting streets searching out the odd architectural detail in the ancient facades. What looks like a crack is really a tiny passage to IJssel.

Deventer was already a bustling mercantile port as far back as AD 800, and it maintained its prosperous trading ties for centuries, evidence of which you'll see everywhere in its sumptuously detailed old buildings. Think of it as the Delft of the east.

Information

Library (☎ 64 99 62; Brink 70; internet access per hr €3; ☽ 11am-9pm Tue & Thu, 11am-5.30pm Wed & Fri, 11am-4pm Sat)

Tourist office (☎ 69 14 10; www.vvvdeventer.nl; Brink 56; ☽ 10am-5pm Tue-Sat, 1-5pm Sun & Mon) Shares space with the museum; has good walking tour maps.

Sights

The **Brink** is the main square and Deventer's commercial heart. The town's famous **Waag**, the 1528 weigh-house in the middle of the square, was recently restored. Look for the cauldron on the north side – a gruesome and well-supported legend tells of a 16th-century clerk boiled alive in it, after he was discovered substituting cheap metals for precious ones in the local money supply.

There's a small **museum** (☎ 69 37 80; adult/child €3/1; ☽ 10am-5pm Tue-Sat, 1-5pm Sun) inside the Waag, with historical displays and the oldest bicycle in Holland. Check out the fish.

The **Grote of Lebuïnuskerk** (admission €2.50; ☽ 1am-5pm Mon-Sat) is the city's main church. It stands on a site where other churches were razed by flames and other catastrophes time and again, before the present Gothic structure was built between 1450 and 1530.

Deventer is so well preserved that most streets will have something to see. On **Assenstraat** and **Polstraat** there are wall carvings and window decorations created over

several centuries. Assenstraat 67-79 is more contemporary, while **Walstraat 20** shows a woman climbing down the wall while hanging by a sheet. In fact, so rich is the detail that the WWII film *A Bridge Too Far,* which was essentially about Arnhem's role in the war, was filmed here (Arnhem, of course, had been levelled by the war).

Bergstraat is another place to find the town's Hanseatic survivors (like Gothic-style No 29). At the top, **Bergkerk** (☎ 61 85 18; admission free; ☽ 11am-5pm Tue-Sun) has landmark towers that date to the 13th century. The medieval equivalent of *Extreme Makeover* gave it a Gothic revamp in the 1400s.

Activities

The banks of the IJssel River are a scenic place for **cycling**. Green panoramas filigreed with water stretch in all directions. Riding national route LF3 36km north to Zwolle is a fine option, while a good 32km round-trip follows the river banks north to Olst, where you can take a ferry across and return along the other side to Deventer. You can do the same thing going south to Zutphen, a 47km loop.

Sleeping

OUR PICK Hotel de Leeuw (☎ 61 02 90; www.hoteldeleeuw .nl; Nieuwstraat 25; r €80-140; ☐) One of the sweetest places to stay in the Netherlands, and not just because it has a candy museum. Every comfort you can think of, right down to the weather forecasts at breakfast, is provided by the charming owner. The lovely building dates back to 1645; the simple rooms (with high-speed internet) are comfy and many have kitchenettes.

Hotel Gilde (☎ 64 18 46; www.gildehotel.nl; Nieuwstraat 41; s/d from €90/120; ☎) This charming 36-room hotel, once a 17th-century convent, celebrates its former architectural glory. With all that weight of history on the trimmings and frills, you know that this is the swishest place in town (despite the austerity of its former tenants).

Other options:

Camping De Worp (☎ 61 36 01; www.stadscamping .eu; Worp 12; camp sites from €14; ☽ May-Sep) Right across the IJssel from the centre of town, about two minutes north of the passenger ferry.

Hotel Royal (☎ 61 18 80; www.royal-deventer.nl; Brink 94; r €60-100) Twenty-three basic but spotless rooms.

Eating & Drinking

Eetcafé De Sjampetter (☎ 61 71 55; Brink 81; meals from €8) The brownest of the gaggle of cafes on the

OVERIJSSEL & GELDERLAND

main square. Long wooden tables inside are good for spreading out a map with your drink while the outside tables are oceanic in scope.

Bouwkunde (☎ 61 40 75; Klooster 4; meals from €25; ✆ dinner Tue-Sun) The best produce from the region is used at this superb brasserie located under a small theatre. The menu combine French accents with Dutch staples: expect fine preparations of simple seafoods and meats. Service is polished – like the silver.

't Arsenaal (☎ 61 64 95; www.restaurantarsenaal .nl; Nieuwe Markt 33-34; menus from €30; ✆ dinner Mon-Sat) This stylish restaurant, next to the Lebuïnuskerk, comes into its own in summer, when the courtyard and alleyway, in the shadow of the old church, make for a grand setting. The seasonal menu has French inspirations for dishes such as lobster ravioli.

ourpick Heksenketel (☎ 61 34 12; Brink 63) At least a dozen brews are on tap at this local favourite where you'll find a jolly mix of regulars, students – and even guidebook writers.

Shopping
The local speciality is Deventer *koek,* a mildly spiced gingerbread made with honey. It's

widely available and so dense that it can sit undisturbed at the bottom of your bag for months. The Saturday market on the Brink attracts food, flower and craft vendors from around the region.

Getting There & Around
The bus area is located to the right as you leave the train station.

BICYCLE
The bicycle shop is in the train station. National bike route LF3 runs 36km north through lush farmlands to Zwolle. Going southwest, the LF3 runs 55km to Arnhem and the gateway to Hoge Veluwe National Park, mostly following wide river banks and dykes.

PARKING
There is parking around the town's periphery, but the best place to park is the free car park on the west bank of the IJssel. To get there, take the free passenger ferry. The voyage takes less than five minutes and operates most of the day and night. The pier on the town side is near Vispoort.

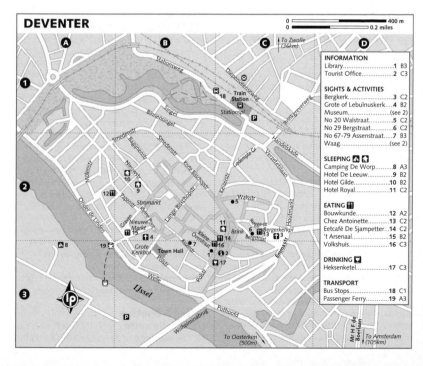

THE HANSEATIC LEAGUE

Although primarily composed of northern German cities such as Lübeck and Hamburg, the Hanseatic League also included several Dutch towns. The powerful trading community was organised in the mid-13th century and its member towns quickly grew rich by the importing and exporting of goods that included grain, ore, honey, textiles, timber and flax. The league was not a government as such, but it did defend its ships from attack and it entered into monopolistic trading agreements with other groups, such as the Swedes. That it achieved its powerful trading position through bribery, boycotts and other methods shouldn't sound too unusual to business students today. The Hanseatic League members did work hard to prevent war among their partners for the simple reason that conflict was bad for business.

Seven Dutch cities along the IJssel River were prosperous members of the league: Hasselt, Zwolle, Kampen, Hattem, Deventer, Zutphen and Doesburg. It's ironic that the Hanseatic League's demise is mostly attributable to the Dutch. The traders of Amsterdam saw a good thing and during the 15th century essentially beat the league at its own game, outmuscling them in market after market.

TRAIN

Deventer sits at the junction of two train lines; service is good in all directions. There are lockers up along track 3.

Destination	Fare (€)	Duration (min)	Frequency (per hr)
Amsterdam	15.50	85	1
Arnhem	7.60	36	2
Nijmegen	10.30	61	2
Zwolle	5.60	24	2

ZWOLLE

☎ 038 / 117,800

Zwolle, the capital of Overijssel, is a compact town that can easily occupy a day of exploration – longer in summer, when the weekend market and a seemingly endless schedule of small festivals keep things bubbling. In the 14th and 15th centuries Zwolle garnered wealth as the main trading port for the Hanseatic League and became a cultural centre of some repute. While those days are long gone, you can still step back in time, courtesy of the moat and ancient fortifications that surround the town.

The **tourist office** (☎ 0900 112 23 75; www.vvvzwolle .nl; Grote Markt 20; ☑ 10am-5pm Mon-Fri, 10am-4pm Sat) is attached to the Grote Kerk.

Sights & Activities

People from Zwolle say they know they're home when they see the Onze Lieve Vrouwetoren (also known as the Peperbus, or Peppermill), the huge former church that dominates the skyline as you approach town. You can climb the **tower** (www.peperbus-zwolle.nl; adult/child €2/1; ☑ 11am-4.30pm Jun-Aug, 1.30-3.30pm Sep-May).

The **Stedelijk Museum Zwolle** (☎ 421 46 50; www .stedelijkmuseumzwolle.nl; Melkmarkt 41; adult/child €5/2.50; ☑ 10am-5pm Tue-Sat, 1-5pm Sun) has a fine collection of items, including a wealth of Hanseatic material. It also hosts numerous special exhibitions a year, ranging from high-art painting retrospectives to contemporary photography and multimedia. The wing in an elegant 16th-century mansion has good displays on local history.

Standing on the Oude Vismarkt, you have a good view of the other two main sights. The **Grote Kerk** is grand but was much grander before the usual series of disasters (three times struck by lightning – do you think it's cursed?) knocked down the tower etc. Much of what's left is from the 15th century. Next door, the **Stadhuis** has a typically Dutch old part (15th century) and a typically oddball (1976) new part.

The 15th-century **Sassenpoort**, situated at the corner of Sassenstraat and Wilhelminasingel, is one of the remaining town gates.

Ecodrome (☎ 421 50 50; www.ecodrome.nl; Willemsvaart 19; adult/child €14/12.50; ☑ 10am-5pm daily Apr-Oct, 10am-5pm Wed, Sat & Sun Nov-Mar) is a science-based, interactive multimedia education centre housed in futuristic-looking buildings. Well suited to travellers with kids in tow, it's a 1km walk turning right from the station.

Sleeping

Accommodation is tight here. Try the tourist office's booking service; there are some excellent B&Bs run by friendly locals, starting from around €20 to €25.

Hanze Hotel Zwolle (☎ 421 81 82; www.hanzehotel .com; Rode Torenplein 10-11; r €70-120; ☑) Virtually

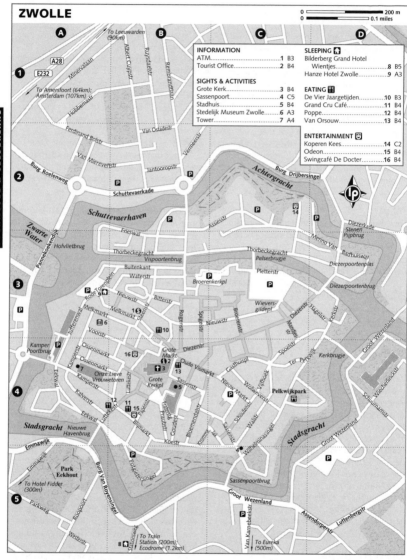

an island of vintage charm, the rooms here are simple but tidy. Sizes vary and those on the third floor are gut-busters for those who overpacked. Good breakfast buffet.

Hotel Fidder (☎ 421 83 95; www.hotelfidder.nl; Koningin Wilhelminastraat 6; r €100-175; 🛜) Three grand late-19th-century homes have been combined into one 21-room family-run

hotel. The gardens are pretty but the real joy comes inside where antiques abound and many rooms have ornate four-poster beds and other frou-frous.

Bilderberg Grand Hotel Wientjes (☎ 425 42 54; www.grandhotelwientjes.nl; Stationsweg 7; r €100-175; 🛜) This stately establishment is a grand, sumptuous 56-room business hotel, with all the usual facilities and service to match. It has a chic cafe and is located next to the station.

Eating

Van Orsouw (☎ 421 68 35; Grote Markt 6; treats from €1) Locally renowned bakery that tempts with its olfactory siren song as you walk past. Get your *blauwvingers* (blue fingers, a local speciality of shortbread dipped in icing) here. The lunch room does not disappoint, with fine sandwiches, soups and more.

Grand Cru Café (☎ 422 66 00; Blijmarkt 23; meals from €8) Housed in an 1817 bank building, this very popular cafe has tables out the front where you can take in the charms of this lovely square or more intimate tables in the courtyard. The menu is classic: salads, soups, sandwiches, hot plates and more.

De Vier Jaargetijden (☎ 421 99 04; Melkmarkt 8; meals €8-20) Of the many cafes in the centre, this one is always the most crowded and for good reason: fast service, tasty chow and a long drinks list. This is *the* place in summer (one of the 'four seasons' in the name) to let the long evening go on and on.

Poppe (☎ 421 30 50; Luttekestraat 66; meals from €32; ⏲ lunch Tue-Fri, dinner Tue-Sun) The golden letters of the name on the vermilion awning tell you that you've arrived, and indeed you have. One of Zwolle's best, the open kitchen issues forth a steady stream of superb seasonal dishes. Spring brings asparagus, summer mussels, autumn…?

Entertainment

Swingcafé De Docter (☎ 421 52 35; www.dedocter.nl; Voorstraat 3) A great place, dark and musty, the swing cafe hosts live rock bands a few nights per week, and has inviting open frontage and ample supplies of Hertog Jan, a great Brabant pilsener.

Odeon (☎ 428 82 80; www.schouwburg-odeon .nl; Blijmarkt 25) This grand building is a multipurpose entertainment venue hosting everything from theatre and dance to live rock and electronica nights.

Koperen Kees (☎ 423 22 24; Spinhuisplein 14; ⏲ 8pm-late Fri & Sat) A popular fashion-victim club with swish cocktails. It's also open any night there is a show in the De Spiegel theatre upstairs (www.odeondespiegel.nl).

Shopping

The market occupies most of the former Melkmarkt, Oude Vismarkt and the star-shaped

centre in general on Friday and Saturday. Fish, fresh fruit and vegetables, clothes – anything goes. You'll also find cheap cheese and bread – a great way to stock up for a picnic. Pelkwijkpark or the area just south of Kerkbrugje are also good areas for picknicking. In summer, crowds surge and it becomes a party.

Diezerstraat is the mainstream strip of chains and big stores.

Getting There & Around

Local buses leave from the right as you exit the station.

BICYCLE

The bicycle shop is to the left of the station. Historic Urk (p170) in Noord Holland is 50km northwest on national bike route LF15, a scenic ride of dykes and rivers. Deventer is 36km south on LF3 and there are a lot of optional routes along the IJssel. Hoge Veluwe National Park is a 40km ride through national forests, parklands and heath. Paths go in all directions so a map is essential for this ride.

TRAIN

Zwolle is a transfer point for trains and has good connections. A new line linking Zwolle to Lelystad via Kampen is set to open in 2012.

Destination	Fare (€)	Duration (min)	Frequency (per hr)
Deventer	5.60	24	2
Groningen	15.90	67	3
Leeuwarden	14.50	60	2
Utrecht	13.40	60	3

KAMPEN

☎ 038 / pop 49,900

Picturesque Kampen, another lovely Hanseatic city, is a perfect day trip, 15km west of Zwolle, about 30 minutes by bicycle and well-linked to national bike routes. Its surrounding parklands are pretty and its historic centre is one of the country's best preserved, boasting no fewer than 500 medieval monuments, including houses, gates and towers. The closing of the Zuiderzee ended Kampen's status as an important port and the long economic decline that followed kept modernisation down and old buildings up.

It's difficult to get lost in Kampen, as it's small and laid out in a linear fashion, parallel to the IJssel.

**THE GRASS IS ALWAYS GREENER...
UP THE TOWER**

Once upon a time a local farmer mistook moss growing atop Nieuwe Toren for grass and wondered aloud if he could get his cows up there to graze. So what he did was he hoisted one of his cows up to the top via a dodgy system of pulleys and ropes. The cheering townspeople below saw the cow's tongue protruding from its mouth and assumed it was indeed having a good old feed. And there was much rejoicing. Unfortunately the poor animal was actually choking to death, a ridiculous episode that made Kampen the butt of Dutch jokes for many, many years.

Plan your day with the help of the **tourist office** (☎ 331 35 00; www.vvvkampen.nl; Oudestraat 151; ⌚ 9.30am-5.30pm Mon-Fri, 10am-4pm Sat), which can also organise private rooms (about €30).

Sights & Activities

The major sights lie along Oudestraat.

The **Nieuwe Toren** is immediately obvious: it's the 17th-century tower with the incredible lean. There's a little statue of a cow here, linked to a rather ludicrous old story (see boxed text, above). Yet another renovation is ongoing.

The **Oude Raadhuis** (Old Town Hall; ☎ 339 29 99; Oudestraat 133) was – surprise, surprise – badly damaged by fire and rebuilt in 1543.

The 14th-century Gothic **Bovenkerk** (☎ 331 64 53; Koornmarkt 28) features an organ with more than 3000 pipes, while the **Gotische Huis** (Gothic House; Oudestraat 158) is a 15th-century merchant's house that's worth a look.

The **Stedelijk Museum** (☎ 331 73 61; www.stedelijke museakampen.nl; Oudestraat 133; adult/child €5/free; ⌚ 10am-5pm Tue-Sat, 1-5pm Sun) has local, historical relics plus a lot of artwork from the past 1000 years. Some of the portraits of rich old Kampens from the 17th century are quite unnerving.

Two 15th-century **city gates** survive along the gorgeous park on Kampen's west side.

Sleeping & Eating

Most people only visit for the day, but the town has a couple of decent options for food and rest if you choose to stay.

Hotel Van Dijk (☎ 331 49 25; home.tiscali.nl/~hotel vandijk; IJsselkade 30-3; r €60-90; 🖵) This solid 18-room family-run place has decor that dates

from an era known as 'the '80s' but it's a real charmers, and cyclists are catered for with a locked storage area.

Café Bar De Pub (☎ 331 55 98; Plantage 18; meals from €6) Best of several cafes on this square off Oudestraat, where on a nice day you may be tempted to stay long enough to join the list of local monuments. There's a good beer selection.

Restaurant de Bottermarck (☎ 331 95 42; Broederstraat 23; meals from €30; ⌚ lunch & dinner Tue-Sat) An innovative couple runs this fine bistro in an old building with thick exposed beams in the ceiling. A few tables out the front add a casual accent to the white tablecloths within. The changing menu is fresh and seasonal.

Getting There & Around
BICYCLE

Kampen is a hub of national bike routes: LF15 northwest to Urk and east to Zwolle (18km); LF 23, which follows the old coast below Flevoland and goes 130km west to Amsterdam; LF22, which also follows the old coast north and west to Friesland; and LF3, which runs south via Zwolle to Arnhem.

TRAIN

Trains make the run between Zwolle and Kampen (€2.90, 10 minutes, two per hour). The beautiful old station has been made 'efficient' by NS, which means no lockers or other services, although there is a small shop for tickets.

NORTHERN OVERIJSSEL

Before the Noordoostpolder was created, the Northern Overijssel region was on the Zuiderzee. Today the former coastal villages are landlocked, but maintain their links to the water through the spider web of canals that criss-cross this marshy area. It's a difficult area to get around without a car or a bike and a set of energetic legs, as buses are infrequent and involve inconvenient connections. Still, it's worth the effort to explore as you'll take in great scenery and feel a sense of detachment from the rest of the Netherlands.

Giethoorn
☎ 0521 / pop 2500

Giethoorn, the region's highlight, is a town with no streets, only canals, walking paths and bike trails (inevitably it's tagged the 'Dutch Venice'). Contrary to most Dutch geography, Giethoorn is built on water crossed by a few bits of land, and farmers even used to move their cows around in row boats filled with hay. This is a sentimental place for the Dutch as it was the setting for *Fanfare*, a popular, funny 1958 film about the local folk, and one of the first to dissect the Dutch psyche.

The entire area is a joy to pedal through and there are countless opportunities for rides via purring electric boats (€15 for one hour) – although communing with a cow will be tougher these days as Giethoorn is hugely popular, appearing in summer to be populated entirely by campervans along the ample canalside space. But in the low season it has an almost mystical charm as you wander its idiosyncratic waterways.

Giethoorn's **tourist office** (☎ 0900 567 46 37; www.vvvgiethoorn.nl; Eendrachtsplein 1; �9am-6pm Mon-Sat, 9am-5pm Sun May-Sep, 9am-5pm Mon-Fri Oct-Apr) is in the centre of things behind the Spar grocery store in the new library, which also has internet access. It can help navigate the maze of sleeping options: camping grounds, B&B and hotel rooms, and rental cabins.

Bus 70 serves Giethoorn on its route between Steenwijk (18 minutes) and Zwolle (one hour). Service is hourly.

It's difficult to get around Giethoorn without a boat, a bike or a combination thereof. The many bike shops hire out per day. The area is about five scenic cycling kilometres off national bike routes LF3, LF9 and LF22.

GELDERLAND

Lush Gelderland looks like a Rorschach test. And each person will see it differently.

Nijmegen's college students look forward to the future, while Arnhem looks forward to escape its infamous WWII past. Zutphen has a few echoes of the Hanseatic League while De Hoge Veluwe National Park echoes with just a few calls of the wild. The latter, of course, is the star of the province, with its natural setting and superb museum.

NIJMEGEN

☎ 024 / pop 162,100

There's a minor rivalry between Nijmegen and Maastricht to claim the title as the oldest city in the Netherlands. Unfortunately the Romans, who would know, are long dead. However, it is known that the Romans conquered the place in 70 AD and promptly burnt it down. A sad taste of things to come.

Nijmegen built itself up as a trading and manufacturing town. It rolled with the many invasions through the centuries right up until WWII, which was devastating. A marshalling point for German forces, it was bombed heavily by the Americans in February 1944. Later that year, it was devastated during the Operation Market Garden fiasco (see boxed text, p264). The postwar years have seen several rebuilding schemes, some better than others.

Nijmegen is home to many fine cafes and it has a lively nightlife, helped along by the 13,000 students at the Netherlands' only Catholic university. It is a good base for exploring Gelderland and the centre is only 10 minutes from the train station. The waterfront along the Waal River has cafes and boat tours.

Orientation & Information

Nijmegen's centre is compact but – get ready for this – is set on hills and you actually get to traverse a few steep streets down to the wide expanse of the Waal.

Library (☎ 327 49 11; Mariënburg 29; internet per hr €3; �2-6pm Mon & Wed, 11am-8pm Tue, Thu & Fri, 10am-5pm Sat; ☎)

Tourist office (☎ 0900 112 23 44; www.vvvnijmegen.nl; Keizer Karelplein 32h; �9.30am-5.30pm Mon-Fri, 10am-5pm Sat) Not one of the better ones; even the shop is a dud.

Sights & Activities

The **Museum het Valkhof** (☎ 360 88 05; www.museum hetvalkhof.nl; Kelfkensbos 59; adult/child €7/3.50; ☎ 10am-5pm Tue-Fri, 11-5pm Sat & Sun) is housed in a striking glass-clad building. The museum's rich collections cover regional history and art and there's a first-rate section of Roman artefacts.

Across from the museum is the **Valkhof**, a lovely park and the site of a few castle ruins. At centre-stage is the 16-sided **Sint Nicolaaskapel**, which dates to the time of Charlemagne. It has been remodelled and reworked in a multitude of styles (depending on who held power in Nijmegen) during its 950-year lifespan. There are good views of the Waal from up here.

Follow the paths down the hillside to the riverfront **Nationaal Fietsmuseum Velorama** (National Cycling Museum; ☎ 322 58 51; www.velorama .nl; Waalkade 107; adult/child €5/3; ☎ 10am-5pm Mon-Sat, 11am-5pm Sun), a small but interesting museum with more than 250 bikes: everything from 19th-century wooden contraptions to hand-propelled bikes, to an entire room devoted to penny farthings, plus more modern – and sane – machines. It's a must-see for anyone

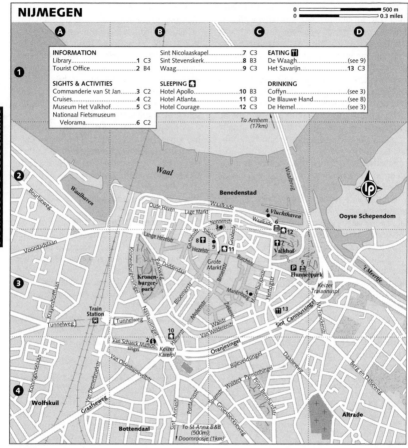

NIJMEGEN

0 ————— 500 m
0 ————— 0.3 miles

INFORMATION
Library..................................1 C3
Tourist Office......................2 B4

SIGHTS & ACTIVITIES
Commanderie van St Jan.......3 C2
Cruises.................................4 C2
Museum Het Valkhof...........5 C3
Nationaal Fietsmuseum
Velorama............................6 C2

Sint Nicolaaskapel................7 C3
Sint Stevenskerk..................8 B3
Waag...................................9 C3

SLEEPING
Hotel Apollo.......................10 B3
Hotel Atlanta......................11 C3
Hotel Courage....................12 C3

EATING
De Waagh.........................(see 9)
Het Savarijn.......................13 C3

DRINKING
Coffyn...............................(see 3)
De Blauwe Hand................(see 8)
De Hemel..........................(see 3)

who's marvelled at the Dutch affinity for two-wheelers.

A few important bits of the old town either survived the war or have been reconstructed. The **Waag** (old weigh-house) on Grote Markt was built in 1612 and has a lovely interior (see opposite). Through an arch, **Sint Stevenskerk** (☎ 360 47 10; tower climb €1; ☼ noon-5pm) dates from the 14th century and has a classic reformist interior: no expense was spared for whitewash. It's 183 steps to the top.

Commanderie van St Jan, near Grote Markt on Franseplaats, was a 15th-century hospital for the knights of St John. Today it still gives life: it houses a brewery (opposite).

Even allowing for the usual air of frivolity commonly associated with such watery zones,

strolling along the **Waalkade**, Nijmegen's waterfront, is delightful, especially if you're into boats and shipping. This stretch of river, Europe's busiest, sees a large barge or ferry plying the waters past Nijmegen every few minutes. Sometimes it's busier than the traffic on the road. Walk or ride a bike along the **Waalbrug** for breath-stealing sunset views of the old town, with the the water and the boats chugging below.

Various **cruises** (☎ 323 32 85; www.tonissen.nl) on the Waal depart from the waterfront along Waalkade. Some go all the way to Rotterdam (Thursdays in August, €42).

Festivals & Events

Nijmegen's big event is the annual **Vierdaagse** (Four Days; www.4daagse.nl), a four-day, 120km- to

200km-long march held in late July. It has a long history: the first one was held in 1909. Thousands walk it, even though the shortest or easiest route is a minimum of 30km a day. Many suffer debilitating blisters, while thousands more endure debilitating hangovers, as the Wandelvierdaagse is the city's excuse for a weeklong party. There are varying route classifications according to gender and age. Completing the walk is considered a national honour and comes with a medal.

Sleeping

Don't think about staying in the region during the time of the Vierdaagse.

Hotel Atlanta (☎ 360 30 00; www.atlanta-hotel.nl; Grote Markt 38-40; s/d from €63/88; ☜) This place is a great-value option with 17 comfy rooms. It's also home to a popular cafe on the Grote Markt. Be warned, though – the central location gets quite noisy at night.

St Anna B&B (☎ 350 18 08; www.sintanna.nl; St Annastraat 208; s/d from €70/90; ▯) Perhaps Nijmegen's most charming accommodation. St Anna's owners also run a travel agency specialising in New Zealand, which explains the sheep motif. It also explains why one of the rooms has pictures of kiwi fruit on the walls and on the bedding. Rooms have high-speed internet.

Hotel Apollo (☎ 322 35 94; www.apollo-hotel -nijmegen.nl; Hamerstraat 14; s/d from €70/90; ☜) A basic, modern place; the 18 rooms are comfortable and have extras such as coffee-makers.

Hotel Courage (☎ 360 49 70; www.hotelcourage.nl; Waalkade 108-112; r €82-120; ☒ ☜) This hotel has a superb location right on the waterfront – in the shadow of the Waalbrug – plus a nice restaurant and bar, and 21 very cosy rooms. The most expensive rooms have grand river views. All guests get direct access to the adjoining cycling museum (p259).

Eating & Drinking

The best way to choose one of the cafes and restaurants on the Waal is to wander the riverfront and let your intuition reign. The Waag is surrounded by cafes; it's the same deal here.

De Waagh (☎ 323 07 57; www.de-waagh.nl; Grote Markt 26; mains €18-25; ☽ lunch & dinner) This is an atmospheric place in which to eat, being as it is the town's 1612 former weigh-house. The interior has been restored to a rich, sumptuous Burgundian ideal. In keeping with the

traditional surrounds, the menu is a hearty showpiece of roasts and more.

Het Savarijn (☎ 323 26 15; Van der Brugghenstraat 14; meals from €30; ☽ lunch Mon-Fri, dinner Mon-Sat) A fine verandah surrounds this bistro, which has a seasonal menu. Local produce is a speciality and you can expect interesting dishes such as soufflés and spicy Med-inspired mains. Go nuts and have the surprise menu (€45). Excellent wine list by the glass.

De Blauwe Hand (Blue Hand; ☎ 360 61 67; Achter de Hoofdwacht 3) The best bar in Nijmegen is also its oldest (1542), an ancient survivor that derives its name from its 17th-century customers: workers at a nearby dye shop. This corner spot is the perfect little Dutch bar (friendly and inviting) as evidenced by its motto: 'A frosty mug of rich beer gives you warmth, joy and sweet pleasure.'

COMMANDERIE VAN ST JAN

The 15th-century hospital (Franseplaats 1) has several places for sustenance.

Coffyn (☎ 329 47 40; treats from €1; ☽ 10am-6pm Tue-Sun) Organic and free-trade coffees and teas are both served and roasted here.

De Hemel (Heaven; ☎ 360 61 67; www.brouwerij dehemel.nl; ☽ noon-10pm Tue-Sun) A brewery with a few notable brews: Luna, a 5% lager and the 'hearty' Nieuw Ligt, which is anything but, being heavy in taste, body and colour – and 10% alcohol quotient. It has a decent cafe with some lovely outside tables in the courtyard.

Entertainment

Doornroosje (☎ 355 98 87; www.doornroosje.nl; Groenewoudseweg 322) Long-running, eclectic multipurpose venue, with live comedy and music ranging from electronica and house to indie-rock and world music.

Getting There & Around

Regional and local buses depart from the area in front of the station.

BICYCLE

The bicycle shop is underground in front of the station. Arnhem is 40km along the sinuous course of national bike route LF3, which follows rivers, including the Waal. Den Bosch is about 70km southwest along the equally curvaceous LF12. The rolling terrain means that you'll want a full range of gears on your bike.

TRAIN

The train station is large and modern with many services. Lockers are near track 1A and are poorly marked.

Destination	Fare (€)	Duration (min)	Frequency (per hr)
Amsterdam	14.60	70	2
Arnhem	3.80	15-20	8
Den Bosch	7.30	30-39	4

ARNHEM

☎ 026 / pop 145,600

With its centre all but levelled during WWII, Arnhem today is a nondescript, though prosperous, township with several museums and attractions around its northern outskirts. Plus it's a desirable launch pad for Hoge Veluwe National Park. Another fact from the war years (fans of Trivial Pursuit take note!): Audrey Hepburn attended Arnhem Conservatory from 1939 to 1945.

The **tourist office** (☎ 370 02 26; www.vvvarnhem.nl; Stationsplein 13; 9.30am-5.30pm Mon-Fri, 9am-5pm Sat) is conveniently just south of the train station.

Sights & Activities

Southeast of the Korenmarkt is the **John Frostbrug**, a replica of the infamous 'bridge too far' (see the boxed text, p264). It's not much to look at, but its symbolic value is immense.

The **Museum voor Moderne Kunst** (☎ 351 24 31; www.mmkarnhem.nl; Utrechtseweg 87; admission €6; 10am-5pm Tue-Fri, 11am-5pm Sat & Sun) has a commanding spot overlooking the Rijn (Rhine) and a fine modern-art collection; at least half of the works on display at any time must be by women.

Get a taste of Arnhem's rich heritage – literally – at the **Historische Museum Het Burgerweeshuis** (☎ 337 53 00; www.hmarnhem.nl; Bovenbeekstraat 21; adult/child €4/free; 10am-5pm Tue-Fri, 11am-5pm Sat & Sun). After a revamp it shows off historical treasures better than ever.

The **Nederlands Openluchtmuseum** (☎ 357 61 11; www.openluchtmuseum.nl; Schelmseweg 89; adult/child €12.90/9; 10am-5pm Apr-Oct) is an open-air museum that showcases a collection of buildings and artefacts from all provinces with everything from farmhouses and old trams to working windmills. Volunteers in period costumes demonstrate traditional skills such as emptying chamber pots out windows – okay not that one… See it with the Zuiderzeemuseum (p157) in Enkhuizen for a complete picture of old Dutch life.

Nearby, **Burgers' Zoo** (☎ 442 45 34; www.burgerszoo.nl; Antoon van Hooffplein 1; adult/child €18/16; 9am-7pm or sunset) tries to re-create the natural environments of its many animals. The creatures mostly don't buy this ruse, given the climate. Bus 3 and 13 serve the zoo and the open-air museum.

Sleeping & Eating

Cafes and fast-food outlets crowd around the station.

Stayokay Arnhem (☎ 442 01 14; www.stayokay.com /arnhem; Diepenbrocklaan 27; d from €24) This hostel, with 181 beds and a pub, is 2km north of town and inconvenient for the centre, but perfectly situated for seeing a lot of the sights on Arnhem's outskirts, especially by bike. Take bus 3 (direction: Alteveer) and get off at Ziekenhuis Rijnstate (hospital).

Hotel Old Dutch (☎ 442 07 92; www.old-dutch.nl; Stationsplein 8; s/d from €80/110;) Conveniently located for transport connections, it's across the road from the main train station with 22 comfortable, striped rooms (with high-speed internet).

Getting There & Around

Buses and public transport leave from in front of the station, although the massive reconstruction sporadically affects this.

BICYCLE

The bike shop moves with the train station construction. This area is one place to invest in a bike map – sights are ideal for visiting by bike and there is a thicket of bike routes. National route LF3 runs 55km northeast to Deventer; Nijmegen is a twisting 40km south along wide rivers; Utrecht is 40km west via LF4.

TRAIN

Arnhem's train station is undergoing a massive reconstruction that should see parts debut in 2011 with the new name 'Arnhem Centraal'. Much of the new facility will be underground and until things are completed later in the decade, expect chaos. Lockers will move about. Some of the grander aspects of the scheme still need funding.

Destination	Fare (€)	Duration (min)	Frequency (per hr)
Amsterdam	14.60	70	2
Deventer	7.60	36	2
Nijmegen	3.80	15-20	8

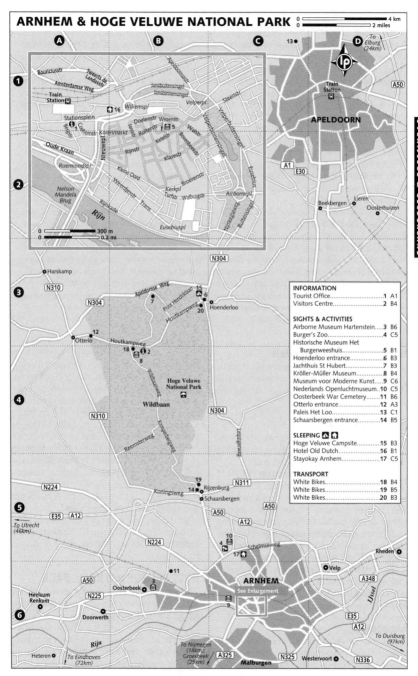

ARNHEM & HOGE VELUWE NATIONAL PARK

0 ———— 4 km
0 ———— 2 miles

OVERIJSSEL & GELDERLAND

INFORMATION
Tourist Office................................**1** A1
Visitors Centre............................**2** B4

SIGHTS & ACTIVITIES
Airborne Museum Hartenstein....**3** B6
Burger's Zoo.................................**4** C5
Historische Museum Het
   Burgerweeshuis.......................**5** B1
Hoenderloo entrance..................**6** B3
Jachthuis St Hubert.....................**7** B3
Kröller-Müller Museum...............**8** B4
Museum voor Moderne Kunst.....**9** C6
Nederlands Openluchtmuseum...**10** C5
Oosterbeek War Cemetery........**11** B6
Otterlo entrance.........................**12** A3
Paleis Het Loo............................**13** C1
Schaarsbergen entrance............**14** B5

SLEEPING
Hoge Veluwe Campsite..............**15** B3
Hotel Old Dutch..........................**16** B1
Stayokay Arnhem........................**17** C5

TRANSPORT
White Bikes.................................**18** B4
White Bikes.................................**19** B5
White Bikes.................................**20** B3

A BRIDGE TOO FAR: OPERATION MARKET GARDEN

The battle they called Operation Market Garden was devised by British General Bernard Montgomery to end WWII in Europe by Christmas 1944. Despite advisers warning that the entire operation was likely to fail, Montgomery pushed on. He had often groused that the Americans under General George Patton were getting all the headlines in their charge across France. The plan was for British forces in Belgium to make a huge push along a narrow corridor to Arnhem in the Netherlands, where they would cut off large numbers of German troops from being able to return to Germany, thereby allowing the British to dash east to Berlin and end the war.

Everything went wrong. The British paratroops were only given two days' rations and the forces from the south had to cross 14 bridges, all of which had to remain traversable and lightly defended for the plan to work. The southern forces encountered some of the German army's most hardened troops and the bridges weren't all completely intact. This, in effect, stranded the Arnhem paratroops. They held out there and in neighbouring Oosterbeek for eight days without reinforcements. The survivors, a mere 2163, retreated under darkness. More than 17,000 other British troops were killed.

The results of the debacle were devastating for the Dutch: Arnhem and other towns were levelled and hundreds of civilians killed. The Dutch resistance, thinking that liberation was at hand, came out of hiding to fight the Germans. But without the anticipated Allied forces supporting them, hundreds were captured and killed.

Finally Montgomery abandoned the country. The winter of 1944–45 came to be known as the 'Winter of Hunger', with starvation rife as no food could be imported from Allied-held Belgium.

Most of the Netherlands was still occupied when the war ended in Europe in May 1945.

Besides the museums and memorials covered here, the Nationaal Oorlogs- en Verzetsmuseum (p280) in North Limburg covers the battle.

AROUND ARNHEM

WWII Museums & Memorials

The tourist offices in Nijmegen and Arnhem can both provide specific information on visits and tours to the many sites in the region. Bike routes cover it all.

OOSTERBEEK

An old suburb 5km west of Arnhem, Oosterbeek was the scene of heavy combat during Operation Market Garden.

The **Airborne Museum Hartenstein** (☎ 333 77 10; www.airbornemuseum.org; Utrechtsweg 232; adult/child & veteran €4.80/3.80; ⏰ 10am-5pm Mon-Sat, noon-5pm Sun) is inside a mansion used by the British as HQ during the battle. New galleries added in 2009 do an excellent job of explaining the complex battle. Take trolleybus 1 serving both Oosterbeek and Arnhem train stations.

The **Oosterbeek War Cemetery** is 200m northeast of Oosterbeek train station (follow the signs). More than 1700 Allied (mostly British and Free Polish) troops are buried here.

GROESBEEK

The small town of Groesbeek, just inside Gelderland's southern border, 10km south of Nijmegen, is home to the **National Liberation Museum 1944–45** (☎ 397 44 04; www.bevrijdingsmuseum.nl; Wylerbaan 4; adult/child €10/5; ⏰ 10am-5pm Mon-Sat, noon-5pm Sun). Using interactive displays and historical artefacts, visitors 'relive' the campaign to liberate the Netherlands (which did not go so well). There's also a heavy dose about why people fight for freedom. Connexxion bus 5 runs here from Nijmegen every 15 minutes. By bike it's a pretty 8km.

Nearby, the **Groesbeek Canadian War Cemetery** is a mausoleum dedicated to the soldiers who fell here during Operation Market Garden. Of the 2610 Commonwealth soldiers commemorated, 2331 are Canadian. A memorial lists those killed but never found.

In the tiny township of Jonkerbos (a short distance from Nijmegen), **Jonkerbos War Cemetery** is the final resting place of mainly British servicemen.

HOGE VELUWE NATIONAL PARK

This **park** (☎ 0318-59 10 41; www.hogeveluwe.nl; adult/child €7/3.50, park & museum €14/7; ⏰ 9am-6pm Nov-Mar, 8am-8pm Apr, 8am-9pm May & Aug, 8am-10pm Jun & Jul, 9am-8pm Sep, 9am-7pm Oct), the largest in the Netherlands, would be a fantastic place to visit for its marshlands, forests and sand dunes alone, but its brilliant museum makes it unmissable.

The park was purchased in 1914 by Anton and Helene Kröller-Müller, a wealthy German-Dutch couple. He wanted hunting grounds, she wanted a museum site. They got both. It was given to the state in 1930, and in 1938 a museum opened for Helene's remarkable art collection. A visit to the park can fill an entire day, and even if you don't have a bike, you can borrow one of the park's hundreds of famous, free white bicycles.

The ticket booths at each of the three entrances at Hoenderloo, Otterlo and Schaarsbergen have basic information and invaluable park maps (€2.50). In the heart of the park, the main **visitors centre** (☒ 9.30am-6pm Apr-Oct, to 5pm Nov-Mar) is an attraction itself. It has displays on the flora and fauna, including one showing the gruesome results of when a deer has a bad day and a crow has a good day.

Roads through the park are limited. There are myriad bike paths and 42km of hiking trails, with three routes signposted. The most interesting area is the **Wildbaan**, south of the Kröller-Müller Museum. At the north edge, **Jachthuis St Hubert** is the baronial hunting lodge that Anton had built. Named after the patron saint of hunting (but not the hunted), you can tour its woodsy interior.

Cyclists in particular will be interested in the **camping ground** (☎ 055-378 22 32; per person €5; ☒ Apr-Oct), which is located at the Hoenderloo entrance. There are 100 sites; you can't reserve but you can call and see what's available.

Kröller-Müller Museum

Among the best museums in Europe, the **Kröller-Müller Museum** (☎ 0318-59 12 41; www.kmm.nl; Houtkampweg 6; ☒ 10am-5pm Tue-Sun) has works by some of the greatest painters of several centuries, from Bruyn the Elder to Picasso. The Van Gogh collection is world class, a stunning collection of the artist's work that rivals the collection in the eponymous Amsterdam museum. Here you'll find *The Potato Eaters* and *Weavers* among many more, all arranged chronologically so you can trace his development as a painter. Impressionists include Renoir, Sisley, Monet and Manet.

A new wing showcases modern sculpture. There's also a sculpture garden featuring works by Rodin, Moore and more. Art lovers can easily spend half a day here and they can recharge at an excellent cafe. If you are cycling to the museum from one of the three park entrances, it's 2.5km from Otterlo, 4km from Hoenderloo and 10km from Schaarsbergen.

Getting There & Around

From Arnhem train station in the south, take bus 2 (15 minutes, every half-hour) to the Schaarsbergen entrance (stop: Koningsweg). From Apeldoorn train station in the north, take Veolia bus 108 to Hoenderloo (26 minutes, hourly). Various buses run inside the park to the museum.

There is car parking at the visitors centre and museum. It costs €6 to take cars into the park, €2 to park them at the entrances. Cars are not admitted after 8pm.

By bike, the park is easily reached from any direction; national route LF4 through Arnhem is the closest major route. You can also wait and use the famous free white bicycles, available at the entrances.

APELDOORN

The rather featureless town of Apeldoorn has one attraction: the **Paleis Het Loo** (☎ 055-577 24 00; www.paleishetloo.nl; Koninklijk Park 1; adult/child €10/3; ☒ 10am-5pm Tue-Sun), built in 1685 for William III; Queen Wilhelmina lived here until 1962. Now it's a magnificent museum celebrating the history of the royal House of Oranje-Nassau. View the royal bed chambers, regal paintings, the lavish dining room dating from 1686, the immense gardens with their maze of hedgerows and pathways.

It's all very impressive, unfortunately it was overshadowed by tragedy in 2009 when a man tried to ram his car into an open vehicle carrying the royal family in a parade to Het Loo on Queen's Day (30 April). Although the royals were unscathed, eight people, including the driver, died in the attack.

Apeldoorn is a junction of train lines to Deventer, Zutphen and Amersfoort. The station has no lockers. Numerous local buses go near the palace.

ELBURG

☎ 0525 / pop 22,200

Gorgeous Elburg has a sculpted, cobbled 16th-century splendour. Compact and gridlike, its centre can be easily explored on foot. One highlight is the old harbour. Continue all the way down Jufferenstraat, through the 14th-century **Vischpoort** at the end of Vischpoortstraat and into the harbour itself, where a small flotilla of pleasure and fishing

OVERIJSSEL & GELDERLAND

boats can take you on a boat tour. There's also an enjoyable market in good weather, where you can help yourself to cheap snacks or local crafts.

Visit the **tourist office** (☎ 68 15 20; www.vvvelburg .nl; Ledige Stede 31; ☼ 9am-5pm Mon-Fri year-round, 10am-4pm Sat May-Aug) for more information.

Getting There & Around

Take bus 100 from Zwolle train station (40 minutes, one to two per hour); it stops about 100m from the beginning of Jufferenstraat, the main drag. Elburg makes a fine rest stop on national bike route LF23; it is a 16km ride south of Kampen.

Noord Brabant & Limburg

The Dutch southeast belies most clichés about the Netherlands: tulips, windmills and dykes are scarce. Although there's still plenty of beer. However the Belgian and German influences are felt. Even the French have influence, especially in the wider array of culinary treats on offer.

Noord Brabant is primarily a land of agriculture and industry peppered with a few pleasant towns, such as Den Bosch. It's also home to the Netherlands' most popular domestic tourist draw, the Efteling theme park, and the biggest street fair in Benelux, the Tilburgse Kermis. It's striped by rivers which make for curvaceous – and bodacious – cycling along their banks.

Meanwhile, Limburg is home to beautiful Maastricht, contender for the title of Finest Dutch City, as well as – drum roll – hills. The one outstanding attraction in these two provinces, Maastricht, is as diametrically different from Amsterdam as it is geographically distant from it except in one key area: its people are just as irreverent and just as interested in fun.

Neither province has its roots in the asceticism of the north, a fact made obvious during *carnaval*, when the streets fill with bands and impromptu parties, with fireworks overhead. And both provinces' proximity to Belgium and all those indulgent Catholic monasteries – most of which double as excellent microbreweries – mean there are many chances to imbibe.

In fact, the Dutch call the southeastern lifestyle *bourgondisch:* like the epicurean inhabitants of Burgundy in France, people in these parts love to eat and drink heartily.

HIGHLIGHTS

- Thrill to the good life in **Maastricht** (p274), a world apart from the north
- Go bonkers at Maastricht's **Carnaval** (p277)
- Explore the unusual canals and charming cafes of lively **Den Bosch** (p268)
- Hop off your bike or train to tour **Breda** (p272) and its boffo church

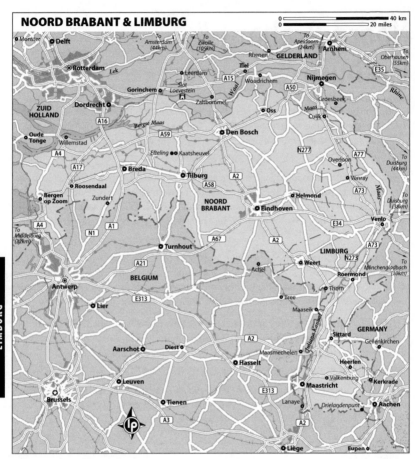

NOORD BRABANT & LIMBURG

NOORD BRABANT & LIMBURG

NOORD BRABANT

The country's largest province, Noord Brabant, spans the bottom of the country, from the water-logged lands of the west to the hilly lands of the east. Den Bosch is its main city and an interesting place to spend the day. Breda is also worth a look. However, despite its size, Noord Brabant won't fill your schedule. It's primarily a land of agriculture and industry.

DEN BOSCH ('S-HERTOGENBOSCH)
☎ 073 / pop 137,800

The full name of Noord Brabant's capital is 's-Hertogenbosch (Duke's Forest), which is understandably not used often. Den Bosch has a remarkable church and a good museum.

It has fun cafes and unique tunnel canals you can explore.

The significance of the city's full name held true in the 12th century when there was a castle and large forest here. Both are long gone. It was hotly contested during the Eighty Years' War and you can still see where the lines of fortifications followed the shape of the canals. It's the birthplace of the 15th-century painter Hieronymous Bosch, who took his surname from the town. Today, Den Bosch (*den boss*) is a regional shopping and industrial town.

Orientation
The town's pedestrianised centre is based around the Markt, 600m east of the train station.

Information

Bosch Medicentrum (☎ 699 20 00; Nieuwstraat 34) Regional hospital.

Library (☎ 612 30 33; Hinthamerstraat 72; internet per hr €3; ☒ 11am-8pm Tue-Fri, noon-4pm Sat & Sun)

Post office (Kerkstraat 67; ☒ 9am-6pm Mon-Fri, 9am-2pm Sat)

Tourist office (☎ 0900 112 23 34; www.vvvdenbosch .nl; Markt 77; ☒ 1-6pm Mon, 9.30am-6pm Tue-Fri, 9am-5pm Sat)

Sights & Activities

The main attraction is **Sint Janskathedraal** (☎ 613 03 14; www.sint-jan.nl; Choorstraat 1; admission free; ☒ 10am-4.30pm), one of the finest churches in the Netherlands. It took from 1336 to 1550 to complete, and there's an interesting contrast between the red-brick tower and the ornate stone buttresses. The interior is also of interest, with late-Gothic stained-glass windows, an impressive statue of the Madonna and an amazing organ case from the 17th century.

Unfortunately, Protestants destroyed the cathedral's paintings in 1566. Recent restorations uncovered a few 15th-century survivors.

Take the opportunity to climb the 73m **tower** (admission €3.50), with its carillon and great views.

The **Stadhuis** (town hall) was given its classical baroque appearance in 1670. The **Noordbrabants Museum** (☎ 687 78 77; www.noord brabantsmuseum.nl; Verwersstraat 41; adult/child €7/free; ☒ 10am-5pm Tue-Fri, noon-5pm Sat & Sun), in the 18th-century former governor's residence, features a sculpture garden and exhibits about Brabant life and art, a Van Gogh and – for those cafe-bound – an inspirational Roman statue of Bacchus. Plans call for a major revamp in 2012.

There are many good bike rides around Den Bosch; see p272 for a few ideas.

Tours

Canals in Den Bosch are different from the others you've been seeing: many have long stretches where they pass under buildings, plazas and roads. These tunnels add spice to the usual canal tours and have inspired more than one Tunnel of Love moment.

Binnendieze (☎ 612 23 34; www.binnendieze.nl; Molenstraat 15a; adult/child €6/3; ☒ tickets 9.30am-5pm

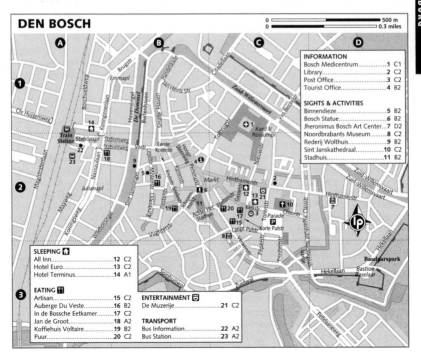

DEN BOSCH

| 0 | 500 m |
| 0 | 0.3 miles |

INFORMATION
Bosch Medicentrum...............1 C1
Library.................................2 C2
Post Office............................3 C2
Tourist Office........................4 B2

SIGHTS & ACTIVITIES
Binnendieze...........................5 B2
Bosch Statue..........................6 B2
Jheronimus Bosch Art Center....7 D2
Noordbrabants Museum..........8 C2
Rederij Wolthuis.....................9 B2
Sint Janskathedraal..............10 C2
Stadhuis.............................11 B2

SLEEPING
All Inn..............................12 C2
Hotel Euro.........................13 C2
Hotel Terminus...................14 A1

EATING
Artisan.............................15 C2
Auberge Du Veste...............16 B2
In de Bossche Eetkamer.......17 C2
Jan de Groot......................18 A2
Koffiehuis Voltaire..............19 B2
Puur................................20 C2

ENTERTAINMENT
De Muzerije.......................21 C2

TRANSPORT
Bus Information..................22 A2
Bus Station........................23 A2

Apr-Oct) runs various fascinating 50-minute tours of the centre's canals. Boats usually leave hourly but on busy summer weekends they depart with a frequency that rivals Disney's *Pirates of the Caribbean* ride.

Rederij Wolthuis (☎ 631 20 48; www.rederijwolthuis .nl; Sint Janssingel; adult/child €7.50/6.50; ☿ noon-3pm Tue-Sun May-Sep) runs large boats in the old defensive and shipping canals that surround the old town (one hour).

Sleeping

Hotel Terminus (☎ 613 06 66; www.hotel-terminus.nl; Boschveldweg 15; s/d €34/65) As its name suggests, it's close to the station. The simple, brightly coloured rooms are decent enough and share bathrooms. There's a cheery bar and regular live folk music.

All Inn (☎ 613 40 57, 0631 36 42 34; home.wanadoo .nl/hotelallin; Gasselstraat 1; s/d from €45/60; ☿ closed Aug & carnaval) Dating from 1905, this *pension* is on the lovably shabby but clean side. Note: there's a midnight curfew.

Hotel Euro (☎ 613 77 77; www.eurohotel-denbosch .com; Kerkstraat 56; s/d from €65/85; ⊠) This business hotel has generic but comfortable rooms that are right out of the Best Western catalogue (the franchiser here). Fans of mauve will appreciate the corporate pastel palette. Good service and central location.

Eating & Drinking

Restaurant-lined Korte Putstraat is as crowded with diners as a Bosch painting is filled with little people.

Try the local speciality, a heart-failure calorie-fest known as the *Bossche bol* (Den Bosch ball). It's a chocolate-coated cake the size of a softball, filled with sweetened cream.

ourpick **Jan de Groot** (☎ 613 38 30; Stationsweg 24; treats from €2; ☿ 8am-6pm Mon-Fri, to 5pm Sat) The crowds know this is *the* place to get local balls; join them! The rest of the bakery cases are filled with alluring goods and there's an excellent cafe for a coffee, snack or meal.

Koffiehuis Voltaire (☎ 613 96 72; Stoofstraat 6; meals from €5; ☿ 10am-6pm Mon-Sat) The definition of funky. Settle into a table out front or amid the multicoloured shambles inside for some fab vegie fare. The affable owner cooks up a mean house special: a grilled sandwich of organic cheese, pesto, arugula, avocado and more. Great fruit shakes. No smoking anything.

Puur (☎ 613 27 76; Verwerstraat 18; meals from €10; ☿ 9am-9pm Sun-Wed, to midnight Thu-Sat) Glide through the creamy interior to the luscious terrace out the back. Scenesters enjoy an eclectic menu of nibbles, from sushi to local cheeses. The drinks list is long, many wines pour forth by the glass.

In de Bossche Eetkamer (☎ 613 28 28; Korte Putstraat 9; mains €21-25; ☿ dinner) A traditional menu of steak and seafood is served in this traditional restaurant with cane chairs at the tables out the front. Competition lines the street.

Artisan (☎ 614 94 87; Verwerstraat 24; menus from €28; ☿ noon-10pm Tue-Sun) Fresh fare sourced locally. Lunches feature imaginative sandwiches, salads and specials. Dinner brings out the kitchen skills with seasonal menus that can range from mussels to roasts. Between meals enjoy a glass of wine in the courtyard.

Auberge de Veste (☎ 614 46 44; www.aubergede veste.nl; Uilenburg 2; meals from €35; ⊙ lunch Mon, Tue, Thu, Fri, dinner Thu-Tue) Slim as a leek, this old brick canal house has a charming little terrace overlooking the tour boats passing by. But there's no traditional stodge here: mains can include locally caught plaice with artichokes and fennel.

Entertainment

De Muzerije (☎ 614 10 84; www.de-muzerije.nl; Hinthamerstraat 74) This all-in-one venue features different kinds of theatre, dance and film.

Shopping

Thursday is the big night for shopping and many lunch places stay open to refresh the hordes. Wednesday and Saturday are big market days on Markt.

Uilenburg has antique shops, while Vughterstraat is lined with interesting boutiques. Hinthamerstraat going east is another fine place for upmarket browsing and creative loafing.

Getting There & Around

Buses leave from the area to the right as you exit the station.

BICYCLE

The bicycle shop is located below the station. National bike route LF12 heads due west over a twisting route through lush countryside, around rivers and through tiny villages some 70km to Dordrecht. It passes Slot Loevestein (p219) and the north side of Biesbosch National Park (p218). LF12 goes northeast 70km to Nijmegen along a twisting river route.

For some freelance fun head north 16km to the little old village of Zaltbommel, then cross the wide Waal and ride another 11km on rural paths north towards Beesd, where you can pick up LF17 and ride west through the beautiful river valley of the Linge in Gelderland.

TRAIN

The modern train station brims with services, including a good grocery store aimed at travellers. Lockers are on the concourse over the tracks. Sample fares and schedules:

Destination	Price (€)	Duration (min)	Frequency (per hr)
Amsterdam	13.40	60	2
Breda	7.30	31-35	4
Maastricht	18.80	85	2
Nijmegen	7.30	30-39	4
Utrecht	8	30	4

EINDHOVEN
☎ 040 / pop 212,300

A mere village in 1900, Eindhoven grew exponentially thanks to Philips, founded here in 1891. During the 1990s the electronics giant found it was having trouble recruiting employees to work in its home town; it solved the problem by moving to Amsterdam, although its research and engineering arms remain here. Electronics aside, Eindhoven is best known for its football team, PSV, which routinely dominates the national league, though it could be said the many budget carriers serving its airport have also brought it frugal fame.

The **tourist office** (☎ 297 91 00; www.vvveindhoven .nl; Stationsplein 17; ⊙ 10am-5.30pm Mon, 9am-5.30pm Tue-Thu, 9am-7pm Fri, 10am-5pm Sat) is next to the train station and will book accommodation.

Eindhoven's main attraction is the excellent **Van Abbemuseum** (☎ 275 52 75; www .vanabbemuseum.nl; Bilderdijklaan 10; adult/child under 12 €8.50/free; ⊙ 11am-5pm Tue-Sun, to 9pm Thu). The first-rate collection of contemporary art includes works by Picasso, Chagall and Kandinsky.

There's an action-packed nightlife district, **Het Stratumseind**, with more than 30 cafes, bars and restaurants on a single stretch of street.

Getting There & Around
AIR
Eindhoven Airport (code EIN; www.eindhovenairport .nl) is 6km west of the centre. It has become a hub for budget airlines. Many flights serve holiday spots in the south such as the Canaries, but there are also some flights to major European cities. Airlines and a selection of their destinations with regular service include the following:

Aer Lingus (www.aerlingus.com) London Gatwick.
Ryanair (www.ryanair.com) London Stansted, Madrid, Rome-Ciampino.
Wizzair (www.wizzair.com) Budapest, Prague.

Bus 401 runs every 10 minutes between the airport and the train station (22 minutes).

BICYCLE

Eindhoven is on the marathon national bike route LF7, which links Maastricht in the south with Amsterdam and on to the north coast. Den Bosch is 45km north.

TRAIN

Budget fliers will easily find train connections to the rest of the Netherlands. The train station has lockers, money exchange and a full range of services.

Sample fares and schedules:

Destination	Price (€)	Duration (min)	Frequency (per hr)
Amsterdam	17.50	80	2
Maastricht	14.90	62	2
Rotterdam	16.10	70	2

TILBURG
☎ 013 / pop 203,000

With one of the highest ratios of students in the Netherlands (almost 15% of the population), you'd expect a more progressive vibe. But Tilburg, a former textile town, is in flux now that the mills have closed due to foreign competition, and its centre bears the scars of unfortunate 1960s' urban renewal schemes (think East Berlin).

People generally make a beeline to Tilburg in the middle of July, when the **Tilburgse Kermis** (Tilburg Fair; www.tilburgsekermis.com) takes place for close to two weeks. Basically an enormous street party, it's a massive celebration of street fair and street fare. Rides, beer, bad music, sugary treats, stalls offering stuffed prizes for games of 'skill'… It's the biggest fair in Benelux, and for that reason alone it's remarkable.

EFTELING

Near Tilburg, in the unassuming town of Kaatsheuvel, is **Efteling** (☎ 0416-28 81 11; www .efteling.nl; Europalaan 1, Kaatsheuvel; admission €28; ☒ 10am-6pm Apr-Oct, to 9pm mid-Jul–Aug), the biggest domestic tourist attraction in the Netherlands. This 'Dutch Disneyland' pulls more than three million visitors annually, proving its five-decade history as a family favourite is undiminished by the emergence of newer competitors, such as Flevoland's Six Flags.

All the usual suspects are here: huge, scary rides; walk-through entertainment with robots; scenes from popular stories and fairytales; live shows performed by 'talent'; sticky

hands; crying kids… (And maybe it's us but the mascots all look a little peaked.)

To get to Efteling take bus 136, 137 or 300 which run between Tilburg (20 minutes) and Den Bosch (one hour) train stations via the park.

BREDA
☎ 076 / pop 172,000

Lovely Breda makes for a good pause on a train or cycling journey. Enjoy interesting streets, flower-filled parks and a commanding main church. Its present peace belies its turbulent past, where its proximity to the Belgian border meant it has been overrun by invading armies many times.

The town centre is 500m southwest of the station through the leafy park, the Valkenberg.

There are two **tourist offices** (www.vvvbreda.nl; ☎ 0900 522 24 44; Grote Markt Grote Markt 38; ☒ 10.30am-5.30pm Wed-Fri, 10.30am-5pm Sat; Willemstraat Willemstraat 17; ☒ 1-5.30pm Mon, 9am-5.30pm Tue-Fri, 10am-4pm Sat). Neither has much beyond maps and brochures for sale.

Sights & Activities

The **Valkenberg** (Falcon Mountain) is the huge park between the station and the centre. It's a good place to lounge around and listen to the splash of the fountains. On the south side is the 12th-century **Begijnhof** (admission to small museum €1; ☒ noon-5pm Tue-Sun), a home that sheltered unmarried women. Breda has wonderfully preserved examples of these homes, which were found throughout the Netherlands.

Breda castle is still an active military base and is off limits. However the surrounds are worth a wander, especially the **Spanjaardsgat** (Spanish gate), a 16th-century survivor of the town's fortified era.

The white stones of the **Grote Kerk** (www .grotekerkbreda.nl; admission €2; ☒ 10am-5pm Mon-Sat, 1-5pm Sun) gleam thanks to a recent restoration. This beautiful Gothic church was built between the 15th and 17th centuries. Its perfect tower is 97m tall and is occasionally open for a climb.

The Dutch tradition of clear visual communications is explored at the **Graphic Design Museum** (☎ 529 99 00; www.graphicdesignmuseum.com; Boschstraat 22; adult/child €7.50/free; ☒ 10am-5pm Tue-Sun). The vintage Philips ads are timeless.

Festivals & Events

The **Bloemencorso** (www.bloemencorsozundert.nl; ☒ 1st Sun in Sep) is a huge annual parade of gorgeously

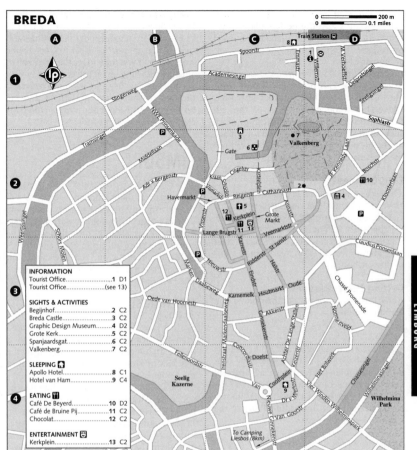

BREDA

decorated, multicoloured floats – each one of them constructed entirely from flowers – that passes through the streets of Zundert, 20km southwest of Breda. Take bus 115 from Breda.

Sleeping

Camping Liesbos (☎ 514 35 14; www.camping-liesbos.nl; Liesdreef 40; camp sites €13; ☾ Apr-Sep; ☞) Near some woods. Take bus 111 (direction: Etten-Leur) to the Boswachterij Liesbos stop and follow the signs for 700m.

Hotel van Ham (☎ 521 52 29; www.hotelvanham.com; Van Coothplein 23; s/d from €50/70) This 100-year-old family-run inn has 10 basic rooms that share bathrooms. The ground floor cafe is a delight.

Apollo Hotel (☎ 522 02 00; www.apollohotelsresorts .com; Stationsplein 14; r from €85; ☒ ☞) Breda's main

post office has been reborn as a stylish mid-range hotel. The 40 rooms are not huge but are colourful, and the hotel is close to everything.

Eating & Drinking

Breda is a great cafe town and on a sunny day it seems the entire population of the region is sitting around having a drink. Good ones can be found along all the pedestrian streets, with a classy bunch right on Kasteelplein.

Café de Bruine Pij (☎ 521 42 85; Kerkplein 7; meals from €8; ☞) Just far enough away from the Markt madness by day; by night you can enjoy the quiet of the square and the bells of the church unless there's a band on.

Café De Beyerd (☎ 521 42 65; www.beyerd .nl; Boschstraat 26; meals from €8) The Beyerd is a highly regarded beer cafe, with more than 120 brews. It's also the perfect place to try some *bitterballen* (small, crumbed, deep-fried pureed meatballs) or other typical snacks to accompany beer.

Chocolat (☎ 533 59 75; Torenstraat 9; mains €15-30; ❤ lunch & dinner) Part of the Hotel Bliss complex, Chocolat is a high-concept bistro-bar where Hollywood stars gaze at you through the namesake-shaded decor. Fresh produce stars on the menu, which is good for a snack with a fine beverage or a meal. In the evenings the vibe changes to a cool lounge.

Entertainment

There's a concentration of places around the Havermarkt, mostly of varying quality.

Kerkplein (www.kerkpleinbreda.nl; Torenstraat 17-19; ❤ 11pm-4am Thu-Sat) The decor here got flocked, – it's all faux luxe in gold and reds. Located right behind the Grote Kerk on Kerkplein, it hums to the wee hours.

Getting There & Around

Buses leave from the area to the right as you exit the station.

BICYCLE

The bicycle shop is right next to the station. National bike route LF11 starts here and runs northwest 110km to Den Haag via Dordrecht and Rotterdam. LF9 runs via Utrecht all the way to the north coast and LF13 runs via Breda straight east from Middelburg to the German border.

TRAIN

The train station has all the usual services; lockers are in the tunnel. Some fares and schedules:

Destination	Price (€)	Duration (min)	Frequency (per hr)
Den Bosch	7.30	31-35	4
Roosendaal	4.55	20	2
Rotterdam	8.30	32	3

WEST NOORD BRABANT

Near the border with Zeeland, Noord Brabant more closely resembles its soggy neighbour: canals and rivers criss-cross the land, and everything is absolutely flat.

Roosendaal is a major rail junction for lines north to Rotterdam, south to Belgium, east to Breda and west to Zeeland.

Bergen op Zoom was plundered at various times by the Spanish, French and even the British. The results are a hodgepodge of buildings and styles. It's an unremarkable place except for one week a year. If you want to see the aftermath of a real party, show up on the Wednesday after Shrove Tuesday. Bergen op Zoom's **carnaval** is the most raucous west of Maastricht, drawing revellers from throughout Europe who basically go on a four-day bender.

LIMBURG

This long, narrow province at times barely seems part of the Netherlands, especially in the hilly south. There are all sorts of amusing notices on the A2 motorway warning drivers of impending 'steep grades' that would be considered mere humps in other countries.

Maastricht is the one star and more than enough reason to make the journey down here form the rest of Holland.

MAASTRICHT

☎ 043 / pop 118,300

Spanish and Roman ruins, sophisticated food and drink, French and Belgian twists in the architecture, a shrugging off of the shackles of Dutch restraint. Are we still in the Netherlands?

Just like that other great afterthought, the appendix, Maastricht hangs down from the rest of the country hemmed in on all sides by Belgium and Germany. It was this very precarious position that saved the town from war damage in the 20th century; the Dutch government didn't bother mounting a defence.

In the centuries before, however, Maastricht was captured at various times by most of Europe's powers. This legacy as a crossroads for invading armies has helped give Maastricht its pan-European flavour. The average Maastricht citizen bounces between Dutch, English, French, German and Flemish with ease. This makes it all the more fitting that the city was the site of two seminal moments in the history of the EU. The first was the signature on 10 December 1991 by the 12 members of the then-European Community of the treaty for economic, monetary and political union. The following February, the nations gathered again to sign the treaty which created the EU.

Maastricht is a lively and energetic place out of proportion to it's size. The people are irreverent, there are hordes of university students and the streets are steeped in history. No visit to the Netherlands is complete without a visit to Maastricht.

Orientation

The centre of Maastricht is quite compact, bisected by the Maas River. The area on the east side is known as Wyck, and to the south of here is Céramique. It's about 750m from the train station to the Vrijthof, the old centre.

Information

BOOKSHOPS

Selexyz n' Dominicanen (☎ 321 08 25; Dominicanenkerkstraat 1) A vast cathedral of books – literally.

INTERNET ACCESS

The main tourist office has a free terminal for a quick email check.

Centre Ceramique Library (☎ 350 56 00; Ave Céramique 50; 🕑 10.30am-8.30pm Tue & Thu, 10.30am-5pm Wed & Fri, 10am-5pm Sat, 1-5pm Sun) A multifaceted cultural centre with free internet access.

Grand Net Internet Café (81 Boschstraat; per hr €2) One of several here.

MEDICAL SERVICES

Academisch Ziekenhuis Maastricht (☎ 387 65 43; P Debyelaan 25) An academic hospital just east of the MECC exposition centre.

POST

Post office (☎ 329 91 99; Statenstraat 4; 🕑 9am-6pm Mon-Fri, 9am-1.30pm Sat) There's another post office at Stationsstraat 60.

TOURIST INFORMATION

ANWB (Wycker Brugstraat 24; 🕑 9.30am-6pm Mon-Fri, to 5pm Sat) Has a tourist office info desk; convenient to the train station.

Tourist office (☎ 325 21 21; www.vvvmaastricht.nl; Kleine Straat 1; 🕑 9am-6pm Mon-Sat year-round, 11am-3pm Sun May-Oct) In the 15th-century Dinghuis; offers excellent walking-tour brochures.

Sights & Activities

Maastricht's delights are scattered along both banks of the Maas. The best approach is to just start strolling. The city's ruins, museums, cafes (and the odd surprise) reward walkers.

BONNEFANTENMUSEUM

The **Bonnefantenmuseum** (☎ 329 01 90; www.bonne fantenmuseum.nl; Ave Céramique 250; adult/child €8/free;

🕑 11am-5pm Tue-Sun) features a 28m tower that's a local landmark. Designed by Aldo Rossi, the museum opened in 1995, and is well laid-out with collections divided into departments, each on its own floor: Old Masters and medieval sculpture are on one floor, contemporary art by Limburg artists on the next. A dramatic sweep of stairs beckons visitors to both floors. Make time for the world-class Neuteling collection of medieval art.

Space is devoted to special exhibitions and shows. The museum is the patron of the major biennial Vincent Van Gogh Award for Contemporary Art in Europe.

VRIJTHOF

The large square of Vrijthof is surrounded by lively cafes and cultural institutions. It's dominated by **Sint Servaasbasiliek** (admission €2; 🕑 10am-5pm Mon-Sat, 12.30-5pm Sun), a pastiche of architecture dating from 1000. Duck around the back to the serene cloister garden and the **Treasury** (schatkamer; adult/child €4/free; 🕑 10am-5pm Mon-Sat, 12.30-5pm Sun) where much of the gold artwork dates from the 12th century. Don't miss the shrine to St Servatius, a Catholic diplomat who died here in 384.

Sint Janskerk (🕑 11am-4pm Mon-Sat) is a small 17th-century Gothic church, one of the most beautiful in the Netherlands. A remarkable red colour, it photographs beautifully. Climb to the top (€2) for sweeping views.

The 16th-century **Spanish Government Museum** (☎ 321 13 27; www.museumspaansgouvernement.nl; Vrijthof 18; adult/child €4/free; 🕑 1-5pm Wed-Sun) is where Philip II outlawed his former lieutenant Willem the Silent at the start of the Eighty Years' War. The exhibits feature statues and 17th-century paintings.

STREETS, SQUARES & BRIDGES

Streets not to miss include those south and east of Vrijthof: you'll be rewarded with a medieval labyrinth punctuated by interesting shops and any number of places for a drink on a shady square.

Onze Lieve Vrouweplein is an intimate cafe-filled square named after its church, the **Onze Lieve Vrouwebasiliek** (treasury adult/child €2/1; 🕑 10am-5pm), which has parts dating from before 1000 and may well be built on the foundations of a Roman cathedral. There is a separate treasury area that houses gaudy jewels and riches; these you can see for a small and worthwhile fee. The shrine to Mary Star of the Sea near the

NOORD BRABANT & LIMBURG

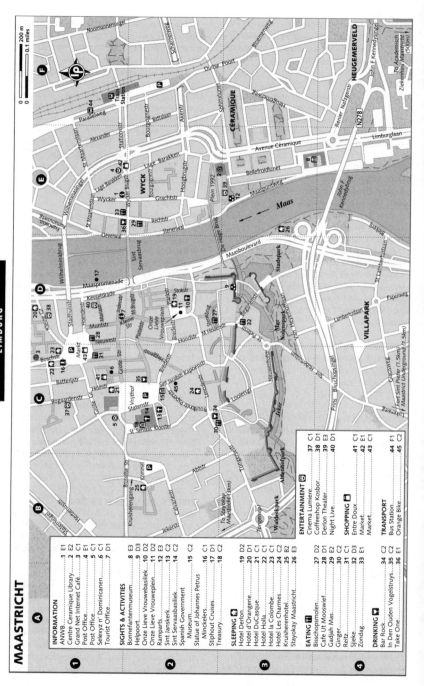

NOORD BRABANT & LIMBURG

MAASTRICHT

DARK AT THE END OF THE TUNNEL

The Romans developed the Sint Pietersberg tunnels by quarrying soft marlstone at a painstaking rate of just four blocks per day, creating an underground system that provided refuge during the numerous occasions when Maastricht found itself under attack.

The portion called the Northern Corridor System Tunnels is an amazing feat of pre-industrial engineering: at one stage there were 20,000 separate passages, adding up to a length of 200km and stretching past the Belgian border.

Walking through the tunnels is an eerie experience and you'll feel a deep chill, not only from the thought of ghosts but also because it's cold (9°C) and dark. People hiding down here during sieges would often die of exposure.

One of the most fascinating aspects of the tunnels is the graffiti from throughout the ages. You can see generations of drawings on the walls, everything from ancient Roman stick figures to wartime depictions of movie stars such as Bette Davis, to '70s hippie nudes (the tunnels were barred from general access from the '80s on, before Dutch rappers could lay down some murals).

---

entrance has been drawing pilgrims for more than 300 years.

At the north end of the **Markt** is a **statue of Johannes Petrus Minckelers**, who holds a flaming rod – he's the chap who invented gaslight.

The busy pedestrian **Sint Servaasbrug** dates from the 13th-century and links Maastricht's centre with the Wyck district.

FORTIFICATIONS

At the end of Sint Bernardusstraat, the **Helpoort** is the oldest surviving town gate in the Netherlands (1229); this area is laced with old walls. The remains of 13th-century **ramparts** and fortifications are across the Maas in the Céramique district. Much of Maastricht is riddled with defensive tunnels dug into the soft sandstone over the centuries. The best place to see the tunnels is **Fort Sint Pieter** (adult/child €5/4), which dates to Roman times and has now been restored to its appearance in 1701. It's 2km south of Helpoort. This is a really beautiful area, pastoral despite the ominous walls – the fort is an arresting sight looming over the charming hillside – and it's a fine walk from town.

The Romans built the Northern Corridor System Tunnels (see the boxed text, above) throughout the hills over a period of 2000 years; at one stage, the tunnels extended under the Netherlands–Belgium border.

Maastricht Underground (☎ 325 21 21; www .maastrichtunderground.nl; adult/child €5/4; ☾ hours vary), which also operates the fort, runs spooky, thrilling, amusing and fascinating tours throughout the year on a constantly shifting schedule. At least one a day is often in English; the entrance is near Fort Sint Pieter.

Tours

The tourist office can arrange walking tours and cycling expeditions.

Stiphout Cruises (☎ 351 53 00; www.stiphout.nl; Maaspromenade 58; adult/child from €8/4.20; ☾ daily Apr-Oct, Sat & Sun Nov-Dec) runs a variety of boat cruises on the Maas.

Festivals & Events

Three events stand out on the busy Maastricht calendar:

European Fine Art Foundation Show (TEFAF; www .tefaf.com) Europe's largest annual art show is held in mid-March. More than 200 exhibitors converge on Maastricht offering masterpieces to those with a few million euros to spare. The event is open to the public.

Carnaval (www.carnavalinmaastricht.nl) Celebrated with gusto in Maastricht to match Venice (Italy), Cologne (Germany) and Sitges (Spain). The orgy of partying and carousing begins the Friday before Shrove Tuesday and lasts until the last person collapses sometime on Wednesday. *Everything* stops for *carnaval*.

Preuvenemint (www.preuvenemint.nl) Each year Maastricht hosts this foodie festival, which takes over the Vrijhof for four days around the last weekend in August. It's touted as the 'largest open-air restaurant in the world'.

Sleeping

Maastricht is a popular weekend destination throughout the year, so reservations are a must. The tourist office has a list of private rooms travellers can book.

BUDGET

Stayokay Maastricht (☎ 750 17 90; www.stayokay.com /maastricht; Maasboulevard 101; dm from €20, r from €55; 🖳) A stunner of a hostel with a large terrace right on the Maas. Choose from one of the 199 beds in dorms and private rooms. It's just south of the centre in a park.

Hotel Holla (☎ 321 35 23; www.hotelholla.nl; Boschstraat 104-106; r €50-90; 💻 🛜) In an elegant 1855 building, the 24 rooms here are freshly decorated and feature stylish linens. Adding to the fine value is the ground-floor cafe, which serves excellent coffee in smart surrounds.

Hotel la Colombe (☎ 321 57 74; www.hotellacolombe .nl; Markt 30; r €65-90) On the Markt in a simple, white building, the Colombe has rooms that are equally unadorned, but all have a TV and bathroom. This unassuming but friendly hotel has a decent cafe on the Markt and it rents out scooters and bikes.

MIDRANGE

Hotel DuCasque (☎ 321 43 43; www.amrathhotels .com; Helmstraat 14; r €80-160; 🛜) There's an air of faded art-deco intrigue in this 45-room hotel close to the shopping district and the Vrijthof. An elevator saves you from the stairs; some rooms on the 4th floor have terraces with views over the town.

Hotel d'Orangerie (☎ 326 11 11; www.hotel -orangerie.nl; Kleine Gracht 4; r €85-160; 🛜) There's a gracious elegance about this hotel in a stately building dating back to 1752. The welcome is genuine. The 22 rooms come in various levels of ornate decor. Take breakfast in the airy courtyard.

Hotel Les Charmes (☎ 321 74 00; www.charmes.nl; Lenculenstraat 18; r €110-160; 🛜) On a very attractive 18th-century street, two 1725 townhouses have been restored to their original glory. The 15 rooms (some on high floors reached only by stairs) are spacious and have sitting areas. The vine-covered inner garden offers green refuge.

TOP END

Kruiseherenhotel (☎ 329 20 20; www.chateauhotels.nl; Kruiserengang 19-23; r from €190; 🍴 💻) This superb option is housed inside the former Crutched Friar monastery complex that dates from 1483. Where there are modern touches, such as moulded furniture and padded walls, they accent the historical surrounds. The 60 sumptuous rooms feature high-speed internet and wall-length paintings.

Hotel Derlon (☎ 321 67 70; www.derlon.com; Onze Lieve Vrouweplein 6; r from €200; 🍴 💻 🛜) The sleekly luxurious and smartly suave Derlon boasts 48 rooms with designer fittings. The breakfast room in the basement is built around

Roman ruins. A pampering and indulgent experience.

Eating

Maastricht has more than its share of excellent places to eat at every price range. Clusters of good places worth browsing include the eastern end of Tongersestraat, Rechtstraat, the little streets near the walls and up around the Vrijthof.

RESTAURANTS

Reitz (☎ 321 57 06; Markt 75; frites €2) Join the queue for this iconic French-fries counter, which has been serving perfectly scrumptious *frites* under the classic neon sign for decades.

Bisschopsmolen (☎ 327 06 13; Stenebrug 1-3; meals €4-10; 🕘 9.30am-6pm Tue-Sat, 11am-5pm Sun) How cool is this? A working water wheel powers a vintage flour mill that supplies an adjoining bakery. The loaves come in many forms and are joined by other tasty treats (direct from the ovens that are on view out the back). The cafe has sandwiches and other house-made creations. Finally, you can self-tour the mill and see how flour's been made for eons.

Ginger (☎ 326 00 22; Tongersestraat 7; mains €10-20; 🕘 lunch & dinner) As carefully arranged as a bento box, Ginger takes inspiration from Thailand to Japan, China to Bali. The menu bursts with goodness and authentic Asian flavours – hence the name.

ourpick **Sjieke** (☎ 380 49 59; St Pieterstraat 13; meals €12-25; 🕘 5-11pm) This cosy corner spot turns out traditional Dutch fare, including hearty stews, roasts, fresh fish and more, with colour and flair. In summer there's a mess of tables in the park across the street. Have a red beer and pick out the stars through the trees. Glorious.

Gadjah Mas (☎ 321 15 68; Rechtstraat 42; mains €17-25; 🕘 dinner) The Rechtstraat, east of the river, is one of the best streets for dining in Maastricht. This small, lovely Indonesian bistro has *rijsttafels* (array of spicy dishes served with rice) that break with the clichéd norm. Flavours are bright and spices are not skimped on.

CAFES

Onze Lieve Vrouweplein is easily the best place for a cafe interlude. Settle back under the trees at one of many cafes that blend together into one.

Cafe Ut Mooswief (☎ 325 40 44; Markt 66; mains €6-15) Closest to the daily market stalls on the Markt, this otherwise unassuming cafe stands out from the plethora of competition first by giving you ultracomfy seats for your bum while providing superb fare for your tum. Among the Dutch classics, the pea soup is a standout.

Zondag (☎ 321 93 00; www.cafezondag.nl; Wycker Brugstraat 42) Funky mellow tunes through the day segue to jazzier, harder sounds at night. It's light, airy, beautifully tiled and the food couldn't be fresher. Choose from a huge range of sandwiches and baked goods by day. The creative drinks list is long.

Drinking

our pick Take One (☎ 321 64 23; www.takeonebiercafe.nl, in Dutch; Rechtstraat 28) Cramped and narrow from the outside, this 1930s' tavern has well over 100 beers from the most obscure parts of the Benelux. It's run by a husband-and-wife team who help you select the beer most appropriate to your taste. The Bink Blonde is sweet, tangy and very good.

In Den Ouden Vogelstruys (☎ 321 48 88; www.vogelstruys.nl; Vrijthof 15) Overlooking the cathedral across the square, this antique bar is a little bit naughty and a little bit nice. The entrance has big, old, heavy, red curtains, while inside the bar there are photos of big, old, heavy men on the wall, big, old, heavy light fittings, and big, old, heavy Trappist beer. (But the local cheese is light and creamy…)

Bar Rock (☎ 06 1514 1235; www.barrock.nl; Tongersestraat 27; ☽ 7pm-2am Thu-Tue) A fun joint with old LPs hanging in the window (that would be large vinyl records, not guidebooks…). You never know what you'll hear at night as the payment policy for bands is a crate of beer. There's also darts and a classic merry Dutch drinking vibe.

Entertainment

Cinema Lumiere (☎ 321 40 80; www.lumiere.nl; Bogaardenstraat 40B) Offbeat and classic films are screened at a cinema located on a street with a name appropriate for films.

Coffeeshop Kosbor (☎ 325 35 49; Kleine Gracht 3; ☽ 11am-midnight) Cheery place known for its good assortment of hash and pot.

Derlon Theater (☎ 350 30 50; www.derlontheater.nl; Plein 1992) Near the library, Derlon has drama and music. The cafe has fine river views from the terrace.

Night Live (☎ 362 82 78; Kesselskade 43; ☽ 11pm-4am Thu-Sat) A nightclub in an old church that opens late at weekends; eclectic musical policy, quick getaway by train.

Shopping

Markets (☽ 8am-1pm) are held on the Markt on Wednesday and Friday. A totally **organic market** (☽ Thu) fills the median of Stationsstraat. A used-everything market fills the same spot Saturday.

The streets leading off Grote Straat are lined with mainstream stores. There's a clutch of luxury retailers around the **Entre Doux** (Helmstraat 3) shopping arcade. Stokstraat has galleries, boutiques and art stores, although you can find surprises all along the little streets in and around the old walls, such as St Pieterstraat.

Across the river, Rechtstraat has the most compelling mix of cafes and shops in the city. Happy browsing!

Getting There & Away
BICYCLE
See p280 for bike rentals. Maastricht is one long ride from the rest of the Netherlands. National bike route LF3 starts here and heads 220km north to Arnhem (where it continues to the north coast), staying east towards Germany much of the way. The initial route along the banks of the Maas is rather pretty, with good vistas as you swing through the innumerable turns.

LF7 runs along waterways northwest all the way to Alkmaar (350km) via Amsterdam. On this route the first major city you reach that's of interest to travellers is Den Bosch (140km northwest).

Both LF3 and LF7 intersect more than a dozen national routes over their course. For an international trip, take LF6 due east 35km to Vaals on the border with Germany. The fun of Aachen is just 5km further on.

BUS
The bus station is to the right as you exit the train station. Eurolines has one bus a day to/from Brussels. Interliner has hourly buses to/from Aachen.

TRAIN
The classic old train station has full services. Lockers are in an alcove off the soaring main hall. Sample train fares and schedules:

Destination	Price (€)	Duration (min)	Frequency (per hr)
Amsterdam	26.60	150	2
Den Bosch	18.80	85	2
Utrecht	23.50	120	2

NOORD BRABANT & LIMBURG

There is an hourly international service to Liege (30 minutes), from where you can catch fast trains to Brussels, Paris and Cologne.

Getting Around

There is car and motorcycle parking in massive underground lots by the river.

The bicycle shop is in a separate building to the left as you exit the station. **Orange Bike** (☎ 311 36 13; www.orangebike.nl; Sint Jacobstraat 4; per day from €10; ☺ 9am-6pm) offers rentals and repairs.

AROUND MAASTRICHT

The hills and forests of southern Limburg make for excellent hiking and biking. The **Drielandenpunt** (the convergence of the Netherlands, Belgium and Germany) is on the highest hill in the country (323m), in Vaals, 26km southeast of Maastricht. It's an excellent driving or biking destination.

Valkenburg

☎ 043 / pop 12,500

This small town in the hills east of Maastricht has possibly the most overcommercialised centre in the Netherlands, attracting hordes of tour buses. But away from the town are excellent trails and cycle paths through the nearby forests.

The **tourist office** (☎ 0900 555 97 98; www.vvvzuid limburg.nl; Th Dorrenplein 5; ☺ 9am-5pm Mon-Sat, 10am-2pm Sun) has a huge selection of maps of the area and can assist with bicycle hire. You might start at the over-restored **castle** (adult/child €3.50/2.50; ☺ 10am-5pm Apr-Oct) above town from where trails radiate out through the countryside. In keeping with the local vibe it has a year-round Christmas market.

ASP Adventure (☎ 604 06 75; www.aspadventure.nl) gives 90-minute guided tours (from €24) of the networks of caves that riddle the soft sandstone of the hills. There are many options, including riding bikes underground.

Valkenburg is easily reached from Maastricht by train (€2.60, 12 minutes, four per hour). The N590 from Maastricht (10km) has

bike paths, however follow the trails through the hills to the north for more fun.

Netherlands American Cemetery & Memorial

In Margraten, 10km southeast of Maastricht, the **Netherlands American Cemetery & Memorial** (☺ sunrise-sunset) is dedicated to US soldiers who died in 'Operation Market Garden' and the general Allied push to liberate the Dutch. It's a sombre memorial with row after row of silent white gravestones – a stark but necessary testament to the futility of war.

Veolia bus 50 runs from Maastricht's train station (20 minutes, four times per hour).

NORTH LIMBURG

Clinging to the Maas river, the northern half of Limburg, barely 30km across at its widest point, is a no-nonsense place of industry and agriculture. **Venlo**, the major town, has a small historic quarter near the train station. Venlo, along with **Thorn** and **Roermond**, is worth a quick look if you are changing trains for the hourly service to Cologne.

Nationaal Oorlogs- en Verzetsmuseum

Overloon, a tiny town on the border with Noord Brabant, was the scene of fierce battles between the Americans, British and the Germans as part of 'Operation Market Garden' in 1944. The heart of the battlefield is now the site of the sober **Nationaal Oorlogs-en Verzetsmuseum** (National War & Resistance Museum; ☎ 0478-64 18 20; www.oorlogsmuseum-overloon.nl; Museumpark 1; adult/child €13/8; ☺ 10am-5pm), a thoughtful place that examines the role of the Netherlands in WWII and the fate of Dutch resistance fighters.

To reach the museum take the half-hourly train to Venray from either Roermond (€7.70, 40 minutes) or Nijmegen (€6.60, 35 minutes). Then take a taxi to the museum, 7km from the station (about €10). Make arrangements with the driver for your return. National bike route LF3 passes by 6km to the east.

Directory

CONTENTS

ACCOMMODATION

The country's wealth of hotels, home stays and hostels provides any traveller – whether they be backpacker or five-star aficionado – with plenty of choice. Hotels and B&Bs are the mainstay of accommodation in the country

---

BOOK YOUR STAY ONLINE

For more accommodation reviews and recommendations by Lonely Planet authors, check out the online booking service at www.lonelyplanet.com/hotels. You'll find the true, insider low-down on the best places to stay. Reviews are thorough and independent. Best of all, you can book online.

---

and, while most are fairly standard and highly functional, a few gems fly the boutique flag or are simply idiosyncratic.

Note that a good part of the country suffers from the 'Amsterdam effect': because transport is so efficient and the city is so popular, many visitors stay in the capital even if they're travelling further afield. Conversely, some savvy folk use easy-to-access charmers such as Haarlem or Delft as their base of operations, visiting the capital as a day – or night – trip (trains on key lines run all night).

B&Bs

Bed-and-breakfasts are an excellent way to meet the friendly locals face to face, and to see the weird, the wacky and the wonderful interior designs of the Dutch firsthand. Unfortunately, they're not abundant in cities, but the countryside is awash with them. Local tourist offices keep a list of B&Bs on file, where costs usually start from €25 per person.

Camping

The Dutch are avid campers, even within their own country. Campgrounds tend to be self-contained communities complete with shops, cafes, playgrounds and swimming pools. Lists of sites with ratings (one to five stars) are available from the ANWB (the Dutch automobile organisation; www.anwb .nl) and tourist offices. If you plan to do a lot of camping, pick up a copy of ANWB's yearly *Campinggids* (€9.95); it's in Dutch, but the listings are easy to follow.

A camp site, which costs anything between €10 and €20, covers two people and a small tent; a car is an extra €2 to €6. Caravans are popular – every one in 15 residents owns one – so there are oodles of hook-ups.

Simple bungalows or *trekkershutten* (hiker huts; from €32) are another option. A typical hiker hut has four bunks, cooking facilities and electricity, but you'll need to bring your own sleeping bags, dishes and utensils. Consult www.trekkershutten.nl.

Rough camping is illegal. To get away from it all, seek out *natuurkampeerterreinen* (nature campgrounds) attached to farms. You'll enjoy

PRACTICALITIES

■ The metric system is used for weights and measures.

■ Buy or watch videos on the PAL system.

■ Keep abreast of things back home in the *International Herald Tribune*, the *Guardian*, or the *Times*, or weeklies such as the *Economist*, *Newsweek* or *Time* on news-stands.

■ If you know a little Dutch, read up on the Netherlands' perspective on the news in *De Telegraaf*, *NRC Handelsblad*, *Het Parool* and *Het Financieele Dagblad*.

■ Read the latest gossip and a smattering of news, in Dutch, for free in *Spits*, *Metro* and *De Pers*, three daily rags available at train stations.

■ Find out what the Dutch are listening to on Noordzee FM (100.7FM), Radio 538 (102FM) and Sky Radio (101.2FM).

■ Listen to the BBC World Service at 648AM. Watch the BBC, CNN and other cable channels in most hotels.

■ Plug your hairdryer into a Continental two-pin adapter before you tap the electricity network (220V to 240V AC, 50Hz).

a simpler and less crowded existence than at the major campgrounds. Reserve through tourist offices or check information online at www.natuurkampeerterreinen.nl.

Hostels

The Dutch youth-hostel association **Stayokay** (www.stayokay.com) still uses the Hostelling International (HI) logo, but the hostels go under the name Stayokay. Most offer a good variety of rooms. Facilities tend to be impressive, with newly built hostels common. Some, like the Rotterdam Stayokay (p210), are in landmark buildings.

A youth-hostel card costs €15 at the hostels, or nonmembers can pay an extra €2.50 per night and thus become a member after six nights. HI members get discounts on international travel and pay less commission on money exchange at GWK offices. Members and nonmembers have the same privileges, and there are no age limits.

Almost all Stayokay hostels have rooms limited to one to eight people. Nightly rates normally range from €20 to €30 per person for dorm beds or from €60 for private rooms. Book ahead, especially in high season.

Amsterdam (p117) has scores of indie hostels. Some quiet, some shambolic, some party central.

Hotels

The Dutch hotel rating system goes up to five stars; accommodation with less than one star can call itself a *pension* or guesthouse

but not a hotel. The stars aren't very helpful because they measure the amenities and the number of rooms but not the quality of the rooms themselves. Hotels tend to be small, with fewer than 20 rooms.

Many establishments have steep stairs but no lifts, which can pose problems for the mobility-impaired (or those not relishing a six-flight mountain climb, as you'll find in Amsterdam). Having said that, most top-end and many midrange hotels do have lifts.

A number of tourist offices can book hotel rooms virtually anywhere in the country for a small fee (usually a few euros). GWK currency-exchange offices take hotel reservations, charging a small fee and 10% of the room charge in advance.

The usual online booking sites can be useful. But you may also find the local website www.hotels.nl often has the best selection and prices, especially for smaller properties not on the chain-dominated big sites. Another good choice for independent hotels is www.best2stay.nl.

Prices vary, but in cities you should expect to pay from €80 for a double room in a budget hotel, up to €160 in a midrange hotel and from €160 for the top end. Prices in Amsterdam may be higher but, conversely, competition also keeps them down.

When booking for two people, be clear whether you want two single (twin) beds or a double bed. And note: Dutch beds are often the softest in the world, ready to swallow the somnolent like a bowl of jelly.

Rental Accommodation
HOLIDAY RENTALS
Renting a flat for a few days can be a fun part of a trip. In Amsterdam it gets you a kitchen and other amenities that make coming 'home' after a hard day having fun that much nicer, while out in the countryside it can be like your own retreat. (And rentals are often priced very competitively with hotels, which give you much less.)

Two websites to check:

www.eurorelais.travel More than 1000 Dutch holiday homes, often near the beach.

www.vrbo.com (Vacation Rentals by Owner) Good for urban areas.

See p117 for more info on short-stay rentals in Amsterdam.

LONG-TERM ACCOMMODATION
Prices for furnished or unfurnished apartments in Amsterdam start at about €750 per month but can easily be triple that. Do take note that long- and short-term affordable housing is in short supply – everyone, including locals, laments the situation. Your best bet as an English-speaker is to check out www.craigslist.org's Amsterdam housing section, the classified ads on www.expatica.com, or to ask the local people you know to spread the word that you're on an apartment hunt.

If time is of the essence, try the following Amsterdam agents:

Amsterdam Apartment (☎ 020-668 26 54; www.amsterdamapartment.nl)

Apartment Services (☎ 020-672 18 40; www.apartmentservices.nl)

IDA Housing (☎ 020-624 83 01; www.idahousing.com)

ACTIVITIES
The most popular outdoor activities are linked to the defining characteristics of the Dutch landscape: flat land and water. There is no shortage of sports clubs and special-interest groups for your favourite pastime, as the Dutch have a penchant for organisation.

DUTCH WEBSITES IN ENGLISH

Many Dutch websites offer English as a language option. For those that don't, Google's translation service works like a charm: translate.google.com.

Boating
It seems as though everyone in the Netherlands is the proud owner of a boat. Stroll by the canals and lakes and you'll see all manner of water craft, some impossibly wacky, often decades old, lovingly maintained and enjoyed in weather fair or foul. Small canoes and sailboats can be hired on lakes throughout the country – the likes of Loosdrechtse Plassen (p179) in Utrecht province, Sneek (p231) in Friesland or the myriad small old waterside towns in Noord Holland such as Monnickendam (p148) make particularly good bases for such an activity.

Sailing on a traditional boat is an unforgettable experience. Named for the boats' ruddy sails, the 'brown fleet' of restored flat-bottomed vessels is a familiar sight on the vast IJsselmeer at weekends. The cheapest rental option are *botters*, old fishing boats with long, narrow leeboards and sleeping berths for up to eight passengers. Larger groups can go for converted freight barges known as *tjalks* (smacks), ancient pilot boats or massive clippers. You'll also find motorboats for gliding through the country canals.

Local tourist offices can be a good source for boat rentals. The **Royal Dutch Watersports Association** (☎ 030-656 65 50; www.watersportverbond.nl) provides advice on boating rules, and has links to relevant websites. ANWB stocks maps of the Netherlands' most popular waterways.

The following companies have typical rates, bearing in mind that everything is negotiable (after all, bargaining is a Dutch tradition):

Flevo Sailing (☎ 0320-26 03 24; www.flevosailing.nl; Oostvaardersdijk 59c, Lelystad) Has a fleet of four- to eight-passenger sailing yachts for rent.

Holiday Boatin Yachtcharter (☎ 0515-41 37 81; www.holidayboatin.nl, Sneek) Rents motorboats for puttering about on Friesland's myriad lakes and canals.

Holland Zeilcharters (see p148).

Hollands Glorie (☎ 0294-27 15 61; www.hollandsglorie.nl; Muiden) Has *tjalks* for rent from a day to a week. Boats depart from harbours around the country, including Amsterdam, Edam, Hoorn, Medemblik and Muiden.

Top of Holland Yacht Charter (www.topofholland.com) Represents companies in Friesland, the IJsselmeer region and Zuid Holland, renting out everything from small sailboats to large cabin cruisers.

Cycling
Cycling is a way of life in the Netherlands and a good basis for a holiday. The country offers easy cycling terrain with many

designated paths, including loads of off-road routes through pastures and woodland. The infrastructure gives priority to bikes over other forms of transportation, and car drivers often yield to cyclists even when the latter are pushing their luck. For more, see p67.

Skating

Ice skating was part of the Dutch psyche long before scarfed figures appeared in Golden Age winterscapes. The first skates were made from cow shanks and ribs, had hand-drilled holes and were tied to the feet. When canals and ponds freeze over, everyone takes to the ice. When a cold snap in 2009 froze canals in the south for the first time in years, it was a de facto regional holiday.

The famous Elfstedentocht (Eleven Cities Race, p234) takes place in Friesland when the canals freeze (the last time was in 1997), and even Crown Prince Willem-Alexander took part in 1986, to be greeted by Queen Beatrix at the finish line. Not surprisingly, the Dutch have had plenty of ice-skating champions.

The Netherlands is practically tailor-made for in-line skating. City parks are breeding grounds for the latest flashy manoeuvres on half-pipes, but the popularity of skating is such that day trips have been mapped throughout the country. The Achterhoek region (the eastern part of Gelderland) combines quiet conditions with a nice variety of landscapes; the Graafschap area in the northwest has seven signposted skating routes with a total length of 200km. The list of places to skate is endless – any dyke top can be perfect for a spin. See **Skatebond Nederland** (Dutch Skating Club; www.skatebond.nl) for more info.

Walking

The Dutch are avid walkers and hikers – in almost any weather and surroundings. The Vierdaagse (Four Days; p260) is the world's largest walking event and attracts more than 40,000 enthusiasts every July.

For salt breezes you might head for the coasts of Friesland, Zeeland or the coastal towns along the IJsselmeer. National parks such as Hoge Veluwe, Weerribben and Biesbosch offer a varied backdrop ranging from bogs to dunes to forest. The pretty, undulating knolls of Limburg can be a welcome change after the flatlands in the rest of the country.

Or for something completely different, you can go walking out across the ocean – well tidal mudflats really (see the boxed text, p246).

Nederlandse Wandelsportbond (Netherlands Hiking Club; ☎ 030-231 94 58; www.nwb-wandelen.nl) is a goldmine of information about the nicest paths and events. Branches of the ANWB motoring club, tourist offices and bookshops have more maps and brochures than you can shake a walking stick at.

Watersports

Abundant water and near-constant breezes make a perfect combination for windsurfing. Most developed beaches along the coast of the North Sea, the IJsselmeer and the Wadden Islands have places that rent windsurfing boards (look for *surfplanken*). In winter the frozen lakes become racecourses for ice-surfing, with breakneck speeds of 100km per hour or more. Websites such as **Windlords** (www .windlords.com/nl) list the most popular locations to windsurf around the country. You can also enquire at any tourist office.

Wherever there's windsurfing, kite-surfing won't be far away. Harder to master but arguably more exhilarating, this relatively new pastime is catching on quickly with lovers of wind and water. If you're interested in giving it a try or want to hone your skills while on holiday, check out www.kitesurf.pagina.nl; it's in Dutch, but the lists of Dutch kite-surfing websites are easy to navigate.

All that placid water sitting around in canals is perfect for paddling. Opportunities abound, and a few places where you can easily rent canoes and kayaks include Enkhuizen (p158) in Noord Holland, the water-logged bogs of Weerribben National Park (p251) in Overijssel, the urban canals of Leiden (p187) and beautiful Biesbosch National Park (p218) near Dordrecht.

The surrounding salt water is also good for paddling. The Frisian Islands such as Vlieland (p235) have places you can rent sea kayaks.

BUSINESS HOURS

As a general rule, opening hours occur as follows:

Banks & Government Offices Open 9.30am to 4pm Monday to Friday.

Bars & Cafes Open 11am to 1am, although some stay open longer at weekends and others won't open for service till the late afternoon.

Businesses Hours are 8.30am to 5pm Monday to Friday.

Clubs Hours vary, but in general clubs open 10pm to 4am Friday and Saturday; some also open on Wednesday, Thursday and Sunday.

Post offices Open 9am to 6pm Monday to Friday.
Restaurants Open 10am or 11am to 10pm, with a break in the afternoon from 3pm to 6pm.
Shops Open noon to 6pm Monday, and 8.30am or 9am to 6pm Tuesday to Saturday. Most towns have *koopavond* (evening shopping), when stores stay open till 9pm on Thursday or Friday. Bigger supermarkets in cities stay open until 8pm. Sunday shopping is becoming more common; large stores are often open from noon to 5pm.

Most museums are closed on Monday.

We only list business hours in this book when they differ from the standard ones outlined above.

CHILDREN

Attitudes to children in the Netherlands are very positive and there is a lot to keep kids occupied. Dutch children tend to be spontaneous and confident, thanks to a relaxed approach to parenting.

Lonely Planet's *Travel with Children* by Brigitte Barta et al is worth reading if you're unsure about travelling with kids.

Practicalities

A few hotels have a no-children policy – check when you book. Most restaurants have high chairs and children's menus. Facilities for changing nappies, however, are limited to the big department stores, major museums and train stations, and you'll pay to use them. Breastfeeding is generally OK in public if done discreetly. Kids are allowed in pubs but aren't supposed to drink until they're 16. Many museums have joined a trend to make admission free for children.

Children aged under four travel free on trains if they don't take up a seat. There's a Railrunner fare (€2) for kids aged four to 11.

Sights & Activities

Dutch museums and attractions do a good job of engaging youngsters. Many have excellent exhibits geared towards younger visitors.

Zaanse Schans (p146) near Amsterdam is a great afternoon out, with its preserved windmill village, traditional Dutch houses, cheese farm and craft centre. Further north, the island of Texel has the Ecomare (p161), with oodles of birds and seals.

A child's fantasies can run wild at Efteling amusement park (p272), especially in the maze or Fairy Tale Forest.

For more ideas, see p22.

CLIMATE CHARTS

Unlike the climate suggested by 17th-century landscapes depicting half-frozen skaters, the Netherlands has a temperate maritime climate with cool winters and mild summers.

Rain is spread evenly over the year, often in the form of endless drizzle, though the statisticians tell us that most of it falls at night (yeah, right). It's best to bring a foul-weather jacket in case of the occasional cold snap or rain storm. Very few hotels have air-conditioning, although higher temperatures due to global warming are slowly forcing a change. December to February is the coldest period, with occasional slushy snow and temperatures around freezing. It rarely freezes hard enough to allow skating on the canals.

For more detailed climate information, see p13.

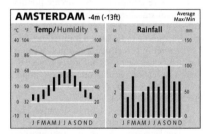

COURSES
Language

Dutch is a close relative of English, but that doesn't make it easy to learn. Standard courses take months, and intensive courses last several weeks. Make enquiries well in advance.

Here are some options for studying the Dutch language in all its guttural glory:

Amsterdam Maastricht Summer University (Map p91; ☎ 620 02 25; www.amsu.edu; Keizersgracht 324) Based in the Felix Meritis building.

British Language Training Centre (Map pp88-9; ☎ 622 36 34; www.bltc.nl; Nieuwezijds Voorburgwal 328e) Offers Dutch and English courses and has a good reputation.

Volksuniversiteit Amsterdam (☎ 626 16 26; www .volksuniversiteitamsterdam.nl; Rapenburgerstraat 73) Well-regarded day and evening courses that don't cost a fortune.

CUSTOMS REGULATIONS

For visitors from EU countries, limits only apply for excessive amounts. See www .douane.nl for details.

Residents of non-EU countries are limited to the following:

DIRECTORY

Coffee 500g of coffee, or 200g of coffee extracts or coffee essences.
Perfume 50g of perfume and 0.25L of eau de toilette.
Tea 100g of tea, or 40g of tea extracts or tea essences.
Tobacco 200 cigarettes or 250g of tobacco (shag or pipe tobacco) or 100 cigarillos or 50 cigars.
Wine 1L spirits, wine or beer

Bringing meat or meat products, flowers, fruit, plants and protected species to the Netherlands is illegal. Tobacco and alcohol may only be imported by people aged 17 and over.

DANGERS & ANNOYANCES

Much of the Netherlands is utterly safe, but caution is advised in the larger cities. Amsterdam (see p84) and Rotterdam require a modicum of big-city street sense but nothing you wouldn't normally do at home.

Cars with foreign registration are popular targets for smash-and-grab theft. Don't leave things in the car: remove registration and ID papers and the radio/stereo if possible.

If something is stolen, get a police report for insurance purposes but don't expect the police to retrieve your property or to apprehend the thief – put the matter down to experience. *Always* lock your bike.

Mosquitoes can be a pain in summer. They breed in stagnant parts of the canals and in water under houses. In parts of the country near lakes or canals people sleep under netting.

Bicycles can be quite a challenge to pedestrians. Remember when crossing the street to look for speeding bikes as well as cars; straying into a bike lane without looking both ways is a no-no.

Intensive urban development means there's often little grass for dog poo, and you may spend more time watching the pavement than the sights.

DISCOUNT CARDS

Teachers, professional artists, museum conservators and certain categories of students may get discounts at a few museums or even be admitted free – it can depend on the person behind the counter. Bring proof of affiliation such as the International Teacher Identity Card (ITIC). People over 65 (and their partners over 60) receive discounts on public transport, museum entry fees, concerts and more. You could try flashing your home-country senior card, but you might have to show your passport too.

Many cities (eg Den Haag and Rotterdam) offer discount card schemes that are good for discounts on museums, attractions and local transport. Ask at tourist offices.

Other discount cards:
Cultureel Jongeren Paspoort (Cultural Youth Passport, Euro<26 Card; www.cjp.nl; €15) Big discounts to museums and cultural events nationwide for people under 30 years.
Hostelling International Card Useful at the official youth hostels (called Stayokay in the Netherlands); provides a €2.50 per night discount.
I Amsterdam Card (per 24/36/72hr €38/48/58) Available at VVV offices and some hotels. Provides admission to many museums, canal boat trips, and discounts and freebies at shops, attractions and restaurants. Also includes a GVB transit pass.
International Student Identity Card (ISIC; www.isic .org) Will get some admission discounts and might pay for itself through discounted air and ferry tickets. The same applies to hostel cards.
Museumkaart (Museum Card; over 25/13-25yr/under 13 €35/17.50/14.95, plus €4.95 for first-time registrants) Free entry to some 400 museums all over the country for one year. Buy one at the ticket counter before you hit an exhibition.

EMBASSIES & CONSULATES

In Amsterdam:
France (Map pp92–3; ☎ 530 69 69; www.ambafrance .nl; Vijzelgracht 2)
Germany (Map pp92–3; ☎ 574 77 00; Honthorststraat 36-8)
UK (Map pp86-7; ☎ 676 43 43; www.britain.nl; Koningslaan 44)
USA (Map pp92–3; ☎ 575 53 30; http://thehague.us embassy.gov; Museumplein 19)

In Den Haag:
Australia (Map p190; ☎ 070-310 82 00; www.nether lands.embassy.gov.au; Carnegielaan 4)
Belgium (Map p192; ☎ 312 34 56; www.diplomatie .be/thehague; Alexanderveld 97)
Canada (Map p192; ☎ 070-311 16 00; www.nether lands.gc.ca; Sophialaan 7)
France (Map p192; ☎ 312 58 00; www.ambafrance.nl; Smidsplein 1)
Ireland (Map p192; ☎ 070-363 09 93; www.irish embassy.nl; Dr Kuyperstraat 9)
New Zealand (Map p190; ☎ 070-346 93 24; www .nzembassy.com; Eisenhowerlaan 77)
UK (Map p192; ☎ 070-427 04 27; www.britain.nl; Lange Voorhout 10)
USA (Map p192; ☎ 070-310 22 09; http://thehague .usembassy.gov; Lange Voorhout 102)

FESTIVALS & EVENTS

Following are the cream of the largest and most important events in the country – they may well be reason for a special trip. More goings-on are listed in destination chapters.

February/March

Carnaval Weekend before Shrove Tuesday. Celebrations with gusto that would do Rio de Janeiro or New Orleans proud, mostly in the Catholic provinces of Noord Brabant, Gelderland and Limburg. Maastricht's party (p277) means days of uninhibited drinking, dancing and street music.

March

European Fine Art Foundation Show (TEFAF) For 10 days in the first half of March in Maastricht (p277). Europe's largest art show is your chance to pick up a Monet, or at least do some serious browsing.

April

Koninginnedag (Queen's Day) On 30 April. Marked throughout the country with the wearing of orange, drinking and flea-market activity. Processions, dances and live music. For more, see the boxed text, p116.

May

Herdenkingsdag & Bevrijdingsdag (Remembrance Day & Liberation Day) On 4 and 5 May. The fallen from WWII are honoured in an Amsterdam ceremony (p115), followed by live music, debate and a market the following day.

Nationale Molendag (National Mill Day; www.nationalemolenengemalendag.nl) Second Saturday in May. About 600 working windmills (p215) throw open their doors to visitors. Look for blue pennants.

June

Holland Festival (www.hollandfestival.nl) Virtually all month. The country's biggest extravaganza for theatre, dance, film and pop music.

De Parade (www.deparade.nl) Mid-June to August. Nationwide inverse-circus tour, where the audience is in the ring while all manner of music, theatre, film and variety performances go on around them.

Oerol (www.oerol.nl) Latter half of June. Outdoor performance festival on Terschelling is revered nationwide as a perfect excuse for going to sea (p236).

Parkpop (www.parkpop.nl) Late June. Some 350,000 ravers descend on Den Haag (p194).

July

North Sea Jazz Festival (www.northseajazz.nl) Mid-July, in Rotterdam (p210). World's largest jazz festival; attracts big names from around the planet, and even bigger crowds.

Dance Valley (www.dancevalley.nl) Mid-July. This outdoor dance technothon draws more than 100 DJs and bands performing to fields of 40,000 or more in Spaarnwoude near Amsterdam.

Vierdaagse (Four Days; www.4daagse.nl) Late July. Four-day, 120km- to 200km-long march held around Nijmegen (p260).

August

Amsterdam Pride Festival First Saturday in August. The only water-borne gay parade in the world, with lots of pride on show on the outlandish floats (see the boxed text, p118).

Dance Parade (www.fitforfreedanceparade.nl) Early August. Turns Rotterdam (p210) into one big open-air club catering to a crowd of around 350,000 people.

Noorderzon (www.noorderzon.nl) Mid-August. Eleven-day arts festival in Groningen (p243) that is huge fun.

Uitmarkt (www.uitmarkt.nl) Late August. The reopening of Amsterdam's cultural season, with three days of free concerts and information booths around the Eastern Docklands.

Lowlands (www.lowlands.nl) Mid-August, in Biddinghuizen (Flevoland). Alternative music and cultural megabash, with campgrounds for the masses.

November

Sinterklaas Intocht Mid-November. Every year the Dutch Santa Claus arrives at a different port 'from Spain' with his staff and Black Pete helpers.

December

Sinterklaas On 5 December. Families exchange small gifts ahead of religious celebrations for Christmas.

FOOD

Prices tend to be high by European standards. As a general rule, snacks and takeaway items cost about €3 to €8, while a three-course sit-down meal at a typical restaurant or cafe will run from €15 to €35. In cities in this book where Eating listings are broken down by price, the following ranges apply for a meal (one or two courses, without drinks):

Budget under €15
Midrange €15-35
Top End over €35

See p47 for more details.

GAY & LESBIAN TRAVELLERS

The best national source of information is **COC** (www.coc.nl). It has branches throughout the country that are happy to offer advice to newcomers.

Partisan estimates put the proportion of gay and lesbian people in Amsterdam at 20% to 30%. This is probably an exaggeration, but Amsterdam is certainly one of the gay capitals of Europe. Mainstream attitudes have always been reasonably tolerant, but it wasn't until the early 1970s that the age of consent for gay sex was lowered to 16. It's now illegal to discriminate against job-seekers on the basis of sexual orientation. In 2001, the Netherlands became the first country to legalise same-sex marriage.

Few countries are as gay-friendly. The government has long subsidised COC, the police advertise in the gay media for applicants, and homosexuals are admitted to the armed forces on an equal footing (in 2009 it was decided that members of the military could march in gay-pride parades in uniform).

In towns outside Amsterdam, however, gay and lesbian bars and clubs often operate behind dark windows. Rotterdam is an exception, as are the university towns with large gay and lesbian populations.

HOLIDAYS
Public Holidays
People take public holidays seriously. Most museums adopt Sunday hours on the days below (except Christmas and New Year) even if they fall on a day when the place would otherwise be closed, such as Monday. Many people treat Remembrance Day (4 May) as a day off.

Carnaval is celebrated with vigour in the Catholic south. Huge lager-fed parties are thrown in the run-up to Shrove Tuesday and little work gets done.

The holidays:

Nieuwjaarsdag (New Year's Day) Parties and fireworks galore.
Goede Vrijdag Good Friday
Eerste Paasdag Easter Sunday
Tweede Paasdag Easter Monday
Koninginnedag (Queen's Day) 30 April
Bevrijdingsdag (Liberation Day) 5 May. This isn't a universal holiday: government workers have the day off, but almost everyone else has to work.
Hemelvaartsdag (Ascension Day) Fortieth day after Easter Sunday.
Eerste Pinksterdag (Whit Sunday; Pentecost) Fiftieth day after Easter Sunday.
Tweede Pinksterdag (Whit Monday) Fiftieth day after Easter Monday.
Eerste Kerstdag (Christmas Day) 25 December
Tweede Kerstdag (Boxing Day) 26 December

School Holidays
School holidays are staggered across three regions (north, central and south) to relieve congestion on the roads and rails. Generally the holidays are scheduled as follows:
Spring holiday Two weeks in mid-February, also known as 'crocus' holiday.
May holiday First week of the month.
Summer holiday July, August and sometimes the first few days of September.
Autumn holiday Second half of October.
Christmas holiday Two weeks through to the first full week of January.

INSURANCE
Travel insurance is a good idea if your policies at home won't cover you in the Netherlands. Although medical or dental costs might already be covered through reciprocal healthcare arrangements, you'll still need cover for theft or loss, and for unexpected changes to travel arrangements (ticket cancellation etc). Check what's already covered by your local insurance policies or credit cards.

Also see the Insurance sections of the Health chapter (p306) and the Transport chapter (p301).

INTERNET ACCESS
Wi-fi is common in hotels and can be found for free in many cafes, some tourist offices and other public places. Open your wireless device and you'll often find paid wi-fi access from KPN (www.kpn.com), the national phone company, and other providers such as T-Mobile (www.t-mobile.nl). Costs can be extortionate: upwards of €16 for a day pass.

Internet cafes have become less common, although storefronts selling cheap phone cards with a few slow terminals can be found near train stations in larger towns. Many libraries, tourist offices, coffeeshops and hotels provide internet terminals (sometimes free) with very fast connections. Expect to pay anything from €2 to €4 per hour.

If you have a G3 phone that works in the Netherlands, you can surf with that, although beware of very high roaming charges.

LEGAL MATTERS
The Dutch police (politie) are a pretty relaxed lot and helpful to travellers. You're unlikely to incite their ire unless you do something instinctively wrong – like chucking litter or smoking a joint under their noses.

Officers can hold you up to six hours for questioning and another six if they can't establish your identity. If the matter's serious, you can be detained for 24 hours. You won't have the right to a phone call, but they'll notify your embassy or consulate. Relax – you're presumed innocent until proven guilty.

Anyone over 14 years of age is required by law to carry ID. Foreigners should carry their passport or a photocopy of the relevant data pages; a driving licence isn't sufficient.

You can drink beer and wine from age 16, and spirits from age 18, although bars and cafes are pretty lenient when it comes to proof of age. Coffeeshops require visitors to be 18 or even 21 to enter and consume soft drugs. The legal driving age is 18.

Drugs

Contrary to what you may have heard, marijuana is illegal. The confusion arises because the authorities distinguish between 'soft' drugs (eg cannabis) and addictive 'hard' drugs such as heroin, crack or cocaine. Possession of soft drugs up to 5g is tolerated, but larger amounts make you a 'dealer' and subject to prosecution. However, if you're caught with, say, 10g, you'll probably only receive a fine.

The key term is *gedogen*. This concept means that officials condemn the action but look the other way if common sense dictates. Hard drugs are treated as a serious crime, but under the unique Dutch drug policy the authorities tend to treat genuine, registered addicts as medical cases rather than hardened criminals.

These tolerant policies attract many drug tourists; drugs are cheaper, more readily available and generally of better quality in the Netherlands than elsewhere. The country has become a major exporter of high-grade marijuana (grown locally) and is the European centre for the production of ecstasy. However the days of tolerance are ending.

WARNING

Never buy drugs on the street: you'll get ripped off or mugged.

Don't light up in view of the police, or in an establishment without checking that it's OK to do so. The Dutch detest tourists who think they can just smoke dope anywhere.

Claiming concerns about gangs and crime, Amsterdam has said it may very well close half of its coffeeshops as licences come up for renewal. Rotterdam and other cities have also announced cutbacks. Border towns such as Roosendaal and Bergen op Zoom have banned coffeeshops from selling marijuana, saying that the streets are clogged with French and Belgians looking to get high on weekends.

There are also proposals to make coffeeshops private clubs or restrict entry to only Dutch citizens – who are a minority of customers overall. No matter how things develop, the days of a Dutch holiday spent high in coffeeshops may be ending.

In 2008 'smartshops', which sell magic mushrooms, had to contend with various government bans and closures.

For more about soft drugs, see the boxed text, p37.

Prostitution

Prostitution is legal in the Netherlands – based on the view that its practitioners are victims rather than criminals. The industry is protected by law, and prostitutes pay tax and even have their own lobby group. Much of this open policy stems from a desire to undermine the role of pimps and the underworld in the sex industry, although this has had limited success: Amsterdam is reducing the amount of legal prostitution (p99). The majority of prostitutes are from the Third World and Eastern Europe. Violent pimps and crime gangs are active and human trafficking is a problem.

In Amsterdam's Red Light District you have little to fear as the streets are well-policed, but the back alleys are more dubious. This also goes for other Dutch cities such as Rotterdam and Den Haag. Even towns such as Leiden and Groningen have red-light areas plopped down amid otherwise quiet streets. For more, see p98.

MAPS

The best road maps of the Netherlands are those produced by Michelin and the Dutch automobile association ANWB. The ANWB also puts out provincial maps detailing cycling paths and picturesque road routes. You'll find a wide variety of maps for sale at any tourist office, as well as at bookstores and news-stands.

Tourist offices sell all forms of maps and often have local walking-tour maps in English for sale. See p67 for sources of cycling maps.

MONEY

Like other members of the EU, the Netherlands currency is the euro (€), which is divided into 100 cents. There are coins for one, two, five, 10, 20 and 50 cents, and €1 and €2. Notes come in denominations of €5, €10, €20, €50, €100, €200 and €500. The one- and two-cent coins are still in circulation but are unofficially being phased out; most shops now round up or down to the nearest five cents.

The Quick Reference page inside the front cover of this book lists exchange rates at time of publication, while the Getting Started chapter (p13) has a rundown of costs.

ATMs

Automated teller machines can be found outside most banks and at airports and most train stations. Credit cards such as Visa and MasterCard/Eurocard are widely accepted, as well as cards from the Plus and Cirrus networks. Know whether you're limited to a maximum withdrawal per day. Also note that using an ATM can be the cheapest way to exchange your money from home – but check with your home bank for service charges before you leave.

You can use your ATM card to keep stocked up with euros throughout the Netherlands so there's no need for currency exchange. However using your ATM card, as opposed to a credit card, to pay for purchases is unlikely to work as the Dutch use PIN cards (right).

Cash

Cash is still common and nothing beats it for convenience – or risk of theft or loss. Plan to pay cash for most daily expenses. Car-hire agencies, however, require a credit card and hotels may want a hefty cash deposit if you don't have a credit card. Keep the equivalent of about €100 separate from the rest of your money as an emergency stash in case of theft or if your ATM card stops working.

Credit Cards

All major international cards are recognised, and you will find that most hotels, restaurants and major stores accept them (although *not* the Dutch railway). But always check first to avoid, as they say, disappointment. Shops may

levy a 5% surcharge (or more) on credit cards to offset the commissions charged by card providers. Note that some vending machines may require that credit cards have the embedded chips common on European-issued cards.

To withdraw money at a bank counter instead of from an ATM, go to a GWK branch (see Moneychangers, below). You'll need to show your passport.

Report lost or stolen cards to the following 24-hour numbers:
American Express (☎ 020-504 86 66)
Diners Club (☎ 0900 03 34)
Eurocard/MasterCard (☎ 030-283 55 55)
Visa (☎ 0800 022 31 10)

International Transfers

GWK (see Moneychangers, below) is an agent for Western Union and money is transferred within 15 minutes of lodgement at the other end. The person making the transfer pays a commission that varies from country to country.

Moneychangers

Generally your best bet for exchanging money is to use **GWK** (☎ 0900 05 66; www.gwk.nl) – note that calls to this number cost €0.25 per minute. Offices are in many medium-sized and most larger train stations (details are given in the city train service listings in this book) as well as at the borders on major highways. Many locations, such as those at Amsterdam's Centraal Station and at Schiphol airport, are open 24 hours. Banks are also a good option; they stick to official exchange rates and charge a sensible commission.

Avoid the private exchange booths dotted around tourist areas. They're convenient and open late hours, but rates or commissions are lousy. The best strategy is to simply avoid needing to change money.

PIN Cards

In the Netherlands you'll notice people gleefully using 'PIN' cards everywhere, from shops to public telephones and cigarette-vending machines. These direct-debit cards look like credit or bank cards with little circuit chips on them, but they won't be of much use to visitors without a Dutch bank account.

Tipping

Tipping is not essential as restaurants, hotels, bars etc include a service charge on their bills.

A little extra is always welcomed though, and it's an excellent way to compliment the service (if you feel it needs complimenting). The tip can be anything from rounding up to the nearest euro to 10% of the bill.

Travellers Cheques

Travellers cheques are uncommon in the Netherlands – you'll be very hard pressed to find a bank that will change them for you.

POST

The national post office in the Netherlands was privatised and renamed TNT Post (www .tntpost.nl) in 2006. The results have been mixed at best. For travellers this means that it can be very hard to find a place to mail something. City centre post offices are being closed at a rapid rate (such as the fairly new and beautiful one in Leeuwarden) to cut costs. When we asked a lady in the Delft tourist office where she went to mail a letter, her answer was brief: 'Rotterdam'.

City post offices are supposedly being replaced by counters offering postal services in supermarkets and other stores. In practice, however, this is problematic. It's hard to figure out which shops might have a postal counter and when you find one the busy employees may not be much help for transactions outside of the Netherlands. In one supermarket three employees shut down the checkout lines while they tried to figure out how to send our package internationally (we had our receipt from a shipment the week before which they finally used as a guide – while shoppers muttered).

The good news is that letters and parcels move efficiently once you find a way to mail them.

Postal Rates

The standard rate ('priority') for letters under 20g is €0.45 within the Netherlands, €0.74 within Europe and €0.90 outside Europe. When you buy stamps, you'll have to buy a booklet of at least five, so stock up on postcards.

SHOPPING

There is seemingly not a lot in the Netherlands that you won't find back home, aside from dope, round after round of cheese, interesting little cookies, rare flower bulbs and even rarer types of *jenever* (Dutch gin). Even the majority of the ubiquitous Delftware – blue-and-white porcelain stocked in every single souvenir

shop – is made in China. Clogs, on the other hand, are one item you normally won't find outside the Netherlands, and they're available in almost every town across the country.

Initial impressions can be deceiving, however. The Dutch still like their little shops and you'll find all manner of interesting places to browse and peruse what is often creative, surprising or idiosyncratic merchandise. Wandering little streets dotted with unusual stores is one of the pleasures of visiting a Dutch town or city. This is true even in Amsterdam, where you can spend day after day exploring its variety of shops (p132).

Large markets are held on central squares of every town on certain days of the week. Besides interesting local foods, you'll find all manner of goods from the cheap and banal to the intriguing and unusual.

SOLO TRAVELLERS

The Dutch are uninhibited when it comes to striking up a conversation with a complete stranger, whether at the next table in a restaurant or in a supermarket queue, and before you know it you'll find yourself in a conversation.

Booking into a group activity such as a walking tour or boat trip is a good recipe for making contacts. Young travellers also hook up with like-minded people at youth hostels or budget hotels. Nightclubs in cities such as Amsterdam and Rotterdam draw a large, fun-loving contingent of foreigners, and many also make their way to beach parties in places such as Bloemendaal or Scheveningen. Single women should try to join forces before hitting the clubs – that's what the Dutch do.

TELEPHONE

The Dutch phone network, **KPN** (www.kpn .com), is efficient, and prices are reasonable by European standards.

Collect call (*collect gesprek;* domestic ☎ 0800 01 01, international ☎ 0800 04 10) Both numbers are free.
International directory enquiries (☎ 0900 84 18; per number €1.15)
National directory enquiries (☎ 1888; per number €1.30)
Operator assistance (☎ 0800 04 10; free call)

Costs

Calls are time-based, anytime and anywhere. KPN Telecom public phone boxes charge €0.10 per 15 seconds for all national calls (minimum charge €0.20), and €0.10 per nine seconds for calling a mobile phone. Phones in cafes, supermarkets and hotel lobbies often charge more. Calling from private phones is considerably cheaper.

The cost of international calls varies with the destination, and changes frequently due to competition. At the time of writing, calls to Britain and the USA cost €0.058 to €0.073 per minute respectively, and Australia €0.20. The connection charge is about €0.10. To all three countries, rates jump to €0.10 every 13 seconds when ringing from a KPN phone box.

Incoming calls to Dutch mobile phones are generally free to the recipient.

Coin phones have made a comeback, but card phones still predominate – when you can find one. You can easily pick up a phonecard (see right). Many public phones accept credit cards, although starting fees are stiff and cards issued outside of the Netherlands may require extra steps during dialling.

Internet Calls

Services such as **Skype** (www.skype.com) and **Google Voice** (www.google.com/voice) can make calling home cheap. Check the websites for details.

Mobile Phones

The Netherlands uses GSM 900/1800, compatible with the rest of Europe and Australia but not with the North American GSM 1900 (some convertible phones work in both places). G3 phones such as iPhones will work fine – but beware of enormous roaming costs, especially for data.

Prepaid mobile phones are available at mobile-phone shops starting from around €35 when on special. You can also buy SIM cards for your own GSM mobile phone that will give you a Dutch telephone number (from €5). Look for Phone House, Orange, T-Mobile and Vodafone shops wherever chain stores gather.

New prepaid phones generally come with a small amount of call time already stored. To top it up, purchase more minutes at one of the branded stores, news dealers or supermarkets, and follow the instructions.

Phone Codes

To phone abroad, dial ☎ 00 followed by the country code for your target country, the area code (you usually drop the leading 0 if there is one) and the subscriber number. The country code for calling the Netherlands is ☎ 31. Drop the leading 0 on city codes if you're call-

ing from outside the Netherlands (eg 20 for Amsterdam instead of 020). Do not dial the city code if you are in the area covered by it.

Free calls (☎ 0800)
Mobile or pager numbers (☎ 06)
Paid information calls (☎ 0900) Cost varies between €0.10 and €1.30 per minute.

Phonecards

For public telephones, cards are available at post offices, train station counters, VVV and GWK offices and tobacco shops for €5, €10 and €20. KPN's card is the most common but there are tonnes of competitors – T-Mobile, Orange and Vodaphone among them – that usually have better rates. Train stations have Telfort phone booths that require a Telfort card (available at GWK offices or ticket counters), although there should be KPN booths nearby.

TIME

The Netherlands is on Central European time, GMT/UTC plus one hour. Noon in Amsterdam is 11am in London, 6am in New York, 3am in San Francisco, 6am in Toronto, 9pm in Sydney and 11pm in Auckland, and then there's daylight-saving time. Clocks are put forward one hour at 2am on the last Sunday in March and back again at 3am on the last Sunday in October.

When telling the time, beware that Dutch uses half to indicate 'half before' the hour. If you say 'half eight' (8.30 in many forms of English), a Dutch person will take this to mean 7.30. Dutch also uses constructions such as *tien voor half acht* (ten to half eight – 7.20) and *kwart over acht* (quarter past eight – 8.15).

TOURIST INFORMATION

Within the Netherlands, tourist information is supplied by the **VVV** (Vereniging voor Vreemdelingenverkeer, Netherlands Tourism Board; www.vvv .nl), which has affiliated tourist offices throughout the country. Although each tourist office is locally run, they all have a huge amount of information that covers not just their area but the rest of the country as well. Most VVV publications cost money and there are commissions for services (eg €3 to €15 to find a room, €2 to €3 for theatre tickets). Tourist offices are usually a very good place to buy all manner of maps and guides.

The Dutch automobile association **ANWB** (☎ 0800 05 03; www.anwb.nl; ☺ 10am-6pm Mon-Sat) has maps and guidebooks for sale. It provides a wide range of useful information and assistance if you're travelling with any type of vehicle (car, bicycle, motorcycle, yacht etc). In some cities the VVV and ANWB share offices. You'll have to show proof of membership of your home automobile club to get free maps or discounts.

TRAVELLERS WITH DISABILITIES

Travellers with restricted mobility will find the Netherlands somewhat accessible despite the limitations of most older buildings. A large number of government offices and museums have lifts or ramps; many hotels, however, are in old buildings where steep, narrow stairs are the only option. Restaurants tend to be on the ground floor, though they sometimes include a few steps up or down.

Train and other public transport stations sometimes have lifts; most train stations and public buildings have toilets for the disabled. The trains themselves have wheelchair access in most instances, and people with a disability get discounted travel on public transport.

Netherlands Railways (NS; ☎ 030-235 78 22; www .ns.nl) has an information line with details of all its services for travellers with disabilities. The website has a section showing what facilities for the disabled are available at each station.

The Dutch national organisation for the disabled is **ANGO** (Algemene Nederlandse Gehandicapten Organisatie, Dutch Society for the Disabled; ☎ 033-465 43 43; www.ango.nl); the blind and deaf can contact **LED** (Landelijk Expertisecentrum Doofblindheid, Association for the Deaf & Blind; ☎ 030-267 92 88; www.doofblind.nl).

VISAS

Tourists from nearly 60 countries – including Australia, Canada, Israel, Japan, New Zealand, Singapore, South Korea, the USA and most of Europe – need only a valid passport to visit the Netherlands for up to three months. EU nationals can enter for three months with just their national identity card or a passport that expired less than five years ago.

Nationals of most other countries need a so-called Schengen visa, valid within the EU member states (except the UK and Ireland), plus Norway and Iceland, for 90 days within a six-month period.

Schengen visas are issued by Dutch embassies or consulates overseas and can take a while to process (up to two months). You'll need a passport valid until at least three months after your visit, and proof that you have sufficient funds for your stay and return journey.

Visa extensions are handled by the **Immigratie en Naturalisatiedienst** (Immigration & Naturalisation Service; ☎ 0900 123 45 61, per min €0.10; www.ind.nl; Postbus 3211, 2280 GE Rijswijk). Study visas must be applied for via your college or university in the Netherlands. For working visas, see below.

WOMEN TRAVELLERS

Equality has long been taken for granted, although far fewer women than men are employed full time, and fewer still hold positions in senior management. The feminist movement is less politicised than elsewhere and certainly more laid-back. Efforts focus on practical solutions such as cultural centres, bicycle repair shops run by and for women, or support systems to help women set up businesses.

There's little street harassment in Dutch cities, where most women will feel safe. Amsterdam is probably as secure as it gets among the major cities of Europe. Just take care in the Red Light District, where it's best to walk with a friend to minimise unwelcome attention.

Most women's organisations are based in Amsterdam. **Centrum voor Seksuele Gezondheid** (Map pp86-7; ☎ 624 54 26; www.acsg.nl; Sarphatistraat 618; ☻ 9am-6pm Mon-Fri, to 9pm Tue) is a clinic offering information and help with sexual problems and birth control, including morning-after pills. Appointments are necessary.

WORK

Work permits must be applied for by your employer in the Netherlands; in general, the employer must prove that the position cannot be filled by someone from within the EU before offering it to a non-EU citizen. Nationals from many countries must apply for a Temporary Entry Permit (MVV or Machtiging tot Voorlopig Verblijf). Citizens of EU countries, Norway and Switzerland are exempt.

You'll need to apply for temporary residence before an employer can ask for your work permit. The process should take five weeks; contact the Dutch embassy or consulate in your home country.

In the Netherlands, residency permits are issued by the **Immigratie en Naturalisatiedienst** (☎ 0900 123 45 61, per min €0.10; www.ind.nl; Postbus 3211, 2280 GE Rijswijk). For details of work permits, contact the **CWI** (Employment Services Authority; ☎ 0800 80 01; Westwaarts 11, 2701 AD Zoetermeer). The CWI also runs a website (www.werk.nl) with up-to-date job offers.

Transport

The Netherlands is an easy place to reach. Amsterdam's Schiphol airport has copious air links worldwide, including many on low-cost European airlines, and the links on high-speed trains are especially good from France, Belgium and Germany. Other land options are user-friendly and the border crossings are nearly invisible thanks to the EU. There are also several ferry links with the UK and Scandinavia.

What's more, once you get to the Netherlands the transport stays hassle-free. Most journeys by rail, car or bus are so short that you can reach most regional destinations before your next meal. And with a country as flat as this, getting around by bicycle is a dream.

THINGS CHANGE...

The information in this chapter is particularly vulnerable to change. Check directly with the airline or a travel agent to make sure you understand how a fare (and ticket you may buy) works and be aware of the security requirements for international travel. Shop carefully. The details given in this chapter should be regarded as pointers and are not a substitute for your own careful, up-to-date research.

GETTING THERE & AWAY

ENTERING THE COUNTRY
Passport
In principle all passengers with passports are allowed entry to the Netherlands. See p293 for details of the relatively few nationalities that need visas.

AIR
Airports & Airlines
SCHIPHOL AIRPORT
Conveniently near Amsterdam, **Schiphol airport** (code AMS; ☎ 020-794 08 00; www.schiphol.nl) is the Netherlands' main international airport and the fourth busiest in Europe. It is the hub of Dutch passenger carrier KLM, which has nonstop service worldwide and, it should be noted, some of the smallest economy seats in the industry.

The airport is like a small city and is well-linked to the rest of the country by train, including the new high-speed line south to Rotterdam and Belgium (p297). For details on getting to Amsterdam from the airport, see (p136).

The airport runs efficiently for its size. There is a huge shopping mall and food court as well as airport hotels. You can store luggage here for up to a week.

Dozens of airlines fly to Schiphol, including the following. Few airlines have city ticket offices anymore.

Aer Lingus (EI; ☎ 0900 265 82 07; www.aerlingus.com)
Air France (AF; ☎ 020-654 57 20; www.airfrance.nl)
BMI (BD; ☎ 020-346 92 11; www.flybmi.com)
British Airways (BA; ☎ 020-346 95 59; www.british airways.com)
Cathay Pacific (CX; ☎ 020-653 20 10; www.cathay pacific.com)
Continental Airlines (CO; ☎ 020-346 93 81; www .continental.com)
Delta Air Lines (DL; ☎ 020-201 35 36; www.delta.com)
easyJet (U2; ☎ 0900 265 80 22; www.easyjet.com)
Japan Airlines (JL; ☎ 020-305 00 75; www.jal.com)
KLM (KL; ☎ 020-474 77 47; www.klm.nl)
Lufthansa (LH; ☎ 0900 123 47 77; www.lufthansa .com)
Malaysia Airlines (MH; ☎ 521 62 50; www.malaysia airlines.com)

CLIMATE CHANGE & TRAVEL

Climate change is a serious threat to the ecosystems that humans rely upon, and air travel is the fastest-growing contributor to the problem. Lonely Planet regards travel, overall, as a global benefit, but believes we all have a responsibility to limit our personal impact on global warming.

Flying & Climate Change

Pretty much every form of motor travel generates CO_2 (the main cause of human-induced climate change) but planes are far and away the worst offenders, not just because of the sheer distances they allow us to travel, but because they release greenhouse gases high into the atmosphere. The statistics are frightening: two people taking a return flight between Europe and the US will contribute as much to climate change as an average household's gas and electricity consumption over a whole year.

Carbon Offset Schemes

Climatecare.org and other websites use 'carbon calculators' that allow jetsetters to offset the greenhouse gases they are responsible for with contributions to energy-saving projects and other climate-friendly initiatives in the developing world – including projects in India, Honduras, Kazakhstan and Uganda.

Lonely Planet, together with Rough Guides and other concerned partners in the travel industry, supports the carbon offset scheme run by climatecare.org. Lonely Planet offsets all of its staff and author travel.

For more information check out our website: lonelyplanet.com.

Singapore Airlines (SQ; ☎ 020-548 88 88; www .singaporeair.com)
United Airlines (UA; ☎ 020-201 37 08; www.united airlines.com)
US Airways (US; www.usairways.com)

OTHER AIRPORTS

The other airports of interest to visitors are Rotterdam Airport (p213) and Eindhoven Airport (p271). Neither has much service, although the latter hosts some budget carriers.

Tickets

Within Europe there are plenty of budget airlines connecting the Netherlands to other countries and these tickets are usually found online.

From other continents, you have many options. Travel agents such as **STA Travel** (www.sta travel.com) and **Trailfinders** (www.trailfinders.com) offer good prices. Airline websites may have fares not found elsewhere while internet booking sites are good for comparison shopping and seeing what choices you have for flying to the Netherlands.

Useful internet booking sites include the following (many have branches specific to countries, eg for Australia add '.au' to the address). For other useful sites, see the geographic-specific listings below.

Expedia (www.expedia.com) Full service.
Hotwire (www.hotwire.com) Cheapo tickets that reveal the airline after you've purchased.
Kayak (www.kayak.com) Excellent site that checks both airline and discount websites.
Orbitz (www.orbitz.com) Full service with the widest range of fares.
Priceline (www.priceline.com) Bid a price and see if an airline accepts.
SideStep (www.sidestep.com) Searches and compares fares on multiple sites.
Travelocity (www.travelocity.com) Full service.

Africa

KLM has numerous services to Africa, including daily flights to Johannesburg, Dar es Salaam and Nairobi.

Rennies Travel (www.renniestravel.com) and **STA Travel** (www.statravel.co.za) have offices throughout Southern Africa. Check their websites for branch locations.

Asia

The major Asian airlines, such as Singapore Airlines, Cathay Pacific, Japan Airlines and Malaysia Airlines, have flights into Amsterdam.

STA Travel proliferates in Asia:
Bangkok (☎ 02-236 0262; www.statravel.co.th)
Singapore (☎ 6737 7188; www.statravel.com.sg)

Another resource in Japan is **No 1 Travel** (☎ 03 3205 6073; www.no1-travel.com); in Hong Kong try **Four Seas Tours** (☎ 2200 7760; www.fourseastravel.com).

Australia

Itineraries from Australia generally go via a Southeast Asian capital such as Kuala Lumpur, Bangkok or Singapore.

For the location of STA Travel branches call ☎ 1300 733 035 or visit www.statravel.com .au. **Flight Centre** (☎ 133 133; www.flightcentre .au) also has offices throughout Australia. For online bookings, try www.travel.com.au.

Canada

From Canada KLM flies from Calgary, Montreal, Toronto and Vancouver. Otherwise you'll fly a US or European carrier and change planes at their respective hubs.

Travel Cuts (☎ 800-667-2887; www.travelcuts.com) is Canada's national student travel agency.

Continental Europe

Amsterdam is well connected to almost all other European cities. KLM and other major airlines have a web of routes to/from important cities across the continent. In addition Eindhoven Airport is an option as it is served by budget airlines.

New Zealand

Reaching Amsterdam from New Zealand usually means you have a choice of transiting via a Southeast Asian city.

Both **Flight Centre** (☎ 0800 243 544; www.flightcentre .co.nz) and **STA Travel** (☎ 0508 782 872; www.statravel .co.nz) have branches throughout the country. Try www.travel.co.nz for online bookings.

UK & Ireland

Options for flying across the channel are many, although the opening of the Dutch high-speed rail line makes the train a viable option (see p299).

To Schiphol, try Aer Lingus, BMI, British Airways, EasyJet and KLM. There are other options to Eindhoven (p271), which is served by Ryanair among others, and Rotterdam (p213).

Popular travel agencies include **STA Travel** (☎ 087-0163 0026; www.statravel.co.uk), with offices throughout the UK. Other recommended agencies include **Trailfinders** (☎ 0845-050 5940; www.trailfinders.com) and **Travelbag** (☎ 087-0607 0620; www.travelbag.co.uk).

USIT (☎ 01-602 1904; www.usitnow.ie) has branches in Ireland and Northern Ireland specialising in student and independent travel.

USA

KLM has nonstop service from several US cities as do Continental Airlines, Delta Air Lines, United Airlines and US Airways. You might save money by flying a European carrier and changing planes in Europe, but what fun is that?

STA Travel (☎ 800-781-4040; www.statravel.com) is found across the USA, although most people book through a website.

LAND
Bicycle

In a land where the humble bicycle is king, bringing your own bike into the Netherlands will cause no problems.

By air, it's possible to first take your bicycle apart and protect it with a bike bag or box before handing it over to the baggage handlers, but it's much easier simply to wheel your bike to the check-in desk, where it should be treated as a piece of baggage. You may have to remove the pedals and turn the handlebars sideways so that it takes up less space in the aircraft's hold; check all this with the airline well in advance, preferably before you pay for your ticket.

Your bike can also travel with you on international trains provided you can disassemble the bike and fit it into a stowage bag that will fit into the normal luggage-storage racks on board.

Or you can ride it! Once you reach the Netherlands, you enter the most bike-friendly place on the planet. See the Bicycle sections that follow for information on cycling from various countries.

If you want to bring your own bike, consider the risk of theft in Amsterdam – rental might be the wiser option in the capital.

Beware of mopeds, which also use bike paths and might be travelling well above their 40km/h speed limit (30km/h in built-up areas). Only competition cyclists and poseurs tend to wear bicycle helmets, but that shouldn't stop you from protecting your own cranium.

For much more on cycling, see p67.

Bus

Amsterdam and Rotterdam, and smaller cities such as Den Haag and Utrecht, are connected to the rest of Europe and North Africa by long-distance bus. See right for information on buses to and from Germany and p298 for details on buses to and from the UK.

The most extensive European bus network is maintained by **Eurolines** (www.eurolines.com), a consortium of coach operators. It offers a variety of passes with prices that vary by time of year, or you can book tickets ahead and save.

Car & Motorcycle

For information about car ferries from England, see p299.

Drivers of cars and riders of motorbikes will need the vehicle's registration papers, third-party insurance and an international driving permit in addition to their domestic licence. It's a good idea to also have complete insurance coverage – be sure to ask for a Green Card from your insurer.

ANWB (p292) provides a wide range of information, maps, advice and services if you can show a membership card from your own automobile association, such as the AA.

Hitching

Hitching is never entirely safe anywhere in the world and we don't recommend it. Travellers who decide to hitch should understand that they are taking a small but potentially serious risk.

Many Dutch students have a government-issued pass allowing free public transport. Consequently, the number of hitchhikers has dropped dramatically and car drivers are no longer used to the phenomenon. Hitchers have reported long waits. Some university towns do have designated hitching spots; ask students for details.

On Channel crossings from the UK, the car fares on the Harwich–Hoek van Holland ferry as well as the shuttle through the Channel Tunnel include passengers, so you can hitch to the continent at no cost to the driver (though the driver will still be responsible if you do something illegal).

Looking for a ride out of the country? Try the noticeboards at universities, public libraries and hostels.

Belgium & Germany
BICYCLE

Long-distance cyclists can choose from a variety of safe, easy, specially designated routes to get to the Netherlands from Belgium and Germany. The bicycle paths are called *lan-*

delijke fietsroutes (LF) and retain that label in northern Belgium. The LF2 route runs 340km from Brussels via Ghent to Amsterdam; the LF4 stretches 300km from Enschede near the German border to Den Haag.

BUS

Eurolines (see left) has buses to the Netherlands from many points in neighbouring countries. There is also a link between Brugge and the Netherlands; see p225 for details.

CAR & MOTORCYCLE

The main entry points from Belgium are the E22 (Antwerp–Breda) and the E25 (Liege–Maastricht). From Germany there are loads of border crossings, but the chief arteries are the E40 (Cologne–Maastricht), the E35 (Düsseldorf–Arnhem) and the A1 (Hanover–Amsterdam).

TRAIN

The Netherlands has good train links to Germany and Belgium and on to France. Train passes good for the Netherlands are valid on Dutch trains, which are mostly operated by **Nederlandse Spoorwegen** (NS; www.ns.nl). See p302 for more about trains within the country.

Major Dutch train stations have international ticket offices, and in peak periods it's wise to reserve seats in advance. You can also buy tickets for local trains to Belgium and Germany at the normal ticket counters.

Hispeed (☎ 0900 9296, per min €0.35; www.nshispeed .nl), the international arm of the Dutch railways, handles international sales. You can book online or visit the Hispeed counter at the largest stations.

To/from Belgium

Trains between Amsterdam and Brussels have experienced much drama (see p298). Assuming the many problems are finally sorted out, a fast hourly service will link Brussels and Antwerp with Rotterdam and Amsterdam (1¾ hours from Brussels, hourly) in 2010. Dubbed **Fyra** (www.fyra.com), the trains are operated by **Hispeed** (www.nshispeed.nl), the international arm of the Dutch railways. Although full fare is likely to be high, advance fares on the Fyra are likely to be cheap.

Thalys (www.thalys.com) operates trains between Paris, Brussels and Amsterdam (3¼ hours from Paris). It also has good advance fares and there is a range of discount schemes.

TRANSPORT

ON THE WRONG TRACK

Built at huge expense (€6 billion and counting), a 125km-long high-speed rail line runs from near Schiphol airport south to Rotterdam and on to Belgium. It was supposed to open in 2007, allowing trains to whiz along at 300km/h through the Netherlands and then continue at that speed on the high-speed lines of Belgium and France. The savings in travel time over the classic route via Den Haag are enormous:

	Old Time	New Time
Amsterdam-Brussels	2:40	1:44
Amsterdam-Paris	4:11	3:13

With a change in Brussels to Eurostar, London would be reachable within four hours. And although the tracks had delays, the decade-long project was mostly finished in 2007. And then what happened? Vines grew on the tracks, the rails rusted and graffiti spread. In a fairly spectacular bit of mismanagement and general buffoonery where blame is shared by myriad parties, there were no trains to run on the new tracks.

New trains ordered to run on the tracks were delivered more than two years late (these were – we are not making this up – initially named 'Albatross' until Fyra was chosen instead) while Thalys, the incumbent operator of trains from Amsterdam to Brussels and Paris, showed little interest in modifying its trains – which run at 300km in Belgium and France – to run fast in Holland. Meanwhile vast amounts of taxpayer money were being spent trying to salvage the entire mess. It was hoped all would finally work in 2010.

In the south there is hourly service between Maastricht and Liege (30 minutes).

To/from Germany
German ICE high-speed trains run six times a day between Amsterdam and Cologne (2½ hours) via Utrecht. Many continue on to Frankfurt (four hours) via Frankfurt Airport.

Advance purchase fares bought on the web are as little as €39. Buy your tickets in advance at either www.nshispeed.nl or www.bahn.de, print them out and present them on the train.

With connections in Cologne or Frankfurt, you can reach any part of Germany fairly easily. Other direct services include several regular trains a day between Amsterdam and Berlin (6½ hours) and a local service from Groningen straight east across the border to tiny Leer, where you can get trains to Bremen and beyond.

From Maastricht you can reach Cologne via Liege in Belgium and Aachen in Germany (1½ to two hours).

UK
BICYCLE
Most cross-Channel ferries don't charge foot passengers extra to take a bicycle. You can also bring your two-wheeler on the train (opposite) where it travels for free if it fits into a bike bag as hand luggage.

BUS
Eurolines (see p297) runs a regular coach service to Amsterdam via Rotterdam and Den Haag or Utrecht from London's Victoria coach station (from UK£18 for adults, 12 hours). Coaches have onboard toilets and reclining seats.

Busabout (☎ 020-7950 1661; www.busabout.com) operates buses that complete set circuits around Europe, stopping at major cities. Its Northern Loop circuit passes through Amsterdam and eventually links up with its western and southern routes in Paris and Munich respectively. Pricing is complex; check the website.

CAR & MOTORCYCLE
Ferries take cars and motorcycles to the Netherlands from several ports in the UK (for details, see opposite). **Eurotunnel** (☎ 0870 535 3535; www.eurotunnel.com) runs a 'drive-on, drive off' shuttle through the Channel Tunnel linking Folkstone, UK, to Calais, France, from where you can drive to the Netherlands. It's a 35-minute journey and cars/motorcycles cost from UK£60/30 with advance reservations.

TRAIN

Eurostar (www.eurostar.com) takes two hours from London St Pancras to Brussels. There you can connect to a Thalys or Fyra high-speed train to the Netherlands and Amsterdam (1¾ hours from Brussels, see p297). And there is speculation that Eurostar will extend its trains to Amsterdam, obviating the change.

Rail Europe (☎ 0870 837 1371; www.raileurope.co.uk) may be able to book you a through ticket from the UK to the Netherlands, however the website at times fails at this simple task. If necessary book the tickets separately. The excellent website www.seat61.com explains all the options.

The **Dutch Flyer** (☎ 08705455455; www.dutchflyer .co.uk) is one of the cheapest ways to reach the Netherlands from the UK. Trains from London (Liverpool Street Station), Cambridge and Norwich connect with ferries sailing from Harwich to Hoek van Holland, where a further train travels on to Rotterdam and Amsterdam. The journey takes around 9½ hours and costs as little as UK£29 one way.

SEA
UK
FERRY

Several companies operate car/passenger ferries between the Netherlands and the UK. Most travel agents have details of the following services but might not always know the finer points. The ferry companies run frequent specials. For information on train-ferry-train services, see above.

Reservations are essential for cars in high season, although motorcycles can often be squeezed in. Most ferries don't charge for a bike and have no shortage of storage space.

Stena Line (☎ 08705 70 70 70; www.stenaline.co.uk) sails between Harwich and Hoek van Holland. The fast HSS ferries take only three hours 40 minutes and depart in each direction twice a day. Overnight ferries take 6¼ hours (one daily), as do normal day ferries (one daily). Foot passengers pay from UK£50 return. Fares for a car and driver range from UK£100 to UK£350 return depending on the season and the day of the week. A motorcycle and driver costs UK£70 to UK£200. Options such as reclining chairs and cabins cost extra and are compulsory on night crossings.

P&O Ferries (☎ 08705 20 20 20; www.poferries.com) operates an overnight ferry every evening (11 hours) between Hull and Europoort (near

Rotterdam). Return fares start at UK£150 for a foot passenger, UK£240 for a car with driver, and UK£220 for a motorcycle and rider. Prices here include berths in an inside cabin; luxury cabins are available.

DFDS Seaways (☎ 08702 52 05 24; www.dfds.co.uk) sails between Newcastle and IJmuiden (p146), which is close to Amsterdam; the 15-hour sailings depart every day. The earlier you book, the lower your fare: return fares start at UK£40 for a foot passenger in an economy berth, plus UK£100 for a car. The fare for a motorcycle and rider is UK£120 one way. Prices go up from there.

GETTING AROUND

The Netherlands is very easy to get around. If you are sticking to all but the most esoteric cities and sights, you won't need a car as the train and bus system blankets the country. Or you can do as the Dutch do and provide your own power on a bike.

See p300 for the many ways you can plan your trip.

AIR

With a country as small as the Netherlands (the longest train journey, between Groningen and Maastricht, takes 4¼ hours), there is no need to fly anywhere.

BICYCLE

The Netherlands is extremely bike-friendly and a *fiets* (bicycle) is the way to go. Many people have the trip of a lifetime using nothing but pedal power. Most modes of transport such as trains and buses are friendly to cyclists and their mounts. Dedicated bike routes go virtually everywhere. Oh and it's mostly flat.

For full details, see p67.

BOAT
Ferry

Ferries connect the mainland with the five Frisian Islands. See the Friesland (p235) and Noord Holland (p164) chapters for details. Passenger ferries span the Westerschelde in the south of Zeeland, providing a link between the southwestern expanse of the country and Belgium. These are popular with people using the Zeebrugge ferry terminal and run frequently year-round (see p225).

The **Waterbus** (☎ 0900 899 8998; www.waterbus.nl; day pass adult/child €11/6.75) is an excellent fast ferry

TRANSPORT

service that links Rotterdam and Dordrecht as well as the popular tourist destinations of Kinderdijk and Biesbosch National Park. Boats leave from Willemskade every 30 minutes.

Many more minor services provide links across the myriad of Dutch canals and waterways.

Hire

Renting a boat is a popular way to tour the many rivers, lakes and inland seas. Boats come in all shapes and sizes from canoes to motor boats to small sailing boats to large and historic former cargo sloops. Prices run the gamut and there are hundreds of rental firms throughout the country. See p283 for more details.

BUS

Buses are used for regional transport rather than for long distances, which are better travelled by train. They provide a vital service, especially in parts of the north and east, where trains are less frequent or nonexistent. The fares are zone-based. You can always buy a ticket from the driver (€2.60 to €5 for modest distances) but most people use other, cheaper, forms of payment (see p304).

There is only one class of travel. Some regions have day passes good for all the buses; ask a driver, they are usually very helpful. For schedule information, see below.

CAR & MOTORCYCLE

Dutch freeways are extensive but prone to congestion. Those around Amsterdam, the A4 south to Belgium and the A2 southeast to Maastricht are especially likely to be jammed at rush hours and during busy travel periods; traffic jams with a total length of 350km or

more aren't unheard of during the holiday season.

Smaller roads are usually well maintained, but the campaign to discourage car use throws up numerous obstacles – two-lane roads are repainted to be one-lane with wide bike lanes or there are barriers, speed-bumps and other 'traffic-calming schemes'.

Parking a car can be both a major headache and expensive. Cities purposely limit parking to discourage car use and rates are high: hotels boast about 'discount' parking rates for overnight guests of €30. Amsterdam has the highest parking rates in the world, averaging €50 per day.

Automobile Associations

For motoring information, contact the **ANWB** (☎ 070-314 71 47; www.anwb.nl); most big towns and cities have an office. Members of auto associations in their home countries (the AA, AAA, CAA, NRMA etc) can get assistance, free maps, discounts and more.

Driving Licence

Visitors are entitled to drive in the Netherlands on their foreign licences for a period of up to 185 days per calendar year. If you stay longer, you must get a Dutch licence (with some exceptions). For all queries, ring the **National Transport Authority** (☎ 0900 07 39, per min €0.10).

You'll need to show a valid driving licence when hiring a car in the Netherlands. An international driving permit (IDP) is not needed.

Fuel

Like much of Western Europe, petrol is very expensive and fluctuates on a regular basis.

PLANNING YOUR TRIP

The website **www.9292ov.nl** is an essential planning resource. It has comprehensive schedules for every train, tram and bus in the country and it can be set for English. You enter details of your journey – everything from mere city names to exact addresses or names of attractions – and it returns a range of options, each specified in exact detail. Time spent walking is even included. What's not included is the cost of the trip, due to the variability of bus and other fares.

Without web access, you can call (☎ 0900 9292, per min €0.70), check with tourist offices or in larger cities there are usually public transport information windows at the train station. Bus stops always list routes and schedules. Many attractions show public transport options on their brochures and websites for the benefit of the green-minded Dutch public.

If you know you are taking only the train, the website of **NS** (www.ns.nl) has an efficient English-language planning function that shows all available trains and fares. If you lack a web connection, call ☎ 0900 9292 or visit a station and ask in person.

ROAD DISTANCES (KM)

	Amsterdam	Apeldoorn	Arnhem	Breda	Den Bosch	Den Haag	Dordrecht	Eindhoven	Enschede	Groningen	Haarlem	Leeuwarden	Leiden	Maastricht	Nijmegen	Rotterdam	Tilburg	Utrecht
Amsterdam	---																	
Apeldoorn	86	---																
Arnhem	99	27	---															
Breda	101	141	111	---														
Den Bosch	88	91	64	48	---													
Den Haag	55	133	118	72	102	---												
Dordrecht	98	133	102	30	65	45	---											
Eindhoven	121	109	82	57	32	134	92	---										
Enschede	161	75	98	212	162	224	200	180	---									
Groningen	203	147	172	260	236	252	248	254	148	---								
Haarlem	19	117	114	121	103	51	94	136	184	204	---							
Leeuwarden	139	133	158	248	222	188	234	240	163	62	148	---						
Leiden	45	125	110	87	99	17	60	132	192	242	42	178	---					
Maastricht	213	201	167	146	124	223	181	86	274	348	228	334	239	---				
Nijmegen	122	63	18	101	44	135	98	62	134	208	135	194	131	148	---			
Rotterdam	73	128	118	51	81	21	24	113	195	251	70	206	36	202	114	---		
Tilburg	114	115	88	25	25	102	60	34	186	260	129	246	117	123	68	81	---	
Utrecht	37	72	64	73	55	62	61	88	139	195	54	181	54	180	85	57	81	---

TRANSPORT

At the time of research it was about €1.45 per litre (about US$6.75 per gallon). Gasoline (petrol) is *benzine* in Dutch, while unleaded fuel is *loodvrij*. Leaded fuel is not sold in the Netherlands but diesel is always available. Liquid petroleum gas can be purchased at petrol stations displaying LPG signs.

Petrol isn't noticeably more or less expensive outside of towns. Cheaper fuel is generally available from cut-rate chains such as Tango or TinQ – just ask the locals.

Hire

The Netherlands is well covered for car hire; all major firms have numerous locations. However, apart from in Amsterdam and Schiphol, the car-hire companies can be in inconvenient locations if you're arriving by train. Check their websites. You can look for local car-rental firms in telephone directories under the heading Autoverhuur. You must be at least 23 years of age to hire a car in the Netherlands. Some car-hire firms levy a small surcharge (€10 or so) for drivers under 25. A credit card is required to rent. Americans should note: less than 4% of European cars have automatic

transmissions, so if you need this, you'll pay a huge surcharge for your rental.

Car rentals are competitive and it pays to do some comparison surfing. Travel booking sites show a range of options but the rental firms often save the best deals for their own sites; some are prepaid and cost well under €20 per day. Checking rates from your home country too can yield greater savings than reserving once in Europe. Try this by alternating '.com' or '.co.uk' with '.nl' in the URL.

Insurance

Collision damage waiver (CDW), an insurance policy that limits your financial liability for damage, is a costly add-on for rentals but may be necessary. Without insurance you'll be liable for damages up to the full value of the vehicle.

But it's common for both credit cards and your home auto insurance policy to offer CDW-type coverage; the key is to make darn certain about this before you decline the costly (from €10 per day) CDW. If you rely on your credit card for cover, take time to review the terms and conditions. In the event of an accident you may be required to pay for repairs out of your own pocket and reclaim the sum from the credit-card company later, a procedure that can be fraught with problems.

Note that at most car-rental firms, CDW does not cover the first €500 to €1000 of damages incurred, but still another add on, an excess cover package for around €10 to €20 per day, is normally available to cover this amount. Again, see what your credit card and home auto insurance cover as you may not need anything extra at all, making that bargain rental an actual bargain.

Road Rules

As in the rest of Continental Europe, traffic travels on the right. The minimum driving age is 18 for vehicles and 16 for motorcycles. Seat belts are required for everyone in a vehicle, and children under 12 must ride in the back if there's room.

The standard European road rules and traffic signs apply. Trams always have the right of way. If you are trying to turn right, bikes have priority. At roundabouts yield to vehicles already travelling in the circle. Full concentration is required because you may need to yield to cars, bikes that appear out of nowhere and pedestrians in quick succession.

Speed limits are 50km/h in built-up areas, 80km/h in the country, 100km/h on major through-roads and 120km/h on freeways (sometimes 100km/h, clearly marked). The blood-alcohol limit is 0.05%, or 0.02% for those who got their licence after 30 March 2002.

HITCHING

For information on hitching in the Netherlands, see p297.

LOCAL TRANSPORT
Bicycle

Any Dutch town you visit is liable to be blanketed with bicycle paths. They're either on the streets or in the form of smooth off-road routes. In many cases the fastest way to get around is by bike. See p67 for more.

Bus, Tram & Metro

Buses and trams operate in most cities, and Amsterdam and Rotterdam have the added bonus of metro networks. See p300 for ways you can plan your trips.

> **BIG BROTHER IS WATCHING**
>
> More than 800 unmanned radar cameras (known as *flitspalen*) watch over Dutch motorways.

Taxi

Usually booked by phone – officially you're not supposed to wave them down on the street – taxis also hover outside train stations and hotels and cost roughly €12 for 5km. Even short trips in town can get expensive quickly. *Treintaxis* (see p305), which operate from many train stations, are a cheaper and more practical bet.

Taxis were deregulated in 2000 and anyone can drive a cab. But this has predictably led to all sorts of abuse and fraud (not to mention drivers who have no idea where they are going) so there are moves afoot for some reregulation.

TOURS

Special interest and luxury tours of the Netherlands are myriad. Some of the most interesting are marketed by museums such as the Smithsonian Institution in the US (www.smithsonianjourneys.org) and have cultural themes with experts as leaders. Here are a few options:

Cycletours Holland (☎ 020-521 84 90; www.cycletours.com) Conducts short tours of up to a week by bicycle and canal barge. Tours cost around €760.

Fiets-Fun (www.fiets-fun.nl) Runs popular and economical bicycle tours lasting one or two weeks that stop each night in rural, car-free campgrounds. Camping equipment is provided.

Hat Tours (☎ 0299-690 771; www.hat-tours.com) Offers similar tours to Cycletours Holland and appeals to cyclists and nature lovers.

Holland Discovery Tour (☎ 348 786 826; www.hollanddiscoverytour.com) Custom arranges tours on land and water for various specialised interests.

TRAIN

Dutch trains are efficient, fast and comfortable. Trains are frequent and serve domestic destinations at regular intervals, sometimes five or six times an hour. It's an excellent system and possibly all you'll need to get around the country, although there are a few caveats.

The national train company **NS** (www.ns.nl) operates all the major lines in the Netherlands. Minor lines in the north and east have been hived off to private bus and train operators such as Arriva and Veolias, although scheduling and fares remain part of the national system.

Bikes are welcome on the train system, see p67 for details.

See the boxed text, p300, for information on how to plan your journey. Stations show departure information but the boards don't show trip duration or arrival times, so planning requires the web or a visit to a ticket or information window.

The system shuts down roughly from midnight to 6am except in the Amsterdam–Schiphol–Rotterdam–Den Haag–Leiden circuit where trains run hourly all night.

Stations

Medium and large railways stations have a full range of services: currency exchange, ATMs, small groceries, food courts, FEBO-like coin-operated hot food vending machines, flower shops and much more.

Smaller stations, however, often have no services at all and are merely hollow – often architecturally beautiful – shells of their former selves. At these there may only be ticket vending machines (see below). This is especially true on non-NS lines.

LOCKERS

Generally these stations also have lockers, much to the delight of day-trippers. These are operated using a credit card, which unusually may be a non-Dutch card. Pick an empty locker, stuff your stuff in, close the door, insert your credit card and a one-day fee (€3.60 to €6 depending on size and location) is deducted and a claim card issued. If you return after more than 24 hours, you have to insert your credit card to pay an extra charge. If it's more than 72 hours, your goods will have been removed and you have to pay a €70 fine.

But note that many stations popular with day-trippers (eg Enkhuizen, Delft et al) do not have lockers. We note this in the train listings for each town in this book.

Tickets

Train travel in the Netherlands is reasonably priced. Tickets cost the same during the day as in the evening and many discounts are available.

PURCHASING TICKETS

There is one important caveat to buying tickets in the Netherlands for visitors: credit cards are not accepted at all. If you don't have a Dutch PIN card it is all cash all the time.

Ticket windows are available at midsize to larger stations. Staff speak English and are often very good at figuring out the lowest fare you need to pay, especially if you have a complex itinerary of day trips in mind. But windows may be closed at night or the lines may be long. In which case there are scores of ticket machines. However they only take Dutch PIN cards. Oops. About 25% do take coins but not bills, so if you have coins for your €13.30 Amsterdam to Rotterdam ticket you are in luck (the machines are touchscreen, can be set for English and are a breeze to use).

If you are at a station with a closed ticket window and don't have the coins for the machines, board the train and find the conductor. Explain your plight (they know where this applies so don't fib) and they will usually sell you a ticket (they take bills) without levying the fine (€35) for boarding without a ticket. If they do fine you, apply for a refund at a ticket window.

RESERVATIONS

For national trains, simply turn up at the station: you'll rarely have to wait more than 30 minutes for a train. Reservations may be required for some international trains.

TICKET TYPES

- *Enkele reis* (one-way) – single one-way ticket; with a valid ticket you can break your journey along the direct route.
- *Dagretour* (day return) – normal day return; 10% to 15% cheaper than two one-way tickets.
- *Weekendretour* (weekend return) – costs the same as a normal return and is valid from 7pm Friday to 4am Monday.
- *Dagkaart* (day pass) – costs €42.90/72.80 for 2nd/1st class and allows unlimited train travel throughout the country. Only good value if you're planning extensive train travel on any one day.
- *OV-dagkaart* (public transport day pass) – €5; bought in conjunction with the *dagkaart* (above), it allows use of trams, buses and metros for one day.
- *Railrunner* – €2; day pass for children aged four to 11.
- *Dagkaart hond* (doggie day pass) – €3; lets Fido ride with you all day.

CHIPS, STRIPS & CASH

Once all the Netherlands was under one system of payment for local transport, the handy *strippenkaart* (strip card). But while it is still in use, it is rapidly being phased out for a new high-tech system, the OV-chipkaart (OV chip card). You may find it all perplexing. Here's a guide to sort through your payment options.

OV-chipkaart

The new universal form of transport payment in the Netherlands, the **OV-chipkaart** (www.ov-chip kaart.nl) is a smartcard that you use in place of cash. Visitors can buy one from vending machines in stations or at ticket windows. Each card stores the value of your payment and deducts the cost of trips as you use it, eg a €5 card gets you that much in rides.

When you board a bus, tram or train, you hold the card against a reader at the doors or station entrance gates. A beep and you are in. When you exit, you must do the same thing. The system then calculates your fare and deducts it from the card. If you are transferring, the system tracks this and always deducts the least amount needed. What's good is that fares for the chip cards are much lower than for cash or even for strips. Tourists can also buy OV-chipkaarts good for unlimited use for one or more days. What's unclear as the card is being rolled out is how easy it will be to recharge your card. Vending machines for adding value use Dutch PIN cards that are different from the ATM or credit cards used elsewhere.

Strippenkaart

Simple, low-tech and recyclable, strip cards will be missed even if visitors often never knew how many strips to use. Starting with the Rotterdam Metro, strip cards are being phased out across the country.

Note that for delays in excess of half an hour – irrespective of the cause – you're entitled to a refund. Delays of 30 to 60 minutes warrant a 50% refund and delays of an hour or more a 100% refund.

International trains require passengers to buy tickets in advance and carry surcharges, but also may have very cheap fares available in advance.

TRAIN PASSES

There are several train passes for people living both inside and outside the Netherlands. These should be purchased before you arrive in the Netherlands. The websites www .raileurope.co.uk and www.raileurope.com offer online purchases.

However the passes don't offer very good value even if you plan on a lot of train travel. The Eurail Benelux pass is good for five days travel in a month on all trains within the Netherlands, Belgium and Luxembourg. It costs US$370/236 1st class/2nd class. A Benelux InterRail pass good for six days in one month costs UK£234/174. In most cases you'll save more with the Voordeelurenabonnement (right), even if you can't pronounce it.

VOORDEELURENABONNEMENT

Not just a mouthful, but a great way to save, the Voordeelurenabonnement (Off-Peak Discount Pass) is fantastic value if you're going to be seeing a lot of the country by train. It costs €55, is valid for one year and provides a 40% discount on train travel on weekdays after 9am, as well as weekends, public holidays and all of July and August. The discount also applies to up to three people travelling with you on the same trip. The card is available at train station counters; you need a passport photo.

Trains

CLASSES

The longest train journey in the Netherlands (Maastricht–Groningen) takes about 4½ hours, but the majority of trips are far shorter. Trains have 1st-class sections, but these are often little different from the 2nd-class areas and, given the short journeys, not worth the extra cost. In fact on the often overcrowded Veolias trains in the east, 1st class is really a cruel joke.

That said, where 1st class is worth the extra money is during busy periods when seats in 2nd class are over-subscribed.

In the meantime, they are available from tobacco shops, post offices and newsagencies and can be bought in denominations of two (€1.60), three (€2.40), 15 (€7.30) and 45 (€21.60) strips. Bus and tram drivers only sell two- and three-strip cards, so you're better off hunting down the larger, more economical strip cards.

To validate your journey just jump on a tram, bus or metro and stamp off a number of strips depending on how many zones you plan to cross. The ticket is then valid on all buses, trams, metro systems and city trains for an hour or longer depending on the number of strips you've stamped. In most towns you punch two strips (one for the journey and one for the zone), with an additional strip for each additional zone.

In the central areas of cities and towns, you usually will only need to stamp two strips – the minimum fee. When riding on trams and metros it's up to you to stamp your card, as fare dodgers can be fined on the spot. The machines are usually located on board trams and at the entrance to metro platforms.

The buses are more conventional, with drivers stamping the strips as you get on. More than one person can use a *strippenkaart,* and children and pensioners get reductions. Note that if you get caught without a properly stamped strip, playing the ignorant foreigner (the 'doofus' strategy) will guarantee that you get fined €40.

Cash

If you're without a chip card or a strip card, you can usually pay cash for your journey, either to the driver of a bus, a conductor on a tram (many in Amsterdam are in ticket booths to the rear of the tram) or at a vending machine outside metro or train station gates. But this is the most expensive way to go, often double of the chip-card rate.

TRANSPORT

TYPES

In descending order of speed:

Thalys (www.thalys.com) Operates French TGV-style high-speed trains from Amsterdam, Schiphol and Rotterdam south to Belgium and Paris. Trains are plush and have wi-fi.

Fyra (www.nshispeed.com) Operates domestic high-speed trains on the line from Amsterdam south to Rotterdam plus service on to Belgium and side jaunts to Den Haag and Breda. Airline-style ticket pricing.

ICE (Intercity Express; www.nshispeed.com, www.bahn .de) German fast trains from Amsterdam to Cologne and onto Frankfurt Airport and Frankfurt. Carries a surcharge for domestic riders.

Intercity The best non-high-speed domestic trains. They run express past small stations on all major lines. Usually air-conditioned double-deck cars.

Sneltrein (fast train) Not an Intercity but not as slow as a stoptrein. May not be air-conditioned.

Stoptrein (stop train) Never misses a stop, never gets up to speed. Cars may be old.

Treintaxi

More than 30 train stations offer an excellent *treintaxi* (train taxi) service that takes you to/from the station within a limited area. The cost per person per ride is €4.60 at a train-station counter or ticketing machine, or €5.50 direct from the driver. The service operates daily from 7am (from 8am Sunday and public holidays) till the evening. There's usually a special call box outside near the normal taxi rank and there's a central information number (☎ 0900 873 46 82, per minute €0.35).

The *treintaxi* service can be very handy for reaching places far from stations that don't have useful local bus services, such as Kamp Westerbork in Drenthe (p248). Unfortunately, most major stations (Amsterdam CS, Den Haag CS or HS, Rotterdam CS) are excluded.

Health

CONTENTS

Travel health depends on your predeparture preparations, your daily health care while travelling and how you handle any medical problem that does develop. For the Netherlands, peace of mind is the first thing to pack, as health care and medical facilities are generally excellent.

BEFORE YOU GO

Prevention is the key to staying healthy while abroad. A little planning before departure, particularly for pre-existing illnesses, will save trouble later: see your dentist before a long trip; carry a spare pair of contact lenses and glasses; and take your optical prescription with you. Bring medications in their original, clearly labelled containers. A signed and dated letter from your physician describing your medical conditions and medications,

---

NATIONAL HEALTH WEBSITES

It's usually a good idea to consult your government's travel-health website before departure, if one is available:
Australia (www.smartraveller.gov.au)
Canada (www.phac-aspc.gc.ca/tmp-pmv/index.html)
UK (www.nhs.uk/healthcareabroad)
US (www.cdc.gov/travel)

---

including generic names, is also a good idea. If carrying syringes or needles, be sure to have a physician's letter documenting their medical necessity.

INSURANCE

If you're an EU citizen, a European Health Insurance Card (EHIC), available from health centres or, in the UK, post offices, covers you for most medical care. It will not cover you for nonemergencies or emergency repatriation. Citizens from other countries should find out if there is a reciprocal arrangement for free medical care between their country and the Netherlands. If you do need health insurance, make sure you get a policy that covers you for the worst possible scenario, such as an accident requiring an emergency flight home. Find out in advance if your insurance plan will make payments directly to providers or reimburse you later for overseas health expenditures.

RECOMMENDED VACCINATIONS

No jabs are required to travel to the Netherlands. The World Health Organization (WHO) recommends that all travellers should be covered for diphtheria, tetanus, measles, mumps, rubella and polio, as well as hepatitis B, regardless of their destination. Since most vaccines don't produce immunity until at least two weeks after they're given, visit a physician at least six weeks before departure.

INTERNET RESOURCES

The WHO's publication *International Travel and Health* is revised annually and is available online at www.who.int/ith/. Other useful websites include the following:
- www.mdtravelhealth.com – Travel-health recommendations for every country.
- www.fitfortravel.nhs.uk – General travel advice.
- www.ageconcern.org.uk – Advice on travel for the elderly.

FURTHER READING

Health Advice for Travellers (currently called the 'T6' leaflet) is an annually updated leaflet produced by the UK Department of Health and available free in post offices. It contains some general information, legally required and recommended vaccines for different countries, reciprocal health agreements and an E111 application form. Lonely Planet's *Travel with Children* includes advice on travel health for younger children. Other recommended references include *Traveller's Health* by Dr Richard Dawood (published by Oxford University Press) and *The Traveller's Good Health Guide* by Ted Lankester (published by Sheldon Press).

IN TRANSIT

DEEP VEIN THROMBOSIS (DVT)

Blood clots may form in the legs during plane flights, chiefly because of prolonged immobility. The longer the flight, the greater the risk. The chief symptom of deep vein thrombosis (DVT) is swelling or pain of the foot, ankle or calf, usually – but not always – on just one side. When a blood clot travels to the lungs it may cause chest pain and breathing difficulties. Travellers with any of these symptoms should immediately seek medical attention.

To prevent the development of DVT on long flights you should walk about the cabin, contract the leg muscles while sitting, drink plenty of fluids, and avoid alcohol and tobacco.

JET LAG & MOTION SICKNESS

To avoid jet lag (which is common when crossing more than five time zones), try drinking plenty of nonalcholoholic fluids and eating light meals. Upon arrival, get exposure to natural sunlight and readjust your schedule (for meals, sleep and so on) to the time zone you're in as soon as possible.

Antihistamines such as dimenhydrinate (Dramamine) and meclizine (Antivert, Bonine) are usually the first choice for treating motion sickness. A herbal alternative is ginger.

IN THE NETHERLANDS

AVAILABILITY & COST OF HEALTH CARE

Good health care is readily available. For minor self-limiting illnesses an *apotheek* (pharmacy) can give valuable advice and sell over-the-counter medication. It can also advise when more specialised help is required and point you in the right direction. The standard of dental care is usually good; how-

ever, it is sensible to have a dental check-up before a long trip.

Hospitals for emergency care are listed for the larger cities in this book.

ENVIRONMENTAL HAZARDS
Heat Exhaustion & Heat Stroke

Heat exhaustion (yes, it can happen, even in the Netherlands!) occurs following excessive fluid loss with inadequate replacement of fluids and salt. Symptoms include headache, dizziness and tiredness. Dehydration is already happening by the time you feel thirsty – aim to drink sufficient water to produce pale, diluted urine. To treat heat exhaustion, replace fluids with water and/or fruit juice, and cool the body with cold water and fans. Treat salt loss with salty fluids such as soup or bouillon, or add a little more table salt than usual to foods.

Heat stroke is much more serious, resulting in irrational and hyperactive behaviour and eventually loss of consciousness and death. Rapid cooling by spraying the body with water and fanning is ideal. Emergency fluid and electrolyte replacement by intravenous drip is recommended.

Insect Bites & Stings

Mosquitoes are found in most parts of Europe and are well represented in the Netherlands. They may not carry malaria but can cause irritation and infected bites. Use a DEET-based insect repellent.

Bees and wasps only cause real problems for those with a severe allergy (anaphylaxis). If you have a severe allergy to bee or wasp stings, carry an Epipen or similar adrenaline injection.

Bed bugs lead to itchy lumpy bites. Applying crawling-insect spray to the mattress after changing the bedding will get rid of them.

Scabies are tiny mites that live in the skin, particularly between the fingers. They cause an intensely itchy rash. It's easily treated with lotion from a pharmacy; other members of the household also need to be treated to avoid spreading scabies between asymptomatic carriers.

LYME DISEASE

Ticks can carry a serious bacterial infection called Lyme disease. A bite from an infected tick may produce a red welt and a 'bull's eye' around the spot within a day or two. Mild flulike symptoms (headache, nausea etc) may or may not follow, but antibiotics are needed to avoid the next stage of the illness – pain in

HEALTH

the joints, fatigue and fever. If left untreated, Lyme disease can cause mental and muscular deterioration.

The most risky places in the Netherlands are the wooded areas of Friesland, Groningen and Drenthe, Hoge Veluwe National Park, parts of Zeeland and on the Wadden Islands. The best prevention is to wear clothing that covers your arms and legs when walking in grassy or wooded areas, to apply insect repellent containing DEET and to check your body for ticks after outdoor activities.

If a tick has attached itself to you, use tweezers to pull it straight out – do not twist it. Do not touch the tick with a hot object such as a cigarette because this can cause the tick to regurgitate noxious saliva into the wound. Do not rub oil or petroleum jelly on it.

TRAVELLING WITH CHILDREN

All travellers with children should know how to treat minor ailments and when to seek medical treatment. Make sure the children are up to date with routine vaccinations, and discuss possible travel vaccines well before departure, as some vaccines are not suitable for children under a year old.

Remember to avoid contaminated food and water. If your child is vomiting or has diarrhoea, lost fluid and salts must be replaced. It may be helpful to take along rehydration powders to reconstitute with boiled water.

Children should be encouraged to avoid and mistrust any dogs or other mammals because of the risk of rabies and other diseases. Any bite, scratch or lick from a warm-blooded, furry animal should immediately be thoroughly cleaned. If there is any possibility that the animal is infected with rabies, immediate medical assistance should be sought.

WOMEN'S HEALTH

Emotional stress, exhaustion and travelling through different time zones can all contribute to an upset in the menstrual pattern. If using oral contraceptives, remember that some antibiotics, diarrhoea and vomiting can stop the pill from working and lead to the risk of pregnancy – remember to take condoms with you just in case. Time zones, gastrointestinal upsets and antibiotics do not affect injectable contraception.

Travelling during pregnancy is usually possible, but there are important things to consider. Always have a medical check-up before planning your trip. The most risky times for travel are during the first 12 weeks of pregnancy and after 30 weeks. Illness during pregnancy can be more severe, so take special care to avoid contaminated food and water and insect and animal bites. A general rule is to only use vaccines, like other medications, if the risk of infection is substantial. Remember that the baby could be in serious danger if you were to contract infections such as typhoid or hepatitis. Some vaccines are best avoided; for example, those that contain live organisms. However, there is very little evidence that damage has been caused to an unborn child when vaccines have been given to a woman very early in pregnancy before the pregnancy was suspected. Take written records of the pregnancy with you. Ensure your insurance policy covers pregnancy, delivery and postnatal care. Always consult your doctor before you travel.

SEXUAL HEALTH

Emergency contraception is most effective if taken within 24 hours after unprotected sex.

When buying condoms, look for a European CE mark, which means they have been rigorously tested, and then keep them in a cool, dry place or they may crack and perish. Condoms are widely available from pharmacies and vending machines in many restaurants and nightclubs.

Free testing for sexually transmitted diseases is available in Amsterdam at the **GGD STD Clinic** (Map p95; Municipal Medical & Health Service; ☎ 555 58 22; www.ggd.amsterdam.nl; Weesperplein 1; ⏰ 8.30-10am & 1.30-4.30pm Mon-Fri). Call for an appointment or arrive early in the morning for same-day testing. If a problem is diagnosed, staff will provide free treatment immediately, but blood-test results take a week (they'll give you the results over the phone between 10.15am and 12.15pm if need be).

Language

Almost every Dutch person from age five onwards seems to speak English, often very well and better than you'll ever learn Dutch, so why bother? That's a good question because you'll rarely get the opportunity to practise: your Dutch acquaintances will launch into English, probably because they relish the opportunity to practise their language skills. Nevertheless, a few words in Dutch show good will, which is always appreciated, and you might even get to understand a bit more of what's going on around you. The phrase *Spreekt u Engels?* (Do you speak English?) before launching into English is best used with older people. The young, thanks to years of English in school, as well as exposure to vast amounts of English-language media (movies are usually subtitled rather than dubbed), will likely look at you like you've gone around the bend if you ask about their English skills.

The people of the northern Friesland province speak their own language. Although Frisian is actually the nearest relative to English, English speakers probably won't be able to make much sense of it, and you'll have to go to a small-town shop or a farm to really hear it. It's not the dominant language in the province, but most of the locals know some as a sign of cultural pride.

Most English speakers use the term 'Dutch' to describe the language spoken in the Netherlands and 'Flemish' for that spoken in the northern half of Belgium. Both are in fact the same language, called *Nederlands* (Dutch). The differences between Dutch and Flemish *(Vlaams)* are similar in degree to those between British and North American English, or between British and Australian English.

Dutch nouns come in one of three genders: masculine, feminine (both with *de* for 'the') and neuter (with *het* for 'the'). Where English uses 'a' or 'an', Dutch uses *een*, regardless of gender.

There's also a polite and an informal version of the English 'you'. The polite form is *u* (pronounced with the lips pursed and rounded), the informal is *je*. As a general rule, people who are older than you should be addressed as *u*.

For a food glossary and cooking terms that will help when dining out, see also p53. For more extensive coverage of Dutch, get a copy of Lonely Planet's comprehensive and user-friendly *Dutch Phrasebook*.

PRONUNCIATION

We have used the letters in the lists below to render the Dutch pronunciation – you can read our pronunciation guides as if they were English and you'll be understood just fine.

Vowels

a	as the 'u' in 'run'
e	as in 'bet'
i	as in 'hit'
o	as in 'pot'
u	pronounced with pursed, rounded lips, as in the French *tu*
uh	as the 'a' in 'ago'
aa	as the 'a' in 'father'
ee	as in 'eel'
oa	as in 'boat'
oo	as in 'zoo'
ow	as in 'cow'
ay	as in 'say'
eu	similar to 'er' in 'her', but without 'r' sound
öy	similar to the sound of 'er-y' in 'her year' (without 'r' sound), not unlike 'eui' in the French *fauteuil*

WHAT'S IN A NAME?

Dutch, like German, strings words together, which can baffle a foreigner trying to decipher (let alone remember) street names. *Eerste Goudsbloemdwarsstraat* (First Marigold Cross Street) is a good example. Chopping a seemingly endless name into its separate components might help a bit. The following terms appear frequently in street names and on signs:

baan – path, way
binnen – inside, inner
bloem – flower
brug – bridge
buiten – outside, outer
dijk – dyke
dwars – transverse
eiland – island
gracht – canal
groot – great, large, big
haven – harbour
hoek – corner
huis – house
kade – quay
kapel – chapel
kerk – church
klein – minor, small
laan – avenue
markt – market

molen – (wind)mill
nieuw – new
noord – north
oost – east
oud – old
plein – square
poort – city gate, gate
sloot – ditch
sluis – sluice, lock
steeg – alley
straat – street
toren – tower
veld – field
(burg)wal – (fortified) embankment
weg – road
west – west
wijk – district
zuid – south

Consonants

Most Dutch consonant sounds are similar to their English counterparts (**b**, **d**, **f**, **g**, **h**, **k**, **l**, **m**, **n**, **p**, **s**, **t**, **v**, **w**, **z**). The few trickier sounds are listed below:

ch	as in 'chip'
g	as in 'go'
kh	a throaty sound like the 'ch' in the Scottish *loch*
ng	as in 'ring'
r	trilled
y	as in 'yes'
zh	as the 's' in 'pleasure'

Word Stress

There are no universal rules on stress in Dutch. Just follow our pronunciation guides in which the stressed syllables are indicated in italics.

ACCOMMODATION

I'm looking for a ... *Ik ben op zoek naar een ...* ik ben op zook naar uhn ...

camping ground	*camping*	*kem*·ping
guest house	*pension*	pen·*syon*
(cheap) hotel	*(goedkoop) hotel*	(khoot·*koap*) ho·*tel*
youth hostel	*jeugdherberg*	*yeukht*·her·berkh

What is the address?
Wat is het adres?   wat is huht a·*dres*

Could you write the address, please?
Kunt u het adres opschrijven alstublieft?   kunt u huht a·*dres op*·skhray·vuhn als·tu·*bleeft*

Do you have any rooms available?
Heeft u een kamer vrij?   hayft u uhn *kaa*·muhr vray

I'd like (a) ...	*Ik wil graag een ...*	ik wil khraakh uhn ...
bed	*bed*	bet
single room	*eenpersoons-kamer*	*ayn*·puhr·soans·*kaa*·muhr
double room	*tweepersoons-kamer*	*tway*·puhr·soans·*kaa*·muhr
room with two beds	*kamer met twee bedden*	*kaa*·muhr met tway *be*·duhn
room with a bathroom	*kamer met badkamer*	*kaa*·muhr met *bat*·kaa·muhr
to share a dorm	*bed op een slaapzaal*	bet op uhn *slaap*·zaal

How much is it per night/person?
Hoeveel is het per nacht/persoon?   hoo·*vayl* is huht puhr nakht/per·*soan*

Is breakfast included?
Is ontbijt inbegrepen?   is ont·*bayt in*·buh·khray·puhn

MAKING A RESERVATION
(for phone or written requests)

To ...	Tot ...
From ...	Van ...
Date	Datum
I'd like to book ...	Ik wil ... reserveren.
	(see also the list under
	'Accommodation')
in the name of ...	op naam van ...
for the night/s of ...	voor de nacht(en) van ...
credit card	kredietkaart
number	nummer
expiry date	vervaldag
Please confirm	Gelieve de prijs en
availability	beschikbaarheid
and price.	te bevestigen.

May I see the room?
Mag ik de kamer zien?   makh ik duh *kaa*·muhr zeen
Where is the bathroom?
Waar is de badkamer?   waar is duh *bat*·kaa·muhr
I'm leaving today.
Ik vertrek vandaag.   ik vuhr·*trek* van·*daakh*
We're leaving today.
Wij vertrekken vandaag.   way vuhr·*tre*·kuhn van·*daakh*

CONVERSATION & ESSENTIALS
Hello.
Dag./Hallo.   dakh/ha·*loa*
Goodbye.
Dag.   dakh
Yes./No.
Ja./Nee.   yaa/nay
Please.
Alstublieft. (pol)   als·tu·*bleeft*
Alsjeblieft. (inf)   a·shuh·*bleeft*
Thank you (very much).
Dank u (wel). (pol)   dangk u (wel)
Dank je (wel). (inf)   dangk yuh (wel)
Thanks.
Bedankt. (pol or inf)   buh·*dangt*
That's fine./You're welcome.
Graag gedaan.   khraakh khuh·*daan*
Excuse me.
Pardon./   par·*don*/
Excuseer mij.   eks·ku·*zayr* may
I'm sorry.
Sorry./Excuses.   so·ree/eks·ku·zuhs
How are you?
Hoe gaat het met   hoo khaat huht met
u/jou? (pol/inf)   u/yow

I'm fine, thanks.
Goed, bedankt.   khoot, buh·*dangt*
See you soon.
Tot ziens.   tot zeens
What's your name?
Hoe heet u? (pol)   hoo hayt u
Hoe heet je? (inf)   hoo hayt yuh
My name is ...
Ik heet ...   ik hayt ...
Where are you from?
Waar komt u vandaan? (pol)   waar komt u van·*daan*
Waar kom je vandaan? (inf)   waar kom yuh van·*daan*
I'm from ...
Ik kom uit ...   ik kom öyt ...
I (don't) like ...
Ik hou (niet) van ...   ik how (neet) van ...
Just a minute.
Een moment.   uhn mo·*ment*

DIRECTIONS
Where is ...?
Waar is ...?   waar is ...
How do I get to ...?
Hoe kom ik bij ...?   hoo kom ik bay ...
(Go) straight ahead.
(Ga) rechtdoor.   (khaa) rekht·*doar*
(Turn) left.
(Ga) naar links.   (khaa) naar lings
(Turn) right.
(Ga) naar rechts.   (khaa) naar rekhs
at the corner
op de hoek   op duh hook
at the traffic lights
bij de verkeerslichten   bay duh vuhr·*kayrs*·
    likh·tuhn
Which street/road is this?
Welke straat/weg   wel·kuh straat/wekh
is dit?   is dit?

SIGNS

Ingang	Entrance
Uitgang	Exit
Informatie/Inlichtingen	Information
Open	Open
Gesloten	Closed
Verboden/Niet	Prohibited
Toegelaten	
Kamers Vrij	Rooms Available
Vol	Full/No Vacancies
Politiebureau	Police Station
WCs/Toiletten	Toilets
Heren	Men
Dames	Women

behind	achter	akh·tuhr
in front of	voor	vor
far (from)	ver (van)	ver (van)
near (to)	dichtbij	dikht·bay
opposite	tegenover	tay·khuhn·oa·vuhr

beach	strand	strant
bridge	brug	brukh
castle	kasteel	kas·tayl
cathedral	kathedraal	ka·tay·draal
island	eiland	ay·lant
main square	stadsplein	stats·playn
market	markt	markt
old city	oude stad	ow·duh stat
palace	paleis	pa·lays
ruins	ruines	rwee·nuhs
sea	zee	zay
square	plein	playn
tower	toren	toa·ruhn

EATING OUT

Sir!/Miss! (when calling waiting staff)
Meneer!/Mevrouw!   muh·*nayr*/muh·*vraw*
May I see the menu/wine list?
Mag ik het menu/   makh ik het muh·*nu*/
de wijnkaart zien?   duh *wayn*·kaart zeen
Do you have a menu in English?
Heeft u een menu   hayft u uhn muh·*nu*
in het Engels?   in het *eng*·uhls
A beer, please.
Een pils/bier, alstublieft.   uhn pils/beer als·tu·*bleeft*
A bottle of wine, please.
Een fles wijn, alstublieft.   uhn fles wayn als·tu·*bleeft*
What would you recommend?
Wat kan u aanbevelen?   wat kan u *aan*·buh·vay·luhn
What's the local speciality?
Wat is het   wat is huht
streekgerecht?   strayk·khuh·rekht
Is that dish spicy?
Is dit gerecht pittig?   is dit khuh·*rekht* pi·*tuhkh*
I'm a vegetarian.
Ik ben vegetariër.   ik ben vay·khay·*taa*·ree·yuhr
Enjoy your meal.
Eet smakelijk.   ayt *sma*·kuh·luhk
It tastes good.
Het smaakt lekker.   het smaakt *le*·kuhr
My compliments to the chef.
Mijn complimenten   mayn kom·plee·*men*·tuhn
aan de chef.   aan duh shef
May I have the bill, please?
Mag ik de rekening,   makh ik duh *ray*·kuh·ning
alstublieft?   als·tu·*bleeft*

EMERGENCIES

Help!
Help!   help
There's been an accident.
Er is een ongeluk   uhr is uhn *on*·khuh·luk
gebeurd.   khuh·*beurt*
I'm lost.
Ik ben de weg kwijt.   ik ben duh wekh kwayt
Go away!
Ga weg!   kha wekh

Call ...!	Haal ...	haal ...
a doctor	een doktor	uhn dok·tuhr
the police	de	duh
	politie	po·leet·see

HEALTH

I need a doctor.	Ik heb een dokter nodig.	ik hep uhn dok·tuhr noa·dikh
Where is the hospital?	Waar is het ziekenhuis?	waar is huht zee·kuhn·höys
I'm ill.	Ik ben ziek.	ik ben zeek
It hurts here.	Het doet hier pijn.	huht doot heer payn

I'm ...	Ik ben ...	ik ben ...
asthmatic	asthmatisch	ast·maa·tis
diabetic	suikerziek	söy·kuhr·zeek

I have epilepsy.
Ik heb epilepsie.   ik hep ay·pee·lep·see

I'm allergic to ...	Ik ben allergisch voor ...	ik ben a·ler·khis voar ...
antibiotics	antibiotica	an·tee·bee·o·tee·ka
aspirin	aspirine	as·pee·ree·nuh
bees	bijen	bay·uhn
penicillin	penicilline	pay·nee·see·lee·nuh
nuts	noten	noa·tuhn

antiseptic	ontsmettings-middel	ont·sme·tings·mi·duhl
aspirin	aspirine	as·pee·ree·nuh
condoms	condooms	kon·doams
constipation	verstopping	vuhr·sto·ping
contraceptive	anticonceptie-middel	an·tee·kon·sep·see·mi·duhl
diarrhoea	diarree	dee·a·ray
medicine	geneesmiddel/medicijn	khuh·nays·mi·duhl/may·dee·sayn
sunscreen	zonnebrandolie	zo·nuh·brant·oa·lee
tampons	tampons	tam·pons
nausea	misselijkheid	mi·suh·luhk·hayt

Language Difficulties
Do you speak English?
Spreekt u Engels?   spraykt u *eng*·uhls
How do you say ... in Dutch?
Hoe zeg je ...   hoo zekh yuh ...
in het Nederlands?   in huht *nay*·duhr·lants
What does ... mean?
Wat betekent ...?   wat buh·*tay*·kuhnt ...
I (don't) understand.
Ik begrijp het (niet).   ik buh·*khrayp* huht (neet)
Please write it down.
Schrijf het alstublieft op.   skhrayf huht als·tu·*bleeft* op
Can you show me (on the map)?
Kunt u het mij tonen   kunt u huht may *toa*·nuhn
(op de kaart)?   (op duh kaart)

NUMBERS
0	*nul*	nul
1	*één*	ayn
2	*twee*	tway
3	*drie*	dree
4	*vier*	veer
5	*vijf*	vayf
6	*zes*	zes
7	*zeven*	*zay*·vuhn
8	*acht*	akht
9	*negen*	*nay*·khuhn
10	*tien*	teen
11	*elf*	elf
12	*twaalf*	twaalf
13	*dertien*	*der*·teen
14	*veertien*	*vayr*·teen
15	*vijftien*	*vayf*·teen
16	*zestien*	*zes*·teen
17	*zeventien*	*zay*·vuhn·teen
18	*achttien*	*akh*·teen
19	*negentien*	*nay*·khuhn·teen
20	*twintig*	*twin*·tuhkh
21	*eenentwintig*	*ayn*·en·twin·tuhkh
22	*tweeëntwintig*	*tway*·en·twin·tuhkh
30	*dertig*	*der*·tuhkh
40	*veertig*	*vayr*·tuhkh
50	*vijftig*	*vayf*·tuhkh
60	*zestig*	*zes*·tuhkh
70	*zeventig*	*zay*·vuhn·tuhkh
80	*tachtig*	*takh*·tuhkh
90	*negentig*	*nay*·khuhn·tuhkh
100	*honderd*	*hon*·duhrt
1000	*duizend*	*döy*·zuhnt
2000	*tweeduizend*	*tway*·döy·zuhnt

PAPERWORK
name	*naam*	naam
nationality	*nationaliteit*	na·syo·na·lee·*tayt*
date of birth	*geboortedatum*	khuh·*boar*·tuh·daa·tuhm
place of birth	*geboorteplaats*	khuh·*boar*·tuh·plaats
passport	*paspoort*	*pas*·poart
sex (gender)	*geslacht*	khuh·*slakht*
visa	*visum*	*vee*·zum

SHOPPING & SERVICES
I'd like to buy ...
Ik wil graag ... kopen.   ik wil khraakh ... *koa*·puhn
How much is it?
Hoeveel is het?   hoo·*vayl* is huht?
I don't like it.
Ik vind het niet leuk.   ik vint huht neet leuk
May I look at it?
Mag ik het zien?   makh ik huht zeen
Can I try it (on)?
Kan ik het eens proberen?   kan ik huht ayns pro·*bay*·ruhn
I'm just looking.
Ik kijk alleen maar.   ik *kayk* a·*layn* maar
It's cheap.
Het is goedkoop.   huht is khoot·*koap*
It's too expensive (for me).
Het is (mij) te duur.   huht is (may) tuh dur
I'll take it.
Ik neem het.   ik naym huht

Do you accept ...?	*Accepteert u ...*	ak·sep·*tayrt* u ...
credit cards	*kredietkaarten*	kray·*deet*·kaar·tuhn
travellers cheques	*reischeques*	*rays*·sheks

more	*meer*	mayr
less	*minder*	*min*·duhr
smaller	*kleiner*	*klay*·nuhr
bigger	*groter*	*khroa*·tuhr

I'm looking for ...	*Ik ben op zoek naar ...*	ik ben op zook naar ...
the bank	*de bank*	duh bangk
a bookshop	*een boekenwinkel*	uhn *boo*·kuhn·wing·kuhl
the chemist/ pharmacy	*de drogist/ apotheek*	duh dro·*khist* a·po·*tayk*
the ... embassy	*de ... ambassade*	duh ... am·ba·*saa*·duh
the exchange office	*het wisselkantoor*	huht *wi*·suhl·kan·toar
the market	*de markt*	duh markt
the post office	*het postkantoor*	huht *post*·kan·toar
a public toilet	*een openbaar toilet*	uhn *oa*·puhn·baar twa·*let*
a supermarket	*een supermarkt*	uhn *su*·puhr·mart
the tourist office	*de VVV*	duh vay·vay·*vay*

What time does it open/close?

Hoe laat opent/	hoo laat oa·puhnt/
sluit het?	slöyt huht

I want to Ik wil ... ik wil ...
change ... wisselen. wi·suh·luhn
  money geld khelt
  travellers reischeques rays·sheks
  cheques

TIME & DATES
What time is it?

Hoe laat is het?	hoo laat is huht

It's (8 o'clock).

Het is (acht uur).	huht is (akht ur)

in the morning	's morgens	smor·khuhns
in the afternoon	's middags	smi·dakhs
in the evening	's avonds	saa·vonts
today	vandaag	van·daakh
tomorrow	morgen	mor·khuhn
yesterday	gisteren	khis·tuh·ruhn

Monday	maandag	maan·dakh
Tuesday	dinsdag	dins·dakh
Wednesday	woensdag	woons·dakh
Thursday	donderdag	don·duhr·dakh
Friday	vrijdag	vray·dakh
Saturday	zaterdag	zaa·tuhr·dakh
Sunday	zondag	zon·dakh

January	januari	ya·nu·aa·ree
February	februari	fay·bru·aa·ree
March	maart	maart
April	april	a·pril
May	mei	may
June	juni	yu·nee
July	juli	yu·lee
August	augustus	ow·gus·tus
September	september	sep·tem·buhr
October	oktober	ok·to·buhr
November	november	no·vem·buhr
December	december	day·sem·buhr

TRANSPORT
Public Transport
What time does the ... leave?

Hoe laat vertrekt ...?	hoo laat vuhr·trekt ...

What time does the ... arrive?

Hoe laat komt ... aan?	hoo laat komt ... aan

boat	de boot	duh boat
bus	de bus	duh bus
plane	het vliegtuig	huht fleekh·töykh
train	de trein	duh trayn
tram	de tram	duh trem

Where is ...? Waar is ...? waar is ...
  the airport de du
  luchthaven lukht·haa·vuhn
  the bus stop de bushalte duh bus·hal·tuh
  the metro het metro- huht may·tro·
  station station sta·syon
  the train het (trein)- huht (trayn·)
  station station sta·syon
  the tram stop de tramhalte duh trem·hal·tuh

I'd like ... Ik wil graag ... ik wil khraakh ...
ticket.
  a one-way een enkele uhn eng·kuh·luh
  reis rays
  a return een retourticket uhn ruh·toor·ti·ket
  a 1st-class eerste klas ayr·stuh klas
  a 2nd-class tweede klas tway·duh klas

I want to go to ...

Ik wil naar ... gaan.	ik wil naar ... khaan

The train has been cancelled/delayed.

De trein is afgelast/	duh trayn is af·khuh·last/
vertraagd.	vuhr·traakht

the first	de eerste	duh ayr·stuh
the last	de laatste	duh laat·stuh
platform	spoor/perron	spoar/pe·ron
number	nummer	nu·muhr
ticket office	loket	loa·ket
timetable	dienstregeling	deenst·ray·khuh·ling

Private Transport
I'd like to hire Ik wil graag een ik wil khraakh uhn
a/an ... ... huren. ... hu·ruhn
  bicycle fiets feets
  car auto ow·to
  motorbike motorfiets mo·tuhr·feets

Is this the road to ...?

Is dit de weg naar ...?	is dit duh wekh naar ...

Where's a service station?

Waar is er een	waar is uhr uhn
benzinestation?	ben·zee·nuh·sta·syon

Please fill it up.

Vol alstublieft.	vol als·tu·bleeft

I'd like (30) litres.

Ik wil graag (dertig) liter.	ik wil khraakh (der·tikh) lee·tuhr

diesel

diesel	dee·zuhl

petrol (gas)

benzine	ben·zee·nuh

(How long) Can I park here?

(Hoe lang) Kan ik hier	(hoo lang) kan ik heer
parkeren?	par·kay·ruhn

Afrit/Uitrit	Exit (from freeway)
Eenrichtingsverkeer	One Way
Gevaar	Danger
Ingang	Entrance
Omleiding	Detour
Oprit	Entrance (to freeway)
Tol	Toll
Uitgang	Exit
Veboden Toegang	No Entry
Verboden in te Halen/	No Overtaking
Inhaalverbod	
Verboden te Parkeren/	No Parking
Parkeerverbod	
Vertragen	Slow Down
Voorrang Verlenen	Give Way
Vrij Houden	Keep Clear

I need a mechanic.
Ik heb een mecanicien   ik hep een may·ka·nee·*sye*
nodig.   noa·dikh
The car/motorbike has broken down (at ...).
Ik heb auto/motorfiets   ik heb *ow*·to/*moa*·tuhr·feets
pech (in ...).   pekh (in ...)
The car/motorbike won't start.
De auto/motorfiets   duh *ow*·to/*moa*·tuhr·feets
wil niet starten.   wil neet *star*·tuhn
I have a flat tyre.
Ik heb een lekke band.   ik heb uhn *le*·kuh *bant*
I've run out of petrol.
Ik zit zonder benzine.   ik zit *zon*·duhr ben·*zee*·nuh
I've had an accident.
Ik heb een ongeluk gehad.   ik hep uhn *on*·khuh·luk khuh·*hat*

TRAVEL WITH CHILDREN

I need (a/an) ...	*Ik heb ... nodig.*	ik hep ... noa·dikh
Do you have	*Heeft u ...?*	hayft u ...
(a/an) ...?		
car baby seat	*een autozitje*	uhn *ow*·to·zi·chuh
	voor de baby	voar duh *bay*·bee
child-minding	*een oppasdienst*	uhn op·pas·*deenst*
service		
children's	*een*	uhn
menu	*kindermenu*	*kin*·duhr·muh·nu
(disposable)	*(wegwerp-)*	(wekh·werp·)
nappies/diapers	*luiers*	*löy*·uhrs
formula (milk)	*melkpoeder*	*melk*·poo·duhr
	(voor	(voar
	zuigflessen)	*zöykh*·fle·suhn)
(English-	*een babysit*	uhn *bay*·bee·sit
speaking)	*(die Engels*	(dee *eng*·uhls
babysitter	*spreekt)*	spraykt)
highchair	*een kinderstoel*	uhn *kin*·der·stool
potty	*een potje*	uhn *po*·chuh
stroller	*een wandel-*	uhn *wan*·duhl·
	wagen	waa·khuhn

Is there a baby change room?
Kan ik hier ergens   kan ik heer *er*·khuhns
de baby verschonen?   duh *bay*·bee vuhr·*skhoa*·nuhn
Do you mind if I breastfeed here?
Stoort het u als ik   stoart huht u als ik
hier de borst geef?   heer duh *borst* gayf
Are children allowed?
Zijn kinderen   zayn *kin*·duh·ruhn
toegelaten?   *too*·khuh·la·tuhn

Also available from Lonely Planet:
Dutch Phrasebook and
Western Europe Phrasebook

Glossary

See the boxed text, p310, for a list of terms commonly encountered in street names and sights.

abdij – abbey
ANWB – Dutch automobile association
apotheek – chemist/pharmacy

benzine – petrol/gasoline
bevrijding – liberation
bibliotheek – library
bos – woods or forest
botter – type of 19th-century fishing boat
broodje – bread roll (with filling)
broodjeszaak – sandwich shop
bruin café – brown cafe; traditional drinking establishment
buurt – neighbourhood

cafe – pub, bar; also known as *kroeg*
coffeeshop – cafe authorised to sell cannabis

dagschotel – dish of the day in Dutch restaurants
drop – salted or sweet liquorice

eetcafé – cafes (pubs) serving meals

fiets – bicycle
fietsenstalling – secure bicycle storage
fietspad – bicycle path

gemeente – municipal, municipality
gezellig – convivial, cosy
GVB – Gemeentevervoerbedrijf; Amsterdam municipal transport authority
GWK – Grenswisselkantoren; official currency-exchange offices

hal – hall, entrance hall
haven – port
hof – courtyard
hofje – almshouse or series of buildings around a small courtyard, also known as *begijnhof*
hoofd – literally 'head', but in street names it often means 'main'
hunebedden – prehistoric rock masses purportedly used as burial chambers

jenever – Dutch gin; also *genever*

kaas – cheese
kantoor – office
koffiehuis – espresso bar; cafe (as distinct from a *coffeeshop*)
klompen – clogs
klooster – cloister, religious house
koningin – queen
koninklijk – royal
korfbal – a cross between netball, volleyball and basketball
kroeg – cafe, pub, bar
kunst – art
kwartier – quarter

LF routes – *landelijke fietsroutes*; national (long-distance) bike routes
loodvrij – unleaded (petrol/gasoline)

markt – town square; market
meer – lake
molen – windmill; mill

NS – Nederlandse Spoorwegen; national railway company

OV-chipkaart – new fare card for Dutch public transit

paleis – palace
polder – area of drained land
postbus – post office box

Randstad – literally 'rim-city'; the urban agglomeration including Amsterdam, Utrecht, Rotterdam and Den Haag
Rijk(s-) – the State

scheepvaart – shipping
schouwburg – theatre
sluis – lock (for boats/ships)
spoor – platform (in train station)
stadhuis – town hall
stedelijk – civic, municipal
stichting – foundation, institute
strand – beach
strippenkaart – strip card, punchable multiticket used on all public transport

terp – mound of packed mud in Friesland that served as a refuge during floods (plural *terpen*)

treintaxi – taxi for train passengers
tuin – garden
tuindersvlet – type of small, open-topped boat
tulp – tulip
turf – peat

verzet – resistance
Vlaams – Flemish
VVV – tourist information office

waag – old weigh-house
wadlopen – mud-walking
weeshuis – orphanage
werf – wharf, shipyard
winkel – shop

zaal – room, hall
zee – sea
ziekenhuis – hospital
zwembad – public swimming pool

The Authors

RYAN VER BERKMOES
Coordinating Author

Ryan Ver Berkmoes worked on the first edition of Lonely Planet's *The Netherlands*, a country where the people pronounce his name better than he can, possibly because his ancestors are lurking about there somewhere. Ryan was thrilled to see it's still the same charming, amusing, idiosyncratic place it was last time. These days he lives in Portland, Oregon, which is another place with very good bars. Learn more at ryanverberkmoes.com. For this edition of *The Netherlands*, Ryan wrote all chapters except Amsterdam.

KARLA ZIMMERMAN
Amsterdam

During her Amsterdam travels, Karla admired art, bicycled crash-free, ate an embarrassing number of Droste chocolates and bent over to take her *jenever* (Dutch gin) like a local. She has been visiting Amsterdam since 1989 – two decades that have seen her trade space cakes for *stroopwafels*, to a much more pleasant effect.

Based in Chicago, Karla writes travel features for newspapers, books, magazines and radio. She has authored or co-authored several Lonely Planet guidebooks covering the USA, Canada, the Caribbean and Europe.

Behind the Scenes

THIS BOOK

This 4th edition of *The Netherlands* was researched and written by Ryan Ver Berkmoes, Karla Zimmerman, with research by Caroline Sieg and additional content by Simon Sellars. The 3rd edition was written by Neal Bedford and Simon Sellars; the 2nd edition was written by Jeremy Gray and Reuben Acciano; and the 1st edition was written by Ryan Ver Berkmoes and Jeremy Gray. This guidebook was commissioned in Lonely Planet's London office, and produced by the following:

Commissioning Editors Caroline Sieg, Lucy Monie
Coordinating Editors Charlotte Harrison, Martine Power
Coordinating Cartographer Jacqueline Nguyen
Coordinating Layout Designer Jacqui Saunders
Managing Editors Katie Lynch, Annelies Mertens
Managing Cartographers David Connolly, Hunor Csutoros, Herman So
Managing Layout Designer Sally Darmody
Assisting Editors David Carroll, Victoria Harrison, Kristin Odijk, Jeanette Wall
Assisting Cartographers Andras Bogdanovits, Mick Garrett, Khanh Luu, Simon Tillema
Cover Naomi Parker, lonelyplanetimages.com
Internal image research Aude Vauconsant, lonelyplanetimages.com
Language Content Laura Crawford

Project Manager Eoin Dunlevy
Thanks to Imogen Bannister, Lucy Birchley, Barbara Delissen, Fayette Fox, Jane Hart, Craig Kilburn, Trent Paton

THANKS

RYAN VER BERKMOES

Thanks to commissioning editor Lucy Monie and crack co-author Caroline Sieg, who transformed herself during the project. Good luck! A full-bodied glass of Palm and a plate of the best Oud Amsterdammer to Charlotte Harrison for turning this book into a masterpiece and a heaping portion of *frites* to Jacqueline Nguyen for the mapping. A double order of *bitterballen* to Karla Zimmerman, who made it worth missing the train that one night. Too many folks to thank in the Netherlands but I have to mention the incomparable Hortance van den Beld in Deventer. Then there's the linguist from whom I finally learned the meaning of my name: 'of the birch tree in the swamp' or something like that. Of course my heart always floats for Erin, who held my hand after I foolishly ate the 'very hot' dish. I needed a swamp then, preferably a very cool one.

KARLA ZIMMERMAN

Many thanks to Constant Broeren, Gennie Freen, Petra, Paul Lodder, Roswitha De Joode, Marko

---

THE LONELY PLANET STORY

Fresh from an epic journey across Europe, Asia and Australia in 1972, Tony and Maureen Wheeler sat at their kitchen table stapling together notes. The first Lonely Planet guidebook, *Across Asia on the Cheap*, was born.

Travellers snapped up the guides. Inspired by their success, the Wheelers began publishing books to Southeast Asia, India and beyond. Demand was prodigious, and the Wheelers expanded the business rapidly to keep up. Over the years, Lonely Planet extended its coverage to every country and into the virtual world via lonelyplanet.com and the Thorn Tree message board.

As Lonely Planet became a globally loved brand, Tony and Maureen received several offers for the company. But it wasn't until 2007 that they found a partner whom they trusted to remain true to the company's principles of travelling widely, treading lightly and giving sustainably. In October of that year, BBC Worldwide acquired a 75% share in the company, pledging to uphold Lonely Planet's commitment to independent travel, trustworthy advice and editorial independence.

Today, Lonely Planet has offices in Melbourne, London and Oakland, with over 500 staff members and 300 authors. Tony and Maureen are still actively involved with Lonely Planet. They're travelling more often than ever, and they're devoting their spare time to charitable projects. And the company is still driven by the philosophy of *Across Asia on the Cheap*: 'All you've got to do is decide to go and the hardest part is over. So go!'

Ciciliani and Spuddy and Richard Luteijn for sharing their knowledge of all things local. Thanks to commissioning editor Lucy Monie and crack co-author Caroline Sieg. Thanks much to Charlotte Harrison for making the text better. An extra-big glass of appreciation is raised to Ryan Ver Berkmoes for the tips, advice and beer drinking. And thanks most of all to Eric Markowitz, the world's best partner for life, who kindly fed me and kept the home fires burning throughout the long days.

OUR READERS

Many thanks to the travellers who used the last edition and wrote to us with helpful hints, useful advice and interesting anecdotes:

Hilde Albregts, Dana Amsbary, Danny Auron, Robert Booms, Frans Bos, John Bosch, Janet Chapman, Mark Collier, Corinne Cook, Amir Cooper, John Davis, Laura Dijkerman, Marije Douma, Wilke Durand, John Earth, Dan Elves, Charlotte Farlow, Andrea Fennell, Charles Grace, Maryska Hellinga, Renno Hokwerda, Muriel Hooft, Celeste Janssen, Christof Kaiser, Ard Karsten, Jitso Keizer, Francois Keulen, Leila Kuzyk, Judy Lehman, Karen Lindup, Irene Lissamore, Roz Lobo, Leon Martakis, Marjanne Meeuwsen, Ali Murat, Daniel Musikant, Sophia Nijburg, Ruth Noyon, Robert Osmundson, Ian Parker, Alan Porter, Anna Ptaszynska, Liesbeth Rijpma, Jennifer Rodehaver, Hans Rood, Jimmy Rowland, Domenico Scarfò, Barbara Scott, Perminder Sethi, Richard Simpson, Pamela Smith, S J Srinivas, Jenny Theresia, Summer Trentin, Selma van der Burgh, Marieke van der Eerden, Angela van der Knaap, Katalijn Ritsema van Eck, Arjan van Grol, Erik van Loon, Willy van Meegen, Peter-Paul van Oosterhout, Luc van Roy, Laura Viteri, Rieke Weel, Jennifer Fay Wendt

SEND US YOUR FEEDBACK

We love to hear from travellers – your comments keep us on our toes and help make our books better. Our well-travelled team reads every word on what you loved or loathed about this book. Although we cannot reply individually to postal submissions, we always guarantee that your feedback goes straight to the appropriate authors, in time for the next edition. Each person who sends us information is thanked in the next edition and the most useful submissions are rewarded with a free book.

To send us your updates – and find out about Lonely Planet events, newsletters and travel news – visit our award-winning website: **lonelyplanet.com/contact**.

Note: we may edit, reproduce and incorporate your comments in Lonely Planet products such as guidebooks, websites and digital products, so let us know if you don't want your comments reproduced or your name acknowledged. For a copy of our privacy policy visit lonelyplanet.com/privacy.

ACKNOWLEDGMENTS

Many thanks to the following for the use of their content:

Globe on title page ©Mountain High Maps 1993 Digital Wisdom, Inc.

Index

INDEX

INDEX

INDEX

GREENDEX

The following businesses have been selected by Lonely Planet authors because they meet our criteria for sustainable tourism.

However, you have to pass a very high bar to receive special mention in the Netherlands as green practices are both deeply entrenched and enthusiastically followed.

For this title we highlighted establishments that have a clear commitment to organic and sustainable foods and/or are especially innovative when it comes to minimising their effects on the environment. If you think we've omitted a listing here, or if you disagree with our choices, contact us at www.lonelyplanet.com/contact. For more information about sustainable tourism, see www.lonelyplanet.com/responsibletravel.

328

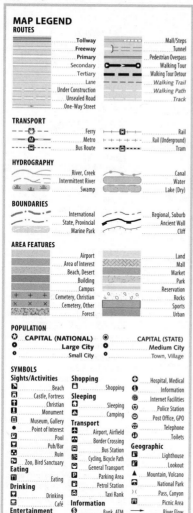

MAP LEGEND
ROUTES

Tollway		Mall/Steps	
Freeway		Tunnel	
Primary		Pedestrian Overpass	
Secondary		Walking Tour	
Tertiary		Walking Tour Detour	
Lane		Walking Trail	
Under Construction		Walking Path	
Unsealed Road		Track	
One-Way Street			

TRANSPORT
Ferry · Rail · Metro · Rail (Underground) · Bus Route · Tram

HYDROGRAPHY
River, Creek · Canal · Intermittent River · Water · Swamp · Lake (Dry)

BOUNDARIES
International · Regional, Suburb · State, Provincial · Ancient Wall · Marine Park · Cliff

AREA FEATURES
Airport · Land · Area of Interest · Mall · Beach, Desert · Market · Building · Park · Campus · Reservation · Cemetery, Christian · Rocks · Cemetery, Other · Sports · Forest · Urban

POPULATION
CAPITAL (NATIONAL) · CAPITAL (STATE) · Large City · Medium City · Small City · Town, Village

SYMBOLS
Sights/Activities Beach, Castle, Fortress, Christian, Monument, Museum Gallery, Point of Interest, Pool, Pub/Bar, Ruin, Zoo Bird Sanctuary
Eating Eating
Drinking Drinking, Café
Entertainment Entertainment
Shopping Shopping
Sleeping Sleeping, Camping
Transport Airport Airfield, Border Crossing, Bus Station, Cycling Bicycle Path, General Transport, Parking Area, Petrol Station, Taxi Rank
Information Bank ATM, Embassy/Consulate, Hospital Medical, Information, Internet Facilities, Police Station, Post Office GPO, Telephone, Toilets
Geographic Lighthouse, Lookout, Mountain Volcano, National Park, Pass Canyon, Picnic Area, River Flow, Shelter Hut

LONELY PLANET OFFICES

Australia (Head Office)
Locked Bag 1, Footscray, Victoria 3011
☎ 03 8379 8000, fax 03 8379 8111
talk2us@lonelyplanet.com.au

USA
150 Linden St, Oakland, CA 94607
☎ 510 250 6400, toll free 800 275 8555
fax 510 893 8572
info@lonelyplanet.com

UK
2nd fl, 186 City Rd,
London EC1V 2NT
☎ 020 7106 2100, fax 020 7106 2101
go@lonelyplanet.co.uk

Published by Lonely Planet Publications Pty Ltd
ABN 36 005 607 983

© Lonely Planet 2010

© photographers as indicated 2010

Cover photograph: Windmill with strips of farmland separated by canals, The Netherlands, Jochem D Wijnands/Getty Images. Many of the images in this guide are available for licensing from Lonely Planet Images: lonelyplanetimages.com.

Mixed Sources
Product group from well-managed forests and other controlled sources
www.fsc.org Cert no. SGS-COC-005002
© 1996 Forest Stewardship Council

read hotel **reviews** ☎ get advice (on everything) ✆ **buy books** ☎ brag to mates • tell stories ✗ check warnings ⁖ read hints ✉ plan adventures ✓ make lists ✆ listen up ✆ get lost ✂ wrestle monkeys ⁖ scam the scammers ➡ learn how to get out of a minefield ✗ complain ⚘ find road–trip buddies ✓ recommend ☞ **get the lowdown** ☎ talk to travellers ✆ meet your soul mate ✈ **practise hippo safety** ⁘ cruise the savanna ☆ take better photos ⚘ wear the right shoes, boots, **sandals** ➒ find restaurant reviews ☾ book a bed $ spare some change ⁙ get challenged ⬥ take the plunge ⚡ download guides ⊛ sell stuff ☛ meet the locals ➡ make a clean escape ♥ find lost love ⁘ chew the fat ✂ save some money ⁖ buy a gift ☆ **get inspired** ⚘ **share a story** ⚘ read hotel reviews ☎ get advice (on everything) ✈ **book flights** ✆ buy books ✉ get DVDs ☎ brag to mates • tell stories **✗ check warnings** ⁖ read hints ✉ get DVDs ✉ plan adventures ✓ make lists ✆ listen up ✉ get lost ✂ wrestle monkeys ⁘ **book flights** ⁘ scam the scammers ➡ learn how to get out of a minefield ✗ complain ⚘ find road-trip buddies ✓ recommend ☞ get the lowdown ☎ talk to travellers ✆ meet your soul mate ✈ practise hippo safety ⁘ **cruise** the savanna ☆ take better photos ⚘ wear the right shoes, boots, sandals ➒ find restaurant reviews ☾ book a bed $ spare some change ⁙ get challenged ⬥ take the plunge ⚡ **download guides** ⊛ sell stuff ☛ **meet the locals** ➡ make a clean escape ♥ find lost love ⁘ **chew the fat** ✂ save some money ⁖ buy a gift ☆ get inspired ☺ share a story ⚘ read hotel reviews ☎ get advice (on everything) ✈ book flights ✆ buy books ✉ **get DVDs** ☎ brag to mates • **tell stories** ✗ check warnings ⁖ read hints ✉ plan adventures ✓ make lists ✉ get lost **✂ wrestle monkeys** ⁘ scam the scammers ➡ learn how to get out of a minefield ✗ complain ⚘ **find road-trip buddies** ✓ recommend ☞ get the lowdown ☎ talk to travellers ✆ meet your **soul** mate ✈ practise hippo safety ⁘ cruise the savanna ☆ take better photos ⚘ wear the right **shoes**, boots, sandals ➒ find restaurant reviews ☾ book a bed $ spare some change ⁙ get **challenged** ⬥ take the plunge ⚡ **download guides** ⊛ sell stuff ☛ meet the locals ➡ make a clean **escape** ♥ find lost love ⁘ chew the fat ✂ save some money ⁖ buy a gift ☆ get inspired ☺ **share** a story ⚘ read hotel reviews ☎ get advice (on everything) ✈ book flights ✆ buy books ✉ get DVDs ☎ brag to mates • tell stories ✗ check warnings ◫ **read hints** ✉ plan adventures ✓ **make lists** ✆ listen up ✉ get lost ✂ wrestle monkeys ⁘ scam the scammers ➡ learn how to get out of a minefield ✗ complain ⚘ **find road-trip buddies** ✓ recommend ☞ get the lowdown ☎ talk to travellers ✆ meet your soul mate ✈ practise hippo safety ⁘ cruise the savanna ☾ take better photos ⚘ wear the right shoes, boots, sandals ➒ find restaurant reviews ☾ book a bed $ spare some change ⁙ get challenged ⬥ take the plunge ⚡ download guides ⊛ **sell stuff** ☛ meet the locals ➡ make a clean escape ♥ find lost love ⁘ chew the fat ✂ save some **money** ⁖ buy a gift ☆ get inspired ☺ share a story ⚘ read hotel reviews ☎ get advice (on **everything**) ✈ book flights ✆ buy books ✉ get DVDs **☎ brag to mates** • tell stories ✗ check warnings ⁖ read hints ✉ plan adventures ✓ make lists ✆ listen up ✉ get lost ✂ wrestle monkeys ⁘ scam the scammers ➡ learn how to get out of a minefield ✗ complain ⚘ find road-trip buddies ✓ recommend ☞ get the lowdown ☎ **talk to travellers** ✆ meet your soul mate ✈ practise **hippo** safety ⁘ cruise the savanna ☆ take better photos ⚘ wear the right shoes, boots, sandals ➒ find restaurant reviews ☾ book a bed $ spare some change ⁙ get challenged ⬥ take the **plunge** ⚡ download guides ⊛ sell stuff ☛ meet the locals ➡ make a clean escape ♥ find lost **love** ⁘ chew the fat ✂ **save some money** ⁖ buy a gift ☆ get inspired ☺ share a story ⚘ **read** hotel reviews ☎ get advice (on everything) ✈ book flights ✆ buy books ✉ get DVDs ☎ **brag** to mates • tell stories ✗ check warnings ⁖ read hints ✉ plan adventures ✓ make lists ✆ listen **up** ✉ get lost ✂ wrestle monkeys ⁘ scam the scammers ➡ learn how to get out of a minefield ✗ complain ⚘ find road-trip buddies ✓ **recommend** ☞ get the lowdown ☎ talk to travellers ✆ meet your soul mate ✈ practise hippo safety ⁘ cruise the savanna ☆ **take** better photos ⚘ wear the right shoes, boots, sandals ➒ find restaurant reviews ☾ book a bed $ spare some **change** ⁙ get challenged ⬥ take the plunge ⚡ download guides ⊛ sell stuff ☛ meet the **locals** ➡ make a clean escape ♥ find lost love ⁘ chew the fat ✂ save some money ◫ **buy a gift** ☆ get inspired ☺ share a story ⚘ read hotel reviews ☎ **get advice (on everything)** ✈ book flights ✆ buy books ✉ get DVDs ☎ brag to mates • tell stories ✗ check warnings ⁖ read hints ✉ **plan adventures** ✓ make lists ✆ listen up ✉ get lost ✂ wrestle monkeys ⁘ scam the scammers ➡ learn how to get out of a minefield ✗ complain ⚘ find road-trip buddies ✓ recommend ☞ get the lowdown ☎ talk to travellers ✆ meet your soul mate ✈ practise hippo safety ⁘ cruise the savanna ☆ **take** better photos ⚘ wear the right shoes, boots, sandals ➒ find restaurant reviews ☾ **book a bed** $ spare some change ⁙ get challenged ⬥ take the plunge ⚡ **download guides**

Almost too much information

INSPIRING colour section on the best of the Netherlands

SELECTED coverage of the best walking, boating and cycling

GREEN INDEX pointing to sustainable listings

Nobody knows the Netherlands like Lonely Planet and our 4th edition helps you uncover the secrets of this gently beautiful country. Cycle along the canals, past sand dunes, windmills, tulips and wild national parks. Reward yourself with warm *appeltaart*, then learn to swallow a raw herring without flinching.

Lonely Planet guides are written by experts who get to the heart of every destination they visit. This fully updated edition is packed with accurate, practical and honest advice, designed to give you the information you need to make the most of your trip.

Content includes:

Also available:

Discover, plan, book and share at:
lonelyplanet.com/the-netherlands

ISBN 978-1-74104-925-1

52299

9 781741 049251

4TH EDITION
Published Mar 2010
First Published Jan 2001

USA $22.99
UK £14.99